Second Edition

s t a t i s t i c s

in Criminal Justice

David Weisburd
University of Maryland and Hebrew University, Jerusalem

Chester L. Britt
Arizona State University West

THOMSON ™

WADSWORTH

Australia Canada Mexico Singapore Spain
United Kingdom   United States

Senior Executive Editor, Criminal Justice: *Sabra Horne*
Senior Acquisitions Editor, Criminal Justice: *Jay Whitney*
Development Editor: *Shelley Murphy*
Assistant Editor: *Dawn Mesa*
Editorial Assistant: *Paul Massicotte*
Technology Project Manager: *Susan DeVanna*
Marketing Manager: *Dory Schaeffer*
Marketing Assistant: *Neena Chandra*
Advertising Project Manager: *Stacey Purviance*
Project Manager, Editorial Production: *Matt Ballantyne*
Print/Media Buyer: *Doreen Suruki*

Permissions Editor: *Bob Kauser*
Production Service: *Lifland et al., Bookmakers*
Copy Editor: *Sally Lifland*
Cover Designer: *Cuttriss & Hambleton*
Cover Image: *People walking*
    © *Teri Dixon/Getty Images; zigzag pattern*
    © *Ryan McVay/Getty Images; grid*
    background © *Chad Baker/Getty Images*
Compositor: *UG / GGS Information Services, Inc.*
Text and Cover Printer: *Phoenix Color Corp*

Library of Congress Control Number: 2002114539

ISBN 0-534-59508-1

Wadsworth/Thomson Learning
10 Davis Drive
Belmont, CA 94002–3098
USA

Asia
Thomson Learning
5 Shenton Way #01-01
UIC Building
Singapore 068808

Australia
Thomson Learning
102 Dodds Street
South Melbourne, Victoria 3205
Australia

Canada
Nelson
1120 Birchmount Road
Toronto, Ontario M1K 5G4
Canada

Europe/Middle East/Africa
Thomson Learning
High Holborn House
50/51 Bedford Row
London WC1R 4LR
United Kingdom

For Bryan, who made the desert bloom, used sun to brighten the night, and brought such joy to family and friends

D. W.

For Teri, Aly, and Lucas

C. B.

Contents

Preface

Oliver Wendell Holmes, the distinguished associate justice of the Supreme Court, was noted for his forgetfulness. On a train leaving Washington, D.C., he is said to have been approached by a conductor who requested his ticket. Holmes, searching through his case and his pockets, could not locate his pass. After a few awkward moments, the conductor recognized the distinctive-looking and well-known jurist and suggested that he just send the rail company the ticket when he found it. Justice Holmes, however, is said to have looked sternly at the conductor and responded, "Young man, the problem is not where is my ticket; the problem is where am I going."

For the student of statistics, a textbook is like a train ticket. Not only does it provides a pass the student can use for entering a new and useful area of study; it also defines the route that will be taken and the goals that are important to achieve. Different textbooks take different approaches and emphasize different types of material. *Statistics in Criminal Justice* emphasizes the uses of statistics in research in crime and justice. This text is meant for students and professionals who want to gain a basic understanding of statistics in this field. In the first chapter, the main themes of the text are outlined and discussed. This preface describes how the text is organized.

The text takes a building-block approach. This means that each chapter helps prepare you for the chapters that follow. It also means that the level of sophistication of the text increases as the text progresses. Basic concepts discussed in early chapters provide a foundation for the introduction of more complex statistical issues later. One advantage to this approach is that it is easy to see, as time goes on, how much you have learned about statistics. Concepts that would have seemed impossible to understand, had they been introduced at the outset, are surprisingly simple when you encounter them later on. If you turn to the final chapters of the book now, you will see equations that are quite forbidding. However, when you come to these equations after covering the material in earlier chapters, you will be surprised at how easy they are to understand.

Throughout the text, there is an emphasis on *comprehension* and not *computation*. The approach is meant to provide readers with an accessible but sophisticated understanding of statistics that can be used to examine real-life criminal justice problems. In the opening chapters of the book, basic themes and materials are presented. Chapter 1 provides an introduction to how we use statistics in criminal justice and the problems we face in applying statistics to real-life research problems. Chapters 2 through 5 introduce basic concepts of measurement and basic methods for graphically representing data and using statistics to describe data. Many of the statistics provided here will be familiar to you; however, remember that the more advanced statistics presented in later chapters build on the themes covered in these early chapters.

One of the fundamental problems researchers face is that they seek to make statements about large populations (such as all U.S. citizens) but are generally able to collect information or data on only a sample, or smaller group, drawn from such populations. In Chapters 6 through 12, the focus is on how researchers use statistics to overcome this problem. What is the logic that underlies the statistics we use for making statements about populations based on samples? What are the different types of statistical procedures or tests that can be used? What special problems are encountered in criminal justice research, and how should the researcher approach them? Some texts skip over the basics, moving students from test to test before they understand the logic behind the tests. The approach here is to focus in greater detail on relatively simple statistical decisions before moving on to more complex ones.

Having examined how we can make statements about populations from information gained from samples, we turn to how we describe the strength of association between variables. In the social sciences, it is often essential not only to determine whether factors are related but also to define the strength and character of those relationships. Accordingly, in Chapters 13 and 14, we look at measures of association, and in Chapters 15 through 17, we examine bivariate and multivariate regression. These are likely to be new topics for you, though they are statistics commonly used in criminal justice.

In the concluding chapters, we look at two special topics. Chapter 18 describes confidence intervals, a method for assessing how much trust you can place in the specific estimates that you obtain from a sample. Because our emphasis is on research in criminal justice, we conclude the text with a chapter that examines methods for evaluating and improving the design of a research project. The statistical concept that is central to Chapter 19—statistical power—follows directly from the concepts developed in prior chapters. Statistical power is often ignored in introductory statistics texts. However, it has become a central concern in criminal justice research and accordingly is given emphasis in this text.

While it is always difficult in statistics to decide where an introductory text should stop, with an understanding of these techniques you will have the basic tools to comprehend and conduct criminal justice research. Of course, these tools constitute a building block for more advanced methods. The goal of the text is not only to bring you to this point in learning statistics, but also to leave you with the confidence and tools to tackle more complex problems on your own.

Each chapter starts with a statement of the basic concepts and problems addressed and ends with a full chapter summary. There is also a list of equations, when relevant, at the end of the chapter. These materials should help you to review what you have learned and to identify the basic knowledge you need to move on to subsequent chapters. All of the chapters contain a list of key terms with short definitions. The key terms appear in boldface the first time they are mentioned in the chapter. Sometimes a term may have been briefly explained in an earlier chapter, but is designated as a key term in the chapter where the concept is more central. A general glossary of key terms appears at the end of the book.

Chapters 2 through 18 each have a set of questions at the end. The questions are designed to make you think about the subjects covered in the chapter. Sometimes they are straightforward, following directly from the text. Sometimes they ask you to develop ideas in slightly different ways than in the text. In constructing the questions, we sought to make working on statistical issues as much fun as possible. In statistics, it is crucial to go over material more than once. The questions are meant to reinforce the knowledge you have gained.

A working knowledge of computers is not required to understand the statistical concepts or procedures presented in the text. However, computers have become a very important part of research in statistics, and thus we provide computer exercises for relevant chapters and a web site where you can access the data needed for those exercises. You are encouraged to use the web site. It will help you to see the connection between the topics discussed in the chapters and statistical computing. An SPSS® Student Version 11.0 CD-ROM is included with this book. It is based on SPSS statistical software, widely used in colleges and universities.

Statistics in Criminal Justice will allow you to approach statistics in a familiar context. It emphasizes the statistics and the problems that are commonly encountered in criminal justice research. It focuses on understanding rather than computation. However, it takes a serious approach to statistics, which is relevant to the real world of research in crime and justice. The text is meant not only as an introduction for students but also as a reference for researchers. The approach taken will help both students who want an introduction to statistics and professionals who seek a straightforward explanation for statistics that have become a routine tool in contemporary criminal justice systems.

Acknowledgments

In the development of any academic enterprise, many students and colleagues provide support and advice. We are particularly indebted to Professor Joseph Naus of the Department of Statistics of Rutgers University, who has played a crucial advisory role in the preparation of both the original edition of this work and this revised and expanded second edition. We owe a special debt as well to Pamela Diamond of Sam Houston University, who prepared the teaching supplement and provided us with useful advice on revising and adding chapters. Cynthia Lum, Laura Wyckoff, and Sue-Ming Yang, doctoral students at the University of Maryland, and Hana Herbst, of the Hebrew University in Jerusalem, helped us in revising and checking the manuscript and provided much-needed assistance in the preparation of the second edition. Finally, we want to again thank Daniel Salem, a graduate of the Institute of Criminology of the Hebrew University, who played a crucial role in assisting in the development of the first edition of this work.

This edition of *Statistics in Criminal Justice* would not have been completed without the continual encouragement and persistence of Sabra Horne, of Wadsworth Publishing. Her faith in the importance of the text and her energy in pursuing it to its completion are much appreciated. We want to thank others as well who have helped in the production of the work, including Matthew Ballantyne of Wadsworth Publishing and Kimberly Shockey. We are especially indebted to Sally Lifland of Lifland et al., Bookmakers, for her careful and thoughtful reading and editing of our work and her attention to the details of its production.

Though anonymous reviewers cannot be thanked at the outset, they always play a major role in improving the quality of scholarly work. We were fortunate to have a large number of reviewers who read and commented on both this edition and the first edition of text. The final product reflects their keen insights and thoughtful suggestions:

Thomas L. Austin, Shippensburg University
Candice Batton, University of Nebraska, Omaha
Steven G. Brandl, University of Wisconsin–Milwaukee
Jerald C. Burns, Alabama State University
Shawn Bushway, University of Maryland
Michael H. Hazlett, Western Illinois University
Frank Horvath, Michigan State University
Edward Latessa, University of Cincinnati
Janet Lauritsen, University of Missouri–St. Louis
Michael D. Maltz, University of Illinois–Chicago
Greg Manco, Rutgers University
Kimberly McCabe, University of South Carolina

Terance D. Miethe, University of Nevada–Las Vegas
Larry S. Miller, East Tennessee State University
Alex Piquero, University of Florida
Albert J. Reiss, Yale University
Richard Sluder, Central Missouri State University
Thomas Tomlinson, Western Illinois University
Joseph Waldron, Youngstown State University
Elin Waring, Lehman College
Alexander Weiss, Indiana University
Mary Ann Zagar, Florida Gulf Coast University

David Weisburd is a leading researcher and scholar in the field of criminal justice. He holds appointments as Professor of Criminology at the Hebrew University Law School in Jerusalem and at the University of Maryland at College Park. He is also a Senior Fellow at the Police Foundation in Washington, DC. Professor Weisburd is a member of the National Academy of Sciences Panel on Police Practices and Policies and sits on the steering committee of the Campbell Collaboration Crime and Justice Group. He also serves on the editorial boards of the *Journal of Research in Crime and Delinquency, Journal of Quantitative Criminology, Advances in Criminological Theory, Policing: An International Journal of Police Strategies and Management,* and *The Israel Law Review.* Professor Weisburd received his Ph.D. from Yale University, where he was a Research Associate at Yale Law School. He has also served as Senior Research Associate at the Vera Institute of Justice in New York and Director of the Center for Crime Prevention Studies at Rutgers University. Professor Weisburd is author or editor of ten books and more than fifty scientific articles. His most recent books are *White Collar Crime and Criminal Careers* (Cambridge University Press, 2001), and *Social Organization and Crime* (Transaction Press, 2002). His articles have appeared in such journals as *Criminology, Justice Quarterly, Journal of Quantitative Criminology, Crime and Justice, Annals of the American Academy of Social and Political Sciences, Law and Social Inquiry,* and *American Sociological Review.*

Chester L. Britt is a researcher and scholar in criminology and criminal justice. He is an Associate Professor in the Department of Administration of Justice at Arizona State University West in Phoenix. After receiving his Ph.D in sociology from the University of Arizona, Professor Britt taught at the University of Illinois and Penn State University. He serves on the editorial board of *Justice Quarterly* and is co-editor of a forthcoming volume on criminological theory entitled *Control Theories of Crime and Delinquency.* His research articles have appeared in such journals as *Law and Society Review, Justice Quarterly, Journal of Quantitative Criminology,* and *Journal of Research in Crime and Delinquency.*

Introduction: Statistics as a Research Tool

initial hurdles

Do Statisticians Have to Be Experts in Mathematics?

Are Computers Making Statisticians Redundant?

key principles

What Is Our Aim in Choosing a Statistic?

What Basic Principles Apply to Different Types of Statistics?

What Are the Different Uses of Statistics in Research?

THE PURPOSE OF STATISTICAL ANALYSIS is to clarify and not confuse. It is a tool for answering questions. It allows us to take large bodies of information and summarize them with a few simple statements. It lets us come to solid conclusions even when the realities of the research world make it difficult to isolate the problems we seek to study. Without statistics, conducting research about crime and justice would be virtually impossible. Yet, there is perhaps no other subject in their university studies that criminal justice students find so difficult to approach.

A good part of the difficulty lies in the links students make between statistics and math. A course in statistics is often thought to mean long hours spent solving equations. In developing your understanding of statistics in criminal justice research, you will come to better understand the formulas that underlie statistical methods, but the focus will be on concepts and not on computations. There is just no way to develop a good understanding of statistics without doing some work by hand. But in the age of computers, the main purpose of doing computations is to gain a deeper understanding of how statistics work.

Researchers no longer spend long hours calculating statistics. In the 1950s, social scientists would work for months developing results that can now be generated on a computer in a few minutes. Today, you do not need to be a whiz kid in math to carry out a complex statistical analysis. Such analyses can be done with user-friendly computer programs. Why then do you need a course in statistics? Why not just leave it to the computer to provide answers? Why do you still need to learn the basics?

The computer is a powerful tool and has made statistics accessible to a much larger group of criminal justice students and researchers. However, the best researchers still spend many hours on statistical analysis. Now that the computer has freed us from long and tedious calculations, what is left is the most challenging and important part of statistical analysis: identifying the statistical tools that will best serve researchers in interpreting their research for others.

The goal of this text is to provide you with the basic skills you will need to choose statistics for research and interpret them. It is meant for students of criminology and criminal justice. As in other fields, there are specific techniques that are commonly used and specific approaches that have been developed over time by researchers who specialize in this area of study. These are the focus of this text. Not only do we draw our examples from crime and justice issues; we also pay particular attention to the choices that criminal justice researchers make when approaching statistical problems.

Before we begin our study of statistics in criminal justice, it is useful to state some basic principles that underlie the approach taken in this text. They revolve around four basic questions. First, what should our purpose be in choosing a statistic? Second, why do we use statistics to answer research questions? Third, what basic principles apply across very different types of statistics? And finally, what are the different uses for statistics in research?

The Purpose of Statistics Is to Clarify and Not Confuse

It sometimes seems as if researchers use statistics as a kind of secret language. In this sense, statistics provide a way for the initiated to share ideas and concepts without including the rest of us. Of course, it is necessary to use a common language to report research results. This is one reason why it is important for you to take a course in statistics. But the reason we use statistics is to make research results easier—not more difficult—to understand.

For example, if you wanted to provide us with a description of three offenders you had studied, you would not need to search for statistics to summarize your results. The simplest way to describe your sample would be just to tell us about your subjects. You could describe each offender and his or her criminal history without creating any real confusion. But what if you wanted to report on 20 offenders? It would take quite a long time to tell us about each one in some detail, and it is likely that we would have difficulty remembering who was who. It would be even more difficult to describe 100 offenders. With thousands of offenders, it would be just about impossible to take this approach.

This is one example of how statistics can help to simplify and clarify the research process. Statistics allow you to use a few summary statements to provide a comprehensive portrait of a large group of offenders. For example, instead of providing the name of each offender and telling us how many crimes he or she committed, you could present a single statistic that described the average number of crimes committed by the people you studied. You might say that, on average, the people you studied committed two to three crimes in the last year. Thus, although it might be impossible to describe each person you studied, you could, by using a statistic, give your audience an overall picture. Statistics make it possible to summarize information about a large number of subjects with a few simple statements.

Given that statistics should simplify the description of research results, it follows that the researcher should utilize the simplest statistics appropriate for answering the research questions that he or she raises. Nonetheless, it sometimes seems as if researchers go out of their way to identify statistics that few people recognize and even fewer understand. This approach does not help the researcher or his or her audience. There is no benefit in using statistics that are not understood by those interested in your research findings. Using a more complex statistic when a simpler one is appropriate serves no purpose beyond reducing the number of people who will be influenced by your work.

The best presentation of research findings will communicate results in a clear and understandable way. When using complex statistics, the researcher should present them in as straightforward a manner as possible. The mark of good statisticians is not that they can mystify their audiences, but rather that they can communicate even complex results in a way that most people can understand.

Statistics Are Used to Solve Problems

Statistics develop because of a need to deal with a specific type of question or problem. In the example above, you were faced with the dilemma that you could not describe each person in a very large study without creating a good deal of confusion. We suggested that an average might provide a way of using one simple statistic to summarize a characteristic of all the people studied. The average is a statistical solution. It is a tool for solving the problem of how to describe many subjects with a short and simple statement.

As you will see in later chapters, statistics have been developed to deal with many different types of problems that researchers face. Some of these may seem difficult to understand at the outset, and indeed it is natural to be put off by the complexities of some statistics. However, the solutions that statisticians develop are usually based on simple common sense. Contrary to what many people believe, statistics follow a logic that you will find quite easy to follow. Once you learn to trust your common sense, learning statistics will turn out to be surprisingly simple. Indeed, our experience is that students who have good common sense, even if they have very little formal background in this area, tend to become the best criminal justice statisticians.

But in order to be able to use common sense, it is important to approach statistics with as little fear as possible. Fear of statistics is a greater barrier to learning than any of the computations or formulas that we will use. It is difficult to learn anything when you approach it with great foreboding. Statistics is a lot easier than you think. The job of this text is to take you step by step through the principles and ideas that underlie basic statistics for criminal justice researchers. At the beginning, we will spend a good deal of time examining the logic behind statistics and illustrating how and why statisticians choose a particular solution to a particular statistical problem. What you must do at the outset is take a deep breath and give statistics a chance. Once you do, you will find that the solutions statisticians use make very good sense.

Basic Principles Apply Across Statistical Techniques

A few basic principles underlie much of the statistical reasoning you will encounter in this text. Stating them at the outset will help you to see how statistical procedures in later chapters are linked one to another. To understand these principles, you do not need to develop any computations or formulas; rather, you need to think generally about what we are trying to achieve when we develop statistics.

The first is simply that *in developing statistics we seek to reduce the level of error as much as possible.* The purpose of research is to provide answers to research questions. In developing these answers, we want to be as accurate as we can. Clearly, we want to make as few mistakes as possible. The best statistic is one that provides the most accurate statement about your study. Accordingly, a major criterion in choosing which statistic to use—or indeed in defining how a statistic is developed—is the amount of error that a statistic incorporates. In statistics, we try to minimize error whenever possible.

Unfortunately, it is virtually impossible to develop any description without some degree of error. This fact is part of everyday reality. For example, we do not expect that our watches will tell perfect time or that our thermostats will be exactly correct. At the same time, we all know that there are better watches and thermostats and that one of the factors that leads us to define them as "better" is that they provide information with less error. Similarly, although we do not expect our stockbroker to be correct all of the time, we are likely to choose the broker who we believe will make the fewest mistakes.

In choosing a statistic, we also use a second principle to which we will return again and again in this text: *Statistics based on more information are generally preferred over those based on less information.* This principle is common to all forms of intelligence gathering and not just those that we use in research. Good decision making is based on information. The more information available to the decision maker, the better he or she can weigh the different options that are presented. The same goes for statistics. A statistic that is based on more information, all else being equal, will be preferred over one that utilizes less information. There are exceptions to this rule, often resulting from the quality or form of the information or data collected. We will discuss these in detail in the text. But as a rule, the best statistic utilizes the maximum amount of information.

Our third principle relates to a danger that confronts us in using statistics as a tool for describing information. In many studies, there are cases that are very different from all of the others. Indeed, they are so different that they might be termed deviant cases or, as statisticians sometimes call them, "outliers." For example, in a study of criminal careers, there may be one or two offenders who have committed thousands of crimes, whereas the next most active criminal in the sample has committed only a few hundred crimes. Although such cases form a natural part of the research process, they often have very significant implications for your choice of statistics and your presentation of results.

In almost every statistic we will study, outliers present a distinct and troublesome problem. A deviant case can make it look as if your offenders are younger or older than they really are—or less or more criminally active than they really are. Importantly, deviant cases often have the most dramatic effects on more complex statistical procedures. And it is precisely here, where the researcher is often preoccupied with other statistical issues, that deviant cases go unnoticed. But whatever statistic is used, the principle remains the same: *Outliers present a significant problem in choosing and interpreting statistics.*

The final principle is one that is often unstated in statistics, because it is assumed at the outset: *Whatever the method of research, the researcher must strive to systematize the procedures used in data collection and analysis.* As Albert J. Reiss, Jr., a pioneer in criminal justice methodologies, has noted, "systematic" means in part "that observation and recording are done according to explicit procedures which permit replication and that rules are followed which permit the use of scientific inference."[1]

---

[1] A. J. Reiss, Jr., "Systematic Social Observation of Social Phenomenon," in Herbert Costner (ed.), *Sociological Methodology* (San Francisco: Jossey Bass, 1971), pp. 3–33.

While Reiss's comment will become clearer as statistical concepts are defined in coming chapters, his point is simply that you must follow clearly stated procedures and rules in developing and presenting statistical findings.

It is important to approach statistics in a systematic way. You cannot be sloppy or haphazard, at least if the statistic is to provide a good answer to the research question you raise. The choice of a statistic should follow a consistent logic from start to finish. You should not jump from statistic to statistic merely because the outcomes are favorable to the thesis you raise. In learning about statistics, it is also important to go step by step—and to be well organized and prepared. You cannot learn statistics by cramming in the last week of classes. The key to learning statistics is to adopt a systematic process and follow it each week.

Statistical procedures are built on all of the research steps that precede them. If these steps are faulty, then the statistics themselves will be faulty. In later chapters, we often talk about this process in terms of the assumptions of the statistics that we use. We assume that all of the rules of good research have been followed up to the point where we decide on a statistic and calculate it. Statistics cannot be disentangled from the larger research process that comes before them. The numbers that we use are only as good as the data collection techniques that we have employed. Very complex statistics cannot hide bad research methods. A systematic approach is crucial not only to the statistical procedures that you will learn about in this text but to the whole research process.

The Uses of Statistics

In the chapters that follow, we will examine three types of statistics or three ways in which statistics are used in criminal justice. The first is called **descriptive statistics,** because it helps in the summary and description of research findings. The second, **inferential or inductive statistics,** allows us to make inferences or statements about large groups from studies of smaller groups, or samples, drawn from them. Finally, we introduce **multivariate statistics** toward the end of the text. Multivariate statistics, as the name implies, allow us to examine a series of variables at one time.

Descriptive Statistics

We are all familiar in some way with descriptive statistics. We use them often in our daily lives, and they appear routinely in newspapers and on television. Indeed, we use them so often that we sometimes don't think of them as statistics at all. During an election year, everyone is concerned about the percentage support that each candidate gains in the primaries. Students at the beginning of the semester want to know what proportion of their grades will be based on weekly exercises. In deciding whether our salaries are fair, we want to know what the average salary is for other people in similar positions. These are all descriptive statistics. They summarize in one simple statement the characteristics of many people. As discussed above in the example concerning criminal histories, descriptive statistics make it possible for us to summarize or describe large amounts of information.

In the chapters that follow, we will be concerned with two types of descriptive statistics: **measures of central tendency** and **measures of dispersion.** Measures of central tendency are measures of typicality. They tell us in one statement what the average case is like. If we could take only one person as the best example for all of the subjects we studied, who would it be? If we could choose only one level of criminal activity to typify the frequency of offending of all subjects, what level would provide the best snapshot? If we wanted to give our audience a general sense of how much, on average, a group of offenders stole in a year, what amount would provide the best portrait? Percentages, proportions, and means are all examples of measures of central tendency that we commonly use. In the coming chapters, you will learn more about these statistics, as well as more complex measures with which you may not be familiar, such as correlation and regression coefficients.

Having a statistic that describes the average case is very helpful in describing research results. However, we might also want to know how typical this average case is of the subjects in our study. The answer to this question is provided by measures of dispersion. They tell us to what extent the other subjects we studied are similar to the case or statistic we have chosen to represent them. Although we don't commonly use measures of dispersion in our daily lives, we do often ask similar questions without the use of such statistics.

For example, in deciding whether our income is fair, we might want to know not only the average income of others in similar positions, but also the range of incomes that such people have. If the range was very small, we would probably decide that the average provides a fairly good portrait of what we should be making. If the range was very large, we might want to investigate more carefully why some people make so much more or less than the average. The range is a measure of dispersion. It tells us about the spread of scores around our statistic. In the chapters that follow, we will look at other measures of dispersion—for example, the standard deviation and variance, which may be less familiar to you. Without these measures, our presentation of research findings would be incomplete. It is not enough simply to describe the typical case; we must also describe to what degree other cases in our study are different from or similar to it.

Inferential Statistics

Inferential statistics allow us to make statements about a population, or the larger group of people we seek to study, on the basis of a sample drawn from that population. Without this very important and powerful tool, it would be very difficult to conduct research in criminal justice. The reason is simple. When we conduct research, we do so to answer questions about populations. But in reality we seldom are able to collect information on the whole population, so we draw a sample from it. Statistical inference makes it possible for us to infer characteristics from that sample to the population.

Why is it that we draw samples if we are really interested in making statements about populations? In good part it is because gaining information on most populations is impractical and/or too expensive. For example, if we seek to examine the attitudes of U.S. citizens toward criminal justice processing, we are interested in how all citizens feel. However, studying all citizens would be a task of gigantic proportion and would cost billions of dollars. Such surveys are done every few years and are called censuses. The last census in the United States took many years to prepare and implement and cost over $5 billion to complete. If every research study of the American population demanded a census, then we would have very few research projects indeed.

Even when we are interested in much smaller populations in the criminal justice system, examination of the entire population is often beyond the resources of the criminal justice researcher. For example, to study all U.S. prisoners, we would have to study over 1 million people. Even if we wanted to look at only the 90,000 or so women prisoners, it would likely cost millions of dollars to complete a simple study of their attitudes. This is because the most inexpensive data collection can still cost tens of dollars for each subject studied. When you consider that the National Institute of Justice, the primary funder of criminal justice research in the United States, provides a total of about $100 million a year for all research, it is clear that criminal justice research cannot rely on studies of whole populations.

It is easy to understand, then, why we want to draw a sample or subset of the larger population to study, but it is not obvious why we should believe that what we learn from that sample applies to the population from which it is drawn. How do we know, for example, that the attitudes toward criminal justice expressed by a sample of U.S. citizens are similar to the attitudes of all citizens? The sample is a group of people drawn from the population; it is not the population itself. How much can we rely on such estimates? And to what extent can we trust such statistics?

You have probably raised such issues already, in regard to either the surveys that now form so much a part of public life or the studies that you read about in your other college classes. When a news organization conducts a survey of 1,000 people to tell us how all voters will vote in the next election, it is using a sample to make statements about a population. The criminal justice studies you read about also base their conclusions about populations—whether of offenders, criminal justice agents, crime-prone places, or criminal justice events—on samples. Statistical inference provides a method for deciding to what extent you can have faith in such results. It allows you to decide when the outcome observed in a sample can be generalized to the population from which it was drawn. Statistical inference is a very important part of statistics and one we will spend a good deal of time discussing in this text.

Taking into Account Competing Explanations: Multivariate Statistics

Multivariate statistics allow us to solve a different type of problem in research. It is often the case that the issue on which we want to focus is confounded by other factors in our study. Multivariate statistics allow us to isolate one factor while taking into account a host of others. For example, a number of criminal justice studies examine the impact of imprisonment on the future criminal behavior of offenders. In general, they compare offenders who are found guilty in court and sentenced to prison with those who are found guilty but do not receive a prison sanction. Such studies focus on whether the criminal behavior of prisoners, once they are released into the community, is different from that of nonprisoners. Researchers conducting these studies face a very difficult research problem. Prisoners and nonprisoners are often very different types of people, and some of these differences are likely to affect their criminal behavior in the community.

For example, prisoners are more likely than nonprisoners to have been arrested before, since a prior arrest is often an important factor in the judge's decision to incarcerate a convicted offender in the first place. And we know from research about criminal careers that people with a prior history of arrest are much more likely than people without such a history to commit a crime in the future. Accordingly, prisoners are more likely to commit a crime in the future, irrespective of the fact that they have served a prison sentence. This makes it very difficult to assess the impact of imprisonment on future offending. If we discover that prisoners, once released into the community, are more likely than nonprisoners to commit a crime, how can we tell whether this was a result of the experience of imprisonment? It might be due to the simple fact that prisoners are more likely than nonprisoners to commit crimes in the first place. Their more serious arrest histories would predict this result.

The complex task facing the criminal justice researcher is to isolate the specific impact of imprisonment itself from all of the other possible explanations for differences in reoffending between prisoners and nonprisoners. Multivariate analysis provides a statistical solution to this problem. It allows the criminal justice researcher to isolate the impact of one factor—in this case, imprisonment—from those of other factors, such as prior criminal history, that might confound the researcher's conclusions.

Chapter Summary

Statistics seem intimidating because they are associated with complex mathematical formulas and computations. Although some knowledge of math is required, an understanding of the concepts is much more important than an in-depth understanding of the computations. Today's computers, which can perform complex calculations in a matter of seconds or fractions of seconds, have drastically cut the workload of the researcher. They cannot, however, replace the key role a researcher plays in choosing the most appropriate statistical tool for each research problem.

The researcher's aim in using statistics is to communicate findings in a clear and simple form. As a result, the researcher should always choose the simplest statistic appropriate for answering the research question. Statistics offer commonsense solutions to research problems. The following principles apply to all types of statistics: (1) In developing statistics, we seek to reduce the level of error as much as possible. (2) Statistics based on more information are generally preferred over those based on less information. (3) Outliers present a significant problem in choosing and interpreting statistics. (4) The researcher must strive to systematize the procedures used in data collection and analysis.

There are three principal uses of statistics discussed in this book. In **descriptive statistics,** the researcher summarizes large amounts of information in an efficient manner. Two types of descriptive statistics that go hand in hand are **measures of central tendency,** which describe the characteristics of the average case, and **measures of dispersion,** which tell us just how typical this average case is. We use **inferential statistics** to make statements about a population on the basis of a sample drawn from that population. Finally, in **multivariate statistics,** we isolate the impact of one factor from others that may distort our results.

Key Terms

descriptive statistics A broad area of statistics that is concerned with summarizing large amounts of information in an efficient manner. Descriptive statistics are used to describe or represent in summary form the characteristics of a sample or population.

inferential, or inductive, statistics A broad area of statistics that provides the researcher with tools for making statements about populations on the basis of knowledge about samples. Inferential statistics allow the researcher to make inferences regarding populations from information gained in samples.

measures of central tendency Descriptive statistics that allow us to identify the typical case in a sample or population. Measures of central tendency are measures of typicality.

measures of dispersion Descriptive statistics that tell us how tightly clustered or dispersed the cases in a sample or population are. They answer the question "How typical is the typical case?"

multivariate statistics Statistics that examine the relationships among variables while taking into account the possible influences of other confounding factors. Multivariate statistics allow the researcher to isolate the impact of one variable from others that may distort his or her results.

Measurement: The Basic Building Block of Research

MEASUREMENT LIES AT THE HEART of statistics. Indeed, no statistic would be possible without the concept of measurement. Measurement is also an integral part of our everyday lives. We routinely classify and assign values to people and objects without giving much thought to the processes that underlie our decisions and evaluations. In statistics, such classification and ordering of values must be done in a systematic way. There are clear rules for developing different types of measures and defined criteria for deciding which are most appropriate for answering a specific research question.

Although it is natural to focus on the end products of research, it is important for the researcher to remember that measurement forms the first building block of every statistic. Even the most complex statistics, with numbers that are defined to many decimal places, are only as accurate as the measures upon which they are built. Accordingly, the relatively simple rules we discuss in this chapter are crucial for developing solid research findings. A researcher can build a very complex structure of analysis. But if the measures that form the foundation of the research are not appropriate for the analyses that are conducted, the findings cannot be relied upon.

We begin Chapter 2 by examining the basic idea of measurement in science. We then turn to a description of the main types of measures in statistics and the criteria used to distinguish among them. We are particularly concerned with how statisticians rank measurement based on the amount of information that a measure includes. This concept, known as levels of measurement, is very important in choosing which statistical procedures are appropriate in research. Finally, we discuss some basic criteria for defining a good measure.

Science and Measurement: Classification as a First Step in Research

Criminal justice research is a scientific enterprise that seeks to develop knowledge about the nature of crimes, criminals, and the criminal justice system. The development of knowledge can, of course, be carried out in a number of different ways. Criminal justice researchers may, for example, observe the actions of criminal justice agents or speak to offenders. They may examine routine information collected by government or criminal justice agencies or develop new information through analyses of the content of records in the criminal justice system. Knowledge may be developed through historical review or even through examination of archaeological records of legal systems or sanctions of ancient civilizations.

The methods that criminal justice researchers use vary. What they have in common is an underlying philosophy about how knowledge may be gained and what scientific research can tell us. This philosophy, which is predominant in scientific study in the modern world, is usually called positivism.[1] At its core is the idea that science is based on facts and not values. Science cannot make decisions about the way the world should be (although scientific observation may inform such decisions). Rather, it allows us to examine and investigate the realities of the world as we know it. The major tool for defining this reality in science is **measurement**.

Measurement in science begins with the activity of distinguishing groups or phenomena from one another. This process, which is generally termed **classification,** implies that we can place units of scientific study—such as victims, offenders, crimes, or crime places—in clearly defined categories. The classification process leads to the creation of **variables**. A variable is a trait, characteristic, or attribute that can be measured. What differentiates measurement in science from measurement in our everyday lives is that there must be systematic criteria for determining both what each category of a variable represents and the boundaries between categories. We now turn to a discussion of these criteria as they relate to different **levels of measurement**.

Levels of Measurement

Classification forms the first step in measurement. There are a number of different ways we can classify the people, places, or phenomena we wish to study. We may be content to simply distinguish one category from another. But we may also be interested in how those categories relate to one another. Do some represent more serious crime or less serious crime? Can we rank how serious various crimes are in a clear and

---

[1]See D. Black, "The Boundaries of Legal Sociology," in D. Black and M. Mileski (eds.), *The Social Organization of Law* (New York: Seminar Press, 1973), pp. 41–47.

| Figure 2.1 | *Ladder of Measurement* |

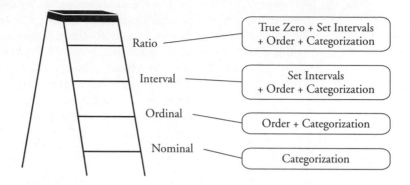

defined order? Is it possible to define exactly how serious one crime is relative to another?

As these types of questions suggest, measurement can be a lot more complex than simply distinguishing one group from another. Recognizing this complexity, statisticians have defined four basic groups of measures, or **scales of measurement,** based on the amount of information that each takes advantage of. The four are generally seen as occupying different positions, or levels, on a ladder of measurement (see Figure 2.1). Following a principle stated in Chapter 1—that statistics based on more information are generally preferred—measures that include more information rank higher on the ladder of measurement.

Nominal Scales

At the bottom of the ladder of measurement are **nominal scales**. Nominal-scale variables simply distinguish one phenomenon from another. Suppose, for example, that you want to measure crime types. In your study, you are most interested in distinguishing between violent crime and other types of crime. To fulfill the requirements of a nominal scale, and thus the minimum requirements of measurement, you need to be able to take all of the crime events in your study and place them in one of two categories: either violent crime or other crime. There can be no overlap. In practice, you might come across many individual events that seem difficult to classify. For example, what would you do with a crime event in which the offender first stole from his victim and then assaulted him? This event includes elements of both violent and property crime. What about the case where the offender did not assault the victim, but merely threatened her? Would you decide to include this in the category of violent crime or other crime?

In measurement, you must make systematic choices that can be applied across events. You cannot decide one way for one event and another way for another. In the situation described above, you might conclude that the major issue in your study was the presence of violence. Thus, all cases with any violent events would be placed in the violent category. Similarly, you might conclude that violence had to include physical victimization. Whatever your choice, to meet the requirements of measurement you must define clearly where all events in your study are to be placed.

In criminology and criminal justice, we often make use of nominal-scale variables. Many of these reflect simple dichotomies, like the distinction between violent and other crime. For example, criminologists often seek to examine differences between men and women in their involvement in criminality or treatment in the criminal justice system. It is common as well to distinguish between those who are sentenced to prison and those who are not or those who commit more than one crime ("recidivists") and those who are only one-shot offenders.

It is often necessary to distinguish among multiple categories of a nominal-level variable. For example, if you wanted to describe legal representation in court cases, you would provide a very simplistic picture if you simply distinguished between those who had some type of legal representation and those who did not. Some of the offenders would be likely to have private attorneys and others court-appointed legal representation. Still others might gain help from a legal aid organization or a public defender. In order to provide a full portrait of legal representation, you would likely want to create a nominal-scale variable with five distinct categories: No attorney, Legal aid, Court appointed, Public defender, and Private attorney. Table 2.1 presents a number of examples of nominal-level scales commonly used in criminal justice.

Nominal-scale measures can include any number of different categories. The Uniform Crime Reporting system, which keeps track of arrests in the United States, includes some 29 categories of crime. These

Table 2.1   Nominal-Scale Variables Commonly Found in Criminal Justice Research

VARIABLE	COMMON CATEGORIES
Gender	Male, Female
Race-Ethnicity	Non-Hispanic Black, Non-Hispanic White, Hispanic (any race)
Marital Status	Single, Married, Separated, Divorced, Widowed
Pretrial Release Status	Detained, Released
Type of Case Disposition	Dismissed, Acquitted, Diverted, Convicted
Method of Conviction	Negotiated guilty plea, Nonnegotiated guilty plea, Bench trial, Jury trial
Type of Punishment	Incarceration, Nonincarceration

range from violent crimes, such as murder or robbery, to vagrancy and vandalism. Although there is no statistical difficulty with defining many categories, the more categories you include, the more confusing the description of the results is likely to be. If you are trying to provide a sense of the distribution of crime in your study, it is very difficult to practically describe 20 or 30 different crime categories. Keeping in mind that the purpose of statistics is to clarify and simplify, you should try to use the smallest number of categories that will accurately describe the research problem you are examining.

At the same time, do not confuse collection of **data** with presentation of your findings. You do not lose anything by collecting information in the most detailed way that you can. If you collect information with a large number of categories, you can always collapse a group of categories into one. For example, if you collect information on arrest events utilizing the very detailed categories of the criminal law, you can always combine them later into more general categories. But if you collect information in more general categories (for example, just violent crime and property crime), you cannot identify specific crimes such as robbery or car theft without returning to the original source of your information.

Though nominal-scale variables are commonly used in criminology and criminal justice, they provide us with very limited knowledge about the phenomenon we are studying. As you will see in later chapters, they also limit the types of statistical analyses that the researcher can employ. In the hierarchy of measurement, nominal-scale variables form the lowest step in the ladder. One step above are **ordinal scales**.

Ordinal Scales

What distinguishes an ordinal from a nominal scale is the fact that we assign a clear order to the categories included. Now not only can we distinguish between one category and another; we also can place these categories on a continuum. This is a very important new piece of information; it allows us to rank events and not just categorize them. In the case of crime, we might decide to rank in order of seriousness. In measuring crime in this way, we would not only distinguish among categories, such as violent, property, and victimless crimes; we might also argue that violent crimes are more serious than property crimes and that victimless crimes are less serious than both violent and property crimes. We need not make such decisions arbitrarily. We could rank crimes by the amount of damage done or the ways in which the general population rates or evaluates different types of crime.

Ordinal-scale variables are also commonly used in criminal justice and criminology. Indeed, many important criminal justice concepts are measured in this way. For example, in a well-known London survey of vic-

Table 2.2	Ordinal Scale Variables Commonly Found in Criminal Justice Research

VARIABLE	COMMON CATEGORIES
Level of Education	Less than high school, Some high school, High school graduation, Some college or trade school, College graduate, Graduate/ professional school
Severity of Injury in an Assault	None, Minor—no medical attention, Minor—medical attention required, Major—medical attention required with no hospitalization, Major—medical attention required with hospitalization
Attitude and Opinion Survey Questions	Strongly disagree, Disagree, No opinion, Agree, Strongly agree; Very high, High, Moderate, Low, Very low
Bail-Release Decision	Released on own recognizance, Released on bail, Detained— unable to post bail, Denied release
Type of Punishment	Probation/community service, Jail incarceration, Prison incarceration, Death sentence

timization, fear of crime was measured using a simple four-level ordinal scale. Researchers asked respondents: "Are you personally concerned about crime in London as a whole? Would you say you are (1) very concerned, (2) quite concerned, (3) a little concerned, or (4) not concerned at all?"[2]

Ranking crime by seriousness and measuring people's fear of crime are only two examples of the use of ordinal scales in criminal justice research. We could also draw examples regarding severity of court sentences, damage to victims, complexity of crime, or seriousness of prior records of offenders, as illustrated in Table 2.2. What all of these variables have in common is that they classify events and order them along a continuum. What is missing is a precise statement about how various categories differ one from another.

Interval and Ratio Scales

Interval scales not only classify and order people or events; they also define the exact differences between them. An interval scale requires that the intervals measured be equal for all of the categories of the scale examined. Thus, an interval-scale measure of prior record would not simply rank prior record by seriousness; it would allow us to say how much more serious one offender's record was than another's in a standard unit of measurement—for example, number of arrests, convictions, or prison stays.

---

[2]See R. Sparks, H. Genn, and D. Dodd, *Surveying Victims: A Study of the Measurement of Criminal Victimization* (New York: Wiley, 1977).

Most criminal justice variables that meet the criteria of an interval scale also meet the criteria of a **ratio scale**. A ratio scale has all of the characteristics of an interval scale but also requires that there be a non-arbitrary, or true, zero value. This means simply that zero represents the absence of the trait under study. To understand how interval scales differ from ordinal scales and from ratio scales, it is useful to examine a concrete example. We commonly measure prior offending in terms of the number of arrests on an offender's criminal history record. If we compare an offender who has 20 arrests with one who has only 5 arrests, we know that the former has 15 more arrests than the latter. We have an important piece of information that we would not have gained with an ordinal scale. Now, not only can we say that the prior record of one offender is more serious than that of another, but we can specify exactly how many more arrests the offender has. This variable thus meets the requirements of an interval scale. But it also meets the additional requirement of a ratio scale that there be a true zero value, since we can state that someone with 20 arrests has 4 times as many arrests as someone with 5 arrests. If the zero value were arbitrary, we could not make this statement.

This fact is best illustrated with an example. Suppose we alter our measure of prior record to focus on the degree to which offenders exceed a specific threshold of prior offending. Let's say that our threshold is 4 prior arrests and we are interested only in offenders who have 4 or more prior arrests. An offender with 5 arrests would gain a score of 1 on this new measure, and an offender with 20 arrests would have a score of 16. An offender with 4 arrests would have a score of 0. This variable meets the criteria of an interval scale because we can distinguish scores, rank them, and define the exact difference between them. A score of 16 represents a more serious prior criminal record than a score of 1. In turn, an offender with a score of 16 has 15 more arrests than an offender with a score of 1. However, we cannot say that the offender with a score of 16 on this measure had 16 times as many prior arrests as the offender with a score of 1. This is because the scale has an arbitrary zero point. Zero represents not the absence of a prior record, but the fact that the offender has 4 prior arrests. Thus, the scale is an interval scale but not a ratio scale.

Nearly all the statistics that we use in criminal justice (and all those that we describe in this text) are also appropriate for interval scales if they are appropriate for ratio scales. For this reason, most statistics texts do not differentiate between the scales in practice, even if they identify how they differ in theory. We follow the same approach. For the rest of the chapter and indeed the rest of this text, we will concentrate on the differences among nominal, ordinal, and *at least* interval scales.

Criminal justice researchers use interval scales to present findings about criminal justice agency resources, criminal sentences, and a whole

| Table 2.3 | Variables Commonly Found in Criminal Justice Research That Are Measured on at Least Interval Scales |

VARIABLE	COMMON CATEGORIES
Age	Years
Education	Years
Income or Salary	Dollars, etc.
Number of Crimes in a City/County State Nation	Count
Crime Rates for a City/County/State/Nation	Count of crimes, adjusted for the size of the population
Self-Reported Delinquent Acts	Count

host of other issues related to crimes and criminals. For example, we can measure the amount spent by criminal justice agencies to pay the salaries of police officers or to pay for the health care costs of prison inmates. We can measure the financial costs of different types of crime by measuring the amount stolen by offenders or the amount of time lost from work by violent crime victims. We can measure the number of years of prison served or sentenced or the age at which offenders were first arrested. Table 2.3 provides examples of criminal justice variables that meet the requirements of at least an interval level of measurement.

Now that we have defined each step in the ladder of measurement, we can summarize. As is illustrated in Table 2.4, as you move up the ladder of measurement, the amount of information that is gained increases. At the lowest level, you have only categorization. At the next level, you add knowledge about the order of the categories included. With interval scales, you not only classify and order your measure but also define how much categories differ one from another. A ratio scale requires all of these characteristics as well as a non-arbitrary, or true, zero value.

| Table 2.4 | Summary of the Information Required for Each Level of Measurement |

LEVEL OF MEASUREMENT	CATEGOR- IZATION	ORDER + CATEGOR- IZATION	SET INTERVALS + ORDER + CATEGORIZATION	TRUE ZERO + SET INTERVALS + ORDER + CATEGORIZATION
Ratio	X	X	X	X
Interval	X	X	X	
Ordinal	X	X		
Nominal	X			

Relating Interval, Ordinal, and Nominal Scales: The Importance of Collecting Data at the Highest Level Possible

One important lesson we can draw from the ladder of measurement is that you should measure variables in a study at the highest level of measurement your data allow. This is because each higher level of measurement requires additional information. And if you fail to collect that information at the outset, you may not be able to add it at the end of your study. In general, variables measured lower on the ladder of measurement cannot be transformed easily into measures higher on the ladder. Conversely, variables measured higher on the ladder of measurement can be transformed easily into measures lower on the ladder.

Take, for example, the measurement of victimization. If you decided to simply compare the types of victimization involved in a crime event, you would measure victimization using a nominal scale. You might choose the following categories: events involving loss of money or property, events including physical harm, a combination of such events, and all other events. But let us assume, for a moment, that at some time after you collected your data, a colleague suggests that it is important to distinguish not only the type of event but also the seriousness of crimes within each type. In this case, you would want to distinguish not only whether a crime included monetary loss or violence but also the seriousness of each loss. However, because your variable is measured on a nominal scale, it does not include information on the seriousness of loss. Accordingly, from the information available to you, you cannot create an ordinal-level measure of how much money was stolen or how serious the physical harm was.

Similarly, if you had begun with information only on the order of crime seriousness, you could not transform that variable into one that defined the exact differences between categories you examined. Let's say, for example, that you received data from the police that ranked monetary victimization for each crime into four ordinally scaled categories: no monetary harm, minor monetary harm (less than $500), moderate monetary harm ($501–10,000), and serious monetary harm ($10,001 and above). If you decide that it is important to know not just the general order of monetary harm but also the exact differences in harm between crimes, these data are insufficient. Such information would be available only if you had received data about harm at an interval level of measurement. In this case, the police would provide information not on which of the four categories of harm a crime belonged to, but rather on the exact amount of harm in dollars caused by each crime.

While you cannot move up the ladder of measurement, you can move down it. Thus, for example, if you have information collected at an interval level, you can easily transform that information into an ordinal-scale measure. In the case of victimization, if you have information on the exact amount of harm caused by a crime in dollars, you could at any point decide to group crimes into levels of seriousness. You would simply define the levels and then place each crime in the appropriate level. For example, if you defined crimes involving harm between $501 and $10,000 as being of moderate victimization, you would take all of the crimes that included this degree of victimization and redefine them as falling in this moderate category. Similarly, you could transform this measure into a nominal scale just by distinguishing between those crimes that included monetary harm and those that did not.

Beyond illustrating the connections among different levels of measurement, our discussion here emphasizes a very important rule of thumb for research. You should always collect information at the highest level of measurement possible. You can always decide later to collapse such measures into lower-level scales. However, if you begin by collecting information lower on the ladder of measurement, you will not be able to decide later to use scales at a higher level.

What Is a Good Measure?

In analysis and reporting of research results, measures that are of a higher scale are usually preferred over measures that are of a lower scale. Higher-level measures are considered better measures, based on the principle that they take into account more information. Nonetheless, this is not the only criterion we use in deciding what is a good variable in research. The researcher must raise two additional concerns. First, does the variable reflect the phenomenon to be described? Second, will the variable yield results that can be trusted?

The first question involves what those who study research methods call **validity**. Validity addresses the question of whether the variable used actually reflects the concept or theory you seek to examine. Thus, for example, collecting information on age in a sample is not a valid way of measuring criminal history. Age, although related to criminal history, is not a measure of criminal history. Similarly, work history may be related to criminality, but it does not make a valid measure of criminality. But even if we restrict ourselves to variables that directly reflect criminal history, there are often problems of validity to address.

Let's say that you wanted to describe the number of crimes that offenders committed over a one-year period. One option you might have is to examine their criminal history as it is recorded on the Federal Bureau of Investigation's (FBI) criminal history record, or rap sheet. The rap sheet includes information on arrests, convictions, and incarcerations. Although each of these variables tells us something about a person's criminal history, they are not all equally valid in terms of answering the research question we have proposed.

The most valid measure of frequency of offending is the one that most directly assesses how many crimes an individual has committed. Associated with each of the three variables included on the rap sheet is some degree of threat to validity. This means that each can be criticized because it does not quite reflect the concept we wish to study. Incarceration, for example, is more a measure of seriousness of crime than frequency of offending. This is because judges may impose a number of different types of sanctions, and they are more likely to impose a prison sentence for more serious crimes. Many crimes that result in a conviction lead not to incarceration but rather to probation, fines, or community service. Thus, if we use incarceration to measure frequency of offending, we are likely to miss many crime events in an offender's criminal record. Accordingly, incarceration provides a biased picture of the number of offenses committed by an offender. It is not a highly valid measure of this concept.

Using this logic, criminologists have generally assumed that arrest is the most valid measure of frequency of offending that can be gained from official data sources, such as the FBI rap sheet. Arrests are much closer in occurrence to the actual behavior we seek to study and are not filtered by the negotiations found at later stages of the legal process. While criminologists have assumed that arrests reflect criminal behavior more accurately than convictions or incarceration, some legal scholars contend that arrests are a less valid measure of criminality precisely because they come before the court reaches a conclusion regarding the innocence or guilt of a defendant. They contend that someone has not committed a crime until the legal system defines an act as such.

Self-report surveys are generally considered to provide the most valid measure of frequency of offending. This is because an individual can be asked directly how many crimes he or she has committed. But self-report studies are often criticized in terms of another concern in measurement, which is termed reliability.

Reliability addresses the question of whether a measure gains information in a consistent manner. Will you get the same result if you repeat measurement of the same case or person? If different people have similar characteristics, will your measure reflect that similarity? Returning to the above example of criminal history, we would ask not whether the measure reflects the concept of frequency of offending, but whether measurement of the concept is reliable across different subjects.

Self-reports, which allow us to ask valid questions about the number of crimes that a person has committed, have been challenged on the basis of their reliability. One problem is that people may lie about their criminal histories. Crime is a sensitive issue, and no matter what efforts the researcher makes to assure subjects of confidentiality, people may be hesitant to talk about crimes in their past. Accordingly, depending on the degree of hesitancy of subjects, a researcher might gain different answers, irrespective of a person's actual criminal history. But even if a person is willing to provide accurate responses to such questions, he or she may not be able to. Some people have better memories than others, and the reliability of this measure depends in part on a person's ability to recall events generally. Such issues of reliability have begun to be addressed directly by criminologists, who are trying to increase the reliability of self-report methods by improving interview techniques and protocols.

Returning to the FBI rap sheets, we can also assess their reliability. In general, not only is arrest assumed to be the most valid of official measures; it is also the measure most reliably recorded on the FBI rap sheets. This is the case in good part because the rap sheets are built around fingerprint records, which police agencies have come to routinely send to the FBI. This helps the police agencies as well, because they often use this information to check the identities of arrestees and to assess their criminal histories. Other types of agencies are less consistent in their transfer of information to the FBI, and as a result convictions and incarcerations are less reliably recorded.

The issues raised in connection with the validity and reliability of criminal history information are good examples of the kinds of problems you will encounter in assessing measures in criminal justice. You should keep in mind that no variable is perfect. Some threat to validity is likely to be encountered, no matter how careful you are. Some degree of unreliability is almost always present in measurement. Your task is to develop or choose the best measure you can. The best measure is the one that most closely reflects the concept you wish to study and assesses it in a consistent and reliable way across subjects or events.

Chapter Summary

In science, we use **measurement** to make accurate observations. All measurement must begin with a **classification** process—a process that in science is carried out according to systematic criteria. This process implies that we can place units of scientific study in clearly defined categories. The end result of classification is the development of **variables.**

There are four **scales of measurement**: nominal, ordinal, interval, and ratio. With a **nominal scale,** information is organized by simple classification. The aim is merely to distinguish between different phenomena. There can be no overlap between categories nor can there be cases that do not fit any one category. There is no theoretical limit to the number of nominal categories possible. With an **ordinal scale,** not only is information categorized, but these categories are then placed in order of magnitude. An **interval scale** is one that, in addition to permitting the processes of categorization and ordering, also defines the exact difference between objects, characteristics, or events. A **ratio scale** is an interval scale for which a non-arbitrary, or true, zero value can be identified.

Data collected at a higher level of measurement may subsequently be reduced to a lower level, but data collected at a lower level may not be transformed to a higher one. For this reason, it is always advisable to collect data at the highest level of measurement possible.

There are three separate factors that affect the quality of a measure. The researcher should strive for a measure that has (1) a high scale of measurement (one that uses the most information); (2) a high level of **validity** (one that provides an accurate reflection of the concept being studied); and (3) a high level of **reliability** (one that provides consistent results across subjects or units of study).

Key Terms

classification The process whereby data are organized into categories or groups.

data Information used to answer a research question.

interval scale A scale of measurement that uses a common and standard unit and enables the researcher to calculate exact differences between scores, in addition to categorizing and ordering data.

levels of measurement Types of measurement that make use of progressively larger amounts of information.

measurement The assignment of numerical values to objects, characteristics, or events in a systematic manner.

nominal scale A scale of measurement that assigns each piece of information to an appropriate category without suggesting any order for the categories created.

ordinal scale A scale of measurement that categorizes information and assigns it an order of magnitude without using a standard scale of equal intervals.

ratio scale A scale of measurement identical to an interval scale in every respect except that, in addition, a value of zero on the scale represents the absence of the phenomenon.

reliability The extent to which a measure provides consistent results across subjects or units of study.

scale of measurement Type of categorization used to arrange or assign values to data.

validity The extent to which a variable accurately reflects the concept being measured.

variable A trait, characteristic, or attribute of a person/object/event that can be measured at least at the nominal-scale level.

Exercises

2.1 For each of the following examples of criminal justice studies, state whether the scale of measurement used is nominal, ordinal, or at least interval (i.e., interval or ratio). Explain your choice.

a. In a door-to-door survey, residents of a neighborhood are asked how many times over the past year they (or anyone in their household) have been the victims of any type of crime.

b. Parole-board members rate inmate behavior on a scale with values ranging from 1 to 10; a score of 1 represents exemplary behavior.

c. One hundred college students are asked whether they have ever been arrested.

d. A researcher checks prison records to determine the racial background of prisoners assigned to a particular cell block.

e. In a telephone survey, members of the public are asked which of the following phrases best matches how they feel about the performance of their local police force: totally dissatisfied, dissatisfied, indifferent, satisfied, or very satisfied.

f. A criminologist measures the diameters (in centimeters) of the skulls of inmates who have died in prison, in an attempt to develop a biological theory of the causes of criminality.

g. Secretaries at a top legal firm are asked the following question: "Over the past year, have you been the victim of sexual harassment—and if so, how many times?" Answers are categorized as follows: never, once, two or three times, more than three times, or refused to answer.

2.2 You have been given access to a group of 12 jurors, with a mandate from your senior researcher to "go and find out about their prior jury experience." Under each of the following three sets of restrictions, devise a question to ask the jurors about the number of experiences they have had with previous juries.

a. The information may be recorded *only* on a nominal scale of measurement.

b. The information may be recorded on an ordinal scale but not on any higher scale of measurement.

c. The information may be recorded on an interval scale.

Your senior researcher subsequently informs you that she wishes to know the answers to the following five questions:

—How many of the jurors have served on a jury before?

—Who is the juror with the most prior experience?

—What is the sum total of previous jury experience?

—Is there anyone on the jury who has served more than three times?

—What is the average amount of prior jury experience for this group?

d. If you had collected data at the nominal level, which (if any) of the above questions would you be in a position to answer?

e. If you had collected data at the ordinal level, which (if any) of the above questions would you be in a position to answer?

f. If you had collected data at the interval level, which (if any) of the above questions would you be in a position to answer?

2.3 You have been asked to measure the public's level of support for using the death penalty. Devise questions to gauge each of the following:

a. Overall support for using the death penalty.

b. Support for using the death penalty if there are other punishment options.

c. Support for using the death penalty if the chances of an innocent person being executed are
    i. 1 in 1,000.
    ii. 1 in 100.
    iii. 1 in 10.

2.4 You are investigating the effects of a defendant's prior record on various punishment decisions made by the court. One variable that you have access to in local court records is the total number of prior felony arrests for each defendant.

a. What kinds of questions would you be able to answer with prior record measured in this way?

b. Explain how you would recode this information on a nominal scale of measurement. What kinds of questions would you be able to answer with prior record measured in this way?

c. Explain how you would recode this information on an ordinal scale of measurement. What kinds of questions would you be able to answer with prior record measured in this way?

2.5   Because the Ministry of Transport (MOT) is concerned about the num-
      ber of road accidents caused by motorists driving too close together, it
      has, on an experimental 2-km stretch of road, painted "chevrons"
      (lane markings) every few meters in each lane. By the roadside it has
      erected a sign that reads: "KEEP YOUR DISTANCE: STAY AT LEAST 3
      CHEVRONS FROM THE CAR IN FRONT!" The MOT has asked you to
      measure the extent to which this instruction is being followed. There
      are a number of possible measures at your disposal. Assess the relia-
      bility and validity of each approach suggested below. Which is the
      best measure?

      a. Stand on a bridge over the experimental stretch of road and count
         how many of the cars passing below do not keep the required
         distance.

      b. Compare police figures on how many accidents were recorded on
         that stretch of road over the periods before and after it was painted.

      c. Study the film from a police camera situated 5 km farther down the
         same stretch of road (after the end of the experimental stretch) and
         count how many cars do not keep a safe distance.

2.6   The police are planning to introduce a pilot "community relations
      strategy" in a particular neighborhood and want you to evaluate
      whether it has an effect on the willingness of citizens to report crimes
      to the police. There are a number of possible measures at your dis-
      posal. Assess the reliability and validity of each approach suggested
      below. Which is the best measure?

      a. Telephone every household and ask respondents to measure, on a
         scale of 1 to 10, how willing they are to report particular types of
         crime to the police. Repeat the experiment after the scheme has
         been in operation six months.

      b. Compare a list of offenses reported by members of the neighbor-
         hood in the six months before introduction of the scheme with a
         similar list for the six months after introduction of the scheme. (It is
         standard procedure for the police to record the details of the com-
         plainant every time a crime is reported to them.)

2.7   You are comparing the psychological condition of three inmates serv-
      ing out long terms in different high-security prisons, and you are in-
      terested in the amount of contact each one has with the outside
      world. You wish to determine how many letters each one has sent
      over the past 12 months. No official records of this exist. There are a
      number of possible measures at your disposal. Assess the reliability
      and validity of each approach suggested below. Which is the best
      measure?

      a. Ask each prisoner how many letters he or she sent over the past
         year.

b. Check the rules in each of the prisons to see how many letters high security prisoners are allowed to send each year.

c. Check the records of the prison postal offices to see how many times each prisoner bought a stamp over the past year.

2.8   The government is interested in the link between employment and criminal behavior for persons released from prison. In a study designed to test for an effect of employment, a group of people released from prison are randomly assigned to a job training program, where they will receive counseling, training, and assistance with job placement. The other offenders released from prison will not receive any special assistance. There are a number of possible measures at your disposal. Assess the reliability and validity of each approach suggested below. Which is the best measure?

a. Eighteen months after their release from prison, interview all the offenders participating in the study and ask about their criminal activity to determine how many have committed criminal acts.

b. Look at prison records to determine how many offenders were returned to prison within 18 months of release.

c. Look at arrest records to determine how many offenders were arrested for a new crime within 18 months of release.

2.9   In a recent issue of a criminology or criminal justice journal, locate a research article on a topic of interest to you. In this article, there should be a section that describes the data. A well-written article will describe how the variables were measured.

a. Make a list of the variables included in the article and how each was measured.

b. What is the level of measurement for each variable—nominal, ordinal, or at least interval? Explain why.

c. Consider the main variable of interest in the article. Assess its reliability and validity.

Computer Exercises

There are a number of statistical software packages available for data analysis. Most spreadsheet programs will also perform statistical analyses of the kind described in this text. The exercises included in this text focus on the use of the software program SPSS, which at the time of this writing was at version 10.1. There are many excellent reference books on the use of SPSS for statistical data analysis, and our intent here is not to repeat what is said in those books. Rather, our goal with the computer exercises is to illustrate some of the power available to you in packages such as SPSS. In real-world situations where you are performing some type of statistical analysis, you will rarely work through a problem by hand, especially if the number of observations is large.

Several SPSS data files are available at the following web address: http://cj.wadsworth.com/weisburd_datafiles. The data file we will use first represents a subset of the data from the National Youth Survey, Wave 1. The sample of 1,725 youth is representative of persons aged 11 to 17 years in 1976, when the first wave of data was collected. While these data are several years old, researchers continue to publish reports based on new findings and interpretations of these data. One of the apparent strengths of this study was its design; the youth were interviewed annually for five years from 1976 to 1980 and then were interviewed again in 1983 and 1987. The data file on our web site was constructed from the full data source available at the Inter-University Consortium of Political and Social Research, which is a national data archive. Data from studies funded by the National Institute of Justice (NIJ) are freely available to anyone with an Internet connection; go to http://www.icpsr.umich.edu/NACJD. All seven waves of data from the National Youth Survey are available, for example.

To begin our exploration of SPSS, we will focus here on some of the data management features available in SPSS version 10. After starting the SPSS program on your computer, you will need to open the National Youth Survey data file from the web site (***nys_1.sav***).

After you start SPSS, the data should appear in a window that looks much like a spreadsheet. Each column represents a different variable, while each row represents a different observation (individual, here). If you scroll down to the end of the data file, you should see that there are 1,725 lines of data.

There are three direct ways to learn about the variables included in this data file. First, notice the lower two tabs. One (which should be in front) is labeled "Data View," and the other is labeled "Variable View." The data view tab presents us with the spreadsheet of values for each observation and variable. If you click on the tab labeled "Variable View," you should now see another spreadsheet, in which variable names are listed in the first column and the other columns contain additional information about each variable. For example, the first column provides the name of the variable (limited to eight characters and/or numbers in SPSS), another column provides a label for the variable (allowing us to add a more informative description of our variable), and an additional column provides value labels. It is from this column that we will be able to learn more about each variable. Click on the cell in this column for the sex variable, and you should see a small gray box appear in the cell. Now click on this small gray box, and you will be presented with a new window that lists possible values for sex and the corresponding labels. Here, we see that males have been coded as "1" and females as "2." If you click on "OK" or "Cancel," the window disappears. You can then perform this same operation for every other variable.

A second way of obtaining information about the variables in an SPSS data file involves using the "Variables" command. To execute this command, click on "Utilities" on the menu bar; then click on "Variables." What you should see is a list of variables on the left and another window on the right that presents information about the highlighted variable. If you click on the sex variable, you should see information on its coding and values in the window on the right. This command is particularly useful if you are working with an SPSS data file and simply need a reminder of how the variables are coded and what categories or values are included. This feature is useful if you are working with a data set and need to know what a particular variable refers to or how it is measured in order to continue working.

A third way of obtaining information about the variables in an SPSS data file involves the "File Info" command. Again, click on "Utilities" on the menu bar; then click on "File Info." This command generates text for the output window in SPSS. This output contains all the information SPSS has on every variable in a data file. Executing this command is equivalent to executing the "Variables" command for every variable in the data set and saving that information in another file. Be aware that using this command on a data file with many variables will produce a very large output file. This command is most useful when you are first working with an SPSS data set that someone else has conveniently set up for you and you need to verify the contents of the data set and the nature of the variables included in the data set.

Using one of the three ways listed above, work through the variables included in this data file:

1. Note the level of measurement for each variable and explain why it is what it is. (*Do not rely on the level of measurement information given in the SPSS data file.*)

2. Note the levels of reliability and validity for each variable and explain why they are what they are.

chapter three

Representing and Displaying Data

THE GRAPHICAL DISPLAY OF DATA is an important tool for presenting statistical results in such a way that the key features or characteristics of an analysis are highlighted. There are many different ways the same data might be displayed. Indeed, many books have been written that focus entirely on graphical presentation of data. In this chapter, we introduce some common ways of representing data in graphical form, along with suggestions for effectively presenting information in an accurate way. We begin by discussing the most basic way of summarizing—and then graphing—data: frequency distributions and histograms. Building on the discussion of histograms, we move on to more general bar charts, noting the variety of information that can be presented in bar and pie charts. Finally, we examine how graphs can be used to represent a series of observations over time.

What Are Frequency Distributions and Histograms?

When we array scores according to their value and **frequency,** we construct what is called a **frequency distribution.** Let's take the following data on previous arrests of 100 known offenders as an example:

14	0	34	8	7	22	12	12	2	8
6	1	8	1	18	8	1	10	10	2
12	26	8	7	9	9	3	2	7	16
8	65	8	2	4	2	4	0	7	2
1	2	11	2	1	1	5	7	4	10
11	3	41	15	1	23	10	5	2	10
20	0	7	6	9	0	3	1	15	5
27	8	26	8	1	1	11	2	4	4
8	41	29	18	8	5	2	10	1	0
5	36	3	4	9	5	10	8	0	7

We first group all of the cases with the same value together. Accordingly, we group together the cases with no prior arrests, one prior arrest, two prior arrests, and so forth, until we have covered all of the potential scores in the distribution. Then we arrange these scores in order of magnitude, as is done in Table 3.1. Looking at the data in this way allows us to get a sense of the nature of the distribution of scores.

In practice, creating a frequency distribution is usually the first step a researcher takes in analyzing the results of a study. Looking at the distribution of scores not only provides a first glance at the results of a study; it also allows the researcher to see whether there are scores that do not make sense. For example, coding errors in the data set may have given rise to impossible scores. In our example, a result of thousands of arrests would be very unlikely and would thus lead the researcher to take another look at that particular case.

Constructing frequency distributions by hand can be very time and labor intensive. Researchers today seldom construct frequency distributions by hand. This task can be done simply and easily with packaged statistical software, such as SPSS.

Table 3.1	Frequency Distribution of Prior Arrests for 100 Known Offenders

VALUE	FREQUENCY
0	6
1	11
2	11
3	4
4	6
5	6
6	2
7	7
8	12
9	4
10	7
11	3
12	3
14	1
15	2
16	1
18	2
20	1
22	1
23	1
26	2
27	1
29	1
34	1
36	1
41	2
65	1
Total	100

If you decide to present a frequency distribution of the results of a study, you must choose what particular format to use. For example, the distribution of prior arrests could simply be presented as in Table 3.1. Or the same information could be presented graphically in what is called a **histogram.** To make a histogram, we take the scores and values from a frequency distribution and represent them in pictorial form. In this case, we use a bar to represent each value in the frequency distribution. The *x*-axis (the horizontal axis) of the histogram represents the values of the variable we are analyzing—here, the number of arrests. The *y*-axis (the vertical axis) captures the height of the bars and indicates the number of scores—the frequency—found in each category. A histogram of the data on prior arrests is provided in Figure 3.1. The information presented in the histogram is identical to the information presented in the frequency distribution in Table 3.1, but the histogram conveys to the reader an immediate sense of the range of values, the location of clusters of cases, and the overall shape of the distribution—information that is not as easily obtainable from a frequency distribution.

It is important to note that the *x*-axis in Figure 3.1 correctly represents the full range of values for the variable. In particular, note that there is a large gap in the distribution from 41 arrests to 65 arrests. Depending on

Figure 3.1   *Histogram of Frequency Distribution*

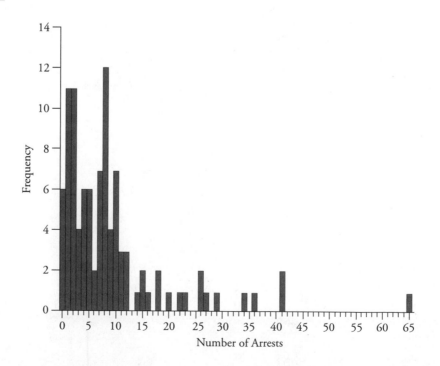

the software used to generate a histogram, this information may or may not be represented. Excluding this information and placing all the bars adjacent to each other essentially means ignoring the level of measurement of the variable and treating the variable as if it were nominal or ordinal. Why would you want to include information about those values that have an observed frequency of zero? If you look at Figure 3.1, you can see that there are relatively few observations for increasingly greater numbers of arrests and that the distance between categories starts to increase. If the bars were adjacent to each other and correctly labeled, it would still be possible for the reader to discern the spread of observations. But when the values with an observed frequency of zero are portrayed as well, it is often easier to interpret the histogram.

Before we get into working with more complex graphs, it is worth noting that frequency distributions of interval-level variables are often dispersed across a large number of values. Thus, in presenting a frequency distribution or histogram, it is often necessary to group scores together into categories that represent a range of values. For example, if we were looking at the incomes of a random sample of thousands of people, we would likely not want to present the simple distribution of income scores. If we did, we might end up with thousands of scores, most of which would include only one or two cases. It would take pages and pages to illustrate these data in the form of either a frequency distribution or a histogram. The solution to this problem is to "group" data together in larger categories—for example, by thousands or tens of thousands of dollars in the case of incomes. Although there is no hard-and-fast rule about how to create such larger groupings, it should be done in a way that fairly represents the raw distribution of scores. Do not create such a small group of categories that important variation in your data is hidden.

A common source of confusion for students of statistics is the fact that statisticians often represent distributions as "curves" rather than histograms or frequency distributions. For example, Figure 3.2 uses a curve to represent the 2001 SAT math scores of over 1.2 million college-bound test takers.[1] What is the relationship between a frequency distribution or histogram and a distribution represented by a curve, such as the one in Figure 3.2?

When we represent a distribution as a curve, it is usually a distribution with a very large number of cases, such as that of SAT math scores of 2001 college-bound seniors. We can represent these distributions as curves because, with a true interval-scale measure, as the number of cases becomes very large, we can construct a histogram in such a way

[1]The College Board, *2001 College-Bound Seniors: A Profile of SAT Program Test Takers,* accessed at http://www.collegeboard.com/sat/cbsenior/yr2001/pdf/NATL.pdf.

| Figure 3.2 | *Smooth Curve Representation of a Histogram:*
SAT Math Scores of 2001 College-Bound Seniors |

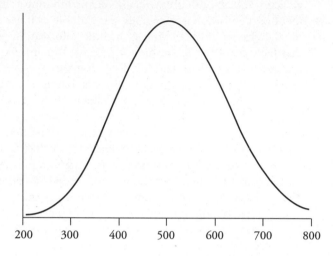

that it begins to approximate a curve. We do this by making the intervals of scores smaller and smaller.

This process is illustrated in Figure 3.3. We begin with a histogram of almost 10,000 cases, in which all of the scores are placed within 10

| Figure 3.3 | *Constructing a Distribution That Approximates a Curve* |

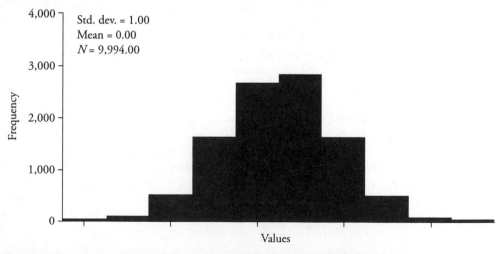

(a) *Distribution with 10 Intervals*

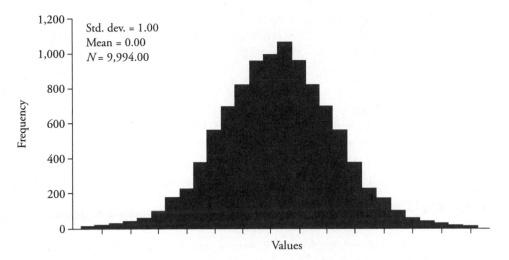

(b) *Distribution with 30 Intervals*

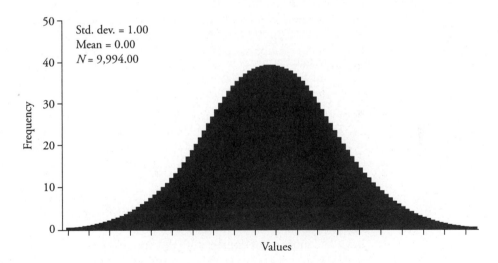

(c) *Distribution with 650 Intervals*

broad categories (see part a). Here each category is represented by one
large bar. When we increase the number of intervals, or categories, in
the histogram to 30 (part b), we can still see the individual bars but the
shape of the distribution is not as jagged. When the number of categories is increased to 650 (part c), the histogram looks more like a
smooth curve than a histogram, although if you look closely you will be

able to identify the bars that make up the curve. If our distribution had included an even larger number of scores and categories, the curve would have become even smoother.

Extending Histograms to Multiple Groups: Using Bar Charts

Although histograms provide a quick and easy way to present data from a frequency distribution, they can be used to present the frequency distribution for only a single group. What happens when we have frequency distributions for the same variable for more than one group? There are many instances where an investigator will want to present results graphically for two or more groups, such as treatment and control groups, males and females, or states. We could simply construct a histogram for each group we were interested in, but we would not be able to make direct comparisons across the groups in the form and shape of the distributions. A simple extension of the histogram to multiple groups makes use of the **bar chart.** Bar charts allow us to present information for multiple groups simultaneously. Bar charts are constructed in much the same way as histograms. The x-axis generally represents the values of the variable, and the y-axis the size of the bar.[2] Most statistical software and spreadsheet packages allow the user to construct bar charts to depict patterns in the various groups. Two of the more common approaches involve placing the bars side by side and on top of each other. Presenting data for each group in adjacent bars gives the reader a sense of the distribution for each group and allows for immediate comparison of distributions across groups.

Table 3.2 presents simulated frequency distributions for numbers of prior convictions among 100 men and 100 women arrested for drug offenses. The frequencies for male and female arrestees suggest that males have had more prior contact with the criminal justice system than the females. Figure 3.4 portrays the male and female frequency distributions in a bar chart.

In addition to being able to incorporate data from more than one group, a bar chart has other benefits. For example, bars may be pre-

---

[2]Most statistical software and spreadsheet packages allow for manipulation of many characteristics of a bar chart, including color, shading, patterning, and dimensions (two vs. three). While this allows for the construction of unique charts, the investigator should be wary of adding so much detail to a chart that the reader loses the point the investigator is trying to make.

| **Table 3.2** | Frequency Distributions of Number of Prior Convictions for Male and Female Drug Arrestees |

| | **FREQUENCY** | |
Number of Prior Convictions	**Male**	**Female**
0	25	40
1	20	25
2	15	15
3	10	7
4	8	4
5	6	0
6	2	3
7	6	3
8	5	1
9	0	2
10	3	0
Total	**100**	**100**

sented either vertically, as in Figure 3.4, or horizontally, as in Figure 3.5. The only difference between the bar charts in Figures 3.4 and 3.5 is that in the latter the axes have been flipped: The *y*-axis now represents the values of the variable (here, the number of prior convictions), and the *x*-axis represents the size of the bar (the frequency). There are no specific rules about which form of bar chart is better. Some people like vertical bar charts because they can draw an imaginary horizontal line across the graph to get a sense of which bars are larger and smaller. Alternatively, other people prefer horizontal bars because looking at them mimics the

| **Figure 3.4** | *Bar Chart for Male and Female Frequency Distributions* |

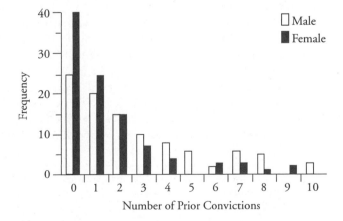

Figure 3.5   *Horizontal Bar Chart for Male and Female Frequency Distributions*

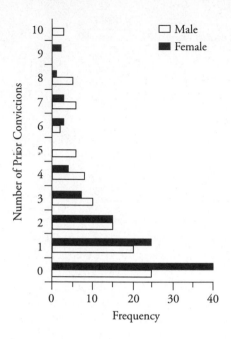

process of reading text from left to right. Since the research on visual perception is mixed about whether vertical or horizontal bars are more effective—there are benefits and drawbacks to both approaches—the preferences of the investigator typically determine which approach is used.[3]

A cautionary note is needed about the use of bar charts for comparing multiple groups. In Figure 3.4, the number of individuals in each group was equal, allowing us to make a direct comparison of each group's frequency distribution. An investigator would run into trouble, however, if the two groups did not have the same number of cases. Say one group had two or three times as many cases as a second group. If we simply presented a bar chart of the observed frequencies, then we would be limited to discussing the shape of each group's distribution; we would be unable to make valid comparisons across the two groups. For example, in the frequency distributions of prior convictions in Table 3.2, sup-

---

[3]For a good discussion of the benefits and drawbacks of various approaches, see Gary T. Henry, *Graphing Data: Techniques for Display and Analysis* (Thousand Oaks, CA: Sage, 1995).

Figure 3.6   *Bar Chart for 200 Male and 100 Female Arrestees*

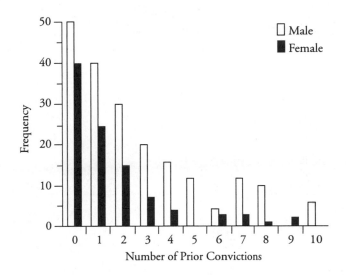

pose that we doubled the frequencies for the male arrestees, giving us a total of 200 males in the sample. In Figure 3.6, the bars representing male arrests are twice as large as they are in Figure 3.4, and one might be tempted to say that more males have zero, one, or two arrests. Strictly speaking, such an observation is correct—the frequency is larger for one group than for the other group—but it misrepresents the relative sizes of the two groups and the relative distribution of cases within each group, which are unchanged by doubling the number of male arrests.

In research on crime and criminal justice, the groups we are interested in comparing rarely have an equal number of cases. For example, Table 3.3 presents the frequency distributions of years of education for capital offenders executed in the United States between 1977 and 1995, distinguished by the recorded race of the offender. These data come from a public data file archived by the Bureau of Justice Statistics.[4] The bar chart for these data is presented in Figure 3.7. It is important to note that whites outnumber African Americans about 3 to 2. This tells us that although we can evaluate the frequency distributions for whites and

---

[4] *Capital Punishment in the United States,* ICPSR Study #6956, available through the National Archive of Criminal Justice Data (NACJD) at http://www.icpsr.umich.edu/NACJD.

Table 3.3

Number of Years of Education Among Offenders Executed in the United States, 1977 to 1995, by Race of Offender

Years of Education	RACE OF OFFENDER	
	White	African American
7	24	7
8	14	17
9	19	16
10	24	20
11	14	18
12	60	31
13	8	1
14	12	2
15	2	0
16	3	0
17	1	0
Total	181	112

Figure 3.7

Bar Chart for Number of Years of Education Among Offenders Executed in the United States, 1977 to 1995, by Race of Offender

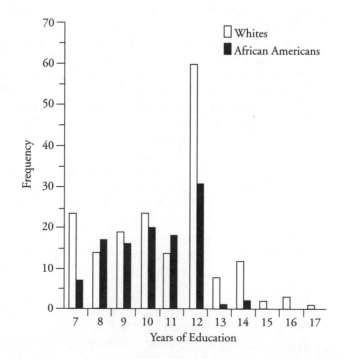

African Americans separately, we should avoid any direct comparisons across the two groups.

How do we address the problem of unequal group sizes? The most direct way is to convert the observed frequencies into proportions or percentages. A **proportion** has a value between 0 and 1 and represents the fraction of all observations that fall into a category. We calculate a proportion as:

$$\text{Proportion} = \frac{N_{\text{cat}}}{N_{\text{total}}}$$

Equation 3.1

where N_{cat} refers to the number of observations in a given category and N_{total} refers to the total number of observations. For example, to find the proportion of whites who had 8 years of education, we would take the number of white offenders who had 8 years of education (14) and divide it by the total number of whites executed (181):

W orking It Out
$$\text{Proportion} = \frac{N_{\text{cat}}}{N_{\text{total}}}$$ $$= \frac{14}{181}$$ $$= 0.077$$

By convention, we generally round a proportion to the second decimal place. (However, as we will discuss in more detail in the next chapter, your decision as to how precisely to present a statistic should be based on the specific research problem you are examining.) The proportion of executed white offenders who had 8 years of education is thus about 0.08.

Sometimes researchers like to transform a proportion into a percentage, because percentages are more commonly used in our everyday lives. We obtain the **percentage** simply by multiplying the proportion by 100:

$$\text{Percentage} = \left(\frac{N_{\text{cat}}}{N_{\text{total}}}\right) \times 100$$

Equation 3.2

For our example of executed white offenders with 8 years of education, we multiply 14/181 by 100:

Working It Out

$$\text{Percentage} = \left(\frac{N_{\text{cat}}}{N_{\text{total}}}\right) \times 100$$

$$= \left(\frac{14}{181}\right) \times 100$$

$$= 7.7\%$$

This tells us that about 8% of executed white offenders had 8 years of education. Table 3.4 presents the observed frequencies and corresponding percentages (calculated to the third decimal place) for every cell in Table 3.3.

At this point, we can graph either the proportions or the percentages in a bar chart. The selection of proportions or percentages does not matter, as it will not have any bearing on the shape of the distributions. The bar chart in Figure 3.8 uses percentages to display years of education among executed offenders in the United States, distinguished by race.

Table 3.4	Frequency Distributions and Percentages for Number of Years of Education Among Executed Offenders, by Race

| | RACE OF OFFENDER | | | |
| | WHITE | | AFRICAN AMERICAN | |
Years of Education	Freq.	%	Freq.	%
7	24	13.260	7	6.250
8	14	7.735	17	15.179
9	19	10.497	16	14.286
10	24	13.260	20	17.857
11	14	7.735	18	16.071
12	60	33.149	31	27.679
13	8	4.420	1	0.893
14	12	6.630	2	1.786
15	2	1.105	0	0.000
16	3	1.657	0	0.000
17	1	0.552	0	0.000
Total	181		112	

Figure 3.8   *Percentages of Executed Offenders with Various Numbers of Years of Education, by Race*

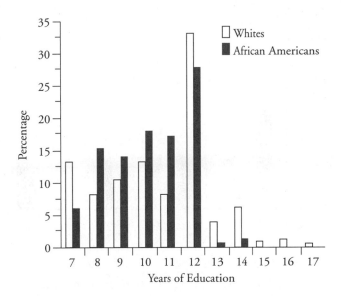

Using Bar Charts with Nominal or Ordinal Data

The previous examples of bar charts and histograms have focused on variables measured at the interval level. Bar charts are also quite useful for visually representing nominally or ordinally measured variables. In much of the research on public opinion about use of the death penalty in the United States, there are sharp differences between the views of whites and those of African Americans. Table 3.5 presents the level of support for using the death penalty for first-degree murderers, distinguished by

Table 3.5   Level of Agreement with Use of the Death Penalty for Convicted First-Degree Murderers

| | RACE OF RESPONDENT | | | |
| | WHITE | | AFRICAN AMERICAN | |
Level of Agreement	Freq.	%	Freq.	%
Strongly agree	567	51.266	57	37.748
Agree	290	26.221	32	21.192
Neutral/no opinion	76	6.872	24	15.894
Disagree	106	9.584	25	16.556
Strongly disagree	67	6.058	13	8.609
Total	1,106		151	

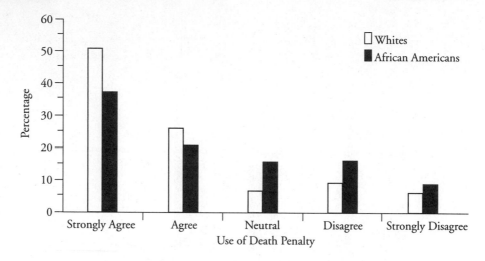

Figure 3.9

Bar Chart for Level of Agreement with Use of the Death Penalty for Convicted First-Degree Murderers

race of the respondent. The data come from the General Social Survey (GSS), administered by the National Opinion Research Center at the University of Chicago. Respondents were asked: "How strongly do you agree with the following statement: The death penalty should be used for persons convicted of first-degree murder." The responses were strongly agree, agree, neutral/no opinion, disagree, and strongly disagree.[5]

To chart these data, we cannot graph the numbers of white and African American respondents in each category and hope to make sense of the patterns, since there are about seven times more white respondents than African American respondents. Again, we construct a bar chart using the proportion or percentage of respondents who fall into each category. A bar chart presenting percentages of white and African American respondents in each category appears in Figure 3.9.

Pie Charts

Pie charts offer another way of displaying data graphically if the number of categories of a variable is relatively small. Each wedge in a pie chart is a proportional representation of the number of cases in that category. When we present data on the percentage or proportion of cases in

---

[5]The entire GSS database is publicly available and can be accessed at http://www. icpsr.umich.edu/GSS. Data presented here are drawn from a 1991 study.

| Figure 3.10 | *Percentage of Agreement with Use of the Death Penalty for Convicted First-Degree Murderers* |

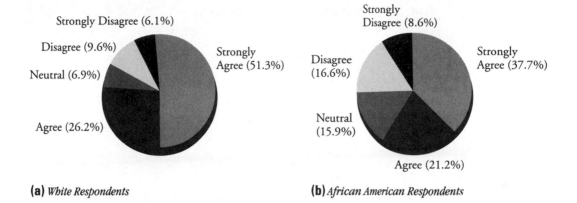

(a) *White Respondents*   **(b)** *African American Respondents*

a pie chart, the information contained in a pie chart is identical to that presented in a bar chart. As with bar charts, most statistical software and spreadsheet packages allow the researcher to manipulate various aspects—size, shape, orientation, dimensions (two or three), position of wedges, colors, shades, and so on.

We will use the death penalty opinion data in Table 3.5 to illustrate the construction of pie charts. Parts a and b of Figure 3.10 present the responses for white and African American respondents, respectively.

The information presented in Figure 3.10 is identical to that in Figure 3.9. But the need for two separate pie charts to represent the data for the two groups of respondents points out one of the limitations of using pie charts for comparing multiple groups. In Figure 3.9, the bars for the two groups of respondents are presented side by side. The reader is able to quickly assess which group is larger, which group is smaller, and the magnitude of the difference. With the two pie charts represented in parts a and b of Figure 3.10, the reader has to go back and forth between the pies, match up the category of interest, and then try to infer the magnitude of the difference in size between the two wedges. Although pie charts are an easy and effective way of representing the relative sizes of different categories of a variable, we discourage the use of pie charts for any type of cross-group comparison, to avoid the potential for confusing or misleading the reader.

Time Series Data

Study of many important issues in crime and criminal justice requires the use of **time series data.** Time series data include measures on the same variable for the same unit of analysis at more than one point in time. For

Table 3.6	Total Crime Rate and Murder Rate in the United States, 1990 to 2000

YEAR	TOTAL CRIME RATE (PER 100,000)	MURDER RATE (PER 100,000)
1990	5,820.300	9.4000
1991	5,897.800	9.8000
1992	5,660.200	9.3000
1993	5,484.400	9.5000
1994	5,373.500	9.0000
1995	5,275.900	8.2000
1996	5,086.600	7.4000
1997	4,930.000	6.8000
1998	4,619.300	6.3000
1999	4,266.800	5.7000
2000	4,124.800	5.5000

example, in a study of adolescents, the same individuals may be interviewed two or more times. Or, in an examination of the effectiveness of a treatment program, information on key characteristics of participants may be collected before and after the treatment, to test for change.

An example of time series data more familiar to many students comes from the Federal Bureau of Investigation's annual *Uniform Crime Reports*.[6] Included in the reports are the "official" crime rates, which tell us the total crime rate, the murder rate, the burglary rate, and so on. We can easily locate a crime rate for the United States—as well as smaller geopolitical units, such as states or counties—for some period of time. Table 3.6 presents the total crime rate and murder rate for the United States per 100,000 people for the years 1990 to 2000.

In a **time series plot,** data are graphed over time, with the measure of time along the *x*-axis. For the data in Table 3.6, the measure of time is years, but in other cases, we may have daily, weekly, monthly, or quarterly data. The *y*-axis then represents the value—here, the crime rate. Figure 3.11 presents a plot of the total crime rate per 100,000 people in the United States for the period 1990 to 2000. As you can see, the time series plot provides a very powerful way to present data over time. The "crime drop" in the United States during this period is clearly illustrated in Figure 3.11.

It is also possible to plot more than one time series on the same graph, but be careful about the values of the different series. If one series has values that are many times larger than those in the other series, you run the risk of generating a plot in which the line of one group looks misleadingly like a straight line. Figure 3.12, which shows total

---

[6]Federal Bureau of Investigation, *Crime in the United States,* available at http://www.fbi.gov/ucr/ucr.htm.

Figure 3.11   *Total Crime Rate (per 100,000 People) in the United States, 1990 to 2000*

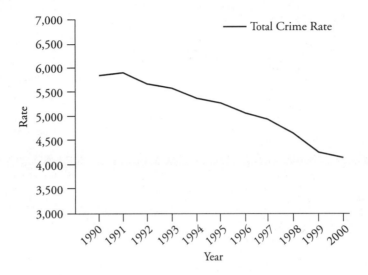

crime rates and murder rates for the 1990 to 2000 period, illustrates this problem. Since the total crime rate ranges between about 4,000 and 6,000 per 100,000 while the murder rate varies between about 5 and 10 per 100,000, the line representing the murder rate appears straight and indeed can hardly be seen. In such a case, one solution is to construct a

Figure 3.12   *Total Crime Rate and Murder Rate (per 100,000 People)*
in the United States, 1990 to 2000: Single Vertical Axis

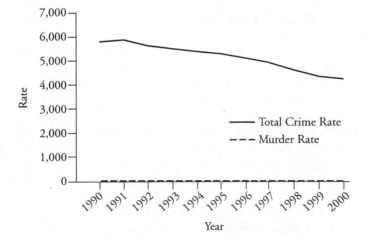

| Figure 3.13 |

*Total Crime Rate and Murder Rate (per 100,000 People) in the United States,
1990 to 2000: Two Vertical Axes*

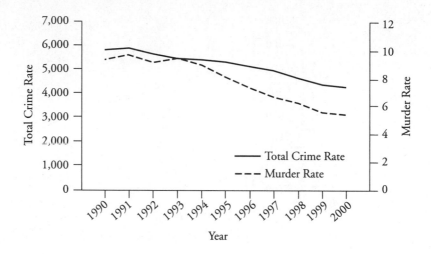

time series plot with a second *y*-axis on the right side of the chart. Figure
3.13 adds a second *y*-axis to account for the smaller values associated
with the murder rate, providing a better depiction of the annual variation
in both rates.

Chapter Summary

A **frequency distribution** is an arrangement of data according to the
frequency with which each value occurs. The data may be represented
in a table or in graphic form in a **histogram,** which uses a bar to represent the frequency for each value.

    Bar charts can be used to represent the **frequencies, percentages,**
or **proportions** of variables, regardless of whether they have been measured at the nominal, ordinal, or interval level. In a vertical bar chart, the
sizes of the bars are indicated along the *y*-axis and correspond to the frequency, the percentage, or the proportion. The values, or categories, of
the variable are represented along the *x*-axis. When comparing two or
more groups in a bar chart, it is important to have the values represent
the percentage or proportion of cases, since the presentation of frequencies could be misleading if the groups are of very different sizes.

    Pie charts are another common way to represent variables with a
small number of categories or values. The size of each wedge in a pie
chart corresponds to the relative size of that category's frequency count.

Pie charts are better suited to describing data from a single sample or group than data from multiple groups.

Time series data may be graphically displayed in a **time series plot,** a line graph that portrays the values of a variable over some period of time, such as days, weeks, months, or years. To allow for the comparison of multiple variables, additional lines can be easily incorporated into the line graph. If the magnitudes of the variables differ by a large degree, it is possible to add an additional y-axis so that the lines can be overlaid and common or unique trends in the plotted variables discerned.

Key Terms

bar chart A graph in which bars represent frequencies, percentages, or proportions for the categories or values of a variable.

frequency The number of times that a score or value occurs.

frequency distribution An arrangement of scores in order from the lowest to the highest, accompanied by the number of times each score occurs.

histogram A bar graph used to represent a frequency distribution.

percentage A relation between two numbers in which the whole is accorded a value of 100 and the other number is given a numerical value corresponding to its share of the whole.

pie chart A graph in which a circle (called a pie) is cut into wedges to represent the relative size of each category's frequency count.

proportion A relation between two numbers in which the whole is accorded a value of 1 and the other number is given a numerical value corresponding to its share of the whole.

time series data Repeated measures of the same variable over some regularly occurring time period, such as days, months, or years.

time series plot A line graph that connects repeated measures of the same variable over some regularly occurring time period, such as days, months, or years.

Symbols and Formulas

N_{cat} Number of cases in a category of a variable

N_{total} Total number of cases

To calculate the proportion of cases falling into a category:

$$\text{Proportion} = \frac{N_{cat}}{N_{total}}$$

To calculate the percentage of cases falling into a category:

$$\text{Percentage} = \left(\frac{N_{cat}}{N_{total}}\right) \times 100$$

Exercises

3.1   A team of researchers observed the behavior of 20 children during breaktime on a school playground. The observers recorded how many times each child performed a "violent act"—be it a push, a kick, or a punch—against another child. The scores of the 20 children were as follows:

2   0   1   0   0   4   0   10   2   1   3   3   0   1   4   11   0   0   2   0

a. Construct a frequency distribution table for the above results.

b. Construct a histogram of the frequency distribution.

c. How might you interpret the results?

3.2   Workers at an inner-city rape crisis center asked all the callers on a given night for their ages. For a total of 50 callers, the results were as follows:

28   39   17   18   22   31   26   27   16   20
34   35   29   26   17   23   22   23   37   28
24   19   14   25   27   19   24   26   41   27
21   24   17   16   35   25   19   23   29   18
23   26   24   43   28   21   21   36   26   27

a. Construct a frequency distribution table for the above results.

b. Based on the frequency distribution, construct three different histograms, with the data grouped in 1-year intervals, 3-year intervals, and 10-year intervals.

3.3   A review of the records of 20 male and 20 female adjudicated delinquents revealed the following numbers of prior arrests for violent crimes:

Male: 0   2   1   7   4   2   2   1   6   5   0   0   1   2   4   1   0   0   2   9
Female: 0   0   1   4   2   3   1   1   5   1   0   0   0   1   0   3   2   1   0   1

a. Construct three frequency distribution tables: one for males, one for females, and one for the male and female data combined.

b. Construct a histogram for each of the three frequency distributions.

c. How might you interpret the results?

3.4 In a survey of 75 offenders convicted through guilty pleas, respondents were asked who had the greatest influence on their decision to plead guilty. Here are their responses: defense attorney ($n = 35$), spouse/partner ($n = 25$), prosecutor ($n = 10$), and judge ($n = 5$).

a. Graph these data on three bar charts using frequencies, proportions, and percentages.

b. Graph these data on a pie chart.

3.5 Suppose a researcher conducted a survey to assess the link between gender and attitudes about the criminal justice system. Among 850 male respondents, the researcher found that 500 thought the punishments given by the courts were "too lenient," 200 thought the punishments were "about right," and the remaining 150 thought the punishments were "too harsh." Among 300 female respondents, the researcher found that 150 thought the punishments were "too harsh," 100 thought the punishments were "about right," and 50 thought the punishments were "too lenient."

a. Present this information graphically in the way that you think is most informative—either for the full sample or for each gender separately.

b. Explain your choice of chart.

c. Describe the patterns that you find in this type of chart.

3.6 The burglary rates for two cities over a 10-year period are reported in the following table:

Year	City A	City B
1991	2,576	875
1992	2,675	966
1993	2,892	1,015
1994	3,014	1,325
1995	2,852	1,779
1996	2,651	1,954
1997	2,443	2,333
1998	2,519	2,121
1999	2,999	2,657
2000	2,840	2,005

a. Present this information in the way that you think is most informative.

b. Explain why you selected this type of chart.

c. Describe the patterns that you observe in this chart.

Computer Exercises

SPSS contains a useful set of graphics tools comparable to those found in many of the better spreadsheet packages. The following computer exercises are intended to guide you through the basic steps in producing graphs in SPSS. The discussion is meant only as a brief overview of some of the capabilities of SPSS. We encourage you to experiment and to explore the range of features available in SPSS's graphics commands.

Before working with the graphics commands in SPSS, open the data file **nys_1.sav**.

Frequency Distributions and Histograms

Frequency distributions and histograms are produced quite easily in SPSS through the use of the "Frequencies" command (Analyze→Descriptive Statistics→Frequencies).

After you click on the "Frequencies" command, you will be presented with a window that lists the variable names on the left and has a blank box on the right. The variable names that you move into the box on the right are the ones for which you will obtain frequency distributions and histograms. Choose one of the delinquency variables from the **nys_1.sav** data file. To obtain a histogram, click on the button at the bottom of this window labeled "Charts," then the circle next to "Histogram," then "Continue," and then "OK." The output window generated by the command should now contain a frequency distribution table and a histogram for these data.

You should note that the default in SPSS is to construct intervals for the values of the variable to be graphed. The size and number of intervals can be modified by editing the chart in SPSS.

The "Histogram" command (Graphs→Histogram) provides an alternative way of obtaining just a histogram, without a frequency distribution. In the window that opens after you execute the "Histogram" command, you will be prompted to move one variable name from the left box into the small box on the right—this is the variable that will be graphed. Choose the same variable that you used in the "Frequencies" command above, and move its name into the box on the right. Click on "OK" to produce the histogram. The histogram produced by this command should be identical to the histogram produced with the "Frequencies" command.

Bar Charts

To have SPSS produce bar charts, all you have to do is execute the "Bar . . ." command (Graphs→Bar . . .). The window that opens will have three options for you to choose from. To generate a simple bar chart for one variable, click on the "Simple" box and the circle next to "Summaries for groups of cases." Then click on "Define." To get a sense of how the bar charts differ from the histograms, it is instructive to use the same variable that you have worked with already. Move the name of this variable into the box for "Category axis." (This defines the x-axis.) Note, in the upper right corner of this window, the variety of things that can be plotted. Be sure that the dot is next to "N of cases." Click on "OK." Your bar chart should look much like the histograms you produced for this same variable, although you may notice a different scaling of the x-axis.

If you want to produce a bar chart that includes bars for multiple groups, there are many different ways of doing this in SPSS. A simple bar chart for multiple groups can be obtained by again executing the "Bar . . . " command. Click on the "Clustered" box rather than "Simple," and then click on "Define." In this window, move a variable name that represents different groups—such as gender or race—into the box "Define clusters by," and move the variable to be graphed into the box "Category axis." Note that the dot is still next to "N of cases," although you might explore the percentage or proportion options. Click on "OK" to produce the chart. If you selected gender as the grouping variable, you should see two sets of bars—one for males and one for females.

Pie Charts

Pie charts are very easy to produce in SPSS with the "Pie . . ." command (Graphs→Pie . . .). When the window opens, select "Summaries for groups of cases" and click on "Define." As with the bar chart command, you simply have to move the variable name from the box on the right into the box labeled "Define slices by." You also have the option of using the number of cases, percentage, or another summary statistic to determine the size of each wedge. As with other charts in SPSS, you can edit various dimensions of the chart after it has been created and presented in the output window.

Line Graphs

To have SPSS produce a line graph, use the "Line . . ." command (Graphs→ Line . . .). To generate a simple line graph, click on "Simple" and "Summaries for groups of cases." To get a sense of how this kind of graph is similar to and different from the previous charts, continue to use the same variable. Note that the dot is next to "N of cases." Click on "OK" to generate the graph. The result will be a line graph that corresponds to the histogram you created previously.

A time plot is also easily obtained through the "Line . . . " command. Open the data file ***crime_ts.sav.*** These are the crime data used for Figures 3.11 to 3.13 in the text. To produce line graphs similar to those in Figures 3.11 and 3.12, do the following:

— Click on "Simple" and then on "Values of individual cases."

— Move the variable "total crime rate" into the box "Line represents."

— Click on the circle next to the word "Variable" (located in the middle of the window). Move the variable "year" into this box. This defines the x-axis.

— Click on "OK." The result should look like Figure 3.11.

— Click on "Graphs→Line . . . " again. Then click on "Multiple."

— Again move the variable "year" into the box next to "Variable."

— Move both crime rate variables into the "Lines represent" box. Click on "OK." The result should look like Figure 3.12.

NOTE: SPSS will *not* produce a line graph with two y-axes. You will need to use a spreadsheet package to produce such a graph.

1. Enter the data from Exercise 3.1.

   a. Produce a frequency distribution table and a histogram.

   b. How does the histogram produced by SPSS differ from the one you constructed?

   c. Experiment with the interval length to see if you can reproduce in SPSS the chart you constructed by hand.

2. Enter the data from Exercise 3.3.

   a. Produce two frequency distribution tables and two histograms, one each for males and for females.

   b. Use the "Bar . . . " command to produce a bar chart that presents the information for males and females simultaneously, in terms of

      i. Number of cases
      ii. Percentage of cases.

3. Enter the data from Exercise 3.6. Produce three time plots:

   a. One for City A

   b. One for City B

   c. One that contains lines representing both City A and City B.

4. Open the *nys_1.sav* data file.

   a. Produce a frequency distribution table and a histogram for each of the delinquency variables.

   b. Describe the shapes of the distributions produced in part a.

   c. Choose one of the delinquency variables.

      i. Produce a bar chart using percentages for each gender. Describe how the patterns are similar and different across gender.

      ii. Produce a bar chart using percentages for each race. Describe how the patterns are similar and different across race.

   d. Select two of the nominal or ordinal variables (excluding gender and race).

      i. Produce pie charts for both variables.

      ii. Produce pie charts for both variables, distinguished by gender.

      iii. Produce pie charts for both variables, distinguished by race.

      iv. Describe how the patterns are similar and different across gender and race.

   e. Use the "Line . . ." command to produce a series of graphs that correspond to the bar charts in part c.

Describing the Typical Case:

Measures of Central Tendency

the mode

How Is It Calculated?

What Information Does It Use?

What Are Its Advantages and Disadvantages?

the median

How Is It Calculated?

What Information Does It Use?

What Are Its Advantages and Disadvantages?

the mean

How Is It Calculated?

What Information Does It Use?

What Are Its Advantages and Disadvantages?

What Are Its Other Unique Properties?

THE NATURAL FIRST STEP in summarizing research is to provide a basic portrait of the characteristics of a sample or population. What is the typical case? If the researcher could choose one case to represent all others, which would it be? When a sample is very small, it is possible merely to show the array of cases and let the reader decide. However, as the number of cases grows, it becomes difficult to make a decision about typicality from the distribution as a whole. This is the function of measures of central tendency in statistics. They provide us with a simple snapshot of our data that can be used to gain a picture of the average case.

In this chapter, three commonly used measures of central tendency are discussed and compared. The first, the mode, is used primarily with nominal-level data. It is the simplest measure of central tendency, drawing information only about the frequency of events in each category. The second measure, the median, takes into account not only frequency but also the order or ranking of study subjects. Finally, the mean adds the additional factor of the exact scores associated with each subject studied. As in the discussion of levels of measurement, we emphasize in this chapter the benefits gained from statistics that use more information. But we also illustrate the importance of looking carefully at the distribution of cases in your study before deciding which measure of central tendency is most appropriate.

The Mode: Central Tendency in Nominal Scales

Faced with a nominal-scale measure, how would you define a typical case? Take as an example Table 4.1. Here you have a nominal scale of legal representation for a sample of offenders convicted of white-collar crimes in U.S. federal courts. Offenders were placed into one of five categories, indicating the type of legal representation they had: no attorney

| Table 4.1 | Legal Representation for White-Collar Crime |

CATEGORY	FREQUENCY (N)
No Attorney	20
Legal Aid	26
Court Appointed	92
Public Defender	153
Private Attorney	380
Total (Σ)	671

present, legal-aid attorney, court-appointed attorney, public defender, and privately retained attorney. The number of individuals who fall in each category—or, in statistical language, the N of cases—is reported.

Clearly, you have very limited information in this example on which to base a choice about typicality. Here, as with other nominal-scale measures, you simply know how many cases fall into one category or another. You would probably choose the category "private attorney" as most representative of this sample, because it contains by far the most cases (380). And indeed, this is precisely how statisticians define typicality for nominal-level variables. We call the category with the largest N, or number of cases, the **mode.** In this sample of white-collar offenders, the modal category for type of representation is "private attorney."

By defining one category as the modal category, we are able to provide a summary of the type of case that is typical of our sample or population. Such statements are common in criminal justice research. We often are interested in the racial category that appears most often in our data or the type of offense that is most common. The modal category can also provide a basis for making comparisons among samples. For example, let's say that a sample of offenders convicted of nonviolent property crimes that would not ordinarily be defined as white collar was compared to this larger sample of offenders convicted of white-collar crimes. For the former group, as is apparent from Table 4.2, the modal category is not "private attorney" but rather "court-appointed attorney." Although this comparison of the two samples is not a complex one, it

| Table 4.2 | Legal Representation for Common Crime |

CATEGORY	FREQUENCY (N)
No Attorney	40
Legal Aid	7
Court Appointed	91
Public Defender	22
Private Attorney	70
Total (Σ)	230

Table 4.3	Financial Harm for a Sample of Convicted Offenders

CATEGORY	FREQUENCY (N)
Less than $100	15
$101–$2,500	92
$2,501–$10,000	20
More than $10,000	19
Total (Σ)	146

illustrates the different backgrounds of the two groups. White-collar offenders are much more likely than common criminals to have the resources to pay for private legal representation.

In general, we do not use the mode to describe central tendency with ordinal or interval scales. The reason, in good part, is that the mode does not take advantage of the additional information that such scales provide. The average case should not be chosen simply on the basis of the frequency of events in a particular category, because higher-level scales also provide information on the order or nature of the differences between categories.

Nonetheless, there are cases where researchers choose to use the mode to describe ordinal- or interval-level measures. Generally this occurs when there is a very large group of cases in one particular category. Table 4.3, for example, provides an ordinal-level measure of the financial harm caused by a sample of convicted offenders. Because almost two-thirds of the individuals studied fall in the category "$101–$2,500," you might want to describe typicality in this case by saying that this category is the modal category. Similarly, if you were examining prior arrests and two-thirds of the offenders in your sample had no prior arrests, you might want to report no arrests as the modal category. Even though this measure is an interval measure, the mode provides a fairly good summary of the typical case in your sample.

The Median: Taking into Account Position

In constructing the **median,** we utilize information not only on the number of cases found in a particular category, but also on the positions of the categories. The median may be defined simply as the middle score in a distribution. For ordinal scales, it is the category in which the middle score lies. For interval scales, the median is the value that splits the distribution of scores in half.

There are two general steps in determining the median for a distribution of scores. First, the values need to be arranged from low to high

| Table 4.4 | Student Views on Public Drunkenness |

CATEGORY	FREQUENCY (*N*)	CUMULATIVE *N*
Not serious at all	73	73
A bit serious	47	120
Somewhat serious	47	167
Serious	27	194
Very serious	26	220
Extremely serious	39	259
Most serious	22	281
Total (Σ)	**281**	

scores. As we saw in Chapter 3, a frequency distribution allows us to represent our data in this way. Table 4.4 presents a frequency distribution of views of public drunkenness, drawn from a survey of students. The students were presented with an ordinal-scale measure that allowed them to rate the seriousness of a series of crimes. The ratings ranged from "not serious at all" to "most serious."

Second, we need to determine which observation splits the distribution. A simple formula, Equation 4.1, allows us to define which observation is the median when the number of observations in the distribution is odd, as is the case with our example of views of public drunkenness.

$$\text{Median observation} = \frac{N + 1}{2}$$

Equation 4.1

In this case, we add 1 to the total number of observations in the sample or population we are studying and then divide by 2. For the frequency distribution in Table 4.4, the median observation is the 141st score:

Working It Out

$$\text{Median observation} = \frac{N + 1}{2}$$

$$= \frac{281 + 1}{2}$$

$$= 141$$

However, because our variable, student views on drunkenness, is measured on an ordinal scale, it does not make sense to simply state that the 141st observation is the median score. To give a substantive meaning to the median, it is important to define which category the median score falls in. The 141st observation in our distribution of ordered scores falls in the category labeled "somewhat serious."

The advantage of the median over the mode for describing ordinal scales is well illustrated by our example of views of public drunkenness. If we used the mode to describe typicality in student assessments of the seriousness of public drunkenness, we would conclude that the typical student did not see drunkenness as at all serious. But even though the "not serious at all" category includes the largest number of cases, almost three-quarters of the students rate this behavior more seriously. The median takes this fact into consideration by placing the typical case in the middle of a distribution. It is concerned with not only the number of cases in the categories, but also their position.

If the number of observations or cases in your distribution is even, then you cannot identify a single observation as the median. While statisticians recognize that the median is ambiguously defined in this case, by convention they continue to use Equation 4.1 to identify the median for an ordinal-level distribution. In practice, this places the median score between two observations. For example, consider the distribution of 146 scores in Table 4.3, representing financial harm in a sample of offenders. Here the number of scores is even, and thus there is not a single observation that can be defined as the median. Using Equation 4.1, we can see that the median is defined as the halfway point between the 73rd and the 74th observation. This means that the median falls in the category defined as $101 to $2,500.[1]

Working It Out

$$\text{Median observation} = \frac{N+1}{2}$$

$$= \frac{146+1}{2}$$

$$= 73.5$$

73rd observation: $101–$2,500

74th observation: $101–$2,500

The median is sometimes used for defining typicality with interval scales. For example, Table 4.5 presents the average number of minutes of public disorder (per 70-minute period) observed in a sample of 31

---

[1]With this method, it is possible that the defined median value will fall between two categories of an ordinally measured variable. In that case, you simply note that the median falls between these two categories.

| Table 4.5 | Hot Spots: Minutes of Public Disorder (A) |

HOT SPOT SCORE	FREQUENCY (*N*)	CUMULATIVE (*N*)
0.35	1	1
0.42	1	2
0.46	1	3
0.47	1	4
0.52	1	5
0.67	1	6
1.00	1	7
1.06	1	8
1.15	1	9
1.19	2	11
1.48	1	12
1.60	1	13
1.63	1	14
2.02	1	15
2.12	1	16
2.21	1	17
2.34	1	18
2.45	1	19
2.66	1	20
3.04	1	21
3.19	1	22
3.23	1	23
3.46	1	24
3.51	1	25
3.72	1	26
4.09	1	27
4.47	1	28
4.64	1	29
4.65	1	30
6.57	1	31
Total (Σ)	31	31

"hot spots of crime," or city blocks with high levels of crime. The hot spots are arranged in ascending order on the basis of the number of minutes of disorder observed. In this case, the distribution has an odd number of observations, and thus the median is the score in the middle of the distribution, or the 16th observation, which has a value of 2.12.

Working It Out

$$\text{Median observation} = \frac{N+1}{2}$$
$$= \frac{31+1}{2}$$
$$= 16$$

Accordingly, using the median, we would describe the average hot spot as having a little more than two minutes of disorder in each 70-minute period.

As noted above, when the number of observations in a distribution is even, the median is ambiguously defined. Let's, for example, delete the hot spot with a score of 6.57 from Table 4.5. In this case, there is no single middle value for the array of cases in the table. If we use Equation 4.1 to define the median observation, we get a value of 15.5.

W orking It Out

$$\text{Median observation} = \frac{N + 1}{2}$$

$$= \frac{30 + 1}{2}$$

$$= 15.5$$

But what is the value or score associated with an observation that lies between two scores in an interval-level scale? If both the 15th and the 16th observation are in the same category, then the solution is easy. You simply define the median as the score associated with both the 15th and the 16th observation. However, it will sometimes be the case with an interval-level variable that each of these observations will have a different value on the scale, as we find here. There is no true median value for this example. By convention, however, we define the median with interval-level measures as the midpoint between the observation directly below and the observation directly above the median observation. In our example, this is the midpoint on our scale between the scores 2.02 and 2.12. The median in this case is defined as 2.07.[2]

W orking It Out

15th case = 2.02

16th case = 2.12

$$\text{Median} = \frac{2.02 + 2.12}{2}$$

$$= 2.07$$

---

[2]Sometimes the median for ordinal-level variables is also calculated using this method. In such cases, the researcher should realize that he or she is treating the variable under consideration as an interval-level measure. Only for an interval-level measure can we assume that the units of measurement are constant across observations.

The median is generally more appropriate than the mode for assessing central tendency for both ordinal- and interval-level measures. However, the median does not take advantage of all the information included in interval-level scales. Although it recognizes the positions of the values of a measure, it does not take into account the exact differences among these values. In many cases, this can provide for a misleading estimate of typicality for interval-level measures.

For example, let's say that the distribution of disorder in hot spots is that represented in Table 4.6. In this case, the median is 1.83. But is 1.83 a good estimate of central tendency for this distribution? The 17th score is 3.34, which is not very close to 1.83 at all. The score of 1.83 is not an ideal estimate of typicality, as it is far below half the scores in the distribution. The median is not sensitive to the gap in our measure between the values of the 16th and 17th cases. This is because it looks only at

| **Table 4.6** | Hot Spots: Minutes of Public Disorder (B) | | |

HOT SPOT SCORE	FREQUENCY (*N*)	CUMULATIVE (*N*)	CUMULATIVE %
0.35	1	1	3.2
0.42	1	2	6.5
0.46	1	3	9.7
0.47	1	4	12.9
0.52	1	5	16.1
0.67	1	6	19.4
1.00	1	7	22.6
1.06	1	8	25.8
1.15	1	9	29.0
1.19	2	11	35.5
1.48	1	12	38.7
1.60	1	13	41.9
1.63	1	14	45.2
1.73	1	15	48.4
1.83	1	16	51.6
3.34	1	17	54.9
3.44	1	18	58.1
3.45	1	19	61.3
3.66	1	20	64.5
4.04	1	21	67.7
4.19	1	22	71.0
4.23	1	23	74.2
4.46	1	24	77.4
4.51	1	25	80.6
4.72	1	26	83.9
5.09	1	27	87.1
5.47	1	28	90.3
5.64	1	29	93.5
5.65	1	30	96.8
5.57	1	31	100.0
Total (Σ)	31	31	100.0

position and not at the size of the differences between cases. The median does not take advantage of all the information provided by interval-level measures.

Another way to describe the median in interval-level measures is to say that it is the 50th percentile score. A percentile score is the point or score below which a specific proportion of the cases is found. The 50th percentile score is the score below which 50% of the cases in a study lie. For the data in Table 4.6, if we defined the median in this way, we again choose 1.83 as the median minutes of disorder observed in the hot spots. In this case, if we add the percentage of cases for all of the scores up until the middle, or 16th, score, we come to a total (or cumulative percentage) of 51.6. At the 15th score, or 1.73, the cumulative percentage is only 48.4, less than 50%.

The Mean: Adding Value to Position

The **mean** takes into account not only the frequency of cases in a category and the positions of scores on a measure, but also the values of these scores. To calculate the mean, we add up the scores for all of the subjects in our study and then divide the total by the total number of subjects. In mathematical language, the mean can be written as a short equation:

$$\overline{X} = \frac{\sum_{i=1}^{N} X_i}{N}$$

Equation 4.2

Even though equations sometimes put students off, they are an important part of statistics. Indeed, equations are the language of statistics. They show how a statistic is constructed and the method we use to calculate it. Equations provide a short way of writing out what would often take a number of sentences to describe in English. One of our tasks in this text is to help you to translate such equations and to become more comfortable with them.

In the case of the mean, we introduce what are for most students of criminal justice some new symbols and concepts. First, to express the mean, statisticians provide us with a shorthand symbol, $\overline{X}$—in English, "X bar." The equation also includes the summation symbol, Σ. Under the symbol is $i = 1$, and above it is N. What this means is that you should start summing your cases with the first subject in the sample and end

Table 4.7	Total Number of Prior Arrests	

TOTAL NUMBER OF ARRESTS	FREQUENCY (*N*)	CUMULATIVE (*N*)
0	4	4
1	1	5
2	2	7
4	3	10
5	3	13
7	4	17
8	2	19
10	1	20

with the last one (represented by *N* because, as we have already discussed, *N* is the number of cases in your sample). But what should you sum? *X* represents the measure of interest—in the case of our example, minutes of disorder. We use the subscript *i* to denote each of the observations of the variable *X*. If, for example, we wrote X_3, we would be referring only to the 3rd observation of the variable. So Equation 4.2 says that you should sum the scores for minutes of disorder from the first to the last case in your study. Then you should divide this number by the total number of cases.

Table 4.7 presents information about the total number of prior arrests for a sample of 20 individuals arrested for felony offenses. To calculate the mean, we first sum all of the scores, as shown in the numerator of Equation 4.2:

W orking It Out

$$\sum_{i=1}^{N} X_i = \sum_{i=1}^{20} X_i$$

$$= 0 + 0 + 0 + 0 + 1 + 2 + 2 + 4 + 4 + 4$$
$$+ 5 + 5 + 5 + 7 + 7 + 7 + 7 + 8 + 8 + 10$$

$$= 86$$

We then take the sum of the values, 86, and divide by the number of observations in the sample.

W orking It Out

$$\overline{X} = \frac{\sum\limits_{i=1}^{N} X_i}{N}$$

$$= \frac{86}{20}$$

$$= 4.3$$

The result, 4.3, tells us that in this sample the typical person arrested for a felony has, on average, 4.3 prior arrests.

As another example, let's take the data from Table 4.5 on minutes of disorder in crime hot spots. According to Equation 4.2, the first step is to sum all of the scores:

W orking It Out

$$\sum_{i=1}^{N} X_i = \sum_{i=1}^{31} X_i$$

$$= 0.35 + 0.42 + 0.46 + 0.47 + 0.52 + 0.67 + 1.00 + 1.06$$
$$+ 1.15 + 1.19 + 1.19 + 1.48 + 1.60 + 1.63 + 2.02 + 2.12$$
$$+ 2.21 + 2.34 + 2.45 + 2.66 + 3.04 + 3.19 + 3.23 + 3.46$$
$$+ 3.51 + 3.72 + 4.09 + 4.47 + 4.64 + 4.65 + 6.57$$

$$= 71.56$$

We then take this number, 71.56, and divide it by N, or 31, the number of cases in our sample.

W orking It Out

$$\overline{X} = \frac{\sum\limits_{i=1}^{N} X_i}{N}$$

$$= \frac{71.56}{31}$$

$$= 2.308387097$$

The result, 2.308387097 (rounded to the ninth decimal place), brings up an issue that often arises in reporting statistics. Do you really need to provide your audience with the level of precision that is given by your statistic? In this case, for example, at what level of precision should minutes of disorder be presented?

A basic rule of thumb is to use your common sense in answering such questions. Don't provide statistics developed out to a large number of decimal places just to impress others. In making this decision, you should ask: What is the simplest presentation of my results that will provide the reader or listener with enough information to understand and evaluate my work? Overall, criminal justice researchers seldom report the mean to more than two decimal places. This is a good choice in our example. Rounding to the second decimal place gives a mean of 2.31. Providing a more precise representation of the mean here would not add important information for the reader.

In some cases, it is useful to develop estimates with much greater precision. In particular, if the values for the cases you are examining are very small in the first place, you will want to present a more precise mean. For example, Lawrence Sherman and his colleagues looked at the mean daily rate of reported domestic violence in a study that compared the impact of arrests versus warnings as a strategy for controlling spouse abusers.[3] Had they reported their findings only to the second decimal place, as recommended above, they would have ended up with a mean daily rate over the longest follow-up period (361–540 days) of 0.00 for short arrest and 0.00 for warning. The difficulty here is that individuals are unlikely to report cases of domestic violence on a very frequent basis. Sherman et al. needed a much higher degree of precision to examine the differences between the two groups they studied. Accordingly, they reported their results to the fourth decimal place. For arrests, the rate was 0.0019, and for warnings it was 0.0009. These differences, though small, were found to be meaningful in their research.

Comparing Results Gained Using the Mean and Median

Returning to the example from Table 4.5, we see that the mean for minutes of disorder, 2.31, is very similar to the median of 2.12 calculated earlier. In this case, adding knowledge about value does not change our portrait of the typical hot spot very much. However, we get a very different sense of the average case if we use the data from Table 4.6. Here, the median provided a less than satisfying representation of the average

---

[3]L. Sherman, J. D. Schmidt, D. Rogan, P. Gartin, E. G. Cohn, D. J. Collins, and A. R. Bacich, "From Initial Deterrence to Long-Term Escalation: Short-Custody Arrest for Poverty Ghetto Domestic Violence," *Criminology* 29 (1991): 821–850.

case. It was not sensitive to the fact that there was a large gap in the scores between the 16th and 17th cases. Accordingly, the median, 1.83, was very close in value to the first half of the cases in the sample, but very far from those hot spots with higher values. The mean should provide a better estimate of typicality here, because it recognizes the actual values of the categories and not just their positions. Let's see what happens when we calculate the mean for Table 4.6.

Following our equation, we first sum the individual cases:

W orking It Out

$$\sum_{i=1}^{N} X_i = \sum_{i=1}^{31} X_i$$

$$= 0.35 + 0.42 + 0.46 + 0.47 + 0.52 + 0.67 + 1.00 + 1.06$$

$$+ 1.15 + 1.19 + 1.19 + 1.48 + 1.60 + 1.63 + 1.73 + 1.83$$

$$+ 3.34 + 3.44 + 3.45 + 3.66 + 4.04 + 4.19 + 4.23 + 4.46$$

$$+ 4.51 + 4.72 + 5.09 + 5.47 + 5.64 + 5.65 + 5.77$$

$$= 84.41$$

We then divide this number by the total number of cases:

W orking It Out

$$\overline{X} = \frac{\sum_{i=1}^{N} X_i}{N}$$

$$= \frac{84.41}{31}$$

$$= 2.7229$$

Here, we gain an estimate of typicality of 2.72 (rounding to the second decimal place). As you can see, this score is much better centered in our distribution than is the median. The reason is simple. The median does not take into account the values of the categories. The mean does take value into account and thus is able to adjust for the gap in the distribution.

There are cases in which the sensitivity of the mean to the values of the categories in a measure can give misleading results. For example, let's say that one case in your study is very different from the others. As noted in Chapter 1, researchers call such a case an **outlier,** because it is very much outside the range of the other cases you studied. Taking the example of minutes of disorder from Table 4.5, let's say that the last case had 70 minutes of disorder (the maximum amount possible) rather than 6.57 minutes. When we calculate the mean now, the sum of the cases is much larger than before:

W orking It Out

$$\sum_{i=1}^{N} X_i = \sum_{i=1}^{31} X_i$$

$$= 0.35 + 0.42 + 0.46 + 0.47 + 0.52 + 0.67 + 1.00 + 1.06$$
$$+ 1.15 + 1.19 + 1.19 + 1.48 + 1.60 + 1.63 + 2.02 + 2.12$$
$$+ 2.21 + 2.34 + 2.45 + 2.66 + 3.04 + 3.19 + 3.23 + 3.46$$
$$+ 3.51 + 3.72 + 4.09 + 4.47 + 4.64 + 4.65 + 70.0$$

$$= 134.99$$

Dividing this sum by the total number of cases provides us with a mean of 4.35 (rounded to the second decimal place):

W orking It Out

$$\bar{X} = \frac{\sum_{i=1}^{N} X_i}{N}$$

$$= \frac{134.99}{31}$$

$$= 4.3545$$

The mean we calculated with the original score was 2.31 (see page 70). Accordingly, merely by changing one score to an outlier, we have almost doubled our estimate of typicality. In this case, the sensitivity of the mean to an extreme value in the distribution led it to overestimate the average case. This illustrates the general principle that the mean is sensitive to outliers. Because the mean is used to develop many other more complex statistics, this principle is relevant not only to the mean itself but also to a number of other important statistical techniques used by researchers.

So what should you do if outliers lead to a misleading conclusion regarding typicality in your study? One solution is simply to exclude the outliers from specific analyses and let your readers or audience know that some cases have been excluded and why. If the number of extreme cases is large enough, you may want to analyze these cases separately. Another solution is to transform the outliers. That is, you may want to replace them with values closer to the rest of the distribution (e.g., the highest value that is not an outlier). In this way, you can include the cases, but minimize the extent to which they affect your estimate of typicality. However, you should be cautious in developing such transformations of your scores, keeping in mind that you are changing the character of the distribution examined in your study.

Other Characteristics of the Mean

Two other traits of the mean are important because they play a role in how we develop other statistics. The first concerns what happens when we look at **deviations** (or differences) **from the mean.** This will become an issue in the next chapter, when we discuss measures of dispersion. The second, often termed the **least squares property** of the mean, will become important to us in Chapter 15, when we discuss regression.

If we take each score in a distribution, subtract the mean from it, and sum these differences, we will always get a result of 0. In equation form, this principle is represented as follows:

$$\sum_{i=1}^{N} (X_i - \overline{X}) = 0 \qquad \qquad \text{Equation 4.3}$$

In English, this equation says that if we sum the deviations from the mean, from the first to the last case, we will always get a result of 0. This principle is illustrated in Table 4.8, using the data on minutes of public disorder from Table 4.5. Here we have taken the 31 scores and subtracted the mean from each one. We then added these differences. Because the positive scores balance out the negative ones, the result is 0. This will always happen when we use the mean.

The second trait, the least squares property, is very important for understanding regression analysis (introduced in Chapter 15), a technique commonly used for describing relationships among variables in criminal justice. For the moment, it is enough to note this fact and that the issues

| Table 4.8 | Deviations from the Mean for Minutes of Public Disorder (A) |

SCORE (X)	DEVIATION FROM THE MEAN ($X_i - \overline{X}$)
0.35	$0.35 - 2.31 = -1.96$
0.42	$0.42 - 2.31 = -1.89$
0.46	$0.46 - 2.31 = -1.85$
0.47	$0.47 - 2.31 = -1.84$
0.52	$0.52 - 2.31 = -1.79$
0.67	$0.67 - 2.31 = -1.64$
1.00	$1.00 - 2.31 = -1.31$
1.06	$1.06 - 2.31 = -1.25$
1.15	$1.15 - 2.31 = -1.16$
1.19	$1.19 - 2.31 = -1.12$
1.19	$1.19 - 2.31 = -1.12$
1.48	$1.48 - 2.31 = -0.83$
1.60	$1.60 - 2.31 = -0.71$
1.63	$1.63 - 2.31 = -0.68$
2.02	$2.02 - 2.31 = -0.29$
2.12	$2.12 - 2.31 = -0.19$
2.21	$2.21 - 2.31 = -0.10$
2.34	$2.34 - 2.31 = 0.03$
2.45	$2.45 - 2.31 = 0.14$
2.66	$2.66 - 2.31 = 0.35$
3.04	$3.04 - 2.31 = 0.73$
3.19	$3.19 - 2.31 = 0.88$
3.23	$3.23 - 2.31 = 0.92$
3.46	$3.46 - 2.31 = 1.15$
3.51	$3.51 - 2.31 = 1.20$
3.72	$3.72 - 2.31 = 1.41$
4.09	$4.09 - 2.31 = 1.78$
4.47	$4.47 - 2.31 = 2.16$
4.64	$4.64 - 2.31 = 2.33$
4.65	$4.65 - 2.31 = 2.34$
6.57	$6.57 - 2.31 = 4.26$
Total (Σ)	0*

*Because of rounding error, the actual column total is slightly less than zero.

we address early on in statistics are often the bases for much more complex types of analysis. "Don't forget the basics" is a good rule. Many mistakes that researchers make in developing more complex statistics come from a failure to think about the basic issues raised in the first few chapters of this text.

The least squares property is written in equation form as follows:

$$\sum_{i=1}^{N} (X_i - \overline{X})^2 = \text{minimum}$$

Equation 4.4

What this says in English is that if we sum the squared deviations from the mean for all of our cases, we will get the minimum possible result. That is, suppose we take each individual's score on a measure, subtract the mean from that score, and then square the difference. If we then sum all of these values, the result we get will be smaller than the result we would have gotten if we had subtracted any other number besides the mean. You might try this by calculating the result for minutes of disorder using the mean. Then try other values and see if you can find some other number of minutes that will give you a smaller result. The least squares property says you won't.

Using the Mean for Noninterval Scales

The mean is ordinarily used for measuring central tendency only with interval scales. However, in practice, researchers sometimes use the mean with ordinal scales as well. Is this wrong? In a pure statistical sense, it is. However, some ordinal scales have a large number of categories and thus begin to mimic some of the characteristics of interval-level measures.

This is particularly true in cases where the movements from one category to another in an ordinal scale can be looked at as equivalent, no matter which category you move from. Taking our example of student attitudes toward public drunkenness in Table 4.4, a researcher might argue that the difference between "somewhat serious" and "a bit serious" is about equivalent to that between "very serious" and "extremely serious," and so forth. Thus, the difference between these categories is not just a difference of position; it is also a movement of equal units up the scale. Taking this approach, we can say that this measure takes into account both position and value, although the values here are not as straightforward as those gained from true interval scales such as number of crimes or dollar amount stolen.

A researcher might argue that the mean is appropriate for presenting findings on views of public drunkenness because this ordinal-scale measure of attitudes is like an interval-scale measure. Although it is easy to see the logic behind this decision, it is important to note that such a decision takes a good deal of justification. In general, you should be very cautious about using the mean for ordinal-level scales, even when the above criteria are met.

Statistics in Practice: Comparing the Median and the Mean

The general rule is that the mean provides the best measure of central tendency for an interval scale. This follows a principle stated in Chapter 1: In statistics, as in other decision-making areas, more information is better than less information. When we use the mean, we take into account not only the frequency of events in each category and their position, but also the values or scores of those categories. Because more information is used, the mean is less likely than other measures of central tendency to be affected by changes in the nature of the sample that a researcher examines. It is useful to note as well that the mean has some algebraic characteristics that make it more easily used in developing other types of statistics.

The mean is generally to be preferred, but when the distribution of a variable is strongly **skewed,** the median provides a better estimate of central tendency than the mean. "Skewed" means that the scores on the variable are very much weighted to one side and that frequencies of extreme values trail off in *one* direction away from the main cluster of cases. A distribution that has extreme values lower than the main cluster of observations (i.e., there is a "tail" to the left in the distribution) is said to be negatively skewed, while a distribution that has extreme values greater than the main cluster of observations (i.e., there is a "tail" to the right in the distribution) is said to be positively skewed.[4]

A good example of a skewed distribution in criminal justice is criminal history as measured by self-reports of prisoners. Horney and Marshall, for example, reported results on the frequency of offending for a sample of prisoners.[5] As is apparent from Figure 4.1, most of the offenders in their sample had a relatively low offending rate—between 1 and 20 offenses in the previous year. But a number of offenders had rates of more than 100, and a fairly large group had more than 200. The mean for this distribution is 175.

Clearly, 175 offenses provides a misleading view of typical rates of offending for their sample. Because the mean is sensitive to value, it is inflated by the very high frequency scores of a relatively small proportion of the sample. One solution suggested earlier to the problem of outliers

---

[4]A formal statistic for measuring the degree of skewness of a distribution is given by the following equation:

$$\text{skewness} = \frac{\Sigma(X_i - \overline{X})^3}{Ns_X^3}$$

In words, this equation tells us to take the deviation between a value and the mean and cube it, then sum these values over all observations; the sum of the cubed deviations is then divided by the sample size (N) multiplied by the standard deviation cubed. The measure of skewness will have a value of 0 if the distribution is symmetrical, a negative value if the distribution is negatively skewed, and a positive value if the distribution is positively skewed. The greater the value of the measure, the greater the degree of positive or negative skewness.

[5]J. Horney and I. H. Marshall, "An Experimental Comparison of Two Self-Report Methods for Measuring Lambda," *Journal of Research in Crime and Delinquency* 29 (1992): 102–121.

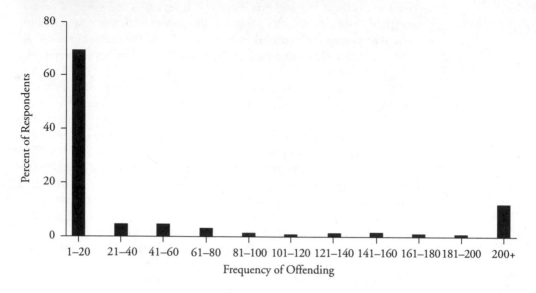

| Figure 4.1 | *Individual Frequency of Offending for a Sample of Offenders: A Case Where the Mean Is a Misleading Measure of Central Tendency* |

was to exclude such cases. But here, this would mean excluding almost 30% of the sample. Thus, these are not outliers in the traditional sense. Another option mentioned earlier is to analyze the "outliers" separately. But again, there is quite a spread of scores even if we look at those above 50 or 100 separately, and the analysis of the outliers might in itself provide a misleading view of central tendency. A common solution used for describing this type of skewed interval-level distribution is to use the median rather than the mean to describe central tendency. The median for this distribution is 4, which is certainly more representative of the average case than is the mean. But even if you choose this solution, it is very important to note to your audience that the distribution is skewed and to tell them a bit about the nature of the distribution.

How should you decide when a distribution is so skewed that it is preferable to use the median as opposed to the mean? You should begin by comparing the mean and the median. When there is a very large difference between them, it may be the result of skewness. In such cases, you should look at the distribution of the scores to see what is causing the mean and median to differ widely. But there is no solid boundary line to guide your choice.

In extreme cases (such as that of prior record in our example) or cases where the mean and median provide relatively close estimates, your choice will be clear. In the former case you would choose the median, and in the latter the mean. However, when your results fall somewhere in between, you will have to use common sense and the experiences of other researchers working with similar data as guidelines. What seems to make sense? What have other researchers chosen to do? One way of being fair to your audience is to provide results for both the mean and the median, irrespective of which you choose as the best measure of typicality.

Chapter Summary

The **mode** is calculated by identifying the category that contains the greatest number of cases. It may be applied to any scale of measurement. Because the mode uses very little information, it is rarely used with scales of measurement higher than the nominal scale. It can occasionally serve as a useful summary tool for higher-level scales, however, when a large number of cases are concentrated in one particular category.

The **median** is calculated by locating the middle score in a distribution and identifying in which category it falls. It is also known as the 50th percentile score, or the score below which 50% of the cases lie. The information used includes both the number of cases in a particular category and the positions of the categories. The median uses more information than does the mode and requires a scale of measurement that is at least ordinal in magnitude.

The **mean** is calculated by dividing the sum of the scores by the number of cases. The information used includes not only the number of cases in a category and the relative positions of the categories, but also the actual value of each category. Such information normally requires at least an interval scale of measurement. For this reason, the researcher should be cautious about using the mean to describe an ordinal scale. The mean uses more information than the mode and the median. It is, however, sensitive to extreme cases—**outliers.** Faced with the distorting effect of outliers, the researcher may choose to keep them, to transform them to other values, or to delete them altogether. If a distribution of scores is substantially **skewed,** then it may be more appropriate to use the median than to use the mean.

The sum derived by adding each score's **deviation from the mean** will always be 0. If the deviation of each score from the mean is squared, then the sum of these squares will be less than it would be if any number other than the mean were used. This is called the **least squares property.**

Key Terms

deviation from the mean The extent to which each individual score differs from the mean of all the scores.

least squares property A characteristic of the mean whereby the sum of all the squared deviations from the mean is a minimum—it is lower than the sum of the squared deviations from any other fixed point.

mean A measure of central tendency calculated by dividing the sum of the scores by the number of cases.

median A measure of central tendency calculated by identifying the value or category of the score that occupies the middle position in the distribution of scores.

mode A measure of central tendency calculated by identifying the score or category that occurs most frequently.

outlier(s) A single or small number of exceptional cases that substantially deviate from the general pattern of scores.

skewed Describing a spread of scores that is clearly weighted to one side.

Symbols and Formulas

X Individual score

$\overline{X}$ Mean

N Number of cases

Σ Sum

To calculate the median observation:

$$\text{Median observation} = \frac{N+1}{2}$$

To calculate the mean:

$$\overline{X} = \frac{\sum_{i=1}^{N} X_i}{N}$$

To show how the sum of the deviations from the mean equals 0:

$$\sum_{i=1}^{N} (X_i - \overline{X}) = 0$$

To express the least squares property:

$$\sum_{i=1}^{N} (X_i - \overline{X})^2 = \text{minimum}$$

Exercises

4.1   Drivers cited for moving violations are required by a state's laws to take a driving safety course taught by the local police department. The sign-in sheet asks individuals to note why they received a ticket. The 14 participants at a recent class noted the following:

Speeding, Running a red light, Running a stop sign, Speeding, Speeding, Running a red light, Tailgating, Speeding, Running a red light, Recklessness, Speeding, Running a red light, Speeding, Running a stop sign

a. Categorize these data and calculate the mode.

b. Explain why the median would not be an appropriate measure of central tendency for these data.

4.2   Calculate the mode, median, and mean for the following data:

a. Number of previous employments held by 25 convicts:

3 3 1 1 0 1 0 2 1 0 8 4 3

1 2 1 9 0 1 7 0 7 2 0 1

b. Weeks of training undergone by 20 prison guards:

10 16 12 16 16 16 10 8 10 12

16 18 12 16 16 8 0 12 10 16

c. Height (in meters) of 30 convicts:

1.72 1.78 1.73 1.70 1.81 1.64 1.76 1.72 1.75 1.74

1.88 1.79 2.01 1.80 1.77 1.79 1.69 1.74 1.75 1.66

1.77 1.73 1.72 1.91 1.80 1.74 1.72 1.82 1.86 1.79

4.3   A researcher checked the response times of police to ten emergency telephone calls. The data below record the number of minutes that elapsed from when the telephone call ended to when the police arrived:

24 26 14 27 198 22 27 17 19 29

a. Calculate the mode, the median, and the mean.

b. Which of these measures is the most suitable for this particular case? Explain your choice.

4.4   Airport officials wished to check the alertness of their security officers over the two busiest weeks of the summer. During this period, they sent out 50 undercover staff carrying suspicious items of hand luggage. Five of them were stopped at the entrance to the airport. Six made it into the airport, but were stopped at check-in. Thirteen more got into the airport and through check-in, only to be stopped at the hand-luggage inspection point. Two passed the airport entrance, check-in, and hand-luggage inspection, but were stopped when presenting their boarding cards at the gate. Four people made it past every one of these stages, only to be stopped when boarding the plane. Twenty of the undercover staff were not detected at all.

a. Categorize the data and calculate the median category.

b. Is the median a good measure of central tendency in this case? Explain your answer. If you think it is not, suggest an alternative and explain why.

4.5   On the first day of the term in a statistics course, the professor administered a brief questionnaire to the students, asking how many statistics courses they had ever taken before the current term. Of the 33 students who answered the question, 17 said none, 9 said one, 3 said two, 2 said three, 1 said four, and 1 said five.

a. Calculate the mode, median, and mean for number of prior statistics classes.

b. Which one of these measures of central tendency best measures the typicality of these data?

4.6   As part of her undergraduate thesis, a criminal justice student asked ten other criminal justice majors to rate the fairness of the criminal justice system. The students were asked to say whether they strongly agreed, agreed, were uncertain, disagreed, or strongly disagreed with the following statement: "The criminal justice system in our country treats all defendants fairly." The ten responses were

Strongly agree, Strongly agree, Strongly disagree, Strongly disagree, Uncertain, Disagree, Disagree, Agree, Strongly disagree, Uncertain

a. Categorize these data and calculate an appropriate measure of central tendency.

b. Explain why this measure of central tendency best represents the typicality of these data.

4.7   There are five prisoners in the high-security wing in a prison—Albert, Harry, Charlie, Dave, and Eddie. Only Eddie's biographical details have been lost. The information available is as follows:

	Age	Previous Convictions
Albert	23	1
Harry	28	4
Charlie	18	1
Dave	41	1
Eddie	?	?

a. Can we compute any of the following for previous convictions of the five prisoners: the mode, the median, or the mean? If any (or all) of these three measures may be calculated, what are their values?

b. If the mean number of previous convictions is 2.0, how many convictions does Eddie have?

c. If we know that the median age for the five prisoners is 28, what does this tell us about Eddie's age? Explain why.

d. If the mean age for the five prisoners is 28.2, how old is Eddie?

4.8 A researcher sat on a bench along the main shopping street of a city center on ten successive Saturdays from 11:00 A.M. to 2:00 P.M.—the three busiest shopping hours of the day—and recorded the number of times a police officer passed by. The results for the ten weeks are as follows:

Week No.:	1	2	3	4	5	6	7	8	9	10
No. of Police Officers Observed:	4	3	6	4	4	5	4	35	3	5

On week 8, local unionists held a demonstration in the city center, and the high number of observations for that week can be explained by the extra officers called in to police the rally.

a. Calculate the mode, median, and mean for the number of police officers observed.

b. Which measure of central tendency best represents typicality for these data? Discuss the issues involved in choosing the most appropriate means of describing the data.

c. Imagine that the unionists had decided to hold a regular demonstration in the city center on alternating weeks. The results recorded for the same study would be as follows:

Week No.:	1	2	3	4	5	6	7	8	9	10
No. of Police Officers Observed:	4	30	6	31	6	52	4	35	4	34

Would the measure of central tendency you recommended in part b still be the best measure of typicality? Explain why.

4.9 On a recent evening, a police crackdown on prostitution solicitation resulted in 19 arrests. The ages of the persons arrested were

17 18 24 37 32 49 61 20 21 21

25 24 24 26 30 33 35 22 19

a. Calculate an appropriate measure of central tendency.

b. Explain why this measure of central tendency best represents typicality for these data.

4.10   Using your answers from part a of Exercise 4.5, calculate

    a. The sum of the deviations from the mean.

    b. The sum of the squared deviations from the mean.

    c. The sum of the squared deviations from the median.

    d. The sum of the squared deviations from the mode.

    e. Which of these sums of squared deviations has the smallest value?

Computer Exercises

There are several different ways of obtaining measures of central tendency in SPSS. Two of the more direct ways of computing measures of central tendency are to use the "Descriptives" command and the "Frequencies" command.

Using the "Descriptives" command

— Click on "Analyze→Descriptive Statistics→Descriptives."

— You should see a window with two boxes. The box on the left contains the names of the variables in the data set; the box on the right is empty. For those variables for which you want a mean, move the variable name from the left box to the right box.

— Click on "OK" to have the descriptive statistics calculated for you. The output window will contain quite a bit of information for each variable that you have selected.

Note: The "Descriptives" command will report only the mean, not the mode or the median. Since the only measure of central tendency this command will calculate is the mean, it is generally useful only for interval-level data. This command is most useful when you are working with a data set that contains almost exclusively interval-level variables.

Using the "Frequencies" command

— Click on "Analyze→Descriptive Statistics→Frequencies."

— As you may recall from the previous chapter's computer exercises, this command will produce frequency distributions for the variables whose names are moved from the list on the left to the box on the right of the window. To obtain measures of central tendency for the variables of interest, click on the box labeled "Statistics" at the bottom of this window.

— In the new window that appears, you will be presented with a menu of statistics that SPSS can calculate on each of the variables. Select (click on the empty square next to) Mode, Median, and Mean.

— Click on "Continue" and then "OK" to have these statistics calculated for you. In the output window, you should see a box labeled "Statistics." Each column of this table refers to a separate variable. As you move down the rows, you should see the reported values for the mode, the median, and the mean.

Caution: Note that the mode and the median are listed as numbers, even though the data may be nominal or ordinal and you have entered value labels. To report correctly the value of the mode or median, you need to report the *category* represented by that number. For example, suppose you had a variable labeled "gender," where males were coded as 1 and females as 2. The mode would be reported by SPSS as either 1 or 2, and it would be up to you to report correctly whether the modal category was male or female.

1. Open the data file **nys_1.sav.** Consider the level of measurement for each variable, and then compute and report appropriate measures of central tendency for each variable.

2. Do any of the variables included in the data file appear to have potential outliers? (You may want to consult your histograms from the Chapter 3 computer exercises or create histograms now for the interval-level variables included in the data file.)

3. If you find one or more potential outliers, take the following steps to investigate their effect on the measures of central tendency.

    a. Use the "Recode" command to create two new variables, one that recodes the outliers as "System Missing" values and one that recodes the outliers as the next smaller value.

    b. Using your variable that recodes the outliers as missing, report how the values of the mean and the median change when potential outliers are removed from the analysis.

    c. Using your variable that recodes the outliers as the next smaller value, report how the values of the mean and the median change when potential outliers are made less extreme.

    d. Which approach to handling potential outliers is more appropriate for analyzing these data? Explain why. Faced with potential outliers, which measure of central tendency would you report?

How Typical Is the Typical Case?:

Measuring Dispersion

measures of dispersion

What Do They Tell Us About Our Data?

**measuring dispersion in nominal
and ordinal scales: proportions,
percentages, and the variation ratio**

How Are They Calculated?

What Are Their Characteristics?

**measuring dispersion in interval scales:
range, variance, and standard deviation**

How Are They Calculated?

What Are Their Characteristics?

MEASURES OF CENTRAL TENDENCY provide a snapshot of the typical case; however, the same statistic may be obtained from samples or populations that are in fact quite dissimilar. For example, a sample of police recruits with a mean or median age of 23 is not likely to include people younger than 18 or older than 30, because most police departments have age requirements for incoming officers. A sample of offenders with a mean or median age of 23, however, will include offenders younger than 18 and much older than 30. In both these samples, the average person studied is 23 years old. But the sample of offenders will include more younger and older people than the sample of police recruits. The ages of the offenders are dispersed more widely around the average age.

Measures of dispersion allow us to fill a gap in our description of the samples or populations we study. They ask the question: How typical is the typical case? They tell us to what extent the subjects we studied are similar to the case we have chosen to represent them. Are most cases clustered closely around the average case? Or, as with the sample of offenders above, is there a good deal of dispersion of cases both above and below the average?

Measures of Dispersion for Nominal- and Ordinal-Level Data

With nominal scales, we define the typical case as the category with the largest number of subjects. Accordingly, in Chapter 4 we chose "private attorney" as the modal category for legal representation for a sample of white-collar offenders. But how would we describe to what extent the use of a private attorney is typical of the sample as a whole? Put another way, to what degree are the cases concentrated in the modal category?

The Proportion in the Modal Category

The most straightforward way to answer this question is to describe the proportion of cases that fall in the modal category. Recall from Chapter 3 that a proportion is represented by the following equation:

$$\text{Proportion} = \frac{N_{\text{cat}}}{N_{\text{total}}}$$

Accordingly, we can represent the proportion of cases in the modal category using Equation 5.1:

$$\text{Proportion} = \frac{N_{\text{modal cat}}}{N_{\text{total}}} \qquad \text{Equation 5.1}$$

That is, we take the number of cases in the modal category and divide it by the total number of cases in the sample.

Taking the example of legal representation, we divide the N of cases in the modal category (private attorney) by the total N of cases in the sample (see Table 5.1):

W orking It Out

$$\text{Proportion} = \frac{N_{\text{modal cat.}}}{N_{\text{total}}}$$

$$= \frac{380}{671}$$

$$= 0.5663$$

Following our earlier suggestions regarding rounding to the second decimal place, we say that the proportion of white-collar offenders in the modal category was about 0.57.

Table 5.1   Legal Representation for White-Collar Crime

CATEGORY	FREQUENCY (N)
No Attorney	20
Legal Aid	26
Court Appointed	92
Public Defender	153
Private Attorney	380
Total (Σ)	671

| **Table 5.2** | Method of Execution in the United States, 1977–2000 |

CATEGORY	FREQUENCY (*N*)
Lethal Injection	518
Electrocution	149
Lethal Gas	11
Hanging	3
Firing Squad	2
Total (Σ)	683

Source: Tracy L. Snell, "Capital Punishment 2000,"
Bureau of Justice Statistics Bulletin, 2001, p. 12.

Table 5.2 presents information about the method of execution used on the 683 persons executed in the United States from 1977 to 2000. The modal category is lethal injection, so the proportion in the modal category is found by dividing the *N* of cases in that category by the total *N* of cases:

W orking It Out

$$\text{Proportion} = \frac{N_{\text{modal cat.}}}{N_{\text{total}}}$$

$$= \frac{518}{683}$$

$$= 0.7584$$

Of persons executed in the United States from 1977 to 2000, the proportion killed through lethal injection was about 0.76.

The Percentage in the Modal Category

Alternatively, we may refer to the percentage in the modal category. Most people find percentages easier to understand than proportions. Recall that a percentage is obtained by taking a proportion and multiplying it by 100. Accordingly, we can take Equation 5.1 and multiply the result by 100 to get the percentage of cases in the modal category.

$$\text{Percentage} = \frac{N_{\text{modal cat.}}}{N_{\text{total}}} \times 100$$

For our legal representation example,

> **W** orking It Out
>
> $$\text{Percentage} = \frac{N_{\text{modal cat.}}}{N_{\text{total}}} \times 100$$
>
> $$= \frac{380}{671} \times 100$$
>
> $$= 56.6319$$

That is, about 57% of the cases in the sample fall in the modal category.

Similarly, for the method of execution example, the percentage in the modal category is

$$\text{Percentage} = \frac{518}{683} \times 100$$

$$= 75.8419$$

About 76% of all executions in the United States from 1977 to 2000 involved the use of lethal injection.

The Variation Ratio

Another way to describe the degree to which the modal category represents the cases in a sample is to use a statistic called the **variation ratio** (VR). The variation ratio is based on the same logic as a proportion, but it examines the extent to which the cases are spread outside the modal category, rather than concentrated within it. The proportion of cases in the modal category is subtracted from 1:

$$\text{VR} = 1 - \left(\frac{N_{\text{modal cat.}}}{N_{\text{total}}} \right)$$

Equation 5.2

For the legal representation example, the variation ratio is

> **W** orking It Out
>
> $$\text{VR} = 1 - \left(\frac{N_{\text{modal cat.}}}{N_{\text{total}}} \right)$$
>
> $$= 1 - \left(\frac{380}{671} \right)$$
>
> $$= 0.4337$$

The variation ratio for legal representation in this sample of white-collar offenders is about 0.43. But what does this say about the extent to which cases in the sample are clustered around the typical case? Is a variation ratio of 0.43 large or small? What rule can we use for deciding more generally whether the distribution we are examining is strongly clustered?

One approach is to define at the outset the upper and lower limits for the variation ratio or proportion for a particular measure. Obviously, the largest proportion, regardless of the study, is 1.0, which would mean that all of the cases were in the modal category. Having all of the cases in the modal category would lead to a variation ratio of 0, indicating no dispersion.

The smallest proportion (or largest VR) depends, however, on the number of categories in your measure. The mode is defined as the category in your measure with the most cases, so it must have at least one more case than any other category. If you have only two categories, then the modal category must include one more than half of the cases in your study. So, in the instance of two categories, the least possible concentration is just over 0.50 of the cases. The least possible dispersion, as measured by the variation ratio, would be 1 minus this proportion, or just under 0.50. If you have four categories, the modal category must have more than one-quarter of the cases. Accordingly, the smallest variation ratio would be a bit smaller than 0.75.

What about our example of legal representation? We have five categories and 671 cases. The smallest number of cases the modal category could have with these numbers is 135. In this instance, each of the other four categories would have 134 cases. This is the maximum amount of dispersion that could exist in this sample, and it amounts to about 20.12% of the total number of cases in the sample, or a variation ratio of 0.7988. As noted earlier, the greatest degree of concentration in the modal category would yield a proportion of 1 and a variation ratio of 0. The estimates we calculated for legal representation (proportion = 0.57; VR = 0.43) lie somewhere between these two extremes.

Is this dispersion large or small? As with many of the statistics we will examine, the answer depends on the context in which you are working. "Large" or "small" describes a value, not a statistical concept. Statistically, you know that your estimate falls somewhere between the largest possible degree of concentration and the largest possible degree of dispersion. But whether this is important or meaningful depends on the problem you are examining and the results that others have obtained in prior research.

For example, if, in a study of legal representation for white-collar crime in England, it had been found that 90% of the cases were concentrated in the private attorney category, then we might conclude that our results reflected a relatively high degree of dispersion of legal representation in the United States. If, in England, only 25% of the cases had been in the modal category, we might conclude that there was a relatively low degree of dispersion of legal representation in the United States.

The proportion and the variation ratio are useful primarily for describing dispersion with nominal-level measures. In some circumstances, however, they can be useful for describing ordinal-level variables as well. This is true primarily when there are just a few categories in a measure or when there is a very high degree of concentration of cases in one category. The problem in using a simple proportion or variation ratio for ordinal-level measures is that the mode, upon which these statistics are based, is often a misleading measure for ordinal scales. As discussed in Chapter 4, the mode does not take into account the positions of scores in a measure, and thus it may provide a misleading view of the average case.

Index of Qualitative Variation

One measure of dispersion that is not based on the mode—and that can be used for both nominal and ordinal scales—is the **index of qualitative variation** (IQV). The IQV compares the amount of variation observed in a sample to the total amount of variation possible, given the number of cases and categories in a study. It is a standardized measure. This means that whatever the number of cases or categories, the IQV can vary only between 0 and 100. An IQV of 0 means that there is no variation in the measure, or all of the cases lie in one category. An IQV of 100 means that the cases are evenly dispersed across the categories.

$$\text{IQV} = \left(\frac{\sum\limits_{i=1}^{k-1} \sum\limits_{j=i+1}^{k} N_{\text{obs}_i} N_{\text{obs}_j}}{\sum\limits_{i=1}^{k-1} \sum\limits_{j=i+1}^{k} N_{\text{exp}_i} N_{\text{exp}_j}} \right) \times 100 \qquad \text{Equation 5.3}$$

Equation 5.3 provides a guide for how to compute the IQV. You are already familiar with the summation symbols within the parentheses. Here we are summing not across cases, but across products of distinct categories. N_{obs} represents the number of cases we observe within a category in our study. N_{exp} represents the number of cases we would expect in a category if the measure were distributed equally across the categories. That is, it is the N we would expect if there were the maximum amount of dispersion of our cases. We use the subscripts i, j, and k as a shorthand way to say that we should multiply all of the potential pairs of categories. Here's how this works: k represents the total number of categories of a variable. In the legal representation example, $k = 5$. Subscripts i and j index the categories of the variable. Use of the subscripts i and j provides us with a way of keeping track and making sure that we have multiplied all possible pairs of observed frequencies from each of the categories.

For example, if a variable had three categories, then the numerator (the measure of observed variation) would be equal to

$$N_{obs_1}N_{obs_2} + N_{obs_1}N_{obs_3} + N_{obs_2}N_{obs_3}$$

If a variable had four categories, then the numerator would be equal to

$$N_{obs_1}N_{obs_2} + N_{obs_1}N_{obs_3} + N_{obs_1}N_{obs_4} + N_{obs_2}N_{obs_3} + N_{obs_2}N_{obs_4} + N_{obs_3}N_{obs_4}$$

A concrete example will make it much easier to develop this statistic in practice. Let's say that we wanted to describe dispersion of an ordinal-scale measure of fear of crime in a college class of 20 students. The students were asked whether they were personally concerned about crime on campus. The potential responses were "very concerned," "quite concerned," "a little concerned," and "not concerned at all." The responses of the students are reported under the "N observed" column in Table 5.3. As you can see, the cases are fairly spread out, although there are more students in the "very concerned" and "quite concerned" categories than in the "a little concerned" and "not concerned at all" categories. The expected number of cases in each category under the assumption of maximum dispersion is 5. That is, if the cases were equally spread across the categories, we would expect the same number in each. Following Equation 5.3, we first multiply the number of cases observed in each category by the number observed in every other category and then sum. We then divide this total by the sum of the number expected in each category

Table 5.3	Fear of Crime Among Students	
CATEGORY	**N OBSERVED**	**N EXPECTED**
Not Concerned at All	3	20/4 = 5
A Little Concerned	4	20/4 = 5
Quite Concerned	6	20/4 = 5
Very Concerned	7	20/4 = 5
Total (Σ)	20	20

multiplied by the number expected in every other category. This amount is then multiplied by 100:

W orking It Out

$$IQV = \frac{\sum\limits_{i=1}^{k-1} \sum\limits_{j=i+1}^{k} N_{\text{obs}_i} N_{\text{obs}_j}}{\sum\limits_{i=1}^{k-1} \sum\limits_{j=i+1}^{k} N_{\text{exp}_i} N_{\text{exp}_j}} \times 100$$

$$= \left(\frac{(3 \times 4) + (3 \times 6) + (3 \times 7) + (4 \times 6) + (4 \times 7) + (6 \times 7)}{(5 \times 5) + (5 \times 5) + (5 \times 5) + (5 \times 5) + (5 \times 5) + (5 \times 5)} \right) \times 100$$

$$= \left(\frac{145}{150} \right) \times 100$$

$$= 96.6667$$

The observed variation is 145. The expected variation is 150, representing the maximum amount of dispersion possible for the measure. The IQV for this measure is 96.67, meaning that the cases studied are very dispersed among the categories of the measure.

Measuring Dispersion in Interval Scales: The Range, Variance, and Standard Deviation

A common method of describing the spread of scores on interval or higher scales is to examine the **range** between the highest and lowest scores. Take, for example, the distribution of cases in Table 5.4. Let's say that this was a distribution of crime calls at hot spots over a one-year period. In describing typicality in this distribution, we would report the mean number of calls for the 12 places, which is 21.50. In describing how dispersed the scores are, we would report that the scores range between 2 and 52, or that the range of scores is 50.

The range is very simple and easy to present. Its attraction lies precisely in the fact that everyone understands what a range represents. However, the range is an unstable statistic because it uses very little of the information available in interval-level scales. It bases its estimate of dispersion on just two observations, the highest and lowest scores. This means that a change in just one case in a distribution can completely

Table 5.4 Crime Calls at Hot Spots in a Year

HOT SPOT NUMBER	NUMBER OF CALLS
1	2
2	9
3	11
4	13
5	20
6	20
7	20
8	24
9	27
10	29
11	31
12	52

alter your description of dispersion. For example, if we changed the case with the most calls in Table 5.4 from 52 to 502, the range would change from 50 to 500.

One method for reducing the instability of the range is to examine cases that are not at the extremes of your distribution. In this way, you are likely to avoid the problem of having the range magnified by a few very large or small numbers. For example, you might choose to look at the range between the 5th and 95th percentile scores, rather than that between the lowest and highest scores. It is also common to look at the range between the 25th and 75th percentile scores or between the 20th and 80th percentile scores. But however you change the points at which the range is calculated, you still rely on just two scores in determining the spread of cases in your distribution. The range provides no insight into whether the scores below or above these cases are clustered together tightly or dispersed widely. Its portrait of dispersion for interval scales is thus very limited.

How can we gain a fuller view of dispersion for interval scales? Remember that we became interested in the problem of dispersion because we wanted to provide an estimate of how well the average case represented the distribution of cases as a whole. Are scores clustered tightly around the average case or dispersed widely from it? Given that we have already described the mean as the most appropriate measure of central tendency for such scales, this is the natural place to begin our assessment. Why not simply examine how much the average scores differ from the mean?

In fact, this is the logic that statisticians have used to develop the main measures of dispersion for interval scales. However, they are faced with a basic problem in taking this approach. As we discussed in Chapter 4, if we add up all of the deviations from the mean, we will always

Table 5.5	Deviations from the Mean for Crime Calls at Hot Spots in a Year

HOT SPOT NUMBER	NUMBER OF CALLS	DEVIATIONS FROM THE MEAN $(X_i - \overline{X})$
1	2	$2 - 21.5 = -19.5$
2	9	$9 - 21.5 = -12.5$
3	11	$11 - 21.5 = -10.5$
4	13	$13 - 21.5 = -8.5$
5	20	$20 - 21.5 = -1.5$
6	20	$20 - 21.5 = -1.5$
7	20	$20 - 21.5 = -1.5$
8	24	$24 - 21.5 = 2.5$
9	27	$27 - 21.5 = 5.5$
10	29	$29 - 21.5 = 7.5$
11	31	$31 - 21.5 = 9.5$
12	52	$52 - 21.5 = 30.5$
		Total $(\Sigma) = $ 0.0

come up with a value of 0. You can see this again by looking at the data on crime calls at hot spots in Table 5.5. If we take the sum of the differences between each score and the mean, written in equation form as

$$\sum_{i=1}^{N}(X_i - \overline{X})$$

the total, as expected, is 0.

As discussed in Chapter 4, when we add up the deviations above and below the mean, the positive and negative scores cancel each other out. In order to use deviations from the mean as a basis for a measure of dispersion, we must develop a method for taking the sign, or direction, out of our statistic. One solution is to square each deviation from the mean. Squaring will always yield a positive result because multiplying a positive number or a negative number by itself will result in a positive outcome. This is the method that statisticians have used in developing the measures of dispersion most commonly used for interval scales.

The Variance

When we take this approach, the **variance** (s^2) provides an estimate of the dispersion around the mean. It is the sum of the squared deviations from the mean divided by the number of cases. Written in equation form, it is

$$s^2 = \frac{\sum_{i=1}^{N}(X_i - \overline{X})^2}{N}$$

Equation 5.4

Table 5.6	Variance for Crime Calls at Hot Spots in a Year

HOT SPOT NUMBER	NUMBER OF CALLS	$(X_i - \overline{X})$	$(X_i - \overline{X})^2$
1	2	$2 - 21.5 = -19.5$	380.25
2	9	$9 - 21.5 = -12.5$	156.25
3	11	$11 - 21.5 = -10.5$	110.25
4	13	$13 - 21.5 = -8.5$	72.25
5	20	$20 - 21.5 = -1.5$	2.25
6	20	$20 - 21.5 = -1.5$	2.25
7	20	$20 - 21.5 = -1.5$	2.25
8	24	$24 - 21.5 = 2.5$	6.25
9	27	$27 - 21.5 = 5.5$	30.25
10	29	$29 - 21.5 = 7.5$	56.25
11	31	$31 - 21.5 = 9.5$	90.25
12	52	$52 - 21.5 = 30.5$	930.25
		Total (Σ) = 0.0	Total (Σ) = 1,839.00

In practice, you must take the following steps to compute the variance (as we do for our example in Table 5.6):

1. Take each case and subtract the mean from it, to get the deviation from the mean. For our example of crime calls at hot spots, we first take the case with 2 calls and subtract the mean of 21.5 from it, to get a score of -19.5.

2. Square each of these scores. For the first case, our result is 380.25.

3. Sum the results obtained in step 2. For our example of hot spots of crime, this yields a total of 1,839.

4. Finally, divide this result by the number of cases in the study. For our 12 cases, this leads to a variance of 153.25.[1]

---

[1]If you are working with SPSS or another computer package, you will notice that the result you get computing the variance by hand using this formula and the result provided by the computer package are slightly different. For example, SPSS computes a variance of 167.18 for the distribution provided in Table 5.6. The difference develops from the computer's use of a correction for the bias of sample variances: 1 is subtracted from the N in the denominator of Equation 5.4. The correction is used primarily as a tool in inferential statistics and is discussed in Chapter 10. Though it is our view that the uncorrected variance should be used in describing sample statistics, many researchers report variances with the correction factor for sample estimates. When samples are larger, the estimates obtained with and without the correction are very similar, and thus it generally makes very little substantive difference which approach is used.

W orking It Out

$$s^2 = \frac{\sum\limits_{i=1}^{N}(X_i - \overline{X})^2}{N}$$

$$= \frac{\sum\limits_{i=1}^{12}(X_i - 21.5)^2}{12}$$

$$= \frac{1,839}{12}$$

$$= 153.25$$

As another example, consider the data presented in Table 5.7 on bail amounts required for a group of 15 defendants. The mean bail amount is $3,263.33. Following the same procedure as before, we subtract the mean from each of the individual observations. These values are presented in the third column. The squared deviations from the mean appear in the fourth column, and the sum of the squared deviations appears at the bottom of the column. When we divide the total by the N of cases, we gain a variance of $6,984,155.56 for the dollar amount of bail.

Table 5.7 Variance for Bail Amounts for a Sample of Persons Arrested for Felonies

DEFENDANT	BAIL AMOUNT	$(X_i - \overline{X})$	$(X_i - \overline{X})^2$
1	500	−2,763.33	7,635,992.69
2	1,000	−2,263.33	5,122,662.69
3	1,000	−2,263.33	5,122,662.69
4	1,000	−2,263.33	5,122,662.69
5	1,200	−2,063.33	4,257,330.69
6	1,500	−1,763.33	3,109,332.69
7	2,500	−763.33	582,672.69
8	2,500	−763.33	582,672.69
9	2,500	−763.33	582,672.69
10	2,750	−513.33	263,507.69
11	5,000	1,736.67	3,016,022.69
12	5,000	1,736.67	3,016,022.69
13	5,000	1,736.67	3,016,022.69
14	7,500	4,236.67	17,949,372.69
15	10,000	6,736.67	45,382,722.69
		Total (Σ) = 0.05	Total (Σ) = 104,762,333.33

> ## W orking It Out
>
> $$s^2 = \frac{\sum\limits_{i=1}^{N}(X_i - \overline{X})^2}{N}$$
>
> $$= \frac{\sum\limits_{i=1}^{15}(X_i - 3,263.33)^2}{15}$$
>
> $$= \frac{104,762,333.33}{15}$$
>
> $$= 6,984,155.56$$

With the variance, we now have a statistic for computing dispersion based on deviations from the mean. However, how can we interpret whether the variance for a distribution is large or small? If you are having trouble making sense of this from our two examples, you are not alone. While squaring solves one problem (the fact that the raw deviations from the mean sum to 0), it creates another. By squaring, we generally obtain numbers that are much larger than the actual units in the distributions we are examining.[2]

The Standard Deviation

Another measure of dispersion based on the variance provides a solution to the problem of interpretation. This measure, the **standard deviation,** is calculated by taking the square root of the variance. Accordingly, it reduces our estimate of dispersion, using a method similar to the one we employed to solve the problem of positive and negative differences from the mean adding to 0. The standard deviation (s) provides an estimate of dispersion in units similar to those of our original scores. It is described in equation form as

$$s = \sqrt{\frac{\sum\limits_{i=1}^{N}(X_i - \overline{X})^2}{N}}$$

Equation 5.5

---

[2]In the special case of a fraction, the result will be smaller numbers.

Although Equations 5.4 and 5.5 provide a useful way of conceptualizing and measuring the variance and standard deviation, you can also use a computing formula that has fewer steps and is less likely to result in computational error. In Table 5.6, we rounded the mean and then calculated squared deviations based on values that were rounded at each step. In an attempt to limit the amount of rounding, and consequently decrease the chances of a mistake, an alternative equation that can be used for the variance is

$$s^2 = \frac{\sum\limits_{i=1}^{N} X_i^2 - \dfrac{\left(\sum\limits_{i=1}^{N} X_i\right)^2}{N}}{N}$$

And an alternative for the standard deviation is

$$s = \sqrt{\frac{\sum\limits_{i=1}^{N} X_i^2 - \dfrac{\left(\sum\limits_{i=1}^{N} X_i\right)^2}{N}}{N}}$$

Let's reconsider the data in Table 5.6 on hot spots. The following table illustrates the key calculations:

HOT SPOT NUMBER	NUMBER OF CALLS (X_i)	X_i^2
1	2	4
2	9	81
3	11	121
4	13	169
5	20	400
6	20	400
7	20	400
8	24	576
9	27	729
10	29	841
11	31	961
12	52	2,704
Total (Σ)	258	7,386

The variance (s^2) is then calculated with the computational equation as

$$s^2 = \frac{7{,}386 - \dfrac{(258)^2}{12}}{12} = 153.25$$

And the standard deviation is simply the square root of the variance:

$$s = \sqrt{153.25} = 12.38$$

Similarly, let's revisit the bail data in Table 5.7 and compute the variance with the computational formula. The following table illustrates the key calculations.

DEFENDANT	BAIL AMOUNT (X_i)	X_i^2
1	500	250,000
2	1,000	1,000,000
3	1,000	1,000,000
4	1,000	1,000,000
5	1,200	1,440,000
6	1,500	2,250,000
7	2,500	6,250,000
8	2,500	6,250,000
9	2,500	6,250,000
10	2,750	7,562,500
11	5,000	25,000,000
12	5,000	25,000,000
13	5,000	25,000,000
14	7,500	56,250,000
15	10,000	100,000,000
Total (Σ)	48,950	264,502,500

The variance is

$$s^2 = \frac{264{,}502{,}500 - \dfrac{(48{,}950)^2}{15}}{15} = 6{,}984{,}155.56$$

And the standard deviation is

$$s = \sqrt{6{,}984{,}155.56} = 2{,}642.76$$

In calculating the standard deviation, we add one step to our calculation of variance: We take the square root of our result. For the example of crime calls at 12 hot spots (where the variance equaled 153.25), we obtain a standard deviation of $\sqrt{153.25} = 12.38$.[3] If you were to define, on average, how much the scores differed from the mean just by looking at these 12 cases, you would probably come to a conclusion close to that provided by the standard deviation. Similarly, if we take the square root of the variance for the bail example above, we come up with a figure that makes much more intuitive sense than the variance. In this case, the standard deviation is $\sqrt{6,984,155.56}$, or $2,642.76.

The standard deviation has some basic characteristics, which relate generally to its use:

1. A standard deviation of 0 means that a measure has no variability. For this to happen, all of the scores on a measure have to be the same. For example, if you examine a group of first-time offenders, there will be no variation in the number of offenses in their criminal records. By definition, because they are all first-time offenders, the standard deviation (and the variance) will be 0.

2. The size of the standard deviation (and the variance) is dependent on both the amount of dispersion in the measure and the units of analysis that are used. When cases are spread widely from the mean, there is more dispersion and the standard deviation will be larger. When cases are tightly clustered around the mean, the standard deviation will be smaller.

   Similarly, when the units of analysis in the measure are large, the standard deviation will reflect the large units. For example, if you report the standard deviation of police salaries in a particular city in dollars, your standard deviation will be larger than if you reported those salaries in units of thousands of dollars. If the standard deviation is 3,350 in dollars, the standard deviation would be 3.35 using the unit of thousands of dollars.

3. Extreme deviations from the mean have the greatest weight in constructing the standard deviation. What this means is that here, as with the mean, you should be concerned with the problem of outliers. In this case, the effect of outliers is compounded because they affect not only the mean itself, which is used in computing the standard deviation, but also the individual deviations that are obtained by subtracting the mean from individual cases.

---

[3]As discussed in footnote 1, SPSS and many other computer packages would provide a slightly different result, based on the use of a correction of -1 in the denominator.

Table 5.8	Duncan SEI for Bribery and Antitrust Offenders

CATEGORY	N	$\bar{X}$	s
Bribery	83	59.27	19.45
Antitrust	112	61.05	11.13
Total (Σ)	195		

The standard deviation is a useful statistic for comparing the extent to which characteristics are clustered or dispersed around the mean in different samples. For example, in Table 5.8, a sample of offenders convicted of antitrust violations is compared to a sample of offenders convicted of bribery. The characteristic examined is social status, as measured by the interval-scale Duncan socioeconomic index (SEI).[4] The index is based on the average income, education, and prestige associated with different occupations. The mean Duncan scores for these two samples are very similar (61.05 for antitrust violators; 59.27 for bribery offenders), but the standard deviation for those convicted of bribery is about twice that of those convicted of antitrust violations.

Figure 5.1 illustrates why these two samples yield similar means but very different standard deviations. The scores for most antitrust offenders are clustered closely within the range of 55 to 75. For bribery offenders, in contrast, the scores are much more widely spread across the distribution, including many more cases between 75 and 90 and below 50. What this tells us is that the antitrust sample includes a fairly homogeneous group of offenders, ranking on average relatively high on the Duncan socioeconomic index. Bribery is a much more diverse category. Although the means are similar, the bribery category includes many more lower- and higher-status individuals than does the antitrust category.

The Coefficient of Relative Variation

For the data on bribery and antitrust offenders in Table 5.8, in which the means of the two groups are fairly similar, a direct comparison of standard deviations provides a good view of the differences in dispersion. When the means of two groups are very different, however, this comparison may not be a fair one. If the mean Duncan score for one group was 10 and for the other was 50, we might expect a larger standard deviation in the latter group simply because the mean was larger and there was

---

[4]See Albert J. Reiss, *Occupations and Social Status* (New York: Free Press, 1961).

Figure 5.1   *Socioeconomic Indices*

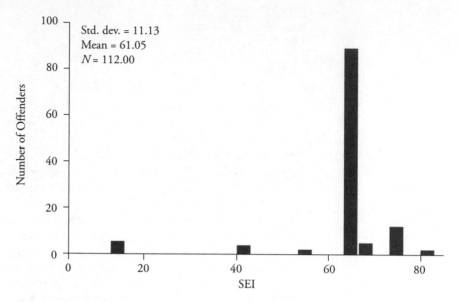

Std. dev. = 11.13
Mean = 61.05
N = 112.00

(a) *Antitrust Offenders*

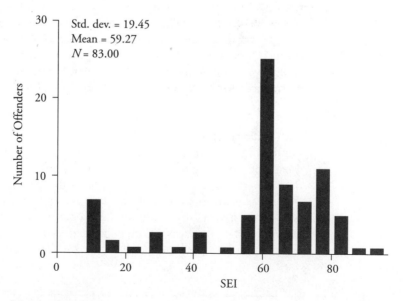

Std. dev. = 19.45
Mean = 59.27
N = 83.00

(b) *Bribery Offenders*

greater potential for dispersion. Similarly, if two measures use different units of analysis—for example, dollars and number of offenses—a direct comparison of standard deviations does not make sense.

One solution to this problem is to use the **coefficient of relative variation** (CRV). The coefficient of relative variation looks at the size of the standard deviation of a measure relative to the size of its mean:

$$CRV = \frac{s}{\overline{X}}$$

Equation 5.6

In the example of the SEI for antitrust offenders, we divide the standard deviation (11.13) by the mean (61.05) to obtain a CRV of 0.18, meaning that the standard deviation is about one-fifth the size of the mean. Because the CRV expresses dispersion in a measure in a standardized form relative to the mean, we can compare the CRV across measures that have widely different means and standard deviations.

A measure that has a CRV of 1, for example, may be considered to include much greater relative variation than is found in our sample of antitrust offenders.

Working It Out

$$CRV = \frac{s}{\overline{X}}$$

$$= \frac{11.13}{61.05}$$

$$= 0.1823$$

A Note on the Mean Deviation

The standard deviation allows us to measure dispersion in interval scales, taking into account the deviation from the mean of each case in our sample or population. But it is not the only measure that allows us to do this. The **mean deviation** takes a similar approach, but relies on absolute values, rather than squaring, to overcome the fact that the sum of the deviations from the mean equals 0. When you take the absolute value of a number, you ignore its sign. Accordingly, -8 and 8 both have an absolute value of 8; in mathematical notation, $|-8| = |8| = 8$.

The equation for the mean deviation is similar to that for the variance. The only difference is that we take the absolute value of the

| | Table 5.9 | | Mean Deviation for Crime Calls at Hot Spots in a Year |

HOT SPOT NUMBER	NUMBER OF CALLS	DEVIATIONS FROM THE MEAN $\|X_i - \overline{X}\|$
1	2	$\|2 - 21.5\| = 19.5$
2	9	$\|9 - 21.5\| = 12.5$
3	11	$\|11 - 21.5\| = 10.5$
4	13	$\|13 - 21.5\| = 8.5$
5	20	$\|20 - 21.5\| = 1.5$
6	20	$\|20 - 21.5\| = 1.5$
7	20	$\|20 - 21.5\| = 1.5$
8	24	$\|24 - 21.5\| = 2.5$
9	27	$\|27 - 21.5\| = 5.5$
10	29	$\|29 - 21.5\| = 7.5$
11	31	$\|31 - 21.5\| = 9.5$
12	52	$\|52 - 21.5\| = 30.5$
		Total (Σ) = 111.0

difference between each score and the mean, rather than the square of the difference:

$$\text{Mean deviation} = \frac{\sum_{i=1}^{N} \left| X_i - \overline{X} \right|}{N}$$

Equation 5.8

Using the data on crime calls in hot spots from Table 5.4, we take the following steps to obtain the mean deviation. We first take the absolute value of the difference between each score and the mean (see Table 5.9). We then sum up the 12 scores. Notice that we obtain a positive number now (111), and not 0, because we are taking the absolute values of the differences. Dividing this sum by the number of cases, N, we get a mean deviation of 9.25.

Working It Out

$$\text{Mean deviation} = \frac{\sum_{i=1}^{N} \left| X_i - \overline{X} \right|}{N}$$

$$= \frac{\sum_{i=1}^{12} \left| X_i - 21.5 \right|}{N}$$

$$= \frac{111}{12}$$

$$= 9.25$$

The mean deviation and the standard deviation provide similar estimates of dispersion, but the mean deviation here is a bit smaller than the standard deviation of 12.38 that we calculated earlier. Which is the better estimate of dispersion? In some sense, the mean deviation is more straightforward. It simply looks at the average deviation from the mean. In obtaining the standard deviation, we first must square the deviations; then later, to return our result to units similar to those of the original distribution, we must take the square root of the variance.

Given our rule that we should use the least complex presentation that is appropriate to answering our research question, you may wonder why the standard deviation is almost always preferred over the mean deviation in criminal justice research. As you will see in the next few chapters, the answer is that the standard deviation is relevant to a number of other statistics that we use in analyzing and describing data.

Chapter Summary

Measures of dispersion describe to what extent cases are distributed around the measure of central tendency. They tell us just how typical the typical case is.

There are several measures of dispersion for nominal and ordinal scales. Proportions and percentages describe the extent to which cases are concentrated in the modal category. The **variation ratio** (VR) describes the extent to which cases are spread outside the modal category. A proportion of 1 (VR of 0) means that all the cases are in the modal category. This represents the least possible amount of dispersion. The value for the greatest possible dispersion can be determined by calculating the minimum possible value of the modal category and then translating that into a proportion or VR value. These measures can, in principle, be used with ordinal-level data, but the results may be misleading, as they take into account only the value of the mode. As an alternative, the **index of qualitative variation** (IQV) is a standardized measure that takes into account variability across all the categories of a nominal- or ordinal-level variable. An IQV of 0 means that there is no variation; an IQV of 100 means that there is maximum variation across the categories.

A different set of measures is used to measure dispersion for interval and ratio scales. The **range** measures the difference between the highest and lowest scores. It has the advantage of simplicity, but it uses very little information (only two scores) and the scores used are taken from the two extremes. It is also very sensitive to outliers. A researcher may instead choose to measure the range between, say, the 95th and the 5th percentile. Such measures, however, are still based on minimal information and thus are generally considered unstable statistics. A more stable statistic for measuring dispersion in interval-level scales is the **variance**. The variance is the sum of the squared deviations of each score from the mean divided by the number of cases. The **standard deviation** (s) is the square root of the variance. The advantage of the standard deviation over the variance is that the results are more easily interpreted. If all the scores in a sample are the same, s will be 0. The more widely the scores are spread around the mean, the greater will be the value of s. Outliers have a considerable impact on the standard deviation.

Comparing the standard deviations of means is problematic when the means are very different or when their units of measurement are different. An alternative measure, the **coefficient of relative variation** (CRV), enables comparisons among samples with different means. A less often used measure of dispersion for interval scales is the **mean deviation.** The mean deviation is computed by taking the sum of the absolute values of the deviations from the mean divided by the number of cases.

Key Terms

coefficient of relative variation A measure of dispersion calculated by dividing the standard deviation by the mean.

index of qualitative variation A measure of dispersion calculated by dividing the sum of the possible pairs of observed scores by the sum of the possible pairs of expected scores (when cases are equally distributed across categories).

mean deviation A measure of dispersion calculated by adding the absolute deviation of each score from the mean and then dividing the sum by the number of cases.

range A measure of dispersion calculated by subtracting the smallest score from the largest score. The range may also be calculated from specific points in a distribution, such as the 5th and 95th percentile scores.

standard deviation A measure of dispersion calculated by taking the square root of the variance.

variance (s^2) A measure of dispersion calculated by adding together the squared deviation of each score from the mean and then dividing the sum by the number of cases.

variation ratio A measure of dispersion calculated by subtracting the proportion of cases in the modal category from 1.

Symbols and Formulas

$N_{\text{modal cat.}}$ Number of cases in the modal category

N_{total} Total number of cases

N_{obs} Number of cases observed in each category

N_{exp} Number of cases expected in each category

s Standard deviation

s^2 Variance

To calculate the proportion of cases falling in the modal category:

$$\text{Proportion} = \frac{N_{\text{modal cat.}}}{N_{\text{total}}}$$

To calculate the percentage of cases falling in the modal category:

$$\text{Percentage} = \frac{N_{\text{modal cat.}}}{N_{\text{total}}} \times 100$$

To calculate the variation ratio:

$$\text{VR} = 1 - \left(\frac{N_{\text{modal cat.}}}{N_{\text{total}}} \right)$$

To calculate the index of qualitative variation:

$$\text{IQV} = \left(\frac{\sum\limits_{i=1}^{k-1} \sum\limits_{j=i+1}^{k} N_{\text{obs}_i}\, N_{\text{obs}_j}}{\sum\limits_{i=1}^{k-1} \sum\limits_{j=i+1}^{k} N_{\text{exp}_i}\, N_{\text{exp}_j}} \right) \times 100$$

To calculate the variance:

$$s^2 = \frac{\sum\limits_{i=1}^{N}(X_i - \overline{X})^2}{N}$$

To calculate the standard deviation:

$$s = \sqrt{\frac{\sum\limits_{i=1}^{N}(X_i - \overline{X})^2}{N}}$$

To calculate the coefficient of relative variation:

$$CRV = \frac{s}{\overline{X}}$$

To calculate the mean deviation:

$$\text{Mean deviation} = \frac{\sum_{i=1}^{N}\left|X_i - \overline{X}\right|}{N}$$

Exercises

5.1 Police records for 105 rape victims were analyzed to determine whether any prior relationship existed between the victim and the offender. The results were as follows:

Spouse   41

Family member other than spouse   14

Acquaintance   22

No prior relationship   28

   a. Calculate the modal proportion and the variation ratio.

   b. What are the minimum and maximum possible values for the variation ratio?

   c. Calculate the index of qualitative variation.

5.2 As part of a larger study on the influence of delinquent peers, a sample of high school youth were asked how much they wanted to be like their best friend. The responses were coded as follows: in every way, 26; in most ways, 36; in some ways, 41; and not at all, 8.

   a. Calculate the variation ratio for these data.

   b. Calculate the index of qualitative variation for these data.

5.3 People convicted of minor traffic offenses who appeared in the magistrate's court of a given locality on a given day were sentenced as follows: conditional discharge, 14; fine, 35; and license disqualification, 11.

   a. Calculate the variation ratio.

   b. Calculate the index of qualitative variation.

   c. Why do these two results differ?

5.4 A sample of women was drawn from town A, and another sample was drawn from town B. All the women were asked how safe or unsafe they felt walking alone at night in their neighborhoods. The results were recorded on a scale as follows: totally unsafe (town A: 40; town B: 25), quite unsafe (town A: 29; town B: 23), quite safe (town A: 10; town B: 15), and totally safe (town A: 21; town B: 17).

a. For each town, describe the typical case, using an appropriate measure of central tendency. Explain why this is the best measure of central tendency for these data.

b. For each town, describe how typical the typical case is, using an appropriate measure of dispersion. Explain why this is the best measure of dispersion for these data.

c. In comparing the measures of central tendency and dispersion for the two towns, what conclusions may be drawn about the attitudes of the women?

5.5   For a sample of 12 offenders convicted of weapons violations, the length of prison sentence in months was recorded as:

6   6   2   12   36   48   60   24   24   20   18   15

a. Calculate the range for these data.

b. Calculate the mean and the variance for these data.

5.6   A group of 20 prisoners in a particular cell block were tested on their knowledge of the rules of the institution. The marks (out of a possible 70) were as follows:

31   28   27   19   18   18   41   0   30   27
27   36   41   64   27   39   20   28   35   30

a. Calculate the range.

b. Remove the largest and smallest scores. Calculate the range for the remaining cases.

c. How do you account for the difference between the values of the above two measures of dispersion?

5.7   Police crack a drug ring of 18 suppliers and discover that of the 18, only 4 have no previous convictions for drug- or theft-related offenses. Eight of those arrested have 1 previous conviction, and the others have 2, 3, 4, 5, 6, and 8, respectively.

a. Calculate the mean and the standard deviation of the 18 cases.

b. If each of the drug suppliers is convicted this time around, does the extra conviction on each of their criminal records affect the mean or the standard deviation in any way? Explain your answer.

5.8   Use the data collected from tests of prisoners' knowledge of institution rules in Exercise 5.6.

   a. Calculate the mean and the standard deviation for these data.

   b. If you remove the two most extreme scores, 0 and 64, what are the new mean and standard deviation?

   c. How do you account for this effect?

5.9   When asked about how often in the last year they drank more than four beers in one evening, a sample of college students reported the following:

Number of Times	Frequency
0	187
1	213
2	162
3	94
4	71
5	55
6	39
7	12
8	9
9	5
10	13

   a. Calculate an appropriate measure of dispersion for these data. Explain why this measure is most appropriate for these data.

   b. Describe one way these data could be recoded to reduce the number of categories. Calculate an appropriate measure of dispersion for the recoded data and explain why this measure is most appropriate.

5.10   A researcher takes a sample of shop owners in Tranquiltown and a sample of shop owners in Violenceville and asks them to estimate the value of goods stolen from their shops in the past 12 months. The mean figure is \$11.50 ($s = $ \$2.50) for Tranquiltown and \$4,754.50 ($s = $ \$1,026.00) for Violenceville. When the study is published, the mayor of Violenceville protests, claiming that the mean sum for his town is a misleading figure. Because the standard deviation for Violenceville is much bigger than that for Tranquiltown, he argues, it is clear that the mean from Violenceville is a much less typical description of the sample than the mean from Tranquiltown.

   a. What statistic might help the researcher to refute this criticism? Why?

   b. Calculate this statistic for each town. What should the researcher conclude?

5.11 A researcher investigating differences in violence among preschool-age boys and girls found that the average number of violent acts per week was 7.6 ($s = 4.8$) for boys and 3.1 ($s = 1.9$) for girls.

   a. Calculate the coefficient of relative variation for boys and for girls.

   b. How can the coefficient of relative variation be used to compare these two groups? What does it tell you?

Computer Exercises

As with measures of central tendency, there are several ways to obtain measures of dispersion for interval-level variables in SPSS. (SPSS does not compute measures of dispersion, such as the index of qualitative variation, for nominal or ordinal variables.)

Using the "Descriptives" Command

The "Descriptives" command (Analyze→Descriptive Statistics→Descriptives) allows you to compute the standard deviation and variance. The default in SPSS is to compute the standard deviation and minimum and maximum values. To obtain the variance and/or range, click on the "Options" button and select these statistics from the window that appears. By default, SPSS uses a correction for the bias of sample measures of variance and dispersion: 1 is subtracted from the N in the denominator of Equations 5.4 and 5.5. The correction is used primarily as a tool in inferential statistics and is discussed in Chapter 10. Though it is our view that the uncorrected variance and standard deviation should be used in describing sample statistics, many researchers report these statistics with the correction factor for sample estimates. When samples are larger, the estimates obtained with and without the correction are very similar, and thus it generally makes very little substantive difference which approach is used.

Using the "Frequencies" Command

The "Frequencies" command (Analyze→Descriptive Statistics→Frequencies) provides similar measures of dispersion through use of the "Statistics" button. You may select from the standard deviation, variance, range, minimum, and maximum. The list of measures of dispersion is the same as for the "Descriptives" command. One benefit of use of the "Frequencies" command is the ability to calculate percentiles, since calculation of percentiles by hand can be very difficult. There are three options for calculating percentiles in SPSS: quartiles (25th, 50th, and 75th percentiles), cut points for some number of equally spaced groups, and specific percentiles that you may be interested in (e.g., 5th, 95th, 99th).

1.   Enter the data from Exercise 5.6 on the 20 prisoners' test scores.

    a. What is the range?

    b. What are the 5th and 95th percentiles? What is the range between the 5th and 95th percentiles?

    c. How does your answer to part b compare to your answer to part b in Exercise 5.6?

2.   Enter the data from Exercise 5.7. (Be sure that you have 18 lines of data, since there are 18 observations listed in the question.)

    a. What are the mean and the standard deviation? How does the standard deviation differ from the value you calculated in Exercise 5.7?

    b. To add 1 to each person's number of prior convictions, use the "Compute" command (Transform→Compute). When the window appears, type a new variable name into the "Target variable" box to distinguish the new variable from the existing variable. The box on the right—"Numeric expression"—is where you type the calculation that you want performed. To increase the value of prior convictions by 1 for each offender, move the variable name representing prior convictions into the numeric expression box and type "+1" (without the quotation marks) after the variable name. Click on "OK," and the calculation will be performed by SPSS. What are the mean and standard deviation for this new variable? What changed? What remained the same?

3.   Open the data file ***nys_1.sav*** into SPSS.

    a. What are the quartiles for the delinquency measures?

    b. What is the range between the 25th and 75th percentiles for each delinquency measure? (This difference is known as the "inter-quartile range.") What do the differences in inter-quartile ranges indicate about the dispersion of self-reported delinquency?

    c. What number of delinquent acts would mark the 15% *least* delinquent youth? The 20% *most* delinquent youth?

    d. Use the mean and the standard deviation calculated by SPSS for each of the delinquency measures. Calculate the coefficient of relative variation for each delinquency variable. What do the values of the coefficient of relative variation for each delinquency variable indicate about the relative dispersion of these variables?

The Logic of Statistical Inference:

Making Statements About Populations

from Sample Statistics

sample distributions and population distributions

How Are They Defined?

What Symbols Are Used?

How Are the Two Interrelated?

asking the research question

What Are the Research and Null Hypotheses?

How Are They Set Up?

answering the research question

How Can a Sample Teach Us About a Population?

What Types of Error Are Possible?

What Is an "Acceptable" Risk of Error?

When Might It Be Necessary to Accept a Different Level of Risk?

IN THIS CHAPTER, we look at an important dilemma that researchers face in conducting criminal justice research. Although they seek to make statements about populations, generally they collect data on samples drawn from such populations. Statistical inference provides a solution to this dilemma: It allows the researcher to make statements, or inferences, about the characteristics of a population from data collected from a sample drawn from the population. We begin our discussion of statistical inference by explaining the dilemma researchers face in making statements about populations from samples. We then examine the logic of statistical inference and the statistical risks associated with using this logic. You will be introduced to how null and research hypotheses are set up, how risks of error are assessed, and how levels of statistical significance are used to limit this error.

The Dilemma: Making Statements About Populations from Sample Statistics

In descriptive statistics, we are concerned with two basic types of distributions. One is the distribution of scores in the **sample,** or the **sample distribution.** The second is the distribution of scores in the **population** from which the sample is drawn. This is referred to as the **population distribution.** One of the fundamental problems in research in criminal justice, as in other fields, is that we want to make statements about the characteristics of the population distribution, but we generally have information only about the distribution of sample scores. For example, when we draw a sample of 2,000 voters in an election survey, we are not interested per se in how those people will vote. Rather, we examine their voting preference to learn something about how all people will vote in the election. In statistical terms, we want to use information on characteristics of the distribution of sample scores to make statements about characteristics of the distribution of population scores.

It is important to note at the outset that populations can be defined in a number of different ways. There is, for example, the population of the entire United States or the population of a particular state. There is the population of all prisoners in the United States or the population of prisoners only in a specific state. Although the population of cases is fixed at any particular time, actual populations are constantly changing across time. For example, we can speak of the population of prisoners on any particular day. But every day new people enter prisons and some prisoners are freed. Since the population of prisoners changes every day, the population of prisoners at any one time is only a sample of the population of prisoners across a longer period of time—for example, a year or two.

Statisticians use different symbols to distinguish statistics on a population from statistics on a sample (see Table 6.1). Population statistics, or **parameters,** are defined using Greek letters. For example, the parameter for the mean in a distribution of population scores is represented by μ and the standard deviation by σ. **Sample statistics** are represented by roman letters. We denote the mean in a distribution of sample scores as $\overline{X}$ and the standard deviation as s.

Why do we study sample statistics if we really want to say something about population parameters? It certainly makes more sense to collect information on the population if that is what is of interest in the long run. In practice, however, it is usually very difficult to gain information on the **universe,** or total group of cases in the population. One reason is simply financial. As was pointed out in Chapter 1, to carry out just one survey of the U.S. population regarding their attitudes toward crime would exhaust the budget of the National Institute of Justice (the major funder of research in criminal justice in the United States) for many years. But beyond the costs of such studies, there is the problem of their management. A study of an entire population will often demand contact with hundreds of thousands or even millions of people. Such an effort is likely to be not just expensive, but difficult to manage and time consuming to complete.

Because of the difficulty of gaining information on the characteristics of an entire population, such parameters are generally unknown. However, when a parameter is available, there is no point in drawing statistics from a sample. In recent years, advances in computer technology

Table 6.1	Representing Population Parameters and Sample Statistics

	MEAN	VARIANCE	STANDARD DEVIATION
Sample distribution	$\overline{X}$	s^2	s
Population distribution	μ	σ^2	σ

and recognition by public officials of the importance of data in making policy decisions about the criminal justice system have led to the development of a number of databases that include information on the population of cases. For example, we now have population parameters on characteristics of sentencing in the federal courts and basic demographic characteristics of offenders held in jails and prisons. Information on the population of arrests and emergency calls to the police is routinely collected and computerized in most cities. One scholar suggests that this trend means that criminologists in the future will have to pay less and less attention to samples and the problems they create for researchers.[1] However, whatever the future will bring, at present criminal justice researchers must rely primarily on sample statistics in trying to say something about the characteristics of a population.

Given our reliance on sample statistics, it is important at the outset to define how they might differ from population parameters. One obvious difference is that sample statistics are generally known—put differently, they can be defined by the researcher in the context of a research study. In contrast, parameters are generally unknown, although, as we noted above, there is a trend toward development of parameters about major issues in criminal justice.

Even though parameters are often unknown, they are assumed to be fixed. By that we mean that there is one true parameter for any measure. For example, there is a true mean age at first arrest for the population of all criminals in the United States at a specific time. In contrast, sample statistics vary from sample to sample. For example, if you were to draw 10 samples from a population, using exactly the same method each time, each sample would likely provide different sample statistics.

This is illustrated in Table 6.2. Ten random samples of 100 offenders were drawn from a population of 1,940 offenders. Sample statistics are presented for mean age and number of prior arrests. Although the sample statistics obtained are generally similar to the population parameters, each sample provides a somewhat different group of estimates, and in some cases the differences are relatively large. In the case of sample 10, for example, the average number of arrests for the sample is more than a third lower than the population score. In sample 4, the average age is more than two years older than the population parameter. This occurs despite the fact that we drew each of the samples using the same technique and from the same population of scores. You might want to try this yourself by drawing a series of samples from your class or dormitory. Using the same method, you will almost always obtain different sample statistics.

---

[1]M. Maltz, "Deviating from the Mean: The Declining Significance of Significance," *Journal of Research in Crime and Delinquency* 31 (1994): 434–463.

Table 6.2	Ten Random Samples of 100 Offenders Drawn from a Population of 1,940 Offenders	

	MEAN AGE	MEAN ARRESTS
Population	39.7	2.72
Sample 1	41.4	2.55
Sample 2	41.2	2.19
Sample 3	38.8	2.09
Sample 4	42.1	3.45
Sample 5	37.9	2.58
Sample 6	41.1	2.62
Sample 7	39.2	2.79
Sample 8	39.2	2.48
Sample 9	37.8	2.55
Sample 10	37.7	1.72

This fact is one of the fundamental problems we face in statistics. We want to make statements about populations, but we generally must rely on sample statistics to do so. If sample statistics vary from sample to sample, how can we use them to make reliable statements about the parameters associated with a population? Put differently, what is the use of most studies in criminal justice, if they are based on samples rather than populations? Fortunately, there is an area of statistics that provides us with a systematic way to make decisions about population parameters based on sample statistics. This area is called **statistical inference,** and in the remaining sections of this chapter we focus on the logic that underlies statistical inference.

The Research Hypothesis

Statistical inference begins with the definition of the questions that the researcher seeks to answer in a research project. Sometimes **research questions** in criminal justice are focused on specific agencies in the criminal justice system. For example, we may want to learn more about the police, the courts, or probation services. Other times research questions revolve around broad theoretical concerns that can be applied across criminal justice agencies. We may, for example, seek to define common features of criminal justice programs that lead to a reduction in recidivism (reoffending). Sometimes our questions relate to offenders, other times to victims of crime or criminal justice agents.

To answer a research question, we have to set up at least one and sometimes several **research hypotheses** related to it. A hypothesis is a proposed answer to our research question that we can then test in the context of a study. Stating a research hypothesis does not mean that we assume that the hypothesis is true. Rather, it focuses our research question in such a way that it can be directly examined in the context of a study. When the research hypothesis does not indicate a specific type of outcome, stating only that there is a relationship or a difference, we say that it is a **nondirectional hypothesis.** However, in those cases where a researcher has a very clear idea of what to expect—based on prior research evidence and/or theory—the research hypothesis may be more precise. In this case, the researcher may specify the nature of the relationship that is expected. Such a research hypothesis is called a **directional hypothesis.** When a directional hypothesis is used, the researcher states at the outset that he or she is interested in a specific type of outcome—for example, that one group has more arrests than another.

Suppose we are interested in comparing the arrest records of drug-involved offenders with those of offenders who do not use drugs. Our research hypothesis might be simply that the arrest records of drug-involved offenders and offenders who do not use drugs are different (a nondirectional hypothesis). But based on prior knowledge of criminal behavior among drug-involved offenders, we might want to state a directional hypothesis—that drug-involved offenders have more serious arrest records than do non–drug-involved offenders. One problem with choosing the latter option is that if we state our research hypothesis as a directional hypothesis, we are stating that we are not interested in outcomes that fall in the opposite direction. In criminal justice research, we can often be surprised by what we learn in a study. Accordingly, researchers generally are cautious in defining a directional research hypothesis.

Having defined a research hypothesis, we want to examine whether it is true for the population in which we are interested. For our example of drug-involved offenders, if we could collect information about all offenders, we could simply look at the parameters drawn from our study to see whether they support the research hypothesis and, if so, to what degree. In this case, we would not need to use the logic of statistical inference. We would collect data directly on the population parameters. But ordinarily we cannot collect information on the population parameters and must rely on the statistics drawn from a sample in making our decision. Our problem is that we cannot come to an absolute conclusion regarding the research hypothesis because we know that statistics vary from sample to sample.

On the basis of a sample, we can never be sure of the true value of a population parameter. Accordingly, we can never be absolutely certain as to whether the research hypothesis is true. But does the fact that we cannot be sure mean that we cannot come to a reasonable conclusion regarding our hypotheses?

In fact, we often make decisions about hypotheses on the basis of samples in our daily lives. For example, let's say that you are deciding whether to sign up for a course taught by an instructor named Professor Justice. One issue that you are particularly concerned about is the impact the course will have on your grade point average. To make an informed decision about the course, you might decide to ask friends of yours who took the course last year how Professor Justice grades in comparison to others at your college. Although you might not think of them quite in this way, your friends represent your sample. In turn, the hypothesis that the professor grades differently from other faculty members in your college is similar to a research hypothesis.

If your friends gave a mixed view or generally were unable to say whether Professor Justice grades more harshly or more easily than other professors, you would likely conclude that the course would not have much impact on your grade point average. Put differently, you would decide that the research hypothesis is probably false. If most of your friends said that the professor is an easy grader or, conversely, that she was a hard grader, you would take this as evidence that the research hypothesis is most likely correct—that the professor grades differently and that the course is likely to have an impact on your grade point average.

Once you have made the decision that Professor Justice is different from others, you are likely to assess how she is different. If your friends define the professor as a hard grader, you might decide to avoid the course because you fear you would get a lower grade than is usual with other professors. If they define the professor as an easy grader, you might be encouraged to take the course, with the expectation that your grade will be higher than usual.

In effect, you make a decision about the research hypothesis based on information that you draw from your "sample" of friends. Your confidence in making a decision will depend greatly on how reliable you believe your friends' observations to be and to what degree they represent other students in the class. This is very similar to the logic we use in making statistical inferences from samples to populations. However, in statistical inference, we test hypotheses not in reference to the research hypothesis but in reference to a type of hypothesis that statisticians call the **null hypothesis.**

The Null Hypothesis

The null hypothesis—or H_0—gains its name from the fact that it usually states that there is no relationship, or no difference. It is the flip side of the research hypothesis (H_1), which usually posits that there is a relationship. In the example of the professor's grading, the null hypothesis would simply be that "there is no difference between the grading of Professor Justice and that of others in the university."

In practice, in statistics, we make decisions about hypotheses in relation to the null hypothesis rather than the research hypothesis. This is because the null hypothesis states that the parameter in which we are interested is a particular value. For example, returning to the comparison of drug-involved and other offenders, your null hypothesis (H_0) might be that there is no difference between the two groups in the average number of crimes committed, or, put differently, that the difference is equal to zero. In the case of Professor Justice's grading, the null hypothesis also states that there is no difference, or again that the difference between the average grade given by Professor Justice and the average grade given by her colleagues is equal to zero.

In contrast, the research hypothesis is ordinarily not stated in exact terms. A number of potential outcomes can satisfy the research hypothesis. In the example of the professor's grading, any average grade that is different from that of other professors in the college is consistent with the research hypothesis. But only one result, that the professor's grading is the same as that of others, is consistent with the null hypothesis. The null hypothesis, accordingly, has the advantage of defining a specific value for the population parameter.[2]

By stating the null and research hypotheses, we have taken a first very important step in making statistical inferences. However, we still have the problem of how to make decisions about these hypotheses on the basis of sample statistics.

Whenever we rely on sample statistics to make statements about population parameters, we must always accept that our conclusions are tentative. The only way to come to a definitive conclusion regarding the population parameter is to actually examine the entire population. This happens more and more with criminal justice data today. However, in most research, we are still able to collect information only about sample statistics.

This means that when we test hypotheses in research, we generally do not ask whether a hypothesis is true or false. To make such a statement would require knowledge about the population parameters. Rather, we ask whether we can make an inference, or draw a conclusion, about our hypotheses based on what we know from a sample. In statistical inference, we use sample statistics to infer to, or draw conclusions about, population parameters.

---

[2]Some statisticians prefer to call the research hypothesis the "alternative" hypothesis, because we can, in theory, choose any value as the null hypothesis, and not just the value of zero or no difference. The alternative hypothesis, in this case, can be defined as all other possible outcomes or values. For example, you could state in your null hypothesis that the professor's grades are, on average, five points higher than those of other professors in the college. The alternative hypothesis would be that the professor's grades are not, on average, five points higher than those of other professors.

In order to understand the logic of making inferences, it will help to return to our example of drug-involved offenders. Let's say we are interested in the number of crimes that offenders commit in a given year. We decide to use arrests as our measure of criminal behavior. We might state our null hypothesis as follows: "Drug-involved offenders and offenders who do not use drugs have, on average, the same number of arrests in a given year." To test our hypothesis, we take a sample of drug-involved offenders and another sample of offenders who do not use drugs. We find that drug-involved offenders in our sample have a mean of five arrests per year, whereas offenders who do not use drugs have a mean of three arrests per year. Should we reject the null hypothesis? Should we conclude that there is a difference in the numbers of arrests in the population based on results from our sample?

As illustrated earlier in regard to Professor Justice's grading, in everyday life we make such decisions through a combination of intuition, prior experience, and guesswork. In statistical inference, we take a systematic approach to this decision making, which begins with the recognition that whatever decision we make has a risk of error.

Risks of Error in Hypothesis Testing

What types of error do we risk when making a decision about a population parameter from a sample? A simple way to examine this question is to compare the potential decisions that can be made about a null hypothesis with the value of the population parameter. For our null hypothesis concerning arrests among drug-involved and non–drug-involved offenders, there are only two possible scenarios for the population. In the first case, the null hypothesis is true, meaning that there is no difference in average number of arrests between offenders in the population who use drugs and those who do not. Alternatively, the null hypothesis may be false, meaning that there is a difference in the population between drug-involved and other offenders. In this case, drug-involved offenders have, on average, either fewer or more arrests in a year than do offenders who do not use drugs.

Based on our sample statistic, we can, as well, come to only two possible conclusions regarding the null hypothesis. We can reject the null hypothesis and infer that there is a difference in the average numbers of arrests of drug-involved and other offenders in the population. Alternatively, we can fail to reject the null hypothesis and state that our sample does not provide sufficient evidence to conclude that there is a difference in the average numbers of arrests of drug-involved offenders and offenders in the population who do not use drugs.

If we cross these two sets of possibilities, we define four possible situations, as represented in Figure 6.1. Two of these are desirable, because they suggest that our decision about the null hypothesis is consistent with the population parameter. In one case (box 1), we fail to reject the null hypothesis, and it is in fact true. In the second (box 4), we reject the null hypothesis on the basis of our sample results, and the null hypothesis is false.

In the remaining situations, however, our decisions are not consistent with the population parameter. In one (box 2), we fail to reject the null hypothesis on the basis of our sample statistic, but it is in fact false. In this case, we have made what statisticians call a **Type II (or beta) error.** A Type II error would occur in our example of arrests among offenders if we did not reject the null hypothesis on the basis of our sample results when in fact the average numbers of arrests for drug-involved and other offenders were different in the population to which we want to infer. We make a **Type I (or alpha) error** (see box 3) when we reject the null hypothesis on the basis of sample statistics but H_0 is true. In this case, we infer from our sample that drug offenders are different from offenders who do not use drugs, when in fact they are similar in the population.

Whenever we make a decision about a population parameter from a sample statistic, we risk one of these two types of statistical error. If we

Figure 6.1 *Types of Error in a Statistical Test*

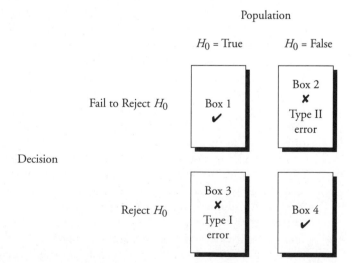

fail to reject the null hypothesis, there is always the possibility that we have failed to reject it when it was false (Type II error). If we reject the null hypothesis, there is always the possibility that we have rejected it when it was true (Type I error). Although we cannot avoid the possibility of error when we study samples, we can decide at the outset how much risk or error we are willing to take in making decisions about hypotheses.

Risks of Error and Statistical Levels of Significance

In statistical inference, we assess the risk of making a wrong decision about the population parameter in reference to Type I error. This is why it is very important in statistical inference that we use the phrase "reject" or "fail to reject" the null hypothesis, rather than the simpler statement that we "reject" or "accept" the null hypothesis. Type I error is concerned with rejection of the null hypothesis when it is true. It does not refer directly to the risk of accepting the null hypothesis when it is false (Type II error). This latter problem will be the focus of a discussion in Chapter 19. For now, it is important to remember that in statistical inference we make a decision either to "reject" or to "fail to reject" the null hypothesis on the basis of the amount of Type I error we are willing to risk.

We define the amount of Type I error we are willing to risk as the **significance level** of a **test of statistical significance.** In a test of statistical significance, we make a decision to reject or to fail to reject the null hypothesis on the basis of a sample statistic. The significance criterion, or level, of a test of statistical significance is ordinarily represented by the symbol α. The estimate of the risk of Type I error that is associated with rejecting the null hypothesis in a test of statistical significance (based on a sample statistic) is called the **observed significance level** and is ordinarily represented by the symbol p. In statistical inference, we first identify the amount of Type I error we are willing to risk, or the significance level of a test. We then estimate the observed significance level from our sample statistics. Finally, we compare the observed significance level gained from our study with the criterion significance level we set at the outset of our test of statistical significance. If the observed significance level is less than the significance criterion, or level, that we set at the outset of the test, we reject the null hypothesis. In the next chapter, we examine how statisticians estimate the observed significance level of a test. At this juncture, it is important to consider how we decide on the amount of Type I error we are willing to risk. How do we choose the significance level in a test of statistical significance?

If we are willing to take a good deal of risk of Type I error, we set a very lenient significance level. This means that we are willing to reject the null hypothesis on the basis of our sample statistic, even if the risk of a Type I error is fairly large. If we set a very strict significance level, this means that we are unwilling to reject the null hypothesis unless we are fairly certain that our decision is correct.

If we return to the example of Professor Justice's grading, the importance of Type I error in making statistical inferences will become clearer. Let's say that every one of the friends you ask reports that the professor is a much easier grader than other professors at your college. In this case, you would probably conclude that the observed significance level, or risk of a Type I error, in your study was very small. It is unlikely that all of your friends would say that the professor was an easy grader if she was in reality very similar to others in the college. Of course, your friends could provide a mistaken view of the professor's grading habits. But you would probably assume that this is not very likely.

But what if your friends provided you with a mixed view of Professor Justice's grading? What if 40% of your friends say that Professor Justice grades similarly to other professors and 60% say that she is easier? Would you be so confident in rejecting the null hypothesis with these results? Overall, the majority of your friends still say the professor is a relatively easy grader. But in this case there is a substantial group reporting that she grades much as other professors do. If you set a strict significance level, you might not be willing to reject the null hypothesis based on your observations (your observed significance level), and you might simply conclude that there is not enough evidence, on the basis of your sample of friends, to say that Professor Justice grades differently.

It might seem at first that we would want to be fairly lenient in setting our significance level. Often, in defining the research hypothesis, we are expressing what we believe to be true. Why, then, would we want to make it difficult to reject the null hypothesis? By rejecting the null hypothesis that there is no difference, we are led to infer that the research hypothesis is correct. This would seem in our best interest. In fact, by convention we set a fairly strict significance level. In order to reject the null hypothesis, we are expected to provide convincing evidence that our conclusions reflect the true population parameters.

What is "convincing evidence"? How much risk of a Type I error should we be willing to take in a test of statistical significance? In criminal justice, and in most of the social sciences, a 5% level of statistical significance is generally considered rigorous enough for tests of hypotheses. This means that if the observed significance level of our test is greater than 0.05, we will fail to reject the null hypothesis. If the observed significance level is less than 0.05, we will reject the null hypothesis.

Departing from Conventional Significance Criteria

In statistics, as in everyday life, it is simplest to follow the accepted conventions. Accordingly, most criminal justice researchers apply the 5% significance level fairly automatically to the research questions they consider. The problem with this approach is that the purposes of the research may be better served by departing from established norms. Sometimes this is the case because our criterion is not cautious enough for the issue we are examining.

For example, a criminal justice agency making a decision about its policies may want you to use a stricter standard than you would ordinarily apply to your research. This may be the case if your conclusions could lead to expensive or time-consuming changes in the structure or activities of the agency. The agency will likely not want to make such changes unless you are very confident that your conclusions are correct. In this situation, you might decide to set your significance level at 0.01 or 0.001, meaning that you are willing to reject the null hypothesis only if the observed significance level of a test is less than 1% or less than 0.1%. Whenever you use a significance level more stringent than 5%, it is important to explain clearly why you have chosen to make it harder to reject the null hypothesis in your study.

Sometimes a researcher may decide to use a more lenient significance level than 5%. This ordinarily occurs when the researcher is particularly concerned with a Type II error rather than a Type I error. In the Minneapolis hot spots experiment, for example, which evaluated the impact of police patrol on street blocks with high crime activity, the principal investigators discussed the dangers of a Type II error at the outset of their study.[3] They argued that conventional significance criteria might be too strict for assessing the effectiveness of new police initiatives. Failure to reject the null hypothesis of no program impact in this case, if it were false, would lead the police not to pursue a potentially effective new method of police patrol. The principal investigators, accordingly, decided to use a 0.10, rather than a 0.05, significance level.

Why would a concern with a Type II error lead us to change the significance level of our test of hypotheses? As we noted earlier, the significance level is based on a Type I error, not a Type II error. However, the two types of statistical error are related. When we increase the risk of a Type I error, we reduce the risk of a Type II error. When we decrease the risk of a Type I error, we increase the risk of a Type II error. This

---

[3]See Lawrence Sherman and David Weisburd, "General Deterrent Effects of Police Patrol in Crime 'Hot Spots': A Randomized Study," *Justice Quarterly* 12:4 (1995): 625–648.

relationship is an obvious one, because setting a stricter significance level (by decreasing the risk of a Type I error) naturally makes it less likely that you will reject the null hypothesis. Similarly, when we make it easier to reject the null hypothesis by increasing the risk of a Type I error, it is that much harder in practice to fail to reject the null hypothesis (and therefore to make a Type II error). The relationship between Type I and Type II error is easy to understand, but it is not directly proportional. As we will discuss in Chapter 19 when we examine the concept of "statistical power," other factors in addition to the significance level of a study affect the risk of a Type II error.

You should always consider carefully the implications of risks of error in your research before setting the significance level of a test of statistical significance. Even though you are likely in the end to rely on the conventional norm of 5%, there are, as discussed above, some cases for which you might want to consider stricter or more lenient levels of significance. If you do choose a level other than 0.05, you must explain to your audience the factors that led you to depart from common practice in criminal justice.

The level of significance in a study should be defined at the outset, and not after your results are in. If you wait until you have your sample data, there will always be the temptation to adjust your significance level to fit your sample statistics. This is particularly important if you decide to use more stringent or more lenient criteria. If you use a more lenient criterion, others might argue that you have made that decision in order to allow rejection of the null hypothesis (and thus support for the research hypothesis). If you use a stricter criterion, others might argue that you are trying to avoid rejecting the null hypothesis. In many funded research studies, researchers specify in their original proposals the significance levels that they intend to apply to tests of hypotheses in order to prevent such criticism later on.

In this chapter, we discussed the logic underlying statistical inference. In the coming chapters, we will examine how statisticians define the risk of Type I error associated with a specific outcome in a study, or the observed significance level of a test. We also detail how such tests are applied to different types of statistics. You should not expect to have a full understanding of statistical inference at this point. We have only begun to develop these ideas and will return to them again and again.

Chapter Summary

In descriptive statistics we are concerned with two types of distributions. The **sample distribution** is the distribution of scores in the **sample.** The **population distribution** is the distribution of scores in the

population from which the sample is drawn. Population statistics are known as **parameters,** and they have symbols different from those which you have encountered so far. The mean in a population distribution is represented by μ and the standard deviation by σ. Parameters are assumed to be fixed and are generally unknown. Sample statistics are by definition known, but they vary from sample to sample. Statisticians are faced with a fundamental dilemma in that they are usually interested in making statements about population parameters, but they generally study sample statistics. **Statistical inference** provides a solution to this dilemma.

Statistical inference begins with the definition of the **research hypothesis** and the **null hypothesis.** These hypotheses are set up by the researcher to answer the broader **research question.** The research hypothesis is the proposed answer to a specific research question. When the research hypothesis does not indicate a specific type of outcome, stating only that there is a relationship or a difference, we say that it is a **nondirectional hypothesis.** When the research hypothesis identifies the nature of the relationship that is expected, it is called a **directional hypothesis.** The null hypothesis generally posits that there is no such relationship or no difference. The null hypothesis is stated in exact terms. The research hypothesis encompasses a range of possible alternatives. It is thus easier to focus decisions on whether to reject the null hypothesis.

Given the difficulties involved in collecting information on an entire population, we are forced to work with samples. The tools of statistical inference enable us to infer from a sample to a population by identifying the risk of making a mistaken decision and determining the amount of risk we are prepared to take. Two possible errors can be made when making decisions about a population from a sample. A researcher who rejects the null hypothesis when it is in fact true has made a **Type I error.** A researcher who fails to reject the null hypothesis when it is in fact false has made a **Type II error.**

In a **test of statistical significance,** we make a decision to reject or to fail to reject the null hypothesis on the basis of a sample statistic. The **significance level** defines the risk of Type I error that a researcher is willing to take in a test of statistical significance. The risk of Type I error associated with a specific sample statistic is the **observed significance level** of a test. A commonly accepted standard significance level is 5%, but researchers may choose to set a lower level if they want it to be more difficult to reject the null hypothesis—or a higher level if they want to make it easier. A researcher who wishes to depart from the accepted standard should explain the reasons for such a decision at the outset. Decreasing the risk of a Type I error increases the risk of a Type II error, and vice versa.

Key Terms

directional hypothesis A research hypothesis that indicates a specific type of outcome by specifying the nature of the relationship that is expected.

nondirectional hypothesis A research hypothesis that does not indicate a specific type of outcome, stating only that there is a relationship or a difference.

null hypothesis A statement that reduces the research question to a simple assertion to be tested by the researcher. The null hypothesis normally suggests that there is no relationship or no difference.

observed significance level The risk of Type I error associated with a specific sample statistic in a test. When the observed significance level is less than the criterion significance level in a test of statistical significance, the researcher will reject the null hypothesis.

parameter A characteristic of the population—for example, the mean number of previous convictions for all U.S. prisoners.

population The universe of cases that the researcher seeks to study. The population of cases is fixed at a particular time (e.g., the population of the United States). However, populations usually change across time.

population distribution The frequency distribution of a particular variable within a population.

research hypothesis The antithesis of the null hypothesis. The statement normally answers the initial research question by suggesting that there is a relationship or a difference.

research question The question the researcher hopes to be able to answer by means of a study.

sample A set of actual observations or cases drawn from a population.

sample distribution The frequency distribution of a particular variable within a sample drawn from a population.

sample statistic A characteristic of a sample—for example, the mean number of previous convictions in a random sample of 1,000 prisoners.

significance level The level of Type I error a researcher is willing to risk in a statistical test of significance.

statistical inference The process of making generalizations from sample statistics to population parameters.

test of statistical significance A test in which a researcher makes a decision to reject or to fail to reject the null hypothesis on the basis of a sample statistic.

Type I error Also known as alpha error. The mistake made when a researcher rejects the null hypothesis on the basis of a sample statistic (i.e., claiming that there is a relationship) when in fact the null hypothesis is true (i.e., there is actually *no* such relationship in the population).

Type II error Also known as beta error. The mistake made when a researcher fails to reject the null hypothesis on the basis of a sample statistic (i.e., failing to claim that there is a relationship) when in fact the null hypothesis is false (i.e., there actually *is* a relationship).

universe The total population of cases.

Symbols and Formulas

H_0 Null hypothesis

H_1 Research hypothesis

α Significance level of a test

μ Population mean

p Observed significance level of a test

σ^2 Population variance

Exercises

6.1   For each of the following random samples, describe the population to which the results could be generalized:

  a. Subscribers to a magazine on hunting are asked about gun legislation.

  b. Youth aged 15 to 19 years in the United States are asked about personal drug use.

  c. Registered voters in Los Angeles are asked whom they will vote for in the next election for mayor.

  d. Visitors to a domestic violence shelter are assessed for psychological distress.

  e. Members of the National Organization for Women (NOW) are asked about sexual harassment in the workplace.

  f. Judges in New Jersey are asked about their sentencing philosophy.

6.2   A foundation sponsored a review of all studies carried out over the past 15 years into the link between smoking and juvenile delinquency. Eric, a criminologist commissioned by the foundation, unearthed five studies that sought to determine at what age delinquents who smoke began their habit. The five studies, conducted at the same time, use identical sampling techniques and sample sizes and draw their samples from a fixed database of delinquents. The mean age, however, is different for each of the samples:

Study sample no. 1: mean age = 12.2

Study sample no. 2: mean age = 11.6

Study sample no. 3: mean age = 14.0

Study sample no. 4: mean age = 11.3

Study sample no. 5: mean age = 12.8

Overall computed mean = 12.38

a. During Eric's presentation, one member of the foundation asks him to explain how it can be that each of the study samples produced a different result: Does this mean that there was something wrong with the sampling techniques used? How should Eric respond?

b. Another foundation member also seems confused. She asks if the overall computed mean is the mean age of the population. How should Eric respond?

6.3   A researcher collects data on the families of 20 delinquent and 20 nondelinquent children from the records of a school and checks how many children from each group come from broken homes.

a. State the null hypothesis.

b. State a nondirectional research hypothesis.

c. State a directional research hypothesis.

6.4   A researcher is interested in whether electronic monitoring of offenders on probation is an effective means of reducing crime. To test for an effect of electronic monitoring, probationers are randomly assigned either to a monitored group or to a control group that has no electronic monitoring.

a. State the null hypothesis.

b. State a nondirectional research hypothesis.

c. State a directional research hypothesis.

6.5   A study published in a distinguished journal reported the results of a series of tests carried out on 50 convicted burglars. One of the claims of the investigators is that the average IQ of convicted burglars is 120.

a. From the following list of options, choose an appropriate null hypothesis and research hypothesis for testing this claim.

$IQ = 120$ $IQ \neq 120$ $IQ > 120$ $IQ < 120$

b. Explain your choice of null and research hypotheses.

6.6   A gang of criminals is planning to rob a supermarket. Eddy, the gang leader, reports that he "staked the store out" the day before and saw the store detective going for a 15-minute coffee break at 9.15 A.M. He suggests that this would be the best time to strike. Clive, a gang member, thinks that this plan is too risky—how do they know that the detective takes his break at the same time each day? Eddy, who is desperate for the money, thinks that the plan is safe enough and wants to carry out the robbery the next day. After an argument, they agree to compromise and watch the supermarket for three more days. On each of the three days, the store detective indeed takes his 15-minute break at 9:15 A.M. The gang decides to go ahead with the robbery on the fourth day.

   The robbers can be seen as having set themselves a research question and having made a statistical decision based on a simple study.

a. How would you frame the robbers' null hypothesis and research hypothesis?

b. Based on these hypotheses, what is their decision?

c. How would the robbers make a Type I error? How would the robbers make a Type II error? What type of statistical error ought the robbers to be most concerned with making? Explain why.

d. How does the argument between Eddy and Clive relate to the concept of statistical significance?

6.7 The government wishes to launch a pre-Christmas advertising campaign warning about the dangers of drunk driving. It suspects that drivers aged 18 to 21 are most likely to drive while under the influence of alcohol and is considering targeting the campaign specifically at this age group. A preliminary study gathers data on the ages of drunk drivers apprehended in a particular district over a six-month period.

a. What are the null and research hypotheses? Explain why the research hypothesis is directional or nondirectional.

b. How might the government make a Type I error?

c. How might the government make a Type II error?

d. The government accepts that targeting this specific age group in the advertising campaign will not cost any extra money. There is a feeling that the new campaign will be "worth a try," even if the study doesn't find enormous differences between the offending rate of 18- to 21-year-olds and that of other ages. How should these considerations affect the researchers' decision on what level of significance to set?

6.8 The head of the police force in the city of Cheadle suspects that increasing the pay of his officers might increase their efficiency. A police researcher is assigned to test whether there is a difference between the crime-solving rates of a group of detectives who have been randomly awarded pay raises and a control group of detectives who have not been awarded pay raises. In writing up his report, the researcher concludes as follows:

> The results show that the observed significance level is 0.14, meaning that rejecting the null hypothesis would run a 14% risk of a Type I error. Although a 5% significance level is considered standard, in light of the potential benefits of salary increases for crime control rates, a higher 15% threshold is justified here, and the H_0 may therefore be rejected.

a. What is the null hypothesis to which the researcher refers?

b. Explain why the researcher's statistical reasoning is problematic.

6.9   A study explored whether there is a link between male aggression and climate. The researcher recorded her results as follows: 5% significance level set, H_0 could not be rejected.

a. Explain these results in plain English.

b. Why is it important for the researcher to set the significance level at the beginning of the research and not at the end?

6.10 A private research foundation claims that increased regulation of handguns would reduce homicides in the United States. To examine this relationship, the foundation funds a study to assess the impact of handgun legislation on homicides in four states that recently passed laws restricting handgun ownership. The foundation expects that the reduced availability of handguns following the change in law will reduce the number of opportunities for lethal violence. The researcher collects data on homicides in the four states for one year before and one year after the change in handgun laws.

a. What are the null and research hypotheses? Explain why the research hypothesis is directional or nondirectional.

b. Explain how the researcher could make a Type I error.

c. Explain how the researcher could make a Type II error.

d. The results show an observed significance level of 0.06. The researcher wants to conclude that the null hypothesis cannot be rejected based on a 5% risk of Type I error. An official from the foundation wants the researcher to increase the significance level of the study to 10% and reject the null hypothesis. Should the researcher increase the significance level of the study? Why?

6.11 A group of researchers at a private think tank claims that the increased use of incarceration in the United States has not been harmful to the social fabric of the country. To support this claim, the researchers conduct a study looking at rates of incarceration and rates of divorce in all fifty states for a 20-year period. The group of researchers tests for a relationship between rates of incarceration and rates of divorce, but does not expect to find a relationship between these two variables.

a. What are the null and research hypotheses? Explain why the research hypothesis is directional or nondirectional.

b. Explain how the research group could make a Type I error.

c. Explain how the research group could make a Type II error.

d. The observed significance level developed in their study is 0.03. The research group initially set a 5% risk of Type I error. One member of the research group suggests that they simply decrease the significance level of the study to 1% and fail to reject the null hypothesis. Should the research group decrease the significance level of the study? Why?

Defining the Observed Significance Level

of a Test: A Simple Example Using

the Binomial Distribution

sampling distributions

What Are They?

What Role Do They Play in Inferential Statistics?

probabilities and probability distributions

How Does One Calculate the Probability of a Given Outcome?

What Are Probability Distributions?

How Are They Used?

the binomial distribution

What Is It?

How Is It Calculated?

What Are Its Characteristics?

W HEN WE MAKE INFERENCES to a population, we rely on a statistic in our sample to make a decision about a population parameter. At the heart of our decision is a concern with Type I error. Before we reject our null hypothesis, we want to be fairly confident that it is in fact false for the population we are studying. For this reason, we want the observed risk of a Type I error in a test of statistical significance to be as small as possible. But how do statisticians calculate that risk? How do they define the observed significance level associated with the outcome of a test?

The methods that statisticians use for calculating the observed significance level of a test of statistical significance vary depending on the statistics examined. Sometimes these methods are very complex. But the overall logic that underlies these calculations is similar, irrespective of the statistic used. Thus, we can take a relatively simple example and use it as a model for understanding how the observed significance level of a test is defined more generally in statistics. This is fortunate for us as researchers, because it means that we do not have to spend all of our time developing complex calculations to define risks of error. Once we understand how risks of error are defined for one problem, we can let statisticians calculate the risks for other more complex problems. Our concern is not with the calculations themselves, but with understanding the general logic that underlies them.

We begin this chapter by discussing a very simple decision. When should we begin to suspect that a coin used in a coin toss is unfair or biased? Ordinarily, we might come to a conclusion based on common sense or intuition. In statistics, we take a more systematic approach, relying on the logic of hypothesis testing and a type of distribution called a sampling distribution. Using this example of the coin toss and a sampling distribution called the binomial distribution, we illustrate how statisticians use probability theory to define the observed significance level, or risk of Type I error, for a test of statistical significance.

The Fair Coin Toss

Imagine that you and your friends play a volleyball game each week against a group of criminal justice students from another school. You always begin the game with a coin toss to decide who will serve the ball first. Your opponents bring an old silver dollar, which you have agreed to use for the toss. They choose heads and continue to choose heads each time you play. At first, this does not seem like a problem. However, each week you play, the coin comes up heads and they serve the ball.

Suppose that this happened for four straight weeks. Would you begin to become suspicious? What if it went on for six weeks? How many times in a row would they have to win the coin toss before you and your team accused them of cheating? Would they have to win for ten or twenty weeks? You might worry about accusing them too quickly, because you know that even if the coin is fair it sometimes happens that someone is lucky and just keeps on winning. You would want to be fairly certain that the coin was biased before concluding that something was wrong and taking some action.

In everyday life, you are likely to make this decision based on intuition or prior experience. If you ask your classmates, each one is likely to come up with a slightly different number of coin tosses before he or she would become suspicious. Some students may be willing to tolerate only four or five heads in a row before concluding that they have enough evidence to accuse their opponents of cheating. Others may be unwilling to reach this conclusion even after ten or fifteen tosses that come up heads. In part, the disagreement comes from personality differences. But more important, guesswork or common sense does not give you a common yardstick for deciding how much risk you take in coming to one conclusion or another.

Sampling Distributions and Probability Distributions

Statistical inference provides a more systematic method for making decisions about risk. The coin toss can be thought of as a simple test of statistical significance. The research hypothesis is that the coin is biased in favor of your opponents. The null hypothesis is that the coin is fair. Each toss of the coin is an event that is part of a sample. If you toss the coin ten times, you have a sample of ten tosses. Recall from Chapter 6 that Type I error is the error of falsely rejecting the null hypothesis that the coin is fair. If you follow the common norm in criminal justice, then you are willing to reject the null hypothesis if the risk of a Type I error is less than 5%.

But how can we calculate the risk of a Type I error associated with a specific outcome in a test of statistical significance, or what we generally term the observed significance level of a test? One simple way to gain an estimate of the risk of unfairly accusing your friends is to check how often a fair coin would give the same result as is observed in your series of volleyball games. For example, let's say that you played ten games in a season and in all ten games the old silver dollar came up heads (meaning that the opposing team won the toss). To check out how often this might happen just by chance when the coin is in fact a fair one, you might go to a laboratory with a fair coin and test this out in practice. One problem you face is deciding how many samples or trials you should conduct. For example, should you conduct one trial or sample by flipping your fair coin just ten times and stopping? Or should you conduct multiple trials or samples, each with ten tosses of the fair coin? Clearly, one trial or sample of ten tosses will not tell you very much. Indeed, one of the reasons you have gone to the laboratory is that you know it sometimes happens that a fair coin will come out heads ten times in a row. What you want to know is how rare an event this is. How often would you gain ten heads in a row in a very large number of samples or trials of a fair coin?

The distribution that is gained from taking a very large number of samples or trials is called a **sampling distribution.** In principle, one could create a sampling distribution by drawing thousands and thousands of samples from a population. For example, in the case of our coin toss, we might conduct thousands of trials of ten flips of a fair coin. If we recorded the outcome for each trial and placed our results in a frequency distribution, we would have a sampling distribution for a sample of ten tosses of a fair coin.

This sampling distribution would allow us to define the risk of a Type I error we would face in rejecting the null hypothesis that the old silver dollar is fair. For example, suppose that in the sampling distribution we gained a result of ten heads in only 1 in 1,000 samples. If we reject the null hypothesis in this case, our risk of making a Type I error, according to the sampling distribution, is only 0.001. This is the observed significance level of our test of statistical significance. In only 1 in 1,000 samples of ten tosses of a fair coin would we expect to gain a result of ten heads. If the old silver dollar was indeed a fair coin, it would seem very unlikely that on our one trial of ten tosses of the coin each toss would come out heads. Of course, in making our decision we cannot be certain that the silver dollar used in the volleyball toss is not a fair coin. While the occurrence of ten heads in ten tosses of a fair coin is rare, it can happen about once in every 1,000 samples.

Building a sampling distribution provides a method for defining our risk of a Type I error. However, it is very burdensome to create a sampling distribution by hand or even in the laboratory. If you try out our example of ten tosses of a fair coin, you will see that developing even 100 samples is not easy. If we had to actually construct a sampling distribution every time we wanted to make a decision about a hypothesis, it would be virtually impossible to make statistical inferences in practice.

Fortunately, there is another method we can use for creating sampling distributions. This method relies on probability theory, rather than a burdensome effort to collect samples in the real world. Because we use probabilities, the distributions that are created using this method are called **probability distributions.** Importantly, though we rely on probability theory because it is very difficult to develop sampling distributions in practice, we do not suffer for our approach. This is because probability theory allows us to calculate the outcomes one would expect in a perfect world. In the real world, we might flip the coin slightly differently as we got tired or the coin might become worn on one side or another, thus affecting the outcomes we gain. In probability theory, we remove the imperfections of the real world from our estimates.

The Multiplication Rule

In order to estimate the risk of a Type I error in the case of a series of tosses of a fair coin, we can use the **multiplication rule,** a simple rule about probabilities drawn from probability theory. The multiplication rule tells you how likely we are to gain a series of events one after another—in this case, a series of outcomes in a toss of a coin. It allows us to estimate theoretically how often we would gain a specific series of events if we drew an infinite number of samples. The multiplication rule generally used to establish probabilities in statistics is based on the assumption that each event in a sample is **independent** of every other event. In the case of the coin toss, this means that the outcome of one toss of a coin is unaffected by what happened on the prior tosses. Each time you toss the coin, it is as if you started with a clean slate. That would seem a fairly reasonable assumption for our problem. What worries us is that the coin is unfair overall, not that it is becoming less or more unfair as time goes on.

An example of a series of events that are not independent is draws from a deck of cards. Each time you draw a card, you reduce the number of cards left in the deck, thus changing the likelihood of drawing any card in the future. For example, let's say that on your first draw from a deck of 52 cards you drew an ace of spades. On your second draw, you cannot draw an ace of spades because you have already removed it from the deck. The likelihood of drawing an ace of spades on the second draw has thus gone from 1 in 52 to 0 in 51. You have also influenced the likelihood of drawing any other card because there are now 51, not 52, cards left in the deck. If you want a series of draws from a deck to be independent of one another, you have to return each card to the deck after you draw it. For example, if you returned the ace of spades to the deck, the chance of choosing it (assuming the deck was mixed again) would be the same as it was on the first draw. The chances of choosing any other card would also be the same because you once again have all 52 cards from which to draw.

The multiplication rule for four independent events is stated in Equation 7.1. It says that the likelihood of any series of events, represented as *A, B, C,* and *D,* happening one after another is equal to the probability of event *A* times the probability of event *B* times the probability of event *C* times the probability of event *D.* The rule can be extended to as many events as you like. We have chosen four here, because this was the number of volleyball games we began with. If you wanted to extend the rule, you would simply include the additional events on the left side of the equation (for example, *E* and *F*) and include the probability of each on the right side of the equation [e.g., $P(E) \cdot P(F)$].

$$P(A \& B \& C \& D) = P(A) \cdot P(B) \cdot P(C) \cdot P(D) \qquad \text{Equation 7.1}$$

Extending this logic to our example of the coin toss is straightforward. The probability of *A* and *B* and *C* and *D* can represent the probability that four tosses in a row come up heads. Our main problem is to establish what the probability is of a head coming up on any particular toss of the coin. In this, we are helped by our null hypothesis, which states that the coin is fair. If the coin is fair, then there should be an even chance of a head or a tail coming up on any particular toss of the coin. Put differently, under the assumption of the null hypothesis that the coin is fair, the likelihood of a head coming up is 0.50.

What, then, does the multiplication rule tell us about the chances of getting four heads in a row on four tosses of a fair coin? In part a of Table 7.1, we calculate that probability by multiplying 0.50 (the likelihood of gaining a head on any toss of a fair coin) by itself four times, to represent four tosses of an unbiased coin. The result is 0.0625. If you had decided at the outset to make a decision about the null hypothesis—that the coin is fair—after four tosses of the coin, then you have conducted a type of test of statistical significance. For this test, the observed significance level (or risk of a Type I error) of rejecting the null hypothesis on the basis of four heads is 0.0625.

If you use the norms of criminal justice research, this is not enough, however, for you to reject the null hypothesis that the coin is fair. Criminal justice researchers generally want the risk of falsely rejecting the null hypothesis to be less than 5%. A bit over 6% is still more than the 5% significance criterion that is used by convention. So if you had decided to

---

Table 7.1   **Probabilities Associated with Tosses of a Fair Coin**

a. $P(A \& B \& C \& D) = P(A) \cdot P(B) \cdot P(C) \cdot P(D) = (0.50)(0.50)(0.50)(0.50) = 0.0625$

b. $P(A \& B \& C \& D \& E) = P(A) \cdot P(B) \cdot P(C) \cdot P(D) \cdot P(E) = (0.50)(0.50)(0.50)(0.50)(0.50) = 0.0313$

c. $P(A \& B \& C \& D \& E \& F \& G \& H \& I \& J) = P(A) \cdot P(B) \cdot P(C) \cdot P(D) \cdot P(E) \cdot P(F) \cdot P(G) \cdot P(H) \cdot P(I) \cdot P(J)$
    $= (0.50)(0.50)(0.50)(0.50)(0.50)(0.50)(0.50)(0.50)(0.50)(0.50) = 0.0010$

make a decision about the fairness of the coin after four coin tosses, you would probably not want to reject the null hypothesis that the coin is fair and confront your opponents. Under this criterion, the likelihood of falsely rejecting the null hypothesis, or the observed significance level of your test, would have to be below 0.05.

What if you had decided at the outset to make a decision about the null hypothesis after five tosses of a coin? Would a result of five heads in a row lead you to reject the null hypothesis? As illustrated in part b of Table 7.1, the multiplication rule tells you that the likelihood of getting five heads in a row if the coin is fair is 0.0313. This is less than our threshold of 0.05, and thus would lead you to reject the null hypothesis. Is this consistent with your earlier commonsense conclusions? Students are usually surprised at how quickly they reach the 0.05 significance threshold in this example.

If you had decided at the outset that you would need ten or fifteen heads in a row, you may want to reconsider, given what we have learned from the multiplication rule. The likelihood of getting ten heads in a row in ten tosses of a fair coin is only 1 in 1,000 (see part c of Table 7.1). The likelihood of getting fifteen heads in a row in fifteen tosses of a fair coin is even lower: about 3 in 100,000. In both of these cases, you would take a very small risk of a Type I error if you rejected the null hypothesis. Nonetheless, the multiplication rule tells us that, even if the coin is fair, it is possible to get ten or even fifteen heads in a row. It just does not happen very often.

The multiplication rule allows us to estimate how often we would expect to get a series of specific outcomes in a very large number of trials or samples, without actually going out and doing the hard work of constructing a sampling distribution in the real world. However, the problem as examined so far assumes that the coin will come up heads every time. What if the coin comes up heads generally, but not all the time? For example, what if you play ten games and the coin comes up heads nine times? The situation here is not as one-sided. Nonetheless, it still seems unlikely that your opponents would win most of the time if the coin were fair. The multiplication rule alone, however, does not allow us to define how likely we are to get such a result.

Different Ways of Getting Similar Results

The multiplication rule allows us to calculate the probability of getting a specific ordering of events. This is fine so far in our coin toss because in each example we have chosen there is only one way to get our outcome. For example, there is only one way to get five heads in five coin

Table 7.2	Arrangements for Nine Successes in Ten Tosses of a Coin

Arrangement 1	●	○	○	○	○	○	○	○	○	○
Arrangement 2	○	●	○	○	○	○	○	○	○	○
Arrangement 3	○	○	●	○	○	○	○	○	○	○
Arrangement 4	○	○	○	●	○	○	○	○	○	○
Arrangement 5	○	○	○	○	●	○	○	○	○	○
Arrangement 6	○	○	○	○	○	●	○	○	○	○
Arrangement 7	○	○	○	○	○	○	●	○	○	○
Arrangement 8	○	○	○	○	○	○	○	●	○	○
Arrangement 9	○	○	○	○	○	○	○	○	●	○
Arrangement 10	○	○	○	○	○	○	○	○	○	●

○ = Head; ● = Tail

tosses or ten heads in ten coin tosses. In each case, your opponents must toss a head before each game. This would be the situation as well if your opponents tossed tails ten times in ten coin tosses. However, for any outcome in between, there is going to be more than one potential way to achieve the same result.

For example, if your opponents tossed nine heads in ten coin tosses, they could win the coin toss nine times (with a head) and then lose the toss in the tenth game (with a tail). Or they could lose the first toss (with a tail) and then win the remaining nine. Similarly, they could lose the second, third, fourth, fifth, sixth, seventh, eighth, or ninth coin toss and win all the others. Each of these possible ordering of events is called an **arrangement.** As is illustrated in Table 7.2, there are ten possible arrangements, or different ways that you could get nine heads in ten coin tosses. In the case of ten heads in ten coin tosses, there is only one possible arrangement.

It is relatively simple to list all of the arrangements for our example of nine heads in ten coin tosses, but listing becomes very cumbersome in practice as the split of events becomes more even. For example, if we were interested in how many ways there are of getting eight heads in ten coin tosses, we would have to take into account a much larger number of arrangements. As Table 7.3 illustrates, it takes a good deal of effort to list every possible arrangement even for eight heads. In the case of a more even split of events—for example, five heads in ten tosses—it becomes extremely cumbersome to list each arrangement one by one. Because of this, we generally use the formula in Equation 7.2 to define the number of arrangements in any series of events.

$$\binom{N}{r} = \frac{N!}{r!(N-r)!}$$

Equation 7.2

On the left side of this equation we have N "choose" r, where N is the number of events in the sample and r is the number of successes in the

Table 7.3	Arrangements for Eight Successes in Ten Tosses of a Coin

```
 1: ●●○○○○○○○○    16: ○●○○○○○○●○    31: ○○○○●●○○○○
 2: ●○●○○○○○○○    17: ○●○○○○○○○●    32: ○○○○●○●○○○
 3: ●○○●○○○○○○    18: ○○●●○○○○○○    33: ○○○○●○○●○○
 4: ●○○○●○○○○○    19: ○○●○●○○○○○    34: ○○○○●○○○●○
 5: ●○○○○●○○○○    20: ○○●○○●○○○○    35: ○○○○●○○○○●
 6: ●○○○○○●○○○    21: ○○●○○○●○○○    36: ○○○○○●●○○○
 7: ●○○○○○○●○○    22: ○○●○○○○●○○    37: ○○○○○●○●○○
 8: ●○○○○○○○●○    23: ○○●○○○○○●○    38: ○○○○○●○○●○
 9: ●○○○○○○○○●    24: ○○●○○○○○○●    39: ○○○○○●○○○●
10: ○●●○○○○○○○    25: ○○○●●○○○○○    40: ○○○○○○●●○○
11: ○●○●○○○○○○    26: ○○○●○●○○○○    41: ○○○○○○●○●○
12: ○●○○●○○○○○    27: ○○○●○○●○○○    42: ○○○○○○●○○●
13: ○●○○○●○○○○    28: ○○○●○○○●○○    43: ○○○○○○○●●○
14: ○●○○○○●○○○    29: ○○○●○○○○●○    44: ○○○○○○○●○●
15: ○●○○○○○●○○    30: ○○○●○○○○○●    45: ○○○○○○○○●●
```

○ = Head; ● = Tail

total number of events. In our case, N is the number of coin tosses and r is the number of times that the coin comes up heads. Put together, this statement establishes our question: How many ways are there of gaining r heads in N tosses of a coin? To answer our question, we need to solve the right side of the equation. Each of the terms in the equation is defined as a **factorial,** indicated by the symbol !. When we take a factorial of a number, we merely multiply it by all of the whole numbers smaller than it. For example, 3! is equal to (3)(2)(1), or 6. Because factorials get very large very quickly, a table of factorials is presented in Appendix 1. Note that 0! = 1. Applied to our problem of nine heads in ten coin tosses, Equation 7.2 is worked out below:

Working It Out

$$\binom{N}{r} = \frac{N!}{r!(N-r)!}$$

$$\binom{10}{9} = \frac{10!}{9!(10-9)!}$$

$$= \frac{10!}{9!\ 1!}$$

$$= \frac{3,628,800}{362,880(1)}$$

$$= 10$$

Using this method, we get the same result as before. There are ten possible arrangements to get nine heads in ten tosses of a coin. When we apply Equation 7.2 to the problem of five heads in ten coin tosses, its usefulness becomes even more apparent. There are 252 different ways of getting five heads in ten tosses. Listing each would have taken us considerably longer than the calculation below.

W orking It Out

$$\binom{N}{r} = \frac{N!}{r!(N-r)!}$$

$$\binom{10}{5} = \frac{10!}{5!(10-5)!}$$

$$= \frac{10!}{5!\,5!}$$

$$= \frac{3,628,800}{120(120)}$$

$$= 252$$

Solving More Complex Problems

Now that we have a method for calculating arrangements, we can return to our original problem, which was to define the probability of your opponents tossing the coin in ten games and getting heads nine times. Because there are ten different ways of getting nine heads in ten coin tosses, you need to add up the probabilities associated with these ten sequences. This is what is done in Table 7.4. The multiplication rule is used to calculate the probability for each sequence, or arrangement, under the assumption of the null hypothesis that the coin is fair. Because our null hypothesis states that the coin is fair, we can assume that the chances of gaining a head and a tail are even. The probability of any event, whether a head or a tail, is 0.50, and the probability of a sequence of ten events is always the same. This makes our task easier. But it is important to note that if the null hypothesis specified an uneven split (for example, 0.75 for a head and 0.25 for a tail), then each of the sequences would have a different probability associated with it. In any case, the likelihood of getting any one of these sequences is about 0.001, rounded to the nearest thousandth. When we add together the ten sequences, we get a probability of 0.010.

Table 7.4	The Sum of Probabilities for All Arrangements of Nine Heads in Ten Tosses of a Fair Coin

											PROBABILITY
Arrangement 1	●	○	○	○	○	○	○	○	○	○	0.001
Arrangement 2	○	●	○	○	○	○	○	○	○	○	0.001
Arrangement 3	○	○	●	○	○	○	○	○	○	○	0.001
Arrangement 4	○	○	○	●	○	○	○	○	○	○	0.001
Arrangement 5	○	○	○	○	●	○	○	○	○	○	0.001
Arrangement 6	○	○	○	○	○	●	○	○	○	○	0.001
Arrangement 7	○	○	○	○	○	○	●	○	○	○	0.001
Arrangement 8	○	○	○	○	○	○	○	●	○	○	0.001
Arrangement 9	○	○	○	○	○	○	○	○	●	○	0.001
Arrangement 10	○	○	○	○	○	○	○	○	○	●	0.001
								Total Probability:			0.01

Probability of throwing each arrangement of 10 throws
$= P(A) \cdot P(B) \cdot P(C) \cdot P(D) \cdot P(E) \cdot P(F) \cdot P(G) \cdot P(H) \cdot P(I) \cdot P(J)$
$= (0.50)(0.50)(0.50)(0.50)(0.50)(0.50)(0.50)(0.50)(0.50)(0.50)$
$= 0.001$

This means that we would expect to get nine heads in ten coin tosses of a fair coin in only about 1 in 100 samples in a very large number of trials of a fair coin. But is this the observed significance level of a test of statistical significance in which we gain nine heads in ten tosses of a coin? Or put in terms of Type I error, is this the total amount of risk we face of falsely rejecting the null hypothesis when we gain nine heads? The answer to this question is no, although it may be difficult at first to understand why. If we are willing to reject the null hypothesis based on an outcome of nine heads in ten trials, then we are, by implication, also willing to reject the null hypothesis if our outcome is ten heads in ten trials. In calculating our total risk of a Type I error, we must add together the risk of all potential outcomes that would lead us to reject the null hypothesis. This is why, when testing hypotheses, we generally do not begin with an estimate of the specific probability associated with a single outcome, but rather with the sampling distribution of probabilities of all possible outcomes.

The Binomial Distribution

To construct a probability or sampling distribution for all of the possible outcomes of ten coin tosses, we could continue to compute the number of permutations and the likelihood of any particular arrangement. However, Equation 7.3 provides us with a more direct method for calculating the probability associated with each of the potential outcomes in our sample. Equation 7.3 is generally defined as the **binomial formula,** and the distribution created from it is called the **binomial distribution.** As the name suggests, the binomial distribution is concerned with events in which there are only two possible outcomes—in our example, heads and tails.

$$P\binom{N}{r} = \frac{N!}{r!(N-r)!} \, p^r (1-p)^{N-r}$$

Equation 7.3

The binomial formula may look confusing, but most of it is familiar from material already covered in this chapter. The left-hand side of the equation represents the quantity in which we are interested—the probability of getting r successes (in our case, r heads) in a sample of N events (for us, ten tosses of a coin). The first part of the equation provides us with the number of arrangements for that number of heads. This quantity is then multiplied by $p^r(1-p)^{N-r}$, where p is the probability of a successful outcome (a head) under the null hypothesis and r is the number of successes. This formula gives us the probability associated with each arrangement. Although this part of the equation looks somewhat different from the multiplication rule we used earlier, it provides a shortcut for getting the same result, as the example below illustrates.

We have already calculated the likelihood of getting nine or ten heads in ten coin tosses if the coin is fair. To complete our sampling distribution, we need to compute probabilities associated with zero through eight heads as well. Let's begin with eight heads in ten coin tosses of an unbiased coin:

$$P\binom{10}{8} = \frac{10!}{8!(10-8)!} (0.50)^8 (1-0.50)^{10-8}$$

Step 1: Calculating the number of arrangements

Working It Out

$$\binom{10}{8} = \frac{10!}{8!(10-8)!}$$

$$= \frac{10!}{8!\,2!}$$

$$= \frac{3,628,800}{40,320(2)}$$

$$= 45$$

In step 1 we simply follow the same method as we did earlier in establishing the number of ways of getting eight heads in ten tosses of a coin. Our conclusion is that there are 45 different arrangements.

Step 2: Calculating the probability of any specific arrangement

---

W orking It Out

$$p^r(1 - p)^{N-r} = (0.50)^8(1 - 0.50)^{10-8}$$

$$= (0.50)^8(0.50)^2$$

$$= (0.50)^{10}$$

$$= 0.00098$$

Step 2 provides us with the likelihood of getting any particular arrangement under the assumption of the null hypothesis that the coin is fair. By the null hypothesis, p is defined as 0.50, and r is the number of successes (heads) in our example, or 8. So p^r is $(0.50)^8$, and $(1 - p)^{N-r}$ is $(1 - 0.50)^{10-8}$, or $(0.50)^2$. The outcome of this part of the equation can be simplified to $(0.50)^{10}$. This in turn is the same outcome that we would obtain using the multiplication rule, because the expression $(0.50)^{10}$ means that we multiply the quantity 0.50 by itself 10 times. Using the multiplication rule, we would have done just that.

Step 3: Combining the two outcomes

W orking It Out

$$P\binom{N}{r} = \frac{N!}{r!(N - r)!} p^r(1 - p)^{N-r}$$

$$P\binom{10}{8} = 45(0.00098)$$

$$= 0.0441$$

Combining the two parts of the equation, we find that the likelihood of tossing eight heads in ten tosses of a fair coin is about 0.044. In Table 7.5, we calculate the probabilities associated with all the potential out-

Table 7.5   Computation of Probability Distribution for Ten Tosses of a Fair Coin

	$\binom{N}{r} = \dfrac{N!}{r!\,(N-r)!}$	$\binom{N}{r} p^r (1-p)^{N-r}$
0 heads	$\dfrac{3{,}628{,}800}{1(10-0)!} = \dfrac{3{,}628{,}800}{3{,}628{,}800} = 1$	$1(0.00098) = 0.0010$
1 head	$\dfrac{3{,}628{,}800}{1(10-1)!} = \dfrac{3{,}628{,}800}{362{,}880} = 10$	$10(0.00098) = 0.0098$
2 heads	$\dfrac{3{,}628{,}800}{2(10-2)!} = \dfrac{3{,}628{,}800}{80{,}640} = 45$	$45(0.00098) = 0.0441$
3 heads	$\dfrac{3{,}628{,}800}{6(10-3)!} = \dfrac{3{,}628{,}800}{30{,}240} = 120$	$120(0.00098) = 0.1176$
4 heads	$\dfrac{3{,}628{,}800}{24(10-4)!} = \dfrac{3{,}628{,}800}{17{,}280} = 210$	$210(0.00098) = 0.2058$
5 heads	$\dfrac{3{,}628{,}800}{120(10-5)!} = \dfrac{3{,}628{,}800}{14{,}400} = 252$	$252(0.00098) = 0.2470$
6 heads	$\dfrac{3{,}628{,}800}{720(10-6)!} = \dfrac{3{,}628{,}800}{17{,}280} = 210$	$210(0.00098) = 0.2058$
7 heads	$\dfrac{3{,}628{,}800}{5{,}040(10-7)!} = \dfrac{3{,}628{,}800}{30{,}240} = 120$	$120(0.00098) = 0.1176$
8 heads	$\dfrac{3{,}628{,}800}{40{,}320(10-8)!} = \dfrac{3{,}628{,}800}{80{,}640} = 45$	$45(0.00098) = 0.0441$
9 heads	$\dfrac{3{,}628{,}800}{362{,}880(10-9)!} = \dfrac{3{,}628{,}800}{362{,}880} = 10$	$10(0.00098) = 0.0098$
10 heads	$\dfrac{3{,}628{,}800}{3{,}628{,}800(10-10)!} = \dfrac{3{,}628{,}800}{3{,}628{,}800} = 1$	$1(0.00098) = 0.0010$

$\Sigma = 1.0^*$

*The total in the last column is in fact slightly greater than 100%. This is due to rounding the numbers to the nearest decimal place in order to make the calculation more manageable.

comes in this binomial distribution. The resulting sampling distribution is displayed in Table 7.6.

The probability or sampling distribution for ten tosses of a fair coin illustrates how likely you are to get any particular outcome. All of the outcomes together add up to a probability of 1.[1] Put differently, there is a 100% chance that in ten tosses of a coin you will get one of these 11 potential outcomes. This is obvious, but the sampling distribution allows you to illustrate this fact. Following what our common sense tells us, it also shows that an outcome somewhere in the middle of the distribution

[1]Because of rounding error, the total for our example is actually slightly larger than 1 (see Table 7.5).

Table 7.6	Probability or Sampling Distribution for Ten Tosses of a Fair Coin

0 heads	0.001
1 head	0.010
2 heads	0.044
3 heads	0.118
4 heads	0.206
5 heads	0.247
6 heads	0.206
7 heads	0.118
8 heads	0.044
9 heads	0.010
10 heads	0.001

is most likely. If the coin is fair, then we should more often than not get about an even split of heads and tails.

The largest proportion (0.247) in the sampling distribution is found at five heads in ten tosses of a coin. As you move farther away from the center of the distribution, the likelihood of any particular result declines. The smallest probabilities are associated with gaining either all heads or no heads. Like many of the distributions that we use in statistics, this distribution is symmetrical. This means that the same probabilities are associated with outcomes on both sides.

In Chapter 6, we talked about the fact that samples vary from one another. This is what makes it so difficult to make inferences from a sample to a population. Based on a sample statistic, we can never be sure about the actual value of the population parameter. However, as illustrated in this sampling distribution, samples drawn from the same population vary in a systematic way in the long run. It is very unlikely to draw a sample with ten heads in ten tosses of a fair coin. On the other hand, it is very likely to draw a sample with four, five, or six heads in ten tosses.

Using the Binomial Distribution to Estimate the Observed Significance Level of a Test

Using the sampling distribution, we can now return to the problem of identifying the risks of error associated with rejecting the null hypothesis that the coin brought by the other volleyball team is fair. Earlier we suggested that you might want to use a 5% significance level for this test, in part because it is the standard or conventional significance level used by most criminal justice researchers. This means that you want the observed significance level (p) of your test, or the risk of making a Type I error by incorrectly rejecting the null hypothesis, to be less than 5% (or $p < 0.05$). Using this level, when would you be willing to reject the null hypothesis that the coin is fair and confront your opponents?

The examples in the text focus on applying the binomial distribution to situations where the probability of a success is equal to 0.5. There are other situations where we are interested in the probability of multiple successes (or failures), but success and failure are not equally likely. For example, many of the games of chance that a person might play at a casino are constructed in such a way that winning and losing are not equally likely—the chances of losing are greater than the chances of winning—but use of the binomial distribution would allow for calculation of the chances of winning over several plays of the game.

Consider the following more detailed example. Suppose that we have a quiz with five questions and we are interested in the probability of a student correctly guessing all of the answers on the quiz. If the only possible answers are true or false, then the probability of guessing the correct response on any single question is $p = 1/2 = 0.5$. We can then apply the binomial in the same way as we have in the previous examples to determine the probability of some number of correct answers. The following table presents the numbers of correct answers and the corresponding probabilities.

Computation of Binomial Probabilities for Five True-False Questions

NUMBER OF CORRECT ANSWERS	$\binom{N}{r}p^r(1-p)^{N-r}$
0 correct	$\frac{5!}{0!(5-0)!}0.5^0(1-0.5)^{5-0} = 0.03125$
1 correct	$\frac{5!}{1!(5-1)!}0.5^1(1-0.5)^{5-1} = 0.15625$
2 correct	$\frac{5!}{2!(5-2)!}0.5^2(1-0.5)^{5-2} = 0.3125$
3 correct	$\frac{5!}{3!(5-3)!}0.5^3(1-0.5)^{5-3} = 0.3125$
4 correct	$\frac{5!}{4!(5-4)!}0.5^4(1-0.5)^{5-4} = 0.15625$
5 correct	$\frac{5!}{5!(5-5)!}0.5^5(1-0.5)^{5-5} = 0.03125$

Now suppose that the questions are worded as multiple-choice items and the student has to choose one answer from four possibilities. For any single question, the probability of guessing the correct answer is $p = 1/4 = 0.25$. Given that we have multiple questions, we can again calculate the probability for the number of correct responses using the binomial distribution, but we need to replace $p = 0.5$ with $p = 0.25$ in the equations to reflect the different probability of a correct answer. The following table presents the numbers of correct responses and the corresponding probabilities for the multiple-choice response set.

Computation
of Binomial
Probabilities
for Five
Multiple-
Choice
Questions

NUMBER OF CORRECT ANSWERS	$\binom{N}{r} p^r (1 - p)^{N-r}$
0 correct	$\dfrac{5!}{0!(5 - 0)!} \, 0.25^0 \, (1 - 0.25)^{5-0} = 0.2373$
1 correct	$\dfrac{5!}{1!(5 - 1)!} \, 0.25^1 \, (1 - 0.25)^{5-1} = 0.3955$
2 correct	$\dfrac{5!}{2!(5 - 2)!} \, 0.25^2 \, (1 - 0.25)^{5-2} = 0.2637$
3 correct	$\dfrac{5!}{3!(5 - 3)!} \, 0.25^3 \, (1 - 0.25)^{5-3} = 0.0879$
4 correct	$\dfrac{5!}{4!(5 - 4)!} \, 0.25^4 \, (1 - 0.25)^{5-4} = 0.0146$
5 correct	$\dfrac{5!}{5!(5 - 5)!} \, 0.25^5 \, (1 - 0.25)^{5-5} = 0.0010$

It is important to note that the distribution presented in the second table is no longer symmetrical, reflecting the fact that the probability of a correct response is no longer equal to the probability of an incorrect response. For the true-false questions, where the probabilities of correct and incorrect answers are the same, we see that the probabilities of zero and five correct responses are equal, the probabilities of one and four correct responses are equal, and the probabilities of two and three correct responses are equal. In contrast, when we look at the probabilities for multiple-choice questions with four possible answers, there is no such symmetry. The most likely outcome is one correct response, with a probability of 0.3955. The probability of guessing four or five correct multiple-choice answers is much lower than the probability of guessing four or five correct true-false answers. In general, the probabilities in the table show that increasing the number of possible answers makes it much more difficult for the student to correctly guess all the answers and increases the chances of getting no correct responses or only one correct response.

At first glance, you might decide to reject the null hypothesis for outcomes of zero, one, two, eight, nine, and ten heads. Each of these is below the threshold of 0.05 that we have suggested. However, at the outset we stated in our research hypothesis that we were concerned not that the coin was biased per se, but that it was biased against your team. This means that we set up our research hypotheses in such a way that we would reject the null hypothesis only if the outcomes were mostly heads. Although tossing zero, one, or two heads is just as unlikely as tossing eight, nine, or ten heads, our research hypothesis states our intention not to consider the former outcomes.

What about the risk of falsely rejecting the null hypothesis in the case of eight, nine, or ten heads? As we noted earlier, in calculating the risk of a Type I error, we must add up the probabilities associated with all the outcomes for which we would reject the null hypothesis. So, for example, if we want to know the risk of falsely rejecting the null hypothesis on the basis of eight heads in ten coin tosses, we have to add together the risks associated with eight, nine, and ten heads in ten tosses. The question we ask is, What is the risk of falsely rejecting the null hypothesis if we gain eight or more heads in ten coin tosses? The total risk, or observed significance level, would be about 0.055 (that is, 0.044 + 0.010 + 0.001), which is greater than our threshold of 0.05 for rejecting the null hypothesis. It is too large an outcome for you to confront your opponents and accuse them of cheating.

In the case of nine heads, the outcome is well below the threshold of a Type I error we have chosen. By adding together the probabilities associated with gaining nine or ten heads in ten coin tosses, we arrive at a risk of 0.011 of falsely rejecting the null hypothesis. If we decided to reject the null hypothesis that the coin is fair on the basis of an outcome of nine heads, then the observed significance value for our test would be 0.011. For ten heads, as we noted earlier, the risk of a Type I error is even lower ($p = 0.001$). Because there are no outcomes more extreme than ten heads in our distribution, we do not have to add any probabilities to it to arrive at an estimate of the risk of a Type I error.

You would take a very large risk of a Type I error if you decided in advance to reject the null hypothesis that the coin is fair based on six heads in ten tosses of a coin. Here, you would have to add the probabilities associated with six (0.206), seven (0.118), eight (0.044), nine (0.010), and ten heads (0.001).

As the coin toss example illustrates, sampling distributions play a very important role in inferential statistics. They allow us to define the observed significance level, or risk of a Type I error, we take in rejecting the null hypothesis based on a specific outcome of a test of statistical significance. Although most sampling distributions we use in statistics are considerably more difficult to develop and involve much more complex mathematical reasoning than the binomial distribution, they follow a logic similar to what we have used here. For each distribution, statisticians use probabilities to define the likelihood of gaining particular outcomes. These sampling distributions provide us with a precise method for defining risks of error in tests of statistical significance.

What you have learned here provides a basic understanding of how sampling distributions are developed from probability theory. In later chapters, we will rely on already calculated distributions. However, you should keep in mind that steps similar to those we have taken here have been used to construct these distributions.

Chapter Summary

Whereas a sample distribution is the distribution of the results of one sample, a **sampling distribution** is the distribution of outcomes of a very large number of samples, each of the same size. A sampling distribution that is derived from the laws of probability (without the need to take countless samples) may also be called a **probability distribution.** A sampling distribution allows us to define the observed significance level of a test of statistical significance, or the estimated risk of a Type I error we take in rejecting the null hypothesis based on sample statistics. To guide our decision as to whether to reject or fail to reject the null hypothesis, we compare the observed significance level with the criterion significance level set at the outset of the test of statistical significance.

By using the **multiplication rule,** we can calculate the probability of obtaining a series of results in a specific order. The number of **arrangements** is the number of different ways of obtaining the same result. The total probability of obtaining any result is the individual probability multiplied by the number of different possible arrangements.

The **binomial distribution** is the sampling distribution for events with only two possible outcomes—success or failure, heads or tails, etc. It is calculated using the **binomial formula.** When deciding whether the result achieved, or observed significance level, passes the desired threshold for rejecting the null hypothesis, it is important to remember to take a cumulative total of risk.

Key Terms

arrangements The different ways events can be ordered and yet result in a single outcome. For example, there is only one arrangement for gaining the outcome of ten heads in ten tosses of a coin. There are, however, ten different arrangements for gaining the outcome of nine heads in ten tosses of a coin.

binomial distribution The probability or sampling distribution for an event that has only two possible outcomes.

binomial formula The means of determining the probability that a given set of binomial events will occur in all its possible arrangements.

factorial The product of a number and all the positive whole numbers lower than it.

independent Describing two events when the occurrence of one does not affect the occurrence of the other.

multiplication rule The means for determining the probability that a series of events will jointly occur.

probability distribution A theoretical distribution consisting of the probabilities expected in the long run for all possible outcomes of an event.

sampling distribution A distribution of all the results of a very large number of samples, each one of the same size and drawn from the same population under the same conditions. Ordinarily, sampling distributions are derived using probability theory and are based on probability distributions.

Symbols and Formulas

!   Factorial

r Number of successes

N Number of trials

p The probability of a success

To determine the probability of events A, B, C, and D occurring jointly under the assumption of independence (the multiplication rule):

$$P(A \& B \& C \& D) = P(A) \cdot P(B) \cdot P(C) \cdot P(D)$$

To determine the number of arrangements of any combination of events:

$$\binom{N}{r} = \frac{N!}{r!(N-r)!}$$

To determine the probability of any binomial outcome occurring in all its possible arrangements (the binomial formula):

$$P\binom{N}{r} = \frac{N!}{r!(N-r)!} p^r(1-p)^{N-r}$$

Exercises

7.1   Calculate the probability for each of the following:

a. Two tails in two tosses of a fair coin.

b. Three heads in three tosses of a fair coin.

c. Four heads in four tosses of an unfair coin where the probability of a head is 0.75.

d. Three sixes in three rolls of a fair die.

e. Five fours in five rolls of an unfair die where the probability of a four is 0.25.

7.2   All of Kate's children are boys.

a. Intuitively, how many boys do you think Kate would have to have in succession before you would be willing to say with some certainty that, for some biological reason, she is more likely to give birth to boys than girls?

b. Now calculate the number of successive births required before you could make such a decision statistically with a 5% risk of error.

c. How many successive boys would have to be born before you would be prepared to come to this conclusion with only a 1% risk of error?

7.3   The Federal Bureau of Investigation trains sniffer dogs to find explosive material. At the end of the training, Lucy, the FBI's prize dog, is let loose in a field with four unmarked parcels, one of which contains Semtex explosives. The exercise is repeated three times, and on each occasion, Lucy successfully identifies the suspicious parcel.

a. What is the chance of an untrained dog performing such a feat? (Assume that the untrained dog would always approach one of the parcels at random.)

b. If there had been five parcels instead of four and the exercise had been carried out only twice instead of three times, would the chances of the untrained dog finding the single suspicious parcel have been greater or less?

7.4   Alex, an attorney, wishes to call eight witnesses to court for an important case. In his mind, he has categorized them into three "strong" witnesses and five "weaker" witnesses. He now wishes to make a tactical decision on the order in which to call the strong and the weaker witnesses.

For example, one of his options is

Strong Weak Weak Strong Weak Weak Weak Strong

  a. In how many different sequences can he call his strong and weaker witnesses?

  b. If Alex decides that one of his three strong witnesses is in fact more suited to the weaker category, how many options does he now have?

7.5   In a soccer match held at a low-security prison, the inmates beat the guards 4 to 2.

  a. How many different arrangements are there for the order in which the goals were scored?

  b. What would your answer be if the final score were 5 to 1?

7.6   At the end of each year, the police force chooses its "Police Officer of the Year." In spite of the fact that there are equal numbers of men and women on the force, in the last 15 years, 11 of the winners have been men and 4 have been women. Paul has been investigating whether women and men are treated differently in the police force.

  a. Do these figures provide Paul with a reasonable basis to suspect that the sex of the officer is an active factor? Explain your answer.

  b. Looking back further into the records, Paul discovers that for the three years before the 15-year span initially examined, a woman was chosen each time. Does this affect his conclusion? Explain your answer.

7.7   Use the binomial distribution to calculate each of the following probabilities:

  a. Three heads in eight tosses of a fair coin.

  b. Six tails in thirteen tosses of a fair coin.

  c. Four fives in five rolls of a fair die.

  d. Two ones in nine rolls of a fair die.

  e. Five sixes in seven rolls of a fair die.

7.8   Tracy, a teacher, gives her class a ten-question test based on the homework she assigned the night before. She strongly suspects that Mandy, a lazy student, did not do the homework. Tracy is surprised to see that of the ten questions, Mandy answers seven correctly. What is the probability that Mandy successfully guessed seven of the ten answers to the questions if

  a. The questions all required an answer of true or false?

  b. The questions were all in the multiple-choice format, with students having to circle one correct answer from a list of five choices?

7.9 After a supermarket robbery, four eyewitnesses each report seeing a man with glasses fleeing from the scene. The police suspect Eddy and make up an identity parade of five men with glasses. Eddy takes his place in the parade alongside four randomly chosen stooges. Of the four eyewitnesses who are brought in, three identify Eddy and the fourth points to one of the stooges. The detective in charge decides that there is enough evidence to bring Eddy to trial.

   a. The detective's superior wishes to know the probability that Eddy would have been chosen by three out of the four eyewitnesses if each witness had chosen a member of the identity parade entirely at random. What is the probability?

   b. What is the probability of Eddy being chosen at random by only two of the four witnesses?

7.10 A gang of five child thieves draws straws each time before they go shoplifting. Whoever draws the short straw is the one who does the stealing. By tradition, Anton, the leader, always draws first. On the four occasions that the gang has performed this ritual, Anton has drawn the short straw three times.

   a. Construct a table to illustrate the binomial distribution of Anton's possible successes and failures for each of the four draws.

   b. Should he accuse his fellow gang members of rigging the draw if
      i. He is willing to take a 5% risk of falsely accusing his friends?
      ii. He is willing to take only a 1% risk of falsely accusing his friends?

7.11 Baron, a gambler, plays 11 rounds at a casino roulette wheel, each time placing a $100 note on either black or red.

   a. Construct a table to illustrate the binomial distribution of Baron's possible successes and failures for each of the 11 rounds.

   b. The casino croupiers have been told to inform the management if a client's winning streak arouses suspicion that he might be cheating. The threshold of suspicion is set at 0.005. How many successes does Baron need on 11 trials to arouse the management's suspicion?

7.12 Nicola is playing roulette on an adjacent table. On 12 successive spins of the wheel, she places a $100 note on either the first third (numbers 1–12), the second third (numbers 13–24), or the final third (numbers 25–36).

   a. Construct a table to illustrate the binomial distribution of Nicola's possible successes and failures for each of the 12 spins.

   b. How many times out of the 12 would Nicola need to win in order to arouse the suspicion of the casino manager that she was cheating, if the management policy is to limit the risk of falsely accusing a customer to 0.001?

7.13 A security consultant hired by store management thinks that the probability of store security detecting an incident of shoplifting is 0.1. Suppose the consultant decides to test the effectiveness of security by trying to steal an item ten different times.

a. Construct a table to illustrate the binomial distribution of possible detections for each of the ten attempted thefts.

b. Store management claims that the chances of detection are greater than 0.1. If the consultant set the threshold for detection at 0.05, how many times would she have to be detected to increase the probability of detection?

7.14 In a crime spree, Joe commits six robberies.

a. If the probability of arrest for a single robbery is 0.7, what is the probability that Joe will be arrested for three of the robberies?

b. If the probability of detection for a single robbery is 0.4, what is the probability that Joe will *not* be arrested for any of his crimes?

7.15 The arrest histories for a sample of convicted felons revealed that, with ten previous arrests, the probability of a drug arrest was 0.25. If an offender has been arrested ten times, what is the probability of

a. two drug arrests?

b. five drug arrests?

c. seven drug arrests?

chapter eight

Steps in a Statistical Test:

Using the Binomial Distribution

to Make Decisions About Hypotheses

statistical assumptions

What Type of Measurement Is Being Used?

Are Assumptions Made About the Population Distribution?

What Sampling Method Is Being Used?

What Are the Hypotheses?

sampling distribution

Which Sampling Distribution Is Appropriate?

significance level

What Is the Rejection Region?

Where Is It Placed?

Should a One-Tailed or a Two-Tailed Test Be Used?

test statistic and decision

What Is the Test Statistic?

How Is a Final Decision Made?

IN THE PREVIOUS CHAPTER, you saw how probability theory is used to identify the observed significance level in a test of statistical significance. But you cannot simply rely on mathematical calculations to determine whether to reject the null hypothesis. You must make sure at the outset that the methods used are appropriate to the problem examined. You must clearly state the assumptions made. You must define the specific hypotheses to be tested and the specific significance criteria to be used. It is best to take a careful step-by-step approach to tests of statistical significance. Using this approach, you will be much less likely to make serious mistakes in developing such tests.

In this chapter, we introduce the basic elements of this step-by-step approach. To place this approach in context, we illustrate each step with a specific research problem that can be addressed using the binomial distribution. Although we use the binomial distribution as an example, you should not lose sight of the fact that our purpose here is to establish a general model for presenting tests of statistical significance, which can be used whichever sampling distribution is chosen.

The Problem: The Impact of Problem-Oriented Policing on Disorderly Activity at Violent-Crime Hot Spots

In Jersey City, New Jersey, researchers developed a problem-oriented policing program directed at violent-crime hot spots.[1] Computer mapping techniques were used to identify places in the city with a very high level of violent-crime arrests or emergency calls to the police. Jersey City police officers, in cooperation with staff of the Rutgers University Center for Crime Prevention Studies, developed strategies to solve violent-crime

---

[1]See Anthony Braga, "Solving Violent Crime Problems: An Evaluation of the Jersey City Police Department's Pilot Program to Control Violent Crime Places," unpublished dissertation, Rutgers University, Newark, NJ, 1996.

| Table 8 .1 | Results at Treatment and Control Locations Derived from Observations of Disorderly Behavior Before and After Intervention |

TRIAL	PLACE	OUTCOME
1	**Journal Square East** Newport Mall	+
2	**Stegman & Ocean** Clerk & Carteret	+
3	**Glenwood & JFK** Journal Square West	−
4	**Bergen & Academy** Westside & Duncan	+
5	**Westside & Clendenny** Franklin & Palisade	+
6	**Belmont & Monticello** MLK & Wade	+
7	**MLK & Atlantic** Neptune & Ocean	+
8	**MLK & Armstrong** Ocean & Eastern	+
9	**Westside & Virginia** JFK & Communipaw	+
10	**Park & Prescott** Dwight & Bergen	+
11	**Old Bergen & Danforth** Bramhall & Arlington	+

Note: Experimental or treatment hot spots are listed in boldface type.
+ = Relative improvement in experimental locations
− = Relative improvement in control locations

problems at a sample of 11 places. The strategies followed a problem-oriented policing (POP) approach, in which police collect a wide variety of information about each hot spot, analyze that information to identify the source of the problem, develop tailor-made responses to do something about the problem, and finally assess whether their approach actually had an impact.[2]

The evaluation involved a number of different components. One part of the research sought to identify whether "disorderly" activity at the hot spots had declined during the period of the study. For example, the researchers wanted to see whether the number of loiterers or homeless people had been reduced as a result of the efforts of the police. The treatment areas were compared to a matched group, or control group, of similar but untreated violent-crime places. Table 8.1 presents the overall

---

[2]Problem-oriented policing is an important new approach to police work formulated by Herman Goldstein of the University of Wisconsin Law School. See H. Goldstein, *Problem-Oriented Policing* (New York: McGraw-Hill, 1990).

results of pre- and posttest comparisons of outcomes for the 11 matched pairs of locations. In 10 of the 11 pairs, the experimental hot spots (those receiving POP intervention) improved relative to the control locations.

The research question asked by the evaluator was whether the POP approach has an impact on disorderly activity at violent-crime hot spots. The statistical problem faced is that the 11 comparisons are only a sample of such comparisons. What conclusions can the researcher make regarding the larger population of violent-crime hot spots? To answer this question, we use a test of statistical significance. The specific test that is appropriate for our problem is based on the binomial sampling distribution.

Assumptions: Laying the Foundations for Statistical Inference

The first step in a test of statistical significance is to establish the **assumptions** on which the test is based. These assumptions form the foundation of a test. No matter how elegant the statistics used and the approach taken, if the assumptions on which they are built are not solid, then the whole structure of the test is brought into question.

Level of Measurement

Our first assumption is related to the type of measurement used. Different types of tests of statistical significance demand different levels of measurement.

Accordingly, it is important to state at the outset the type of measurement required by a test. For the binomial test, which is based on the binomial distribution, a nominal-level binary measure is required. A binary measure has only two possible outcomes, as was the case with the coin toss example in Chapter 7. The type of outcome measure used to evaluate the impact of problem-oriented policing on disorderly activity—whether the treatment hot spot improved (or got worse) relative to the control location—fits this assumption. In stating our assumptions (as is done at the end of this section), we include a specific definition of the level of measurement required:

Level of Measurement: Nominal binary scale.

Shape of the Population Distribution

The second assumption refers to the shape of the population distribution. In statistical inference, we are generally concerned with two types of tests. In the first type—termed **parametric tests**—we make an assumption about the shape of the population distribution. For example, in a number of tests we will examine in later chapters, there is a requirement that for the population to which you infer, the scores on the variable be normally distributed.

The second type of test of statistical significance does not make a specific assumption regarding the population distribution. These tests are called **nonparametric tests** or **distribution-free tests.** The advantage of nonparametric tests is that we make fewer assumptions. The disadvantage is that nonparametric tests do not allow us to analyze data at higher levels of measurement. They are generally appropriate only for nominal and ordinal scales. The binomial test is a nonparametric test. Accordingly, in stating our assumptions we write

Population Distribution: No assumption made.

Sampling Method

The third assumption concerns the sampling method used. When we conduct a test of statistical significance, we want our sample to be a good representation of the population from which it is drawn. Put in statistical terms, we want our study to have high **external validity.**

Let's suppose you are interested in attitudes toward the death penalty. Would a sample of your friends provide an externally valid sample of all Americans? Clearly not, because a sample of only your friends is not likely to include age or ethnic or class differences that typify the U.S. population. Even if we used your friends as a sample of U.S. college students, we could still identify threats to the external validity of the study. Colleges have differing criteria for admission, so it is not likely that one college will be representative of all colleges. Even as a sample of students at your college, your friends may not provide a valid sample. They may be drawn primarily from a specific year of college or have other characteristics that make them attractive as friends but also mean that they are a poor representation of others in the college.

How can we draw a **representative sample?** The most straightforward approach is to choose cases at random from the population. This type of sampling is called **random sampling.** Random samples are assumed to have high external validity compared with what may be termed **convenience samples.** A convenience sample consists of whatever subjects are readily available to the researcher. Your friends form a convenience sample of students at your college or of all college students.

It is important to note that convenience samples are not always bad samples. For example, if you choose to examine prisoners in one prison on the assumption that prisoners there provide a cross section of the different types of prisoners in the United States, you might argue that it is a representative sample. However, if you use a convenience sample, such as prisoners drawn from a single prison, you must always be wary of potential threats to external validity. Convenience samples are prone to systematic biases precisely because they are convenient. The characteristics that make them easy for the researcher to define are likely as well to differentiate them in one way or another from the population the researcher seeks to study.

Statistical tests of significance generally assume that the researcher has used a type of random sampling called **independent random sampling.** Independent random sampling requires not only that cases be identified at random, but also that the selection of cases be independent. As discussed in the previous chapter, two events are statistically independent when the occurrence of one does not affect the occurrence of the other. In sampling, this means that the choice of one case or group of cases will not have any impact on the choice of another case or group of cases. This is a useful assumption in assuring the external validity of a study because it prevents biases that might be brought into the process of sampling.

For example, suppose you want to select 1,000 prisoners from the population of all prisoners in the United States. Each time you select a prisoner for your sample, you use a random method of selection. However, prison officials have told you that if you select one prisoner from a cell then you cannot select any other prisoner from that cell. Accordingly, after each selection of a prisoner, you must remove all of his cellmates from your **sampling frame,** or universe of eligible cases. The result is that there are now systematic reasons why you might suspect that your sample is not representative of the population.

In order to ensure independent random sampling, the same population of cases must be used in drawing each case for a sample. As we discussed in Chapter 7, if we want each draw from a deck of cards to be independent, we have to return the card chosen on any specific draw to the deck. If we didn't replace the card, we would influence the likelihood of a specific card being chosen on the next draw from the deck. For example, if we started with a full deck of 52 cards, the likelihood of getting the queen of spades would be 1 in 52. However, if we drew, say, a jack of hearts and didn't return it to the deck, what would be the likelihood of getting a queen of spades on our next draw? This time we would have only 51 cards to draw from, so our likelihood would change to 1 in 51. In order to gain a fully independent random sample, we must use a method of sampling called **sampling with replacement.** This means that we must use the same population each time we select a case. For every selection, the sampling frame must remain exactly the same. In this way, we can ensure that the choice of one case cannot have any impact on the choice of another.

Though this method ensures independence, it also means that a particular case may be selected more than once. For example, suppose you choose a particular prisoner as case number five in your sample. Because you must use the same sampling frame each time you select a case, that prisoner is returned to the sampling frame after selection. Later in your study, you might choose that prisoner again. Accordingly, while sampling with replacement, or returning sampled cases to the sampling frame after each selection, makes statistical sense, it often does not make practical sense when you are carrying out research in the real world. If you are conducting an interview study, for example, independent random sampling would allow individuals to be interviewed more than once. It is likely that subjects would find it strange to be reinterviewed using the same interview schedule. Moreover, their responses would likely be influenced by their knowledge of the survey. Similarly, if a subject or place is chosen twice in a study that involves a specific treatment or intervention, then that subject or place should be given the treatment after each selection. Here there is the difficulty that it may be harmful to provide the treatment more than once.

Even when there are no specific practical barriers to sampling with replacement, it is difficult to explain to practitioners or even many researchers why an individual may appear twice in the same sample. As a result, many, if not most, criminal justice studies do not replace individuals in the sampling frame once they have been selected. Although this represents a formal violation of the assumptions of your test, in most cases its impact on your test result is negligible. This is because samples are generally very small relative to populations, and thus in practice there is little chance of selecting a case more than once even when sampling with replacement. If, however, your sample reaches one-fifth or more of the size of your population, you may want to include a correction factor in your test.[3]

For this test of statistical significance, we assume that researchers in the Jersey City POP study sampled cases randomly from a large population of hot spots during the sample selection month. Because it would not have been practical to implement treatments more than once at any site, the researchers did not sample with replacement.

---

[3]The correction factor adjusts your test to account for the fact that you have not allowed individuals to be selected from the population more than once. Not including a correction factor makes it more difficult to reject the null hypothesis. That is, the inclusion of a correction factor will make it easier for you to reject the null hypothesis. One problem criminal justice scholars face in using a correction factor is that they often want to infer to populations that are beyond their sampling frame. For example, a study of police patrol at hot spots in a particular city may sample 50 of 200 hot spots in the city during a certain month. However, researchers may be interested in making inferences to hot spots generally in the city (not just those that exist in a particular month) or even to hot spots in other places. For those inferences, it would be misleading to adjust the test statistic based on the small size of the sampling frame. For a discussion of how to correct for sampling without replacement, see Paul S. Levy and Stanley Lemeshow, *Sampling of Populations: Methods and Applications* (New York: Wiley, 1991).

The binomial test, however, like most tests of statistical significance examined in this book, assumes independent random sampling. Accordingly, in stating our assumptions, it is important to note both the requirement for this test and our failure to meet that requirement. Therefore we state our assumption:

Sampling Method: Independent random sampling (no replacement; sample is small relative to population).

Throughout this text, we state the assumptions of a test and then place any violations of assumptions in parentheses. This is good practice, as it will alert you to the fact that in many studies there are violations of one type or another of assumptions. Some of these violations are not important. For example, not sampling with replacement in this study does not affect the test outcome because the population of hot spots is assumed to be very large relative to the sample. However, you will sometimes find more serious violations of assumptions. In those cases, you will have to take a more critical view of the results of the test.

It is good practice to define not only the sampling method used but also the sampling frame of your study. In our example, we can make inferences based on our random sample to the population of hot spots in Jersey City during the month of sample selection. Accordingly, we state in our assumptions:

Sampling Frame: Hot spots of violent crime in one month in Jersey City.

Our sampling frame reminds us of the specific population to which our sample infers. However, researchers usually want to infer beyond the specific population identified by their sampling frame. For example, the population of interest for the POP study is likely to be hot spots throughout the year, not just those in a specific month. Researchers may even want to infer to violent-crime hot spots generally, not just those in Jersey City.

We cannot assume that our sample is a representative sample for these inferences based on our sampling method, since these populations did not constitute our sampling frame. However, we can ask whether our sample is likely to provide valid inferences to those populations. In the case of hot spots in Jersey City, we would need to question whether there is any reason to suspect that hot spots chosen in the month of study were different from those that would be found in other months of the year. For inferences to the population of hot spots in other locations, we would have to assume that Jersey City hot spots are similar to those in other places and would respond similarly to POP interventions. In making any inference beyond your sampling frame, you must try to identify all possible threats to external validity.

The Hypotheses

The final assumptions we make in a test of statistical inference refer to the hypotheses of our study. As discussed in Chapter 6, hypotheses are developed from the research questions raised in a project. Hypotheses must be stated before the researcher collects outcome data for a study. If hypotheses are stated only after data have been collected and analyzed, the researcher might be tempted to make changes in the hypotheses that unfairly affect the tests of statistical significance that are conducted.

As discussed in Chapter 6, the researcher ordinarily begins by defining the research hypothesis. In the problem-oriented policing study, we might state our research hypothesis in three different ways:

Hypothesis 1. Incivilities in treatment hot spots decline relative to incivilities in control hot spots after POP intervention.

Hypothesis 2. Incivilities in treatment hot spots increase relative to incivilities in control hot spots after POP intervention.

Hypothesis 3. The level of incivilities in treatment hot spots relative to incivilities in control hot spots changes after POP intervention.

Recall from Chapter 6 that we distinguish directional from nondirectional hypotheses. The first two research hypotheses are directional hypotheses because they specify the direction, or type of relationship, that is expected. For example, hypothesis 1 is concerned only with whether the POP program is successful in *reducing* incivilities. If the researcher adopts this hypothesis, then he or she is stating that the statistical test employed will not be concerned with the second hypothesis—that the intervention makes matters worse and *increases* incivilities. The third hypothesis is a nondirectional hypothesis. In this case, the researcher is interested in testing the possibility that the intervention improves hot spots or makes them worse.

In the POP study, researchers wanted to assess both positive and negative outcomes. Although they believed that problem-oriented policing should reduce incivilities at violent-crime hot spots, they did not want to preclude at the outset a finding that the program actually made matters worse. Accordingly, they used a nondirectional research hypothesis: "The level of incivilities in treatment hot spots relative to incivilities in control hot spots changes after POP intervention." The null hypothesis is "The level of incivilities in treatment hot spots does not change relative to incivilities in control hot spots after POP intervention."

In practice, the null hypothesis may be stated in terms of probabilities, just as we could state the coin toss hypothesis in the last chapter in terms of probabilities. In this study, the researchers examined (for each matched pair of hot spots) whether the hot spot that received the problem-oriented policing intervention improved or worsened relative to the control location. The null hypothesis suggests that the treatment and control hot spots are equally likely to improve. Put in terms of probabilities, there is a 0.50 chance of success ($P = 0.50$) for the intervention under the null hypothesis. The research hypothesis represents all other possible outcomes ($P \neq 0.50$). Remember that our hypotheses are statements about the populations examined. Accordingly, in stating the hypotheses, we use symbols appropriate for population parameters—in this case P rather than p. Stating our assumptions, we write

Hypotheses:

H_0: The level of incivilities in treatment hot spots does not change relative to incivilities in control hot spots after POP intervention, $P = 0.50$.

H_1: The level of incivilities in treatment hot spots relative to incivilities in control hot spots changes after POP intervention, $P \neq 0.50$.

Stating All of the Assumptions

Our assumptions may be stated as follows:

Assumptions:

Level of Measurement: Nominal binary scale.

Population Distribution: No assumption made.

Sampling Method: Independent random sampling (no replacement; sample is small relative to population).

Sampling Frame: Hot spots of violent crime in one month in Jersey City.

Hypotheses:

H_0: The level of incivilities in treatment hot spots does not change relative to incivilities in control hot spots after POP intervention, $P = 0.50$.

H_1: The level of incivilities in treatment hot spots relative to incivilities in control hot spots changes after POP intervention, $P \neq 0.50$.

Selecting a Sampling Distribution

In stating our hypotheses, we already noted the specific requirements of the binomial sampling distribution. Now we must state why we have chosen the binomial distribution and identify the specific characteristics of the sampling distribution that will be used to assess the risk of falsely rejecting the null hypothesis in our problem-oriented policing example. Choosing a sampling distribution is one of the most important decisions that researchers make in statistical inference. As we will show in later chapters, there are a number of different types of sampling distributions. Moreover, as with the binomial distribution, a single type of sampling distribution may have different forms depending on the problem examined. If the sampling distribution used is inappropriate for the research problem examined, then the conclusion reached will be suspect.

Because our measure is nominal and binary (see assumptions), we selected the binomial distribution for our test. The specific distribution that we use is based on our null hypothesis and the size of our sample. As illustrated in Chapter 7, the binomial distribution provides the likelihood of gaining a particular number of successes (heads in the example of the coin toss) in a fixed number of trials. In order to assess that likelihood, we also need to know what the probability of a success or failure is on any particular trial.

In our example, there are 11 trials, or 11 matched comparisons. Our null hypothesis states that the likelihood of a success for any comparison is 0.50. To build our sampling distribution, we apply the binomial formula to each of the 12 possible outcomes that could be gained in our study, under the assumption that $P = 0.50$. This is done in Table 8.2. The resulting distribution is presented in Table 8.3.

Table 8.2	Computation of Sampling Distribution of Success or Failure in 11 Trials

	$\dbinom{N}{r} = \dfrac{N!}{r!(N-r)!}$	$\dbinom{N}{r} p^r (1-p)^{N-r}$
0 successes	$\dfrac{39{,}916{,}800}{1(11-0)!} = \dfrac{39{,}916{,}800}{39{,}916{,}800} = 1$	$1(0.00049) = 0.00049$
1 success	$\dfrac{39{,}916{,}800}{1(11-1)!} = \dfrac{39{,}916{,}800}{3{,}628{,}800} = 11$	$11(0.00049) = 0.00537$
2 successes	$\dfrac{39{,}916{,}800}{2(11-2)!} = \dfrac{39{,}916{,}800}{725{,}760} = 55$	$55(0.00049) = 0.02686$
3 successes	$\dfrac{39{,}916{,}800}{6(11-3)!} = \dfrac{39{,}916{,}800}{241{,}920} = 165$	$165(0.00049) = 0.08057$
4 successes	$\dfrac{39{,}916{,}800}{24(11-4)!} = \dfrac{39{,}916{,}800}{120{,}960} = 330$	$330(0.00049) = 0.16113$
5 successes	$\dfrac{39{,}916{,}800}{120(11-5)!} = \dfrac{39{,}916{,}800}{86{,}400} = 462$	$432(0.00049) = 0.22638^*$
6 successes	$\dfrac{39{,}916{,}800}{720(11-6)!} = \dfrac{39{,}916{,}800}{86{,}400} = 462$	$432(0.00049) = 0.22638^*$
7 successes	$\dfrac{39{,}916{,}800}{5{,}040(11-7)!} = \dfrac{39{,}916{,}800}{120{,}960} = 330$	$330(0.00049) = 0.16113$
8 successes	$\dfrac{39{,}916{,}800}{40{,}320(11-8)!} = \dfrac{39{,}916{,}800}{241{,}920} = 165$	$165(0.00049) = 0.08057$
9 successes	$\dfrac{39{,}916{,}800}{362{,}880(11-9)!} = \dfrac{39{,}916{,}800}{725{,}760} = 55$	$55(0.00049) = 0.02686$
10 successes	$\dfrac{39{,}916{,}800}{3{,}628{,}800(11-10)!} = \dfrac{39{,}916{,}800}{3{,}628{,}800} = 11$	$11(0.00049) = 0.00537$
11 successes	$\dfrac{39{,}916{,}800}{39{,}916{,}800(11-11)!} = \dfrac{39{,}916{,}800}{39{,}916{,}800} = 1$	$1(0.00049) = 0.00049$

*Probabilities contain rounding error.

Table 8.3	Sampling Distribution of Success or Failure in 11 Trials

OUTCOME OF TRIALS	OVERALL PROBABILITY
0 successes	0.00049
1 success	0.00537
2 successes	0.02686
3 successes	0.08057
4 successes	0.16113
5 successes	0.22559
6 successes	0.22559
7 successes	0.16113
8 successes	0.08057
9 successes	0.02686
10 successes	0.00537
11 successes	0.00049

Significance Level and Rejection Region

Having selected the distribution that will be used to assess Type I error, we are ready to define the outcomes that will lead us to reject the null hypothesis. Our first step is to choose the significance level of our test. As described in Chapter 6, the significance level of a test is the amount of Type I error we are willing to risk in rejecting the null hypothesis. By convention, criminal justice researchers use a 5% significance threshold. But, as discussed in Chapter 6, we should consider at the outset whether a more lenient or more stringent significance level is appropriate for our study.

As researchers in the problem-oriented policing study do not present any special reason for altering conventionally accepted levels of significance, we will set a 5% significance threshold for our test of statistical significance. As noted in Chapter 6, in articles and books the significance level is often expressed by the Greek letter α. For our test, $\alpha = 0.05$.

The significance level defines the Type I error we are willing to risk in our test. But it does not tell us directly what outcomes in our sample would lead us to reject the null hypothesis. For this, we need to turn to our sampling distribution and define an area within it called a **rejection region.** The rejection region of a test is the area in the sampling distribution that includes those outcomes that would lead to rejection of the null hypothesis. If the observed significance level of a test, or the p value of the test, falls within the rejection region, then the researcher rejects the null hypothesis and concludes that the outcome is statistically significant. The area covered by the rejection region is equivalent to the significance level of a test. The point at which the rejection region begins is called the **critical value** because it is the point at which the test becomes critical and leads the researcher to reject the null hypothesis.

In the problem-oriented policing example, the rejection region includes 5% of the sampling distribution. Our initial problem is to define which 5%. Should we define the rejection region to be in the middle of the distribution represented in Table 8.3—for example, at 5 or 6 successes in 11 comparisons? Or should we look only at the extreme values on the positive side of the distribution, where there are mostly successes? Or should we include the area on the negative side of the distribution, where there are no successes?

Choosing a One-Tailed or a Two-Tailed Rejection Region

The answer to our questions comes in part from common sense and in part from our assumptions. It just would not make sense to place the rejection region in the middle of the sampling distribution. We are trying to decide whether the outcomes observed in our sample are very different from the outcomes that would be expected if problem-oriented policing had no impact. Putting the rejection region in the middle of the distribution would place it among those outcomes that are most likely under the null hypothesis. Clearly, we want the rejection region to be on the edges of the distribution, or in what statisticians call the **tails of the distribution.** These are the unlikely events—those that we would not expect if the null hypothesis were true. As indicated in our sampling distribution in Table 8.3, we would expect to get 11 successes in a row in about 5 of 10,000 samples if the program had no impact on the population. This is a very unlikely event and one that would lead us to reject the null hypothesis.

But zero successes is also an unlikely event, with the same probability of occurrence as 11 successes. Should we include only one tail of the distribution in our rejection region—the tail that assesses whether the program was a success? Or should we also include the opposite side of the distribution, which suggests that the program led to more disorder? Our answer is drawn from the research hypothesis that we stated in our assumptions. We chose a nondirectional research hypothesis, meaning that we are interested in evaluating both the possibility that the experimental sites improved relative to the control hot spots and the potential outcome that they got worse relative to the control hot spots. In terms of the sampling distribution, our research hypothesis suggests that the rejection region for our test should be split between both tails of the distribution.

This type of test is called a **two-tailed test of significance.** If we had stated a directional research hypothesis, we would be concerned with outcomes on only one side of the sampling distribution. Such a test is called a **one-tailed test of significance.** For example, if our research hypothesis were that incivilities in treatment hot spots decrease relative to incivilities in control hot spots after POP intervention, we would be concerned only with outcomes on the side of the distribution that shows program success.

The choice of a one-tailed or two-tailed test of statistical significance has important implications for the types of study outcomes that will lead to rejection of the null hypothesis. Because our test is a two-tailed test, the rejection region must be divided between both sides of the sampling distribution. This means in practice that the total significance level of 0.05 must be divided in half. Half of the rejection region, or 0.025, is found in the tail associated with success of the program, and half, or 0.025, in the tail associated with failure.

What outcomes would lead to rejection of the null hypothesis in our example? When we add 0 and 1 successes or 10 and 11 successes, we gain a probability value of 0.00586 (in each tail of the distribution, 0.00049 + 0.00537). This is less than the 0.025 value that we have defined as the rejection region for each tail of our test. Accordingly, an outcome of 0, 1, 10 or 11 would lead to an observed significance level less than the significance level of 0.05 that we have set, and thus we would reject the null hypothesis ($p < 0.05$). However, including 2 or 9 successes, each of which has a probability value of 0.027, increases the area of the distribution to 0.066. This area is larger than our rejection region. An outcome of 9 or 2 would result in an observed significance level greater than 0.05, and thus we would fail to reject the null hypothesis. Figure 8.1 presents the binomial probabilities for our example and highlights the two tails of the distribution that are used to test our nondirectional hypothesis.

Figure 8.1

Outcomes That Would Lead to Rejecting the Null Hypothesis for a Two-Tailed Test of Significance ($\alpha = 0.05$)

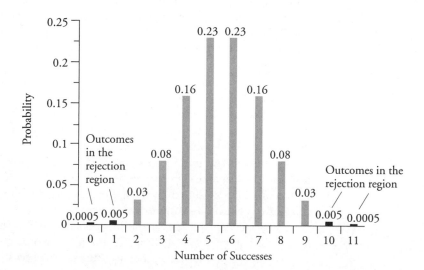

But what if we state a directional research hypothesis? How does this affect our rejection region? In this case, we calculate the area of the rejection region on only one side of the sampling distribution. Parts a and b of Figure 8.2 present the binomial probabilities for our two distinct directional hypotheses and highlight the tail of the distribution that is potentially of interest. For example, if our research hypothesis is that incivilities in treatment hot spots decline relative to incivilities in control hot spots after POP intervention, we look at outcomes only on the tail of the distribution that shows program success (Figure 8.2b). Because we are concerned only about these outcomes, all 5% of the rejection region is placed in this one tail of the distribution. We do not have to split the area of the rejection region. In this example, outcomes of 9, 10, and 11 successes are all within the rejection region, because adding their probabilities results in a value of 0.033 (0.00049 + 0.00537 + 0.02686). An outcome of 9, 10, or 11 results in an observed significance level that is less than the 5% significance threshold of our test (see Figure 8.2b). Adding the probability of 8 successes (or 0.08057) puts us above that threshold. If our research hypothesis is that incivilities increase in treatment hot spots relative to control hot spots, then we look at outcomes only on the opposite tail of the distribution (Figure 8.2a). In this case, outcomes of 0, 1, and 2 successes lead us to reject the null hypothesis.

This example reinforces a rule described earlier: It is important to state the research hypothesis before you gain study outcomes. What if the problem-oriented policing hot spots improved relative to control locations in nine comparisons? With a one-tailed test, the result would fall within our rejection region and lead to rejection of the null hypothesis. With a two-tailed test, the result would be outside our rejection region. The choice of a directional or nondirectional research hypothesis can have an important impact on our conclusions. Merely by stating the research hypothesis a bit differently, we can change the outcome of the test.

A one-tailed test makes it easier to reject the null hypothesis based on outcomes on one side of a sampling distribution because it precludes rejection of the null hypothesis based on outcomes on the opposite side. The price of a larger rejection region in one-tail of the sampling distribution is no rejection region in the other tail. Similarly, the price of being able to examine outcomes on both sides of the distribution, as is the case with a two-tailed test, is that the rejection region will be smaller on each side. The benefit is that you can assess results in both directions. If you already know the outcomes of a test, you might be tempted to adjust the direction of the test according to the observed outcomes of a study. Taking such an approach unfairly adjusts the rejection region to your advantage.

Figure 8.2

Outcomes That Would Lead to Rejecting the Null Hypothesis for a One-Tailed Test of Significance ($\alpha = 0.05$)

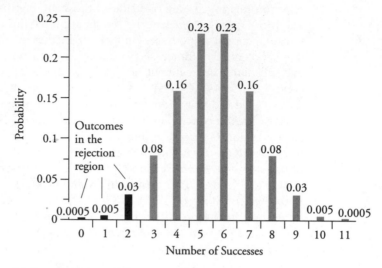

(a) *Focus on Program Failures*

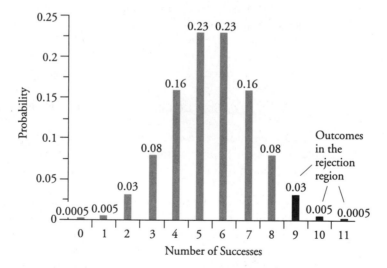

(b) *Focus on Program Successes*

The Test Statistic

In most tests of statistical significance, it is necessary to convert the specific outcome of a study to a **test statistic.** A test statistic expresses the value of your outcome in units of the sampling distribution employed in your test. For the binomial distribution, the units are simply the number of successes in the total number of trials. The test statistic for our POP intervention example is 10.

Making a Decision

The final step in a test of statistical significance is making a decision. If you have laid out all of the steps discussed above, then your choice should be easy. If your test statistic falls within the rejection region, then you reject the null hypothesis. This means in practice that the observed significance level of your test is less than the criterion significance level that you set when you defined the significance level and rejection region for your test. If the test statistic does not fall in the rejection region, you cannot reject the null hypothesis. In our example, the test statistic (10) does fall in the rejection region, which includes 0, 1, 10, and 11 successes. In this case, our observed significance level is less than the 0.05 threshold we set earlier. Our decision, then, is to reject the null hypothesis that incivilities in treatment hot spots do not change relative to incivilities in control hot spots after POP intervention. We conclude that the differences observed are **statistically significant.**

But what does this mean? When we say that a result is statistically significant, we are not claiming that it is substantively important. The importance of a result depends on such issues as whether the research affects real-life criminal justice decision making or whether it contributes new knowledge to a specific area of criminology or criminal justice. We also are not stating that we are certain that the null hypothesis is untrue for the population. Without knowledge of the population parameter, we cannot answer this question with certainty. Statistical significance has a very specific interpretation. The fact that an outcome is statistically significant means that it falls within the rejection region of your test. This happens when the observed significance level for a test is smaller than the significance criterion, or significance level, set at the outset of the test. A statistically significant result is one that is unlikely if the null hypothesis is true for the population. Whenever we make a statement that a result is statistically significant, we do it with the recognition that we are risking a certain level of Type I error. In this test, as in most tests of statistical significance in criminal justice, we were willing to take a 5% risk of falsely rejecting the null hypothesis.

Chapter Summary

The first stage in a test of statistical significance is to state one's **assumptions.** The first assumption is about the type of measurement used. The second assumption concerns the shape of the population distribution. A **parametric test** is one that makes assumptions about the shape of the population distribution. A **nonparametric test** makes no such assumptions. Although nonparametric tests have the advantage of making fewer assumptions, they are generally used only for nominal and ordinal scales. The third assumption relates to the sampling method. A **random sample** is generally considered to be more representative, or to have greater **external validity,** than a **convenience sample. Independent random sampling** is the most accepted form of sampling. To ensure the independence of the sampling, it is in theory necessary to return the subject to the **sampling frame** after selection. **Sampling with replacement** creates practical problems, however, and is generally not required if the sample is small relative to the population. The fourth assumption states the null and research hypotheses. Care should be taken in framing them and in deciding whether the research hypothesis should be directional.

The second stage is to select an appropriate sampling distribution. The third stage is to select a significance level. The significance level determines the size of the **rejection region** and the location of the **critical values** of the test. If a test result falls within the rejection region, the researcher is prepared to reject the null hypothesis. This means that the observed significance level of the test is less than the significance level the researcher set at the outset of the test. If the hypotheses are directional, then the researcher will be concerned only with one **tail of the distribution,** and the entire rejection region will be placed on one side of the distribution (a **one-tailed test of significance**). If the hypotheses are nondirectional, then the researcher is concerned with results in both tails, and the rejection region will be divided equally between both sides of the distribution (a **two-tailed test of significance**).

The fourth stage involves calculating a **test statistic.** The study result is now converted into the units of the sampling distribution. Finally, a decision is made: The null hypothesis will be rejected if the test statistic falls within the rejection region. When such a decision can be made, the results are said to be **statistically significant.**

Key Terms

assumptions Statements that identify the requirements and characteristics of a test of statistical significance. These are the foundations on which the rest of the test is built.

convenience sample A sample chosen not at random, but according to criteria of expedience or accessibility to the researcher.

critical value The point at which the rejection region begins.

distribution-free tests Another name for nonparametric tests.

external validity The extent to which a study sample is reflective of the population from which it is drawn. A study is said to have high external validity when the sample used is representative of the population to which inferences are made.

independent random sampling A form of random sampling in which the fact that one subject is drawn from a population in no way affects the probability of drawing any other subject from that population.

nonparametric tests Tests of statistical significance that make no assumptions as to the shape of the population distribution.

one-tailed test of significance A test of statistical significance in which the region for rejecting the null hypothesis falls on only one side of the sampling distribution. One-tailed tests are based on directional research hypotheses.

parametric tests Tests of statistical significance that make assumptions as to the shape of the population distribution.

random sampling Drawing samples from the population in a manner that ensures every individual in that population an equal chance of being selected.

rejection region The area of a sampling distribution containing the test statistic values that will cause the researcher to reject the null hypothesis.

representative sample A sample that reflects the population from which it is drawn.

sampling frame The universe of eligible cases from which a sample is drawn.

sampling with replacement A sampling method in which individuals in a sample are returned to the sampling frame after they have been selected. This raises the possibility that certain individuals in a population may appear in a sample more than once.

statistically significant Describing a test statistic that falls within the rejection region defined by the researcher. When this occurs, the researcher is prepared to reject the null hypothesis and state that the outcome or relationship is statistically significant.

tails of the distribution The extremes on the sides of a sampling distribution. The events represented by the tails of a sampling distribution are those deemed least likely to occur if the null hypothesis is true for the population.

test statistic The outcome of the study, expressed in units of the sampling distribution. A test statistic that falls within the rejection region will lead the researcher to reject the null hypothesis.

two-tailed test of significance A test of statistical significance in which the region for rejecting the null hypothesis falls on both sides of the sampling distribution. Two-tailed tests are based on nondirectional research hypotheses.

Exercises

8.1   Answer the following conceptual questions:

    a. Is it better to have more or fewer assumptions at the beginning of a test of statistical significance? Explain your answer.

    b. Why is it important to state all of the assumptions at the outset of the test?

    c. In what sense can stating the null and research hypotheses be seen as making assumptions?

8.2   Gatley University is an elite university of 1,000 students. Nadia, a student studying Chinese at the university, wishes to determine the average IQ of students at Gatley. She has decided that her sample size will be 50, and she is considering several different sampling methods. For each method, state the sampling frame and discuss whether the sampling method is random and whether it is independent.

    a. Nadia chooses 50 names at random from the list of language students at the university.

    b. Nadia asks 50 of her acquaintances at the university if they would mind taking an IQ test.

    c. Nadia chooses the first two students from the alphabetical list of each of the 25 university departments.

    d. Nadia takes all 1,000 names and puts them into a hat. She draws out a name, writes it down, and then puts it back in the hat and draws again. This procedure is repeated 50 times.

8.3   Hale Prison is renowned for its poor internal discipline. The new prison governor wants to tackle this problem and decides to investigate whether removing prisoners' visiting privileges will act as a deterrent against future misbehaving. From 100 prisoners who recently took part in a violent prison riot, he selects the 25 inmates with the worst disciplinary records, removes their visiting privileges, and begins to monitor their progress relative to the others.

    a. Does this method meet the criteria of independent random sampling?

    b. Is independent sampling possible in this case?

    c. Describe a more appropriate sampling method.

8.4   For each of the following hypotheses, state whether a one-tailed or a two-tailed test of statistical significance would be appropriate. In each case, explain your choice.

    a. H_1: Citizens over the age of 50 are more likely to be the victims of assault than citizens under the age of 50.

b. H_1: Children raised by adopted parents have rates of delinquency different from those of children raised by their biological parents.

c. H_1: The experience of imprisonment has an impact on the chances of an ex-convict reoffending.

d. H_1: Women are more likely than men to support increased sentences for rapists.

e. H_1: Persons who are not victims of assault have lower levels of anger than persons who have been victims of assault.

f. H_1: White offenders are less likely to be sentenced to prison than Hispanic offenders.

g. H_1: Teenagers have rates of crime that are different from adult rates of crime.

h. H_1: Defendants charged with property crimes have different rates of pretrial misconduct than defendants charged with violent crimes.

i. H_1: Male defendants are more likely to be held on bail than female defendants.

j. H_1: Women are more supportive of capital punishment than men.

k. H_1: States with higher unemployment rates have higher rates of property crime.

l. H_1: The level of poverty in a neighborhood affects the neighborhood's crime rate.

m. H_1: Democrats are less supportive of cutting taxes than Republicans.

n. H_1: Graduates from private law schools are more likely to become federal judges than graduates from state law schools.

8.5 In Chapter 7, we constructed a binomial distribution showing the chances of success and failure for ten tosses of a fair coin. The distribution was as follows:

0 heads 0.001
1 head   0.010
2 heads 0.044
3 heads 0.118
4 heads 0.206
5 heads 0.247
6 heads 0.206
7 heads 0.118
8 heads 0.044
9 heads 0.010
10 heads 0.001

Consider the following alternative hypotheses:

Alternative 1: H_0: The coin is fair.
                    H_1: The coin is biased.

Alternative 2: H_0: The coin is fair.
                    H_1: The coin is biased in favor of heads.

a. Would a one-tailed or a two-tailed test be more appropriate for a researcher who chose alternative 1? Explain why.

b. For a sequence of ten throws, what results would cause a researcher operating under the hypotheses listed under alternative 1 to reject the null hypothesis at a significance level of 5%?

c. Would a one-tailed or a two-tailed test be more appropriate for a researcher who chose alternative 2? Explain why.

d. For a sequence of ten throws, what results would cause a researcher operating under the hypotheses listed under alternative 2 to reject the null hypothesis at a significance level of 5%?

8.6   Use the following binomial distribution showing the chances of success and failure for 12 trials.

Number of Successes	Probability
0 successes	0.00118
1 success	0.01065
2 successes	0.04418
3 successes	0.11110
4 successes	0.18857
5 successes	0.22761
6 successes	0.20032
7 successes	0.12953
8 successes	0.06107
9 successes	0.02048
10 successes	0.00463
11 successes	0.00064
12 successes	0.00004

Using a significance level of 0.05, what outcomes would lead you to reject the null hypothesis for each of the following pairs of hypotheses?

a. H_0: $P = 0.50$
   H_1: $P \neq 0.50$

b. H_0: $P = 0.50$
   H_1: $P < 0.50$

c. H_0: $P = 0.50$
H_1: $P > 0.50$

d. If you changed the significance level to 0.01, how would your answers to parts a, b, and c change?

8.7 Use the following binomial distribution showing the chances of success and failure for 15 trials.

Number of Successes	Probability
0 successes	0.00000
1 success	0.00000
2 successes	0.00001
3 successes	0.00006
4 successes	0.00042
5 successes	0.00228
6 successes	0.00930
7 successes	0.02928
8 successes	0.07168
9 successes	0.13650
10 successes	0.20051
11 successes	0.22313
12 successes	0.18210
13 successes	0.10288
14 successes	0.03598
15 successes	0.00587

Using a significance level of 0.05, what outcomes would lead you to reject the null hypothesis for each of the following pairs of hypotheses?

a. H_0: $P = 0.50$
H_1: $P \neq 0.50$

b. H_0: $P = 0.50$
H_1: $P < 0.50$

c. H_0: $P = 0.50$
H_1: $P > 0.50$

d. If you changed the significance level to 0.01, how would your answers to parts a, b, and c change?

8.8 Locate a research article in a recent issue of a criminology or criminal justice journal.

a. State the research hypotheses tested by the researcher(s).

b. Describe the sampling method, the sample, and the sampling frame used by the researcher(s).

Computer Exercises

The "Binomial" command (Analyze → Nonparametric Tests → Binomial) will use a two-tailed test to calculate an observed significance level for a binary variable (e.g., success vs. failure). The default probability in the "Binomial" command is $p = 0.50$, meaning that this command tests the following hypotheses:

H_0: $P = 0.50$
H_1: $P \neq 0.50$

After you execute the "Binomial" command, the window that appears will have a list of variables in the box on the left. Simply move the names of the variables of interest into the box on the right side of this window. Click on "OK" to compute the results.

To try out the "Binomial" command, open the data file **ox_8_1.sav.** This small data file contains the data from Table 8.1 in the text. Relative decreases in postintervention crime are indicated by a value of 1, and relative increases in postintervention crime are indicated by a value of 0. Execute the "Binomial" command for this variable.

In the output window, you will be presented with a table of results that indicates the proportion of cases in each category and the observed significance level (labeled "Exact Significance" in the table). You will see from this output window that the observed significance level is 0.012, which is identical to the value calculated on p. 172 in the text.

1. The director of a special drug treatment program claims to have found a cure to drug addiction. As supporting evidence, the director produces information on a random sample of 13 former clients who were followed for 12 months after completing the program. Here is how the director classified each former client:

   Success, Failure, Success, Success, Success, Success, Success, Failure, Success, Success, Failure, Success, Success

   Enter these data into SPSS.

   a. State all the assumptions of the test.

   b. What is the test statistic?

   c. What decision can be made about the null hypothesis? (Assume the significance level is 0.05.)

   d. Can the director conclude that the program is effective? Explain why.

2. A group of researchers wanted to replicate previous research on hot spot interventions in another city, using a sample of 25 hot spots. When comparing postintervention crime levels, they classified the 25 locations as follows:

   Decrease, Decrease, Increase, Decrease, Decrease, Increase, Increase, Decrease, Decrease, Decrease, Decrease, Decrease, Decrease,

Decrease, Decrease, Increase, Increase, Decrease, Decrease, Decrease, Decrease, Decrease, Increase, Decrease, Decrease

Enter these data into SPSS.

a. State all the assumptions of the test.

b. What is the test statistic?

c. What decision can be made about the null hypothesis? (Assume the significance level is 0.05.)

d. Did this study show a postintervention change in crime?

e. If the significance level had been set at 0.01, would the researchers have come to the same conclusion? Explain why.

choosing the chi-square distribution

When Is the Chi-Square Distribution Appropriate?

What Are Degrees of Freedom?

How Do Degrees of Freedom Affect the Distribution?

calculating the chi-square statistic

How Is the Chi-Square Statistic Calculated?

How Does One Interpret a Chi-Square Statistic?

substantive examples using the chi-square test

How Is the Chi-Square Test Carried Out When There Is Only One Nominal-Scale Measure?

How Is the Chi-Square Test Applied in the Case of the Relationship Between Two Nominal-Scale Variables?

Can the Chi-Square Test Be Used to Examine the Relationship Between Ordinal-Level Variables?

THE BINOMIAL TEST provides a good introduction to the problem of statistical inference because it examines relatively simple statistical decisions. Using the binomial test, we illustrated how statisticians build a sampling distribution from probabilities. But the binomial distribution can be applied only to a single binary variable. In this chapter, we look at a more commonly used nonparametric test of statistical significance for nominal-level measures: chi-square. The chi-square test allows the researcher to examine multicategory nominal-level variables as well as the relationship between nominal-level measures.

We begin our discussion of chi-square with an example similar to the one used to introduce the binomial distribution in Chapter 7. In this case, we examine the problem of a fair roll of a die. We then turn to applications of the chi-square test in criminal justice.

Testing Hypotheses Concerning the Roll of a Die

In Chapter 7, we examined how you might make a decision about whether to challenge the fairness of a coin used to decide who would serve first in a weekly volleyball match. But what if you had the same question regarding a die used in a friendly game of chance at a local club? Each week, you and a few friends go down to the club and play a game of chance that involves the toss of a die. Let's say that the house (the club) wins whenever you roll a two or a six. You win whenever you roll a three or a four, and no one wins when you roll a one or a five. Over the month, you have played the game 60 times. Of the 60 rolls of the die, you have lost 24, rolling six 20 times and rolling two 4 times (see Table 9.1). You have won 10 times in total, rolling three 6 times and rolling four 4 times. The remaining 26 rolls of the die were split, with 16 ones and 10 fives.

| Table 9.1 | Frequency Distribution for 60 Rolls of a Die |

1	No winner	16
2	You lose	4
3	You win	6
4	You win	4
5	No winner	10
6	You lose	20
Total		60

As in the case of the coin toss, you and your friends have begun to be suspicious. Does it make sense that there should be such an uneven split in the outcomes of the game if the die is fair? Should you raise this issue with the club and suggest that they change their die? You don't want to appear to be a sore sport. Nonetheless, if the distribution of rolls of the die that you observed is very unlikely given a fair die, you would be willing to make a protest.

The Chi-Square Distribution

You cannot use the binomial distribution to assess the fairness of the die because the binomial distribution assumes that there are only two potential outcomes for each event—for example, a head or tail on each toss of a coin. For the die, there are six potential outcomes: a roll of one, two, three, four, five, or six. In such cases, you can make use of another sampling distribution, called the **chi-square** (χ^2) **distribution.** Like the binomial distribution, which varies depending on the number of trials conducted, the chi-square distribution varies from problem to problem. However, the chi-square distribution varies not according to the number of trials that are conducted but according to the number of **degrees of freedom** (df) associated with a test. The number of degrees of freedom refers to how much a mathematical operation is free to vary, or take on any value, after an agreed-upon set of limitations has been imposed.

In the chi-square distribution, these limitations are associated with the number of categories, or potential outcomes, examined. To define the degrees of freedom of a chi-square test, we ask how many categories would have to be known for us to predict the remaining categories with certainty. For example, if we know that there are 60 rolls of the die and we also know the precise number of events that fall in five of the six categories, we will be able to predict the sixth category simply by subtracting from the total number of events (60) the number in the five known categories (see Table 9.2). If two categories are blank, we can predict the total of both, but not the exact split between them. Accordingly, the number of degrees of freedom for this example is 5. Once we know the number of events or observations in five categories,

Table 9.2	Frequency Distribution for 60 Rolls of a Die with Information Missing

1	No winner	16
2	You lose	4
3	You win	6
4	You win	4
5	No winner	10
6	You lose	?
Total		60

Frequency of category 6 = (total frequency) − (sum of categories 1 to 5)
$$20 = 60 - 40$$

we can predict the number in the sixth with certainty. More generally, you can identify the degrees of freedom for a one-variable chi-square distribution using the equation df $= k - 1$, where k equals the number of categories in your measure (for our example, $6 - 1 = 5$).

Figure 9.1 shows how chi-square distributions vary according to the number of degrees of freedom. The height of the distribution represents the proportion of cases found at any specific value of the **chi-square statistic.** As the number of degrees of freedom grows, the height of the chi-square distribution decreases, with a longer and longer tail to the right. This means that the proportion of cases found above higher values of the chi-square statistic grows as the number of degrees of freedom increases. To understand what this means substantively, as well as how the chi-square distribution is used in making decisions about hypotheses, it is important to see how the chi-square statistic is calculated.

Figure 9.1	*Chi-Square Distributions for Various Degrees of Freedom*

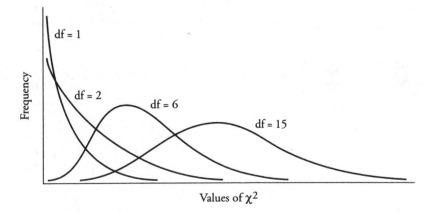

Calculating the Chi-Square Statistic

The formula for the chi-square statistic is presented in Equation 9.1.

$$\chi^2 = \sum_{i=1}^{k} \frac{(f_o - f_e)^2}{f_e}$$

Equation 9.1

The summation symbol in the body of the equation has $i = 1$ below it and k above it. This means that we sum the quantity that follows the summation symbol for each category from the first to the kth, or last, category. Since there are six categories in our example, we will have to carry out the same calculation six times, once for each of the six potential outcomes of the roll of a die.

The quantity that follows the summation symbol includes two symbols, f_o and f_e. The symbol f_o represents the frequency of the events observed in a category, or the **observed frequencies.** For example, in 20 of the 60 trials, a six was rolled (see Table 9.1). The observed frequency for a roll of six is 20. The symbol f_e represents the **expected frequency** of a category. The expected frequencies are ordinarily defined by the null hypothesis. In our example, they represent the number of events that would be expected in each category in the long run if the die were fair. Because a fair die is one for which there is an equal chance of obtaining any of the six potential outcomes, we divide the 60 observations evenly across the six categories. This leads to an expected frequency of 10 for each potential outcome. Table 9.3 shows the expected and observed frequencies for our example.

To calculate the chi-square statistic, Equation 9.1 tells us first to subtract the expected frequency from the observed frequency in each category. We then square the result and divide that quantity by the expected frequency of the category. For example, for a roll of six, we subtract 10 (the expected frequency) from 20 (the observed frequency). We then square that quantity (to get 100) and divide the result by 10. This gives us 10 for a roll of six. After carrying out this computation for each category, as is done in Table 9.4, we add up the results for all six categories

Table 9.3   Expected and Observed Frequencies for 60 Rolls of a Fair Die

	f_e	f_o
1	10	16
2	10	4
3	10	6
4	10	4
5	10	10
6	10	20
Total	60	60

| Table 9.4 | | Computation of Chi-Square for 60 Rolls of a Die | | | |

OUTCOME A	f_o	f_e	$(f_o - f_e)$	$(f_o - f_e)^2$	$\dfrac{(f_o - f_e)^2}{f_e}$
1	16	10	6	36	3.6
2	4	10	−6	36	3.6
3	6	10	−4	16	1.6
4	4	10	−6	36	3.6
5	10	10	0	0	0
6	20	10	10	100	10.0
					$\Sigma = 22.4$

to obtain the total chi-square statistic. The chi-square statistic for this example is 22.4.

The chi-square statistic measures how much the observed distribution differs from that expected under the null hypothesis. If the observed frequencies are similar to the expected frequencies, the chi-square statistic is small. If the observed frequencies are the same as the expected frequencies, the chi-square statistic equals 0. The more the observed frequencies differ from the expected frequencies, the larger the chi-square statistic will be. What does this mean in terms of making a decision about the fairness of the die? To find out, we have to turn to a table of probabilities associated with the chi-square distribution.

Linking the Chi-Square Statistic to Probabilities: The Chi-Square Table

In Chapters 7 and 8, we used the binomial formula to calculate the probability associated with each of the possible outcomes in our sample. For other tests of statistical significance, including chi-square, we can take advantage of already calculated probability distributions. Appendix 2 presents a table of probabilities associated with chi-square distributions with degrees of freedom from 1 to 30. The chi-square table does not give us the probability associated with every possible outcome, but rather provides probabilities and then lists the chi-square statistics associated with them.

As illustrated in the chi-square table in Appendix 2, a larger chi-square statistic is associated with a smaller significance level, or α value. For example, under one degree of freedom, a statistic of 2.706 is associated with a significance level of 0.10, a statistic of 3.841 with an α value of 0.05, and a statistic of 10.827 with an α value of 0.001. This also means that the larger the chi-square statistic obtained in a test, the less likely it is that the observed distribution is drawn from the expected distribution. This logic makes good common sense. For our example of the roll of a die, it is reasonable to become more suspicious about the fairness of the die as the number of events in the different categories

190   CHAPTER NINE: CHI-SQUARE

becomes more uneven. If we expect 10 events in each category and actually get one with 20, one with 16, and two others with only 4, this should begin to make us suspicious. If one or two categories have 25 cases and two or three have none, it seems even more likely that the die is not a fair one. But if each category has about 10 cases, which is to be expected in the long run with 60 rolls of a fair die, both common sense and chi-square give us little reason to suspect a biased die.

Notice as well in Appendix 2 that as the number of degrees of freedom gets larger, a larger chi-square statistic is needed to arrive at the same probability value. For example, with one degree of freedom, a chi-square statistic of 3.841 is associated with an α value of 0.05. With 30 degrees of freedom, a statistic of 43.773 is needed to achieve the same threshold. This reflects the difference in the shape of chi-square distributions with different degrees of freedom and makes good sense if you consider how the chi-square statistic is calculated. A separate addition is made to the chi-square statistic for each possible category. Accordingly, it makes sense to demand a larger statistic as the number of categories in the test increases.

What about our decision regarding the roll of the die? Looking at Appendix 2, we can see that with five degrees of freedom a chi-square statistic of 11.070 is associated with a significance level of 0.05. This means that in the long run we would expect to obtain a chi-square statistic of 11.070 in only 5 in 100 samples if the die is fair. In fact, we obtained a chi-square statistic of 22.4. This number is even larger than that needed for a significance level of 0.001. Accordingly, the observed significance level for this test is less than 0.001 ($p < 0.001$). If the die were fair, the probability of getting a distribution like the one observed in our 60 rolls of a die would be less than 1 in 1,000. Given this result, we would likely come to the conclusion that the die was not a fair one and call for the club to use a new one.

A Substantive Example: The Relationship Between Assault Victims and Offenders

We can illustrate the chi-square test for a single variable by considering the responses from a random sample survey of Illinois residents.[1] One of the primary purposes of the survey was to examine the effect of victimization on the physical and mental health of adults. Each respondent was asked about a variety of possible victimization experiences. When the person claimed to have experienced a crime, a series of follow-up questions were asked about the circumstances of the event. Table 9.5 presents the frequency distribution of the responses to a question about the

[1]See Chester L. Britt, "Health Consequences of Criminal Victimization," *International Review of Victimology* 8 (2001): 63–73 for a description of the study.

Table 9.5	Relationship Between Assault Victim and Offender

CATEGORY	FREQUENCY (N)
Stranger	166
Acquaintance	61
Friend	35
Boyfriend/girlfriend	38
Spouse	66
Other relative	44
Total (Σ)	410

relationship between the victim and the offender for those persons who claimed to have been assaulted.

A simple research question using these data might focus on whether the victim-offender relationship was unevenly distributed among the population of assault victims. To answer our research question, we follow the form of a statistical test introduced in Chapter 8.

We begin by stating the assumptions of our chi-square test. The level of measurement required for chi-square is nominal. We make no specific assumptions regarding the shape of the population distribution, as the chi-square test is a nonparametric test of statistical significance. Although the chi-square test ordinarily requires a fully independent random sample, this sample was selected without replacement.[2] This is not a serious violation of our assumptions because the sample is very small relative to the population of interest. Note that our null hypothesis is that the victim-offender relationship in the population is evenly or randomly distributed across the categories examined. The research hypothesis is that the victim-offender relationship is not randomly or evenly distributed in the population.

Assumptions:

Level of Measurement: Nominal scale.

Population Distribution: No assumption made.

Sampling Method: Independent random sampling (no replacement; sample is small relative to population).

Sampling Frame: Persons aged 18 and over in the state of Illinois.

Hypotheses:

H_0: The type of victim-offender relationship for assault victims is randomly distributed.

H_1: The type of victim-offender relationship for assault victims is not randomly distributed.

---

[2]There are certain specific situations in which the chi-square test does not require sampling with replacement; see B. S. Everitt, *The Analysis of Contingency Tables* (London: Chapman and Hall, 1997).

The Sampling Distribution   Since we are analyzing the distribution of cases for a nominal variable, the chi-square distribution provides an appropriate means of assessing whether the observations are randomly distributed across the six categories of victim-offender relationships. For a single nominal variable, the number of degrees of freedom for the chi-square test is df $= k - 1 = 6 - 1 = 5$.

Significance Level and Rejection Region   Since we have no reason to impose a stricter or more lenient level of statistical significance on our analysis, we will use a significance level (α) of 0.05. Given that the number of degrees of freedom associated with this chi-square test is 5 and the significance level is 0.05, we see from Appendix 2 that the corresponding critical value of the chi-square distribution is 11.070. Accordingly, if the calculated value of the chi-square statistic in our example is greater than 11.070, we will reject the null hypothesis and conclude that type of victim-offender relationship among assault victims is not randomly distributed.

The Test Statistic   Equation 9.1 provides the formula for calculating the chi-square statistic to test for random assignment of cases to each category or value. We begin by calculating the expected frequency (f_e) for each cell in the table. Again, as in the example of the die, we would expect under the null hypothesis that there would be an equal number of cases in each of the categories examined. To calculate the expected frequency mathematically, we divide the total N of cases by the number of categories. This is done below, where we get an expected value for each category of 68.333:

$$f_e = \frac{N}{k} = \frac{410}{6} = 68.333$$

After calculating the expected frequency, we can proceed to calculate the chi-square statistic. Table 9.6 presents the observed and expected frequencies for each cell and the appropriate calculations for determining the value of the chi-square statistic. We find the value of the test statistic to be 178.85.

Table 9.6   Computation of Chi-Square for Type of Victim-Offender Relationship

CATEGORY	f_o	f_e	$(f_o - f_e)$	$(f_o - f_e)^2$	$\frac{(f_o - f_e)^2}{f_e}$
Stranger	166	68.333	97.667	9,538.843	139.593
Acquaintance	61	68.333	−7.333	53.773	0.787
Friend	35	68.333	−33.333	1,111.089	16.260
Boyfriend/girlfriend	38	68.333	−30.333	920.091	13.465
Spouse	66	68.333	−2.333	5.443	0.080
Other relative	44	68.333	−24.333	592.095	8.665
					$\Sigma = 178.849$

The Decision   The critical value for our test of statistical significance was 11.070, meaning that a calculated chi-square statistic greater than this critical value would lead to rejection of the null hypothesis. The value of our test statistic is 178.85, which is much larger than our critical chi-square value. Accordingly, the observed significance level of our test is less than the significance criterion we set at the outset ($p < 0.05$). On the basis of this outcome, we reject the null hypothesis and conclude that type of victim-offender relationship among assault victims is not randomly distributed. Of course, we cannot be certain that the null hypothesis is false for the population we are examining. We make our decision with a set risk of a Type I error defined at the outset of our test.

Relating Two Nominal-Scale Measures in a Chi-Square Test

In criminal justice and criminology, we seldom examine research issues like the fairness of a die or the randomness of type of victim-offender relationship, which are concerned with outcomes on only one measure. More often, we are interested in describing the relationships among two or more variables. For example, we may want to assess whether men and women are likely to be placed in different types of treatment facilities or whether different ethnic groups receive different types of sanctions. For each of these examples, two measures must be assessed at the same time. In the former, we examine both gender and type of treatment facility. In the latter, we examine type of sentence and ethnicity. Below, we use the example of a study of white-collar criminals to illustrate the use of chi-square in making inferences about the relationship between two variables: recidivism and sanction type.

A Substantive Example: Type of Sanction and Recidivism Among Convicted White-Collar Criminals

In a study of white-collar offenders, data on reoffending from FBI records over a ten-year period were examined. The sample included offenders from seven U.S. district courts, convicted of eight different white-collar crimes (antitrust violations, securities fraud, mail and wire fraud, false claims and statements, credit and lending institution fraud, bank embezzlement, income tax fraud, and bribery). The sample was chosen randomly without replacement.[3] The research question concerned whether imprisonment of white-collar offenders impacted upon reoffending.

---

[3]In this case, a stratified random sample was selected in order to ensure a broad sampling of white-collar offenders. For our example here, we treat the sample as a simple random sample. See David Weisburd, Elin Waring, and Ellen Chayet, "Specific Deterrence in a Sample of Offenders Convicted of White Collar Crimes," *Criminology* 33 (1995): 587–607.

The likelihood of rearrest for a group of offenders who received a prison sanction was compared with that of a matched group who did not receive a prison sanction. The researchers found that 33.0% of the prison group ($N = 100$) was rearrested during the follow-up period, in contrast to 28.4% of the no-prison group ($N = 67$). What conclusions can we come to concerning white-collar criminals generally?

To answer our research question, we follow the standard format of a test of statistical significance. We begin by stating our assumptions. Remember that to state the assumptions you must choose the type of test you will use. In this case, we have chosen a chi-square test for relating two nominal-level measures.

Assumptions:

Level of Measurement: Nominal scales.

Population Distribution: No assumption made.

Sampling Method: Independent random sampling (no replacement; sample is small relative to population).

Sampling Frame: Offenders from seven federal judicial districts convicted of eight different white-collar crimes.

Hypotheses:

H_0: There is no difference in the likelihood of rearrest among similar white-collar offenders sentenced or not sentenced to prison. (Or, likelihood of rearrest and imprisonment are independent.)

H_1: There is a difference in the likelihood of rearrest among similar white-collar offenders sentenced or not sentenced to prison. (Or, likelihood of rearrest and imprisonment are not independent.)

The level of measurement required for a chi-square test is nominal. Our example includes two variables: rearrest and type of sanction. Each is measured as a binary nominal variable. For rearrest, we examine those rearrested versus those not rearrested in the follow-up period. For type of sanction, we differentiate between those who were sentenced to prison and those who did not receive a prison sanction. In regard to the population distribution, chi-square is a nonparametric test and therefore requires no specific assumption.

The sample was selected randomly, but as is the case with most criminal justice studies, the investigators did not sample with replacement. At the same time, the population from which the sample was drawn is very large relative to the sample examined, and thus we have no reason to suspect that this violation of the assumptions will affect our test result.

The sampling frame includes offenders from seven federal judicial districts convicted of eight different white-collar crimes. Accordingly, our inferences relate directly to the population of those offenses and those districts. As discussed in Chapter 8, it is necessary to explain why your sample is representative of a broader population of cases if you want to make inferences beyond your sampling frame. In this study, the seven districts examined were seen as providing a sample with geographic spread throughout the United States, and the selected white-collar offenses were defined as offering a "broad sampling of white-collar offenders."

In most applications of the chi-square test, one cannot assign a directional research hypothesis. This is because chi-square requires a nominal level of measurement, which does not assign order or value to the categories examined. Nonetheless, in the special case of two binary variables, as examined here, the researcher can choose between a directional and a nondirectional research hypothesis. In our example, a directional hypothesis would be that the prison group is more likely than the no-prison group to be rearrested or that the no-prison group is more likely than the prison group to be rearrested. The research hypothesis stated by the investigators in this study was nondirectional. It stated simply that the two groups (prison and no-prison) differ in terms of likelihood of rearrest during the follow-up period. The null hypothesis was that there is no difference between the prison and no-prison groups.

Researchers often state the hypotheses of a chi-square test in terms of the independence of the variables that are examined. Stated this way, the null hypothesis would be that prison group (prison or no-prison) is independent, or unrelated to rearrest, in the follow-up period. The research hypothesis is that prison group is not independent. While this method of stating the hypotheses for your test sounds different, it leads to the same conclusions. If the two groups differ in terms of likelihood of rearrest in the follow-up period, then prison group and recidivism are related and thus not independent. If there is no difference, then prison group is unrelated to, or independent of, recidivism in the follow-up period.

The Sampling Distribution Because we are examining the relationship between two nominal-scale variables, the chi-square distribution provides an appropriate sampling distribution for our test. However, our decision about degrees of freedom is not as straightforward as that in the example of a roll of a die. In this case, we must take into account the

Table 9.7 Recidivism Among 167 White-Collar Criminals According to Whether They Did or Did Not Receive Prison Sentences

	Imprisoned	Not imprisoned	Row margin
Subsequently arrested	Cell A 33	Cell B 19	52
Not subsequently arrested	Cell C 67	Cell D 48	115
Column margin	100	67	167

joint distribution of our measures. This is illustrated in Table 9.7, which shows two potential outcomes for the prison variable and two potential outcomes for the arrest variable. We have four **cells,** or four possible combined outcomes. Cell A is for offenders who received a prison sanction and were arrested in the follow-up period. Cell B is for offenders who did not receive a prison sanction and were arrested in the follow-up period. Cell C is for offenders who received a prison sanction and were not arrested in the follow-up period. Cell D is for offenders who did not receive a prison sanction and were not arrested in the follow-up period.

If we sum across and down the cells, we gain two row **marginals** and two column marginals. The row marginals represent the totals for the rows: 52 for those arrested and 115 for those not arrested. The column marginals represent the totals for the columns: $N - 100$ for the prison group, and $N = 67$ for the no-prison group. If you know the row and column marginals, as is assumed in computing the degrees of freedom for chi-square, you can predict with certainty the remaining cells, once the value of any one cell is known (see Table 9.8). Degrees of freedom for a two-variable chi-square can be gained more simply through the formula $df = (r - 1)(c - 1)$, where r represents the number of rows and c the number of columns. For our example, there are two rows and two columns, so $df = (2 - 1)(2 - 1) = 1$.

Significance Level and Rejection Region   We stated no reason at the outset for choosing for our example a stricter or more lenient significance threshold than is used by convention. Accordingly, we use a significance level of 0.05 for our test. Our rejection region is defined by the chi-square table (see Appendix 2). Importantly, the chi-square distribution is not concerned with the direction of outcomes in a test. It tells us to what extent the observed frequencies in our example differ from those that would be expected under the null hypothesis of no difference. Whether they differ in one direction or another, the chi-square statistic will always be positive.

Table 9.8	Predicting the Missing Cells in a Two-Variable Chi-Square Test

			Row margin
	Cell A 33	Cell B ?	52
	Cell C ?	Cell D ?	115
Column margin	100	67	167

Given that cell A = 33:
Cell B = (52 − 33) = 19
Cell C = (100 − 33) = 67
Cell D = (115 − 67) = 48

The terms "directional" and "nondirectional" are very tenuous ones in a chi-square test. Chi-square assumes nominal-scale variables, which by definition do not provide information about the order of values in a measure. If we cannot specify the order of two measures, we cannot speak of the direction of their relationship. As noted earlier, in most situations a directional hypothesis is not appropriate for a chi-square test. In the special case of two binary variables, however, researchers do sometimes use chi-square to examine directional research hypotheses. For example, we might have stated our research hypothesis as "The likelihood of arrest in the follow-up period for white-collar offenders sentenced to prison is lower than that of similar white-collar offenders not sentenced to prison."

However, our research hypothesis is nondirectional, as is the table of chi-square values. To define our rejection region, we turn to the row of the table associated with one degree of freedom. Under a significance level (α) of 0.05, we see a score of 3.841. For us to reject the null hypothesis, our test statistic will have to be greater than this value.[4]

The Test Statistic   To apply chi-square to the two-variable case, we need to adapt our original equation. The formula for the chi-square statistic for relating two measures is presented in Equation 9.2.[5]

$$\chi^2 = \sum_{i=1}^{r} \sum_{j=1}^{c} \frac{(f_\text{o} - f_\text{e})^2}{f_\text{e}}$$

Equation 9.2

The only difference between Equation 9.2 and Equation 9.1 is that we have an additional summation symbol. In this case, we do not sum simply across the categories of one measure; rather, we sum across each row (r) and column (c) of the joint distribution of two measures. Accordingly, Equation 9.2 reminds us that we must examine the expected and observed frequencies for every potential outcome we can observe—or, in terms of the chi-square equation, for every cell in our table.

---

[4]What if we had defined a directional research hypothesis? In this case, we look to the column of the table for twice the value of the desired significance level, since we now have placed all risk of falsely rejecting the null hypothesis in only one direction. For example, for a 0.05 significance level, we turn to the test statistic for a 0.10 level.
[5]When a chi-square test has only one degree of freedom, it is recommended that a correction factor be added if the expected frequencies of any cell fall below 20. The correction provides a more conservative, or smaller, chi-square statistic:

$$\chi^2 = \sum_{i=1}^{r} \sum_{j=1}^{c} \frac{(|f_\text{o} - f_\text{e}| - 0.5)^2}{f_\text{e}}$$

For our example, this means we must sum across cells A, B, C, and D. As before, we want to compare the observed frequency to the expected frequency in each cell. The observed frequencies are those gained in our research. The expected frequencies are defined through the null hypothesis. The null hypothesis states that there is no difference in arrest rates between the prison and no-prison groups. If this is true, then we should expect the same proportion of arrests in both groups. To calculate the expected frequencies, accordingly, we first need to define the overall proportion of offenders arrested in the follow-up period.

The proportion of offenders arrested overall in the sample in the follow-up period is obtained by dividing the total number of offenders arrested ($N_{cat} = 52$) by the total number of offenders in the sample ($N_{total} = 167$):

$$\text{Proportion} = \frac{N_{cat}}{N_{total}} = \frac{52}{167} = 0.3114$$

To get the expected frequency for cell A, we multiply this proportion by the marginal total of 100 ($f_e = 31.14$). For the no-prison group, we have a total of 67 offenders. Applying the proportion of the total sample to this group, we multiply 0.3114 by 67 and get an expected frequency of 20.86 for cell B. In practice, we do not need to compute the expected frequencies for the remaining two cells, C and D. Indeed, we could have assigned all of the cells expected frequencies based on knowledge of only one cell. This is what the number of degrees of freedom for this example tells us. If you know the number of cases in one cell, you can predict with certainty the rest. The expected and observed frequencies for our example are shown in Table 9.9.

Now that we have calculated the observed and expected frequencies for each potential outcome, or cell, we can calculate the chi-square statistic. To do this, we first square the difference of the observed and ex-

Table 9.9

Expected and Observed Frequencies of Recidivism and Nonrecidivism for White-Collar Offenders According to Whether They Received Prison Sentences

	Imprisoned	Not imprisoned	Row margin
Subsequently arrested	Cell A $f_o = 33$ $f_e = 31.14$	Cell B $f_o = 19$ $f_e = 20.86$	52
Not subsequently arrested	Cell C $f_o = 67$ $f_e = 68.86$	Cell D $f_o = 48$ $f_e = 46.14$	115
Column margin	100	67	167

Table 9.10	Computation of Chi-Square for 167 White-Collar Criminals

CELL	f_o	f_e	$(f_o - f_e)$	$(f_o - f_e)^2$	$\dfrac{(f_o - f_e)^2}{f_e}$
A	33	31.14	1.86	3.4596	0.1111
B	19	20.86	−1.86	3.4596	0.1658
C	67	68.86	−1.86	3.4596	0.0502
D	48	46.14	1.86	3.4596	0.0750
					$\Sigma = 0.4021$

pected frequencies for each cell, and then we divide this quantity by the expected frequency of the cell:

$$\frac{(f_o - f_e)^2}{f_e}$$

This is done in Table 9.10 for each of the four cells in our problem. Using cell A as an example, we first subtract the expected frequency of 31.14 from the observed frequency of 33. We then square this quantity (1.86), obtaining a result of 3.4596. Dividing this result by the expected frequency in the cell (31.14) gives us 0.1111. The sum of all four cells, 0.4021, is our test statistic.

The Decision   Our rejection region was defined as including any chi-square statistic greater than 3.841. The test statistic for our example is only 0.402. Accordingly, we choose not to reject the null hypothesis. The observed significance level for our test is greater than the significance level, or threshold, we set at the outset ($p > 0.05$). We conclude that there is no significant difference in the likelihood of recidivism between white-collar offenders who have and have not been sentenced to prison. Our inferences are made directly to the specific offenses and judicial districts defined in the sampling frame.

Extending the Chi-Square Test to Multicategory Variables: The Example of Cell Allocations in Prison

The previous example illustrates the use of chi-square in the case of two binary variables. We now turn to an extension of the chi-square test to an example including a multicategory nominal-level variable. Our example is drawn from a study of the relationship between prisoners' race and their cell assignments in a large state prison in the northeastern

Table 9.11   Proportions of Non-Hispanic White Prisoners in Seven Cell Blocks

	Non-Hispanic whites	Nonwhites	Total
Cell block C	48 18.7%	208 81.3%	256 100%
Cell block D	17 31.5%	37 68.5%	54 100%
Cell block E	28 25.0%	84 75.0%	112 100%
Cell block F	32 28.8%	79 71.2%	111 100%
Cell block G	37 12.2%	266 87.8%	303 100%
Cell block H	34 60.7%	22 39.3%	56 100%
Cell block I	44 14.1%	268 85.9%	312 100%
Total	240 19.9%	964 80.1%	1,204 100%

United States.[6] We examine the placement of non-Hispanic white and "nonwhite" inmates (including Hispanics) into seven cell blocks. The sample includes all prisoners in the general prison population for a single day. The distribution of cases is presented in Table 9.11.

If cell assignments were made on considerations unrelated to race, we would expect to find the proportion of non-Hispanic whites in each cell block roughly equivalent to the proportion of non-Hispanic whites in the general prison population (19.9%; see the marginal for non-Hispanic whites in Table 9.11). Such equivalence is not evident. In block G, for example, non-Hispanic whites constituted 12.2% of the inmates. In block H, they comprised 60.7%. Do results for this sample allow us to conclude that there is disparity in cell-block assignments more generally in the prison?

Assumptions:

Level of Measurement: Nominal scales.

Population Distribution: No assumption made.

Sampling Method: Independent random sampling (the entire sampling frame is examined).

Sampling Frame: All prisoners in the general prison population on a specific day.

---

[6]See Douglas McDonald and David Weisburd, "Segregation and Hidden Discrimination in Prisons: Reflections on a Small Study of Cell Assignments," in C. Hartchen (ed.), *Correctional Theory and Practice* (Chicago: Nelson Hall, 1991).

Hypotheses:

H_0: Cell-block assignment and race are independent.

H_1: Cell-block assignment and race are not independent.

As in our previous example, we assume a nominal level of measurement for our test and do not make assumptions regarding the form of the population distribution. Prisoner race is measured at the binary nominal level, and cell block is a multicategory nominal scale.

The sample includes all cases in the sampling frame. Accordingly, we do not need to use statistical inference to make statements about that population. However, the study was designed not only to describe prison-cell allocations on that day, but also to make more general statements about cell allocations in the prison studied throughout the year. This is not an uncommon scenario in criminal justice research, in good part because the realities of the criminal justice system often preclude sampling beyond specific institutions or outside of specific time frames. This means, however, that the researchers seek to make inferences beyond their sampling frame.

If cell allocations on the day examined in this study are representative of cell allocations more generally throughout the year, then the inferences made on the basis of the test will be reliable. If not, then the test will not provide for valid inferences. In our example, the investigators argue:

There was no reason to suspect that the cell assignments of prisoners on that day differed substantially from assignments on other days. Moreover, these cell assignments represented the results of decisions made over the course of months and perhaps years prior to the date of drawing the sample. There was every reason to believe, consequently, that cell assignments on that date constituted a valid representation of cell assignment decisions made during the several months prior to that day.

Our research question asks whether we would be likely to obtain the distribution we observe in our sample if assignment to cell blocks were colorblind in the population. Stated in the form of hypotheses, we ask whether race and cell-block assignment are independent. If they are independent, as proposed in our null hypothesis, then we would expect about the same proportion of nonwhite and non-Hispanic white prisoners in each cell block. Our research hypothesis is nondirectional. It states that race and cell-block assignment are not independent. In this example, as in most chi-square tests, use of nominal-scale measures, which do not assign order or value to categories, means that one cannot define a directional research hypothesis.

The Sampling Distribution   Because we are examining the relationship between two nominal variables, one binary and one multicategory, we use the chi-square sampling distribution. The number of degrees of freedom for our problem is defined as in the previous example:

W orking It Out

$$\text{df} = (r - 1)(c - 1)$$
$$= (7 - 1)(2 - 1)$$
$$= 6$$

In this case, we have seven categories for our row variable (cell block) and two categories for our column variable (ethnicity). The number of degrees of freedom for our sampling distribution is six.

Significance Level and Rejection Region   As we have no reason to propose more lenient or stricter significance criteria than are used by convention, we will set a 0.05 significance level. To define our rejection region, we turn to the row of the chi-square table associated with six degrees of freedom. Under the 0.05 column, a chi-square statistic of 12.592 is listed. If the test statistic is greater than this critical value, then it falls within the rejection region of the test.

The Test Statistic   To calculate the test statistic in this multicategory example, we follow the same procedure used for the two-by-two table in the previous section. Our first task is to define the expected frequency for each cell of the table. We do this, as before, by dividing a marginal of the table by the total proportion of cases. Taking the overall number of non-Hispanic whites in the sample, we obtain a proportion of 0.1993:

W orking It Out

$$\text{Proportion} = \frac{N_{\text{cat}}}{N_{\text{total}}}$$
$$= \frac{240}{1,204}$$
$$= 0.199335$$

| Table 9.12 | Observed Frequencies and Expected Frequencies for Non-Hispanic White and Nonwhite Prisoners in Seven Cell Blocks |

	Non-Hispanic whites	Nonwhites	Total
Cell block C	$f_o = 48$ $f_e = 51.030$	$f_o = 208$ $f_e = 204.970$	256
Cell block D	$f_o = 17$ $f_e = 10.764$	$f_o = 37$ $f_e = 43.236$	54
Cell block E	$f_o = 28$ $f_e = 22.326$	$f_o = 84$ $f_e = 89.674$	112
Cell block F	$f_o = 32$ $f_e = 22.126$	$f_o = 79$ $f_e = 88.874$	111
Cell block G	$f_o = 37$ $f_e = 60.399$	$f_o = 266$ $f_e = 242.601$	303
Cell block H	$f_o = 34$ $f_e = 11.163$	$f_o = 22$ $f_e = 44.837$	56
Cell block I	$f_o = 44$ $f_e = 62.193$	$f_o = 268$ $f_e = 249.807$	312
Total	240	964	1,204

To calculate the expected frequency in each cell in the non-Hispanic whites column, we multiply this proportion by the marginal total for each row. So, for example, for cell block C, we multiply 256 by 0.199335, leading to an expected frequency for non-Hispanic whites of 51.030. We then replicate this procedure for each of the six other cells in the non-Hispanic whites column. To calculate the expected frequencies for the nonwhites column, we simply subtract the expected frequency for the non-Hispanic whites column from the row marginal. So, for example, for nonwhites in cell block C, the expected frequency is 256 (the marginal total) minus 51.030 (the expected frequency for non-Hispanic whites for that cell block), or 204.970. Table 9.12 includes the expected and observed frequencies for the 14 cells in our example.

To obtain the test statistic, we use Equation 9.2, which may be applied to any two-variable chi-square problem:

$$\chi^2 = \sum_{i=1}^{r} \sum_{j=1}^{c} \frac{(f_o - f_e)^2}{f_e}$$

Again we begin by subtracting the expected frequency from the observed frequency in each cell and squaring the result. This quantity is then divided by the expected frequency of the cell. The chi-square statistic is found by summing the result across all 14 cells. The full set of calculations for the test statistic is presented in Table 9.13. The chi-square score for our example is 88.3610.

Table 9.13	Computation of Chi-Square for Non-Hispanic White (W) and Nonwhite (NW) Prisoners in Seven Cell Blocks

CELL BLOCK	RACE	f_o	f_e	$(f_o - f_e)$	$(f_o - f_e)^2$	$\dfrac{(f_o - f_e)^2}{f_e}$
C	W	48	51.030	−3.030	9.1809	0.1799
C	NW	208	204.970	3.030	9.1809	0.0448
D	W	17	10.764	6.236	38.8877	3.6128
D	NW	37	43.236	−6.236	38.8877	0.8994
E	W	28	22.326	5.674	32.1943	1.4420
E	NW	84	89.674	−5.674	32.1943	0.3590
F	W	32	22.126	9.874	97.4959	4.4064
F	NW	79	88.874	−9.874	97.4959	1.0970
G	W	37	60.399	−23.399	547.5132	9.0649
G	NW	266	242.601	23.399	547.5132	2.2568
H	W	34	11.163	22.837	521.5286	46.7194
H	NW	22	44.837	−22.837	521.5286	11.6317
I	W	44	62.193	−18.193	330.9852	5.3219
I	NW	268	249.807	18.193	330.9852	1.3250
						$\Sigma = 88.3610$

The Decision　　The outcome of 88.3610 is much greater than the critical value for our test of 12.592. Accordingly, we reject the null hypothesis that race and cell-block allocation are independent (using a 5% significance level). We conclude that there is a statistically significant relationship between the distribution of prisoners across cell blocks and their race.

Extending the Chi-Square Test to a Relationship Between Two Ordinal Variables: Identification with Fathers and Delinquent Acts

The examples of the application of the chi-square test presented so far have used only nominal-scale variables. This is consistent with the assumptions of the chi-square test. But in practice researchers sometimes use chi-square to test for independence when one or both of the variables have been measured at the ordinal level of measurement. This test for independence can provide important information to the researcher. However, because the chi-square test assumes a nominal scale of measurement, it does not pay attention to the order of the categories in an ordinal scale. This means that a statistically significant finding can tell the researcher only that the distribution of scores observed is different from that expected had there been no relationship. It cannot test for whether the values of one variable increase as the values of the other increase or, conversely, whether the scores on one measure increase as those on the

Table 9.14	Affectional Identification with Father by Number of Delinquent Acts

AFFECTIONAL IDENTIFICATION WITH FATHER	DELINQUENT ACTS			
	None	One	Two or More	Total
In every way	77 63.636%	25 20.661%	19 15.702%	121 100%
In most ways	263 65.099%	97 24.010%	44 10.891%	404 100%
In some ways	224 57.881%	97 25.065%	66 17.054%	387 100%
In just a few ways	82 47.674%	52 30.233%	38 22.093%	172 100%
Not at all	56 40.580%	30 21.739%	52 37.681%	138 100%
Total	702 57.447%	301 24.632%	219 17.921%	1,222 100%

other decrease. When you use the chi-square test for ordinal-scale variables, the test itself treats the variables as if they were simply composed of a group of nominal categories.

Table 9.14 presents data from the Richmond Youth Survey report on the relationship between number of delinquent acts and affectional identification with one's father. The distribution of cases presented refers only to the white males who responded to the survey.[7] The sample was a random sample (drawn without replacement) for all high school–age white males in Richmond, California, in 1965. The size of the sample is small relative to the sampling frame.

If delinquency were unrelated to attachment to one's family—here indicated by the level of affectional identification with one's father—we would expect to find the distribution of cases for each level of delinquency to be roughly equal across levels of identification. The distribution of cases provides some indication that these variables are not, in fact, independent. For example, among the youths who wanted to be like their father in every way, 63% reported that they had not committed a delinquent act. This was true for only 41% of those who did not want to be at all like their fathers. Our question is whether the differences we observe in our sample are large enough for us to conclude that identification with one's father and delinquency are related in the population from which our sample has been drawn.

---

[7]David F. Greenberg, "The Weak Strength of Social Control Theory," *Crime and Delinquency* 45:1 (1999): 66–81.

Assumptions:

Level of Measurement: Nominal scales (our study examines two ordinal-scale measures).

Population Distribution: No assumption made.

Sampling Method: Independent random sampling (no replacement; sample is small relative to population).

Sampling Frame: High school–age white males in Richmond, California, in 1965.

Hypotheses:

H_0: Affectional identification with father and delinquency are independent.

H_1: Affectional identification with father and delinquency are not independent.

The Sampling Distribution   Although we are using two ordinal-scale measures rather than two nominal-scale measures, we have chosen to use the chi-square sampling distribution to test for a relationship. This violation of the nominal-scale assumption for the chi-square test is acceptable. However, by placing the violation of the assumption in parentheses next to the test requirement of a nominal level of measurement, we remind ourselves that chi-square is not concerned with the order of the categories in the measures examined. It treats the two ordinal-scale measures as if they were nominal-scale measures and simply tests for whether the distributions among the categories depart from what we would expect under an assumption of independence. As we did in the two previous examples, we calculate degrees of freedom as follows:

Working It Out

$$df = (r - 1)(c - 1)$$
$$= (5 - 1)(3 - 1)$$
$$= 8$$

Significance Level and Rejection Region   There is no reason to propose a more lenient or stricter significance level for this analysis, so we will stick with a 0.05 significance level. Given that we have eight degrees of freedom and a significance level of 0.05, we can consult the chi-square table and determine that our critical value of the chi-square statistic is 15.507. If the test statistic is greater than this value, it falls in the rejection region of the test, and we can conclude that delinquency is significantly related to affectional identification.

The Test Statistic   To determine the expected frequency for each cell in the table, we follow the same format we have used in the previous two examples. As before, we start with the calculation of the marginal for no delinquent acts and divide by the total number of cases, which gives us a value of 0.574468:

W orking It Out

$$\text{Proportion} = \frac{N_{\text{cat}}}{N_{\text{total}}}$$

$$= \frac{702}{1,222}$$

$$= 0.574468$$

To calculate the expected frequency for each cell in the no delinquent acts column, we take this proportion and multiply it by the marginal total for the row. For the first row, we multiply 0.574468 by 121, which gives us an expected frequency of 69.511. Similarly, for the second row, we multiply 0.574468 by 404, giving us an expected frequency of 232.085. We continue this procedure for the remaining three rows in the no delinquent acts column.

For the second column, we need to determine the marginal proportion for those cases with one delinquent act. Since there are 301 cases in the marginal for one delinquent act, the corresponding proportion is (301/1,222) = 0.246318. To obtain the expected frequencies for this second column, we multiply 0.246318 by the corresponding row marginal. So, for the first row of the second column, the expected frequency is obtained by multiplying 0.246318 by 121, which gives us 29.804. This procedure is repeated to complete the remaining cells in the second column.

Finally, to determine the expected frequencies for the cells in the third column, we simply add the expected frequencies for the first two columns and subtract that sum from the row marginal. For example, in the first row, the two expected frequencies obtained thus far are 69.511 and 29.804. If we add these two values (69.511 + 29.804 = 99.315) and subtract this sum from the row marginal (121), we find that the expected frequency for the cell in the third column of the first row is equal to (121 − 99.315) = 21.685. To complete the table of expected frequencies,

Observed and Expected Frequencies for Affectional Identification with Father and Number of Delinquent Acts

AFFECTIONAL IDENTIFICATION WITH FATHER	DELINQUENT ACTS			
	None	**One**	**Two or More**	**Total**
In every way	$f_o = 77$ $f_e = 69.511$	$f_o = 25$ $f_e = 29.804$	$f_o = 19$ $f_e = 21.685$	121
In most ways	$f_o = 263$ $f_e = 232.085$	$f_o = 97$ $f_e = 99.512$	$f_o = 44$ $f_e = 72.403$	404
In some ways	$f_o = 224$ $f_e = 222.319$	$f_o = 97$ $f_e = 95.325$	$f_o = 66$ $f_e = 69.355$	387
In just a few ways	$f_o = 82$ $f_e = 98.809$	$f_o = 52$ $f_e = 42.367$	$f_o = 38$ $f_e = 30.824$	172
Not at all	$f_o = 56$ $f_e = 79.277$	$f_o = 30$ $f_e = 33.992$	$f_o = 52$ $f_e = 24.731$	138
Total	702	301	219	1,222

we repeat this operation for the remaining cells in the third column. Table 9.15 contains all the observed and expected frequencies.

To obtain the test statistic, we again use Equation 9.2, which may be applied to any two-variable chi-square problem:

$$\chi^2 = \sum_{i=1}^{r} \sum_{j=1}^{c} \frac{(f_o - f_e)^2}{f_e}$$

Again we begin by subtracting the expected from the observed frequency in each cell and squaring the result. This quantity is then divided by the expected frequency of the cell. The chi-square statistic is found by summing the result across all cells. The full set of calculations necessary for obtaining the value of the chi-square test statistic appears in Table 9.16. The chi-square statistic for our test has a value of 61.532.

The Decision

The calculated chi-square statistic of 61.532 is much larger than the critical value of 15.507 for the chi-square distribution with eight degrees of freedom. This means that the observed significance level for our test is less than the criterion significance level we set at the outset ($p < 0.05$). Thus, we reject the null hypothesis that affectional identification with father is not related to number of delinquent acts (at a 5% significance level). In turn, we conclude that for adolescent males there is a statistically significant relationship between delinquency and affectional identification with father. Importantly, this statistical inference refers directly to our sampling frame: high school–age white males in Richmond, California, in 1965.

Table 9.16	Computation of Chi-Square for Affectional Identification with Father and Delinquency					

IDENTIFICATION	DELINQUENCY	f_o	f_e	$(f_o - f_e)$	$(f_o - f_e)^2$	$\dfrac{(f_o - f_e)^2}{f_e}$
Every way	None	77	69.511	7.489	56.085	0.807
Every way	One	25	29.804	−4.804	23.078	0.774
Every way	Two or more	19	21.685	−2.685	7.209	0.332
Most ways	None	263	232.085	30.915	955.737	4.118
Most ways	One	97	99.512	−2.512	6.310	0.063
Most ways	Two or more	44	72.403	−28.403	806.730	11.142
Some ways	None	224	222.319	1.681	2.826	0.013
Some ways	One	97	95.325	1.675	2.806	0.029
Some ways	Two or more	66	69.355	−3.355	11.256	0.162
Few ways	None	82	98.809	−16.809	282.543	2.859
Few ways	One	52	42.367	9.633	92.795	2.190
Few ways	Two or more	38	30.824	7.176	51.495	1.671
Not at all	None	56	79.277	−23.277	541.819	6.835
Not at all	One	30	33.992	−3.992	15.936	0.469
Not at all	Two or more	52	24.731	27.269	743.598	30.067
						$\Sigma = 61.532$

The Use of Chi-Square When Samples Are Small: A Final Note

The chi-square test is often used by criminal justice researchers. However, it has a very important limitation in its application to studies with small or highly skewed samples. When more than one in five (20%) of the cells in your table has an expected frequency of five or less, it is generally considered inappropriate to use a chi-square test. In such situations, it is recommended that you combine categories of your variables until you meet the minimum expected-frequencies requirement.

Chapter Summary

Whereas the binomial distribution is relevant only for binary variables, the **chi-square distribution** can be used to examine a variable with more than two categories.

The shape of the chi-square distribution chosen depends on the **degrees of freedom** associated with the test. The formula for degrees of freedom defines how many categories would have to be known for us to be able to predict the remaining categories with certainty. The greater the number of degrees of freedom, the flatter the distribution. In practical terms, as the number of degrees of freedom increases, a larger chi-square statistic is required to reject the null hypothesis.

The chi-square test of statistical significance is a nonparametric test. To calculate the test statistic, the researcher must first identify the **observed frequency** and the **expected frequency** of each category. The expected frequencies are those one would expect under the assumption of the null hypothesis. They are distributed in the same proportions as the **marginal frequencies.** The chi-square formula is then applied to each category, or **cell,** in the table. If the observed frequencies differ substantially from the expected frequencies, then the **chi-square statistic** will be large. If the observed frequencies are similar to the expected frequencies, then the chi-square statistic will be small. If the two frequencies are the same, the statistic will be 0. The larger the statistic (and the smaller the number of degrees of freedom), the easier it will be to reject the null hypothesis. The chi-square statistic is always positive. Because the chi-square test relies on nominal nonordered data, it is not concerned with the direction of outcomes.

Key Terms

cells The various entries in a table, each of which is identified by a particular row and column. When we use a table to compare two variables, it is convenient to refer to each combination of categories as a cell.

chi-square distribution A sampling distribution that is used to conduct tests of statistical significance with binary or multicategory nominal variables. The distribution is nonsymmetrical and varies according to degrees of freedom. All the values in the distribution are positive.

chi-square statistic The test statistic resulting from applying the chi-square formula to the observed and expected frequencies for each cell. This statistic tells us how much the observed distribution differs from that expected under the null hypothesis.

degrees of freedom A mathematical index that places a value on the extent to which a particular operation is free to vary after certain limitations have been imposed. Calculating the degrees of freedom for a chi-square test determines which chi-square probability distribution we use.

expected frequency The number of observations one would predict for a cell if the null hypothesis were true.

marginal The value in the margin of a table that totals the scores in the appropriate column or row.

observed frequency The observed result of the study, recorded in a cell.

Symbols and Formulas

χ^2 Chi-square

df   Degrees of freedom

f_o Observed frequency

f_e Expected frequency

c Number of columns

r Number of rows

k Number of categories

To determine the degrees of freedom for a chi-square test including only one variable:

$$df = k - 1$$

To determine the degrees of freedom for a chi-square test including two variables:

$$df = (r - 1)(c - 1)$$

To determine the chi-square statistic for one variable:

$$\chi^2 = \sum_{i=1}^{k} \frac{(f_o - f_e)^2}{f_e}$$

To determine the chi-square statistic for two variables:

$$\chi^2 = \sum_{i=1}^{r} \sum_{j=1}^{c} \frac{(f_o - f_e)^2}{f_e}$$

Exercises

9.1   Local community leaders are concerned about the distribution of homicides in their small town. The local police department broke the city into six recognizable neighborhoods of the same size and discovered the following distribution of homicides:

Neighborhood	Number of Homicides
A	14
B	9
C	17
D	3
E	7
F	10

Community leaders would like to know whether the homicides are randomly distributed across these six neighborhoods.

a. Use a 5% level of significance and outline each of the steps required in a test of statistical significance.

b. What can you conclude about the distribution of homicides across these six neighborhoods?

9.2   Sergeant Bob is in charge of the duty roster at Gatley police station. Every week, it is his responsibility to randomly assign the five beat officers, including his son Bob Jr., to patrol in each of the five zones that make up the city of Gatley. Zones A and D are favored by all the officers because they are usually quiet. Of the others, Zone C is notoriously dangerous. The officers have recently begun to suspect Sergeant Bob of favoritism toward his son. In the last 30 weeks, Bob Jr. has been assigned to Zone A 12 times, Zone B and Zone C 2 times each, Zone D 9 times, and Zone E 5 times.

a. Do the other officers have reason to believe that Sergeant Bob is not assigning zones in a random manner? Use a 5% level of significance and outline each of the steps required in a test of statistical significance.

b. Would your answer be any different if a 1% level of significance were used?

9.3   In the past 100 years, there have been more than 250 successful breakouts from Didsbury Prison. Mike is a researcher who has been hired by the prison governor to investigate the phenomenon. Details are available only for those breakouts that took place in the past ten years—a total of 30. Using the records of these 30 breakouts as a sample, Mike decides to break the figures down to see whether breakouts were more common in certain wings of the prison than in others. It transpires that of the 30 breakouts, 4 have been from A-Wing, 8 from B-Wing, 15 from C-Wing, and 3 from D-Wing.

a. Does Mike have enough evidence to conclude that, over the 100-year period, breakouts were more (or less) likely to occur from certain wings than from others? Use a 5% level of significance and outline each of the steps required in a test of statistical significance.

b. Would your answer be any different if a 1% level of significance were used?

c. Are there any problems with Mike's choice of a sample? Explain your answer.

9.4   A study of death penalty cases (all first-degree murder charges with aggravating circumstances) revealed the following relationship between the victim's race and the chances the offender was sentenced to death: In 100 cases involving white victims, 20 offenders were sentenced to death. In 100 cases involving black victims, 10 offenders were sentenced to death.

a. Is there a relationship between the race of the victim and the likelihood an offender was sentenced to death? Use a 5% level of significance and outline each of the steps required in a test of statistical significance.

b. Would your answer be different if a 1% level of significance were used?

9.5   At a local school, 46 children were accused of cheating on exams over the course of a semester. In an innovation, the principal decided that every second child accused of cheating would be brought before a "peer jury" to decide guilt or innocence. In all other cases, the decision would be made by the examiners as usual. Of the 30 children who were adjudged guilty over the course of the semester, 18 were convicted by the peer jury, and the rest were convicted by the examiners. Of the children who were adjudged not guilty, 5 were acquitted by their peers.

a. The principal is mainly interested in the educational value of the experiment, but he will discontinue it if it becomes clear that the peer jury and the examiners make different decisions to a statistically significant degree. He is willing to take a 5% risk of error. Should the scheme be continued? Outline each of the steps of a test of statistical significance.

b. Could the principal base the test on a directional hypothesis? If so, what would that hypothesis be, and would it make a difference in his final decision?

9.6   In the course of a year, Jeremy, a law student, observed a total of 55 cases in which an accused male pleaded guilty to a serious traffic offense. He observed that of the 15 who were sentenced to prison, 6 wore a shirt and tie in court. Of the 40 who were not sentenced to prison, 8 wore a shirt and tie in court.

a. Can Jeremy conclude that there is a link between the physical appearance of the accused and whether he is imprisoned? Use a 5% level of significance and outline each of the steps required in a test of statistical significance.

b. What level of significance would be required for his decision to be reversed?

9.7   Sasha was interested in the extent to which people are prepared to intervene to help a stranger and whether the race of the stranger is relevant to the likelihood of intervention. She hired four male actors: one of African ancestry, one of Asian ancestry, one of European ancestry, and one of Indian ancestry. The actors were each told to fake a fall in a busy shopping street and pretend to be in some pain. Sasha observed from nearby and recorded whether, within five minutes of the actor's fall, anyone had stopped to see if he was okay. Each actor repeated the experiment 40 times.

The results were as follows:

Ancestry	√	×
African	4	36
Asian	0	40
European	20	20
Indian	8	32

(√ = Intervention within 5 mins; × = no intervention)

a. Can Sasha conclude that there is a link between race of victim and readiness to intervene? Use a 5% level of significance and outline each of the steps required in a test of statistical significance.

b. Would your answer be any different if a 1% level of significance were used?

9.8 Dave takes a random sample of the speeches, interviews, and official statements given by the prime minister and the interior minister of a particular country over the course of a year in which reference is made to "prison policy." He analyzes the content of the statements in his sample and discovers five different types of justification for the government's prison policy. Dave then records each time the prime minister or interior minister refers to any of the five justification types. The results are as follows:

Justification Type	Prime Minister	Interior Minister
Incapacitation or protecting society	6	16
Specific deterrence	2	14
General deterrence	4	20
Rehabilitation	0	15
Retribution	13	10

a. Is there a statistically significant difference between the policy statements of the prime minister and those of the interior minister? Use a 5% level of significance and outline each of the steps required in a test of statistical significance.

b. Would your answer be any different if a 1% level of significance were used?

9.9 The Television Complaints Board monitors the standards of morality for a nation's TV channels. It has recently set up a telephone hotline for viewers who wish to complain about sex, violence, or foul language on any of the nation's three TV channels. In its first month of operation, the board received the following complaints:

	Channel 1	Channel 2	Channel 3
Sex	2	8	10
Violence	10	12	10
Foul language	3	10	15

a. Which of the following questions would a chi-square test of these results seek to answer?

    i. Is there a statistically significant difference between the number of complaints made against each channel?

    ii. Is there a statistically significant difference between the number of each type of complaint made?

    iii. Is there a statistically significant difference between the types of different complaints received about the three different stations?

b. Answer the question you chose in part a by running a chi-square test at a 5% level of significance. Should the null hypothesis be overturned?

9.10 A survey of public opinion about the criminal justice system asked respondents to complete the following statement: "The criminal justice system treats offenders. . . ." The researchers found the following distribution of responses by gender of the respondent:

Gender of Respondent	Too Lenient	About Right	Too Harsh
Female	15	50	35
Male	40	35	25

a. Is there a relationship between the gender of the respondent and perceptions of punishment severity? Use a 5% level of significance and outline each of the steps required in a test of statistical significance.

b. Would your answer be different if the significance level were 0.01?

c. What can you conclude about the relationship between gender and perceptions of punishment severity?

9.11 A researcher is interested in the link between the type of offense a defendant is charged with and the manner in which a conviction is obtained. An examination of court records of a random sample of convicted offenders reveals the following distribution of cases:

Type of Charge Offense	How Conviction Was Obtained		
	Jury Trial	Bench Trial	Guilty Plea
Violent	19	13	67
Property	5	8	92
Drug	8	11	83
Other	10	6	74

a. Is there a relationship between type of charge offense and method of conviction? Use a 5% level of significance and outline each of the steps required in a test of statistical significance.

b. Would your answer be any different if a 1% level of significance were used?

c. What can you conclude about the relationship between type of charge offense and method of conviction?

Computer Exercises

Entering Tabular Data

Before we look at how to obtain chi-square statistics from SPSS, it is useful to become familiar with a feature in SPSS that allows you to enter tabular data, such as data from the tables in the text and exercises above.

The most direct way of entering tabular data is to think of the rows and columns in a table as two separate variables and the number of cases in each cell of the table as a third variable (which represents a count). For example, consider the data presented in Table 9.7:

	Imprisoned	Not Imprisoned	Row Margin
Subsequently arrested	33	19	52
Not subsequently arrested	67	48	115
Column margin	100	67	167

We can enter the information from this table as three variables: the row, the column, and the count. For now, we will simply name the row variable "arrested" (to represent whether or not the person was subsequently arrested), the column variable "prison" (to represent whether or not the person had been imprisoned), and the number of cases in each cell "count." Upon entering these data into SPSS, you would have three variables and four lines of data like the following:

arrest	prison	count
1.0000	1.0000	33.0000
1.0000	2.0000	19.0000
2.0000	1.0000	67.0000
2.0000	2.0000	48.0000

If you were to begin working with SPSS at this point, you would not obtain the correct results, since SPSS will treat these data as representing only four observations. To have SPSS recognize the 167 observations represented by these four lines, you need to use the "Weight cases" command (Data → Weight cases). This command tells SPSS that you have entered data in tabular form.

After execution of the "Weight cases" command, you will be presented with a window informing you that there is no weighting of the cases. Click on the circle next to "Weight cases by . . ."; the adjacent box under the "Frequency Variable" label will become highlighted. Move the name of the count variable into this box and click on "OK" to run the command. SPSS will now treat the four lines of data that you entered as 167 observations.

Obtain the Chi-Square Statistic

The chi-square statistic is obtained by using the "Crosstabs" command (Analyze → Descriptive Statistics → Crosstabs). After executing this command, you will be presented with a window that asks for the names of the row and column variables. In general, you move the names of the variables for which you want to produce tables into the "Row(s)" and "Column(s)" boxes.

To obtain the chi-square statistic, click on the button labeled "Statistics," located at the bottom of this window. A new window will appear that prompts you for the statistics you would like to have calculated. Click on the box next to "Chi-square" and then click on "Continue" and "OK" to run the command.

To continue our example using the data from Table 9.7, enter the "arrest" variable name in the "Row" box and the "prison" variable name in the "Column" box. The output produced by executing this command will contain a cross-tabulation of the data that should be identical to Table 9.7. Immediately below this table will be another table labeled "Chi-square tests." The "Pearson Chi-Square" is the name of the chi-square statistic that you have learned to calculate in this chapter. The value reported by SPSS is 0.403, which differs from the value reported above (0.402) by 0.001, which can be attributed to rounding error above.

1. Input the data on race and cell-block assignment from Table 9.11 into SPSS. Compute the value of the chi-square statistic for these data. How does it compare to the value reported in the text?

2. Input the data on affectional identification with father and delinquency from Table 9.14 into SPSS. Compute the value of the chi-square statistic for these data. How does it compare to the value reported in the text?

3. Enter the data from Exercise 9.7 into SPSS. Compute the value of the chi-square statistic for these data. How does it compare with the value that you calculated for this exercise?

4. Enter the data from Exercise 9.11 into SPSS. Compute the value of the chi-square statistic for these data. How does it compare with the value that you calculated for this exercise?

5. Open the ***nys_1.sav*** data file. Use a 5% level of significance and outline each of the steps required in a test of statistical significance for each of the following relationships:

   a. Is ethnicity related to grade point average?

   b. Is marijuana use among friends related to the youth's attitudes about marijuana use?

c. Is the importance of going to college related to the importance of having a job?

d. Is grade point average related to the importance of having a job?

e. Is the sex of the youth related to the importance of having friends?

f. Is the importance of having a job related to the youth's attitudes about marijuana use?

g. SPSS notes at the bottom of each cross-tabulation the number and percentage of all cells that had expected frequencies less than 5. For parts a through f, are there any cross-tabulations that produce expected frequencies of less than 5 for 20% or more of all cells in the table? If so, what are the consequences for interpreting the chi-square statistic? Explain how the categories of one or more variables could be combined to produce a table that has fewer cells with expected frequencies of less than 5.

parametric tests for a normal population distribution

What Are the Characteristics of the Normal Frequency Distribution?

What Is the *z*-Score?

When Can We Use the Normal Sampling Distribution?

What Are the Assumptions of the One-Sample *z*-Test for Means?

using the normal sampling distribution when population parameters are unknown

How Can We Make Assumptions About an Unknown Population?

What Is the Central Limit Theorem?

When Can It Be Used?

two examples

How Can We Define a Sampling Distribution When the Parameters Are Unknown?

What Is the *z*-Test for Proportions?

What Is the *t*-Test for Means?

I N CHAPTERS 8 AND 9, tests of statistical significance were presented that did not make assumptions about the population distribution of the characteristics studied. We now turn to a different type of test of statistical significance in which the researcher must make certain assumptions about the population distribution. These tests, called parametric tests, are widely used in criminal justice and criminology because they allow the researcher to test hypotheses in reference to interval-level scales.

We begin by introducing the normal sampling distribution and its application to tests of significance for measures that are normally distributed in the population. We then turn to a basic dilemma faced by researchers in the use of parametric tests. The purpose of statistical inference is to make statements about populations from what is known about samples. However, parametric tests require that we make assumptions about the population at the outset. If population parameters are generally unknown, how can we make assumptions about them? In this chapter, we examine this dilemma in the context of two types of parametric tests that are based on the normal distribution.

The Normal Frequency Distribution, or Normal Curve

In Chapter 3, we noted that frequency distributions may take many different forms. Sometimes there is no pattern to a distribution of scores. This is the case for the example in Figure 10.1, in which the frequency of scores goes up and down without consistency. But often a distribution begins to take a specific shape. For example, Floyd Allport suggested more than half a century ago that the distribution of deviant behavior is shaped like a J.[1] His J curve, represented in Figure 10.2, fits many types

---

[1] F. H. Allport, "The J-Curve Hypothesis of Conforming Behavior," *Journal of Social Psychology* 5 (1934): 141–183.

| Figure 10.1 | *Random Frequency Distribution* |

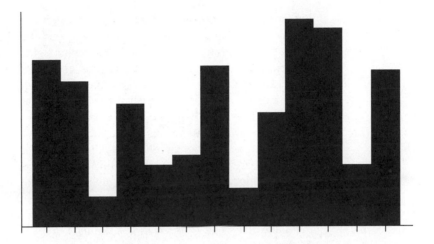

of rule-breaking behavior and suggests a theory of deviance in which social control leads most people to conform more or less to societal rules. Allport fit a J curve to behaviors as diverse as parking violations, conformity to religious rituals in church, and stopping at a stop sign.

The most widely utilized distributional form in statistics is what is defined as the **normal frequency distribution** or **normal curve.** The normal distribution is the basis for a number of parametric statistical

| Figure 10.2 | *The J Curve* |

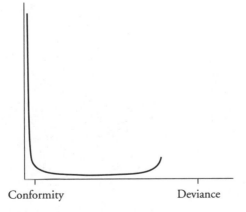

Conformity   Deviance

tests. This is the case in good part because of a set of special characteristics associated with the normal curve.

Characteristics of the Normal Frequency Distribution

A normal distribution is always symmetrical and bell shaped. By that we mean that it is shaped exactly the same on both sides of its mean. If you represent a normal distribution as a curve, you can fold it over at its mean and gain two half-curves that are exactly alike. Of course, there are many different potential bell-shaped curves that are symmetrical, as illustrated in Figure 10.3. The curve in part a of Figure 10.3, for example, is fairly flat. What this means is that the scores are fairly widely spread around the mean. The curve in part b, in contrast, is very peaked. Here, the scores are tightly clustered around the mean. In the statistical language developed in earlier chapters, we can say that the standard deviation of the first distribution is much larger than that of the second.

In a true normal distribution, the mean, mode, and median are always the same. This can be seen in the normal curves in Figure 10.3. If the distribution is completely symmetrical, then the 50th percentile score, or the median, must be right in the middle of the distribution. In turn, since

Figure 10.3   *Two Examples of Normal Curves*

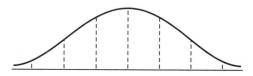

(a) *Normal Curve with a Large Standard Deviation*

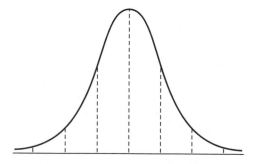

(b) *Normal Curve with a Small Standard Deviation*

the middle of the distribution represents its highest peak, and thus the largest frequency of scores, it is also the location of the mode for the normal distribution. Finally, given that there is an exactly equal distribution of scores below and above that peak, the same value must also be the mean for a normal distribution.

All of these traits help to define a normal distribution. However, the most useful characteristic of a normal distribution develops from the fact that the percentage of cases between its mean and points at a measured distance from the mean is always fixed. The measure in this case is the **standard deviation unit.** A standard deviation unit is simply the standard deviation for the particular distribution being examined. For example, let's say that you were examining the results of a standardized test for assessing adjustment of prisoners and that the distribution obtained was a normal distribution. You obtained a mean score of 90 and a standard deviation of 10 for your sample. The standard deviation unit of this distribution would be 10. That is, if you measured one standard deviation unit from the mean in either direction, you would move 10 points from the mean, to 100 and 80. If you measured two standard deviation units from the mean, you would move 20 points, to 110 and 70.

In a normal distribution, 68.26% of the cases in the distribution are found within one standard deviation unit above and below the mean (see Figure 10.4). Because the normal distribution is symmetrical, this means that 34.13% of the cases lie within one standard deviation unit to either the right (positive side) or the left (negative side) of the mean.

Figure 10.4   *Percentage of Cases Under Portions of the Normal Curve*

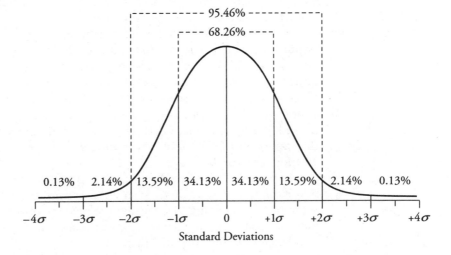

Fully 95.46% of the cases are found within two standard deviation units above and below the mean. Virtually all of the cases in a distribution with a normal form are within three standard deviation units of the mean, although in theory the tails (or extremes) of this distribution go on forever. For the sample of inmates discussed above, we thus know that slightly more than two-thirds have adjustment scores of between 80 and 100 (one standard deviation unit above and below the mean). Very few members of the sample have adjustment scores above 120, which represents a score that is three standard deviation units from the mean.

z-Scores

Using a simple equation, we can convert all normal distributions, irrespective of their particular mean or standard deviation, to a single **standard normal distribution.** This distribution can then be used to identify the exact location of any score. We do this by converting the actual scores in our sample or population to **z-scores,** which represent standard deviation units for the standard normal distribution. This distribution has a mean of 0 and a standard deviation unit of 1. The formula for converting a specific score to a z-score is represented by Equation 10.1.

$$z = \frac{X_i - \mu}{\sigma}$$

Equation 10.1

For this equation, we take the score of interest and subtract from it the mean score for the population distribution (represented by μ). We then divide that result by the standard deviation of the population distribution we are examining (represented by σ). In practice, what this formula does is allow us to convert any specific score in any normal distribution to a z-score in a standard normal distribution. We can then use a standardized table to identify the location of that score. A concrete example will make this conversion easier to understand.

Intelligence quotient (IQ) scores are normally distributed in the U.S. population, with a mean of 100 and a standard deviation of about 15. Suppose a probation officer is writing a report on a young offender. She finds that the young man has an IQ of 124. She wants to give the sentencing judge a good sense of what this means in terms of how this young man compares to others. She can do this by transforming the mean IQ of the offender (124) to a z-score and then identifying where this z-score fits in the standard normal distribution. We use Equation 10.1 for this purpose.

As shown in the numerator of the equation, we subtract the population mean (μ) of IQ scores, which we already noted was 100, from the score of 124. By doing this we shift the position of our score. We now have its location if the mean of our distribution were 0—the mean of a standard normal distribution.

If the mean were 0, then the score for this offender would be 24 (and not 124). As a second step, we divide this result by 15, the standard deviation (σ) of IQ scores in the U.S. population. This is equivalent to converting our sample standard deviation unit to 1, the standard deviation of the standard normal distribution, since each score of 15 is equivalent to one z standard deviation unit. The result is 1.60.

Working It Out

$$z = \frac{X_i - \mu}{\sigma}$$

$$= \frac{124 - 100}{15}$$

$$= 1.60$$

Our final step is to compare this z-score to an already prepared table of the standard normal distribution, provided in Appendix 3. You will notice that the z table goes up to only 0.50. This is because it provides us with only half of the normal curve. On this half of the normal curve, our z-score of 1.60 is equivalent to 0.4452, meaning that 44.52% of the scores lie between 0 and +1.60 standard deviations from 0. In Figure 10.5, our result is illustrated in the context of the normal curve. Because our result is a positive score, we place the value on the right-hand side of the normal distribution.

| Figure 10.5 | *IQ Score of Young Prisoner Compared to Average IQ Score of the General Population* |

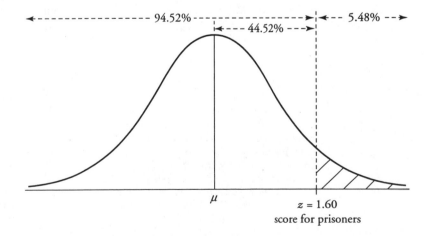

To identify the percentage of people in the general population with IQ scores higher than that of the young offender, we subtract our result of 0.4452 from 0.50 (the proportion of cases in this half of the curve). Our result of 0.0548 means that only a bit more than 5% of the general population has higher IQ scores than this offender. Conversely, almost 95% of the population has lower IQ scores than this offender. By converting the offender's score to a score on the standard normal distribution, we are able to place his intelligence in context. From our finding, we can see that he is indeed a highly intelligent young man, based on his IQ score.

Developing Tests of Statistical Significance Based on the Standard Normal Distribution: The Single-Sample z-Test for Known Populations

The normal distribution can also be used as a sampling distribution. However, in order to use a normal distribution as a sampling distribution for a test of statistical significance, we must assume that the underlying population distribution for the sample or samples is also distributed normally. This is the case for the IQ test, so we will continue to use it as an example. Let's say that you were interested in whether American prisoners differ from Americans generally in terms of average IQ scores. The population characteristics for all Americans are, as discussed above, known. The mean score for the population is 100, and the standard deviation of the population mean is 15. You conduct a study of 125 prisoners selected through an independent random sampling procedure from the population of American prisoners. You find that the mean IQ in your sample is 90.[2] This mean is different from the mean of the American population. But we know that samples vary, and thus you might get a mean of 90 even if the mean for American prisoners were the same as that for the general population. What we want to know is how likely we are to get such an outcome in our sample if the distribution of American prisoners is the same as that of the general American population.[3] Be-

---

[2]Our hypothesized results mirror those found in prior studies; see R. J. Hernstein, "Some Criminogenic Traits of Offenders," in J. Q. Wilson (ed.), *Crime and Public Policy* (San Francisco: Institute for Contemporary Studies, 1983). Whether these differences mean that offenders are, on average, less intelligent than nonoffenders is an issue of some controversy in criminology, in part because of the relationship of IQ to other factors, such as education and social status.

[3]By implication, we are asking whether it is reasonable to believe that our sample of prisoners was drawn from the general population. For this reason, the z-test can also be used to test for random sampling. If you have reason to doubt the sampling methods of a study, you can conduct this test, comparing the observed characteristics of your sample with the known parameters of the population from which your sample was drawn.

cause the population parameters of the American population are known, a **single-sample *z-test*** for known populations is appropriate.

We set up our test of statistical significance the same way we did other tests in previous chapters.

Assumptions:

Level of Measurement: Interval scale.

Population Distribution: Normal distribution.

Sampling Method: Independent random sampling.

Sampling Frame: The American prison population.

Hypotheses:

H_0: The mean IQ of the population from which our sample of prisoners was drawn is the same as the mean IQ of the general population of Americans ($\mu = 100$).

H_1: The mean IQ of the population from which our sample of prisoners was drawn is not the same as the mean IQ of the general population of Americans ($\mu \neq 100$).

As required by the single-sample z-test for known populations, IQ scores are measured at an interval level. As already noted, IQ is also normally distributed in the general population, meaning that it is appropriate to use a normal sampling distribution to conduct our test of statistical significance. Our sample, as required by our test, is drawn randomly with replacement from the American prison population. Our null hypothesis is that the mean IQ of American prisoners is the same as the mean IQ of the general American population ($\mu = 100$). Our research hypothesis is that the mean IQ of prisoners is different from that of the average American ($\mu \neq 100$).

The Sampling Distribution   The mean of the sampling distribution we use for our test of statistical inference is defined, as in other tests, by our null hypothesis. In this case, it is 100, or the mean IQ for the American population. The standard deviation is drawn from our knowledge of the standard deviation of the population distribution of scores. However, we cannot simply take the standard deviation of scores for the population distribution and apply it to the sampling distribution for our test, because the standard deviation of the sampling distribution is influenced by the number of observations in a sample. This is illustrated in Figure 10.6, which presents three different sampling distributions for the same population distribution of scores. In the first, there are only 10 cases in the samples from which the sampling distribution is developed. In the second, there are 25 cases in each sample. Finally, in the third distribution, there are 100 cases in each sample. What is clear here is

Figure 10.6   *Normal Distribution of Scores from Samples of Varying Sizes: N = 10, N = 25, and N = 100*

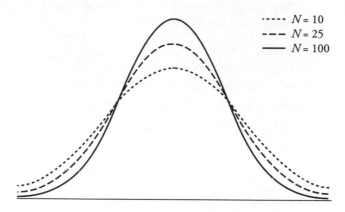

$$\cdots\cdots N = 10$$
$$---- N = 25$$
$$\underline{\quad\quad} N = 100$$

that the spread of scores is reduced as the size of samples in the distribution increases. This fact is a very important one in statistics and follows what our common sense tells us: Our estimates become more tightly clustered around the mean of the distribution as N increases. This implies, in practice, that we are less likely to draw deviant samples (those far from the mean of the sampling distribution) as the N of cases in our samples increases. Put in lay terms, larger samples are more trustworthy or more likely to reflect the true population score, all else being equal, than are smaller samples.

In order to differentiate between the standard deviation of a population distribution of scores and that of a sampling distribution, statisticians call the standard deviation of a sampling distribution the **standard error**. Using Equation 10.2, we adjust our standard error for the fact that the dispersion of sample means decreases as sample size increases. In order to distinguish the standard deviation (σ) from the standard error in this text, we will use the subscripts sd (for sampling distribution) whenever we refer to the standard error of a sampling distribution. Accordingly, the standard error of a sampling distribution is represented as σ_{sd} in Equation 10.2.

$$\text{Standard error} = \sigma_{sd} = \frac{\sigma}{\sqrt{N}} \qquad \textbf{Equation 10.2}$$

For our example, we find the standard error of the sampling distribution by dividing the population standard deviation of IQ, 15, by the square root of our sample N. The result is 1.342.

> ### W orking It Out
>
> $$\text{Standard error} = \frac{\sigma}{\sqrt{N}}$$
>
> $$= \frac{15}{\sqrt{125}}$$
>
> $$= 1.342$$

Significance Level and Rejection Region   Given that no special concerns have been stated in regard to the risk of either a Type I or a Type II error, we use a conventional 0.05 significance threshold. As our research hypothesis is nondirectional, we use a two-tailed test. What this means for our rejection region is illustrated in Figure 10.7. On the right-hand side of the distribution are outcomes greater than the average American IQ of 100. On the left-hand side of the distribution are outcomes less than the average. Because our research hypothesis is not directional, we split our total rejection region of 5% between both tails of the distribution. This is represented by the shaded area. Each shaded area represents half the total rejection region, or 0.025.

Figure 10.7

Rejection Region on a Normal Frequency Distribution for a 0.05 Two-Tailed Significance Test

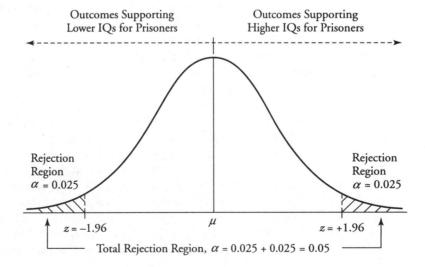

To define the z-score that corresponds with our rejection region, we must turn to the table of probability values associated with the z distribution in Appendix 3. As discussed earlier in the chapter, the z table represents only half of the normal curve. We look at the value associated with 0.4750 (0.5000 − 0.0250) in the table, which is 1.96. If we observe a test statistic either greater than 1.96 or less than −1.96, we will reject the null hypothesis of our test (see Figure 10.7). In this case, our observed significance level would be less than the 0.05 criterion for our test.

If we had stated a directional research hypothesis, we would place the entire rejection region ($\alpha = 0.05$) in one of the two tails of the normal distribution. In this case, we would conduct a one-tailed statistical test. Parts a and b of Figure 10.8 represent the rejection regions for two different one-tailed tests of statistical significance. If our research hypothesis stated that average IQs for prisoners were less than those for the U.S. population, we would place the entire rejection region of 0.0500 in the left tail of the distribution (see Figure 10.8a). We again consult the z table in Appendix 3 to identify the z-score associated with a value of 0.4500 (0.5000 − 0.0500). We observe that 0.4500 falls exactly halfway between two values in the table —0.4495 and 0.4505—corresponding to z-scores of −1.64 and −1.65, respectively. How do we determine the value of z in such a case? The most accurate value for z would be found by interpolating between −1.64 and −1.65, which would give −1.645, since the value we are looking for is halfway between the two proportions reported in the z table. In this case, if our test statistic is less than −1.645, then we reject our null hypothesis and conclude that the average IQ for prisoners is less than the U.S. average. If our research hypothesis stated that the average IQ of prisoners was greater than the U.S. average, we would place the rejection region on the right side of the distribution (see Figure 10.8b). In such a case, our critical value would be +1.645, meaning that if our test statistic was greater than 1.645, we would reject the null hypothesis and conclude that the average IQ for prisoners was greater than the U.S. average.

The Test Statistic   To calculate our test statistic, we can use the same formula we did in examining the relative position of a score in the standard normal distribution, with two important differences. In this case, we have to take into account the fact that sampling distributions become more tightly spread around their mean as the N of sample cases becomes larger. As discussed in defining the sampling distribution above, we need to adjust the standard deviation of the population distribution by dividing it by the square root of the N of our sample. This provides us with the standard error (σ_{sd}) for our distribution. We also need to subtract the

Figure 10.8   *Rejection Region on a Normal Frequency Distribution for a 0.05 One-Tailed Significance Test*

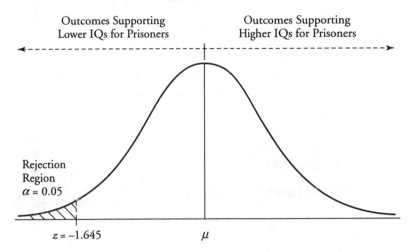

(a) *Lower IQs for Prisoners*

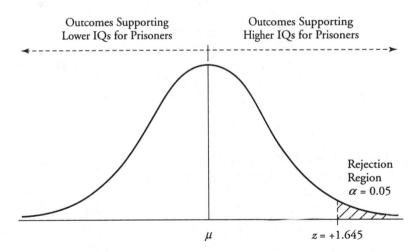

(b) *Higher IQs for Prisoners*

mean (μ) of the population score from $\overline{X}$, rather than X_i. These adjustments are made in Equation 10.3.

$$z = \frac{\overline{X} - \mu}{\sigma_{sd}} = \frac{\overline{X} - \mu}{\sigma/\sqrt{N}}$$

Equation 10.3

Inserting into our equation the mean value of our sample and its N of cases and the mean and standard deviation for the population of scores, we obtain a z-test statistic of -7.453.

W orking It Out

$$z = \frac{\overline{X} - \mu}{\sigma/\sqrt{N}}$$

$$= \frac{90 - 100}{15/\sqrt{125}}$$

$$= -7.453$$

The Decision   Because our test statistic is less than our negative critical value ($-7.453 < -1.96$) and falls in the rejection region, we reject the null hypothesis. We conclude on the basis of our study that the mean IQ of the population from which our sample was drawn is different from that of the general American population.

Applying Normal Sampling Distributions to Nonnormal Populations

The example of IQ presents a case where the single-sample z-test can be used to test hypotheses involving interval-scale measures. However, it requires that the population distribution for the measure be normal. In some fields in the social sciences, measures are constructed in such a way that they are normally distributed in practice.[4] But in criminology, there

---

[4]In principle, any distribution may be arranged in such a way that it conforms to a normal shape. This can be done simply by ranking scores and then placing the appropriate number within standard deviation units appropriate for constructing a standard normal distribution.

has been much less use of distributions that are standardized in normal form, in part because the distributions of the behaviors and populations that we confront do not often conform to the shape of a normal curve. Even measures that do begin to approximate the shape of the normal distribution seldom meet all the requirements of a true normal distribution.

How, then, can parametric tests based on the normal distribution be widely used to make statistical inferences? Not only do they demand that we make an assumption about a population we usually know little about, but the assumption we are being asked to make does not make very much sense for criminal justice measures. The answer may be found in an important distinction between population distributions on the one hand and sampling distributions on the other. While we have every reason to be hesitant in assuming that the population distribution of scores is normal for criminal justice measures, we can assume with a good deal of confidence that the sampling distributions for such measures are approximately normal. Using the toss of a fair coin as an example, we can provide a simple illustration of this fact.

In Figure 10.9, we overlay the distribution of scores for a population of 1,000 tosses of a fair coin over the normal distribution. As is apparent, outcomes in a coin toss are not distributed normally. This makes good sense, since there are only two possible scores for the coin toss: heads and tails. No matter what the outcome, it is impossible for a coin toss to approximate the form of the normal distribution.

But let's now turn to a sampling distribution for the coin toss. In this case, we want to know the likelihood of gaining a specific number of heads in a set number of coin tosses. This is the logic we used

Figure 10.9   *Distribution of 1,000 Tosses of a Fair Coin Contrasted to the Normal Distribution*

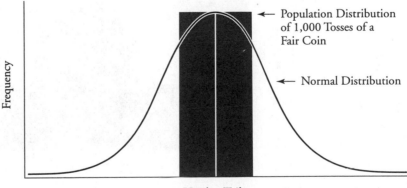

in developing the binomial probability distribution in Chapter 7. Figure 10.10 presents the binomial distribution for different-size samples of the coin toss under the null hypothesis that the coin is fair.

For a sample size of 1 (Figure 10.10a), the shape of the sampling distribution is the same as the shape of the population distribution of scores. However, notice what happens as the size of the samples used to construct the sampling distributions grows. For a sample of 10 (Figure 10.10b), the histogram for the distribution of scores is still jagged, but it has begun to take a shape similar to the normal distribution. Importantly, for a sample of 10, we do not have two potential outcomes, which

Figure 10.10   *Sampling Distribution of Coin Tosses*

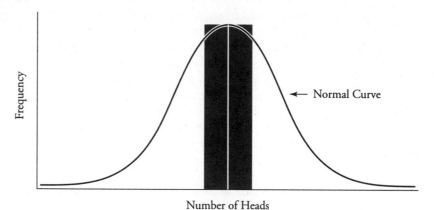

(a) *1 Toss of a Fair Coin*

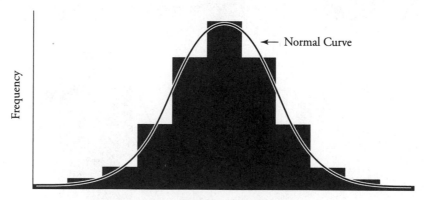

(b) *10 Tosses of a Fair Coin*

Figure 10.10   *Sampling Distribution of Coin Tosses (cont.)*

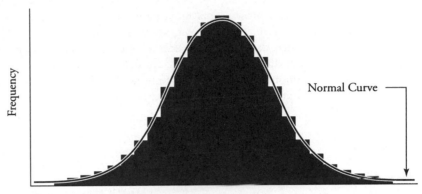

Normal Curve

Number of Heads

(c) *100 Tosses of a Fair Coin*

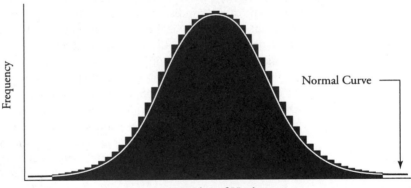

Normal Curve

Number of Heads

(d) *400 Tosses of a Fair Coin*

would make a normal shape impossible, but 11 potential outcomes (no heads, one head, two heads, three heads, four heads, . . . to ten heads). This is the case because we are flipping the coin ten times for each sample. The sampling distribution is telling us the number of times we would expect to gain a specific number of heads in ten tosses of a fair coin in a very large number of trials. For a sample of 100 flips of a fair coin (Figure 10.10c), the sampling distribution even more closely approximates the normal curve. By the time we get to a sample of 400 flips of the coin (Figure 10.10d), the sampling distribution of a fair coin is almost indistinguishable from the normal curve.

The population distribution of scores for a fair coin is very far from a normal form. Yet sampling distributions for the same population begin to approximate the normal distribution as the size of the sample of coin tosses grows. This remarkable fact is summarized in a very important theorem, or statement, about sampling distributions called the **central limit theorem.** The central limit theorem allows us to overcome our initial dilemma because it says that under many circumstances we can use a normal sampling distribution for making inferences about a population that is not normal in shape.

Central Limit Theorem
If repeated independent random samples of size N are drawn from a population, then as N grows large, the sampling distribution of sample means will be approximately normal.

The central limit theorem tells us that when the number of cases in a sample is large, we can assume that the sampling distribution of sample means is approximately normal even if the population distribution itself is not normal. This is what is meant by the statement "then as *N* grows large, the sampling distribution of sample means will be approximately normal." However, the theorem does not provide us with a clear statement about how large the number of cases in a sample must be before we can make this assumption.

One reason for this ambiguity is that the number of cases needed before the sampling distribution begins to approximate normality depends in part on the actual distribution of the measure examined in the population. As can be seen from the example of the coin toss, even when the population distribution departs markedly from the normal distribution, the sampling distribution fits fairly closely to the normal curve with a sample size of 100. For this reason, you will find wide agreement that a normal sampling distribution can be assumed for samples of 100 or more, irrespective of the distribution of scores in a population.

There is much less agreement about what to do when a sample is smaller than 100 cases. Some statisticians argue that with 50 cases you can be fairly confident that the central limit theorem applies in most circumstances. Others apply this yardstick to 25 or 30 cases, and still others argue that under certain circumstances—for example, when prior studies suggest a population distribution fairly close to normality—only 15 cases is enough. In conducting research in criminal justice, you should recognize that there is no hard and fast rule regarding sample size and the central limit theorem. In practice, in criminal justice, researchers generally assume that 30 cases is enough for applying the central limit theorem. However, when a distribution strongly departs from normality, as is the case with a proportion, it is safer to require more than 100 cases.

While the central limit theorem solves a major problem in applying normal distribution tests to criminological questions, we are still faced with a barrier in actually carrying out such tests. As we saw earlier (see Equation 10.3), the standard error of the *z* sampling distribution is gained from knowledge about the standard deviation of the population distribution. How can we identify the standard error of a sampling distribution if we do not know the standard deviation of the population distribution? In the following sections, we illustrate two methods for defining σ for an unknown population. In the first, we take advantage of a special relationship between the mean and the standard deviation of a proportion. In the second, we estimate the unknown parameter based on information gained in our sample.

Comparing a Sample to an Unknown Population: The Single-Sample *z*-Test for Proportions

One implication of the central limit theorem is that we can use a normal sampling distribution to test hypotheses involving proportions. This might seem strange at first, since we estimate the shape of a normal distribution through knowledge of its mean and standard deviation. As discussed in Chapter 4, the mean and standard deviation are not appropriate statistics to use with a nominal-level measure such as a proportion.

Nonetheless, as illustrated in the previous section, the sampling distribution of a proportion—in our example, the coin toss (see Figure 10.10)—begins to approximate a normal distribution when the number of cases for the sample becomes large. The central tendency of this distribution and its dispersion are measured by the mean and standard error, just as in distributions that develop from interval-level data. Accordingly, although it would be inappropriate to use the mean and standard deviation to describe a sample or population distribution of a proportion, the mean and standard error are appropriate statistics for describing the normal sampling distribution that is associated with the same proportion.

Computing the Mean and Standard Deviation
for the Sampling Distribution of a Proportion

How do we compute the mean and standard deviation of a proportion? One way to do this would be to simply apply the formula for the mean and the standard deviation to the scores associated with a proportion. However, there is a simpler way to arrive at the same result. It turns out that the mean of a proportion is equal to the proportion itself. This is illustrated in Table 10.1, which shows an example in which the mean and proportion are calculated for five heads in ten tosses of a coin.

| Table 10.1 | Calculating the Mean and Proportion of 5 Heads in 10 Tosses of a Coin |

CALCULATING THE MEAN FOR FIVE HEADS	CALCULATING THE PROPORTION FOR FIVE HEADS
$\bar{X} = \dfrac{\sum\limits_{i=1}^{N} X_i}{N} = \dfrac{1 + 1 + 1 + 1 + 1 + 0 + 0 + 0 + 0 + 0}{10} = 0.5$	$\text{Proportion} = \dfrac{N_{successes}}{N_{total}} = \dfrac{5}{10} = 0.5$

Note: Head = 1: tail = 0

For the numerator of the mean, we sum the scores on the ten trials (five ones and five zeros) and get 5. The numerator of a proportion is the N of cases in the category of interest. If the category is heads, then we also get a result of 5. The denominators for both equations are the same (10), and thus the outcomes are also the same. As a general rule, we state that for a proportion $\mu = P$.

What about the standard deviation of a proportion? It turns out that we can calculate the standard deviation with knowledge of only the proportion itself. This is illustrated in Table 10.2.

Taking the sum of the squared deviations from the mean and dividing it by N, we get a result of 0.25. But we can get this same result by multiplying the proportion of heads (P) by the proportion of tails (Q)—in our case, multiplying 0.5 by 0.5. Accordingly, we can substitute $P \cdot Q$ for

$$\frac{\sum\limits_{i=1}^{N} (X_i - \bar{X})^2}{N}$$

| Table 10.2 | Calculating the Standard Deviation of 5 Heads in 10 Tosses of a Coin |

CALCULATING THE STANDARD DEVIATION FROM THE RAW SCORES	CALCULATING THE STANDARD DEVIATION FROM P AND Q
$\sigma = \sqrt{\dfrac{\sum\limits_{i=1}^{N} (X_i - \bar{X})^2}{N}}$ $= \sqrt{\dfrac{0.25 + 0.25 + 0.25 + 0.25 + 0.25 + 0.25 + 0.25 + 0.25 + 0.25 + 0.25}{10}}$ $= \sqrt{0.25} = 0.5$	$\sigma = \sqrt{PQ} = \sqrt{(0.5)(0.5)} = \sqrt{0.25} = 0.5$

in the equation for the standard deviation for the mean:

$$\sigma = \sqrt{\frac{\sum_{i=1}^{N} (X_i - \overline{X})^2}{N}} = \sqrt{PQ}$$ **Equation 10.4**

Because of this relationship between the mean and the standard deviation of a proportion, when we state the proportion of successes expected under the null hypothesis, we also state by implication the mean and the standard deviation for the population distribution of scores. So if we state in the null hypothesis that the proportion of successes in the population is 0.50, we know that the mean of the population distribution of scores for our test of the null hypothesis is 0.50 and its standard deviation is 0.25 ($\sigma = \sqrt{PQ} = \sqrt{(0.50)(0.50)} = \sqrt{0.25} = 0.50$).

What this means in practice is that we need not have any a priori knowledge of the shape of the population distribution to construct a sampling distribution for our test of proportions. With a large N, we can assume a normal sampling distribution, irrespective of the actual form of the population distribution. Through our null hypothesis, we can define both the mean and the standard deviation of the population distribution for our test. We are now ready to use the normal distribution to test hypotheses about unknown population parameters.

Testing Hypotheses with the Normal Distribution:
The Case of a New Prison Program

Suppose that you were asked to evaluate a new prison education program. The foundation sponsoring the effort sought to achieve a program success rate of 75% among the 100,000 prisoners enrolled in the program. Success was defined as completion of a six-month course supported by the foundation. Managers of the program claim that the success rate is actually much greater than the criteria set by the foundation. However, a recent newspaper exposé claims that the success rate of the program is actually much below 75%. You are able to collect information on 150 prisoners, selected using independent random sampling. You find that 85% of your sample successfully completed the course. What conclusions can you make, based on your sample results, about the claims of managers and the newspaper exposé?

Assumptions:

Level of Measurement: Interval scale (program success is measured as a proportion).

Population Distribution: Normal distribution (relaxed because N is large).

Sampling Method: Independent random sampling.

Sampling Frame: 100,000 prisoners in the program.

Hypotheses:

H_0: The success rate of the program is 0.75 ($P = 0.75$).

H_1: The success rate of the program is not 0.75 ($P \neq 0.75$).

Because the number of cases in our sample is greater than the threshold of 100 suggested for invoking the central limit theorem in the case of a proportion, we can ignore—or, in statistical terms, **relax—assumptions** regarding the shape of the population distribution. In the special case of a proportion, we can also relax the assumption of an interval scale of measurement.[5] Our sample, as assumed by our test, is drawn randomly with replacement from the sampling frame of 100,000 prisoners in the program.

Our research hypothesis is nondirectional. Managers of the program claim that the program has a success rate of greater than 0.75 ($P > 0.75$). The newspaper exposé claims that the success rate is much below 75% ($P < 0.75$). Accordingly, we want to be able to examine both of these potential outcomes in our test. The null hypothesis is that the rate of success for the program is 0.75 ($P = 0.75$).

The Sampling Distribution   In calculating the mean and standard deviation or standard error for our sampling distribution, we rely on our null hypothesis. Our null hypothesis states that the proportion of successes in the population is 75%. This means that the mean of the sampling distribution is also 0.75. We can calculate the standard error of the sampling

---

[5]It would not make sense, however, to use a normal distribution test for nominal-scale measures with more than two categories. The normal distribution assumes scores above and below a mean. The sampling distribution of a proportion follows this pattern because it includes only two potential outcomes, which then are associated with each tail of the distribution. In a multicategory nominal-scale measure, we have more than two outcomes and thus cannot fit each outcome to a tail of the normal curve. Because the order of these outcomes is not defined, we also cannot place them on a continuum within the normal distribution. This latter possibility would suggest that the normal distribution could be applied to ordinal-level measures. However, because we do not assume a constant unit of measurement between ordinal categories, the normal distribution is often considered inappropriate for hypothesis testing with ordinal scales. In the case of a proportion, there is a constant unit of measurement between scores simply because there are only two possible outcomes (e.g., success and failure).

distribution by adjusting Equation 10.2 to the case of a proportion, as illustrated in Equation 10.5:

$$\sigma_{sd} = \frac{\sigma}{\sqrt{N}} = \frac{\sqrt{PQ}}{\sqrt{N}} = \sqrt{\frac{PQ}{N}}$$

Equation 10.5

Applying this equation to our problem, we obtain a standard error of 0.035 for the normal sampling distribution associated with our null hypothesis:

Working It Out

$$\sigma_{sd} = \sqrt{\frac{PQ}{N}}$$

$$= \sqrt{\frac{(0.75)(0.25)}{150}}$$

$$= \frac{\sqrt{0.1875}}{\sqrt{150}}$$

$$= \frac{0.433}{12.25}$$

$$= 0.0353$$

In order to test our hypothesis, we will convert this sampling distribution, with mean 0.75 and standard error 0.035, to the standard normal distribution (or z), which has a mean of 0 and a standard deviation or standard error of 1. This calculation is done when we calculate the test statistic below.

Significance Level and Rejection Region   Given that no special concerns have been stated in regard to the risk of either a Type I or a Type II error, we use a conventional 0.05 significance threshold. As our research hypothesis is nondirectional, we use a two-tailed test. As our level of significance is the same as in our previous problem, we follow the same procedure and arrive at a critical value of 1.96. If we observe a test statistic either greater than 1.96 or less than −1.96, we will reject the null hypothesis of our test.

The Test Statistic   We can rely on the same formula used in the single-sample z-test for known populations, presented earlier in Equation 10.3. However, in Equation 10.6, we express the formula with proportions rather than means:

$$z = \frac{\overline{X} - \mu}{\sigma_{sd}} = \frac{\overline{X} - \mu}{\sigma/\sqrt{N}} = \frac{p - P}{\sqrt{PQ/N}}$$

Equation 10.6

The mean of the sample (p) is 0.85, since this is the outcome of the study. The mean of the sampling distribution P (0.75) is taken from our null hypothesis. The standard error of the sampling distribution (σ_{sd}) was calculated earlier based on our null hypothesis that the proportion of successes was 0.75. Our result is a z-score of 2.833.

W orking It Out

$$z = \frac{p - P}{\sigma/\sqrt{N}}, \quad \text{where } \sigma = \sqrt{PQ} = \sqrt{(0.75)(.025)}$$

$$= \frac{0.85 - 0.75}{\sqrt{(0.75)(0.25)}/\sqrt{150}}$$

$$= \frac{0.10}{0.0353}$$

$$= 2.8329$$

The Decision   Our test statistic is well within the rejection region of our test (which includes scores greater than 1.96 or less than -1.96), meaning that our observed significance level is less than the significance level we set for our test at the outset ($p < 0.05$). We therefore reject the null hypothesis at a 0.05 significance level. We come out on the side of the managers of the program. Our sample results support their position that the overall program has exceeded the criterion for success of the foundation.

Comparing a Sample to an Unknown Population: The Single-Sample *t*-Test for Means

The proportion provides us with a special case in which we can calculate the standard error of our sampling distribution based on our null hypothesis. But this is not possible when our null hypothesis relates to a mean of an interval-level measure. In this case, there is not one specific variance or standard deviation associated with a mean but an infinite number of potential variances or standard deviations. How, then, can we test hypotheses about unknown parameters in the case of the mean?

One obvious method is to simply use the variance of our sample as a "guesstimate" of the variance of the population distribution. The problem with this solution is that the variance of a sample is a somewhat biased estimate of the variance of the population. By this we mean that the average of repeated observations of the variance (s^2) tends in the long run not to be equivalent to the value of σ^2. We can transform s^2 to a better estimate of σ^2 through a very small correction to the equation for the variance. This new statistic (expressed as $\hat{\sigma}^2$ since it is an estimate of σ^2) is represented in Equation 10.7.[6] An estimate of the standard deviation ($\hat{\sigma}$) can be gained by taking the square root of this value.

$$\hat{\sigma}^2 = \frac{\sum_{i=1}^{N} (X_i - \overline{X})^2}{N - 1}$$

Equation 10.7

In order to use this new statistic to test hypotheses, we must also use a slightly different sampling distribution, called the t distribution. It is sometimes called Student's t because its inventor, W. S. Gossett (1876–1936), first described the distribution under the pen name Student in 1908.

The t distribution (Appendix 4) is very similar to the z distribution (Appendix 3). However, as with the chi-square test, the shape of the t distribution is dependent on the number of degrees of freedom. The number of degrees of freedom for a single-sample t-test is defined as $N - 1$. When the number of cases in a sample is greater than 500, then the t and z distributions are virtually identical. However, as the number of cases in a sample gets smaller and smaller, and so accordingly does the number of degrees of freedom, the t distribution becomes flatter and a larger and larger test statistic is needed to reject the null hypothesis.

This fact can be illustrated by looking at the t table in Appendix 4. As you can see, the t table lists the critical values associated with six significance thresholds for both one- and two-tailed tests. Let's focus on the fourth column, which is the critical value associated with a two-tailed, 5% significance level. When the number of degrees of freedom is 500, the critical value for the t-statistic is the same as for the z distribution: 1.960. At 120, the t value needed to reject the null hypothesis is still almost the same: 1.980. At 100, the value is 1.982: at 50, it is 2.008; and at 25, it is 2.060. The largest differences come for even smaller degrees of freedom.

---

[6]As noted on page 97 (footnote 1), computerized statistical analysis packages, such as SPSS, use this corrected estimate in calculating the variance and standard deviation for sample estimates.

The t distribution presents a new problem as well in making inferences to unknown populations. Relaxing the assumption of normality is generally considered more risky in a t-test than in a z-test. This makes good sense because we are now using an estimate of σ rather than the actual population parameter. As the number of cases increases, our confidence in this estimate grows.[7] How large should N be before you are willing to use a t-test? With samples of more than 30 cases, your statistical conclusions are not likely to be challenged. However, the t distribution is particularly sensitive to outliers. Conclusions based on smaller samples should be checked carefully to make sure that one or two observations are not the cause of a very large statistical outcome.

Testing Hypotheses with the t Distribution

We are now ready to turn to a practical example. Suppose that the study described earlier also examined the average test scores for those prisoners who had completed the program. The foundation set a standard of success of 65 on the test. Program managers say that prisoners who have completed the program achieve average scores much higher than this. The newspaper exposé again claims that the average scores are considerably lower than those expected by the foundation. In this case, you are able to take an independent random sample of 51 prisoners who have completed the test. You find that the test mean for the sample is 60, and the standard deviation is 15. What conclusions about the larger population of prisoners can you come to based on your sample results?

Assumptions:

Level of Measurement: Interval scale.

Population Distribution: Normal distribution (relaxed because N is large).

Sampling Method: Independent random sampling.

Sampling Frame: Prisoners who have completed the program.

Hypotheses:

H_0: The mean test score for prisoners who have completed the program is 65 ($\mu = 65$).

H_1: The mean test score for prisoners who have completed the program is not 65 ($\mu \neq 65$).

---

[7]Our statistical problem is that we assume that μ and σ are independent in developing the t distribution. When a distribution is normal, this is indeed the case. However, for other types of distributions, we cannot make this assumption, and when N is small, a violation of this assumption is likely to lead to misleading approximations of the observed significance level of a test.

Following the assumptions of our test, we use an interval scale (the mean of test scores) and an independent random sampling method. We relax the assumption of normality because N is larger than the minimum threshold of 30 recommended for interval-level measures. Our research hypothesis is once again nondirectional so that we can examine the positions of both the managers of the program and the newspaper exposé. The null hypothesis is that the mean test score for the population of prisoners completing the program is 65 (the foundation standard), or that $\mu = 65$.

The Sampling Distribution   Because σ is unknown and cannot be deduced from our null hypothesis, we will use the t distribution. The number of degrees of freedom for our example is defined as $N - 1$, or $51 - 1 = 50$.

Significance Level and Rejection Region   Again, we have no reason in this example to depart from the 0.05 significance threshold. Because our research hypothesis is not directional, we use a two-tailed test. Turning to the t table, we find that a t-score of 2.008 is associated with a two-tailed, 5% significance threshold (at 50 degrees of freedom). This means that we will reject our null hypothesis if we obtain a test statistic greater than 2.008 or less than -2.008. For these observed values of our test statistic, the observed significance level of our test is less than the criterion of 0.05 that we have selected.

The Test Statistic   The test statistic for the t distribution is similar to that for the z distribution. The only difference is that we now use an estimate of the standard deviation ($\hat{\sigma}$) rather than σ itself.

$$t = \frac{\overline{X} - \mu}{\sigma_{\text{sd}}} = \frac{\overline{X} - \mu}{\hat{\sigma}/\sqrt{N}}$$

Equation 10.8

Although we can get an estimate of σ by adjusting the calculation for s, the formula for t may also be written in a way that allows us to calculate t from the unadjusted sample standard deviation.

$$t = \frac{\overline{X} - \mu}{\hat{\sigma}/\sqrt{N}} = \frac{\overline{X} - \mu}{\sqrt{\dfrac{\sum\limits_{i=1}^{N} (X_i - \overline{X})^2}{N - 1}} \Big/ \sqrt{N}}$$

$$= \frac{\overline{X} - \mu}{\sqrt{\dfrac{\sum\limits_{i=1}^{N} (X_i - \overline{X})^2}{N}} \Big/ \sqrt{N - 1}}$$

This means that we can simplify the equation for the t-test as follows:

$$t = \frac{\overline{X} - \mu}{s/\sqrt{N-1}}$$

Equation 10.9

Applying the t formula to our example, we use the mean of the sample, 60, as $\overline{X}$; μ is defined by the null hypothesis as 65; s is our sample standard deviation of 15; and N is the number of cases for our sample (51).

W **orking It Out**

$$t = \frac{\overline{X} - \mu}{s/\sqrt{N-1}}$$

$$= \frac{60 - 65}{15/\sqrt{51-1}}$$

$$= \frac{-5}{15/\sqrt{50}}$$

$$= \frac{-5}{2.1213}$$

$$= -2.3570$$

The Decision   Because the test statistic of -2.3570 is less than -2.008, we reject the null hypothesis and conclude that the result is significantly different from the goal set by the foundation. In this case, our decision is on the side of the newspaper exposé. We can conclude from our sample (with a 5% level of risk of falsely rejecting the null hypothesis) that the test scores in the population of prisoners who have completed the program are below the foundation goal of 65.

Chapter Summary

Parametric tests of statistical significance allow us to make inferences about a population from samples using interval-level data. In a parametric test, we make certain assumptions about the shape of the population distribution at the outset.

The **normal distribution,** or **normal curve,** is widely used in statistics. It is symmetrical and bell shaped. Its mean, mode, and median are always the same. There will always be a set number of cases between the mean and points a measured distance from the mean. The measure of this distance is the **standard deviation unit.** All normal distributions, irrespective of their mean or standard deviations, can be converted to a single standard normal distribution by converting the actual scores in the sample or population to z-scores. To use a normal sampling distribution for a test of statistical significance, we must assume that the characteristic studied is normally distributed in the population.

An important dilemma in statistical inference is created by this assumption. How can we make assumptions about the population distribution when its characteristics are generally unknown? The **central limit theorem** describes an important fact that allows us to solve this problem. As stated in the theorem, when the number of cases in a sample is large, the sampling distribution will be approximately normal in shape, even if the population distribution itself is not. In the field of criminal justice, it is generally assumed that the central limit theorem can be applied where the sample size is 30 or greater. When dealing with proportions, though, it is safer to require a sample size of at least 100. In such circumstances, we may **relax the assumption** of normality. We can now make inferences using a normal sampling distribution, even though the shape of the population distribution is unknown.

In order to define the sampling distribution, we need information about the population parameters—information that is not usually available. In the case of a test involving proportions, the null hypothesis can be used to define both the mean and the standard error of the population distribution. Once the population parameters have been defined by the null hypothesis, we can apply the formula for the z-test of statistical significance. In the case of a test of means, the null hypothesis cannot be used directly to define the standard error. We may, however, use the t sampling distribution, which relies on an estimate of the standard error.

Key Terms

central limit theorem A theorem that states: "If repeated independent random samples of size N are drawn from a population, as N grows large, the sampling distribution of sample means will be approximately normal." The central limit theorem enables the researcher to make inferences about an unknown population using a normal sampling distribution.

normal curve A normal frequency distribution represented on a graph by a continuous line.

normal frequency distribution A bell-shaped frequency distribution, symmetrical in form. Its mean, mode, and median are always the same. The percentage of cases between the mean and points at a measured distance from the mean is fixed.

relaxing an assumption Deciding that we need not be concerned with that assumption. For example, the assumption that a population is normal may be relaxed if the sample size is sufficiently large to invoke the central limit theorem.

single-sample _t_-test A test of statistical significance that is used to examine whether a sample is drawn from a specific population with a known or hypothesized mean. In a _t_-test, the standard deviation of the population to which the sample is being compared is unknown.

single-sample _z_-test A test of statistical significance that is used to examine whether a sample is drawn from a specific population with a known or hypothesized mean. In a _z_-test, the standard deviation of the population to which the sample is being compared either is known or—as in the case of a proportion— is defined by the null hypothesis.

standard deviation unit A unit of measurement used to describe the deviation of a specific score or value from the mean in a _z_ distribution.

standard error The standard deviation of a sampling distribution.

standard normal distribution A normal frequency distribution with a mean of 0 and a standard deviation of 1. Any normal frequency distribution can be transformed into the standard normal distribution by using the _z_ formula.

_z_-score Score that represents standard deviation units for a standard normal distribution.

Symbols and Formulas

---

p Proportion of successes (sample)

P Proportion of successes (population)

Q Proportion of failures (population)

σ_{sd} Standard error of sampling distribution

t _t_-score

$\hat{\sigma}$ Estimate of σ

To determine the _z_-score for a single observation:

$$z = \frac{X_i - \mu}{\sigma}$$

To determine the standard error of a sampling distribution:

$$\sigma_{sd} = \frac{\sigma}{\sqrt{N}}$$

To determine the z-score for a sample mean:

$$z = \frac{\overline{X} - \mu}{\sigma_{sd}} = \frac{\overline{X} - \mu}{\sigma/\sqrt{N}}$$

To determine the standard deviation of a proportion:

$$\sigma_p = \sqrt{PQ}$$

To determine the z-score for a sample proportion:

$$z = \frac{\overline{X} - \mu}{\sigma_{sd}} = \frac{\overline{X} - \mu}{\sigma/\sqrt{N}} = \frac{p - P}{\sqrt{PQ/N}}$$

To estimate the value of σ from data in a sample:

$$\hat{\sigma} = \sqrt{\frac{\sum_{i=1}^{N} (X_i - \overline{X})^2}{N - 1}}$$

To determine the value of t:

$$t = \frac{\overline{X} - \mu}{s/\sqrt{N - 1}}$$

Exercises

10.1 In which of the following circumstances would a researcher be justified in using a normal sampling distribution? Explain how or why for each case.

    a. A sample of 10 subjects is drawn to study a variable known to be normally distributed in the population.

    b. A sample of 50 subjects is drawn to study a variable known to be normally distributed in the population.

    c. A sample of 10 subjects is drawn to study a variable. The shape of the distribution of this variable in the population is unknown.

    d. A sample of 50 subjects is drawn to study a variable. The shape of the distribution of this variable in the population is unknown.

    e. A sample of 50 subjects is drawn to study a proportion. The shape of the distribution of this proportion in the population is unknown.

10.2 A team of psychologists has created an index they claim measures an individual's "ability to control anger." The index is calculated from the answers to a detailed questionnaire and is normally distributed among U.S. adult males, with a mean of 100 and a standard deviation of 30. Researchers assess a group of ten prisoners, all of whom have been convicted for violent rapes. They discover that the mean score for the group is 50.8.

   a. What percentage of U.S. adult males would be expected to obtain a score equal to or less than that of the rapists?

   b. The psychologists who constructed the index consider the bottom 10% of U.S. adult males on their distribution to be "strongly inclined to use violence to solve social problems." Albert is a respectable businessman who scores 60.6 on the scale. Is Albert included in this category? Explain why.

   c. What percentage of U.S. adult males would be expected to score between 110 and 120 on the "anger index"?

10.3 A teacher gives the following assignment to 200 students: Check the local newspaper every morning for a week and count how many times the word "gun" is mentioned on the "local news" pages. At the end of the week, the students report their totals. The mean result is 85, with a standard deviation of 8. The distribution of scores is normal.

   a. How many students would be expected to count fewer than 70 cases?

   b. How many students would be expected to count between 80 and 90 cases?

   c. Karen is a notoriously lazy student. She reports a total of 110 cases at the end of the week. The professor tells her that he is convinced she has not done the assignment, but has simply made up the number. Are his suspicions justified?

10.4 The professors who teach the Introduction to Psychology course at State University pride themselves on the normal distributions of exam scores. After the first exam, the current professor reports to the class that the mean for the exam was 73, with a standard deviation of 7.

   a. What proportion of student would be expected to score above 80?

   b What proportion of students would be expected to score between 55 and 75?

   c. What proportion of students would be expected to score less than 65?

   d. If the top 10% of the class receive an A for the exam, what score would be required for a student to receive an A?

   e. If the bottom 10% of the class fail the exam, what score would earn a student a failing grade?

10.5 A noted criminologist, Leslie Wilkins, has suggested that the distribution of deviance in the population follows a normal bell-shaped curve, with "sinners" at one extreme, "saints" at the other, and most of us falling somewhere in between the two. Working on the basis of this theory, a researcher constructs a detailed self-report survey whereby individuals are given a score based on the offenses they have committed in the past year, with the score weighted according to the relative triviality or seriousness of each offense. The lower the score, the nearer the individual approximates "sinner" status, and the higher the score, the closer he or she is to being a "saint." From his initial sample of 100 adults in a specific state, the researcher computes a mean score of 30, with a standard deviation of 5.

    a. If the researcher's model is correct, below which score should he expect to find the 5% of U.S. society with the greatest propensity to deviance?

    b. In his sample of 100, the researcher is surprised to discover that 50 subjects score greater than 35 on the deviance test. How many cases would be expected under the assumption of a normal distribution of saints and sinners? What does this suggest about the original theory?

10.6 An established test measuring "respect for authority" has a mean among U.S. adults of 73 and a standard error of 13.8. Brenda gives the test to 36 prison inmates and finds the mean score to be 69.

    a. Is this enough evidence to suggest that the prisoners belong to a population that has significantly less respect for authority than the general U.S. adult population?

    b. Assuming there is enough information, test whether this sample differs significantly from the population. Use a significance level of 5% and outline each of the stages of a test of statistical significance.

10.7 The governor of Stretford Prison has a biographical record of all the inmates. The mean age of all the inmates is 22, with a standard deviation of 7.5. A recent survey by a hostile researcher makes damaging criticisms of the educational standards in the prison. The prison governor suspects that the 50 prisoners interviewed for the study were not chosen at random. The mean age of the prisoners chosen is 20. Show how a test for statistical significance can be used by the governor to cast doubt on the sampling method of the survey. Use a significance level of 5% and outline each of the stages of a test of statistical significance.

10.8 A hundred years ago, an anonymous scientist wrote a famous indictment of a notoriously cruel prison somewhere in the United States. Without ever referring to the prison by name, the scientist checked the records of all those who were imprisoned over its 50-year history and found that 15% of those who entered died within. Henry, a historian, is intrigued by the old report and publishes an article in a historical journal in which he states his conviction that the report was referring to Grimsville Prison, which existed about that time. In a subsequent issue of the journal, a rival historian claims that Henry has shown no evidence to support his theory.

Henry finds the records from Grimsville, and from a sample of 80 prisoner records he discovers that 11% of the prisoners died inside. Can he use this information to substantiate his claim that the object of the report is indeed Grimsville? Use a significance level of 5% and outline each of the stages of a test of statistical significance.

10.9 Every pupil at Foggy Lane College was asked a series of questions, which led to an overall score grading "satisfaction" with the college's discipline procedures. The overall mean score was 65. Roger suspects that the black students at the college feel differently. He takes a random sample of 25 black students from the college and finds that their mean satisfaction score is 61, with a standard deviation of 8.

Are the black students' views on discipline significantly different from those of the general student population? Use a significance level of 1% and outline each of the stages of a test of statistical significance.

10.10 A special police unit has spent several years tracking all the members of a large child-abuse ring. In an interview with a daily newspaper, a junior detective on the unit claims that the ringleaders have been tracked down and will shortly be arrested. In response to questions from the interviewer about the makeup of the child-abuse ring, the detective replies, "We have gathered details on every last member of this criminal group—they come from very varied backgrounds and their average age is 36."

X is the chairperson of a charitable club, which is in fact a front for a substantial child-abuse circle. He reads the newspaper article and fears that it might refer to him and his group. He looks through the club's membership files and draws a sample of 50 members, finding an average age of 40 with a standard deviation of 9.

Can X be confident that the detective interviewed in the newspaper was not referring to *his* criminal group?

10.11 A civil rights group is concerned that Hispanic drug offenders are being treated more severely than all drug offenders in Border State. A state government web site reports that all drug offenders were sentenced to an average of 67 months in prison. The group conducts a small study by taking a random sample of public court records. For the 13 Hispanic drug offenders in the sample, the average sentence was 72 months ($s = 8.4$). Use a 5% significance level and test whether Hispanic drug offenders in Border State are sentenced more severely. Be sure to outline the steps in a test of statistical significance.

10.12 A researcher believes that offenders who are arrested for committing homicides in her city are younger than the national average. A review of FBI arrest statistics for recent years indicates that the mean age of homicide offenders is 18.7. The researcher collects information on a random sample of 25 persons arrested for homicide in her city and finds the mean age to be 16.8, with a standard deviation of 4.1. Can the researcher conclude that homicide offenders in her city are younger than the national average? Use a significance level of 0.05. Be sure to outline the steps in a test of statistical significance.

10.13 Following a revolution, the new leadership of the nation of Kippax decides to hold a national referendum on whether the practice of capital punishment should be introduced. In the buildup to the referendum, a leading army general wishes to gauge how the people are likely to vote so that he can make a public statement in line with popular feeling on the issue. He commissions Greg, a statistician, to carry out a secret poll of how people expect to vote. The results of Greg's poll are as follows: The sample proportion in favor of introducing capital punishment is 52%.

   Do the results indicate that the majority of the population favors introducing capital punishment? Use a significance level of 5% and outline each of the stages of a test of statistical significance.

10.14 The Silver Star Treatment Center claims to be effective at reducing drug addiction among the persons who go through its treatment regimen. As evidence of the effectiveness of the Silver Star treatment, the director claims that 63% of all drug users nationally have a relapse within 12 months of treatment, but in a random sample of 91 cases treated by Silver Star, only 52% had a relapse within 12 months of completing the treatment. Use a 1% level of significance to test whether Silver Star's treatment is effective at reducing drug use. Be sure to outline the steps in a test of statistical significance.

10.15 A federal judge issues an opinion claiming that nonviolent drug offenders should make up no more than 20% of the local jail population. If a jail is found to have more than 20% nonviolent drug offenders, the jail will fall under court order and be required to release inmates until the composition of the jail population conforms to the judge's standard. The local sheriff draws a random sample of 33 inmates and finds that 23% have been convicted of nonviolent drug offenses. Should the sheriff be concerned about the jail coming under court supervision? Use a significance level of 0.05. Be sure to outline the steps in a test of statistical significance.

chapter eleven

Comparing Means and Proportions in Two Samples

comparing sample means

What Is the Two-Sample *t*-Test for Means?

What Are the Assumptions of the Test?

How Is the Test Carried Out?

comparing sample proportions

What Is the Two-Sample *t*-Test for Proportions?

What Are the Assumptions of the Test?

How Is the Test Carried Out?

comparing means in samples that are not independent

What Is the *t*-Test for Dependent Samples?

What Are the Assumptions of the Test?

How Is the Test Carried Out?

IN CHAPTER 10, we used parametric significance tests to compare the mean or proportion of a single sample with a population goal or parameter. In this chapter, we turn to a more commonly used application of parametric tests of statistical significance: comparisons between samples. Let's say, for example, that you are interested in whether there is a difference in the mean salaries of male and female police officers or in the proportions of African Americans and others arrested last year. Your question in either of these cases is not whether the population parameters have particular values, but whether the parameters for the groups examined in each case are different. This involves comparing means and proportions for two populations. If you take samples from these populations, you can make inferences regarding the differences between them by building on the normal distribution tests covered in Chapter 10.

Comparing Sample Means

The Case of Anxiety Among Police Officers and Firefighters

In a study conducted by University of Washington researchers, police officers were compared to firefighters in terms of the amount of stress and anxiety they experienced on the job.[1] One measure the researchers used was derived by creating an interval-scale index from questions about the occurrence on the job of symptoms of anxiety, such as sweating and "the jitters." The researchers drew a sample of police officers by going to police stations and asking officers to be paid participants in their study. For firefighters, the researchers randomly selected subjects. The final sample,

---

[1]Michael Pendleton, Ezra Stotland, Philip Spiers, and Edward Kirsch, "Stress and Strain among Police, Firefighters, and Government Workers: A Comparative Analysis," *Criminal Justice and Behavior* 16 (1989): 196–210.

all drawn from one city, included 127 firefighters and 197 police officers. For this sample, the researchers found that the mean anxiety-on-the-job score for police officers was 12.8 ($s_1 = 2.76$), whereas that for firefighters was 8.8 ($s_2 = 2.85$). What conclusions regarding the larger populations of firefighters and police officers can the researchers draw from these sample statistics?

As in other problems involving comparisons between the means of two groups, we are not able to define the standard deviations of the population distributions for our test. Indeed, we conduct a test of statistical significance for the differences between the two samples precisely because we do not have information on the population parameters. Accordingly, we turn again to the t-test introduced in Chapter 10. In this case, we use a **two-sample t-test** for means.

Assumptions:

Level of Measurement: Interval scale.

Population Distribution: Normal distribution in both populations (relaxed because N is large).

Sampling Method: Independent random sampling (a nonrandom sampling technique was used for police officers; random sampling without replacement was used for firefighters).

Sampling Frame: All police officers and firefighters in one city.

Hypotheses:

H_0: The mean anxiety-on-the-job score for the population of police officers is the same as that for the population of firefighters ($\mu_1 = \mu_2$).

H_1: The mean anxiety-on-the-job score for the population of police officers is different from that for the population of firefighters ($\mu_1 \neq \mu_2$).

The assumptions for the two-sample t-test are similar to those for the one-sample t-test. An interval level of measurement is assumed, and indeed the characteristic being examined, anxiety on the job, is measured at the interval-scale level. The two-sample t-test also requires that both population distributions be normal in form. When this is the case, the sampling distribution of the difference between means—the focus of our test—is also normally distributed. Even when the populations examined are not normally distributed, the sampling distribution of the difference between the sample means will be normally distributed if the N of cases for both samples is large.

The definition of how large samples must be to invoke the central limit theorem is again a matter of debate. In Chapter 10, we noted that a sample size of 30 or more was generally large enough to apply the central limit theorem in a single-sample test for means. For a two-sample test, we need a minimum of 30 cases in each sample. In our example, both samples include a much larger number of subjects, and thus we can relax the assumption of normality.

As with other tests we have examined, here we are required to use an independent random sampling method. For a two-sample *t*-test, we must assume that both samples are independent random samples. In practice, researchers do not ordinarily use separate sampling procedures to identify the samples representing each population of interest. Rather, they draw a random sample from all members of a population and then assume that specific samples within the larger sample are also independent and random. For example, researchers interested in attitudes toward crime in the United States generally draw an independent random sample of all U.S. residents. They may, however, also have an interest in comparing attitudes of men and women or of college graduates and non–college graduates. If the larger sample has been drawn as an independent random sample, the subsamples are also independent random samples.[2]

The one practical difficulty with this assumption arises when the number of subjects in a particular subpopulation is small. For example, in a survey of U.S. residents, a very small group of Jews or Muslims is likely to be sampled when researchers draw a simple independent random sample. Thus, even though such a subsample will still be independent and random (if the larger sample is independent and random), researchers may not end up with many cases because such a group represents a small proportion of the U.S. population. When there is interest in a subpopulation that is small, researchers often identify such groups for special attention and attempt to draw larger samples from them.

For the firefighters in our example, the researchers used a random sampling method, but they did not sample with replacement. This violation of assumptions is not serious because the sample of firefighters drawn was small relative to the number of subjects in the sampling frame. The method of sampling for police officers represents a more serious violation of the assumptions of the two-sample *t*-test. The researchers did not draw a random sample. Nonetheless, they argued that

---

[2]The logic here follows simple common sense. If you select each case independently and randomly from a population, on each selection you have an equal probability of choosing any individual, whether male or female, college-educated or not, and so on. From the perspective of a particular group—for example, males—each time you choose a man, the method can be seen as independent and random. That is, the likelihood of choosing any male from the sample is the same each time you draw a case. Of course, sometimes you will draw a female. However, within the population of males, each male has an equal chance of selection on each draw. And if the sampling method is independent, then each male has an equal chance of being selected every time a case is selected.

their sample was still representative of the population of police officers in the city:

Participant officers were compared with nonparticipant officers on available data (which were acquired by the police department independently of the study). These data included entrance psychological tests, current departmental physical fitness tests, age, sex, and so on. . . . The participant and nonparticipant groups did not differ significantly on 25 comparison variables.

The validity of our inferences to the larger population of police officers in the city depends on how persuasive we find the researchers' claims that their sample was representative. But irrespective of the generalizability of these samples to the population of police officers and firefighters in the city, the researchers also want to infer their findings beyond their sampling frame to police officers and firefighters more generally. For this inference to be justified, the researchers would have to explain why firefighters and police officers in this city are representative of firefighters and police officers in other cities.

The null hypothesis for a difference of means test is generally that there is no difference, and this was the case in the University of Washington research. The null hypothesis stated simply that the mean anxiety-on-the-job score for the populations of police officers (μ_1) and firefighters (μ_2) is the same ($\mu_1 = \mu_2$). The research hypothesis was that there is a difference ($\mu_1 \neq \mu_2$). The researchers did not define the direction of this difference. Their research hypothesis allows the possibility that police officers experience more anxiety at work than firefighters as well as the option that firefighters experience more anxiety at work than police officers.

The Sampling Distribution   For a difference of means test, we use the t sampling distribution. The number of degrees of freedom for the distribution is obtained by adding the numbers of cases in the two samples and subtracting 2: df $= N_1 + N_2 - 2$. For our example, the number of degrees of freedom is 322.

df $= N_1 + N_2 - 2$

$\quad = 197 + 127 - 2$

$\quad = 322$

The mean of the sampling distribution is defined, as in the case of a difference of proportions test, by the null hypothesis. It is represented by $\mu_1 - \mu_2$, or the hypothesized difference between the means of the two populations studied. Since the null hypothesis states that $\mu_1 = \mu_2$, the mean of the sampling distribution is 0.

In defining the standard error of the sampling distribution for comparing two samples, we take into account the variances of the two populations. Accordingly, the standard error of a sampling distribution of the difference of sample means ($\sigma_{sd(\bar{X}_1 - \bar{X}_2)}$) is the square root of the sum of the two sample variances, each divided by its sample N:

$$\sigma_{sd(\bar{X}_1 - \bar{X}_2)} = \sqrt{\frac{\sigma_1^2}{N_1} + \frac{\sigma_2^2}{N_2}}$$ **Equation 11.1**

In calculating this standard error, we can use either of two approaches. The first assumes that the two population distributions not only have equal means but also have equal variances. In this case, we are assuming that the two population distributions are the same. This is often called the **pooled variance** method. The assumption we make in this approach, a common one in statistical tests, is often referred to as **homoscedasticity** (from the Greek for "same scatter [or spread]"). It can be written in mathematical form as follows:

$$\sigma_1^2 = \sigma_2^2 = \sigma^2 \qquad \text{or} \qquad \sigma_1 = \sigma_2 = \sigma$$

A second approach, called the **separate variance** method, does not make a specific assumption that the variances of the two populations are equal. You should note, however, that when samples are very small or one sample is much larger than the other, the simple estimate of degrees of freedom noted above must be corrected if the separate variance method is used. The correction commonly employed involves a good deal of computation.[3] For our problem, which involves large samples of relatively similar size, it is unnecessary to take this approach.

Given that the pooled variance method requires an additional assumption, that of homoscedasticity, you might question why researchers would choose this approach to analyze the statistical significance of their study results. One advantage of the pooled variance method is that you will generally get a more efficient estimate of the standard error of your sampling distribution. This means that the pooled variance method often leads to a larger t-statistic (though this is not always the case, as illustrated later in the chapter). But should you take advantage of this method if it means that you add the risk of violating an additional assumption?

The separate variance method should be used in most circumstances. As a general rule, it is better to make fewer assumptions, because this creates less potential for violating them and coming to a mistaken conclusion. Nonetheless, sometimes your sample results or prior research suggests

---

[3]See H. M. Blalock, *Social Statistics* (New York: McGraw-Hill, 1979), p. 231.

strongly that an assumption of equal variances can be made. For example, if there is little difference in the standard deviations you find in your samples, you may be able to conclude with confidence that the population standard deviations do not differ.[4] If, in turn, prior studies show that the standard deviations between the groups studied are very similar, this might also lead you to apply this assumption in your test. Most statistical analysis computer programs provide test outcomes for both of these options with the correct degrees of freedom applied.

How are the two methods different in practice? Let's start with the pooled variance approach.

If we assume that the two populations of interest have equal variances, we can simplify Equation 11.1, which defines the standard error of the sampling distribution ($\sigma_{sd(\overline{X}_1 - \overline{X}_2)}$) for a difference of means test. This simplification process is outlined in the box on page 261. The simplified formula is given in Equation 11.2.

$$\sigma_{sd(\overline{X}_1 - \overline{X}_2)} = \sigma \sqrt{\frac{N_1 + N_2}{N_1 N_2}} \qquad \textbf{Equation 11.2}$$

Because we do not know the actual value of σ, we rewrite the equation, substituting an estimate of σ, or $\hat{\sigma}$, as shown in Equation 11.3.

$$\hat{\sigma}_{sd(\overline{X}_1 - \overline{X}_2)} = \hat{\sigma} \sqrt{\frac{N_1 + N_2}{N_1 N_2}} \qquad \textbf{Equation 11.3}$$

This, of course, creates another problem for us. How do we calculate $\hat{\sigma}$? We now have two estimates of the sample variance, one from each sample. And we also need to take into account the bias associated with using s^2 to estimate $\hat{\sigma}$, as discussed in Chapter 10. Our solution to the former problem is to weight the two sample variances by the N of cases in each sample. This is only fair, because the larger sample is likely to provide a better estimate of the joint standard deviation than the smaller sample. We include a correction for bias of the sample variances directly in our estimate of σ by subtracting 2 (1 for each sample) in the denominator of the equation, as shown in Equation 11.4.

$$\hat{\sigma} = \sqrt{\frac{N_1 s_1^2 + N_2 s_2^2}{N_1 + N_2 - 2}} \qquad \textbf{Equation 11.4}$$

---

[4]A test of statistical significance may be performed to assess differences in variances. It is based on the F distribution, which is discussed in detail in Chapter 12. The test takes a ratio of the two variances being examined:

$$F = \frac{\hat{\sigma}^2_{\text{larger variance}}}{\hat{\sigma}^2_{\text{smaller variance}}}$$

To work out the pooled variance method for our example, we first estimate the pooled standard deviation for the two populations, which provides a result of 2.8043. We then calculate the standard error ($\hat{\sigma}_{\text{sd}(\bar{X}_1 - \bar{X}_2)}$) for our sampling distribution. Our result is 0.3191.

W orking It Out

$$\hat{\sigma} = \sqrt{\frac{N_1 s_1^2 + N_2 s_2^2}{N_1 + N_2 - 2}}$$

$$= \sqrt{\frac{(197)(2.76)^2 + (127)(2.85)^2}{197 + 127 - 2}}$$

$$= \sqrt{\frac{2{,}532.22}{322}}$$

$$= \sqrt{7.86405}$$

$$= 2.8043$$

W orking It Out

$$\hat{\sigma}_{\text{sd}(\bar{X}_1 - \bar{X}_2)} = \hat{\sigma}\sqrt{\frac{N_1 + N_2}{N_1 N_2}}$$

$$= 2.804\sqrt{\frac{197 + 127}{(197)(127)}}$$

$$= 2.804\sqrt{0.01295}$$

$$= 0.3191$$

How does the pooled variance method differ from the separate variance method? We once again begin with Equation 11.1. Because σ_1^2 and σ_2^2 are unknown, we use s_1^2 and s_2^2 to gain an estimate of $\hat{\sigma}_{sd(\overline{X}_1 - \overline{X}_2)}$. In turn, as before, the variances of our samples are not considered unbiased estimates of the variances of the population distributions. Accordingly, in order to obtain an unbiased estimate of the standard error using this method, we need once more to adjust the equations—in this case, by subtracting 1 from the denominator of each variance estimate, as shown in Equation 11.5.

$$\hat{\sigma}_{sd(\overline{X}_1 - \overline{X}_2)} = \sqrt{\frac{s_1^2}{N_1 - 1} + \frac{s_2^2}{N_2 - 1}}$$ **Equation 11.5**

Based on the sample variances of police officers and firefighters in our example, we get 0.321 as an estimate of the standard error of the two-sample t-text using the separate variance method.

Working It Out

$$\hat{\sigma}_{sd(\overline{X}_1 - \overline{X}_2)} = \sqrt{\frac{s_1^2}{N_1 - 1} + \frac{s_2^2}{N_2 - 1}}$$

$$= \sqrt{\frac{(2.76)^2}{197 - 1} + \frac{(2.85)^2}{127 - 1}}$$

$$= 0.3214$$

As you can see, the result found using the pooled variance method (0.319) is very similar to that found using the separate variance method (0.321). This will often be the case, especially when samples are relatively large or evenly divided between the two groups. Nonetheless, even small differences can sometimes affect the conclusions you reach in a two-sample t-test.

Significance Level and Rejection Region   The University of Washington researchers used a 0.05 significance level and a two-tailed significance test. The two-tailed test was based on their nondirectional research hypothesis, which stated simply that there is a difference in anxiety-on-the-job scores between firefighters and police officers.

Interpolating from the t table (see Appendix 4), we find that a t-value of about 1.97 is associated with a two-tailed 5% significance threshold (with 322 degrees of freedom). This means that a test statistic greater than 1.97 or less than −1.97 is needed to reject the null hypothesis.

The Test Statistic   To define the t-score appropriate for our test, we must alter the single-sample t-test equation to account for the fact that we are comparing two samples. First, we must adjust the numerator to reflect our comparisons of the differences in the means observed in our study with those defined in the null hypothesis. Second, we must adjust the denominator to reflect the standard error of the difference between means. Because we now have two methods for defining the standard error of the sampling distribution, we have two separate equations. The first reflects the difference of means test using a separate variance estimate (11.6a), and the second the difference of means test using a pooled variance estimate (11.6b).

$$t = \frac{(\overline{X}_1 - \overline{X}_2) - (\mu_1 - \mu_2)}{\sqrt{\dfrac{s_1^2}{N_1 - 1} + \dfrac{s_2^2}{N_2 - 1}}}$$

Equation 11.6a
Separate Variance Method

$$t = \frac{(\overline{X}_1 - \overline{X}_2) - (\mu_1 - \mu_2)}{\hat{\sigma}\sqrt{\dfrac{N_1 + N_2}{N_1 N_2}}}$$

Equation 11.6b
Pooled Variance Method

Both Equation 11.6a and Equation 11.6b have two quantities in the numerator. The first is the difference between the two sample means (represented by $\overline{X}_1 - \overline{X}_2$). The second is the difference between the two population means ($\mu_1 - \mu_2$) as defined by the null hypothesis. Because the null hypothesis is that the two populations are equal, this quantity is equal to 0.

In the denominator in each equation, the standard error used for a sampling distribution when comparing a sample mean to a population mean has been replaced with the standard error used when comparing sample means drawn from two populations. This quantity was defined in our discussion of the sampling distribution.

The t-score for this problem is 12.461 using the separate variance estimate and 12.539 using the pooled variance estimate. As recommended (although the differences are small in this case), we use the separate variance method in making our decision.

Working It Out   **Separate Variance**

$$t = \frac{(\overline{X}_1 - \overline{X}_2) - (\mu_1 - \mu_2)}{\sqrt{\dfrac{s_1^2}{N_1 - 1} + \dfrac{s_2^2}{N_2 - 1}}}$$

$$= \frac{(12.8 - 8.8) - 0}{\sqrt{\dfrac{(2.76)^2}{197 - 1} + \dfrac{(2.85)^2}{127 - 1}}}$$

$$= \frac{4}{0.3214}$$

$$= 12.4456$$

Working It Out   **Pooled Variance**

$$t = \frac{(\overline{X}_1 - \overline{X}_2) - (\mu_1 - \mu_2)}{\hat{\sigma}\sqrt{\dfrac{N_1 + N_2}{N_1 N_2}}}, \quad \text{where } \hat{\sigma} = \sqrt{\frac{N_1 s_1^2 + N_2 s_2^2}{N_1 + N_2 - 2}}$$

$$t = \frac{(\overline{X}_1 - \overline{X}_2) - (\mu_1 - \mu_2)}{\sqrt{\dfrac{N_1 s_1^2 + N_2 s_2^2}{N_1 + N_2 - 2}}\sqrt{\dfrac{N_1 + N_2}{N_1 N_2}}}$$

$$= \frac{(12.8 - 8.8) - 0}{\sqrt{\dfrac{(197)(2.76)^2 + (127)(2.85)^2}{197 + 127 - 2}}\sqrt{\dfrac{197 + 127}{(197)(127)}}}$$

$$= \frac{4}{0.3191}$$

$$= 12.5353$$

The Decision   Because our test statistic of 12.4456 is larger than the critical value of our rejection region of 1.97, we reject the null hypothesis that there is no difference in anxiety-on-the-job scores between the populations of police officers and firefighters to which our test infers. For our test, the observed significance level is less than the significance threshold we set at the outset ($p < 0.05$).

Bail in Los Angeles County: Another Example of the Two-Sample t-Test for Means

As a second example of the two-sample t-test for means, we will examine a study of bail setting in Los Angeles County in the 1990s. The *State Court Processing Statistics* database represents a random sample of felony defendants from more than 50 urban court districts in the United States. Since Los Angeles County participated in the study throughout the 1990s, data are available for 1990, 1992, 1994, and 1996.[5]

An important issue in criminal justice decision making has been the impact of the defendant's race or ethnicity on the type of decision made. We can focus on the amount of bail set as one way to begin to test for racial or ethnic differences in criminal case processing. In Los Angeles County in the 1990s, a sample of 1,121 African Americans were required to post a mean bail amount of $50,841 ($s = 115,565$). A sample of 1,798 Hispanics of any race were required to post a mean bail amount of $66,552 ($s = 190,801$). Although the difference in mean bail amounts for these two samples of defendants appears to be large (approximately $16,000$), can we conclude that this difference is statistically significant?

Assumptions

Level of Measurement: Interval scale.

Population Distribution: Normal distribution in both populations (relaxed because N is large).

Sampling Method: Independent random sampling.

Sampling Frame: All felony arrestees in Los Angeles County in the 1990s.

Hypotheses:

H_0: The mean bail amount set for the population of African American felony defendants is the same as the mean bail amount set for the population of Hispanic felony defendants of any race ($\mu_1 = \mu_2$).

H_1: The mean bail amount set for the population of African American felony defendants is different from the mean bail amount set for the population of Hispanic felony defendants of any race ($\mu_1 \neq \mu_2$).

---

[5]These data are available through the National Archive of Criminal Justice Data and can be accessed at http://www.icpsr.umich.edu/NACJD.

The Sampling Distribution Because we are interested in comparing means and σ for the population distributions is unknown, we use a t-test for means. Since the number of cases in each sample is large, we can relax the normality assumption for this test. The number of degrees of freedom for the test is df $= N_1 + N_2 - 2 = 1{,}121 + 1{,}798 - 2 = 2{,}917$.

Significance Level and Rejection Region Let's assume that we want to set a fairly strict level of statistical significance for this test—say, 0.01. We might argue that we are particularly concerned with a Type I error in this example, since concluding that there are racial differences may have very important implications for the criminal justice system. At the same time, there is no stated reason for expecting one group to have higher bail amounts than the other group, so we use a two-tailed test. Given that we have 2,917 degrees of freedom, a significance level of 0.01, and a two-tailed test, we can consult the t distribution table and determine that our critical values for this analysis are ± 2.576. If the test statistic is greater than $+2.576$ or less than -2.576, then it falls into the rejection region for the test, and we will conclude that bail amounts set are not equal across the two felony groups of defendants.

The Test Statistic We calculate the test statistic using both the separate variance and the pooled variance methods. As we demonstrate below, the t-score is -2.7694 using the separate variance method and -2.4863 using the pooled variance method. Following the earlier recommendation, we will use the separate variance method in making our decision about the null hypothesis.

Working It Out   **Separate Variance Method**

$$t = \frac{(\bar{X}_1 - \bar{X}_2) - (\mu_1 - \mu_2)}{\sqrt{\dfrac{s_1^2}{N_1 - 1} + \dfrac{s_2^2}{N_2 - 1}}}$$

$$= \frac{(50{,}841 - 66{,}552) - 0}{\sqrt{\dfrac{115{,}565^2}{1{,}121 - 1} + \dfrac{190{,}801^2}{1{,}798 - 1}}}$$

$$= \frac{-15{,}711}{5{,}673.02}$$

$$= -2.7694$$

> ### **W**orking It Out   Pooled Variance Method
>
> $$t = \frac{(\overline{X}_1 - \overline{X}_2) - (\mu_1 - \mu_2)}{\hat{\sigma}\sqrt{\dfrac{N_1 + N_2}{N_1 N_2}}}, \quad \text{where } \hat{\sigma} = \sqrt{\frac{N_1 s_1^2 + N_2 s_2^2}{N_1 + N_2 - 2}}$$
>
> $$= \frac{(\overline{X}_1 - \overline{X}_2) - (\mu_1 - \mu_2)}{\sqrt{\dfrac{N_1 s_1^2 + N_2 s_2^2}{N_1 + N_2 - 2}}\sqrt{\dfrac{N_1 + N_2}{N_1 N_2}}}$$
>
> $$= \frac{(50{,}841 - 66{,}552) - 0}{\sqrt{\dfrac{(1{,}121)(115{,}565)^2 + (1{,}798)(190{,}801)^2}{1{,}121 + 1{,}798 - 2}}\sqrt{\dfrac{1{,}121 + 1{,}798}{(1{,}121)(1{,}798)}}}$$
>
> $$= \frac{-15{,}711}{6{,}319.07}$$
>
> $$= -2.4863$$

The Decision   Because our test statistic of -2.7694 is less than the critical value of -2.576, we reject the null hypothesis that there is no difference in bail amounts set for African Americans and Hispanics of any race in Los Angeles County. In this case, it is interesting to note that if we had used the pooled variance method, we would have failed to reject the null hypothesis. This points to the importance of making your assumptions before you see the study results.

Comparing Sample Proportions: The Two-Sample *t*-Test for Differences of Proportions

As we noted in Chapter 10, one implication of the central limit theorem is that we can use a normal sampling distribution to test hypotheses involving proportions. While the mean and standard deviation are not appropriate statistics to use with a nominal-level measure such as a proportion, the sampling distribution of a proportion begins to approximate a normal distribution when the number of cases for the sample becomes large. The central tendency of this distribution and its dispersion are measured by the mean and standard error, just as for distributions that develop from interval-level data. In a difference of proportions test, our interest is in the difference between the populations studied. This difference is also a proportion. Though it would be inappropriate to use the mean and standard deviation to describe the sample or population distribution of this proportion, the mean and standard error are appropriate statistics for describing the normal sampling distribution that is associated with this proportion.

At the same time, we generally cannot use the z-test for conducting a difference of proportions test. Rather, as in the previous examples, we rely on the t distribution to test our null hypothesis. You may wonder why we use the t-test rather than the z-test for making statistical inferences in the case of a difference of proportions. A t-test is used when the standard deviation of the population distribution is unknown and must be estimated. In Chapter 10, we noted that when we stated the proportion of successes expected under the null hypothesis, we also stated by implication the mean and the standard deviation of the population distribution of scores and thus the mean and the standard error of the sampling distribution for our test. Why can't we just rely on the same logic to produce the mean and the standard error for a test comparing two proportions?

In fact, we again define the mean of the sampling distribution for such a test through the null hypothesis. For a difference of proportions test, the null hypothesis is ordinarily that there is no difference between the proportions of the two populations to which we seek to infer. This null hypothesis defines the mean of our sampling distribution: no difference, or zero.

As noted earlier in the chapter, in defining the standard error of our sampling distribution, we take into account the variances of the two populations. Our problem is that defining the standard error requires knowing the values of P and Q for each of the two populations we are interested in. (This is the case because we obtain the variance of a proportion by taking the product of P and Q; see Chapter 10, page 238.) But the null hypothesis states only that the proportions of the two populations are equal; it does not tell us the value of those proportions. Because of this, when testing for differences of proportions, the researcher must apply a t rather than a z distribution to his or her test.[6] If the standard deviations for each distribution were known, it would not be neces-

---

[6]In practice, many statistics texts use the z-test for examples involving proportions. Generally this is done because a difference of proportions test is appropriate only for larger samples, and with larger samples, there is substantively little difference between the outcomes of these two normal distribution tests. We illustrate a difference of proportions problem using a t-test because it follows the logic outlined in Chapter 10. That is, in the case where σ is unknown, a t-test should be used. Moreover, most packaged statistical programs provide outcomes only in terms of t-tests.

sary for the researcher to conduct a statistical test of significance at all. In this case, the value of the proportion for each of the two populations would be known by implication.

The Case of Drug Testing and Pretrial Misconduct

In a study conducted in Maricopa County, Arizona, criminal justice researchers examined whether drug testing of defendants released before trial had an impact on pretrial misconduct.[7] They compared two groups of defendants who were released before trial. The first group was monitored through drug testing twice a week. The second group was released without subsequent drug testing. The sample was chosen over a six-month period. The researchers identified subjects for the study through identification numbers kept in a computerized case-management system. Defendants with odd identification numbers were placed in the drug-testing group. Defendants with even identification numbers were placed in the control, or no-drug-testing, group. The drug-testing group had 118 subjects. The control group had 116 subjects.

The researchers followed up on both of these groups of defendants for 90 days. One measure of pretrial misconduct was failure to appear at a hearing during the follow-up period. A total of 38% of the control group and 30% of the drug-testing group failed to appear at a hearing during this period. The question the researchers wanted to answer was whether they could infer from the difference between these two samples that there was in fact a difference in pretrial misconduct between the populations these samples represent. A two-sample t-test is an appropriate statistical test with which to answer this question.

Assumptions:

Level of Measurement: Interval scale (failure to appear is measured as a proportion).

Population Distribution: Normal distribution in both populations (relaxed because N is large).

Sampling Method: Independent random sampling (all cases for six months are selected).

Sampling Frame: Defendants released before trial for a six-month period in Maricopa County, Arizona.

[7]See Chester Britt III, Michael Gottfredson, and John S. Goldkamp, "Drug Testing and Pretrial Misconduct: An Experiment on the Specific Deterrent Effects of Drug Monitoring Defendants on Pretrial Release," *Journal of Research in Crime and Delinquency* 29 (1992): 62–78.

Hypotheses:

H_0: The two populations do not differ in terms of the proportion who fail to appear for a pretrial hearing ($P_1 = P_2$).

H_1: Defendants subject to drug testing will be more likely to appear for a pretrial hearing ($P_1 < P_2$).

The two-sample *t*-test requires an interval level of measurement, as well as a normal population distribution for each of the two samples examined. The actual level of measurement for our example (as stated in parentheses in our assumptions) is nominal—we compare two proportions. As with a single-sample test of proportions, when the sample sizes are large, we can relax assumptions regarding the level of measurement used and the shape of the populations examined. Because we have two samples and not just one, the central limit theorem applies only if both samples are large. The definition of how large samples must be to invoke the central limit theorem in the case of a difference of proportions test is a matter of debate. However, when each sample includes more than 100 cases, as is true for the Arizona study, there will be little argument regarding the use of this parametric test for proportions.

We must again assume that both samples are independent random samples. In our example, the researchers did not draw an independent random sample for either the drug-testing group or the control group. Rather, as was the case with the cell-allocation study examined in Chapter 9, they sampled all defendants released before trial in Maricopa County for a specific period of time—in this case, six months. In order to create the two samples, the researchers assigned the defendants to the groups according to their identification numbers: Even-numbered subjects were assigned to the control group, and odd-numbered subjects to the drug-testing group.

In making statistical inferences, the researchers were clearly interested in inferring beyond their sampling frame (defendants released before trial during the six-month period), not only to other time periods in Maricopa County but also to other jurisdictions and other programs similar to the one they studied.[8] They argued that their findings were likely to apply to other "sophisticated and experienced pretrial services agencies." They also noted that it "is reasonable to assume that the programs that were implemented are comparable to the programs that are likely to be implemented in similar agencies." When drawing conclusions from this research, we would have to consider whether the sample used can in fact be seen as representative of these larger populations.

---

[8]In fact, although we do not examine their findings here, Britt and colleagues conducted their study in two Arizona counties.

Our final assumptions relate to the hypotheses. The null hypothesis, as for earlier tests, is that there is no difference. It assumes that those monitored through drug testing and those not so monitored (the control group) will have the same proportion of defendants who fail to appear. Another way of expressing this is to say that the proportion of failures to appear in the drug-tested population (P_1) of released defendants is the same as that in the population that is not drug-tested (P_2), or that $P_1 = P_2$. The researchers chose a directional research hypothesis because they were concerned only with the possibility that the program decreased the likelihood that offenders would fail to appear for a pretrial hearing. Accordingly, the research hypothesis was stated as $P_1 < P_2$. The researchers were interested in testing whether drug testing would increase compliance.

The Sampling Distribution Because N is large for both samples, we can use a t distribution as the sampling distribution for testing the difference between proportions. The number of degrees of freedom for the distribution is obtained by adding the numbers of cases in the two samples and subtracting 2: df $= N_1 + N_2 - 2$. In our example, the number of degrees of freedom equals $118 + 116 - 2$, or 232.

As we noted earlier, the null hypothesis defines the mean of the sampling distribution we will use for our test. The mean of the sampling distribution is $P_1 - P_2$, or simply 0, because the null hypothesis states that the two population proportions are the same.

In defining the standard error of the sampling distribution, we can rely on the pooled variance approach. This is always the case when we are examining differences between proportions. When we assume in the null hypothesis that the two population proportions are the same, then by implication we also assume that the two standard deviations for these population distributions are also equal. This fact derives from the method by which the population variances are calculated. As noted in Chapter 10, the variance of a proportion is

$$\sigma^2 = PQ$$

and the standard deviation of a proportion is

$$\sigma = \sqrt{PQ}$$

Accordingly, if P is the same for two populations, then we can also assume that the variances of those populations are equal. In statistical terms, as we noted earlier, this is defined as the assumption of homoscedasticity.

Significance Level and Rejection Region   The researchers in the Maricopa County study decided to use "conventional levels" of statistical significance—that is, a rejection region of $\alpha = 0.05$. Following their research hypothesis, they also used a one-tailed test of statistical significance. Given that we have 232 degrees of freedom, a significance level of 0.05, and a one-tailed test, we can consult the t distribution table and determine that the critical value for this analysis is -1.654. If the test statistic is less than -1.654, then it falls into the rejection region for this test.

The Test Statistic   To define the t-score appropriate for our test, we must alter the formula for a t-test of means to take into account the fact that we are examining sample proportions. Accordingly, we replace the difference between the sample means $(\overline{X}_1 - \overline{X}_2)$ with the difference between the sample proportions $(p_1 - p_2)$. We also replace the assumed differences between the population means with $(P_1 - P_2)$, as stated by the null hypothesis. Because the null hypothesis states that the two populations are equal, this quantity is equal to 0. Equation 11.7 presents a modified formula for calculating the t-statistic for proportions.

$$t = \frac{(p_1 - p_2) - (P_1 - P_2)}{\hat{\sigma}\sqrt{\dfrac{N_1 + N_2}{N_1 N_2}}}, \quad \text{where } \hat{\sigma} = \sqrt{\frac{N_1 s_1^2 + N_2 s_2^2}{N_1 + N_2 - 2}} \qquad \text{Equation 11.7}$$

$$= \frac{(p_1 - p_2) - (P_1 - P_2)}{\sqrt{\dfrac{N_1 s_1^2 + N_2 s_2^2}{N_1 + N_2 - 2}}\sqrt{\dfrac{N_1 + N_2}{N_1 N_2}}}$$

Below we calculate the t-statistic for our test. Note that we must first calculate the variance for each of the sample proportions. To calculate the variance of a sample proportion, we use the formula $s^2 = pq$. This formula is identical to that presented above for the variance of a population proportion. The only difference here is the use of the symbols p, q, and s to represent sample rather than population estimates. For our example, $s_1^2 = (0.3)(0.7) = 0.21$ and $s_2^2 = (0.38)(0.62) = 0.2356$.

After inserting the values for the two sample variances (s_1^2 and s_2^2) into Equation 11.7, we obtain a t-statistic equal to -1.29.

W orking It Out   Pooled Variance Method

$$t = \frac{(p_1 - p_2) - (P_1 - P_2)}{\hat{\sigma}\sqrt{\dfrac{N_1 + N_2}{N_1 N_2}}}, \quad \text{where } \hat{\sigma} = \sqrt{\frac{N_1 s_1^2 + N_2 s_2^2}{N_1 + N_2 - 2}}$$

$$= \frac{(p_1 - p_2) - (P_1 - P_2)}{\sqrt{\dfrac{N_1 s_1^2 + N_2 s_2^2}{N_1 + N_2 - 2}}\sqrt{\dfrac{N_1 + N_2}{N_1 N_2}}}$$

$$= \frac{(0.30 - 0.38) - 0}{\sqrt{\dfrac{(118)(0.21) + (116)(0.2356)}{118 + 116 - 2}}\sqrt{\dfrac{118 + 116}{(118)(116)}}}$$

$$= \frac{-0.08}{0.062}$$

$$= -1.29$$

The Decision   Because our test statistic of -1.29 is greater than the critical value of -1.654, we fail to reject the null hypothesis that there is no difference in failure to appear at hearings for the drug testing and control populations. Based on these and other similar results, the researchers in this study concluded that "systematic drug testing and monitoring in the pretrial setting, in programs such as those described above [i.e., examined in this research], is not likely to achieve significant" change in pretrial misconduct.

The *t*-Test for Dependent Samples

One of the requirements of the two-sample *t*-test is that the samples examined be independent. However, sometimes criminal justice researchers examine samples that are not independent. For example, subjects may be matched and placed in like pairs based on such characteristics as social status, education, gender, age, and IQ. Dependent samples will also result when a researcher takes measurements on the same subject or unit of analysis over time. For example, a researcher may examine the attitudes of juvenile delinquents before and after participation in a specific program or may study changes at specific crime hot spots before and after some type of police intervention. Sometimes the same individuals are compared at different ages or stages in their development. Even though in such instances the researcher has two samples of observations—for example, before and after the program—the samples are not independent.

The *t*-test for dependent samples is commonly used in such situations.[9] It focuses on the differences between the pairs in developing the sampling distribution of the test statistic. Each pair in a *t*-test for dependent samples is considered a single observation.

The Effect of Police Presence Near High-Crime Addresses

Let's suppose that a police department took an independent random sample of 35 high-crime addresses from all high-crime addresses in a city. The department then assigned a police officer to walk the beat on each block where one of the addresses was located for a full month. Assume we are asked to assess whether the strategy was effective in reducing calls for police service. We have data on the number of emergency calls for police service for the month before the officer walked the beat and for the month during which the officer walked the beat. These data are given in Table 11.1. The mean number of calls for service the month before was 30, and the mean for the month when the officer was present was 20. Can we conclude from this that the program would be effective in reducing calls for service if applied generally to high-crime addresses?

Assumptions:

Level of Measurement: Interval scale.

Population Distribution: Normal distribution (relaxed because N is large).

Sampling Method: Independent random sampling.

Sampling Frame: All high-crime addresses in the city.

Hypotheses:

H_0: There is no difference in the number of calls for service at high-crime addresses whether an officer walks the beat or not ($\mu_1 = \mu_2$).

H_1: There are fewer calls for service at high-crime addresses when an officer walks the beat ($\mu_1 > \mu_2$).

---

[9]Here we examine the *t*-test for dependent samples only in reference to mean differences for interval-level data. However, this test may also be used for dichotomous nominal-level data. Suppose you were assessing the absence or presence of some characteristic or behavior at two points in time. If each observation were coded as 0 or 1, then you would calculate the mean difference ($\bar{X}_d$) and the standard deviation of the difference (s_d) using the same equations as in this section. The only difference from the example discussed in the text is that you would work only with zeros and ones.

| Table 11.1 | | | Emergency Calls to Police for the Month Before and the Month During Which an Officer Walked the Beat | | |

LOCATION	CALLS BEFORE	CALLS DURING	LOCATION	CALLS BEFORE	CALLS DURING
1	29	14	19	18	22
2	50	28	20	27	24
3	14	8	21	42	16
4	16	6	22	31	14
5	11	20	23	51	30
6	31	17	24	28	8
7	33	4	25	26	11
8	37	22	26	14	19
9	21	20	27	29	21
10	40	27	28	39	26
11	30	29	29	40	20
12	22	30	30	30	20
13	30	18	31	26	11
14	36	20	32	30	28
15	30	22	33	27	13
16	29	26	34	33	20
17	24	19	35	35	34
18	41	33	Σ	1,050	700
			$\overline{X}$	30	20
			s	9.21	7.52

Number of calls for service is an interval-scale measure, as required by the *t*-test. The test also requires that the population of differences between pairs be normally distributed. Because our sample is large (greater than 30), we are able to relax this assumption for our test.

A *t*-test for dependent samples requires that the pairs examined be selected randomly and independently from the target population of pairs. Accordingly, although the scores for the subjects in the pairs are dependent (i.e., they are related to one another), the pairs themselves are independent from one another. Because we began with an independent random sample of high-crime addresses, we can assume that the paired observations taken before and during the police intervention are random and independent.

Our null hypothesis states that there is no difference in the number of calls for police service at high-crime addresses whether a police officer walks the beat or not. Because the police department is concerned only with whether the presence of a police officer walking the beat is effective in reducing emergency calls for service, we use a directional research hypothesis. It states that the number of calls for police service will be lower when a police officer walks the beat.

The Sampling Distribution   The number of degrees of freedom for a t-test for dependent samples is obtained by taking the number of pairs studied and subtracting 1: df $= N - 1$. In our example, which involves paired observations for the same subjects over two time periods, the number of degrees of freedom is $35 - 1$, or 34. If we had examined subjects matched by common traits, the degrees of freedom would also be obtained by taking the number of pairs of subjects and subtracting 1.

The mean of the sampling distribution is defined by the null hypothesis. It is represented by μ_d, or the mean of the population of differences between crime calls when a police officer is and is not walking the beat. Because the null hypothesis states that there is no difference in crime calls during these time periods, μ_d for the sampling distribution is 0. The estimated standard error of the sampling distribution ($\hat{\sigma}_{sd}$) is found using Equation 11.8.

$$\hat{\sigma}_{sd} = \sqrt{\frac{s_d^2}{N-1}}$$

Equation 11.8

Using the estimates of variance calculated in Table 11.2, we find that the estimated standard error for the sampling distribution is 1.559.

W orking It Out

$$\hat{\sigma}_{sd} = \sqrt{\frac{s_d^2}{N-1}}$$

$$= \sqrt{\frac{82.6857}{35-1}}$$

$$= 1.5595$$

Significance Level and Rejection Region   Following conventional norms, we use a 0.05 level of statistical significance. However, our research hypothesis suggests a directional test, which means that we place the entire rejection region on one side of the t distribution. Because the research hypothesis states that the period during which a police officer is walking the beat will have a lower number of crime calls, we are interested in the negative area of the t distribution below the mean. Looking at the t table (Appendix 4) under a one-tailed significance test with 34 degrees of freedom, we see that a critical value of t less than -1.691 is needed to place the score in the rejection region.

| Table 11.2 | | | | Calculation of the Standard Deviation for the Differences Between the Two Sets of Dependent Observations | | | | |

LOCATION	DURING	BEFORE	DIFFER-ENCE X_i	$(X_i - \bar{X}_d)^2$	LOCATION	DURING	BEFORE	DIFFER-ENCE X_i	$(X_i - \bar{X}_d)^2$
1	14	29	−15	25	19	22	18	+4	196
2	28	50	−22	144	20	24	27	−3	49
3	8	14	−6	16	21	16	42	−26	256
4	6	16	−10	0	22	14	31	−17	49
5	20	11	+9	361	23	30	51	−21	121
6	17	31	−14	16	24	8	28	−20	100
7	4	33	−29	361	25	11	26	−15	25
8	22	37	−15	25	26	19	14	+5	225
9	20	21	−1	81	27	21	29	−8	4
10	27	40	−13	9	28	26	39	−13	9
11	29	30	−1	81	29	20	40	−20	100
12	30	22	+8	324	30	20	30	−10	0
13	18	30	−12	4	31	11	26	−15	25
14	20	36	−16	36	32	28	30	−2	64
15	22	30	−8	4	33	13	27	−14	16
16	26	29	−3	49	34	20	33	−13	9
17	19	24	−5	25	35	34	35	−1	81
18	33	41	−8	4		Totals (Σ)		−350	2,894

$$\bar{X}_d = \frac{\sum_{i=1}^{N} X_i}{N}$$

$$= \frac{-350}{35}$$

$$= -10$$

$$s_d^2 = \frac{\sum_{i=1}^{N}(X_i - \bar{X}_d)^2}{N}$$

$$= \frac{2,894}{35}$$

$$= 82.6857$$

The Test Statistic To define the *t*-score appropriate for our test, we alter Equation 10.9 (used for the single-sample test of means in Chapter 10) to take into account the fact that we are now concerned with the mean difference between pairs of observations. Accordingly, instead of comparing the mean of one sample to the hypothesized population parameter $(\bar{X} - \mu)$, we now compare the mean of the observed differences between the pairs with the hypothesized difference between the pairs based on the null hypothesis $(\bar{X}_d - \mu_d)$. As discussed in the section on the sampling distribution, the hypothesized difference is 0. We also adjust the denominator of the equation to reflect the standard error of the differences between the pairs of observations. The revised formula is presented in Equation 11.9.

$$t = \frac{\bar{X}_d - \mu_d}{\sqrt{\dfrac{s_d^2}{N - 1}}}$$

Equation 11.9

Substituting the values from our example, we obtain a t-score of -6.412.

W orking It Out

$$t = \frac{\overline{X}_d - \mu_d}{\sqrt{\dfrac{s_d^2}{N-1}}}$$

$$= \frac{-10 - 0}{\sqrt{\dfrac{82.6857}{35-1}}}$$

$$= -6.4123$$

The Decision   Because our test statistic of -6.4123 is less than the critical value of our rejection region, -1.691, we reject the null hypothesis. The observed significance level of our test is less than the criterion significance level we set when defining the significance level and rejection region for our test ($p < 0.05$). We can conclude that there is a statistically significant decrease in the number of calls for police services at high-crime addresses when a police officer is walking the beat.

A Note on Using the t-Test for Ordinal Scales

Ordinal scales create a special problem in conducting tests of statistical significance. Most tests we have examined so far assume either a nominal or an interval level of measurement. There are nonparametric tests for ordinal-level measures; however, these generally assume that the researcher can rank order all scores in a distribution.[10] Typically, with ordinal measures, there are a limited number of ordinal categories and many observations, so such tests are not appropriate.

There is no simple guideline for deciding which test to use for ordinal-scale variables. In practice, when there are a number of categories in an

---

[10]See Chapter 12 for an example of a rank-order test (the Kruskal-Wallis one-way analysis of variance).

ordinal scale, researchers use the t-test for means to calculate statistical significance. When N is large and the number of categories is more than five, this approach is generally accepted. However, you should keep in mind when you use this approach that the t-test assumes not only that the categories in the scale are ordered but also that the intervals represented by the categories are equal for all of the categories. To the extent that this can be assumed, you will be on more solid ground using the t-test for ordinal scales. When the number of categories is less than five, it may be better to use the chi-square statistic, discussed in Chapter 9. In Chapter 13, we will discuss other descriptive statistics and associated significance tests that are often appropriate for ordinal-level scales.

Chapter Summary

The **two-sample t-test** is a parametric test of statistical significance that may be used to test for equality of two population means or proportions. Although the test requires an interval level of measurement and normal population distributions, it is nonetheless appropriate for unknown populations and for proportions when N is sufficiently large for both samples.

Like other tests of statistical significance examined in previous chapters, the two-sample t-test requires independent random sampling. The null hypothesis states that the population means or proportions for the two samples studied are the same. A critical value for the test is identified on the t sampling distribution, after first determining the degrees of freedom. The mean of the sampling distribution is again defined with reference to the null hypothesis. There are two options for calculating the standard error of the sampling distribution for a difference of means test. The first is termed the **pooled variance** method; it generally provides a more efficient statistical estimate but requires the additional assumption of **homoscedasticity**—that the standard deviations of the two groups are the same. The second is called the **separate variance** method because it does not make an assumption about the equality of variances between the two population distributions. For a difference of proportions test, the pooled variance method is always used.

When the two samples examined are not independent, the **t-test for dependent samples** should be used. The calculation of this statistic is based on the mean difference between pairs of samples and the standard deviation of the differences between the pairs.

Key Terms

homoscedasticity A statement that the variances and standard deviations of two or more populations are the same.

pooled variance A method of obtaining the standard error of the sampling distribution for a difference of means test. The pooled variance method requires an assumption of homoscedasticity.

separate variance A method of obtaining the standard error of the sampling distribu-

tion for a difference of means test. The separate variance method does not require an assumption of homoscedasticity.

t-test for dependent samples A test of statistical significance that is used when two samples are not independent.

two-sample t-test A test of statistical significance that examines the difference observed between the means or proportions of two samples.

Symbols and Formulas

$\hat{\sigma}$ Estimate of the standard deviation of a population

$\hat{\sigma}_{sd}$ Estimate of the standard error of a sampling distribution

To calculate degrees of freedom for the two-sample t-test:

$$df = N_1 + N_2 - 2$$

To calculate an unbiased estimate of the standard error for the sampling distribution in a two-sample t-test (separate variance method):

$$\hat{\sigma}_{sd(\bar{X}_1 - \bar{X}_2)} = \sqrt{\frac{s_1^2}{N_1 - 1} + \frac{s_2^2}{N_2 - 1}}$$

To estimate a pooled joint standard deviation of two populations for the pooled variance method:

$$\hat{\sigma} = \sqrt{\frac{N_1 s_1^2 + N_2 s_2^2}{N_1 + N_2 - 2}}$$

To estimate the standard error for the sampling distribution in a two-sample t-test (pooled variance method):

$$\hat{\sigma}_{sd(\bar{X}_1 - \bar{X}_2)} = \hat{\sigma} \sqrt{\frac{N_1 + N_2}{N_1 N_2}}$$

To calculate the two-sample *t*-test statistic for means (separate variance method):

$$t = \frac{(\bar{X_1} - \bar{X_2}) - (\mu_1 - \mu_2)}{\sqrt{\dfrac{s_1^2}{N_1 - 1} + \dfrac{s_2^2}{N_2 - 1}}}$$

To calculate the two-sample *t*-test statistic for means (pooled variance method):

$$t = \frac{(\bar{X_1} - \bar{X_2}) - (\mu_1 - \mu_2)}{\hat{\sigma}\sqrt{\dfrac{N_1 + N_2}{N_1 N_2}}}$$

To calculate the variance of a sample proportion:

$$s^2 = pq$$

To calculate the two-sample *t*-test statistic for proportions:

$$t = \frac{(p_1 - p_2) - (P_1 - P_2)}{\sqrt{\dfrac{N_1 s_1^2 + N_2 s_2^2}{N_1 + N_2 - 2}}\sqrt{\dfrac{N_1 + N_2}{N_1 N_2}}}$$

To calculate the two-sample *t*-test statistic for means of dependent samples:

$$t = \frac{\bar{X_d} - \mu_d}{\sqrt{\dfrac{s_d^2}{N - 1}}}$$

Exercises

11.1 Test the following pairs of hypotheses using the information given. Assume that the variable has been measured at the interval level and the cases have been selected at random. For each test, answer the following questions:

— Does the test require a one-tailed or a two-tailed test of statistical significance?

— What is (are) the critical value(s) for the stated level of significance?

— What is the value of the test statistic?

— What is the decision regarding the null hypothesis?

— Does the sample size suggest the need for caution in drawing conclusions?

a. H_0: $\mu_1 = \mu_2$
   H_1: $\mu_1 \neq \mu_2$
   $\alpha = 0.05$

$\overline{X}_1 = 24$	$\overline{X}_2 = 30$
$s_1 = 4$	$s_2 = 6$
$N_1 = 14$	$N_2 = 18$

b. H_0: $\mu_1 = \mu_2$
   H_1: $\mu_1 < \mu_2$
   $\alpha = 0.01$

$\overline{X}_1 = 10$	$\overline{X}_2 = 20$
$s_1 = 8$	$s_2 = 10$
$N_1 - 11$	$N_2 = 41$

c. H_0: $\mu_1 = \mu_2$
   H_1: $\mu_1 > \mu_2$
   $\alpha = 0.05$

$\overline{X}_1 = 33$	$\overline{X}_2 = 28$
$s_1 = 6$	$s_2 = 6$
$N_1 = 122$	$N_2 = 215$

d. H_0: $\mu_1 = \mu_2$
   H_1: $\mu_1 \neq \mu_2$
   $\alpha = 0.05$

$\overline{X}_1 = 15$	$\overline{X}_2 = 6$
$s_1 = 2$	$s_2 = 3$
$N_1 = 29$	$N_2 = 33$

e. H_0: $\mu_1 = \mu_2$
   H_1: $\mu_1 > \mu_2$
   $\alpha = 0.01$

$\overline{X}_1 = 45$	$\overline{X}_2 = 32$
$s_1 = 35$	$s_2 = 25$
$N_1 = 513$	$N_2 = 476$

f. H_0: $\mu_1 = \mu_2$
   H_1: $\mu_1 < \mu_2$
   $\alpha = 0.05$

$\overline{X}_1 = 2$	$\overline{X}_2 = 4$
$s_1 = 1$	$s_2 = 2$
$N_1 = 85$	$N_2 = 93$

11.2 Greg wishes to investigate whether there is any difference in the amount of violent crowd behavior that supporters of two soccer teams report having seen in one season. He distributes questionnaires at random to season-ticket holders at United and at City. The mean number of matches at which the sample of 110 United fans remember seeing violent incidents is 15 ($s = 4.7$). For the sample of 130 City fans, the mean number of such matches is 8 ($s = 4.2$).

a. Can Greg conclude that there are differences in the amount of violent crowd behavior observed between the two populations of season-ticket holders? Outline all the steps required in the test of statistical significance. Choose an appropriate level of significance and calculate the *t*-test statistic according to the separate variance method.

b. Would Greg's conclusion be any different if he were to use the pooled variance method?

c. Which of the two methods is preferred in this case?

11.3   To see if there is truth in the claim by a prominent graduate of the police academy that white officers are awarded more promotions than African American officers, an independent random sample is drawn from the 1,000 police officers in Bluesville who graduated from the academy ten years earlier. For the 42 white officers sampled, the mean number of promotions received in the ten years since graduation was 3.2 ($s = 0.8$). For the 20 African American officers sampled, the mean number of promotions received was 2.8 ($s = 0.65$).

a. From these data, can you conclude that white officers who graduated ten years ago have been awarded more promotions than their African American counterparts? Use the separate variance method and set a 5% significance level.

b. Would your answer be any different if you used the pooled variance method?

c. If the level of significance had been set at 1%, would there be any difference in the decisions you would make based on the separate variance and pooled variance methods?

d. Does the sample size have any relevance to the extent to which you can rely on the results?

11.4   By surveying a random sample of 100 students from Partytime High School and 100 students from Funtime High School, a researcher learns that those from Partytime High School have smoked marijuana an average of 9.8 times ($s = 4.2$) in the last six months, while those from Funtime High School have smoked marijuana an average of 4.6 times ($s = 3.6$) in the last six months. Can the researcher conclude that use of marijuana differs between Partytime and Funtime high schools? Use the separate variance method and set a significance level of 0.01. Be sure to state the assumptions of the statistical test.

11.5 Test the following pairs of hypotheses using the information given. Assume that the variable has been measured at the nominal level, the value reported is the proportion, and the cases have been selected at random. For each test, answer the following questions:

— Does the test require a one-tailed or a two-tailed test of statistical significance?

— What is (are) the critical value(s) for the stated level of significance?

— What is the value of the test statistic?

— What is the decision regarding the null hypothesis?

— Does the sample size suggest the need for caution in drawing conclusions?

a. $H_0: P_1 = P_2$
$H_1: P_1 > P_2$
$\alpha = 0.05$
$p_1 = 0.80 \qquad p_2 = 0.60$
$N_1 = 6 \qquad N_2 = 8$

b. $H_0: P_1 = P_2$
$H_1: P_1 < P_2$
$\alpha = 0.01$
$p_1 = 0.73 \qquad p_2 = 0.75$
$N_1 = 211 \qquad N_2 = 376$

c. $H_0: P_1 = P_2$
$H_1: P_1 \neq P_2$
$\alpha = 0.05$
$p_1 = 0.46 \qquad p_2 = 0.54$
$N_1 = 86 \qquad N_2 = 76$

d. $H_0: P_1 = P_2$
$H_1: P_1 \neq P_2$
$\alpha = 0.01$
$p_1 = 0.28 \qquad p_2 = 0.23$
$N_1 = 192 \qquad N_2 = 161$

e. $H_0: P_1 = P_2$
$H_1: P_1 > P_2$
$\alpha = 0.01$
$p_1 = 0.12 \qquad p_2 = 0.10$
$N_1 = 57 \qquad N_2 = 45$

f. $H_0: P_1 = P_2$
$H_1: P_1 < P_2$
$\alpha = 0.05$
$p_1 = 0.88 \qquad p_2 = 0.94$
$N_1 = 689 \qquad N_2 = 943$

11.6 After a long political battle, certain categories of prisoners in Rainy State have been given the right to vote in upcoming local elections. Carolyn wishes to know whether there is any difference between the proportion of eligible prisoners and the proportion of eligible nonprisoners in Rainy State who will take advantage of their right to vote. She draws two random independent samples—one of 125 prisoners, and the other of 130 nonprisoners. The samples are drawn from the entire eligible prisoner and nonprisoner populations of Rainy State. She finds that 60% of her prisoner sample and 44% of her nonprisoner sample intend to vote.

a. Why is a statistical test of significance necessary here?

b. Carry out a test of statistical significance, remembering to outline each step carefully. Can Carolyn conclude that the two populations are different in terms of their respective members' intentions to vote?

11.7 Eric takes a random sample of 200 offenders convicted of bribery and a random sample of 200 offenders convicted of robbery over the past five years in Sunny State. By checking court records, he finds that 9% of the bribery offenders and 1% of the robbery offenders in his samples have university educations.

a. By using a two-tailed test with a significance level of 0.01, can Eric conclude that the differences he observes are statistically significant?

b. What steps would you recommend that Eric take if he wishes to extend his conclusions to the prisoner population of neighboring Rainy State?

11.8 Three hundred prisoners, all convicted of violent crimes against persons, have enrolled in a six-month course in anger control. A random sample of 41 of the prisoners are chosen to complete the same questionnaire on two separate occasions—once during the first lesson and once during the last lesson. The questionnaire measures how likely respondents are to resort to violence to solve problems. The results are translated into an index from 0 to 10, with higher scores indicating a higher tendency to seek nonviolent solutions to problems. The 41 prisoners' scores are shown in the table on page 286.

a. What is the mean change in scores?

b. What is the standard deviation for the differences between scores?

c. Carry out a test of statistical significance, remembering to outline all of the steps required by the test. Can you reject the null hypothesis for the test on the basis of the differences observed?

Subject	First Lesson	Last Lesson	Subject	First Lesson	Last Lesson
1	1	2	22	6	6
2	2	4	23	4	4
3	1	6	24	9	6
4	3	2	25	9	7
5	4	5	26	0	1
6	7	9	27	1	4
7	6	6	28	1	4
8	4	3	29	3	3
9	4	7	30	2	2
10	1	1	31	2	4
11	2	1	32	1	1
12	3	4	33	0	3
13	4	9	34	4	5
14	6	7	35	4	5
15	7	8	36	6	7
16	2	2	37	6	6
17	2	7	38	7	7
18	3	3	39	3	6
19	1	4	40	1	1
20	6	4	41	1	2
21	2	4			

11.9 A random sample of adults in a midwestern state were interviewed twice over a period of two years. Each time, as part of the survey, they were asked how many times their home had been burglarized in the previous 12 months. The numbers of burglaries reported by 27 of the respondents in each interview are shown in the table on page 287.

a. What is the mean change in scores?

b. What is the standard deviation for the differences between scores?

c. Carry out a test of statistical significance. Use a significance level of 5% and outline all of the steps required by the test. Can you reject the null hypothesis for the test on the basis of the differences observed?

d. Would your answer have been any different if you had used a significance level of 1%? Explain why.

Respondent	First Interview	Second Interview
1	0	2
2	1	1
3	2	0
4	1	0
5	0	1
6	0	0
7	3	0
8	0	0
9	0	1
10	5	1
11	2	2
12	2	2
13	1	0
14	1	0
15	0	0
16	0	2
17	0	1
18	0	1
19	1	3
20	0	1
21	1	0
22	2	0
23	0	0
24	0	0
25	2	1
26	0	2
27	1	0

Computer Exercises

Before beginning these exercises on using SPSS to obtain *t*-statistics, open the data file ***nys_1.sav.*** Having this data file open prior to working with the different commands will make some of the instructions less confusing.

The two-sample *t*-test for differences in group means is performed by using the "Independent Samples T Test" command (Analyze → Comparing Means → Independent Samples T Test). At a minimum, when executing this command, you will need two variables: the variable of primary interest (e.g., delinquency, arrest) and the variable that denotes the different groups (e.g., sex, race).

After you execute the command, a window will appear that lists all the variables in the data file in the box on the left. Move the name of one of the delinquency variables into the box on the right. Below this box is another box labeled "Grouping Variable." Move the name of the race variable into this box, and then click on the button "Define Groups." In the new window that opens, you will need to enter the numbers representing the two categories you are interested in comparing. The race variable presents an interesting choice, since it has five categories. For now, enter "1" for group 1 (denoting whites) and "2" for group 2 (denoting African Americans). If you wanted to compare any other combination of race groups, you would simply have to change the numbers representing the groups. Clicking on "Continue" and "OK" will run the command.

The output window generated by the "Independent Samples T Test" command will contain two lines in the main results table. The first line will present the *t*-test results using the pooled variance method, while the second line will present the *t*-test results using the separate variance method.

A dependent samples *t*-test is obtained using the "Paired Samples T Test" command in SPSS (Analyze → Comparing Means → Paired Samples T Test). After you execute this command, a window will appear that lists all the variables in the box on the left. Just below the list of variables is a box labeled "Current Selections," which lists the current pair of variables to be compared. To have SPSS perform the analysis, move the highlighted names to the box on the right (both variable names should appear in the box labeled "Paired Variables"). The output window will give the mean difference (listing the variables in the calculation, such as "var1 − var2"), the standard deviation of the difference, and the corresponding *t*-statistic.

Note that in SPSS paired samples are calculated in only one way. SPSS uses the order of appearance of the variable names in the data file to determine which variable is listed as the "First variable" and which is listed as the "Second variable." Try clicking on a pair of variables in different orders, and see how SPSS rearranges the names to correspond to order of appearance in the data file. The difficulty with this feature of SPSS is that you may want the variable that appears second, such as a post-treatment measure, to be used first in the calculation. The easiest and most straightforward way of dealing with this aspect of SPSS is to change the sign of the mean of the difference if the calculation performed by SPSS is the reverse of what you want. *But be very careful—ensure from the output table that the calculation performed is opposite to the one you want performed.*

1. Open the SPSS data file ***labail.sav***. This data file contains the values used for the bail example in the text. There are only two variables included in this data set: bail amount and race (coded as 1 = African Americans and 2 = Hispanics). Use the "Independent Samples T Test" command to reproduce the results on pages 266 and 267 in the text.

2. Open the data file ***nys_1.sav.*** Use the "Independent Samples T Test" command to test the hypotheses listed below. For each hypothesis test, use a significance level of 5%, state each of the assumptions, and explain whether there is a statistically significant difference between the two groups.

    a. The number of times a youth has stolen something valued at $5 to $50 is different for whites and African Americans.

b. The number of times a youth has smoked marijuana is greater for males than for females.

c. The number of times a youth has physically attacked another student is different for males and females.

d. The number of times a youth has hit his or her parents is greater for 17-year-olds than for 12-year-olds.

e. The number of times a youth has cheated on schoolwork is greater for students earning mostly C's than for students earning mostly A's.

3. Enter the data from Exercise 11.8. Test for a significant change using the "Paired Samples T Test" command. How do these results compare to those you obtained for Exercise 11.8?

4. Enter the data from Exercise 11.9. Test for a significant change using the "Paired Samples T Test" command. How do these results compare to those you obtained for Exercise 11.9?

Comparing Means Among More

Than Two Samples: Analysis of Variance

analysis of variance (ANOVA)

What Is the Logic Underlying ANOVA?

What Are the Assumptions of the Test?

How Is the Test Carried Out?

How Can the Strength of the Relationship Be Defined?

How Does One Make Comparisons Between the Groups?

the Kruskal-Wallis test

When Is the Test Used?

How Is the Test Carried Out?

IN CHAPTER 11, we used the t distribution to test hypotheses about means from two independent samples. But what if we are interested in looking at more than two samples at a time? This is a common problem in criminology and criminal justice, where many important questions can be raised across a number of different samples. For example, race is a central concern in criminal justice and criminology, and often it does not make sense to restrict comparisons involving race to just two groups. Similarly, in many criminal justice studies, a number of interventions are compared simultaneously. In such studies, researchers want to compare not just two but three or more means in the context of one statistical test.

Analysis of variance (ANOVA) is a commonly used parametric test of statistical significance that allows the researcher to compare multiple groups on specific characteristics. ANOVA also provides an opportunity to introduce several important statistical concepts used in more complex types of analysis. In this chapter, we examine in this context the concepts of explained and unexplained variation and consider how they relate to the total variation found in a specific measure. This chapter also introduces a nonparametric test, the Kruskal-Wallis test, which can be used for comparisons across multiple groups when the assumptions underlying ANOVA are difficult to meet.

Analysis of Variance

Analysis of variance is based on a simple premise. As the differences between the means of samples become larger relative to the variability of scores within each sample, our confidence in making inferences grows. Why is this the case? Certainly it makes sense that the more the mean differs from one sample to another, the stronger the evidence supporting the position that there are differences between the population means. All else being equal, the larger the differences between the samples, the more confident we are likely to be in rejecting the position that the population means are equal.

But we are faced with a problem in making such an inference. How much confidence can we place in the observed means of our samples? As we have stated many times in this book, sample estimates vary from sample to sample. If the sample means are likely to vary considerably, then we want to be cautious in drawing strong conclusions from our study. If the sample means are not likely to vary greatly, we can have more confidence in conclusions drawn from them. Analysis of variance uses the variability within the observed samples to come to conclusions about this variability.

Suppose, for example, that you are examining two separate studies, each including three samples. In the first study, the scores are widely dispersed around the mean for each group. In contrast, in the second study, the scores are tightly clustered around the group means. If you take the variability you observe in these samples as an indication of the variability in the populations from which they were drawn, you are likely to have more confidence in estimates gained from the second study than from the first. Those estimates appear to be more stable, evidencing much less variability.

This is precisely the approach taken in analysis of variance. The variability *between* the groups studied is contrasted with the variability *within* these groups to produce a ratio:

Variability between groups
─────────────────────────
 Variability within groups

The larger this ratio—the larger the differences between the groups relative to the variability within them—the more confidence we can have in a conclusion that the population means are not equal. When the ratio is smaller, meaning that the differences between the groups are small relative to the variability within them, we have less reason to conclude that differences exist in the populations to which we want to infer.

Developing Estimates of Variance Between and Within Groups

The first step in analysis of variance is to define the variability between and within the groups studied. To make this process more concrete, let's use a hypothetical study of depression among 12 prison inmates drawn from high-, moderate-, and low-security prisons (see Table 12.1).

Table 12.1   Depression Scores for 12 Prison Inmates Drawn
from High-, Moderate-, and Low-Security Prisons

LOW SECURITY (GROUP 1)	MODERATE SECURITY (GROUP 2)	HIGH SECURITY (GROUP 3)
3	9	9
5	9	10
4	8	7
4	6	10
$\sum = 16$	$\sum = 32$	$\sum = 36$
$\overline{X} = 4$	$\overline{X} = 8$	$\overline{X} = 9$

To calculate the grand mean: $\overline{X}_g = \dfrac{\sum_{i=1}^{N} X_i}{N} = \dfrac{84}{12} = 7$

Between-group variability is measured by first subtracting the **grand mean,** or **overall mean,** of the three samples from the mean of each sample. This difference must then be adjusted to take into account the number of scores or observations in each sample. Equation 12.1 represents this process in mathematical language. The sample (or category) means are represented by $\overline{X}_c$, the overall mean (or grand mean) is represented by $\overline{X}_g$, N_c represents the number of scores or observations in the sample (or category), and $\sum_{c=1}^{k}$ tells us to sum the results from the first sample (or category) mean ($c = 1$) to the last sample (or category) mean ($c = k$).

$$\sum_{c=1}^{k} [N_c(\overline{X}_c - \overline{X}_g)]$$ **Equation 12.1**

As illustrated in Table 12.1, the overall, or grand, mean is found by adding up all the scores in the three samples and dividing by the total number of scores ($N = 12$). To calculate the amount of between-group variability for our example, we take just three quantities—the mean depression score of high-security inmates ($\overline{X} = 9$) minus the overall mean, the mean depression score of moderate-security inmates ($\overline{X} = 8$) minus the overall mean, and the mean depression score of low-security inmates ($\overline{X} = 4$) minus the overall mean—and multiply each by its sample size.

Within-group variability is identified by summing the difference between each subject's score and the mean for the sample in which the subject is found. In Equation 12.2, X_i represents a score from one of the three samples and, as before, $\overline{X}_c$ represents the mean for that sample. Here we sum from $i = 1$ to N, or from the first to the last score in the overall study.

$$\sum_{i=1}^{N} (X_i - \overline{X}_c)$$

Equation 12.2

For within-group variability, we have four calculations to carry out for each sample (group). For the first subject in the low-security prison sample, for example, we subtract from the subject's score of 3 the mean score of low-security inmates in the study (4). The same is done for each of the other three members of this sample. For the moderate-security sample, we repeat the process, starting with the first subject, with a score of 9, and using the mean of 8 for the group as a whole. The same is done for the high-security sample.

When we add up the deviations between the groups and those within them, as is done in Tables 12.2 and 12.3, we find that both are 0. This does not mean that there is an absence of variability either within or between the samples we are examining. Rather, this outcome reflects a rule stated in Chapter 4: The sum of the deviations from a mean equals 0. Clearly, we cannot use the sum of the deviations from the mean as an indicator of variation. As in other similar problems, it makes sense to square the deviations from the mean. The squares of all the deviations from the mean will be positive or 0.

The result when we square these quantities and then add them is commonly referred to as a **sum of squares.** The variability between groups measured in this way is called the **between sum of squares (BSS).** It is calculated by taking the sum of the squared deviation of each sample mean $(\overline{X}_c)$ from the overall mean $(\overline{X}_g)$ multiplied by the number of cases (N_c) in that sample.

$$BSS = \sum_{c=1}^{k} [N_c(\overline{X}_c - \overline{X}_g)^2]$$

Equation 12.3

Table 12.2 Summing the Deviations of the Group Means from the Grand Mean for the Three Groups in the Inmate Depression Study

$\overline{X}_c$	$\overline{X}_g$	$(\overline{X}_c - \overline{X}_g)$	$N_c(\overline{X}_c - \overline{X}_g)$
4	7	−3	−12
8	7	1	4
9	7	2	8
		$\sum = 0$	$\sum = 0$

| Table 12.3 | **Summing the Deviations of the Scores from the Group Means Within the Three Groups in the Inmate Depression Study** |

X_i	$\bar{X}_c$	$(X_i - \bar{X}_c)$
3	4	−1
5	4	1
4	4	0
4	4	0
9	8	1
9	8	1
8	8	0
6	8	−2
9	9	0
10	9	1
7	9	−2
10	9	1
		$\Sigma = 0$

To calculate the between sum of squares for our hypothetical study, we take the same approach as is shown in Table 12.2. The one difference is that after we subtract the overall mean from a category mean, we square the result. Our final result is 56.

Working It Out

$$BSS = \sum_{c=1}^{k} [N_c(\bar{X}_c - \bar{X}_g)^2]$$

$$= 4(4 - 7)^2 + 4(8 - 7)^2 + 4(9 - 7)^2$$

$$= 56$$

When we measure variability within groups using this method, the result is defined as the **within sum of squares (WSS).** The within sum of squares is obtained by taking the sum of the squared deviation of each score from its category mean, as represented in Equation 12.4. As before, we first take the score for each subject and subtract from it the sample mean. However, before adding these deviations together, we square each one. The within sum of squares for our hypothetical example is equal to 14.

$$WSS = \sum_{i=1}^{N} (X_i - \bar{X}_c)^2$$

Equation 12.4

W orking It Out

$$WSS = \sum_{i=1}^{N} (X_i - \overline{X}_c)^2$$

$$= (3 - 4)^2 + (5 - 4)^2 + (4 - 4)^2 + (4 - 4)^2 + (9 - 8)^2$$
$$+ (9 - 8)^2 + (8 - 8)^2 + (6 - 8)^2 + (9 - 9)^2 + (10 - 9)^2$$
$$+ (7 - 9)^2 + (10 - 9)^2$$

$$= 14$$

Partitioning Sums of Squares

We can also calculate a third type of variability for our inmate depression study: **total sum of squares (TSS).** The total sum of squares takes into account all of the variability in our three samples. It is calculated by taking the sum of the squared deviation of each score from the overall mean of scores for the three groups, as shown in Equation 12.5.

$$TSS = \sum_{i=1}^{N} (X_i - \overline{X}_g)^2 \qquad \text{Equation 12.5}$$

In practice, we first take the deviation of a score from the overall mean and then square it. For example, the first subject in the low-security prison sample has a score of 3. We subtract from this score the overall mean of 7 and then square the result (-4), to obtain a value of 16. To arrive at the total sum of squares, we do this for each of the 12 scores in the study and then sum the results.

W orking It Out

$$TSS = \sum_{i=1}^{N} (X_i - \overline{X}_g)^2$$

$$= (3 - 7)^2 + (5 - 7)^2 + (4 - 7)^2 + (4 - 7)^2$$
$$+ (9 - 7)^2 + (9 - 7)^2 + (8 - 7)^2 + (6 - 7)^2 + (9 - 7)^2$$
$$+ (10 - 7)^2 + (7 - 7)^2 + (10 - 7)^2$$

$$= 70$$

The quantity obtained is equivalent to the sum of the between sum of squares and the within sum of squares. That is, the total variability across all of the scores is made up of the variability between the samples and the variability within the samples. More generally, the three types of variability discussed so far may be expressed in terms of a simple formula that partitions the total sum of squares into its two component parts: the between sum of squares and the within sum of squares.

Total sum of squares = between sum of squares
                       + within sum of squares   **Equation 12.6**

(For our example, 70 = 56 + 14.)

Another way to express the relationship among the three types of sums of squares is to partition the total sum of squares into explained and unexplained components:

Total sum of squares = explained sum of squares
                       + unexplained sum of squares   **Equation 12.7**

In this equation, the between sum of squares is represented by the **explained sum of squares (ESS)** because the between sum of squares represents the part of the total variability that is accounted for by the differences between the groups. For our hypothetical example, this is the proportion of the total variability in depression that is "explained" by the type of prison in which the subject is incarcerated.

The within sum of squares is represented in Equation 12.7 by the unexplained variability, or the **unexplained sum of squares (USS).** This is the part of the total variability that differences between the groups do not explain. We usually do not know the cause of this variability.

Developing Estimates of Population Variances

So far we have defined the sums of squares associated with between-group and within-group variability. But analysis of variance, as its name implies, is concerned with variance, not just variability. Accordingly, we have to adjust our sums by taking into account the appropriate number of degrees of freedom. In Chapter 5, when we developed estimates of variance, we divided the squared deviations from the mean by the number of cases in the sample or population. For analysis of variance, we divide the between and within sums of squares by the appropriate degrees of freedom.

For the between-group estimate of variance, we define the number of degrees of freedom as $k - 1$, where k is the number of samples or categories examined. If we are comparing three sample means, the number of degrees of freedom associated with the between-group estimate of variance is thus 2. As illustrated by Equation 12.8, an estimate of the

Representing Sums of Squares: ANOVA Notation in Different Formats

The ANOVA model is often presented using a different set of statistical notation than that used in this text. In this book, we define the total sum of squares as equal to the sum of the within sum of squares and the between sum of squares:

$$\sum_{i=1}^{N}(X_i - \overline{X}_g)^2 = \sum_{i=1}^{N}(X_i - \overline{X}_c)^2 + \sum_{c=1}^{k}[N_c(\overline{X}_c - \overline{X}_g)^2]$$

In many other statistics texts, the following equation is used for the decomposition of the total sum of squares:

$$\sum_{i=1}^{N}\sum_{j=1}^{k}(X_{ij} - \overline{X}..)^2 = \sum_{i=1}^{N}\sum_{j=1}^{k}(X_{ij} - \overline{X}_{\cdot j})^2 + \sum_{i=1}^{N}\sum_{j=1}^{k}(\overline{X}_{\cdot j} - \overline{X}..)^2$$

The double summation symbols indicate that we need to first sum over each group—denoted by the subscript j—and then sum over each individual observation—denoted by the subscript i. In terms of this book's notation, $\overline{X}.. = \overline{X}_g$ and $\overline{X}_{\cdot j} = \overline{X}_c$.

Although we have reduced the number of summation signs to one for each sum of squares, the calculations with the two equations are identical for the total sum of squares and the within sum of squares. The one difference between the two equations lies in the calculation of the between sum of squares. The notation we offer simplifies this calculation by taking into account the fact that all of the individual scores in a single group (N_c) will have the same value. Rather than repeat the same calculation for all the individuals in the same group, we produce the identical answer by multiplying the squared difference of the sample mean and the overall mean by the number of observations in the corresponding sample.

between-group variance ($\hat{\sigma}^2_{bg}$) is obtained by dividing the between sum of squares by $k - 1$.

$$\hat{\sigma}^2_{bg} = \frac{\sum_{c=1}^{k}[N_c(\overline{X}_c - \overline{X}_g)^2]}{k - 1}$$

Equation 12.8

The number of degrees of freedom for the within-group estimate of variance is $N - k$, or the number of cases in the sample minus the number of samples or categories examined. The within-group variance estimate ($\hat{\sigma}^2_{wg}$) is calculated by dividing the within sum of squares by $N - k$ (see Equation 12.9).

$$\hat{\sigma}^2_{wg} = \frac{\sum_{i=1}^{N}(X_i - \overline{X}_c)^2}{N - k}$$

Equation 12.9

A Substantive Example: Age and White-Collar Crimes

Now that we have defined the two types of variance that are compared in analysis of variance, let's look at a substantive problem. Table 12.4 presents data on age for three samples of offenders convicted of white-collar crimes in seven federal district courts over a three-year period.[1]

Table 12.4

Ages of 30 White-Collar Criminals Convicted of Three Different Offenses

OFFENSE 1 BANK EMBEZZLEMENT	OFFENSE 2 BRIBERY	OFFENSE 3 ANTITRUST VIOLATION
19	28	35
21	29	46
23	32	48
25	40	53
29	42	58
30	48	61
31	58	62
35	58	62
42	64	62
49	68	75
$\overline{X} = 30.4$	$\overline{X} = 46.7$	$\overline{X} = 56.2$
$s = 8.98$	$s = 13.99$	$s = 10.54$
Grand mean ($\overline{X}_g$) = 1333/30 = 44.43		

[1]The data are drawn from S. Wheeler, D. Weisburd, and N. Bode, *Sanctioning of White Collar Crime, 1976–1978: Federal District Courts* (Ann Arbor, MI: Inter-University Consortium for Political and Social Research, 1988).

The first sample was drawn from offenders convicted of bank embezzlement, the second from offenders convicted of bribery, and the third from offenders convicted under criminal antitrust statutes. Ten subjects were drawn randomly from each of these populations.

The values listed in Table 12.4 represent the ages of the sampled offenders. The mean age of the bank embezzlers is 30.4 years; of the bribery offenders, 46.7 years; and of the antitrust offenders, 56.2 years. Can we conclude from the differences found among these samples that there are differences among the means of the populations from which these samples were drawn?

Assumptions:

Level of Measurement: Interval scale.

Population Distribution: Normal distribution for each population (the shape of the population distributions is unknown, and the sizes of the samples examined are small).

Sampling Method: Independent random sampling (no replacement; sample is small relative to population).

Sampling Frame: All white-collar offenders convicted of the crimes examined in seven federal judicial districts over a three-year period.

Population variances are equal ($\sigma_1^2 = \sigma_2^2 = \sigma_3^2$).

Hypotheses:

H_0: Population means of age for bank embezzlers, bribery offenders, and antitrust offenders are equal ($\mu_1 = \mu_2 = \mu_3$).

H_1: Population means of age for bank embezzlers, bribery offenders, and antitrust offenders are not equal ($\mu_1 \neq \mu_2 \neq \mu_3$).

Like other parametric tests of statistical significance, analysis of variance requires that an interval level of measurement be used for the scores to be examined. Our example meets this assumption because age is an interval measure. Some statisticians add an assumption of nominal measurement because a comparison of means across samples requires that we define categories (or samples) for comparison. For example, in the case of age and white-collar crime, the three samples represent three categories of offenses. Our interest in this case is in the relationship between age (an interval-scale variable) and category of crime (a nominal-scale variable). In the hypothetical study discussed earlier in this chapter, we were interested in the relationship between depression (measured at an interval level) and type of prison (a nominal-scale variable).

Analysis of variance also requires that the populations underlying the samples examined be normally distributed. For our example, this is the most troubling assumption. We do not have evidence from prior studies that age is distributed normally within categories of crime. Nor are our samples large enough to allow us to invoke the central limit theorem. For ANOVA, as for the two-sample t-test, we want to have at least 30 cases per sample in order to relax the normality assumption. Because the computations for analysis of variance are complex, having only ten cases in each sample makes it easier to learn about ANOVA. However, our test will provide valid results only if the population distributions we infer to are in fact normally distributed.

We must also assume that the samples being compared were drawn randomly and independently. In practice, as we discussed in Chapter 11, researchers often make comparisons between groups within a single larger sample. For example, we might draw an independent random sample of white-collar offenders and then compare the means found in this larger sample for bank embezzlement, bribery, and antitrust offenders. As explained in Chapter 11, if the larger sample was drawn as an independent random sample, then we may assume that subsamples consisting of offenders convicted of different types of crimes are also independent random samples. In this study, random samples were drawn independently from each category of crime. Although the researchers did not sample with replacement, we can assume that this violation of assumptions is not serious because the sample drawn is very small relative to the population of offenders in the districts studied.

For analysis of variance, we must also assume that the population variances of the three groups are equal. This assumption of homoscedasticity is similar to that introduced for the two-sample t-test (using the pooled-variance method) in Chapter 11. However, in contrast to the t-test, ANOVA has no alternative test if we cannot assume equal variances between the groups. Although this seems at first to be an important barrier to using analysis of variance, in practice it is generally accepted that violations of this assumption must be very large before the results of a test come into question.[2]

One reason researchers, as opposed to statisticians, are not very concerned about the assumption of homoscedasticity is that even large

---

[2]For example, see G. Hornsnell, "The Effect of Unequal Group Variances on the *F* Test for Homogeneity of Group Means," *Biometrika* 40 (1954): 128–136; G. E. P. Box, "Some Theorems on Quadratic Forms Applied in the Study of Analysis of Variance Problems. I. Effect of Inequality of Variance in the One Way Classification," *Annals of Mathematical Statistics* 25 (1954): 290–302.

violations of this assumption affect the estimates of statistical significance to only a small degree. Sometimes it is suggested that you simply define a more conservative level of statistical significance when you are concerned with a serious violation of the homoscedasticity assumption.[3] Accordingly, you might select a 1% significance threshold as opposed to the more conventional 5% threshold. In general, large deviations in variance are not likely to occur across all of the groups studied. If one group is very different from the others, you might choose to conduct your test two ways—both including the group that is very different from the others and excluding it—and compare your results. In our example, the variances do not differ widely one from another (see Table 12.4).

Our final assumptions for this analysis relate to the null and research hypotheses. For analysis of variance, the null hypothesis is that the means of the groups are the same. In our example, the null hypothesis is that the mean ages of offenders in the populations of the three crime categories are equal. Our research hypothesis is that the means are not equal. As is true for ANOVA more generally, our research hypothesis is nondirectional. If we are making inferences to three or more populations, it is not possible to define the direction of the differences among them.[4]

The Sampling Distribution   The sampling distribution used for making decisions about hypotheses in analysis of variance is called the F distribution, after R. A. Fisher, the statistician who first described it. The shape of the F distribution varies, depending on the number of degrees of freedom of the variance estimates being compared. The number of degrees

---

[3]Most packaged statistical programs provide a test for equivalence of variances as an option with their ANOVA program. However, be careful not to automatically reject use of analysis of variance on the basis of a statistically significant result. In smaller studies, with samples of less than 50 per group, a finding of a statistically significant difference should make you cautious about using analysis of variance. In such a study, you may want to adjust the significance level, as suggested here, or consider alternative nonparametric tests (discussed later in the chapter). With larger samples, a statistically significant result at conventional significance levels should not necessarily lead to any adjustments in your test. For such adjustments to be made, the difference should be highly significant and reflect large actual differences among variance estimates.

[4]However, in the special case of analysis of variance with only two samples, the researcher can use a directional research hypothesis. This will sometimes be done in experimental studies when the researcher seeks to examine differences across experimental and control groups, taking into account additional factors [e.g., see L. W. Sherman and D. Weisburd, "General Deterrent Effects of Police Patrol in Crime 'Hot Spots.' A Randomized Study," *Justice Quarterly* 12 (1995): 625–648.]

of freedom is represented by $k - 1$ for the between-group variance and $N - k$ for the within-group variance:

W orking It Out

df for between-group variance $= k - 1 = 3 - 1 = 2$

df for within-group variance $= N - k = 30 - 3 = 27$

Because we need to take into account two separate degrees of freedom at the same time, a different table of probability estimates is given for each significance threshold. Accordingly, Appendix 5 provides F tables for 0.05, 0.01, and 0.001 significance levels.

Each table provides the F-scores, adjusted for degrees of freedom, that correspond to the particular significance threshold. Thus, for example, in the table for $\alpha = 0.05$, the values given are the critical values for the test. For all tests using the F distribution, we need to obtain an F-score greater than this critical value to reject the null hypothesis of equal means. Looking at the table for $\alpha = 0.05$, we can identify two interesting characteristics of the F distribution.

First, the F distribution is unidirectional, consisting only of positive values. Consistent with the fact that the research hypothesis in analysis of variance with three or more population means states simply that the means are not equal, the F distribution is concerned only with the absolute size of the statistic obtained.

Second, as the number of degrees of freedom associated with the within-group variance grows, the F-value needed to reject the null hypothesis gets smaller. Remember that the number of degrees of freedom for the within-group variance is equal to $N - k$. Accordingly, as the number of cases in the sample gets larger, the number of degrees of freedom also gets larger. Why should the F-value needed to reject the null hypothesis be related to the size of the sample? As with a t-test, as the number of cases increases, so too does our confidence in the estimate we obtain from an F-test.[5]

Significance Level and Rejection Region   Given that no special concerns have been stated in regard to the risk of either a Type I or a Type II error, we use a conventional 0.05 significance level. Looking at the F table for $\alpha = 0.05$ (Appendix 5), with 2 and 27 degrees of freedom,

---

[5]Indeed, note that the values of F with 1 degree of freedom for the between sum of squares are simply the values of t squared.

respectively, we find a critical value of 3.35. This tells us that we need an F-score greater than 3.35 to reject our null hypothesis of no difference between the population means. An observed F-score greater than 3.35 means that the observed significance level for our test is less than the 0.05 criterion level we have set.

The Test Statistic   To calculate the F-ratio, we must compute estimates of the between-group and within-group population variances based on our three samples. Computing the between-group variance is relatively easy. As noted earlier, the formula for between-group variance ($\hat{\sigma}^2_{bg}$) is

$$\hat{\sigma}^2_{bg} = \frac{\sum_{c=1}^{k}[N_c(\overline{X}_c - \overline{X}_g)^2]}{k - 1}$$

Applying this formula to our example, we first take the mean for each group, subtract from it the overall mean of the three groups (44.43), square the result, and multiply by 10—the number of observations in each group. After this process has been carried out for each of the three groups, the totals are then added together and divided by the degrees of freedom for the between-group variance (2). These calculations are illustrated below. The between sum of squares for our example is 3,405.267. Dividing it by the number of degrees of freedom (2) results in a between-group variance estimate of 1,702.634.

W orking It Out

$$\hat{\sigma}^2_{bg} = \frac{\sum_{c=1}^{k}[N_c(\overline{X}_c - \overline{X}_g)^2]}{k - 1}$$

$$= \frac{10(30.4 - 44.43)^2 + 10(46.7 - 44.43)^2 + 10(56.2 - 44.43)^2}{3 - 1}$$

$$= \frac{3,405.267}{2}$$

$$= 1,702.6335$$

Applying the formula for within-group variance is more difficult in large part because the calculation of a within-group sum of squares demands a good deal of computation even for small samples. For that reason, some texts provide an alternative estimating technique for the within-group sum of squares (see the box on p. 298). However, because it is probably safe to assume that you will turn to statistical computing packages when conducting research in the future and the purpose here is to gain a better understanding of analysis of variance, we will focus on the raw computation. Although cumbersome, it illustrates more directly the logic behind ANOVA.

As discussed earlier, the formula for within-group variance ($\hat{\sigma}^2_{wg}$) is

$$\hat{\sigma}^2_{wg} = \frac{\sum_{i=1}^{N}(X_i - \overline{X}_c)^2}{N - k}$$

For our example, we first take each individual score as illustrated in Table 12.5, and subtract from it the mean for its group: $(X - \overline{X}_c)$. We then square this quantity: $(X - \overline{X}_c)^2$. This is done for all 30 individual scores, and the results are then summed. The within-group sum of squares is 3,874.1. When we divide this quantity by the correct degrees of freedom ($N - k$, or 27), we obtain a within-group variance estimate of 143.485.

To obtain the F-statistic for our example, we simply calculate the ratio of the between- and within-group variances (see Equation 12.10), obtaining 11.866.

$$F = \frac{\text{between-group variance}}{\text{within-group variance}}$$

Equation 12.10

> **W**orking It Out
>
> $$F = \frac{\text{between-group variance}}{\text{within-group variance}}$$
>
> $$F = \frac{1,702.6335}{143.4852}$$
>
> $$= 11.8663$$

Table 12.5 Calculating the Within-Group Sum of Squares

OFFENSE 1 BANK EMBEZZLEMENT $\overline{X} = 30.4$			OFFENSE 2 BRIBERY $\overline{X} = 46.7$			OFFENSE 3 ANTITRUST VIOLATION $\overline{X} = 56.2$		
X	$(X_i - \overline{X}_c)$	$(X_i - \overline{X}_c)^2$	X	$(X_i - \overline{X}_c)$	$(X_i - \overline{X}_c)^2$	X	$(X_i - \overline{X}_c)$	$(X_i - \overline{X}_c)^2$
19	−11.4	129.96	28	−18.7	349.69	35	−21.2	449.44
21	−9.4	88.36	29	−17.7	313.29	46	−10.2	104.04
23	−7.4	54.76	32	−14.7	216.09	48	−8.2	67.24
25	−5.4	29.16	40	−6.7	44.89	53	−3.2	10.24
29	−1.4	1.96	42	−4.7	22.09	58	1.8	3.24
30	−0.4	0.16	48	1.3	1.69	61	4.8	23.04
31	0.6	0.36	58	11.3	127.69	62	5.8	33.64
35	4.6	21.16	58	11.3	127.69	62	5.8	33.64
42	11.6	134.56	64	17.3	299.29	62	5.8	33.64
49	18.6	345.96	68	21.3	453.69	75	18.8	353.44
							$\sum$	= 3,874.1

Computational Formulas for the Within-Group Sum of Squares

While it is important for you to understand the concepts underlying the equations used in the computations for ANOVA, the actual calculation of the within-group sum of squares can be quite tedious. Since it is often easier to calculate the total sum of squares and the between-group sum of squares, the simplest way of obtaining the within-group sum of squares is to rely on the relationship stated in Equation 12.6:

Total sum of squares = between-group sum of squares
+ within-group sum of squares

This equation can be rearranged and solved for the within-group sum of squares:

Within-group sum of squares = total sum of squares
− between-group sum of squares

A formula for computing the total sum of squares is

$$\text{TSS} = \sum_{i=1}^{N} X_i^2 - \frac{\left(\sum_{i=1}^{N} X_i\right)^2}{N}$$

This equation tells us to square the value of each observation and add the resulting squared values together $\left(\sum_{i=1}^{N} X_i^2\right)$. From this quantity, we then subtract the square of the sum of all the values divided by the total number of observations $\left(\left(\sum_{i=1}^{N} X_i\right)^2 / N\right)$.

For an illustration of the use of this formula, we can turn to the data on the ages of white-collar criminals in Table 12.4. In the following table, we take each offender's age (X) and square it (X^2). We then sum each column.

To calculate the total sum of squares, we just enter the two sums into the computational formula:

$$\text{TSS} = \sum_{i=1}^{N} X_i^2 - \frac{\left(\sum_{i=1}^{N} X_i\right)^2}{N}$$

$$= 66,509 - \frac{(1,333)^2}{30}$$

$$= 7,279.367$$

Age (X)	Age Squared (X^2)
19	361
21	441
23	529
25	625
29	841
30	900
31	961
35	1,225
42	1,764
49	2,401
28	784
29	841
32	1,024
40	1,600
42	1,764
48	2,304
58	3,364
58	3,364
64	4,096
68	4,624
35	1,225
46	2,116
48	2,304
53	2,809
58	3,364
61	3,721
62	3,844
62	3,844
62	3,844
75	5,625
$\sum = 1,333$	$\sum = 66,509$

At this point, since we know the total sum of squares (7,279.367) and have already calculated the between-group sum of squares (3,405.267), we can easily see that the within-group sum of squares is 3,874.1:

$$
\begin{aligned}
\text{Within-group sum of squares} &= \text{total sum of squares} \\
&\quad - \text{between-group sum of squares} \\
&= 7{,}279.367 - 3{,}405.267 \\
&= 3{,}874.1
\end{aligned}
$$

The Decision   Because the test statistic for our example (11.866) is larger than 3.35, the critical value of the rejection region, our result is statistically significant at the 0.05 level. Accordingly, we reject the null hypothesis of no difference between the population means and conclude (with a conventional level of risk of falsely rejecting the null hypothesis) that the average age of offenders differs across the three types of crime examined. However, given our concern about violating the assumption of normality, our conclusion will be valid only if age is indeed normally distributed in the three populations studied.

Another ANOVA Example: Race and Bail Amounts Among Felony Drug Defendants

Table 12.6 presents data on bail amounts set for three samples of felony drug defendants in large urban court districts in the United States in the 1990s.[6] The first sample is taken from non-Hispanic whites, the second sample from non-Hispanic African Americans, and the third sample from Hispanics of any race. Twelve defendants were drawn at random from the population of each group. The mean bail amount is $4,833.33 for non-Hispanic whites, $8,833.33 for non-Hispanic African Americans, and $30,375.00 for Hispanics of any race. Do

Table 12.6   Bail Amounts (in Dollars) for 36 Felony Drug Defendants

NON-HISPANIC WHITES	NON-HISPANIC BLACKS	HISPANICS OF ANY RACE
1,000	1,000	1,000
1,000	1,000	2,000
1,500	2,000	4,000
2,000	2,500	5,000
2,500	3,000	10,000
3,000	4,000	12,500
5,000	5,000	25,000
7,000	10,000	25,000
7,500	12,500	25,000
7,500	20,000	40,000
10,000	20,000	65,000
10,000	25,000	150,000
$\bar{X} = 4,833.33$	$\bar{X} = 8,833.33$	$\bar{X} = 30,375.00$
$s = 3,287.18$	$s = 8,201.46$	$s = 42,028.74$

Grand mean $(\bar{X}_g) = 14,680.56$

[6]The data are taken from *State Court Processing Statistics: 1990, 1992, 1994, 1996* and can be accessed through the National Archive of Criminal Justice Data web site at http://www.icpsr.umich.edu/NACJD.

Most statistical analysis software presents the results of an analysis of variance in the form of an ANOVA table. An ANOVA table provides a compact and convenient way to present the key elements in an analysis of variance. In addition to ensuring that the researcher has all the necessary information, it also allows the researcher to reproduce the estimates of the variance and the F-statistic. The general form of an ANOVA table is as follows:

Source	df	Sum of Squares	Mean Square	F
Between	$k-1$	$\sum_{c=1}^{k}[N_c(\bar{X}_c - \bar{X}_g)^2]$	$\dfrac{\text{BSS}}{k-1}$	$\dfrac{\hat{\sigma}_{bg}^2}{\hat{\sigma}_{wg}^2}$
Within	$N-k$	$\sum_{i=1}^{N}(X_i - \bar{X}_c)^2$	$\dfrac{\text{WSS}}{N-k}$	
Total	$N-1$	$\sum_{i=1}^{N}(X_i - \bar{X}_g)^2$		

Each row gives the pieces of information needed and the formulas for the calculations. For example, the "Between" row gives the corresponding degrees of freedom and the formulas for calculating between-group variability, between-group variance (in the "Mean Square" column), and the F-statistic. The "Within" row gives the corresponding degrees of freedom and the formulas for calculating within-group variability and within-group variance.

Following is the ANOVA table for the results of our calculations using the data on the ages of white-collar criminals:

Source	df	Sum of Squares	Mean Square	F
Between	2	3,405.267	1,702.6335	11.8663
Within	27	3,874.100	143.4852	
Total	29	7,279.367		

the differences in sample means indicate that there are differences in the population means?

Assumptions:

Level of Measurement: Interval scale.

Population Distribution: Normal distribution for each population (the shape of the population distributions is unknown, and the sizes of the samples examined are small).

Sampling Method: Independent random sampling (no replacement; samples are small relative to populations).

Sampling Frame: Felony drug defendants in large urban court districts in the United States in the 1990s.

Population variances are equal ($\sigma_1^2 = \sigma_2^2 = \sigma_3^2$).

Hypotheses:

H_0: Population means of bail amounts set for felony drug defendants who are non-Hispanic whites, non-Hispanic African Americans, and Hispanics of any race are equal ($\mu_1 = \mu_2 = \mu_3$).

H_1: Population means of bail amounts set for felony drug defendants who are non-Hispanic whites, non-Hispanic African Americans, and Hispanics of any race are not equal ($\mu_1 \neq \mu_2 \neq \mu_3$).

The Sampling Distribution   We again use the F distribution to test for differences among our three sample means. Recall that we need two indicators of degrees of freedom: one for the between-group variance and one for the within-group variance.

df for between-group variance = $k - 1 = 3 - 1 = 2$

df for within-group variance = $N - k = 36 - 3 = 33$

Significance Level and Rejection Region   As in the preceding example, we do not have any particular concerns about the risk of a Type I or Type II error, so we can use the conventional 0.05 significance level. Given that we have degrees of freedom equal to 2 and 33 with a 0.05 significance level, the critical value of the F-statistic is about 3.29. If our calculated F-statistic is greater than 3.29, then we will reject our null hypothesis of equal means.

The Test Statistic   We begin our calculation of the F-statistic by computing estimates of the between-group variance and the within-group variance. Applying the formula for between-group variance, we find the estimate of $\hat{\sigma}_{bg}^2$ to be 2,264,840,905.56.

W orking It Out

$$\hat{\sigma}^2_{\text{bg}} = \frac{\sum_{c=1}^{k} [N_c(\overline{X}_c - \overline{X}_g)^2]}{k-1}$$

$$= \frac{\left(\begin{array}{c} 12(4{,}833.33 - 14{,}680.56)^2 \\ + 12(8{,}833.33 - 14{,}680.56)^2 + 12(30{,}375.00 - 14{,}680.56)^2 \end{array}\right)}{3-1}$$

$$= \frac{4{,}529{,}681{,}811.11}{2}$$

$$= 2{,}264{,}840{,}905.56$$

The value of the within-group variance ($\hat{\sigma}^2_{\text{wg}}$) is 617,193,813.13. Table 12.7 presents the calculation of the within-group sum of squares, which turns out to be equal to 20,367,395,833.33. We then divide the value of the within-group sum of squares by the corresponding degrees of freedom ($N - k = 36 - 3 = 33$), which gives us an estimate for the within-group variance of 617,193,813.13.

W orking It Out

$$\hat{\sigma}^2_{\text{wg}} = \frac{\sum_{i=1}^{N} (X_i - \overline{X}_c)^2}{N-k}$$

$$= \frac{20{,}367{,}395{,}833.33}{36-3}$$

$$= 617{,}193{,}813.13$$

The value of the F-statistic is obtained by dividing the estimate of between-group variance by the estimate of within-group variance. For our example, F is found to be 3.67.

W orking It Out

$$F = \frac{\text{between-group variance}}{\text{within-group variance}}$$

$$= \frac{2{,}264{,}840{,}905.56}{617{,}193{,}813.13}$$

$$= 3.67$$

| Table 12.7 | Calculating the Within-Group Sum of Squares |

NON-HISPANIC WHITES		NON-HISPANIC BLACKS		HISPANICS OF ANY RACE	
X	$(X_i - \bar{X}_c)^2$	X	$(X_i - \bar{X}_c)^2$	X	$(X_i - \bar{X}_c)^2$
1,000	14,694,418.89	1,000	61,361,058.89	1,000	862,890,625.00
1,000	14,694,418.89	1,000	61,361,058.89	2,000	805,140,625.00
1,500	11,111,088.89	2,000	46,694,398.89	4,000	695,640,625.00
2,000	8,027,758.89	2,500	40,111,068.89	5,000	643,890,625.00
2,500	5,444,428.89	3,000	34,027,738.89	10,000	415,140,625.00
3,000	3,361,098.89	4,000	23,361,078.89	12,500	319,515,625.00
5,000	27,778.89	5,000	14,694,418.89	25,000	28,890,625.00
7,000	4,694,458.89	10,000	1,361,118.89	25,000	28,890,625.00
7,500	7,111,128.89	12,500	13,444,468.89	25,000	28,890,625.00
7,500	7,111,128.89	20,000	124,694,518.89	40,000	92,640,625.00
10,000	26,694,478.89	20,000	124,694,518.89	65,000	1,198,890,625.00
10,000	26,694,478.89	25,000	261,361,218.89	150,000	14,310,140,625.00

$$\Sigma = 20,367,395,833.33$$

The Decision   Since our test statistic of 3.67 is greater than the critical value of 3.29 for the F distribution, we reject the null hypothesis of equal population means; we conclude that there is a statistically significant relationship between bail amount and race of defendant. However, as in our example concerning age and white-collar crime, we began our test with strong doubts about whether we could meet a core assumption of analysis of variance. The samples examined are not large, and thus we cannot relax the normality assumption for our test. In turn, we do not have strong reason to believe that the populations to which we want to infer actually meet the criteria of this assumption. As has been noted throughout the text, statistical conclusions are only as solid as the assumptions the researchers make. In this case, our statistical conclusions clearly do not stand on solid ground.

Defining the Strength of the Relationship Observed

Even though analysis of variance is concerned with comparing means from independent samples, in practice the samples are usually defined as representing a multicategory nominal-level variable. For example, as noted earlier, in comparing three samples of white-collar criminals, we could define each as one category in a nominal-scale measure of type of white-collar crime. Similarly, in our example concerning the relationship between bail amount and race, we spoke about differences among three samples of offenders: non-Hispanic whites, non-Hispanic blacks, and

Hispanics of any race. Nonetheless, these three samples can be seen as three groups in a nominal-level measure of race of defendant.

Accordingly, one question we might ask after finding a statistically significant result is "How strong is the overall relationship we have identified?" The simplest way to answer this question is to look at the differences between the means of the samples. With just three samples, we can get a pretty good sense of the strength of a relationship using this method. But even with three samples, it is difficult to summarize the extent of the relationship observed because we must look at three separate comparisons (that between group 1 and group 2, that between group 2 and group 3, and that between group 3 and group 1). With four samples, the number of comparisons is six; for seven samples, there are 21 comparisons. Clearly, it is useful, especially as the number of samples grows, to have a single statistic for establishing the strength of the observed relationship.

A commonly used measure of association for ANOVA is a statistic called **eta (η).** Eta relies on the partialing of sums of squares to establish the relationship, or **correlation,** between the interval-level variable in ANOVA and the nominal-level variable. To calculate eta, we simply take the square root of the ratio of the between sum of squares to the total sum of squares (see Equation 12.11).

$$\eta = \sqrt{\frac{\text{BSS}}{\text{TSS}}}$$

Equation 12.11

Although it might not seem so at first glance, this measure makes good sense. Understanding eta, however, will be easier if we start with another statistic, **eta squared (η^2),** which is sometimes referred to as the **percent of variance explained** (see Equation 12.12).

$$\eta^2 = \frac{\text{BSS}}{\text{TSS}}$$

Equation 12.12

Eta squared is the proportion of the total sum of squares that is accounted for by the between sum of squares. As previously noted, the between sum of squares is also defined as the explained sum of squares because it represents the part of the total variation that is accounted for by the differences between the samples. Eta squared thus identifies the proportion of the total sum of squares that is accounted for by the explained sum of squares—hence its identification as the percent of variance explained.

The larger the proportion of total variance that is accounted for by the between sum of squares, the stronger the relationship between the nominal- and interval-level variables being examined. When the means of the samples are the same, eta squared will be 0. This means that there is no relationship between the nominal- and interval-level measures the study is examining. The largest value of eta squared is 1, meaning that all of

Table 12.8	Comparing Eta Squared with Eta

η^2	η
0.00	0.00
0.01	0.10
0.02	0.14
0.03	0.17
0.04	0.20
0.05	0.22
0.10	0.32
0.25	0.50
0.50	0.71
0.75	0.87
1.00	1.00

the variability in the samples is accounted for by the between sum of squares. In practice, as eta squared increases in value between 0 and 1, the relationship being examined gets stronger.

The square root of eta squared is a measure more sensitive to small relationships. For example, a value for eta squared of 0.04 is equal to a value for eta of 0.20, and a value for eta squared of 0.1 is equivalent to a value for eta of 0.32, as shown in Table 12.8. In criminal justice, where the relationships examined are often not very large, measures such as this one, which allow us to distinguish relatively small values more clearly, are particularly useful.

Turning to our example concerning age and white-collar crime, we can see that the differences between the groups account for a good deal of the variability in the total sum of squares. Taking the between sum of squares for that example and dividing it by the total sum of squares gives a value for eta squared of 0.468.

W orking It Out

$$BSS = 3{,}405.267$$

$$TSS = BSS + WSS$$

$$= 3{,}405.267 + 3{,}874.100$$

$$= 7{,}279.367$$

$$\eta^2 = \frac{BSS}{TSS}$$

$$= \frac{3{,}405.267}{7{,}279.367}$$

$$= 0.4678$$

By taking the square root of this value, we obtain a correlation coefficient, or eta, of 0.684.

W orking It Out

$$\eta = \sqrt{\frac{\text{BSS}}{\text{TSS}}} = \sqrt{\frac{3{,}405.267}{7{,}279.367}}$$

$$= \sqrt{0.4678}$$

$$= 0.6840$$

Does an eta of 0.684 signify a large or small relationship? To some extent, differentiating between "large" and "small" in this context is a value judgment rather than a statistical decision. We might decide whether a particular value of eta is large or small based on results from other studies in other areas of criminal justice or perhaps similar studies that drew different samples. There is no clear yardstick for making this decision. One psychologist suggests that any value for eta greater than 0.371 represents a large effect.[7] A moderate-size effect is indicated by a value of 0.243. Using this criterion, we would define the relationship between age and type of white-collar crime as very strong. However, in this example, we should be cautious about relying on the results obtained. With small samples, the values of eta are not considered very reliable.[8]

Making Pairwise Comparisons Between the Groups Studied

Once you have established through an analysis of variance that there is a statistically significant difference across the samples studied, you may want to look at differences between specific pairs of the samples. To do this, you make comparisons between two sample means at a time. Such comparisons within an analysis of variance are often called **pairwise comparisons.**

---

[7]See Jacob Cohen, *Statistical Power Analysis for the Behavorial Sciences* (Hillsdale, NJ: Lawrence Erlbaum, 1988), pp. 285–287.

[8]Once again, there is no universally accepted definition of what is "small." There will be little question regarding the validity of your estimate of eta if your samples meet the 30 cases minimum defined for invoking the central limit theorem. Some statisticians suggest that you will gain relatively reliable estimates even for samples as small as 10 cases.

| Table 12.9 | The 21 Separate Pairwise Comparisons To Be Made for an Analysis of Variance with Seven Samples (Categories) |

SAMPLE	1	2	3	4	5	6	7
1							
2	✓						
3	✓	✓					
4	✓	✓	✓				
5	✓	✓	✓	✓			
6	✓	✓	✓	✓	✓		
7	✓	✓	✓	✓	✓	✓	

It would seem, at first glance, that you could simply apply the two-sample t-test discussed in Chapter 11 to test hypotheses related to such comparisons. However, you are faced with a very important statistical problem. If you run a number of t-tests at the same time, you are unfairly increasing your odds of obtaining a statistically significant finding along the way. For example, let's say that you have conducted an analysis of variance comparing seven samples and obtained a statistically significant result. You now want to look at the pairwise comparisons to see which of the specific comparisons are significantly different from one another. There are a total of 21 separate comparisons to make (see Table 12.9). For each test, you set a significance level of 0.05, which means that you are willing to take a 1 in 20 chance of falsely rejecting the null hypothesis. Thus, if you run 20 tests, you might expect to get at least one statistically significant result just by chance.

Here a finding of a significant result could simply be attributed to the fact that you have run a large number of tests. Accordingly, to be fair, you should adjust your tests to take into account the change in the probabilities that results from looking at a series of pairwise comparisons. A number of different tests allow you to do this; many are provided in standard statistical packages.[9] One commonly used test is the **honestly significant difference (HSD) test** developed by John Tukey (see Equation 12.13).

$$\text{HSD} = P_{\text{crit}} \sqrt{\frac{\hat{\sigma}^2_{\text{wg}}}{N_c}}$$

Equation 12.13

HSD defines the value of the difference between the pairwise comparisons that is required to reject the null hypothesis at a given level of statistical significance.

---

[9]For a discussion of pairwise comparison tests, see A. J. Klockars and G. Sax, *Multiple Comparisons* (*Quantitative Applications in the Social Science,* Vol. 61) (London: Sage, 1986).

For our white-collar crime example, with a conventional 5% signifi-cance threshold, we first identify the critical value (P_{crit}) associated with that significance threshold by looking at Appendix 6. With three samples and 27 degrees of freedom in the within sum of squares estimate, the critical value is about 3.51. We then multiply this value by the square root of the within-group variance estimate ($\hat{\sigma}^2_{wg}$) divided by the number of cases in each sample (N_c)—in our example, 10.[10] Our result is 13.296, meaning that the absolute value of the difference in mean age between the pairwise comparisons must be greater than 13.296 to reject the null hypothesis of no difference (using a 5% significance threshold).

W orking It Out

$$HSD = P_{crit} \sqrt{\frac{\hat{\sigma}^2_{wg}}{N_c}}$$

$$= 3.51 \sqrt{\frac{143.49}{10}}$$

$$= 13.296$$

Table 12.10 shows the absolute differences found for the three com-parisons between means. Two of the three comparisons are statistically significant at the 5% level—the absolute differences are greater than 13.296 for the difference between bank embezzlers and bribery offend-ers and for that between bank embezzlers and antitrust offenders. How-ever, for the difference between bribery and antitrust offenders, our re-sult just misses the value needed to reject the null hypothesis. We would have to conclude that our sample results do not provide persuasive evi-dence for stating that the mean ages of bribery and antitrust offenders are different in the larger populations from which these two samples were drawn.

---

[10]Most pairwise comparison tests, including Tukey's HSD test, require that the sample sizes of the groups examined be equal. While most statistical software packages pro-vide adjustments of these tests to account for unequal sample sizes, there is still de-bate over whether the estimates gained can be relied upon [e.g., see Robert R. J. Sokal and F. J. Rohlf, *Biometry: The Principles and Practice of Statistics in Biological Re-search*, 3rd ed. (New York: W. H. Freeman, 1995), Chap. 9]. Irrespective of this de-bate, when unequal sample sizes are examined, the adjusted estimates are to be pre-ferred over the unadjusted estimates.

| Table 12.10 | Results of the Pairwise Comparison Tests | | |

	OFFENSE 1 BANK EMBEZZLEMENT	OFFENSE 2 BRIBERY	OFFENSE 3 ANTITRUST VIOLATION
Offense 1 Bank Embezzlement			
Offense 2 Bribery	16.300*		
Offense 3 Antitrust Violation	25.800*	9.500	

$*p < 0.5$

The comparisons we have made so far have been based on a statistically significant overall result for ANOVA. Should such comparisons be made if the overall differences across the means are not statistically significant? In general, it is not a good idea to look for pairwise comparisons if the overall analysis of variance is not statistically significant. This is a bit like going fishing for a statistically significant result. However, sometimes one or another of the pairwise comparisons is of particular interest. Such interest should be determined before you develop your analyses. However, if you do start off with a strong hypothesis for a pairwise comparison, it is acceptable to examine it, irrespective of the outcomes of the larger test. In such circumstances, it is also acceptable to use a simple two-sample t-test to examine group differences.

A Nonparametric Alternative: The Kruskal-Wallis Test

For studies where you cannot meet the parametric assumptions of the analysis of variance test, you may want to consider a nonparametric **rank-order test.** In performing a rank-order test, you lose some crucial information because you focus only on the order of scores and not on the differences in values between them. However, such tests have the advantage of not requiring assumptions about the population distribution.

One rank-order test is the **Kruskal-Wallis test.** As a nonparametric test of statistical significance, it requires neither a normal distribution nor equal variances between the groups studied. The test asks simply whether the distribution of ranked scores in the three groups is what would be expected under a null hypothesis of no difference. When the number of cases in each group is greater than 5, the sampling distribution of the Kruskal-Wallis test score, denoted H, is approximately chi-square.

As an illustration, let's examine whether this nonparametric test suggests significant differences in terms of age across the white-collar crime categories of our earlier example.

Assumptions:

Level of Measurement: Ordinal scale.

Population Distribution: No assumption made.

Sampling Method: Independent random sampling (no replacement; sample is small relative to population).

Sampling Frame: All white-collar offenders convicted of the crimes examined in seven federal judicial districts over a three-year period.

Hypotheses:

H_0: The distribution of ranked scores is identical in the three populations.

H_1: The distribution of ranked scores differs across the three populations.

In this test, we use an ordinal-level measure: the rank order of ages in the sample. To obtain this measure, we simply rank the 30 subjects studied according to age, with the youngest offender given a rank of 1 and the oldest a rank of 30 (see Table 12.11). In the case of ties, subjects share a rank. For example, the two subjects aged 29 share the rank of 6.5 (the average of ranks 6 and 7), and the three subjects aged 62 share the rank of 26 (the average of ranks 25, 26, and 27).

Table 12.11   White-Collar Offenders Ranked According to Age

OFFENSE 1 BANK EMBEZZLEMENT		OFFENSE 2 BRIBERY		OFFENSE 3 ANTITRUST VIOLATION	
Age	Rank	Age	Rank	Age	Rank
19	1	28	5	35	11.5
21	2	29	6.5	46	16
23	3	32	10	48	17.5
25	4	40	13	53	20
29	6.5	42	14.5	58	22
30	8	48	17.5	61	24
31	9	58	22	62	26
35	11.5	58	22	62	26
42	14.5	64	28	62	26
49	19	68	29	75	30
	$\sum = 78.5$		$\sum = 167.5$		$\sum = 219$

Our null hypothesis is that the distribution of ranked scores in the three populations is identical. Our research hypothesis is that it is not identical across the three populations.

Sampling Distribution   The sampling distribution H is distributed approximately according to chi-square because the number of cases in each group is greater than 5. The number of degrees of freedom for the distribution is defined as $k - 1$, where k refers to the number of samples (or categories). Because our example involves three samples, the number of degrees of freedom for the chi-square distribution is $3 - 1$, or 2.

Significance Level and Rejection Region   Consistent with our earlier choice of a 0.05 significance threshold, we turn to the 0.05 value with 2 degrees of freedom in the chi-square table (see Appendix 2). The critical value identified is 5.991.

The Test Statistic   The formula for H given in Equation 12.14 looks complex. However, it is relatively simple to compute if broken into pieces.

$$H = \left[\left(\frac{12}{N(N+1)} \right) \left(\sum_{c=1}^{k} \frac{\left(\sum_{i=1}^{N_c} R_i \right)^2}{N_c} \right) \right] - 3(N+1) \qquad \text{Equation 12.14}$$

There is only one complex term in the equation. It is

$$\sum_{c=1}^{k} \frac{\left(\sum_{i=1}^{N_c} R_i \right)^2}{N_c}$$

This term tells us to take the sum of the ranks in each sample, square it, and divide it by the number of cases in the sample; then we sum these values for all the samples.[11] The H-score obtained for our problem is 13.038.

---

[11]Most statistical computing packages provide an alternative calculation that adjusts for ties. In practice, the differences between using this correction procedure and performing the unadjusted test are generally small. For our example, where there are a large number of ties relative to the sample size (14/30), the difference in the observed significance level is only 0.0001.

W orking It Out

$$H = \left[\left(\frac{12}{N(N+1)} \right) \left(\sum_{c=1}^{k} \frac{\left(\sum_{i=1}^{N_c} R_i \right)^2}{N_c} \right) \right] - 3(N+1)$$

$$= \left(\frac{12}{30(31)} \right) \left(\frac{(78.5)^2}{10} + \frac{(167.5)^2}{10} + \frac{(219)^2}{10} \right) - 3(31)$$

$$= \left(\frac{12}{930} \right) 8{,}217.95 - 3(31)$$

$$= 13.038$$

The Decision   As with the F-test, our score exceeds the critical value needed to reject the null hypothesis of no difference. The observed significance level of our test is thus less than the criterion significance level we set at the outset ($p < 0.05$). From the Kruskal-Wallis test, we can again conclude that there is a statistically significant relationship between type of white-collar crime and age of offender. This time, however, we can have more confidence in our conclusion because the assumptions of the test are met more strictly.

Chapter Summary

ANOVA is a parametric test of statistical significance that allows a researcher to compare means across more than two groups. It takes into account not only variability between groups but also variability within groups. The larger the differences between the groups relative to the variability within them, the more confidence the researcher can have in a conclusion that differences exist among the population means. Between-group variability is measured by the **between sum of squares** (or **explained sum of squares**). Within-group variability is measured by the **within sum of squares** (or **unexplained sum of squares**). The **total sum of squares** is equal to the sum of the between and within sums of squares. To develop estimates of population variances, the sums of squares are divided by the appropriate degrees of freedom. ANOVA requires the following assumptions: interval scales, normal population distributions, independent random sampling, and homoscedasticity. The sampling distribution for ANOVA is denoted as F.

The F-value needed to reject the null hypothesis gets smaller as the within-group degrees of freedom grows. The F-statistic is calculated by dividing the between-group variance by the within-group variance.

The strength of the relationship observed is measured by the statistic **eta squared,** or **percent of variance explained.** Eta squared is the ratio of the between sum of squares to the total sum of squares. An eta squared value of 0 indicates that there is no relationship between the nominal and interval variables (i.e., the means are the same). An eta squared value of 1 represents a perfect relationship between the nominal and interval variables. The correlation coefficient, or eta, is obtained by taking the square root of eta squared.

A researcher who wishes to compare means of pairs of specific samples within a larger test makes a **pairwise comparison.** Running a series of two-sample t-tests, however, unfairly increases the odds of getting a statistically significant result. The **honestly significant difference (HSD) test** is a pairwise comparison test that corrects for this bias.

When the assumptions underlying ANOVA are difficult to meet, the researcher may choose a nonparametric alternative—the **Kruskal-Wallis test.** This test does not require an assumption of normal population distributions or homoscedasticity. As a **rank-order test,** however, it does not use all of the information available from interval-level data.

Key Terms

analysis of variance (ANOVA) A parametric test of statistical significance that assesses whether differences in the means of several samples (groups) can lead the researcher to reject the null hypothesis that the means of the populations from which the samples are drawn are the same.

between sum of squares (BSS) A measure of the variability between samples (groups). The between sum of squares is calculated by taking the sum of the squared deviation of each sample mean from the grand mean multiplied by the number of cases in that sample.

correlation A measure of the strength of a relationship between two variables.

eta A measure of the degree of correlation between an interval-level and a nominal-level variable.

eta squared The proportion of the total sum of squares that is accounted for by the between sum of squares. Eta squared is sometimes referred to as the percent of variance explained.

explained sum of squares (ESS) Another name for the between sum of squares. The explained sum of squares is the part of the total variability that can be explained by visible differences between the groups.

grand mean The overall mean of every single case across all of the samples.

honestly significant difference (HSD) test A parametric test of statistical significance, adjusted for making pairwise comparisons. The HSD test defines the difference between the pairwise comparisons required to reject the null hypothesis.

Kruskal-Wallis test A nonparametric test of statistical significance for multiple groups, requiring at least an ordinal scale of measurement.

overall mean See *grand mean.*

pairwise comparisons Comparisons made between two sample means extracted from a larger statistical analysis.

percent of variance explained The proportion of the total sum of squares that is accounted for by the explained sum of squares; eta squared.

rank-order test A test of statistical significance that uses information relating to the relative order, or rank, of variable scores.

sum of squares The sum of squared deviations of scores from a mean or set of means.

total sum of squares (TSS) A measure of the total amount of variability across all of the groups examined. The total sum of squares is calculated by summing the squared deviation of each score from the grand mean.

unexplained sum of squares (USS) Another name for the within sum of squares. The unexplained sum of squares is the part of the total variability that cannot be explained by visible differences between the groups.

within sum of squares (WSS) A measure of the variability within samples (groups). The within sum of squares is calculated by summing the squared deviation of each score from its sample mean.

Symbols and Formulas

X_i	Individual subject or score
$\overline{X}_c$	Sample or category mean
$\overline{X}_g$	Grand or overall mean
N_c	Number of cases in each sample
k	Number of categories or samples
η	Correlation coefficient eta
η^2	Percent of variance explained; eta squared
P_{crit}	Critical value for HSD test
R_i	Individual rank of score

To calculate the between sum of squares:

$$\text{BSS} = \sum_{c=1}^{k} [N_c(\overline{X}_c - \overline{X}_g)^2]$$

To calculate the within sum of squares:

$$\text{WSS} = \sum_{i=1}^{N}(X_i - \overline{X}_c)^2$$

To calculate the total sum of squares:

$$\text{TSS} = \sum_{i=1}^{N}(X_i - \overline{X}_g)^2$$

To partition the total sum of squares:

Total sum of squares = between sum of squares
+ within sum of squares

$$\text{TSS} = \text{BSS} + \text{WSS}$$

To estimate between-group variance:

$$\hat{\sigma}_{\text{bg}}^2 = \frac{\sum_{c=1}^{k}[N_c(\overline{X}_c - \overline{X}_g)^2]}{k - 1}$$

To estimate within-group variance:

$$\hat{\sigma}_{\text{wg}}^2 = \frac{\sum_{i=1}^{N}(X_i - \overline{X}_c)^2}{N - k}$$

To calculate F:

$$F = \frac{\text{between-group variance}}{\text{within-group variance}}$$

To calculate eta:

$$\eta = \sqrt{\frac{\text{BSS}}{\text{TSS}}}$$

To calculate eta squared:

$$\eta^2 = \frac{\text{BSS}}{\text{TSS}}$$

To perform the HSD test:

$$\text{HSD} = P_{\text{crit}}\sqrt{\frac{\hat{\sigma}_{\text{wg}}^2}{N_c}}$$

To perform the Kruskal-Wallis test:

$$H = \left[\left(\frac{12}{N(N+1)}\right)\left(\sum_{c=1}^{k}\frac{\left(\sum_{i=1}^{N_c}R_i\right)^2}{N_c}\right)\right] - 3(N+1)$$

Exercises

12.1 Dawn, a criminal justice researcher, gives 125 pretrial defendants scores based on a questionnaire that assesses their ability to understand the court process. The defendants were selected from five separate counties. Dawn took an independent random sample of 25 defendants from each county. The scores for the five populations are normally distributed. Dawn runs an ANOVA test on her results, which produces a test statistic of 3.35.

 a. Would Dawn be able to reject her null hypothesis that there is no difference between the populations in their ability to comprehend the court process if she were to set a 5% significance level?

 b. Would she be able to reject the null hypothesis using a 1% significance level?

 c. Would your answer to either part a or part b be different if Dawn's sample had consisted of five equally sized groups of 200 subjects each?

12.2 Random samples of individuals were drawn from three neighborhoods by a policing research foundation to study the level of public support for the local police department. The research foundation constructed a complicated interval-level measure of police support, in which higher values indicated more support. The researchers found the following pattern across the three neighborhoods: The mean level of support in neighborhood A was 3.1 ($N = 15$); in neighborhood B, it was 5.6 ($N = 17$); and in neighborhood C, 4.2 ($N = 11$). The measure of between-group variance was 4.7, and the measure of within-group variance was 1.1.

 a. If the significance level is 0.05, can the research foundation conclude that there are different levels of support for the police department across neighborhoods? Write out all of the steps of a test of statistical significance, including any violations of assumptions.

 b. What if the significance level is 0.01?

12.3 Random sampling of individuals with four different majors at a university found the following grade point averages (GPAs) for the four groups:

Major A: GPA = 3.23 ($N = 178$)
Major B: GPA = 2.76 ($N = 64$)
Major C: GPA = 2.18 ($N = 99$)
Major D: GPA = 3.54 ($N = 121$)

If the between-group variance is 5.7 and the within-group variance is 1.5, are the GPAs different for the four majors? Use a significance level of 0.01, and write out all of the steps of a test of statistical significance, including any violations of assumptions.

12.4   Random sampling offenders convicted of minor drug possession in Border County found the average jail sentence for white offenders to be 86 days ($N = 15$), for African American offenders to be 99 days ($N = 10$), and for Hispanic offenders to be 72 days ($N = 7$). Further analysis of jail sentence lengths by race found the between sum of squares to be 250 and the within sum of squares to be 1,300. Are the jail sentence lengths significantly different across race categories?

   a. Use a significance level of 0.05. Write out all of the steps of a test of statistical significance, including any violations of assumptions.

   b. Would the conclusion be any different if the significance level had been set at 0.01?

12.5   Listed below is a set of data identifying previous convictions for any offense of 40 inmates serving prison sentences for robbery, rape, murder, and drug dealing.

Robbery	Rape	Murder	Drug Dealing
1	1	0	5
0	1	0	3
2	1	0	7
6	0	6	4
4	0	2	8
5	2	7	0
3	2	1	6
1	1	4	2
5	0	2	1
3	2	3	4

Calculate the following values:

   a. $\overline{X}_g$

   b. df for between-group variance

   c. df for within-group variance

   d. the four values of $\overline{X}_c$

   e. the total sum of squares

   f. the between sum of squares

   g. the within sum of squares

12.6   Convicted drug dealers held in Grimsville Prison are placed in cell block A, B, or C according to their city of origin. Danny (who has little knowledge of statistics) was once an inmate in the prison. Now released, he still bears a grudge against the prison authorities. Danny wishes to make up a series of statistics to show that the convicts in the various blocks are treated differently. According to his fictitious sample, the mean number of hours of exercise per week given to the inmates is 10 hours for block A offenders, 20 hours for block B offenders, and 30 hours for block C offenders. Shown below are two fictitious sets of results.

Fictitious study 1:

Block A	Block B	Block C
9	21	30
10	19	29
9	20	31
11	19	29
11	21	31
$\overline{X} = 10$	$\overline{X} = 20$	$\overline{X} = 30$

Fictitious study 2:

Block A	Block B	Block C
18	16	37
16	18	36
10	2	7
2	31	41
4	33	29
$\overline{X} = 10$	$\overline{X} = 20$	$\overline{X} = 30$

a. From simply looking at the numbers, without running any statistical tests, which of the two fictitious studies would you expect to provide stronger backing for Danny's claim? Explain your answer.

b. Calculate the between sum of squares and the within sum of squares for study 1.

c. Calculate the between sum of squares and the within sum of squares for study 2.

d. Calculate the value of eta for each study. How do you account for the difference?

12.7 A researcher takes three independent random samples of young pickpockets and asks them how old they were when they first committed the offense. The researcher wishes to determine whether there are any differences among the three populations from which the samples were drawn—those who have no siblings, those who have one or two siblings, and those with three or more siblings.

Age at first theft:

0 Siblings	1 or 2 Siblings	3+ Siblings
10	14	15
8	15	15
16	15	10
14	13	13
7	12	16
8	9	15

a. Show that the total sum of squares is equal to the between sum of squares plus the within sum of squares.

b. What is the value of eta?

c. Can the researcher reject the null hypothesis on the basis of the differences observed? Run an F-test using a 5% significance level. Remember to outline all of the steps of a test of statistical significance, including any violations of assumptions.

12.8   Using independent random sampling, Sophie draws samples from three different populations: psychologists, police officers, and factory workers. She gives each subject a hypothetical case study of a drug dealer who has been found guilty and awaits sentencing. The subjects are then asked to suggest how many years the drug dealer should serve in prison. The results are presented below:

Psychologists	Police	Factory Workers
2	3	5
1	2	6
0	3	4
0	3	8
1	4	7
2.5	1	7
2	1.5	6
1.5	0	2
4	0.5	3
1	7	2

a. Can Sophie conclude that the three populations are different in terms of their attitudes toward punishing convicted drug dealers? Run an F-test using a 5% significance level. Remember to outline all of the steps of a test of statistical significance, including any violations of assumptions.

b. Would Sophie's decision be any different if she chose a 1% or a 0.1% level of significance?

c. Calculate the value of eta for the results above. Is the relationship a strong one?

12.9 For the data in Exercise 12.4, run a Kruskal-Wallis test using a 5% level of statistical significance. Remember to outline all of the steps of a test of statistical significance, including any violations of assumptions. Are you able to reject the null hypothesis?

Computer Exercises

Before you try out the ANOVA commands in SPSS, open the data file *ex12_1.sav,* which contains the data presented in Table 12.4 in the text.

ANOVA

In SPSS, the "One-Way ANOVA" command (Analyze → Compare Means → One-Way ANOVA) performs a quick and easy test for differences in group means. After you execute the command, you will be presented with a window that lists all the variables in the data file in a box on the left. On the right side of the window is a box labeled "Dependent List," which will hold the names of the interval level variables you are interested in testing for differences across groups. Below this box is a smaller box for the grouping variable, labeled "Factor," which is where you put the name of the variable that represents the different categories or groups in the sample.

Move the age variable into the "Dependent List" box and the crime type variable into the "Factor" box. Click on "OK" to run the command. The output window will present the ANOVA table (discussed in the box on p. 309), where you should see that the value of the *F*-test reported by SPSS matches that reported on page 305.

ANOVA results can also be obtained with the "Means" command (Analyze → Compare Means → Means). After you execute this command, you will be presented with a window that lists all the variables in the data file in a box on the left. The two boxes on the right are labeled "Dependent List" and "Independent List." The "Dependent List" box will contain the names of the interval-level variables you are testing, and the "Independent List" box will contain the name(s) of the grouping variable(s). Enter the age variable as the dependent variable and the crime type variable as the independent variable.

To obtain the ANOVA table with the "Means" command, you need to click on the "Options" button located in the lower right corner of the window. In the next window that opens, click on the box next to "ANOVA Table and Eta." Then click on "Continue" and "OK" to run the command.

The output from this command will consist of the ANOVA table (check that the values here are identical to those obtained using the "One-Way ANOVA" command) and a table that provides the value of eta. *Note:* Eta is not available through the "One-Way ANOVA" command.

Tukey's HSD

SPSS's "One-Way ANOVA" command will perform a wide range of additional calculations on data; Tukey's HSD statistic is included in this package. To obtain Tukey's HSD statistic, execute the "One-Way ANOVA" command. You will see a button labeled "Post Hoc . . ." at the bottom center of the resulting window. After clicking on this button, you will be presented with a new window that lists many different statistics SPSS can compute. Locate the line labeled "Tukey," and click on the small white box next to the label; then click on "Continue" and "OK" to run the command.

The output presented will contain the ANOVA table and an additional table that lists all possible comparisons of group means. The three major rows in this table represent the three samples of offenders. Within each major row are two smaller rows that represent contrasts between the groups. So, for example, in the first major row (the embezzlement sample), there are calculations for the mean of this group minus the mean of the second group (the bribery sample) in the first line, followed by calculations for the mean of the first group minus the mean of the third group (the antitrust sample) in the second line. The values for Tukey's HSD reported in the first major row match those reported in Table 12.10. In the second major row (the bribery sample), the second line represents the difference between this group's mean and the mean for the third group (the antitrust sample), and the value for Tukey's HSD again matches that reported in Table 12.10.

Sometimes the labels in the table of results for Tukey's HSD can be confusing, so you will need to pay attention to the lines you are working with. Keep in mind that the variable listed in the first column of each major row has the mean for every other group (listed in the second column) subtracted from its mean.

Kruskal-Wallis Test

The Kruskal-Wallis test is available in SPSS through use of the "K Independent Samples" command (Analyze → Nonparametric Tests → K Independent Samples). After you execute this command, you will be presented with a window that lists all the variables in a box on the left. As with the "One-Way ANOVA" command, there is a box labeled "Test Variable List" (enter the age variable here) and a box labeled "Grouping Variable" (enter the crime type variable here). The "Grouping Variable" box requires an additional piece of information. After entering a variable name in this box, you will need to click on the button just below, labeled "Define Range." In the window that opens after this button has been clicked, you will need to enter numbers for the minimum and maximum values for the crime type variable: Enter 1 for the minimum and 3 for the maximum. Click on "Continue" and "OK" to run the command.

The output window will contain two small tables. The first table lists each group or category and its average rank. The second table presents the results for the Kruskal-Wallis test. Note that the value of the test statistic reported by SPSS differs slightly from that reported in the text (SPSS: 13.0729; text: 13.038). The reason for this difference was noted in footnote 11: SPSS corrects the calculation of the test statistic by adjusting for ties in rank, and the formula in the text does not make such a correction.

1. Input the data from Table 12.6 as two variables: bail amount and race (use 1 = non-Hispanic white, 2 = non-Hispanic African American, and 3 = Hispanic of any race).

    a. Reproduce the ANOVA results in the text.

    b. Compute the HSD for these data. What can you conclude about the pairwise comparisons across race categories?

    c. Perform the Kruskal-Wallis test. How do the results from the Kruskal-Wallis test compare to the ANOVA results in part a? Do the results from the Kruskal-Wallis test alter the conclusions obtained through the use of ANOVA?

2. Enter the data from Exercise 12.5. Use the "One-Way ANOVA" command to test for differences in group means.

    a. Write out the assumptions of the test, the critical value of the test statistic, the value of the computed test statistic, and the decision regarding the null hypothesis.

    b. Compute the HSD for each of the group comparisons. What can you conclude about pairwise comparisons for each group?

    c. Use the Kruskal-Wallis test to test for differences in rank order across groups. Write out the assumptions of the test, the critical value of the test statistic, the value of the computed test statistic, and the decision regarding the null hypothesis.

3. Enter the data from Exercise 12.6. Use the "One-Way ANOVA" command to test for differences in group means.

    a. Write out the assumptions of the test, the critical value of the test statistic, the value of the computed test statistic, and the decision regarding the null hypothesis.

    b. Compute the HSD for each of the group comparisons. What can you conclude about pairwise comparisons for each group?

    c. Use the Kruskal-Wallis test to test for differences in rank order across groups. Write out the assumptions of the test, the critical value of the test statistic, the value of the computed test statistic, and the decision regarding the null hypothesis.

4. Open the data file ***nys_1.sav***. Carry out the following statistical analyses for each of the research questions in parts a through e:

    a. Does the mean number of thefts valued at $5 to $50 vary across academic ability?

    b. Does the mean number of times drunk vary across race?

c. Does the level of marijuana use vary across amount of contact with delinquent peers?

d. Does the mean number of attacks on other students vary across victimization experience?

e. Does the mean number of times cheating on schoolwork vary across grade point average?

— Use ANOVA to test for differences in group means. For each hypothesis test, write out the assumptions of the test, the critical value of the test statistic, the value of the computed test statistic, and the decision regarding the null hypothesis.

— Compute the HSD for each of the pairwise comparisons. What can you conclude about pairwise comparisons for each research question?

— Use the Kruskal-Wallis test to test for differences in rank order across groups. For each hypothesis test, write out the assumptions of the test, the critical value of the test statistic, the value of the computed test statistic, and the decision regarding the null hypothesis.

Measures of Association

for Nominal and Ordinal Variables

CHAPTER 12 INTRODUCED eta (η) and the more general concept of measures of association. Eta is a descriptive statistic that allows us to define how strongly the categorical variable or sample in an analysis of variance is related to the interval-level variable or trait we examined across the samples. But there are many other useful measures of association that allow us to define relationships among variables. Over the next few chapters, we will focus on some of these that are particularly useful in studying criminal justice. We will still be concerned with statistical significance in these chapters, but we will examine not only whether a measure is statistically significant but also how strong the relationship is.

In this chapter, our focus is on nominal- and ordinal-level measures of association. We begin with a discussion of why it is important to distinguish between statistical significance and strength of association. While statistical significance can tell us whether we can make reliable statements about differences in a population from observations made from samples, it does not define the size of the relationship observed. It is important to define the strength of the relationship between variables being examined because that puts us in a better position to decide whether results that are statistically significant are also substantively important.

Distinguishing Statistical Significance and Strength of Relationship: The Example of the Chi-Square Statistic

In Chapter 9, we explored the chi-square statistic as a way to determine whether there was a statistically significant relationship between two nominal-level variables. The chi-square statistic is useful as a way of testing for such a relationship, but it is not meant to provide a measure of the strength of the relationship between the variables. It is tempting to look at the value of the chi-square statistic and the observed significance level associated with a particular chi-square value and infer from these statistics the strength of the relationship between the two variables. If we follow such an approach, however, we run the risk of an interpretive error.

Table 13.1 Observed Frequencies (f_o) and Expected Frequencies (f_e) for Two Outcomes of an Experimental Condition with 200 Cases

EXPERIMENTAL CONDITION	OUTCOME		Total
	Failure	Success	
Treatment	$f_o = 40$ $f_e = 50$	$f_o = 60$ $f_e = 50$	100
Control	$f_o = 60$ $f_e = 50$	$f_o = 40$ $f_e = 50$	100
Total	100	100	200

The problem with using the chi-square statistic—or outcomes of other tests of statistical significance—in this way is that the size of the test statistic is influenced not only by the nature of the relationship observed but also by the number of cases in the samples examined. As we have noted a number of times in the text, this makes good sense. Larger samples, all else being equal, are likely to be more trustworthy. Just as we feel more confident in drawing inferences from a sample of 10 or 20 coin tosses than from a sample of 2 or 3 tosses, our confidence in making a decision about the null hypothesis grows as the sizes of the samples examined using a chi-square statistic increase.

The following example will help to illustrate this problem. Suppose we have a sample of 200 cases that cross-tabulate experimental condition with an outcome measure, as shown in Table 13.1. We see that 60% of those in the treatment group have an outcome classified as a success, while only 40% of those in the control group have an outcome classified as a success. Our calculated value of chi-square for these data is 8.00 with df = 1, which has an observed significance level less than 0.01 (see Appendix 2). See Table 13.2 for detailed calculations for obtaining the chi-square statistic.

Table 13.2 Calculations for Obtaining Chi-Square Statistic for the Example in Table 13.1

EXPERIMENTAL CONDITION	OUTCOME	f_o	f_e	$f_o - f_e$	$(f_o - f_e)^2$	$\dfrac{(f_o - f_e)^2}{f_e}$
Treatment	Failure	40	50	-10	100	2
Treatment	Success	60	50	10	100	2
Control	Failure	60	50	10	100	2
Control	Success	40	50	-10	100	2
						$\Sigma = 8.0$

Without changing the proportional distribution of cases for this example—keeping success at 60% for the treatment group and 40% for the control group—suppose we multiply the number of cases by 10. We now have 2,000 total observations, as shown in Table 13.3, but the relationship between experimental condition and outcome is the same. Our calculated chi-square statistic, however, now has a value of 80.00 (see Table 13.4) with df = 1, and the observed significance level is less than 0.0001. So, simply by increasing the size of the sample, we increase the value of chi-square and decrease the corresponding observed significance level.

This feature of the chi-square statistic applies to all tests of statistical significance. Irrespective of the observed relationship between measures, as the sample size increases, the observed significance level associated with that relationship will also increase. This simple rule regarding the relationship between statistical significance and sample size will be examined in more detail in the discussion of statistical power in Chapter 19. The rule does not raise any new questions regarding the meaning of statistical significance. It simply reminds us that, all else being equal, we can be more confident in making statistical inferences from larger samples. It also emphasizes the importance of distinguishing between statistical significance and the size or strength of a relationship between variables.

To allow researchers to define the strength of a relationship among nominal-level or ordinal-level variables, statisticians have developed a variety of measures of association. Some of these measures are based on the value of the chi-square statistic; others are based on unique transformations of the counts or distributions of cases within a table. All the measures of association that we discuss share a standardized scale: A value of 0 is interpreted as no relationship, and a value of 1.0 (or, in the case of ordinal scales, +1 or −1) is interpreted as a perfect relationship between the two variables. The discussion that follows describes some of the more frequently used measures of association for nominal and ordinal variables.

Table 13.3 Observed Frequencies (f_o) and Expected Frequencies (f_e) for Two Outcomes of an Experimental Condition with 2,000 Cases

| EXPERIMENTAL CONDITION | OUTCOME | | Total |
	Failure	Success	
Treatment	$f_o = 400$ $f_e = 500$	$f_o = 600$ $f_e = 500$	1,000
Control	$f_o = 600$ $f_e = 500$	$f_o = 400$ $f_e = 500$	1,000
Total	1,000	1,000	2,000

| Table 13.4 | Calculations for Obtaining Chi-Square Statistic for the Example in Table 13.3 |

EXPERIMENTAL CONDITION	OUTCOME	f_o	f_e	$f_o - f_e$	$(f_o - f_e)^2$	$\dfrac{(f_o - f_e)^2}{f_e}$
Treatment	Failure	400	500	−100	10,000	20
Treatment	Success	600	500	100	10,000	20
Control	Failure	600	500	100	10,000	20
Control	Success	400	500	−100	10,000	20
						$\Sigma = 80.0$

Measures of Association for Nominal Variables

Measures of Association Based on the Chi-Square Statistic

The preceding example illustrated how the chi-square statistic is affected by sample size. With a 2 × 2 table (i.e., two rows and two columns), one straightforward way of measuring the strength of a relationship between two variables that adjusts for the influence of sample size is to transform the value of the chi-square statistic by adjusting for the total number of observations. One measure of association that does this is **phi (ϕ).** Phi is obtained simply by dividing the chi-square statistic by the total number of observations (N) and taking the square root of this value (see Equation 13.1).

$$\phi = \sqrt{\frac{\chi^2}{N}}$$

Equation 13.1

Phi will have a value of 0 if the value of the chi-square statistic is 0 and there is no relationship between the two variables. Phi will have a value of 1 if the chi-square statistic takes on a value equal to the sample size, which can occur only when there is a perfect relationship between two categorical variables. It is important to note that phi is appropriate only for analyses that use a 2 × 2 table. If the number of rows or columns exceeds two, then it is possible for phi to take on values greater than 1.0, eliminating the possibility of any kind of meaningful interpretation.

Consider the two chi-square statistics that we calculated above for the data in Tables 13.1 and 13.3: 8.00 and 80.00, respectively. If we insert these values for chi-square and the sample size, we find that the value of phi for *both* tables is 0.20.

W orking It Out

$$\phi = \sqrt{\frac{8.00}{200}} = 0.20 \qquad \text{and} \qquad \phi = \sqrt{\frac{80.00}{2,000}} = 0.20$$

We now have a measure of association that is not influenced by sample size. For both of our examples, in which the proportion of cases in each group was similar, we have the same phi statistic. However, is the relationship large or small? As noted in Chapter 12, defining "large" and "small" is a matter of judgment and not statistics. In judging the importance of a result, researchers can compare it with other findings from prior studies. Or they may examine the importance of the policy implications that could be drawn from the result. For example, a very small change in rates of heart attacks in the population could save many lives, and thus a small relationship may still be important. According to a standard measure of effect size suggested by Jacob Cohen, a phi of 0.10 is considered to indicate a small relationship, one of 0.30 a medium relationship, and one of 0.50 a large relationship.[1]

Our examples suggest why we might be misled if we used the chi-square statistic and its corresponding significance level as an indicator of the strength of the relationship between two variables. If we had tried to infer the strength of the relationship between experimental condition and outcome from the value of the chi-square statistic, we would have been tempted to conclude that Table 13.3 showed a stronger relationship than Table 13.1. However, once we take into account the size of the sample, we see that the two tables reflect the same relationship between the two variables. The data in Table 13.3 lead to a higher observed significance level because the samples examined are larger. However, the strength of the relationship observed in the two tables is the same.

For tables with more than two rows or two columns, we cannot use phi. Instead, we use a measure of association known as **Cramer's V,** which is also based on the value of the chi-square statistic but makes an adjustment for the number of categories in each variable. Equation 13.2 presents the formula for calculating Cramer's V.

$$V = \sqrt{\frac{\chi^2}{N \times \min(r - 1, \, c - 1)}}$$

Equation 13.2

In Equation 13.2, the chi-square statistic (χ^2) is divided by the product of the total number of observations (N), and the smaller of two numbers,

---

[1]See Jacob Cohen, *Statistical Power Analysis for the Behavioral Sciences* (Hillsdale, NJ: Lawrence Erlbaum, 1988), pp. 215–271.

$r - 1$ or $c - 1$ (i.e., the minimum of these two values), where r is the number of rows in the table and c is the number of columns. For example, if we had a table with two rows and three columns, we would have $r - 1 = 2 - 1 = 1$ and $c - 1 = 3 - 1 = 2$. The value for $r - 1$ is the smaller of these two numbers, so we would use that value (1) for $\min(r - 1, c - 1)$ in the denominator of the formula. If we were working with a larger table with, say, five rows and four columns, we would have $r - 1 = 5 - 1 = 4$ and $c - 1 = 4 - 1 = 3$. Since 3 is less than 4, we would use the value 3 for $\min(r - 1, c - 1)$ in the denominator.

Let's consider an example. Table 13.5 reproduces the data from Table 9.9 on cell-block assignment and race of prisoner. Recall from Chapter 9 that the chi-square statistic for this cross-tabulation was 88.2895, and with df = 6, the observed significance level was less than 0.001. We can use the data in this table to illustrate the calculation of V. The table has seven rows ($r = 7$) and two columns ($c = 2$), meaning that $r - 1 = 7 - 1 = 6$ and $c - 1 = 2 - 1 = 1$. The smaller of these two values is 1, which we substitute for $\min(r - 1, c - 1)$ in the denominator of the formula for V. After inserting the other values into Equation 13.2, we find that $V = 0.2708$.

W orking It Out

$$V = \sqrt{\frac{\chi^2}{N \times \min(r - 1, c - 1)}}$$

$$= \sqrt{\frac{88.2895}{(1{,}204)(1)}}$$

$$= 0.2708$$

Table 13.5   Assignment of Non-Hispanic White and Nonwhite Prisoners in Seven Prison Cell Blocks

CELL BLOCK	NON-HISPANIC WHITES	NONWHITES	TOTAL
C	48	208	256
D	17	37	54
E	28	84	112
F	32	79	111
G	37	266	303
H	34	22	56
I	44	268	312
Total	240	964	1,204

The value of Cramer's V may be interpreted in the same way as that of phi. Accordingly, a value for V of 0.2708 is suggestive of a moderate relationship between cell-block assignment and race of prisoner.

Proportional Reduction in Error Measures: Tau and Lambda

Some measures of association that are appropriate for nominal-level variables are based on the idea of **proportional reduction in error,** or **PRE.** Such measures indicate how much knowledge of one variable helps to reduce the error we make in defining the values of a second variable. If we make about the same number of errors when we know the value of the first variable as when we don't, then we can conclude that the PRE is low and the variables are not strongly related. However, if knowledge of one variable helps us to develop much better predictions of the second variable, then we have a high PRE and the variables may be assumed to be strongly related.

Two of the more common measures of association between nominal variables, **Goodman and Kruskal's tau (τ)** and **lambda (λ)** are both PRE measures. Both of these measures require that we identify at the outset which variable is the **dependent variable** and which variable is the **independent variable.** A dependent variable is an outcome variable—it represents the phenomenon that we are interested in explaining. It is "dependent" on other variables, meaning that it is influenced—or we expect it to be influenced—by other variables. Any variable that affects, or influences, the dependent variable is referred to as an independent variable. The values of Goodman and Kruskal's tau (τ) and lambda (λ) will generally differ depending on which variable is identified as the dependent variable and which as the independent variable.

For most research projects, a body of prior research and/or theory will indicate which variables are dependent and which are independent. For example, for the study in Table 13.1, the independent variable is the experimental condition: the treatment or the control group. Whether the person participated in the treatment or the control group is generally theorized to influence outcome success or failure, which is the dependent variable. In other words, the experiment tests whether success or failure is due, at least in part, to participation in some kind of treatment.

PRE measures of association, such as tau and lambda, require the use of two decision rules. The first decision rule—the *naive decision rule*—involves making guesses about the value of the dependent variable without using any information about the independent variable. The second decision rule—the *informed decision rule*—involves using information about how the cases are distributed within levels or categories of the independent variable. The question becomes "Can we make better predictions about the value of the dependent variable by using information about the independent variable?" Will the informed decision rule provide

| Table 13.6 | Hypothetical Distribution of 200 Cases for Two Nominal Variables |

(a) PRE Measure of Association = 0.0

| | **VARIABLE 2** | | |
VARIABLE 1	**Category 1**	**Category 2**	**Total**
Category 1	50	50	100
Category 2	50	50	100
Total	100	100	200

(b) PRE Measure of Association = 1.0

| | **VARIABLE 2** | | |
VARIABLE 1	**Category 1**	**Category 2**	**Total**
Category 1	0	100	100
Category 2	100	0	100
Total	100	100	200

better predictions than the naive decision rule? PRE measures of association have a value of 0 when there is no relationship between the two variables and a value of 1 when there is a perfect relationship between the two variables. Table 13.6 presents two hypothetical distributions illustrating PRE measures showing no relationship (part a) and a perfect relationship (part b). In part a, we see that knowledge of one variable does not help us make predictions about the second variable, since the cases are evenly distributed across all possible cells of the table. In the perfect relationship shown in part b, knowledge of one variable determines, without error, the value of the second variable.

A key advantage to PRE measures of association is the interpretation of values between 0 and 1. Any value greater than 0 may be interpreted as a proportionate reduction in error achieved by using information on the independent variable. Alternatively, we can multiply the PRE measure by 100 and interpret the value as the percent reduction in errors. For example, a PRE measure of 0.50 indicates a percent reduction in prediction errors of 50% when information about the independent variable is used.

For an illustration of the calculation of tau and lambda, consider the data presented in Table 13.7. These data come from responses to a survey by adult residents of the state of Illinois.[2] Respondents who reported that they had experienced an assault were asked a series of follow-up

---

[2]For a description of the study, see Chester L. Britt, "Health Consequences of Criminal Victimization," *International Review of Victimology,* 8 (2001): 63–73.

Table 13.7   Data on Victim-Offender Relationship and Location of Assault

VICTIM-OFFENDER RELATIONSHIP	LOCATION OF ASSAULT				
	Home	Neighborhood	Work	Someplace Else	Total
Stranger	10	49	18	89	166
Acquaintance/friend	21	22	7	46	96
Partner	77	5	3	19	104
Relative	31	1	2	10	44
Total	139	77	30	164	410

questions about the most recent event. Two of these questions addressed the relationship between the victim and the offender and the location of the assault. Here we have classified the victim-offender relationship into four categories: stranger, acquaintance/friend, partner (includes spouse and boyfriend or girlfriend), and relative. Location of the assault is also classified into four categories: home, neighborhood, work, and someplace else. For this analysis, we assume that the victim-offender relationship is the independent variable and the location of the assault is the dependent variable. Our research question is "What is the strength of the relationship between victim-offender relationship and location of an assault?"

Goodman and Kruskal's tau uses information about the marginal distributions of the two variables to test whether knowledge of the independent variable reduces prediction errors for the dependent variable. The first step in computing this statistic is to ask how many errors we would expect to make, on average, if we did not have knowledge about the victim-offender relationship. This is our naive decision rule, where we are effectively trying to guess what category of the dependent variable an observation might belong to, without using any information about the independent variable. For our example, we begin by looking at the column totals in Table 13.7, which reflect the categories of the dependent variable. Of the 410 assaults, we see that 139 occurred in the home, 77 in the neighborhood, 30 at work, and 164 someplace else. We use these column totals to help us determine the average number of errors we would expect to make if we assigned cases without any information about the victim-offender relationship.

Let's begin with assaults in the home. Of the 410 total assaults, 139 belong in the assaulted-in-the-home category, while 271 do not belong in this category (i.e., the assault occurred elsewhere). Proportionally, 0.6610 (271 of 410) of the cases do not belong in the assaulted-in-the-home category. If we randomly assigned 139 of the 410 cases to the assaulted-in-the-home category, we would expect 0.6610 of these 139 cases to be assigned incorrectly. To obtain the number of cases assigned incorrectly—the number of prediction errors—we multiply the proportion of cases not in the category by the number of cases assigned to that category. For assaulted in the home, this is $(0.6610 \times 139) = 92$. The value 92 represents the number of prediction errors we would expect to make, on average, in assigning cases to the assaulted-in-the-home category without any knowledge of the victim-offender relationship.[3]

Turning to assaults in the neighborhood, we see that 77 cases belong in this category, and the remaining 333 do not belong in this category. As a proportion, 0.8122 of the cases (333 of 410) do not belong in the assaulted-in-the-neighborhood category. This means that we would expect to make $0.8122 \times 77 = 63$ prediction errors, on average, in assigning cases to this category without any knowledge of the victim-offender relationship. For assaults at work, 30 cases belong in this category and 380 do not, meaning that we would expect to make $(380/410) \times 30 = 28$ prediction errors, on average, in assigning cases to the assaults-at-work category without any information about the victim-offender relationship. There are 164 cases that belong to the assaulted-someplace-else category, meaning that 246 cases do not belong in this category. We would expect to make $(246/410) \times 164 = 98$ prediction errors, on average, in assigning cases to this category without any information about the victim-offender relationship. To determine the total number of prediction errors we would make without any knowledge of the victim-offender relationship, we add these four values together: $92 + 63 + 28 + 98 = 281$ total prediction errors.

If we then use information about the victim-offender relationship—whether the victim and offender were strangers, acquaintances/friends, partners, or relatives—we can test whether this information improves our ability to predict the location of the assault. This reflects the use of our informed decision rule: Does our assignment of cases to categories of the dependent variable improve when we use information about the category of the independent variable? In other words, does knowing the category of the independent variable (victim-offender relationship) reduce the number of prediction errors we make about the category of the dependent variable (location of assault)? To the extent that the independent variable has a relationship with the dependent variable, the number of prediction errors should decrease.

The logic behind calculating the prediction errors is the same as before, except that we focus on the row totals in the table, rather than the total number of cases in each category of the dependent variable. We start with the first category of the independent variable (i.e., the first row of Table 13.7) and note that 166 cases involved offenders who were strangers to

---

[3]For all calculations of prediction errors, we have rounded the result to the nearest integer.

the victim. In a process similar to our earlier analysis, we begin by noting the placement of cases within this row: 10 assaults occurred at home, 49 in the neighborhood, 18 at work, and 89 someplace else. Starting with the assignment of cases to assaulted-in-the-home, we note that 10 cases belong in this category and 156 do not belong in this category. As a proportion, 0.9398 of the cases (156 of 166) do not belong in the assaulted-in-the-home category when the offender is a stranger. Thus, if we randomly assigned 10 of the 166 cases in this row to the assaulted-in-the-home category, we would expect to make $0.9398 \times 10 = 9$ prediction errors, on average. Turning to the assaulted-in-the-neighborhood category, we note that 49 cases belong in this category and 117 do not belong in this category, which means that we would expect to make $(117/166) \times 49 = 35$ prediction errors. For the assaulted-at-work category, we would expect to make $(148/166) \times 18 = 16$ prediction errors, and for the assaulted-someplace-else category, we would expect to make $(77/166) \times 89 = 41$ prediction errors. The total number of prediction errors in assigning cases involving offenders who were strangers is 101 (that is, $9 + 35 + 16 + 41$).

To determine the prediction errors for each of the remaining categories of the independent variable (assaults involving offenders who were acquaintances/friends, partners, or relatives), we use the same approach with the three remaining rows of Table 13.7. Table 13.8 presents all the calculations of prediction errors necessary for obtaining tau.

We obtain the total number of prediction errors made using information about the victim-offender relationship by summing the errors across each category of relationship. For cases involving an offender who was a stranger, we would expect to make 101 prediction errors; for cases involving an acquaintance or friend, we would expect to make 63 prediction errors; for cases involving partners, 44 prediction errors; and for cases involving a relative, 20 prediction errors (see the bottom row of Table 13.8). Altogether, we would expect to make 228 (that is, $101 + 63 +$

Table 13.8   Calculations of Prediction Errors for Obtaining Tau for a Relationship Between Victim-Offender Relationship and Location of Assault

LOCATION OF ASSAULT	PREDICTION ERRORS: No Knowledge of Victim-Offender Relationship	PREDICTION ERRORS: Offender Was a Stranger	PREDICTION ERRORS: Offender Was an Acquaintance or a Friend	PREDICTION ERRORS: Offender Was a Partner	PREDICTION ERRORS: Offender Was a Relative
Home	139(271/410) = 92	10(156/166) = 9	21(75/96) = 16	77(27/104) = 20	31(13/44) = 9
Neighborhood	77(333/410) = 63	49(117/166) = 35	22(74/96) = 17	5(99/104) = 5	1(43/44) = 1
Work	30(380/410) = 28	18(148/166) = 16	7(89/96) = 6	3(101/104) = 3	2(42/44) = 2
Someplace else	164(246/410) = 98	89(77/166) = 41	46(50/96) = 24	19(85/104) = 16	10(34/44) = 8
Total	$\Sigma = 281$	$\Sigma = 101$	$\Sigma = 63$	$\Sigma = 44$	$\Sigma = 20$

44 + 20) prediction errors using information about the victim-offender relationship to predict location of assault.

Goodman and Kruskal's tau is a measure of the reduction in prediction errors achieved by using knowledge of the independent variable—which, again, in our example is the victim-offender relationship. Equation 13.3 presents the general formula for calculating tau.

$$\tau = \frac{\left(\begin{array}{l}\text{number of errors} \\ \text{without knowledge of} \\ \text{independent variable}\end{array}\right) - \left(\begin{array}{l}\text{number of errors} \\ \text{with knowledge of} \\ \text{independent variable}\end{array}\right)}{\text{number of errors without knowledge of independent variable}}$$

Equation 13.3

For our example, tau is equal to 0.1886. If we multiply this proportion by 100%, we can discern that knowledge of the victim-offender relationship reduced our prediction errors by 18.86%, which implies a weak to moderate relationship between victim-offender relationship and location of assault.

W **orking It Out**

$$\tau = \frac{281 - 228}{281} = 0.1886$$

Lambda (λ) is a measure of association that is conceptually very similar to Goodman and Kruskal's tau in that it is a PRE measure. However, rather than using the proportional distribution of cases to determine prediction errors, lambda uses the mode of the dependent variable. We begin with the naive decision rule, placing all possible observations in the modal category of the dependent variable and counting as errors the number of cases that do not belong in that modal category. We then use information about the value of the independent variable (the informed decision rule), making assignments of cases based on the mode of the dependent variable within each category of the independent variable.

Equation 13.4 shows that lambda is calculated in a manner similar to that used to calculate tau.

$$\tau = \frac{\left(\begin{array}{l}\text{number of errors} \\ \text{using modes of} \\ \text{dependent variable}\end{array}\right) - \left(\begin{array}{l}\text{number of errors} \\ \text{using mode of} \\ \text{dependent variable} \\ \text{by level of} \\ \text{independent variable}\end{array}\right)}{\text{number of errors using mode of independent variable}}$$

Equation 13.3

The calculation of lambda is less tedious, since we use only information on the modal category overall and then within each level of the independent variable. Without knowledge of the victim-offender relationship, we would assign all 410 cases to the assaulted-someplace-else category, resulting in $410 - 164 = 246$ classification errors.

What about the number of classification errors when we use knowledge of the victim-offender relationship? For assaults where the offender was a stranger, we would assign all 166 cases to the assaulted-someplace-else category, resulting in $166 - 89 = 77$ classification errors. For assaults where the offender was an acquaintance or friend, we would assign all 96 cases to the assaulted-someplace-else category, resulting in $96 - 46 = 50$ classification errors. All 104 partner offenders and 44 relative offenders would both be assigned to the home category, resulting in $104 - 77 = 27$ and $44 - 31 = 13$ classification errors, respectively. We have a sum of 167 prediction errors when we use knowledge of the victim-offender relationship, compared to 246 prediction errors made without any knowledge of the victim-offender relationship. The value of lambda is 0.3211, meaning that knowledge of the modal location of assault for each type of victim-offender relationship reduces our errors in predicting location of assault by 32.11%.

Working It Out

$$\lambda = \frac{246 - 167}{246} = 0.3211$$

As can be seen from our example, different measures of association may lead to somewhat different interpretations of the relationship between two variables. This occurs because different measures use different strategies in coming to a conclusion about that relationship. Which is the best measure of association for assessing the strength of the relationship between two nominal-level variables? Researchers often prefer the two PRE measures—tau and lambda—over phi and V, since PRE measures have direct interpretations of values that fall between 0 and 1. However, to use PRE measures, a researcher must assume that one measure (the independent variable) affects a second (the dependent variable). Of tau and lambda, tau is often defined as the better measure of association for two reasons. First, if the modal category of the dependent variable is the same for all categories of the independent variable, lambda will have a value of 0, implying that there is no relationship between the two variables. Since tau relies on the marginal distributions of observations both overall and within each category of the independent variable, tau can still detect a relationship between the independent and the dependent variables. Second, and this is again related to the marginal distributions, the value of lambda is sensitive to marginal totals (i.e., row or column totals). When row or column totals are not approximately equal, the value of lambda may be artificially high or low. The reliance on marginal distributions in the calculation of tau allows that measure of association to account for the size of the marginal totals directly and causes it not to be as sensitive to differences in marginal totals.

Statistical Significance of Measures of Association for Nominal Variables

The statistical significance of each of the nominal measures of association just discussed can be assessed with the results of a chi-square test. When the chi-square statistic has a value of 0, each of the four coefficients will also have a value of 0. The null hypothesis for each of the four coefficients is simply that the coefficient is equal to 0. The research hypothesis is simply that the coefficient is not equal to 0.

We illustrate the steps of a hypothesis test for tau and lambda, using the data on victim-offender relationship and location of assault.

Assumptions:

Level of Measurement: Nominal scale.

Population Distribution: No assumption made.

Sampling Method: Independent random sampling.

Sampling Frame: Adults aged 18 years and older in the state of Illinois.

Hypotheses:

H_0: There is no association between victim-offender relationship and location of assault ($\tau_p = 0$).

H_1: There is an association between victim-offender relationship and location of assault ($\tau_p \neq 0$).

or

H_0: There is no association between victim-offender relationship and location of assault ($\lambda_p = 0$).

H_1: There is an association between victim-offender relationship and location of assault ($\lambda_p \neq 0$).

The Sampling Distribution Since we are testing for a relationship between two nominal-level variables, we use the chi-square distribution, where degrees of freedom = $(r - 1)(c - 1) = (4 - 1)(4 - 1) = 9$.

Table 13.9   Observed Frequencies and Expected Frequencies for Victim-Offender Relationship and Location of Assault

VICTIM-OFFENDER RELATIONSHIP	LOCATION OF ASSAULT				Total
	Home	Neighborhood	Work	Someplace Else	
Stranger	$f_o = 10$ $f_e = 56.2780$	$f_o = 49$ $f_e = 31.1756$	$f_o = 18$ $f_e = 12.1463$	$f_o = 89$ $f_e = 66.4000$	166
Acquaintance/friend	$f_o = 21$ $f_e = 32.5463$	$f_o = 22$ $f_e = 18.0293$	$f_o = 7$ $f_e = 7.0244$	$f_o = 46$ $f_e = 38.4000$	96
Partner	$f_o = 77$ $f_e = 35.2585$	$f_o = 5$ $f_e = 19.5317$	$f_o = 3$ $f_e = 7.6098$	$f_o = 19$ $f_e = 41.6000$	104
Relative	$f_o = 31$ $f_e = 14.9171$	$f_o = 1$ $f_e = 8.2634$	$f_o = 2$ $f_e = 3.2195$	$f_o = 10$ $f_e = 17.6000$	44
Total	139	77	30	164	410

Table 13.10   Calculations of Chi-Square for Victim-Offender Relationship and Location of Assault

VICTIM-OFFENDER RELATIONSHIP	LOCATION OF ASSAULT	f_o	f_e	$f_o - f_e$	$(f_o - f_e)^2$	$\frac{(f_o - f_e)^2}{f_e}$
Stranger	Home	10	56.2780	−46.2780	2141.6578	38.0549
Stranger	Neighborhood	49	31.1756	17.8244	317.7089	10.1909
Stranger	Work	18	12.1463	5.8537	34.2653	2.8210
Stranger	Someplace else	89	66.4000	22.6000	510.7600	7.6922
Friend	Home	21	32.5463	−11.5463	133.3180	4.0963
Friend	Neighborhood	22	18.0293	3.9707	15.7667	0.8745
Friend	Work	7	7.0244	−0.0244	0.0006	0.0001
Friend	Someplace else	46	38.4000	7.6000	57.7600	1.5042
Partner	Home	77	35.2585	41.7415	1742.3498	49.4164
Partner	Neighborhood	5	19.5317	−14.5317	211.1705	10.8117
Partner	Work	3	7.6098	−4.6098	21.2499	2.7924
Partner	Someplace else	19	41.6000	−22.6000	510.7600	12.2779
Other relative	Home	31	14.9171	16.0829	258.6605	17.3399
Other relative	Neighborhood	1	8.2634	−7.2634	52.7572	6.3844
Other relative	Work	2	3.2195	−1.2195	1.4872	0.4619
Other relative	Someplace else	10	17.6000	−7.6000	57.7600	3.2818
						$\Sigma = 168.0005$

Significance Level and Rejection Region   We use the conventional 5% significance level for this example. From Appendix 2, we see that the critical value of chi-square associated with a significance level of 5% and df = 9 is 16.919. If the calculated chi-square statistic is greater than 16.919, we will reject the null hypotheses and conclude that the association between victim-offender relationship and location of assault is statistically significant.

The Test Statistic   The chi-square statistic for the data in Table 13.7 is 168.001. See Table 13.9 for the expected and observed frequencies and Table 13.10 for the detailed calculations.

The Decision   Since our calculated chi-square statistic of 168.001 is much larger than our critical chi-square of 16.919, we reject the null hypotheses and conclude that there is a statistically significant relationship between victim-offender relationship and location of assault.

Measures of Association for Ordinal-Level Variables

The preceding discussion described several measures of association for nominal variables, where there is no rank ordering of the categories of each variable. With ordinal-level variables, we can use the ordering of the categories to measure whether there is a positive or a negative relationship between two variables. A positive relationship would be indicated by higher ranks on one variable corresponding to higher ranks on a second variable. A negative relationship would be indicated by higher ranks on one variable corresponding to lower ranks on a second variable. The measures of association for ordinal-level variables all have values that range from -1.0 to $+1.0$. A value of -1.0 indicates a perfect negative relationship, a value of $+1.0$ indicates a perfect positive relationship, and a value of 0.0 indicates no relationship between the two variables.

Table 13.11 illustrates these variations in the strength of the relationship between two ordinal variables with a hypothetical distribution of 450 cases. Part a presents a pattern of no association between the two variables. Since the cases are evenly distributed across all the cells of the table, knowledge of the level of one ordinal variable does not provide any information about the level of the second ordinal variable. Parts b and c show perfect negative and positive relationships, respectively, where knowledge of the level of one ordinal variable determines, without error, the level of the second ordinal variable.

The calculation of ordinal measures of association is tedious to perform by hand. When doing data analysis, you would likely rely on a statistical

| Table 13.11 | Hypothetical Distribution of 450 Cases for Two Ordinal Variables |

(a) Measure of Association = 0.0

| | VARIABLE 2 | | | |
VARIABLE 1	Low	Medium	High	Total
Low	50	50	50	150
Medium	50	50	50	150
High	50	50	50	150
Total	150	150	150	450

(b) Measure of Association = −1.0

| | VARIABLE 2 | | | |
VARIABLE 1	Low	Medium	High	Total
Low	0	0	150	150
Medium	0	150	0	150
High	150	0	0	150
Total	150	150	150	450

(c) Measure of Association = +1.0

| | VARIABLE 2 | | | |
VARIABLE 1	Low	Medium	High	Total
Low	150	0	0	150
Medium	0	150	0	150
High	0	0	150	150
Total	150	150	150	450

software package to perform the calculations for you. Most common statistical software packages will compute the measures of association for ordinal variables described here (see, for example, the computer exercises at the end of this chapter). The following discussion is intended to help you understand how these various measures are calculated.

There are four common measures of association for ordinal variables: **gamma (γ)**, **Kendall's γ_b**, **Kendall's γ_c**, and **Somers' d**. Common to all four is the use of **concordant pairs** and **discordant pairs of observations.** The logic behind using concordant and discordant pairs of observations is that we take each possible pair of observations in a data set and compare the relative ranks of the two observations on the two variables examined. Concordant pairs are those pairs of observations for which the rankings are consistent: One observation is ranked high on both variables, while the other observation is ranked low on both variables. For example, one observation is ranked 1 (of five ranked categories) on the first variable and 2 (of five ranked categories) on the second variable, while the other observation is ranked 4 on the first variable and 3 on the second variable. Discordant pairs refer to those pairs of observations for which the rankings are inconsistent: One observation is ranked high on the first variable and low on the second variable, while the other observation is ranked low on the first variable and high on the second variable. For example, one observation is ranked 1 on the first variable and 5 on the second variable, while the other observation is ranked 4 on the first variable and 2 on the second variable. A pair of observations that has the same rank on one or both of the variables is called a **tied pair of observations (tie).**[4] Somers' d is the only one of the four measures for which specification of the dependent and the independent variables is required. The value of d will generally be different depending on which variable is specified as the dependent variable.

How do we decide whether a pair of observations is a concordant pair, a discordant pair, or a tied pair? Let's look at the determination of concordant, discordant, and tied pairs for the data presented in Table 13.12, which represents a cross-tabulation of two ordinal variables, each with three categories: low, medium, and high.

Table 13.12   Cross-Tabulation of Two Ordinal Variables

INDEPENDENT VARIABLE	DEPENDENT VARIABLE		
	Low	Medium	High
Low	Cell A 12	Cell B 4	Cell C 3
Medium	Cell D 5	Cell E 10	Cell F 6
High	Cell G 3	Cell H 5	Cell I 14

[4]All the measures of association for ordinal variables that we discuss here are for grouped data that can be represented in the form of a table. In Chapter 14, we discuss another measure of association for ordinal variables—Spearman's r (r_s)—that is most useful in working with ungrouped data, such as information on individuals. The difficulty we confront when using Spearman's r on grouped data is that the large number of tied pairs of observations complicates the calculation of this measure of association. Spearman's r is a more appropriate measure of association when we have ordinal variables with a large number of ranked categories for individual cases or when we take an interval-level variable and rank order the observations (see Chapter 14).

We begin by determining the concordant pairs—those pairs of observations that have consistent relative rankings. Let's start with Cell A. We remove from consideration the row and column that Cell A is located in, since the cases in the same row or column will have the same ranking on the independent and dependent variables, respectively, and thus represent ties. We then look for cases located *below* and to the *right* of the cell of interest. For Cell A, the cells we will use to determine concordant pairs are Cells E, F, H, and I, since the ranks are consistently lower on both the independent and the dependent variables. To determine the number of pairs of observations that are concordant for observations in Cell A, we begin by summing the number of observations in Cells E, F, G, and I: $10 + 6 + 5 + 14 = 35$. This tells us that for a single observation in Cell A, there are 35 concordant pairs of observations. Since there are 12 observations in Cell A, we multiply the number of cases in Cell A (12) by the sum of the cases in Cells E, F, H, and I. For Cell A, there are 420 concordant pairs.

W orking It Out

$12(10 + 6 + 5 + 14) = 420$

Continuing to work across the first row of Table 13.12, we move to Cell B. The cells located below and to the right of Cell B are Cells F and I, so the number of concordant pairs is $4(6 + 14) = 80$. When we move to Cell C, we see there are no cells below and to the right, so we drop down to the next row and start with Cell D. The cells located below and to the right of Cell D are Cells H and I, so the number of concordant pairs is $5(5 + 14) = 95$. Moving to Cell E, we see that only Cell I is below and to the right, so the number of concordant pairs is $10(14) = 140$. The remaining cells in the table—F, G, H, and I—have no other cells located below and to the right, so they are not used in the calculation of concordant pairs. After calculating concordant pairs for all cells in the table, we sum these values to get the number of concordant pairs for the table. For Table 13.12, the total number of concordant pairs is 735 (that is, $420 + 80 + 95 + 140$).

W orking It Out

Cell A: $12(10 + 6 + 5 + 14) = 420$
Cell B: $4(6 + 14) = 80$
Cell D: $5(5 + 14) = 95$
Cell E: $10(14) = 140$

Sum $= 420 + 80 + 95 + 140 = 735$

To calculate discordant cells, we begin in the upper right corner of Table 13.12 (Cell C), locate cells that are positioned *below* and to the *left* of the cell of interest, and perform calculations similar to those for concordant pairs. Beginning with Cell C, we multiply the number of cases in Cell C by the sum of cases in Cells D, E, G, and H, which are located below and to the left of Cell C. The number of discordant pairs for Cell C is 69.

W orking It Out

$3(5 + 10 + 3 + 5) = 69$

Moving from right to left in the top row of Table 13.12, we shift our attention to Cell B. The discordant pairs for Cell B are calculated by multiplying the number of cases in Cell B by the sum of cases in Cells D and G. We find the number of discordant pairs for Cell B to be $4(5 + 3) = 32$. Since there are no cells located below and to the left of Cell A, it is not used to calculate discordant pairs, and we move on to Cell F. The cells located below and to the left of Cell F are Cells G and H, so the number of discordant pairs is $6(3 + 5) = 48$. For Cell E, the only cell located below and to the left is Cell G, so the number of discordant pairs is $10(3) = 30$. There are no cells located below and to the left of Cells D, G, H, and I, so no further calculations are performed. As with the concordant pairs, we sum our discordant pairs for Table 13.12 and find the sum to be 179 (that is, $69 + 32 + 48 + 30$).

W orking It Out

Cell C: $3(5 + 10 + 3 + 5) = 69$
Cell B: $4(5 + 3) = 32$
Cell F: $6(3 + 5) = 48$
Cell E: $10(3) = 30$

Sum $= 69 + 32 + 48 + 30 = 179$

To calculate ties in rank for pairs of observations, we have to consider the independent and dependent variables separately. We denote ties on the independent variable as T_X and ties on the dependent variable as T_Y. Since the independent variable is represented by the rows in Table 13.12, the pairs of observations that will be defined as ties on the independent variable will be those cases located in the same row of Table 13.12. To calculate the number of ties in each row, we use Equation 13.5.

$$T_X = \frac{1}{2} \sum N_{\text{row}}(N_{\text{row}} - 1)$$

Equation 13.5

where T_X is the number of ties on the independent variable and N_{row} is the row total. Equation 13.5 tells us to calculate the product of the number of observations in a row and the number of observations in a row minus 1 for all rows. We then sum the products calculated for each row and multiply the sum by $\frac{1}{2}$.

For Table 13.12, the three row totals are 19 (row 1), 21 (row 2), and 22 (row 3). When we insert these values into Equation 13.5, we find the number of ties on the independent variable to be 612.

W orking It Out

$$T_X = \frac{1}{2} \sum N_{\text{row}}(N_{\text{row}} - 1)$$

$$= \frac{1}{2} [(19)(19 - 1) + (21)(21 - 1) + (22)(22 - 1)]$$

$$= \frac{1}{2} [(19)(18) + (21)(20) + (22)(21)]$$

$$= \frac{1}{2} (342 + 420 + 462) = \frac{1}{2} (1{,}224)$$

$$= 612$$

The ties on the dependent variable are found in a similar manner. Since the dependent variable is represented in the columns, we perform the same type of calculation, but using column totals rather than row totals. Equation 13.6 presents the formula for calculating ties on the dependent variable.

$$T_Y = \frac{1}{2} \sum N_{\text{col}}(N_{\text{col}} - 1)$$

Equation 13.6

In Equation 13.6, T_Y is the number of ties on the dependent variable and N_{col} is the total number of observations in the column.

In Table 13.12, the column totals are 20 (column 1), 19 (column 2), and 23 (column 3). After inserting these values into Equation 13.6, we find the number of ties on the dependent variable to be 614.

W orking It Out

$$T_Y = \frac{1}{2} \sum N_{col}(N_{col} - 1)$$

$$= \frac{1}{2} [(20)(20 - 1) + (19)(19 - 1) + (23)(23 - 1)]$$

$$= \frac{1}{2} [(20)(19) + (19)(18) + (23)(22)]$$

$$= \frac{1}{2} (380 + 342 + 506) = \frac{1}{2} (1{,}228)$$

$$= 614$$

Gamma

Once we have calculated the numbers of concordant pairs and discordant pairs, gamma (γ) is the simplest of the ordinal measures of association to calculate, since it does not use information about ties in rank. Gamma has possible values that range from -1.0 to $+1.0$. Gamma may also be interpreted as a PRE measure: We can interpret the value of gamma as indicating the proportional reduction in errors in predicting the dependent variable, based on information about the independent variable.

Equation 13.7 presents the formula for calculating gamma. Gamma is the difference between the number of concordant (C) and discordant (D) pairs, ($C - D$), divided by the sum of the concordant and discordant pairs, ($C + D$).

$$\gamma = \frac{C - D}{C + D} \qquad \qquad \textbf{Equation 13.7}$$

For the data in Table 13.12, gamma is equal to 0.6083. The positive value of gamma tells us that as we move from lower ranked to higher ranked categories on the independent variable, the category of the dependent variable also tends to increase. In regard to the relative strength of the relationship, a value of 0.6083 suggests a strong relationship between the independent and dependent variables, since knowledge of the independent variable reduces our errors in predicting the dependent variable by 60.83%.

W orking It Out

$$\gamma = \frac{C - D}{C + D}$$

$$= \frac{735 - 179}{735 + 179}$$

$$= \frac{556}{914}$$

$$= 0.6083$$

Kendall's τ_b and τ_c

Kendall's tau measures—τ_b and τ_c—also assess the strength of association between two ordinal variables.[5] The two measures are conceptually very similar in that they use information about concordant and discordant pairs of observations. But they also utilize information about tied pairs on both the independent and the dependent variables. Both tau measures have possible values ranging from -1.0 to $+1.0$. There are two important differences between τ_b and τ_c: First, τ_b should be applied *only* to a table where the number of rows is equal to the number of columns; τ_c should be applied to a table where the number of rows is not equal to the number of columns. When the number of rows is equal to the number of columns, τ_c will have a value close to that of τ_b. Second, τ_b may be interpreted as a PRE measure, but τ_c may not. The differences in the application and interpretation of each measure suggest that knowing the dimensions of the table is important in deciding which measure is most appropriate.

Equations 13.8 and 13.9 present the formulas for calculating τ_b and τ_c, respectively.

$$\tau_b = \frac{C - D}{\sqrt{[N(N - 1)/2 - T_X][N(N - 1)/2 - T_Y]}}$$ **Equation 13.8**

In Equation 13.8, C and D represent the concordant and the discordant pairs, respectively; N represents the total number of cases; T_X represents the number of ties on the independent variable; and T_Y represents the number of ties on the dependent variable.

---

[5]These two tau measures are different from Goodman and Kruskal's tau, which measures the strength of association between two nominal variables.

Let's return to the data presented in Table 13.12. We have already calculated the number of concordant pairs to be 735, the number of discordant pairs to be 179, the total number of cases to be 62, the number of ties on the independent variable to be 612, and the number of ties on the dependent variable to be 614. After inserting these values into Equation 13.6, we find τ_b to be 0.4351. This indicates that knowledge of the independent variable reduces our prediction errors by 43.51%.

W orking It Out

$$\tau_b = \frac{C - D}{\sqrt{[N(N - 1)/2 - T_X][N(N - 1)/2 - T_Y]}}$$

$$= \frac{735 - 179}{\sqrt{[62(62 - 1)/2 - 612][62(62 - 1)/2 - 614]}}$$

$$= \frac{556}{\sqrt{[1,891 - 612][1,891 - 614]}}$$

$$= \frac{556}{\sqrt{(1,279)(1,277)}}$$

$$= 0.4351$$

Equation 13.9 presents the formula for calculating τ_c. We do not calculate τ_c for Table 13.12, since the number of rows is equal to the number of columns. We do, however, illustrate its calculation below with another example.

$$\tau_c = \frac{C - D}{\frac{1}{2} N^2[(m - 1)/m]}$$

Equation 13.9

where $m = \min(r, c)$

In Equation 13.9, C and D represent the concordant and the discordant pairs, respectively; N represents the total number of cases; and m is the smaller of the number of rows (r) and the number of columns (c). Suppose, for example, that we had a table with five rows ($r = 5$) and four columns ($c = 4$). The number of columns is smaller than the number of rows, so m would be 4.

Somers' *d*

The fourth measure of association for ordinal variables that we present here—Somers' *d*—is similar to the tau measures, but instead of using information about ties on both the independent and the dependent variables, Somers' *d* uses information on ties on only the independent variable. It is important to remember that the statistic you get for Somers' *d* may vary, depending on which variable is defined as the dependent variable. The formula for calculating Somers' *d* is given in Equation 13.10.

$$d_{YX} = \frac{C - D}{N(N - 1)/2 - T_X}$$ **Equation 13.10**

In Equation 13.10, where C, D, N, and T_X represent the concordant pairs, the discordant pairs, the total number of cases, and the number of ties on the independent variable, respectively. The subscript YX on d denotes the dependent and the independent variables, in order.

For Table 13.12, we have already calculated values for C, D, N, and T_X. After inserting these values into Equation 13.10, we find Somers' *d* to be 0.4347.

Working It Out

$$d_{YX} = \frac{C - D}{N(N - 1)/2 - T_X}$$

$$= \frac{735 - 179}{62(62 - 1)/2 - 612}$$

$$= \frac{556}{1,891 - 612}$$

$$= \frac{556}{1,279}$$

$$= 0.4347$$

A Substantive Example: Affectional Identification with Father and Level of Delinquency

Table 9.14 presented a cross-tabulation of two ordinal variables: affectional identification with father and delinquency. Identification with father was determined by the youth's responses to a question about how much they wanted to grow up and be like their fathers. The responses were classified into five ordered categories: in every way, in most

| Table 13.13 | | Affectional Identification with Father by Number of Delinquent Acts | | | |

AFFECTIONAL IDENTIFICATION WITH FATHER	NUMBER OF DELINQUENT ACTS			
	None	**One**	**Two or more**	**Total**
In every way	Cell A 77	Cell B 25	Cell C 19	121
In most ways	Cell D 263	Cell E 97	Cell F 44	404
In some ways	Cell G 224	Cell H 97	Cell I 66	387
In just a few ways	Cell J 82	Cell K 52	Cell L 38	172
Not at all	Cell M 56	Cell N 30	Cell O 52	138
Total	702	301	219	1,222

ways, in some ways, in just a few ways, and not at all. Delinquent acts were classified into three ordered categories: none, one, and two or more. The data came from the Richmond Youth Survey report, and the distribution of cases presented refers only to the white males who responded to the survey.[6] We reproduce this cross-tabulation in Table 13.13.

In our earlier analysis of the data in this table (see Chapter 9), we found a statistically significant relationship between affectional identification with father and delinquency. However, the chi-square statistic told us nothing about the direction of the effect or the strength of the relationship between these two variables. We can use the measures of association for ordinal variables to test the strength of the relationship between identification with father and level of delinquency.

We begin by calculating the numbers of concordant pairs, discordant pairs, and tied pairs of observations. The number of concordant pairs of observations is 201,575; the number of discordant pairs is 125,748; the number of pairs tied on the independent variable is 187,516; and the number of pairs tied on the dependent variable is 315,072.

---

[6]David F. Greenberg, "The Weak Strength of Social Control Theory," *Crime and Delinquency* 45:1 (1999): 66–81.

W orking It Out

Concordant Pairs:

Cell A: 77(97 + 44 + 97 + 66 + 52 + 38 + 30 + 52) = 36,652

Cell B: 25(44 + 66 + 38 + 52)   =   5,000

Cell D: 263(97 + 66 + 52 + 38 + 30 + 52)   = 88,105

Cell E: 97(66 + 38 + 52)   = 15,132

Cell G: 224(52 + 38 + 30 + 52)   = 38,528

Cell H: 97(38 + 52)   =   8,730

Cell J: 82(30 + 52)   =   6,724

Cell K: 52(52)   =   2,704

Sum = 36,652 + 5,000 + 88,105 + 15,132 + 38,528 + 8,730
        + 6,724 + 2,704

    = 201,575

Discordant Pairs:

Cell C: 19(263 + 97 + 224 + 97 + 82 + 52 + 56 + 30) = 17,119

Cell B: 25(263 + 224 + 82 + 56)   = 15,625

Cell F: 44(224 + 97 + 82 + 52 + 56 + 30)   = 23,804

Cell E: 97(224 + 82 + 56)   = 35,114

Cell I: 66(82 + 52 + 56 + 30)   = 14,520

Cell H: 97(82 + 56)   = 13,386

Cell L: 38(56 + 30)   =   3,268

Cell K: 52(56)   =   2,912

Sum = 17,119 + 15,625 + 23,804 + 35,114 + 14,520 + 13,386
       + 3,268 + 2,912

    = 125,748

Pairs Tied on the Independent Variable:

$$T_X = (\tfrac{1}{2})[(121)(120) + (404)(403) + (387)(386) \\ + (172)(171) + (138)(137)]$$

$$= (\tfrac{1}{2})(14{,}520 + 162{,}812 + 149{,}382 + 29{,}412 + 18{,}906)$$

$$= (\tfrac{1}{2})(375{,}032)$$

$$= 187{,}516$$

Pairs Tied on the Dependent Variable:

$$T_Y = (\tfrac{1}{2})[(702)(701) + (301)(300) + (219)(218)]$$

$$= (\tfrac{1}{2})(492{,}102 + 90{,}300 + 47{,}742)$$

$$= (\tfrac{1}{2})(630{,}144)$$

$$= 315{,}072$$

After calculating the concordant pairs, discordant pairs, and pairs tied on the independent and dependent variables, we can calculate the measures of association for ordinal variables. We find the value of gamma to be 0.2317. Don't be confused by the fact that for affectional identification movement from lower to higher ordered categories represents movement from more to less identification with the father. Substantively, what this value of gamma tells us is that as the level of affectional identification with father decreases (i.e., as we move down the rows of the table), the youth are likely to report higher levels of delinquency. The value of gamma also indicates that we reduce our prediction errors about level of delinquency by 23.17% when we use information about the level of affectional identification with father. If affectional identification in this example had been measured from less to more identification with father (rather than more to less identification), gamma would have been negative. As a general rule, it is important to look carefully at the ordering of the categories of your measure in order to make a substantive interpretation of your result.

W orking It Out

$$\gamma = \frac{C - D}{C + D}$$

$$= \frac{201{,}575 - 125{,}748}{201{,}575 + 125{,}748}$$

$$= \frac{75{,}827}{327{,}323}$$

$$= 0.2317$$

Recall that there are two tau measures: τ_b and τ_c. If the number of rows were equal to the number of columns, then we would use τ_b. Since the number of rows is different from the number of columns in Table 13.13, we use τ_c. For the data presented in Table 13.13, τ_c has a value of 0.1523, meaning that as the level of affectional identification with father decreases, the level of delinquency increases. However, since τ_c is not a PRE measure, we cannot interpret this result in terms of proportional reduction in error.

W orking It Out

$$\tau_c = \frac{C - D}{\frac{1}{2} N^2 \left(\frac{m - 1}{m} \right)}, \quad \text{where } m = \min(r, c) = \min(5, 3) = 3$$

$$= \frac{201{,}575 - 125{,}748}{\frac{1}{2} (1{,}222)^2 \left(\frac{3 - 1}{3} \right)}$$

$$= \frac{75{,}827}{497{,}761.3333}$$

$$= 0.1523$$

Our third measure of association for ordinal variables, Somers' d, has a value of 0.1358. The interpretation is the same as that for gamma and τ_c: Lower levels of affectional identification with father are associated with higher levels of delinquency. In this case, knowledge of level of affectional identification with father reduces our prediction errors about level of delinquency by 13.58%.

W orking It Out

$$d_{YX} = \frac{C - D}{N(N - 1)/2 - T_X}$$

$$= \frac{201{,}575 - 125{,}748}{[(1{,}222)(1{,}222 - 1)/2] - 187{,}516}$$

$$= \frac{75{,}827}{558{,}515}$$

$$= 0.1358$$

Note on the Use of Measures of Association for Ordinal Variables

As illustrated in our example, the values for gamma, Kendall's tau measures, and Somers' d will generally not be the same. The difference in values can be attributed primarily to whether the measure accounts for tied pairs of observations. Gamma does not account for tied pairs of observations and thus is sometimes criticized for overestimating the strength of association between two ordinal variables. Somers' d accounts for only the pairs of observations tied on the independent variable, while Kendall's tau measures account for tied pairs of observations on both variables.

Which of these measures is best to use in which situations? As in our discussion of measures of association for nominal variables, to begin to address this question, we need to consider the dimensions of the table and our desire for a PRE measure. If the number of rows is equal to the number of columns, then τ_b is likely the best overall measure of association for two reasons: First, it has a PRE interpretation, meaning that values falling between 0 and 1 have direct interpretations in terms of reduction of error. Second, since τ_b accounts for pairs of observations tied on both the independent and the dependent variables, it will provide a more conservative estimate than gamma. If the number of rows is not equal to the number of columns, Somers' d is sometimes considered a better measure of association than τ_c, since it has a PRE interpretation and τ_c does not. Somers' d offers the additional advantage of being an appropriate measure of association for those situations where we have clearly defined independent and dependent variables.

Statistical Significance of Measures of Association for Ordinal Variables

Each of the four measures of association for ordinal variables can be tested for statistical significance with a z-test. The general formula for calculating the z-score is given in Equation 13.11, where we divide the measure of association by the standard error of the measure of association.

$$z = \frac{\text{measure of association}}{\text{standard error of measure of association}}$$

Equation 13.11

What will differ for each of the measures of association for ordinal variables is the calculation of the standard error. Equations 13.12, 13.13, and 13.14 present *approximate* standard errors for gamma, Kendall's tau measures, and Somers' *d*, respectively.[7]

$$\hat{\sigma}_{\gamma} = \sqrt{\frac{4(r + 1)(c + 1)}{9N(r - 1)(c - 1)}}$$

Equation 13.12
Approximate Standard Error for
Gamma

$$\hat{\sigma}_{\tau} = \sqrt{\frac{4(r + 1)(c + 1)}{9Nrc}}$$

Equation 13.13
Approximate Standard Error for
Kendall's Tau Measures

$$\hat{\sigma}_{d} = \sqrt{\frac{4(r^2 - 1)(c + 1)}{9Nr^2(c - 1)}}$$

Equation 13.14
Approximate Standard Error for
Somers' d

In all three equations, N is the total number of observations, r is the number of rows, and c is the number of columns in the table.

Assumptions:

Level of Measurement: Ordinal scale.

Population Distribution: Normal distribution for the relationship examined (relaxed because N is large).

Sampling Method: Independent random sampling.

Sampling Frame: High school–age white males in Richmond, California, in 1965.

Hypotheses:

H_0: There is no association between affectional identification with father and delinquency ($\gamma_p = 0$).

H_1: There is an association between affectional identification with father and delinquency ($\gamma_p \neq 0$).

---

[7]For a more detailed discussion of these issues, see Jean Dickson Gibbons, *Nonparametric Measures of Association* (Newbury Park, CA: Sage, 1993).

or

H_0: There is no association between affectional identification with father and delinquency ($\tau_{c(p)} = 0$).

H_1: There is an association between affectional identification with father and delinquency ($\tau_{c(p)} \neq 0$).

or

H_0: There is no association between affectional identification with father and delinquency ($d_p = 0$).

H_1: There is an association between affectional identification with father and delinquency ($d_p \neq 0$).

The Sampling Distribution We use the normal distribution to test whether the measures of ordinal association differ significantly from 0. As with our earlier examples using a normal sampling distribution, the N of cases must be large in order for us to relax the normality assumption. When examining the relationship between two ordinal-level variables, we recommend a sample of at least 60 cases.

Significance Level and Rejection Region We use the conventional 5% significance level for our example. From Appendix 3, we can determine that the critical values for z are ± 1.96. If the calculated z-score is greater than 1.96 or less than -1.96, we will reject the null hypotheses and conclude that the measure of association between affectional identification with father and delinquency is significantly different from 0.

The Test Statistic Since we have three different measures of association—γ, τ_c, and d—we need to calculate three separate test statistics. We first need to calculate the approximate standard error for gamma, using Equation 13.12. We find the standard error for gamma to be 0.0330.

W orking It Out

$$\hat{\sigma}_\gamma = \sqrt{\frac{4(r + 1)(c + 1)}{9N(r - 1)(c - 1)}}$$

$$= \sqrt{\frac{4(5 + 1)(3 + 1)}{(9)(1,222)(5 - 1)(3 - 1)}}$$

$$= \sqrt{\frac{96}{87,984}}$$

$$= \sqrt{0.00109}$$

$$= 0.0330$$

Using the standard error for gamma, we then calculate the z-score using Equation 13.11. In our example, we find the z-score for gamma to be 7.0212.

W orking It Out

$$z = \frac{\gamma}{\hat{\sigma}_\gamma}$$

$$= \frac{0.2317}{0.0330}$$

$$= 7.0212$$

Turning to τ_c, we calculate the standard error using Equation 13.13. For our example, the standard error for τ_c is 0.0241.

W orking It Out

$$\hat{\sigma}_\tau = \sqrt{\frac{4(r + 1)(c + 1)}{9Nrc}}$$

$$= \sqrt{\frac{4(5 + 1)(3 + 1)}{(9)(1,222)(5)(3)}}$$

$$= \sqrt{\frac{96}{164,970}}$$

$$= \sqrt{0.00058}$$

$$= 0.0241$$

Using the standard error for τ_c and Equation 13.11, we find the z-score to be 6.3195.

W orking It Out

$$z = \frac{\tau_c}{\hat{\sigma}_\tau}$$

$$= \frac{0.1523}{0.0241}$$

$$= 6.3195$$

For Somers' *d,* we follow the same process, calculating the standard error for *d* and then using the standard error to calculate the *z*-score for *d*. For our example, the standard error for *d* is 0.0264 and the corresponding *z*-score is 5.1439.

W orking It Out

$$\hat{\sigma}_d = \sqrt{\frac{4(r^2 - 1)(c + 1)}{9Nr^2(c - 1)}}$$

$$= \sqrt{\frac{4(5^2 - 1)(3 + 1)}{(9)(1{,}222)(5^2)(3 - 1)}}$$

$$= \sqrt{\frac{384}{549{,}900}}$$

$$= \sqrt{0.00070}$$

$$= 0.0264$$

W orking It Out

$$z = \frac{d}{\hat{\sigma}_d}$$

$$= \frac{0.1358}{0.0264}$$

$$= 5.1439$$

The Decision   All three of the calculated *z*-scores are greater than 1.96, meaning that we reject the null hypotheses and conclude in the case of each test that there is a statistically significant relationship between affectional identification with father and delinquency.

Choosing the Best Measure of Association for Nominal- and Ordinal-Level Variables

Because we have covered so many different measures in this chapter, we thought it would be useful to recap them in a simple table that can be used in deciding which measure of association is appropriate

Table 13.14	Summary of Measures of Association for Nominal and Ordinal Variables

MEASURE OF ASSOCIATION	LEVEL OF MEASUREMENT	PRE MEASURE?	DIMENSIONS OF TABLE (ROWS BY COLUMNS)
ϕ	Nominal	No	2×2
V	Nominal	No	Any size
λ	Nominal	Yes	Any size
τ	Nominal	Yes	Any size
γ	Ordinal	Yes	Any size
τ_b	Ordinal	Yes	Number of rows = Number of columns
τ_c	Ordinal	No	Number of rows $\neq$ Number of columns
d	Ordinal	Yes	Any size

for which specific research problem. Table 13.14 presents summary information on the measures of association for nominal and ordinal variables discussed in this chapter. The first column of Table 13.14 gives the measure of association, the second column notes the appropriate level of measurement for the two variables, the third column tells whether the measure of association is also a PRE measure, and the fourth column lists any restrictions on the size of the table used in the analysis. Thus, for any given pair of nominal or ordinal variables, you should be able to determine which measure of association best suits your needs.

Chapter Summary

Measures of association for nominal and ordinal variables allow researchers to go beyond a simple chi-square test for independence between two variables and assess the strength of the relationship. The measures of association discussed in this chapter are the most commonly used measures of association for nominal and ordinal variables.

Two of the measures of association for nominal variables are based on the value of the chi-square statistic. **Phi (ϕ)** adjusts the value of chi-square by taking into account the size of the sample, but is useful only for 2×2 tables. **Cramer's V** is also based on the value of the chi-square statistic, but makes an additional adjustment for the numbers of rows and columns in the table. One of the difficulties with the interpretation of phi and V is that a value that falls between 0 and 1 does not have a precise interpretation. We can infer that as values approach 0, there is a weak relationship between the two variables. Similarly, as values approach 1, there is a strong (or near perfect) relationship between the two variables.

Goodman and Kruskal's tau and **lambda** are measures of association that are not based on the value of the chi-square statistic and instead use different decision rules for classifying cases. Tau relies on the proportional distribution of cases in a table, while lambda relies on the modal values of the dependent variable overall and within each level or category of the independent variable. Tau and lambda offer an improvement over phi and V in that a value between 0 and 1 can be interpreted directly as the proportional reduction in errors made by using information about the independent variable. More generally, this characteristic is called **proportional reduction in error,** or **PRE.** PRE measures tell us how much knowledge of one measure helps to reduce the errors we make in defining the values of a second measure. Both measures require that we define at the outset which variable is the **dependent variable** and which variable is the **independent variable.** The dependent variable is the outcome variable—the phenomenon that we are interested in explaining. As it is dependent on other variables, it is influenced—or we expect it to be influenced—by other variables. The variables that affect, or influence, the dependent variable are referred to as the independent variables.

There are four common measures of association for ordinal variables: **gamma (γ), Kendall's τ_b and τ_c,** and **Somers' d.** Measures of association for ordinal variables are all based on **concordant pairs** and **discordant pairs** of observations. Concordant pairs are pairs of observations that have consistent rankings on the two variables (e.g., high on both variables or low on both variables), while discordant pairs are those pairs of observations that have inconsistent rankings on the two variables (e.g., high on one variable and low on the other variable). Gamma uses information only on the concordant and discordant pairs of observations. The remaining measures of association— Kendall's tau measures and Somers' d—use information about pairs of observations that have tied rankings. All four of the measures of association for ordinal variables discussed in this chapter have values ranging from -1.0 to 1.0, where a value of -1.0 indicates a perfect negative relationship (i.e., as we increase the value of one variable, the other variable decreases), a value of 1.0 indicates a perfect positive relationship (i.e., as we increase the value of one variable, the other variable also increases), and a value of 0.0 indicates no relationship between the two variables. Gamma (γ), Kendall's τ_b, and Somers' d all have PRE interpretations.

Key Terms

concordant pairs of observations Pairs of observations that have consistent rankings on two ordinal variables.

Cramer's V A measure of association for two nominal variables that adjusts the chi-square statistic by the sample size. V is appropriate when at least one of the nominal variables has more than two categories.

dependent variable The outcome variable; the phenomenon that we are interested in explaining. It is dependent on other variables in the sense that it is influenced—or we expect it to be influenced—by other variables.

discordant pairs of observations Pairs of observations that have inconsistent rankings on two ordinal variables.

gamma (γ) PRE measure of association for two ordinal variables that uses information about concordant and discordant pairs of observations within a table. Gamma has a standardized scale ranging from -1.0 to 1.0.

Goodman and Kruskal's tau (τ) PRE measure of association for two nominal variables that uses information about the proportional distribution of cases within a table. Tau has a standardized scale ranging from 0 to 1.0. For this measure, the researcher must define the independent and dependent variables.

independent variable A variable assumed by the researcher to affect or influence the dependent variable.

Kendall's τ_b PRE measure of association for two ordinal variables that uses information about concordant pairs, discordant pairs, and pairs of observations tied on both variables examined. τ_b has a standardized scale ranging from -1.0 to 1.0 and is appropriate only when the number of rows equals the number of columns in a table.

Kendall's τ_c A measure of association for two ordinal variables that uses information about concordant pairs, discordant pairs, and pairs of observations tied on both variables examined. τ_c has a standardized scale ranging from -1.0 to 1.0 and is appropriate when the number of rows is not equal to the number of columns in a table.

lambda (λ) PRE measure of association for two nominal variables that uses information about the modal category of the dependent variable for each category of the independent variable. Lambda has a standardized scale ranging from 0 to 1.0.

phi (ϕ) A measure of association for two nominal variables that adjusts the chi-square statistic by the sample size. Phi is appropriate only for nominal variables that each have two categories.

proportional reduction in error (PRE) The proportional reduction in errors made when the value of one measure is predicted using information about the second measure.

Somers' d PRE measure of association for two ordinal variables that uses information about concordant pairs, discordant pairs, and pairs of observations tied on the independent variable. Somers' d has a standardized scale ranging from -1.0 to 1.0.

tied pairs of observations (ties) Pairs of observation that have the same ranking on two ordinal variables.

Symbols and Formulas

C Number of concordant pairs of observations

D Number of discordant pairs of observations

N_{row} Total number of observations for each row

N_{col} Total number of observations for each column

T_X Number of pairs of observations tied on the independent variable

T_Y Number of pairs of observations tied on the dependent variable

ϕ Phi; measure of association for nominal variables

V Cramer's V; measure of association for nominal variables

λ Lambda; measure of association for nominal variables

τ Goodman and Kruskal's tau; measure of association for nominal variables

γ gamma; measure of association for ordinal variables

τ_b Kendall's τ_b; measure of association for ordinal variables

τ_c Kendall's τ_c; measure of association for ordinal variables

d Somers' d; measure of association for ordinal variables

To calculate phi (ϕ):

$$\phi = \sqrt{\frac{\chi^2}{N}}$$

To calculate Cramer's V:

$$V = \sqrt{\frac{\chi^2}{N \times \min(r-1,\ c-1)}}$$

To calculate Goodman and Kruskal's tau:

$$\tau = \frac{\begin{pmatrix}\text{number of errors} \\ \text{without knowledge of} \\ \text{independent variable}\end{pmatrix} - \begin{pmatrix}\text{number of errors} \\ \text{with knowledge of} \\ \text{independent variable}\end{pmatrix}}{\text{number of errors without knowledge of independent variable}}$$

To calculate lambda:

$$\tau = \frac{\begin{pmatrix}\text{number of errors} \\ \text{using modes of} \\ \text{dependent variable}\end{pmatrix} - \begin{pmatrix}\text{number of errors} \\ \text{using mode of} \\ \text{dependent variable} \\ \text{by level of} \\ \text{independent variable}\end{pmatrix}}{\text{number of errors using mode of independent variable}}$$

To calculate the number of tied pairs of observations on the independent variable:

$$T_X = \frac{1}{2}\sum N_{\text{row}}(N_{\text{row}} - 1)$$

To calculate the number of tied pairs of observations on the dependent variable:

$$T_Y = \frac{1}{2}\sum N_{\text{col}}(N_{\text{col}} - 1)$$

To calculate gamma:

$$\gamma = \frac{C - D}{C + D}$$

To calculate τ_b:

$$\tau_b = \frac{C - D}{\sqrt{[N(N-1)/2 - T_X][N(N-1)/2 - T_Y]}}$$

To calculate τ_c:

$$\tau_c = \frac{C - D}{\frac{1}{2}N^2[(m-1)/m]}, \text{ where } m = \min(r, c)$$

To calculate Somers' d:

$$d_{YX} = \frac{C - D}{N(N-1)/2 - T_X}$$

To calculate the z-score:

$$z = \frac{\text{measure of association}}{\text{standard error of measure of association}}$$

To calculate the standard error for gamma:

$$\hat{\sigma}_\gamma = \sqrt{\frac{4(r + 1)(c + 1)}{9N(r - 1)(c - 1)}}$$

To calculate the standard error for Kendall's tau measures:

$$\hat{\sigma}_\tau = \sqrt{\frac{4(r + 1)(c + 1)}{9Nrc}}$$

To calculate the standard error for Somers' *d*:

$$\hat{\sigma}_d = \sqrt{\frac{4(r^2 - 1)(c + 1)}{9Nr^2(c - 1)}}$$

Exercises

13.1 A researcher studies the link between race of offender and death sentence decision in a state by selecting a random sample of death penalty cases over a 20-year period. The researcher finds the following distribution of death sentence decisions by race:

Race	Sentenced to Death	Not Sentenced to Death
White	8	73
African American	16	52

a. Calculate phi for these data.

b. Calculate Goodman and Kruskal's tau for these data.

c. Using the values that you calculated for phi and tau, how strongly related are the race of the offender and receiving a death sentence?

13.2 Silver Bullet Treatment Services claims to have an effective system for treating criminal offenders. As evidence for the effectiveness of its program, a spokesperson from the organization presents information on rearrest within one year for 100 individuals randomly assigned to the treatment program and for 100 individuals randomly assigned to a control group. The distribution of cases follows:

Experimental Condition	Not Rearrested	Rearrested
Treatment group	75	25
Control group	40	60

a. Calculate phi for these data.

b. Calculate Goodman and Kruskal's tau for these data.

    c. Calculate lambda for these data.

    d. Based on these three measures of association, what can you conclude about the strength of the relationship between the treatment and rearrest?

13.3 A graduate student is interested in the relationship between the gender of a violent crime victim and the victim's relationship to the offender. To study this relationship, the student analyzes survey data collected on a random sample of adults. Among those persons who had been victims of violent crimes, the student finds the following distribution of cases by gender:

Relationship of Offender to Victim

Gender	Stranger	Friend	Partner
Male	96	84	21
Female	55	61	103

    a. Calculate V for these data.

    b. Calculate Goodman and Kruskal's tau for these data.

    c. Calculate lambda for these data.

    d. Based on these three measures of association, what can you conclude about the strength of the relationship between gender and the victim's relationship to a violent offender?

13.4 In an attempt to explore the relationship between type of legal representation and method of case disposition, a student working on a research project randomly selects a small sample of cases from the local court. The student finds the following distribution of cases:

Method of Case Disposition

Type of Legal Representation	Convicted by Trial	Convicted by Guilty Plea	Acquitted
Privately retained	10	6	4
Public defender	3	17	2
Legal aid	3	13	1

    a. Calculate V for these data.

    b. Calculate Goodman and Kruskal's tau for these data.

    c. Calculate lambda for these data.

    d. Based on these three measures of association, what should the student conclude about the relationship between type of legal representation and method of case disposition?

13.5 A researcher interested in the link between attacking other students and being bullied by other students at school used data from a self-report survey administered to a random sample of teenagers. The distribution of responses was as follows:

	Attacked Another Student		
Bullied	Never	Once	Two or More Times
Never	59	22	19
Once	31	44	52
Two or more times	25	29	61

a. Calculate gamma for these data.

b. Calculate τ_b for these data.

c. Calculate Somers' d for these data.

d. Interpret each of the three measures of association. What can you conclude about the relationship between being bullied and attacking other students?

13.6 In response to an increasing reluctance of individuals to serve on juries, a study is commissioned to investigate what might account for the public's change of heart. Wondering whether prior jury experience has any effect on how favorably the jury system is viewed, a researcher constructs the following table:

	"How would you rate the current jury system?"			
Served on a jury	Very Unfavorable	Unfavorable	Favorable	Very Favorable
Never	22	20	21	26
Once	11	19	12	13
Two or three times	18	23	9	6
Four or more times	21	15	7	4

a. Calculate gamma for these data.

b. Calculate τ_b for these data.

c. Calculate Somers' d for these data.

d. Interpret each of the three measures of association. What can you conclude about the relationship between serving on a jury and attitudes about the jury system?

13.7 A researcher interested in the relationship between attitudes about school and drug use analyzed data from a delinquency survey administered to a random sample of high school youth. The researcher was particularly interested in how well the youth liked school and their use of marijuana. A cross-tabulation of responses revealed the following distribution of cases:

I Like School	Smoked Marijuana in the Last Year		
	Never	Once or Twice	Three or More Times
Strongly agree	52	20	12
Agree	48	26	20
Disagree	31	32	33
Strongly disagree	35	45	50

a. Calculate gamma for these data.

b. Calculate τ_c for these data. Explain why τ_b is not appropriate for these data.

c. Calculate Somers' d for these data.

d. Interpret each of the three measures of association. What can you conclude about the relationship between liking school and smoking marijuana?

13.8   A public opinion poll asked respondents whether punishments for convicted criminals should be made more severe, made less severe, or kept about the same. The respondents were also asked to state whether their political views were liberal, moderate, or conservative. A cross-tabulation of the responses to these two questions shows the following distribution of cases:

Political Views	Criminal punishments should be . . .		
	More Severe	About the Same	Less Severe
Liberal	8	54	79
Moderate	35	41	37
Conservative	66	38	12

a. Calculate gamma for these data.

b. Calculate τ_c for these data. Explain why τ_b is not appropriate for these data.

c. Calculate Somers' d for these data.

d. Interpret each of the three measures of association. What can you conclude about the relationship between views about politics and attitudes about criminal punishments?

Computer Exercises

Each measure of association discussed in this chapter is available with the "Crosstabs" command (Analyze → Descriptive Statistics → Crosstabs) in SPSS (see also the computer exercises in Chapter 9). After executing this command, you will be presented with a window that asks for the names of the row and column variables. In general, you move the names of the variables for which you want to produce tables into the "Row(s)" and "Column(s)" boxes.

To obtain the measures of association discussed in this chapter, click on the button labeled "Statistics" located at the bottom of this window. A new window will appear that prompts you for the statistics you would like to have calculated. Note that the measures are grouped by level of measurement—nominal and ordinal. Although it is not listed under the measures of association for nominal variables, Goodman and Kruskal's tau is obtained by clicking on the box next to "Lambda." Click on the box next to the measure(s) of association that you would like to have SPSS calculate; then click on "Continue" and "OK" to run the command.

To try this command, enter the data from Table 13.5 on race and assignment to different cell blocks. Recall that you will need to enter the data from Table 13.5 as three variables—race, cell block, and count—and that you will need to use the "Weight cases" command. (See the computer exercises in Chapter 9 for a review of this command.) Using the "Crosstabs" command, move the cell-block variable name into the "Row(s)" box and the race variable name into the "Column(s)" box. Click on the "Statistics" button to obtain the list of association measures and then click on the boxes next to "Lambda" and "Phi and Cramer's V." Click on "Continue" and "OK" to run the command.

In the output window, you will be presented with the cross-tabulation of the two variables, followed by two additional tables that give the various measures of association. Note that there are three measures of lambda and two measures of Goodman and Kruskal's tau reported. The key to reading the correct values for lambda and tau is to know which variable is the dependent variable. Recall in the discussion of the cell-block assignment data that we treated cell block as the dependent variable. The value reported for lambda in the line for cell block as the dependent variable will match the value reported in the text. The value reported for Goodman and Kruskal's tau in the line for cell block as the dependent variable will differ slightly from that reported in the text because SPSS does not round the prediction errors to the nearest integer; instead, it records prediction errors with digits after the decimal.

1. Enter the data from Table 13.7 into SPSS. Compute the values of *V*, tau, and lambda for these data. How do the values of these measures of association compare to those reported in the text?

2. Enter the data from Table 13.13 into SPSS. Compute the values of gamma, τ_c, and Somers' *d* for these data. How do the values of these measures of association compare to those reported in the text? Test the statistical significance of each of the measures of association.

3.   Enter the data from Exercise 13.2 into SPSS. Compute the values of phi, tau, and lambda. How do these measures of association compare to the values that you calculated for this exercise? Test the statistical significance of each of the measures of association.

4.   Enter the data from Exercise 13.6 into SPSS. Compute the values of gamma, τ_b, and Somers' d. How do these measures of association compare to the values that you calculated for this exercise?

5.   Open the **nys_1.sav** data file into SPSS. Each pair of variables listed below was tested for a relationship using the chi-square test in the computer exercises at the end of Chapter 9. For each pair of variables, determine the level of measurement (nominal or ordinal) and the dependent and the independent variables; then compute appropriate measures of association. Interpret each of the measures of association that you have computed. Test the statistical significance of each of the measures of association. What can you conclude about the relationship between each pair of variables?

a. What is the relationship between ethnicity and grade point average?

b. What is the relationship between marijuana use among friends and the youth's attitudes about marijuana use?

c. What is the relationship between the importance of going to college and the importance of having a job?

d. What is the relationship between grade point average and the importance of having a job?

e. What is the relationship between the youth's sex and the importance of having friends?

f. What is the relationship between the importance of having a job and the youth's attitudes about having a job?

Measuring Association for Interval-Level

Data: Pearson's Correlation Coefficient

the linear correlation coefficient

What Does a Correlation Coefficient Describe?

What Are the Characteristics of Pearson's r?

When Might Pearson's r Provide Misleading Results?

What Are the Characteristics of Spearman's r?

testing for statistical significance

What Is the Test of Statistical Significance for Pearson's r?

What Is the Test of Statistical Significance for Spearman's r?

THIS CHAPTER INTRODUCES the linear correlation coefficient, a widely used descriptive statistic that enables the researcher to describe the relationship between two interval-level measures. This situation is encountered often in criminal justice research. For example, researchers may want to establish whether number of prior arrests is related to age, education, or monthly income. Similarly, it is common in criminal justice research to ask whether the severity of a sanction measured on an interval scale (e.g., number of years sentenced to imprisonment or amount of a fine) is related to such variables as the amount stolen in an offense or the number of prior arrests or convictions of a defendant. We also examine an alternative rank-order measure of association that may be used when the linear correlation coefficient will lead to misleading results.

Measuring Association Between Two Interval-Level Variables

It may not be intuitively obvious why we need to go to the trouble of examining a new statistic to describe the relationship between two interval-level measures. Why can't we just use the means, as we did when we examined interval-level measures in Chapters 11 and 12? Suppose, for example, that we are presented with the data in Table 14.1. Can we find a simple way of expressing the relationship between these two variables?

For each of the 15 young offenders in our sample, we have information regarding age and number of arrests over the last year. The mean age of the sample overall is 17.1 years. The mean number of arrests is 4.9. These statistics describe the characteristics of our sample overall, but, importantly, they do not help us to understand the relationship between age and arrests in the study.

One way to understand this relationship is to change one of these measures into a categorical variable. For example, we might divide the

Table 14.1	Age and Number of Arrests over the Last Year for 15 Young Offenders	

SUBJECT	NUMBER OF ARRESTS	AGE
1	0	14
2	1	13
3	1	15
4	2	13
5	2	14
6	3	14
7	3	17
8	4	19
9	4	21
10	6	19
11	8	16
12	9	18
13	9	20
14	10	21
15	11	22
	$\overline{X} = 4.8667$	$\overline{X} = 17.0667$

offenders into two groups—one consisting of offenders under age 18 and the other of offenders 18 and older. Then we could use the same approach taken in earlier chapters and simply compare the means for the younger and older groups, as shown in Table 14.2. On average, the older offenders appear to have more arrests than the younger offenders ($\overline{X} = 7.571$ versus $\overline{X} = 2.500$).

Similarly, we could divide arrests into categories and compare the mean age of offenders in each category. For example, Table 14.3 divides arrests into three categories: low number of arrests (less than 3), moderate number of arrests (3–8), and high number of arrests (9 and above). This table again shows that, on average, older offenders have more arrests than younger ones. In this case, the mean age for the high-arrest

Table 14.2	Mean Numbers of Arrests for Offenders Under Age 18 versus Those Age 18 and Older

NUMBER OF ARRESTS (UNDER AGE 18)	NUMBER OF ARRESTS (AGE 18 AND OLDER)
0	4
1	4
1	6
2	9
2	9
3	10
3	11
8	
$\overline{X} = 2.5000$	$\overline{X} = 7.5714$

Table 14.3	Mean Ages for Offenders with Low, Moderate, and High Numbers of Arrests		

LOW NUMBER OF ARRESTS (0–2)	MODERATE NUMBER OF ARRESTS (3–8)	HIGH NUMBER OF ARRESTS (9+)
14	14	18
13	17	20
15	19	21
13	21	22
14	19	
	16	
$\bar{X} = 13.8000$	$\bar{X} = 17.6667$	$\bar{X} = 20.2500$

group was 20.3 and those for the moderate- and low-arrest groups were 17.7 and 13.8, respectively.

Although this approach allowed us to come to a general conclusion regarding the relationship between age and arrests in our sample, it forced us to convert one measure from an interval- to a nominal-level variable. In each example, we had to take a step down the ladder of measurement, which means that we did not use all of the information provided by our data. This, of course, violates one of the general principles stated earlier in the text: Statistics based on more information are generally preferred over those based on less information.

But how can we describe the relationship between two interval-level variables without converting one to a nominal scale? A logical solution to this dilemma is provided by a coefficient named after Karl Pearson, a noted British statistician who died in 1936. **Pearson's *r*** estimates the correlation, or relationship, between two measures by comparing how specific individuals stand relative to the mean of each measure. **Pearson's correlation coefficient** (*r*) has become one of the most widely used measures of association in the social sciences.

Pearson's Correlation Coefficient

Pearson's *r* is based on a very simple idea. If we use the mean of each distribution as a starting point, we can then see how specific individuals in the sample stand on each measure relative to its mean. If, in general, people who are above average on one trait are also above average on another, we can say that there is a generally positive relationship between the two traits. That is, being high, on average, on one trait is related to being high, on average, on the other. If, in contrast, people who are higher, on average, on one trait tend to be low, on average, on the other, then we conclude that there is a negative relationship between those traits.

To illustrate these relationships, let's use the data presented in Table 14.1. If we put a plus next to each subject whose average age or number of arrests is above the mean for the sample overall and a minus next to those whose average is below the mean, a pattern begins to emerge (see Table 14.4). When a subject is above average in number of arrests, the subject is also generally above average in age. This is true for five of the six subjects above average in number of arrests (subjects 10, 12, 13, 14, and 15). Conversely, when a subject is below average in number of arrests, the subject is generally below the mean age for the sample. This is true for seven of the nine subjects below average in number of arrests (subjects 1 through 7).

Accordingly, for this sample, subjects generally tend to stand in the same relative position to the mean for both age and arrests. When individuals in the sample have a relatively high number of arrests, they also tend to be relatively older. When they have fewer arrests, they tend to be younger than average for the sample. A simple mathematical way to express this relationship is to take the product of the signs. By doing this, we find that for 12 of the 15 subjects, the result is a positive value (see Table 14.4). Put simply, 12 of the cases move in the same direction relative to the mean. The relationship observed in this case is generally positive.

Table 14.4 A Positive Relationship Between Age and Number of Arrests for 15 Young Offenders Relative to the Means

SUBJECT	NUMBER OF ARRESTS	ABOVE OR BELOW THE MEAN?	AGE	ABOVE OR BELOW THE MEAN?	PRODUCT OF THE SIGNS
1	0	−	14	−	+
2	1	−	13	−	+
3	1	−	15	−	+
4	2	−	13	−	+
5	2	−	14	−	+
6	3	−	14	−	+
7	3	−	17	−	+
8	4	−	19	+	−
9	4	−	21	+	−
10	6	+	19	+	+
11	8	+	16	−	−
12	9	+	18	+	+
13	9	+	20	+	+
14	10	+	21	+	+
15	11	+	22	+	+
	$\bar{X} = 4.8667$		$\bar{X} = 17.0667$		

Table 14.5   A Negative Relationship Between Age and Number
of Arrests for 15 Young Offenders Relative to the Means

SUBJECT	NUMBER OF ARRESTS	ABOVE OR BELOW THE MEAN?	AGE	ABOVE OR BELOW THE MEAN?	PRODUCT OF THE SIGNS
1	11	+	14	−	−
2	10	+	13	−	−
3	9	+	15	−	−
4	9	+	13	−	−
5	8	+	14	−	−
6	6	+	14	−	−
7	4	−	17	−	+
8	4	−	19	+	−
9	3	−	21	+	−
10	3	−	19	+	−
11	2	−	16	−	+
12	2	−	18	+	−
13	1	−	20	+	−
14	1	−	21	+	−
15	0	−	22	+	−
	$\overline{X} = 4.8667$		$\overline{X} = 17.0667$		

A generally negative relationship can be illustrated by reversing the scores for arrests in Table 14.4. That is, the first subject does not have 0 arrests, but 11; the second does not have 1 arrest, but 10; and so forth. If we now indicate each subject's placement relative to the mean, we obtain the set of relationships listed in Table 14.5. In this table, subjects who are above average in number of arrests are generally below average in age, and subjects who are below average in number of arrests are generally above average in age. The products of these signs are mostly negative. Put differently, the scores generally move in opposite directions relative to the mean. There is still a relationship between age and number of arrests, but in this case the relationship is negative.

This is the basic logic that underlies Pearson's *r*. However, we need to take into account two additional pieces of information to develop this correlation coefficient. The first is the values of scores. Using plus (+) and minus (−) divides the scores into categories and thus does not take full advantage of the information provided by interval-level measures. Accordingly, instead of taking the product of the signs, we take the product of the difference between the actual scores and the sample means. This measure is termed the **covariation** of scores and is expressed mathematically in Equation 14.1.

Covariation of scores $= \displaystyle\sum_{i=1}^{N}(X_{1i} - \overline{X}_1)(X_{2i} - \overline{X}_2)$ **Equation 14.1**

Table 14.6 illustrates what we gain by including the values of the scores. We now have not only a measure of the subjects' placement on both variables relative to the mean—the sign of the relationship— but also an estimate of how strongly the scores vary from the mean. In general, for this distribution, the stronger the deviation from the mean on one variable, the stronger the deviation on the second variable. For example, if we look at the scores most distant in value from the mean in terms of number of arrests over the last year, we also find the scores most distant in terms of age. Those subjects with either zero or one arrest are not just younger, on average, than other subjects; they are among the youngest offenders overall in the sample. Similarly, those with the most arrests (10 or 11) are also the oldest members of the sample (ages 21 and 22).

The covariation of scores provides an important piece of information for defining Pearson's r. However, the size of the covariation between two measures depends on the units of measurement used. To permit comparison of covariation across variables with different units of measurement, we must standardize the covariation between the two

---

Table 14.6 Covariation of Number of Arrests (X_1) and Age (X_2) for 15 Young Offenders

SUBJECT	NUMBER OF ARRESTS X_1	$X_{1i} - \bar{X}_1$	AGE X_2	$X_{2i} - \bar{X}_2$	$(X_{1i} - \bar{X}_1)(X_{2i} - \bar{X}_2)$
1	0	−4.8667	14	−3.0667	14.9247
2	1	−3.8667	13	−4.0667	15.7247
3	1	−3.8667	15	−2.0667	7.9913
4	2	−2.8667	13	−4.0667	11.6580
5	2	−2.8667	14	−3.0667	8.7913
6	3	−1.8667	14	−3.0667	5.7246
7	3	−1.8667	17	−0.0667	0.1245
8	4	−0.8667	19	1.9333	−1.6756
9	4	−0.8667	21	3.9333	−3.4090
10	6	1.1333	19	1.9333	2.1910
11	8	3.1333	16	−1.0667	−3.3423
12	9	4.1333	18	0.9333	3.8576
13	9	4.1333	20	2.9333	12.1242
14	10	5.1333	21	3.9333	20.1908
15	11	6.1333	22	4.9333	30.2574

$$\bar{X}_1 = 4.8667 \qquad \bar{X}_2 = 17.0667 \qquad \sum_{i=1}^{N}(X_{1i} - \bar{X}_1)(X_{2i} - \bar{X}_2) = 125.1332$$

variables according to the variability within each. This is done by taking the square root of the product of the sums of the squared deviations from the mean for the two variables. Pearson's r is then the ratio between the covariation of scores and this value (see Equation 14.2). The numerator of the equation is the covariation of the two variables. The denominator of the equation standardizes this outcome according to the square root of the product of the variability found in each of the two distributions, again summed across all subjects.

$$\text{Pearson's } r = \frac{\sum_{i=1}^{N}(X_{1i} - \overline{X}_1)(X_{2i} - \overline{X}_2)}{\sqrt{\left(\sum_{i=1}^{N}(X_{1i} - \overline{X}_1)^2\right)\left(\sum_{i=1}^{N}(X_{2i} - \overline{X}_2)^2\right)}}$$

Equation 14.2

This ratio will be positive when the covariation between the variables is positive (i.e., when subjects' scores vary in the same direction relative to the mean). It will be negative when the covariation between the variables is negative (i.e., when subjects' scores vary in opposite directions relative to the mean). The ratio will be largest when there is a good deal of covariation of the variables and when the variability of scores around each mean is small. The ratio will be smallest when there is little covariation and a good deal of variability in the measures. The range of possible values of r is between -1 and $+1$.

The Calculation

Calculating Pearson's r by hand takes a good deal of work. For that reason, in the future you will probably enter the data into a computer and then use a packaged statistical program to calculate correlation coefficients. But it will help you to understand r better if we take the time to calculate an actual example. We will use the data on number of arrests and age presented in Table 14.1. The calculations needed for Pearson's r are shown in Table 14.7.

To calculate the numerator of Equation 14.2, we must first take the simple deviation of each subject's score from the mean number of arrests (Table 14.7, column 3) and multiply it by the deviation of the subject's age from the mean age of the sample (column 6). The result, the covariation between the measures, is presented in column 8. So, for the first subject, the product of the deviations from the means is 14.9247; for the second, it is 15.7247; and so on. The covariation for our problem, 125.1332, is gained by summing these 15 products.

To obtain the denominator of the equation, we again begin with the deviations of subjects' scores from the mean. However, in this case we

Table 14.7								
	Calculations for the Correlation of Number of Arrests (X_1) and Age (X_2) for 15 Young Offenders							

Calculations for the Correlation of Number of Arrests (X_1) and Age (X_2) for 15 Young Offenders

SUBJECT	NUMBER OF ARRESTS			AGE				
	X_1	$X_{1i} - \bar{X}_1$	$(X_{1i} - \bar{X}_1)^2$	X_2	$X_{2i} - \bar{X}_2$	$(X_{2i} - \bar{X}_2)^2$	$(X_{1i} - \bar{X}_1)(X_{2i} - \bar{X}_2)$	
(1)	(2)	(3)	(4)	(5)	(6)	(7)	(8)	
1	0	−4.8667	23.6848	14	−3.0667	9.4046	14.9247	
2	1	−3.8667	14.9514	13	−4.0667	16.5380	15.7247	
3	1	−3.8667	14.9514	15	−2.0667	4.2712	7.9913	
4	2	−2.8667	8.2180	13	−4.0667	16.5380	11.6580	
5	2	−2.8667	8.2180	14	−3.0667	9.4046	8.7913	
6	3	−1.8667	3.4846	14	−3.0667	9.4046	5.7246	
7	3	−1.8667	3.4846	17	−0.0667	0.0044	0.1245	
8	4	−0.8667	0.7512	19	1.9333	3.7376	−1.6756	
9	4	−0.8667	0.7512	21	3.9333	15.4708	−3.4090	
10	6	1.1333	1.2844	19	1.9333	3.7376	2.1910	
11	8	3.1333	9.8176	16	−1.0667	1.1378	−3.3423	
12	9	4.1333	17.0842	18	0.9333	0.8710	3.8576	
13	9	4.1333	17.0842	20	2.9333	8.6042	12.1242	
14	10	5.1333	26.3508	21	3.9333	15.4708	20.1908	
15	11	6.1333	37.6174	22	4.9333	24.3374	30.2574	

$$\sum_{i=1}^{N}(X_{1i} - \bar{X}_1)^2 = 187.7333 \qquad \sum_{i=1}^{N}(X_{2i} - \bar{X}_2)^2 = 138.9326 \qquad \sum_{i=1}^{N}(X_{1i} - \bar{X}_1)(X_{2i} - \bar{X}_2) = 125.1332$$

$$\bar{X}_1 = 4.8667 \qquad\qquad \bar{X}_2 = 17.0667$$

do not multiply the two scores for each subject. Rather, we first square the deviations from each mean (columns 4 and 7) and then sum the squared deviations for each variable. The sum of the squared deviations of each score from the mean number of arrests is equal to 187.7333; the sum of the squared deviations of each score from the mean age is equal to 138.9326. Next we take the product of those deviations, and finally we take the square root of that product.

W orking It Out

$$\sqrt{\left(\sum_{i=1}^{N}(X_{1i} - \bar{X}_1)^2\right)\left(\sum_{i=1}^{N}(X_{2i} - \bar{X}_2)^2\right)} = \sqrt{(187.7333)(138.9326)}$$

$$= \sqrt{26,082.2755}$$

$$= 161.5001$$

This leaves us with a value of 161.5001 for the denominator of our equation.

We are now ready to calculate Pearson's r for our example. We simply take the covariation of 125.1332 and divide it by 161.5001, to get 0.7748:

W orking It Out

$$\text{Pearson's } r = \frac{\sum_{i=1}^{N}(X_{1i} - \overline{X}_1)(X_{2i} - \overline{X}_2)}{\sqrt{\left(\sum_{i=1}^{N}(X_{1i} - \overline{X}_1)^2\right)\left(\sum_{i=1}^{N}(X_{2i} - \overline{X}_2)^2\right)}}$$

$$= \frac{125.1332}{\sqrt{(187.7333)(138.9326)}}$$

$$= \frac{125.1332}{161.5001}$$

$$= 0.7748$$

Our correlation is about 0.77, meaning that the correlation between age and number of arrests is a positive one. As number of arrests increases, so does the average age of the offenders in our sample. But what is the strength of this relationship? Is it large or small? As discussed in Chapter 12 when we examined the correlation coefficient eta, whether something is large or small is in good measure a value judgment. The answer depends in part on how the result compares to other research in the same area of criminal justice. For example, if other studies produced correlations that were generally much smaller, we might conclude that the relationship in our sample was a very strong one. Jacob Cohen suggests that a correlation of 0.10 may be defined as a small relationship; a correlation of 0.30, a moderate relationship; and a correlation of 0.50, a large relationship.[1] On this yardstick, the relationship observed in our example is a very strong one.

A Substantive Example: Crime and Unemployment in California

An area of study that has received extensive attention from criminologists is the relationship between crime rates and other social or economic indicators, such as unemployment. An example of such data is provided in Table 14.8, which presents the burglary rate and the unem-

---

[1]See Jacob Cohen, *Statistical Power Analysis for the Behavioral Sciences* (Hillsdale, NJ: Lawrence Erlbaum, 1988), pp. 79–80. In Chapter 19, we discuss in greater detail how statisticians develop standardized estimates of "effect size."

Table 14.8

Unemployment Rate and Burglary Rate
for 58 California Counties in 1999

COUNTY	UNEMPLOYMENT RATE (X_1)	BURGLARY RATE (PER 100,000) (X_2)
Alameda	3.5	837.89
Alpine	9.1	2,037.49
Amador	4.6	818.55
Butte	6.8	865.04
Calaveras	6.9	989.76
Colusa	15.9	520.06
Contra Costa	3.0	664.73
Del Norte	8.0	1,200.91
El Dorado	3.9	509.87
Fresno	13.4	924.10
Glenn	11.2	845.29
Humboldt	6.4	1,027.79
Imperial	23.4	1,526.40
Inyo	5.7	511.12
Kern	11.4	960.18
Kings	13.1	649.22
Lake	7.7	1,333.21
Lassen	7.0	361.24
Los Angeles	5.9	610.28
Madera	11.5	929.32
Marin	1.9	526.98
Mariposa	7.4	775.92
Mendocino	6.7	843.92
Merced	13.3	1,214.69
Modoc	8.5	325.08
Mono	6.7	957.95
Monterey	9.6	570.14
Napa	3.3	477.54
Nevada	4.1	455.37
Orange	2.6	464.52
Placer	3.2	646.12
Plumas	9.0	1,030.58
Riverside	5.4	1,049.18
Sacramento	4.2	925.61
San Benito	8.0	845.75
San Bernadino	4.8	883.02
San Diego	3.1	539.82
San Francisco	3.0	744.81
San Joaquin	8.8	896.85
San Luis Obispo	3.2	540.79
San Mateo	2.0	355.82
Santa Barbara	3.9	444.07
Santa Clara	3.0	347.57
Santa Cruz	6.3	647.73
Shasta	7.0	823.95
Sierra	9.2	699.71
Siskiyou	10.3	575.09
Solano	4.6	769.30
Sonoma	2.7	555.44
Stanislaus	10.5	1,057.99
Sutter	13.0	859.11
Tehama	6.7	816.55
Trinity	11.5	676.23
Tulare	16.5	1,047.32
Tuolumne	6.5	908.79
Ventura	4.8	491.86
Yolo	4.3	591.28
Yuba	11.6	1,366.76

| Table 14.9 | Calculations for the Correlation of Unemployment Rate (X_1) and Burglary Rate (X_2) for 58 California Counties |

UNEMPLOYMENT RATE		BURGLARY RATE		
X_{1i}	$(X_{1i} - \bar{X}_1)^2$	X_{2i}	$(X_{2i} - \bar{X}_2)^2$	$(X_{1i} - \bar{X}_1)(X_{2i} - \bar{X}_2)$
3.5	15.2639	837.89	2,208.9342	−183.6216
9.1	2.8666	2,037.49	1,554,009.8148	2,110.6173
4.6	7.8787	818.55	765.0369	−77.6369
6.8	0.3683	865.04	5,498.1187	−45.0012
6.9	0.2569	989.76	39,548.9985	−100.8068
15.9	72.1327	520.06	73,349.2681	−2,300.1922
3.0	19.4208	664.73	15,916.5222	555.9776
8.0	0.3518	1,200.91	168,115.8264	243.1824
3.9	12.2983	509.87	78,972.6338	985.5115
13.4	35.9172	924.10	17,744.7176	798.3367
11.2	14.3876	845.29	2,959.2838	208.3420
6.4	1.0138	1,027.79	56,121.2783	−238.5339
23.4	255.7792	1,526.40	540,973.9304	11,763.0738
5.7	2.9135	511.12	78,271.6446	477.5406
11.4	15.9448	960.18	28,658.8671	675.9891
13.1	32.4114	649.22	20,070.5872	−806.5455
7.7	0.0859	1,333.21	294,110.2232	158.9538
7.0	0.1656	361.24	184,599.7240	174.8249
5.9	2.2707	610.28	32,620.2250	272.1623
11.5	16.7535	929.32	19,162.6711	566.6050
1.9	30.3259	526.98	69,648.8576	1,453.3298
7.4	0.0000	775.92	224.1219	0.1033
6.7	0.4997	843.92	2,812.1067	−37.4864
13.3	34.7286	1,214.69	179,605.8467	2,497.4917
8.5	1.1949	325.08	216,979.6082	−509.1777
6.7	0.4997	957.95	27,908.8097	−118.0942
9.6	4.8097	570.14	48,730.8716	−484.1284
3.3	16.8666	477.54	98,188.6612	1,286.9000
4.1	10.9356	455.37	112,574.1401	1,109.5334
2.6	23.1063	464.52	106,517.8338	1,568.8313
3.2	17.6980	646.12	20,958.5556	609.0359
9.0	2.5380	1,030.58	57,450.9605	381.8490
5.4	4.0276	1,049.18	66,713.3625	−518.3608
4.2	10.2842	925.61	18,149.2898	−432.0313
8.0	0.3518	845.75	3,009.5428	32.5371
4.8	6.7959	883.02	8,487.8079	−240.1719
3.1	18.5494	539.82	63,036.4964	1,081.3364
3.0	19.4208	744.81	2,123.4309	203.0730
8.8	1.9407	896.85	11,227.3733	147.6119
3.2	17.6980	540.79	62,550.3601	1,052.1486
2.0	29.2346	355.82	189,286.5140	2,352.3838
3.9	12.2983	444.07	120,284.5979	1,216.2655
3.0	19.4208	347.57	196,533.2430	1,953.6700
6.3	1.2252	647.73	20,494.9860	158.4646
7.0	0.1656	823.95	1,092.9173	−13.4518
9.2	3.2152	699.71	8,313.9201	−163.4961
10.3	8.3700	575.09	46,569.9421	−624.3330
4.6	7.8787	769.30	466.1583	60.6029
2.7	22.1549	555.44	55,437.0321	1,108.2429
10.5	9.5673	1,057.99	71,342.0361	826.1648
13.0	31.2828	859.11	4,653.8729	381.5574

(continued on next page)

| Table 14.9 | Calculations for the Correlation of Unemployment Rate (X_1) and Burglary Rate (X_2) for 58 California Counties (*Continued*) |

UNEMPLOYMENT RATE		BURGLARY RATE		
X_{1i}	$(X_{1i} - \bar{X_1})^2$	X_{2i}	$(X_{2i} - \bar{X_2})^2$	$(X_{1i} - \bar{X_1})(X_{2i} - \bar{X_2})$
6.7	0.4997	816.55	658.3997	−18.1386
11.5	16.7535	676.23	13,147.0761	−469.3177
16.5	82.6845	1,047.32	65,755.9859	2,331.7373
6.5	0.8225	908.79	13,900.2449	−106.9229
4.8	6.7959	491.86	89,419.3595	779.5431
4.3	9.6528	591.28	39,844.4316	620.1705
11.6	17.5821	1,366.76	331,625.4507	2,414.6776

$$\sum_{i=1}^{N} = 1{,}010.3570 \qquad \sum_{i=1}^{N} = 5{,}659{,}402.5114 \qquad \sum_{i=1}^{N} = 37{,}128.9297$$

$$\bar{X_1} = 7.4069 \qquad\qquad \bar{X_2} = 790.8907$$

ployment rate for all 58 counties in California in 1999. The burglary rate represents the number of burglaries per 100,000 population, and the unemployment rate represents the percentage of persons actively looking for work who have not been able to find employment.

Table 14.9 presents the detailed calculations for the unemployment and burglary data from California. The sum of the covariations is 37,128.9297, the sum of the squared deviations for the unemployment rate is 1,010.3570, and the sum of the squared deviations for the burglary rate is 5,659,402.5114. After inserting these values into Equation 14.2, we find that $r = 0.4910$. The positive correlation between the unemployment rate and the burglary rate means that counties with higher rates of unemployment also tended to have higher rates of burglary, while counties with lower rates of unemployment tended to have lower rates of burglary.

W orking It Out

$$r = \frac{\sum_{i=1}^{N}(X_{1i} - \bar{X_1})(X_{2i} - \bar{X_2})}{\sqrt{\left(\sum_{i=1}^{N}(X_{1i} - \bar{X_1})^2\right)\left(\sum_{i=1}^{N}(X_{2i} - \bar{X_2})^2\right)}}$$

$$= \frac{37{,}128{,}9297}{\sqrt{(1{,}010.3570)(5{,}659{,}402.5114)}}$$

$$= 0.4910$$

Nonlinear Relationships and Pearson's *r*

Pearson's *r* allows us to assess the correlation between two interval-level measures, taking into account the full amount of information that these measures provide. However, it assesses the strength of only a **linear relationship.** If the correlation between two variables is not linear, then Pearson's *r* will give very misleading results.

A simple way to see this is to look at **scatterplots,** or **scatter diagrams,** representing different types of relationships. A scatterplot positions subjects according to their scores on both variables being examined. Figure 14.1 represents the subjects in our example concerning age and number of arrests. The first case (age = 14, arrests = 0) is represented by the dot with a 1 next to it. The overall relationship in this example is basically linear and positive. That is, the dots move together in a positive direction (as age increases, so too do arrests). A scatterplot of the data in Table 14.5, where the highest number of arrests is found among younger rather than older subjects, is presented in Figure 14.2. In this case, the scatterplot shows a negative relationship (as age increases, number of arrests decreases).

But what would happen if there were a **curvilinear relationship** between age and number of arrests? That is, what if the number of arrests for both younger and older subjects was high, and the number for those of average age was low? This relationship is illustrated in Figure 14.3. In

Figure 14.1	*Scatterplot Showing a Positive Relationship Between Age and Number of Arrests for 15 Subjects*

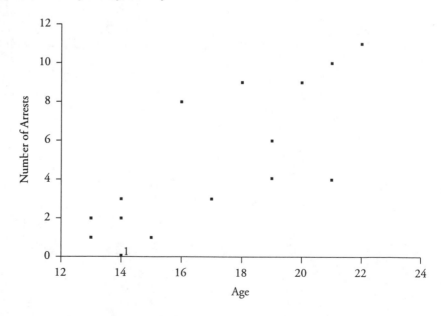

Figure 14.2

*Scatterplot Showing a Negative Relationship
Between Age and Number of Arrests for 15 Subjects*

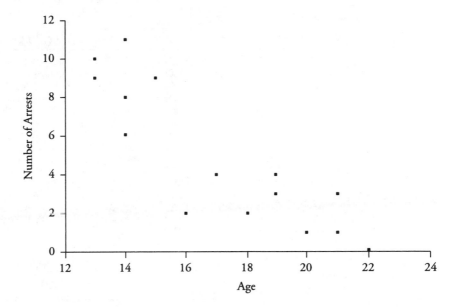

Figure 14.3

*Scatterplot Showing a Curvilinear Relationship
Between Age and Number of Arrests for 15 Subjects*

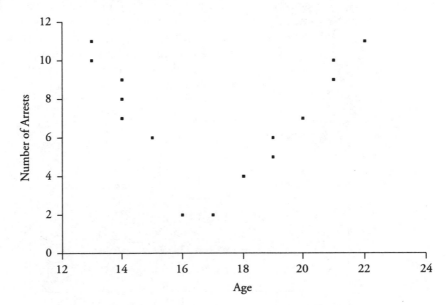

Table 14.10	Curvilinear Relatonship: Calculations for the Correlation of Number of Arrests (X_1) and Age (X_2) for 15 Young Offenders

	NUMBER OF ARRESTS			AGE			
SUBJECT	X_1	$X_{1i} - \overline{X}_1$	$(X_{1i} - \overline{X}_1)^2$	X_2	$X_{2i} - \overline{X}_2$	$(X_{2i} - \overline{X}_2)^2$	$(X_{1i} - \overline{X}_1)(X_{2i} - \overline{X}_2)$
1	9	1.8667	3.4846	14	−3.0667	9.4046	−5.7246
2	11	3.8667	14.9514	13	−4.0667	16.5380	−15.7247
3	6	−1.1333	1.2844	15	−2.0667	4.2712	2.3422
4	10	2.8667	8.2180	13	−4.0667	16.5380	−11.6580
5	8	0.8667	0.7512	14	−3.0667	9.4046	−2.6579
6	7	−0.1333	0.0178	14	−3.0667	9.4046	0.4088
7	2	−5.1333	26.3508	17	−0.0667	0.0044	0.3424
8	5	−2.1333	4.5510	19	1.9333	3.7376	−4.1243
9	9	1.8667	3.4846	21	3.9333	15.4708	7.3423
10	6	−1.1333	1.2844	19	1.9333	3.7376	−2.1910
11	2	−5.1333	26.3508	16	−1.0667	1.1378	5.4757
12	4	−3.1333	9.8176	18	0.9333	0.8710	−2.9243
13	7	−0.1333	0.0178	20	2.9333	8.6042	−0.3910
14	10	2.8667	8.2180	21	3.9333	15.4708	11.2756
15	11	3.8667	14.9514	22	4.9333	24.3374	19.0756

$$\sum_{i=1}^{N}(X_{1i} - \overline{X}_1)^2 = 123.7338 \qquad \sum_{i=1}^{N}(X_{2i} - \overline{X}_2)^2 = 138.9326 \qquad \sum_{i=1}^{N}(X_{1i} - \overline{X}_1)(X_{2i} - \overline{X}_2) = 0.8668$$

$$\overline{X}_1 = 7.1333 \qquad\qquad \overline{X}_2 = 17.0667$$

this scatterplot, the relationship is clear: The number of arrests declines until age 17 and then increases. However, Pearson's r for these data is close to 0. If there is a relationship, why does this happen? Table 14.10 shows why. Subjects who are either much above or much below the mean for age have large numbers of arrests. The covariance for these subjects is accordingly very high. However, for those below the mean in age, the covariance is negative, and for those above the mean, the covariance is positive. If we add these scores together, they cancel each other out. As a result, Pearson's r for this example is close to 0.

Working It Out

$$\text{Pearson's } r = \frac{\sum_{i=1}^{N}(X_{1i} - \overline{X}_1)(X_{2i} - \overline{X}_2)}{\sqrt{\left(\sum_{i=1}^{N}(X_{1i} - \overline{X}_1)^2\right)\left(\sum_{i=1}^{N}(X_{2i} - \overline{X}_2)^2\right)}}$$

$$= \frac{0.8668}{\sqrt{(123.7338)(138.9326)}}$$

$$= 0.0066$$

Pearson's r will provide a good estimate of correlation when the relationship between two variables is approximately linear. However, a strong nonlinear relationship will lead to a misleading correlation coefficient. Figure 14.4 provides examples of a number of nonlinear relationships. These examples illustrate why it is important to look at the scatterplot of the relationship between two interval-level measures to establish that it is linear before calculating Pearson's correlation coefficient. Linear relationships are much more common in criminal justice than nonlinear ones. But you would not want to conclude, based on r, that there was a very small relationship between two variables when in fact there was a very strong nonlinear correlation between them.

What can you do if the relationship is nonlinear? Sometimes the solution is simply to break up the distribution of scores. For example, Figure 14.3 shows a nonlinear relationship that results in an r of 0.007. If we break this distribution at the point where it changes direction, we can calculate two separate Pearson's correlation coefficients, each for a linear relationship. The first would provide an estimate of the relationship for younger offenders (which is negative), and the second an estimate of the relationship for older offenders (which is positive).

For some nonlinear relationships, you may want to consider using alternative statistics. For example, it may be worthwhile to break up your

Figure 14.4   *Examples of Nonlinear Relationships*

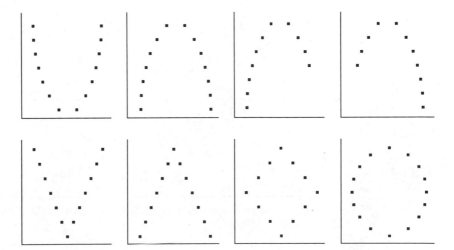

sample into a number of groups, or categories, and then look at the means for each. In some cases, it may be possible to change the form of the variables and, in doing so, increase the linearity of the relationship being examined. Although such transformations are beyond the scope of this text, you should be aware that they provide one solution to problems of nonlinearity.[2]

Beware of Outliers

For Pearson's r, as for other statistics based on deviations from the mean, outliers can have a strong impact on results. For example, suppose we add to our study of age and number of arrests (from Table 14.1) one subject who was very young (12) but nonetheless had an extremely large number of arrests over the last year (25), as shown in the scatterplot in Figure 14.5. If we take the covariation for this one relationship (see sub-

Figure 14.5 · *Scatterplot Showing the Relationship Between Age and Number of Arrests for 16 Subjects, Including an Outlier*

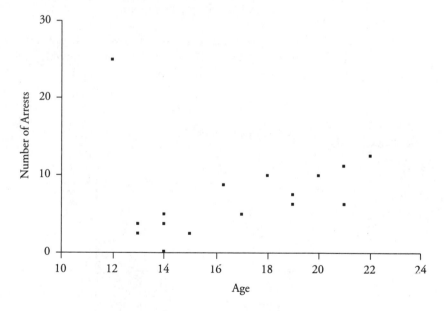

[2]For a discussion of this issue, see. J. Fox, *Linear Statistical Models and Related Methods* (New York: Wiley, 1994).

Table 14.11	Calculations for the Correlation of Number of Arrests (X_1) and Age (X_2) for 16 Young Offenders

	NUMBER OF ARRESTS			AGE			
SUBJECT	X_1	$X_{1i} - \bar{X}_1$	$(X_{1i} - \bar{X}_1)^2$	X_2	$X_{2i} - \bar{X}_2$	$(X_{2i} - \bar{X}_2)^2$	$(X_{1i} - \bar{X}_1)(X_{2i} - \bar{X}_2)$
1	0	−6.1250	37.5156	14	−2.7500	7.5625	16.84375
2	1	−5.1250	26.2656	13	−3.7500	14.0625	19.21875
3	1	−5.1250	26.2656	15	−1.7500	3.0625	8.96875
4	2	−4.1250	17.0156	13	−3.7500	14.0625	15.46875
5	2	−4.1250	17.0156	14	−2.7500	7.5625	11.34375
6	3	−3.1250	9.7656	14	−2.7500	7.5625	8.59375
7	3	−3.1250	9.7656	17	0.2500	0.0625	−0.78125
8	4	−2.1250	4.5156	19	2.2500	5.0625	−4.78125
9	4	−2.1250	4.5156	21	4.2500	18.0625	−9.03125
10	6	−0.1250	0.0156	19	2.2500	5.0625	−0.28125
11	8	1.8750	3.5156	16	−0.7500	0.5625	−1.40625
12	9	2.8750	8.2656	18	1.2500	1.5625	3.59375
13	9	2.8750	8.2656	20	3.2500	10.5625	9.34375
14	10	3.8750	15.0156	21	4.2500	18.0625	16.46875
15	11	4.8750	23.7656	22	5.2500	27.5625	25.59375
16	25	18.8750	356.2656	12	−4.7500	22.5625	−89.65625

$$\bar{X}_1 = 6.1250 \qquad \sum_{i=1}^{N}(X_{1i} - \bar{X}_1)^2 \qquad \bar{X}_2 = 16.7500 \qquad \sum_{i=1}^{N}(X_{2i} - \bar{X}_2)^2 \qquad \sum_{i=1}^{N}(X_{1i} - \bar{X}_1)(X_{2i} - \bar{X}_2)$$

$$= 567.7496 \qquad\qquad\qquad = 163.000 \qquad = 29.5000$$

ject 16 in Table 14.11), we see that it is very large relative to that of other subjects in our analysis. Because it is negative, it cancels out the positive covariation produced by the other subjects in the sample. Indeed, with this subject included, the correlation decreases from 0.77 to 0.10.

> ## W orking It Out
>
> $$\text{Pearson's } r = \frac{\sum_{i=1}^{N}(X_{1i} - \bar{X}_1)(X_{2i} - \bar{X}_2)}{\sqrt{\left(\sum_{i=1}^{N}(X_{1i} - \bar{X}_1)^2\right)\left(\sum_{i=1}^{N}(X_{2i} - \bar{X}_2)^2\right)}}$$
>
> $$= \frac{29.5000}{\sqrt{(567.7496)(163)}}$$
>
> $$= 0.0970$$

What should you do when faced with outliers? When you have just a few deviant cases in your sample, the best decision may be to exclude them from your analysis. If you take this approach, it is important to clearly state that certain cases have been excluded and to explain why. Before excluding outliers, however, you should compare the correlations with and without them. When samples are large, deviant cases may have a relatively small impact; thus, including them may not lead to misleading results.

When there are a relatively large number of outliers that follow the general pattern of relationships in your data, it may be better to choose an alternative correlation coefficient rather than exclude such cases. For example, suppose we add to our study of age and arrests three different subjects for whom the relationships are similar to those noted previously, but the number of arrests and the average age are much higher (see subjects 16, 17, and 18 in Table 14.12). These data are depicted in the scat-

<table>
<tr><th>Table 14.12</th><th colspan="8">Calculations for the Correlation of Number of Arrests (X_1) and Age (X_2) for 18 Young Offenders</th></tr>
<tr><th></th><th colspan="3">NUMBER OF ARRESTS</th><th colspan="4">AGE</th><th></th></tr>
<tr><th>SUBJECT</th><th>X_1</th><th>$X_{1i} - \bar{X_1}$</th><th>$(X_{1i} - \bar{X_1})^2$</th><th>X_2</th><th>$X_{2i} - \bar{X_2}$</th><th>$(X_{2i} - \bar{X_2})^2$</th><th>$(X_{1i} - \bar{X_1})(X_{2i} - \bar{X_2})$</th></tr>
<tr><td>1</td><td>0</td><td>−11.2778</td><td>127.1888</td><td>14</td><td>−8.5556</td><td>73.1983</td><td>96.4883</td></tr>
<tr><td>2</td><td>1</td><td>−10.2778</td><td>105.6332</td><td>13</td><td>−9.5556</td><td>91.3095</td><td>98.2105</td></tr>
<tr><td>3</td><td>1</td><td>−10.2778</td><td>105.6332</td><td>15</td><td>−7.5556</td><td>57.0871</td><td>77.6549</td></tr>
<tr><td>4</td><td>2</td><td>−9.2778</td><td>86.0776</td><td>13</td><td>−9.5556</td><td>91.3095</td><td>88.6549</td></tr>
<tr><td>5</td><td>2</td><td>−9.2778</td><td>86.0776</td><td>14</td><td>−8.5556</td><td>73.1983</td><td>79.3771</td></tr>
<tr><td>6</td><td>3</td><td>−8.2778</td><td>68.5220</td><td>14</td><td>−8.5556</td><td>73.1983</td><td>70.8215</td></tr>
<tr><td>7</td><td>3</td><td>−8.2778</td><td>68.5220</td><td>17</td><td>−5.5556</td><td>30.8647</td><td>45.9881</td></tr>
<tr><td>8</td><td>4</td><td>−7.2778</td><td>52.9664</td><td>19</td><td>−3.5556</td><td>12.6423</td><td>25.8769</td></tr>
<tr><td>9</td><td>4</td><td>−7.2778</td><td>52.9664</td><td>21</td><td>−1.5556</td><td>2.4199</td><td>11.3213</td></tr>
<tr><td>10</td><td>6</td><td>−5.2778</td><td>27.8552</td><td>19</td><td>−3.5556</td><td>12.6423</td><td>18.7675</td></tr>
<tr><td>11</td><td>8</td><td>−3.2778</td><td>10.7440</td><td>16</td><td>−6.556</td><td>42.9759</td><td>21.4879</td></tr>
<tr><td>12</td><td>9</td><td>−2.2778</td><td>5.1884</td><td>18</td><td>−4.5556</td><td>20.7535</td><td>10.3767</td></tr>
<tr><td>13</td><td>9</td><td>−2.2778</td><td>5.1884</td><td>20</td><td>−2.5556</td><td>6.5311</td><td>5.8211</td></tr>
<tr><td>14</td><td>10</td><td>−1.2778</td><td>1.6328</td><td>21</td><td>−1.5556</td><td>2.4199</td><td>1.9877</td></tr>
<tr><td>15</td><td>11</td><td>−0.2778</td><td>0.0772</td><td>22</td><td>−0.5556</td><td>0.3087</td><td>0.1543</td></tr>
<tr><td>16</td><td>36</td><td>24.7222</td><td>611.1872</td><td>40</td><td>17.4444</td><td>304.3071</td><td>431.2639</td></tr>
<tr><td>17</td><td>40</td><td>28.7222</td><td>824.9648</td><td>50</td><td>27.4444</td><td>753.1951</td><td>788.2635</td></tr>
<tr><td>18</td><td>54</td><td>42.7222</td><td>1,825.1864</td><td>60</td><td>37.4444</td><td>1,402.0831</td><td>1,5999.7071</td></tr>
<tr><td colspan="2">$\bar{X_1} = 11.2778$</td><td></td><td>$\sum_{i=1}^{N}(X_{1i} - \bar{X_1})^2$</td><td colspan="2">$\bar{X_2} = 22.5556$</td><td>$\sum_{i=1}^{N}(X_{2i} - \bar{X_2})^2$</td><td>$\sum_{i=1}^{N}(X_{1i} - \bar{X_1})(X_{2i} - \bar{X_2})$</td></tr>
<tr><td colspan="2"></td><td></td><td>$= 4,065.6116$</td><td colspan="2"></td><td>$= 3,050.4446$</td><td>$= 3,472.2214$</td></tr>
</table>

| Figure 14.6 | *Scatterplot Showing the Relationship Between Age and Number of Arrests for 18 Subjects, Including Three Outliers Who Follow the General Pattern* |

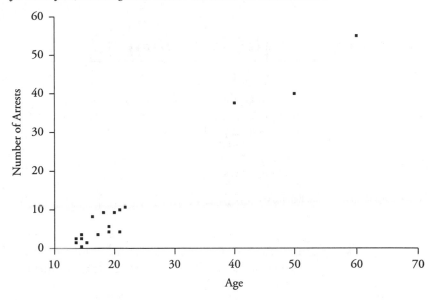

terplot in Figure 14.6. In such situations, Pearson's r is likely to give a misleading view of the relationship between the two variables. For our example, the correlation changes from 0.77 to 0.99.

Working It Out

$$\text{Pearson's } r = \frac{\sum_{i=1}^{N}(X_{1i} - \overline{X}_1)(X_{2i} - \overline{X}_2)}{\sqrt{\left(\sum_{i=1}^{N}(X_{1i} - \overline{X}_1)^2\right)\left(\sum_{i=1}^{N}(X_{2i} - \overline{X}_2)^2\right)}}$$

$$= \frac{3,472.2214}{\sqrt{(4,065.6116)(3,050.4446)}}$$

$$= 0.9859$$

In such situations, you may want to use a rank-order correlation coefficient called **Spearman's r**. Pearson's r is generally more appropriate for interval-level data. However, where a number of outliers are found in the distribution, **Spearman's correlation** coefficient can provide a useful alternative.

Spearman's Correlation Coefficient

Spearman's r compares the rank order of subjects on each measure rather than the relative position of each subject to the mean. Like Pearson's r, its range of possible values is between -1 and $+1$. It is calculated using Equation 14.3.

$$r_s = 1 - \frac{6\sum_{i=1}^{N} D_i^2}{N(N^2 - 1)}$$

Equation 14.3

Let's calculate r_s for our original example with 15 cases (from Table 14.1), and for the example with the additional three outliers (from Table 14.12). To carry out the calculation, we must first rank order the cases, as

Table 14.13	Calculation of Difference in Rank (D) for Spearman's r for 15 Young Offenders

SUBJECT	NUMBER OF ARRESTS	RANK ARRESTS Rk_1	AGE	RANK AGE Rk_2	D $(Rk_1 - Rk_2)$	D^2
1	0	1	14	4	−3	9
2	1	2.5	13	1.5	1	1
3	1	2.5	15	6	−3.5	12.25
4	2	4.5	13	1.5	3	9
5	2	4.5	14	4	0.5	0.25
6	3	6.5	14	4	2.5	6.25
7	3	6.5	17	8	−1.5	2.25
8	4	8.5	19	10.5	−2	4
9	4	8.5	21	13.5	−5	25
10	6	10	19	10.5	−0.5	0.25
11	8	11	16	7	4	16
12	9	12.5	18	9	3.5	12.25
13	9	12.5	20	12	0.5	0.25
14	10	14	21	13.5	0.5	0.25
15	11	15	22	15	0	0
	$\bar{X}_1 = 4.8667$		$\bar{X}_2 = 17.0667$			$\sum_{i=1}^{N} D_i^2 = 98$

| Table 14.14 | Calculation of Difference in Rank (D) for Spearman's r for 18 Young Offenders | | | | | |

SUBJECT	NUMBER OF ARRESTS	RANK ARRESTS Rk_1	AGE	RANK AGE Rk_2	D $(Rk_1 - Rk_2)$	D^2
1	0	1	14	4	−3	9
2	1	2.5	13	1.5	1	1
3	1	2.5	15	6	−3.5	12.25
4	2	4.5	13	1.5	3	9
5	2	4.5	14	4	0.5	0.25
6	3	6.5	14	4	2.5	6.25
7	3	6.5	17	8	−1.5	2.25
8	4	8.5	19	10.5	−2	4
9	4	8.5	21	13.5	−5	25
10	6	10	19	10.5	−0.5	0.25
11	8	11	16	7	4	16
12	9	12.5	18	9	3.5	12.25
13	9	12.5	20	12	0.5	0.25
14	10	14	21	13.5	0.5	0.25
15	11	15	22	15	0	0
16	36	16	40	16	0	0
17	40	17	50	17	0	0
18	54	18	60	18	0	0
	$\overline{X}_1 = 11.2778$		$\overline{X}_2 = 22.5556$			$\sum_{i=1}^{N} D_i^2 = 98$

shown in Tables 14.13 and 14.14. We then take the squared difference in ranks for each subject on the two measures and sum it across all the cases in our example. This value is multiplied by 6, and then divided by $N(N^2 - 1)$. The final figure is then subtracted from 1.

W orking It Out   No Outliers

$$r_s = 1 - \frac{6 \sum_{i=1}^{N} D_i^2}{N(N^2 - 1)}$$

$$= 1 - \frac{(6)(98)}{(15)(224)}$$

$$= 1 - \frac{588}{3360}$$

$$= 1 - 0.1750$$

$$= 0.8250$$

W orking It Out   With Outliers

$$r_s = 1 - \frac{6\sum_{i=1}^{N} D_i^2}{N(N^2 - 1)}$$

$$= 1 - \frac{(6)(98)}{(18)(323)}$$

$$= 1 - \frac{588}{5814}$$

$$= 1 - 0.1011$$

$$= 0.8989$$

The correlation coefficients for our two distributions (without outliers and with outliers) are similar. In the case without the outliers, $r_s = 0.83$; in the case with them, $r_s = 0.90$. The outliers here do not have as much of an impact because Spearman's correlation coefficient does not take into account the actual values of the scores, but only their ranks in the distribution. Note that the correlation coefficient obtained here for the 15 cases, $r_s = 0.83$, is a bit larger than, although similar to, $r = 0.77$. Which is the better estimate of the correlation between these two variables? In the case without the outliers, Pearson's r would be preferred because it takes into account more information (order as well as value). In the case with the outliers, however, Spearman's r would be preferred because it is not affected by the extreme values of the three outliers, but only by their relative positions in the distributions.

Testing the Statistical Significance of Pearson's *r*

As in Chapter 13, our emphasis in this chapter has been not on statistical inference but rather on statistical description. Our concern has been to describe the strength or nature of the relationship between two interval-level variables. Nonetheless, it is important here, as before, to define whether the differences observed in our samples can be inferred to the populations from which they were drawn.

Statistical Significance of *r*: The Case of Age and Number of Arrests

We can use the t-distribution introduced in Chapter 10 to test for the significance of Pearson's r. We begin by conducting a test of statistical significance for our example of the correlation between age and number of arrests.

Assumptions:

Level of Measurement: Interval scale.

Population Distribution: Normal distribution of Y around each value of X (must be assumed because N is not large).

Homoscedasticity.

Linearity.

Sampling Method: Independent random sampling.

Sampling Frame: Youth in one U.S. city.

Hypotheses:

H_0: There is no linear relationship between age and number of arrests in the population of young offenders ($r_p = 0$).

H_1: There is a linear relationship between age and number of arrests in the population of young offenders ($r_p \neq 0$).

The t-test for Pearson's r assumes that the variables examined are measured on an interval scale. In practice, researchers sometimes use ordinal-scale measures for calculating these coefficients, particularly when an interval-level measure is related to an ordinal-scale variable. There is no simple answer to the question of which statistic is most appropriate in such cases, and Pearson's r is often considered a good solution. Nonetheless, you should keep in mind that Pearson's r, like other statistics that require an interval level of measurement, assumes that the categories are not only ranked but also equal to one another. When there are clear differences between the categories, the meaning of r becomes ambiguous. For example, suppose you were interested in the relationship between amount stolen in robberies and age, where amount stolen in robberies was measured on an ordinal scale, with the first category as $1–50, the second as $51–200, and subsequent intervals also of unequal size. If the real relationship between amount stolen and age was truly linear, with every year of age related to a measured increase in amount stolen, you would likely get a misleading correlation coefficient. In this case, an interval-scale measurement would allow you to represent the linear relationship between amount stolen and age. The ordinal scale we have described might mask or misrepresent that relationship. In practice, you should also be wary of using Pearson's correlation coefficient when the number of categories is small (for example, less than 5). While r is sometimes used when the researcher wants to represent the relationship between an ordinal-scale measure and an interval-level variable, it should not be used to define the relationship between two ordinal-level measures or when nominal-scale measurement is involved. As noted in earlier chapters, other statistics are more appropriate for measuring such relationships.

Figure 14.7   *Scatterplot Showing Normal Distribution and Homoscedasticity*

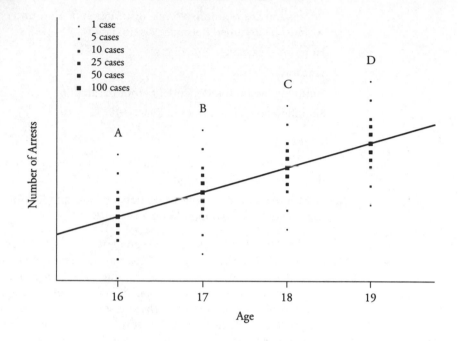

Cross Sections:

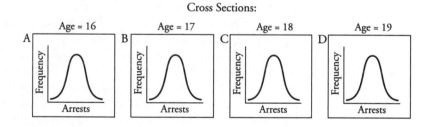

Because our test of the statistical significance of *r* is a parametric test of significance, we must also make assumptions regarding the population distribution. For tests of statistical significance with *r*, we must assume a normal distribution. However, in this case, it is useful to think of this distribution in terms of the joint distribution of scores between X_1 and X_2. Assume that the scatterplot in Figure 14.7 represents the relationship between age and number of arrests for ages 16–19 for the population of scores. The relationship, as in our sample, is linear. Notice how the points in the scatterplot are distributed. Suppose we put an imaginary line through the scatter of points (shown as a real line in Figure 14.7). There is a clustering of points close to the line, in the middle of the distribution. As we move away from the center of the distribution of number of arrests for each age (represented by the imaginary line), there are fewer points. The distribution of number of arrests for each value of age is basically normal in form, as illustrated in the cross section for each of the four ages examined. This imaginary population distribution meets the normality assumption of our test.

One problem in drawing conclusions about our assumptions is that they relate to the population and not to the sample. Because the population distribution is usually unknown, we generally cannot come to solid conclusions regarding our assumptions about the population. In the case of an assumption of normality, the researcher is most often aided by the central limit theorem. When the number of cases in a sample is greater than 30, the central limit theorem can be safely invoked. For our example, we cannot invoke the central limit theorem. Accordingly, our test results cannot be relied on unless the assumption of a normal distribution is true for the population to which we infer.

For our t-test, we must also assume that the variances of the joint distribution of scores are equal. In our example, this means that the spread of number of arrests around each value of age should be about the same. This is the assumption of homoscedasticity. To visualize this assumption, it is useful to look again at the scatterplot in Figure 14.7.

We can see that for each age examined, the variance in the distribution of scores for number of arrests is about equal. That is, the spread of the scores around our imaginary line for each value of age in this population distribution is about equal, whether we look at the cases associated with the youngest subjects (on the left side of the scatterplot), those associated with average-age subjects (in the middle of the scatterplot), or those associated with the oldest offenders (on the right side of the scatterplot). With regard to the assumption of homoscedasticity, researchers generally use the scatterplot of sample cases as an indication of the form of the population distribution. As with analysis of variance, we are generally concerned with only marked violations of the homoscedasticity assumption. Given the small number of cases in our sample distribution of scores, it is very difficult to examine the assumption of homoscedasticity. Nonetheless, if you look back at Figure 14.1, it seems reasonable to conclude that there are no major violations of this assumption.

What would a joint distribution of the relationship between arrests and age look like if both the normality and the homoscedasticity assumption were violated? In the scatterplot in Figure 14.8 (page 406), the points for each age category are not clustered in the center of the distribution of scores for number of arrests. Indeed, they form a type of bimodal distribution, with peaks above and below our imaginary line (see the cross section for each age group). **Heteroscedasticity** (or unequal variances), rather than homoscedasticity, is also represented in the scatterplot in Figure 14.8. For subjects aged 17 and 19, the scores

Figure 14.8   *Scatterplot Showing Nonnormal Distribution and Heteroscedasticity*

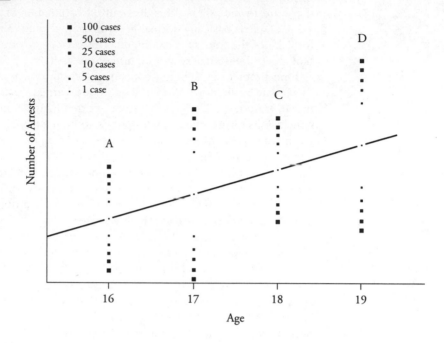

Cross Sections:

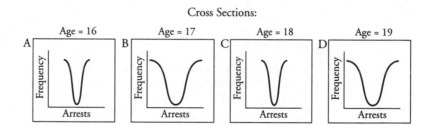

are scattered widely. For subjects aged 16 and 18, however, the scores are tightly clustered around the imaginary line. If this were the population distribution of the variables under study, you would want to be very cautious in applying the *t*-test to your correlation coefficient.

As with other tests of statistical significance, we assume independent random sampling. Pearson's correlation coefficient adds one new assumption to our test—that of linearity. Our null hypothesis is simply that there is no linear relationship between age and number of arrests, or that the population correlation coefficient (r_p) is equal to 0. The research hypothesis is nondirectional; that is, we simply test for a linear relationship between age and number of arrests (i.e., $r_p \neq 0$). However, we might have proposed a directional research hypothesis—for example, that there is a positive relationship between age and number of arrests in the population, or that $r_p > 0$.

The Sampling Distribution   The sampling distribution is t, with $N - 2$ degrees of freedom. For our example, df $= 15 - 2 = 13$.

Significance Level and Rejection Region   With a two-tailed 0.05 significance threshold, the critical value for the t-test (with 13 degrees of freedom) is 2.160 (see Appendix 4). We will reject the null hypothesis if the t-score is greater than 2.160 or less than -2.160. In these cases, the observed significance level of the test will be less than the criterion significance level we have chosen.

The Test Statistic   It is important to note that there is more than one way to test statistical significance for r. Equation 14.4 provides a straightforward estimate of t, based on our calculation of r.

$$t = r \sqrt{\frac{N - 2}{1 - r^2}}$$ **Equation 14.4**

Inserting our sample estimates, we calculate that the t-statistic for r is 4.4188:

W orking It Out

$$t = r \sqrt{\frac{N - 2}{1 - r^2}}$$

$$= 0.7748 \sqrt{\frac{15 - 2}{1 - (0.7748)^2}}$$

$$= 0.7748 \sqrt{32.5256}$$

$$= 4.4188$$

The Decision   Since 4.419 is greater than our critical value of t (2.160), we reject the null hypothesis and conclude that there is a statistically significant relationship between age and number of arrests. However, because we cannot strongly support the assumption of normality in this test or relax that assumption because N is large, we cannot place strong reliance on our test result.

Statistical Significance of *r*:
Unemployment and Crime in California

In our analysis of unemployment and burglary rates in California counties, we found $r = 0.4910$. We can test the statistical significance of this result by following the same approach we used in the previous example. We start by outlining our assumptions and hypotheses.

Assumptions:

Level of Measurement: Interval scale.

Population Distribution: Normal distribution of Y (i.e., burglary rate) around each value of X (i.e., unemployment rate) (relaxed because N is large).

Homoscedasticity.

Sampling Method: Independent random sampling (the 58 counties represent all counties in California in 1999).

Sampling Frame: California counties.

Linearity.[3]

Hypotheses:

H_0: There is no linear relationship between unemployment rate and burglary rate ($r_p = 0$).
H_1: There is a linear relationship between unemployment rate and burglary rate ($r_p \neq 0$).

Since we have data for all counties in California for a given year, you might question why we would choose to conduct a statistical test of significance. Why do we need to make inferences? We already have the population of scores. One reason might be that we want to look at data for the year observed as a sample of the relationships that occur over a number of years. Similarly, we might want to use the data in California to represent other states. For either of these inferences, we would need to explain why this sample was representative of the population. Another reason we might choose to conduct a statistical test of significance is to see whether the correlation observed is likely to be a chance occurrence. We would expect differences across the counties simply as a product of the natural fluctuations that occur in statistics. A significance test in this case can tell us whether the relationship observed is likely to be the result of such chance fluctuations or whether it is likely to represent a real relationship between the measures examined.

---

[3] It is good practice to examine the sample scatterplot of scores to assess whether this assumption is likely to be violated. We find no reason to suspect a violation of the assumption when we examine this scatterplot (see Chapter 15, Figure 15.2).

The Sampling Distribution   The sampling distribution is t, with $N - 2$ degrees of freedom. For this example, df $= 58 - 2 = 56$.

Significance Level and Rejection Region   With a two-tailed 0.05 significance level and 56 degrees of freedom, interpolation yields estimates of $+2.003$ and -2.003 for the critical values of the t-test.[4]

The Test Statistic   We again use Equation 14.4 to calculate a t-value to test the significance of r. Inserting the values for our data, we find the value of the t-statistic to be 4.2177:

$$t = r\sqrt{\frac{N-2}{1-r^2}}$$

$$= 0.491\sqrt{\frac{58-2}{1-(0.491)^2}}$$

$$= 0.491\sqrt{73.789165}$$

$$= 4.2177$$

The Decision   Since 4.218 is greater than our critical value of 2.003, we reject the null hypothesis and conclude that there is a statistically significant relationship between the unemployment rate and the burglary rate.

Testing the Statistical Significance of Spearman's *r*

For Spearman's r, we use a nonparametric statistical test. With $N \leq 30$, we use an exact probability distribution constructed for the distribution of differences between ranked pairs (see Appendix 7). For larger samples, a normal approximation of this test is appropriate. It is constructed by taking the difference between the observed value of r_s and the parameter value under the null hypothesis ($r_{s(p)}$). This value is then divided by 1 divided by the square root of $N - 1$, as shown in Equation 14.5.

$$z = \frac{r_s - r_{s(p)}}{\dfrac{1}{\sqrt{N-1}}}$$
                                                                    Equation 14.5

---

[4]The table does not list a t-value for df $= 56$. We therefore interpolate from the values of df $= 55$ (2.004) and df $= 60$ (2.000).

Because we are examining less than 15 cases, we will use the exact probability table presented in Appendix 7.

Assumptions:

Level of Measurement: Ordinal scale.

Population Distribution: No assumption made.

Sampling Method: Independent random sampling.

Sampling Frame: Youth in one U.S. city.

Hypotheses:

H_0: There is no linear relationship between the rank order of scores in the population ($r_{s(p)} = 0$).

H_1: There is a linear relationship between the rank order of scores in the population ($r_{s(p)} \neq 0$).

Because we use a nonparametric test, we do not need to make assumptions regarding the population distribution. The null hypothesis is the same as for the correlation coefficient r; however, it is concerned with ranks rather than raw scores.

The Sampling Distribution   Because N is small, we use the exact probability distribution constructed for Spearman's r in Appendix 7.

Significance Level and Critical Region   As earlier, we use the conventional 0.05 significance threshold. Since our research hypothesis is not directional, we use a two-tailed rejection region. From Appendix 7, under a two-tailed 0.05 probability value and an N of 15, we find that an r_s greater than or equal to 0.525 or less than or equal to -0.525 is needed to reject the null hypothesis.

The Test Statistic   In the case of the exact probability distribution, the test statistic is simply the value of r_s. As calculated earlier in this chapter (see page 401), r_s equals 0.825.

The Decision   Because the observed r_s is larger than 0.525, we reject the null hypothesis and conclude that there is a statistically significant linear relationship between ranks of age and number of arrests in the population. The observed significance level of our test is less than the criterion significance level we set at the outset ($p < 0.05$).

Chapter Summary

Linear correlation coefficients describe the relationship between two interval-level measures, telling us how strongly the two are associated. **Pearson's r** is a widely used linear correlation coefficient. It examines the placement of subjects on both variables relative to the mean and estimates how strongly the scores move together or in opposite directions relative to the mean. The **covariation,** which is the numerator of the Pearson's r equation, is positive when both scores vary in the same direction relative to the mean and negative when they vary in opposite directions. Dividing the covariation by the denominator of the Pearson's r equation serves to standardize the coefficient so that it varies between -1 and $+1$. Pearson's r will produce a misleading correlation coefficient if there is a nonlinear relationship between the variables.

Outliers have a strong impact on Pearson's r. If there are several outliers that follow the general pattern of relationships in the data, **Spearman's r** may provide less misleading results. Spearman's r also varies between -1 and $+1$. It compares the rank order of subjects on each measure.

The t distribution may be used to test significance for Pearson's correlation coefficient. It is assumed that the variables examined are measured on an interval scale. There is also an assumption of normality and a requirement of homoscedasticity. These assumptions relate to the joint distribution of X_1 and X_2. The researcher must also assume linearity. For Spearman's r, a nonparametric test of statistical significance is used.

Key Terms

covariation A measure of the extent to which two variables vary together relative to their respective means. The covariation between the two variables serves as the numerator for the equation to calculate Pearson's r.

curvilinear relationship An association between two variables whose values may be represented as a curved line when plotted on a scatter diagram.

heteroscedasticity A situation in which the variances of scores on two or more variables are not equal. Heteroscedasticity violates one of the assumptions of the parametric test of statistical significance for the correlation coefficient.

linear relationship An association between two variables whose joint distribution may be represented in linear form when plotted on a scatter diagram.

Pearson's correlation coefficient See *Pearson's r.*

Pearson's r A commonly used measure of association between two variables. Pearson's *r* measures the strength and direction of linear relationships on a standardized scale from −1.0 to 1.0.

scatter diagram See *scatterplot.*

scatterplot A graph whose two axes are defined by two variables and upon which a point is plotted for each subject in a sample according to its score on the two variables.

Spearman's correlation coefficient See *Spearman's r.*

Spearman's r (r_s) A measure of association between two rank-ordered variables. Spearman's *r* measures the strength and direction of linear relationships on a standardized scale between −1.0 and 1.0.

Symbols and Formulas

r Pearson's correlation coefficient

r_s Spearman's correlation coefficient

D Difference in rank of a subject on two variables

To calculate the covariation of scores for two variables:

$$\text{Covariation of scores} = \sum_{i=1}^{N}(X_{1i} - \overline{X_1})(X_{2i} - \overline{X_2})$$

To calculate Pearson's correlation coefficient:

$$\text{Pearson's } r = \frac{\sum_{i=1}^{N}(X_{1i} - \overline{X_1})(X_{2i} - \overline{X_2})}{\sqrt{\left(\sum_{i=1}^{N}(X_{1i} - \overline{X_1})^2\right)\left(\sum_{i=1}^{N}(X_{2i} - \overline{X_2})^2\right)}}$$

To calculate Spearman's correlation coefficient:

$$r_s = 1 - \frac{6\sum_{i=1}^{N}D_i^2}{N(N^2 - 1)}$$

To test statistical significance for Pearson's *r*:

$$t = r\sqrt{\frac{N-2}{1-r^2}}$$

To test statistical significance for Spearman's *r* where *N* is large:

$$z = \frac{r_s - r_{s(p)}}{\frac{1}{\sqrt{N-1}}}$$

Exercises

14.1 A researcher draws four random samples of ten offenders, aged between 30 and 35 years, all of whom are currently serving out a term of imprisonment and all of whom have been in prison before. For each sample, she compares the subjects on the following pairs of variables:

Sample 1	1	2	3	4	5	6	7	8	9	10
X_1: Number of convictions	3	5	1	7	6	2	4	9	10	8
X_2: Average sentence	2	2.5	0.5	3	3	1	2	4.5	5	3.5

Sample 2	1	2	3	4	5	6	7	8	9	10
X_1: Years of education	9	12	17	16	9	14	10	17	17	9
X_2: Age at first offense	14	17	14	16	10	17	16	10	12	12

Sample 3	1	2	3	4	5	6	7	8	9	10
X_1: Age at first offense	13	17	10	16	14	11	18	19	15	12
X_2: Number of convictions	7	3	10	4	6	9	1	1	6	8

Sample 4	1	2	3	4	5	6	7	8	9	10
X_1: Age at first offense	11	16	18	12	15	17	13	20	20	13
X_2: Average sentence	3	5	1.5	1	1	4	4.5	5	3	2.5

a. Calculate the mean scores of both variables for Samples 1, 2, 3, and 4.

b. Display the data for the four samples in four frequency distribution tables. For each score, add a positive or negative sign to indicate the direction in which the score differs from the mean (as done in Tables 14.4 and 14.5). Add an extra column in which you record a plus or a minus for the product of the two signs.

c. Draw four scatterplots, one for each sample distribution. State whether each scatterplot shows a positive relationship, a negative relationship, a curvilinear relationship, or no relationship between the two variables.

d. Would you advise against using Pearson's correlation coefficient as a measure of association for any of the four samples? Explain your answer.

14.2 Jeremy, a police researcher, is concerned that police officers may not be assigned to areas where they are needed. He wishes to find out whether there is a connection between the number of police officers assigned to a particular block and the number of violent incidents reported on that block during the preceding week. For ten different blocks (designated A through J), the number of patrolling officers assigned and the number of prior violent incidents reported are as follows:

	A	B	C	D	E	F	G	H	I	J
X_1: Violent incidents	7	10	3	9	8	0	4	4	2	8
X_2: Officers assigned	6	9	3	10	8	1	4	5	2	7

a. Calculate the covariance for the data recorded above.

b. Calculate the value of Pearson's r for the data recorded above.

c. On an 11th block—block K—there are no police officers patrolling, yet in the previous week 11 violent incidents were reported there. What effect would it have on Pearson's r if Jeremy included block K in his calculations?

d. How do you explain this difference?

14.3 Seven subjects of different ages are asked to complete a questionnaire measuring attitudes about criminal behavior. Their answers are coded into an index, with scores ranging from 1 to 15. The subjects' scores are as follows:

X_1: Age	12	22	10	14	18	20	16
X_2: Score	6	3	3	9	9	6	13

a. Calculate Pearson's correlation coefficient for the two variables listed above.

b. Illustrate the sample distribution on a scatterplot.

c. Divide the scatterplot into two sections, and calculate the value of Pearson's r for each section.

d. Explain the difference between the r values you obtained in parts a and c.

14.4 Eight homeowners in the inner-city neighborhood of Moss Tide are asked how long they have been living in the neighborhood and how many times during that period their house has been burglarized. The results for the eight subjects are listed below:

X_1: Years in neighborhood	2	1.5	3.5	28	1	5	20	3
X_2: Number of burglaries	2	1	5	55	0	4	10	3

a. Calculate Pearson's r for the two variables recorded above.

b. Calculate Spearman's r for the same data.

c. Illustrate the sample distribution on a scatterplot.

d. Which of the two correlation coefficients is more appropriate, in your opinion, for this case? Refer to the scatterplot in explaining your answer.

14.5 Eleven defendants arrested for violent offenses were all required to post bail. The judge said that the amount of bail assigned was related to the total number of prior arrests. The results for the 11 defendants are as follows:

X_1: Number of
prior arrests   0   3   9   13   2   7   1   4   7   20   5

X_2: Amount of
bail assigned   100   500   2,500   10,000   1,000   10,000   100   7,500   5,000   100,000   4,000

   a. Calculate Pearson's r for the two variables recorded above.

   b. Calculate Spearman's r for the same data.

   c. Illustrate the sample distribution on a scatterplot.

   d. Which of the two correlation coefficients is more appropriate, in your opinion, for this case? Refer to the scatterplot in explaining your answer.

14.6 Researchers looking at age and lifetime assault victimization interviewed nine adults and found the following values:

X_1: Age   18   20   19   25   44   23   67   51   33

X_2: Number of times
assaulted in lifetime   1   4   8   0   6   2   9   3   10

   a. Calculate Pearson's r for the two variables recorded above.

   b. Calculate Spearman's r for the same data.

   c. Illustrate the sample distribution on a scatterplot.

   d. Which of the two correlation coefficients is more appropriate, in your opinion, for this case? Refer to the scatterplot in explaining your answer.

14.7 In a study looking at the relationship between truancy and theft, a sample of ten youth were asked how many times in the last year they had skipped school and how many times they had stolen something worth $20 or less. Their responses were

X_1: Number of times
skipped school   9   2   4   0   0   10   6   5   3   1

X_2: Number of thefts
valued at $20 or less   25   10   13   0   2   24   31   20   1   7

   a. Calculate Pearson's r for the two variables recorded above.

   b. Use a 5% level of significance and outline each of the steps required in a test of statistical significance of r.

14.8 A study investigating the link between child poverty and property crime rates gathered information on a random sample of 13 counties. The values for the percentage of children under 18 living in poverty and property crime rates (given per 100,000) are

X_1: Percentage of children living in poverty	10	8	43	11	27	18	15	22	17	17	20	25	35
X_2: Property crime rate	1,000	2,000	7,000	4,000	3,000	4,500	2,100	1,600	2,700	1,400	3,200	4,800	6,300

a. Calculate Pearson's r for the two variables recorded above.

b. Use a 5% level of significance and outline each of the steps required in a test of statistical significance of r.

Computer Exercises

Obtaining Correlation Coefficients in SPSS

Both correlation coefficients discussed in this chapter—Pearson's r and Spearman's r—can be obtained with the same command. The easiest way to have SPSS compute these correlations is with the bivariate correlation command (Analyze → Correlate → Bivariate). After you execute this command, you will be presented with a window that lists all the variables in the data file in a box on the left and has an empty box on the right labeled "Variables." Move the names of all the variables for which you want correlations to the box on the right.

Just below the list of variables in the data file is a list of three correlation coefficients that this command will compute: Pearson's r, Kendall's tau_b (discussed in Chapter 13), and Spearman's r. The default is Pearson's r, but simply clicking on the box located next to the other correlation coefficients will result in their being computed. After selecting the variables and the correlation coefficients, click on "OK" to run the command.

The output window will present a matrix (grid) of correlations for all the variables whose names appear in the box on the right side of the previous window. It is much more efficient to have SPSS compute all the correlations simultaneously, rather than select several specific pairs that you might be most interested in seeing. You should also note that this matrix of correlations is symmetric; running from the upper left to the lower right corner of the matrix is a diagonal that is made up of 1s (the correlation of the variable with itself). The correlations that appear above the diagonal will be a mirror image of the correlations that appear below the diagonal. Thus, to locate the value of the correlation coefficient you are most interested in, you simply find the row that corresponds to one of the variables and the column that corresponds to the other variable. It does not matter which variable you select for the row or for the column; the correlation coefficient reported in the matrix will be the same.

To try out this command, enter the data on age and arrests from Table 14.1 into SPSS. Execute the bivariate correlation command, moving the two variable names into the box on the right. Be sure that both Pearson's r and Spearman's r are selected, and click on "OK" to compute the correlations. The output window should present two tables—one for Pearson's r and one for Spearman's r—that display correlations identical to those reported in the text.

Obtaining Scatterplots in SPSS

As noted in Chapter 3, SPSS has a wide range of graphics commands. One of the graphs that SPSS can produce is a scatterplot, which is obtained with the "Scatter" command (Graphs $\rightarrow$ Scatter). After executing the command, you will be presented with a window that lists four different types of scatterplots that SPSS can produce. Select the "Simple" scatterplot, and then click on "Define." The next window that appears will list all the variables in the data file on the left and prompt you for other information on the right. You must enter information in the two boxes on the right labeled "Y Axis" (the vertical axis) and "X Axis" (the horizontal axis). Insert the names of the variables that you want to represent in the scatterplot. If you want to add titles to the graph produced by SPSS, click on the "Titles" button located in the bottom of the window and enter that information. Click on "OK" to run the command and produce the scatterplot.

To try out this command, use the age and arrest data from Table 14.1 again. Execute the "Scatter" command, entering the age variable in the "X Axis" box and the arrest variable in the "Y Axis" box. Click on "OK" to produce the scatterplot. The output should be very similar to Figure 14.1.

1. Open the ***caucr_99.sav*** data file. These are the data presented in Table 14.8. Compute Pearson's r for these data and note that it matches the value reported in the text.

    a. Compute Spearman's r for these data.

    b. How does the value of Pearson's r compare to that for Spearman's r? What might account for this?

    c. Generate a scatterplot for these data.

2. Enter the data from Exercise 14.2.

    a. Compute both Pearson's r and Spearman's r for these data.

    b. Add the extra case presented in part c of Exercise 14.2. Recompute Pearson's r and Spearman's r for these data.

    c. Compare your answers from parts a and b. How do you explain this pattern?

    d. Generate a scatterplot for the 11 cases.

3. Enter the data from Exercise 14.8.

    a. Compute Spearman's *r* for these data.

    b. How does the value of Pearson's *r* compare to that for Spearman's *r?* What might account for this?

    c. Generate a scatterplot for these data.

4. Open the ***nys_1.sav*** data file into SPSS. Use a 5% level of significance and outline each of the steps required in a test of statistical significance for each of the following relationships:

    a. Age and number of thefts valued at less than $5 in the last year.

    b. Number of times drunk and number of thefts valued at $5 to $50 in the last year.

    c. Frequency of marijuana use and number of times the youth has hit other students in the last year.

    d. Number of times the youth has hit a parent and number of thefts valued at more than $50 in the last year.

    e. Number of times the youth has been beaten up by parent and number of times the youth has hit a teacher in the last year.

5. Generate a scatterplot for each pair of variables listed in Computer Exercise 4.

An Introduction to Bivariate Regression

IN THE PREVIOUS CHAPTER, we asked how strongly two interval-level variables were correlated. In this chapter, we ask a related question that is central to much statistical analysis in criminology and criminal justice: Can we predict the level of one interval-level variable from the value of another? As in the description of specific measures of association for nominal and ordinal variables in Chapter 13, in regression analysis we must define which variable is the independent variable, or predictor variable, and which variable is the dependent variable, or the variable being predicted. We also introduce the idea of regression modeling in this chapter. Our discussion focuses on how regression analysis is used to create a prediction model and the statistics that researchers use to evaluate such models.

Estimating the Influence of One Variable on Another: The Regression Coefficient

By making only a slight change to the equation for Pearson's correlation coefficient, we can construct the **regression coefficient b**—a statistic that estimates how much one variable influences another. As with Goodman and Kruskal's tau, lambda, and Somers' d (see Chapter 13), in developing this measure we again make a very important assumption about the relationship between the variables examined. We assume that the **independent variable (X)** influences or predicts the **dependent variable (Y).**

The regression coefficient b asks how much impact one variable (the independent variable) has on another (the dependent variable). It answers this question not in standardized units, but in the specific units of the variables examined. The specific interpretation of a regression coefficient will depend on the units of measurement used. Nonetheless, b has a general interpretation in terms of X, the symbol for the independent variable, and Y, the symbol for the dependent variable:

A change of one unit in X produces a change of b units in the estimated value of Y.

Let's take a concrete example. Suppose that you are studying the relationship between education and reoffending. You assume that education has an impact on reoffending and thus define years of education as the independent variable, X, and number of arrests as the dependent variable, Y. You calculate the regression coefficient b and find that it has a value of -2. You can interpret this coefficient as meaning that a one-year change (or increase) in education produces, on average, a two-unit change—in this case, reduction—in number of rearrests. If b had been positive, we would have concluded that a one-year increase in education produces, on average, an increase of two arrests.

This interpretation of the regression coefficient reminds us that we are once again concerned with linear relationships. If we say that a unit change in X results in b units of change in Y, we are also saying that the change produced by X is constant. By "constant" we mean that the change produced in Y is always the same, irrespective of other factors such as the value of Y itself. In our example, the regression coefficient predicts that a one-year increase in education produces a reduction of two arrests, irrespective of how much education an offender already has. If the change is constant, then the result is a linear relationship. This is illustrated in Figure 15.1. Importantly, linearity is a central assumption of regression analysis. As with linear correlation coefficients, you should always examine the scatterplot of the relationship between the variables to be sure that the relationship you are estimating is a linear one.

You can see from this example why regression analysis is such a widely used tool in criminal justice and criminology. Contrary to what students often fear, regression coefficients are very easy to understand and make good intuitive sense. The regression coefficient in this case

Figure 15.1   *Hypothetical Regression Line of the Relationship Between Number of Arrests and Years of Education*

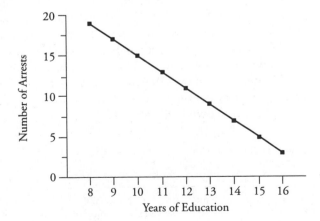

tells us that education reduces reoffending. It also tells us by how much. For each year of education, there is a reduction of about two arrests. Often, criminologists use regression coefficients to estimate how much crime-control benefit is gained from a particular strategy or from the addition of criminal justice resources. In a recent report to the federal government, for example, a group of researchers from the University of Nebraska used regression coefficients to estimate how much each dollar spent on additional police in the United States during the 1990s influenced crime rates in American cities.[1] Clearly, a statistic that can tell us how much each change in one variable influences another can be very useful in deciding on criminal justice strategies or policies.

Calculating the Regression Coefficient

The calculation for the regression coefficient b (Equation 15.1) is very similar to that for the correlation coefficient r (Equation 14.2). Once again, the covariation between the two variables examined is in the numerator, although the two variables are expressed as X and Y rather than X_1 and X_2. The difference is in the denominator of the equation. Instead of standardizing this value according to the variability found in both measures, we now contrast the covariation of the relationship of X and Y with the variability found only in X.

$$b = \frac{\sum_{i=1}^{N} (X_i - \overline{X})(Y_i - \overline{Y})}{\sum_{i=1}^{N} (X_i - \overline{X})^2}$$

Equation 15.1

By taking the example of age and number of arrests over the last year from Table 14.1, we can see how a regression coefficient is calculated in practice (see Table 15.1). Our first step, as noted above, is to examine the scatterplot of points to make sure that the relationship we are estimating is linear. This was done in Chapter 14, so we will not repeat that step here. The next step is to define X and Y. In this case, age is the independent variable (X), and number of arrests is the dependent variable (Y). Our assumption here is that age influences the number of arrests on an offender's record over the previous year. As with the correlation coefficient, we first calculate the covariation between age (X) and number of arrests (Y), as shown in Equation 15.2.

$$\text{Covariation of } X \text{ and } Y = \sum_{i=1}^{N} (X_i - \overline{X})(Y_i - \overline{Y})$$

Equation 15.2

---

[1] Jihong Zhao and Quint Thurman, "A National Evaluation of the Effect of COPS Grants on Crime from 1994–1999," unpublished manuscript, University of Nebraska, December, 2001.

| Table 15.1 | | | | | |

Calculations for the Regression Coefficient
of Age and Number of Arrests for 15 Young Offenders

AGE			ARRESTS		
X (1)	$X_i - \bar{X}$ (2)	$(X_i - \bar{X})^2$ (3)	Y (4)	$Y_i - \bar{Y}$ (5)	$(X_i - \bar{X})(Y_i - \bar{Y})$ (6)
14	−3.0667	9.4046	0	−4.8667	14.9247
13	−4.0667	16.5380	1	−3.8667	15.7247
15	−2.0667	4.2712	1	−3.8667	7.9913
13	−4.0667	16.5380	2	−2.8667	11.6580
14	−3.0667	9.4046	2	−2.8667	8.7913
14	−3.0667	9.4046	3	−1.8667	5.7246
17	−0.0667	0.0044	3	−1.8667	0.1245
19	1.9333	3.7376	4	−0.8667	−1.6756
21	3.9333	15.4708	4	−0.8667	−3.4090
19	1.9333	3.7376	6	1.1333	2.1910
16	−1.0667	1.1378	8	3.1333	−3.3423
18	0.9333	0.8710	9	4.1333	3.8576
20	2.9333	8.6042	9	4.1333	12.1242
21	3.9333	15.4708	10	5.1333	20.1908
22	4.9333	24.3374	11	6.1333	30.2574

$\bar{X} = 17.0667$ $\bar{Y} = 4.8667$

$$\sum_{i=1}^{N}(X_i - \bar{X})^2 = 138.9326 \qquad \sum_{i=1}^{N}(X_i - \bar{X})(Y_i - \bar{Y}) = 125.1332$$

Our result (calculated in column 6 in Table 15.1) is the same as the result for the correlation coefficient: 125.1332. The calculation of the denominator, however, involves less work than before. In this case, we simply take the sum of the squared deviations of each subject's age from the mean for age. The result, calculated in column 3 of Table 15.1, is 138.9326. Our regression coefficient is obtained by dividing these two sums.

Working It Out

$$b = \frac{\sum_{i=1}^{N}(X_i - \bar{X})(Y_i - \bar{Y})}{\sum_{i=1}^{N}(X_i - \bar{X})^2}$$

$$= \frac{125.1332}{138.9326}$$

$$= 0.9007$$

This result of 0.9007 can be interpreted as meaning that a one-year increase in age produces, on average, a 0.90 increase in number of arrests.

A Substantive Example: Unemployment and Burglary in California

In Chapter 14, in an analysis of unemployment and burglary rates for counties in the state of California in 1999, we reported that the correlation between unemployment rates and burglary rates was $r = 0.4910$. We can continue to work with these data to provide another illustration of regression analysis. While the correlation of 0.49 suggests a linear relationship between unemployment rates and burglary rates, it is good practice in regression to start by examining a scatterplot (see Figure 15.2). Our interest is in confirming that the relationship between unemployment rates and burglary rates in California counties is linear. The scatterplot in Figure 15.2 provides no strong evidence to suggest that the relationship is not linear.

In Table 14.9, we reported the two results needed to calculate the regression coefficient b. The covariation between the unemployment rate and the burglary rate is 37,128.9297, and the variability of the unemployment rate is 1,010.3570 (see the bottom of Table 14.9). Inserting these values into Equation 15.1, we find that $b = 36.7483$.

$$b = \frac{\sum_{i=1}^{N} (X_i - \overline{X})(Y_i - \overline{Y})}{\sum_{i=1}^{N} (X_i - \overline{X})^2}$$

$$= \frac{37128.9297}{1010.3570}$$

$$= 36.7483$$

Figure 15.2   *Scatterplot of Unemployment Rates and Burglary Rates in California, 1999*

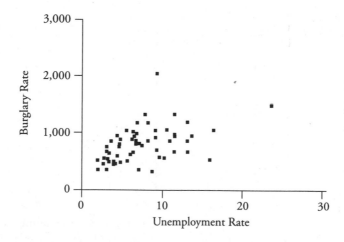

This coefficient tells us that, on average, for every one-unit increase in the unemployment rate, the burglary rate increases by about 36.75 crimes (per 100,000).

Prediction in Regression: Building the Regression Line

The regression coefficient provides a method for estimating how change in an independent variable influences change in a dependent variable. However, by itself, it does not allow the researcher to predict the actual values of the dependent variable. For example, we found in our examination of age and number of arrests that a one-year increase in age in our sample of young offenders was associated with a 0.9007 increase in number of arrests over the last year. Accordingly, based on our analysis, we would predict that a 14-year-old would have about 0.9 more arrests than a 13-year-old. Someone 15 years old would be expected to have about 1.8 more arrests over the last year than someone 13 years old. This is because our regression coefficient suggests that for each year of age, we can expect about 0.9 more arrests. Similarly, for the unemployment rate and burglary rate analysis, we would expect a county with an unemployment rate of 5.0 to have a burglary rate that was about 36.75 (per 100,000) higher than that of a county with an employment rate of 4.0. A county with an unemployment rate of 6.0 would be expected to have a burglary rate that was about 36.75 (per 100,000) higher than that of the county with an unemployment rate of 5.0.

But this still does not tell us how many arrests overall a person 13, 14, or 15 years old would be expected to have over the last year. Nor can we define the rate of burglary in a county with an unemployment rate of 4.0, 5.0, or 6.0. To answer these questions, we need another piece of information: a starting point from which to calculate change. That starting point is provided by a statistic called the Y-intercept.

The Y-Intercept
The **Y-intercept,** or b_0, is the expected value of Y when X equals 0.[2] It is calculated by taking the product of b and the mean of X, and subtracting it from the mean of Y (Equation 15.3).

$$b_0 = \overline{Y} - b\overline{X}$$ **Equation 15.3**

---

[2]Note that there is no single accepted convention for representing the Y-intercept. Some researchers use the symbol α (alpha), while others prefer to use a.

Let's begin with our example of age and number of arrests. We get the value of b_0 by first taking the product of b (0.9007) and the mean for age (17.0667; see Table 15.1) and then subtracting that value (15.3720) from 4.8667, the mean for arrests in the sample. The result is -10.5053.

W **orking It Out**

$b_0 = \overline{Y} - b\overline{X}$

$\quad = 4.8667 - (0.9007)(17.0667)$

$\quad = 4.8667 - 15.3720$

$\quad = -10.5053$

The Regression Line

By looking at a scatterplot (see Figure 15.3), we can see how the Y-intercept helps in developing predictions of number of arrests (Y) from age (X). If we put the value -10.5053 on the line where the value of age is 0, we can then use the regression coefficient b to draw a line of pre-

Figure 15.3

Scatterplot and Regression Line Showing the Relationship Between Age and Number of Arrests for 15 Subjects

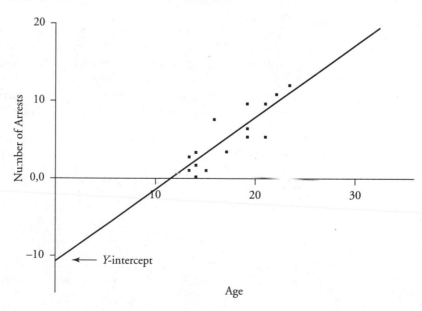

diction, called the **regression line.** The regression coefficient tells us that for each increase of one year in age, there is a corresponding increase of 0.9007 arrest. This means that when age is about 1, number of arrests should be b_0 + 0.9007, or −10.5053 + 0.9007 = −9.6046. For 2 years of age, the number of arrests should be b_0 + 0.9007 + 0.9007, and so forth. By plotting these values, we can draw the regression line for our example. This is done in Figure 15.3, which also includes the scatterplot of the 15 sample scores (from Table 15.1).

The predicted values of Y, designated $\hat{Y}$, can also be found through a simple equation. In this case, $\hat{Y}$ is equivalent to the Y-intercept plus the regression coefficient times the value of X (Equation 15.4).

$$\hat{Y} = b_0 + bX \hspace{4cm} \text{Equation 15.4}$$

For our example, this equation may be represented as shown in Equation 15.5.

Predicted number of arrests = −10.5053 + (0.9007)(age) **Equation 15.5**

We now have a method for predicting the number of arrests based on the age of subjects in our sample. For example, looking at our regression line, we would predict that someone 13 years old would have had about one arrest over the last year. To obtain the exact prediction, we simply insert age 13 in Equation 15.5. The result is 1.2038:

W orking It Out

$$\text{Predicted number of arrests} = -10.5053 + (0.9007)(\text{age})$$
$$= -10.5053 + (0.9007)(13)$$
$$= 1.2038$$

For someone 16 years old, we would predict about four arrests.

W orking It Out

$$\text{Predicted number of arrests} = -10.5053 + (0.9007)(\text{age})$$
$$= -10.5053 + (0.9007)(16)$$
$$= 3.9059$$

For someone 20 years old, we would predict between seven and eight arrests.

W orking It Out

Predicted number of arrests $= -10.5053 + (0.9007)(\text{age})$

$$= -10.5053 + (0.9007)(20)$$

$$= 7.5087$$

Predictions Beyond the Distribution Observed in a Sample

Are our predictions good ones? We will turn a bit later in the chapter to methods of evaluating how well the regression line predicts or fits the data in our sample. Nonetheless, at this point it is useful to look at Figure 15.3 and evaluate on your own how well we have done. I think you will agree that we have done a fairly good job of drawing a line through the data points in our sample. For the most part, the points are close to the line, meaning that our prediction of number of arrests based on age of the offender is fairly close to the actual scores in our sample. But what about predicting beyond our sample scores? Can we use our regression line to predict number of arrests for those 30 or 40 years old? What about for offenders younger than 13?

This approach should be used with caution. In order to predict beyond the data points in your sample, you must assume that the relationships are similar for offenders your study has not examined. As is always the case when you try to make inferences beyond your sampling frame, your conclusions cannot be justified directly from the statistics you develop. You must explain why you expect the relationships observed to continue for populations that have not been represented. In our case, for example, we would have to explain why we think that the relationship between age and number of arrests continues for both older and younger offenders. What we know about offending in criminology suggests that this approach would not be a good one to use for older offenders. A number of studies have shown that offending rates often decrease as offenders get older.[3] Certainly our predictions of number of arrests for those younger than age 12 are to be viewed with caution. Our

---

[3]For a discussion of the relationship between age and crime, see David F. Farrington, "Age and Crime," in *Crime and Justice: An Annual Review of Research,* Vol. 7 (Chicago: University of Chicago Press, 1986), pp. 189–250.

regression line predicts negative values of arrests for these young offenders. This example illustrates a very important limitation of regression analysis. You should be very cautious about predicting beyond the distribution observed in your sample. As a general rule, regression can provide good estimates of predictions for the range of offenders represented by the data; however, it often does not provide a solid basis for predictions beyond that range.

Predicting Burglary Rates from Unemployment Rates in California

What would our prediction model look like for the case of the unemployment rate and burglary rate data from counties in California? First, we need to define the Y-intercept by using Equation 15.3. The value of b is 36.7483, the mean unemployment rate is 7.4069, and the mean burglary rate is 790.8907 (see Table 14.9). The Y-intercept has a value of 518.6997.

W orking It Out

$$b_0 = \overline{Y} - b\overline{X}$$
$$= 790.8907 - (36.7483)(7.4069)$$
$$= 518.6997$$

Once we know the Y-intercept, we can develop the regression line. For our unemployment and burglary example, we write the regression equation as shown in Equation 15.6.

Burglary rate $= 518.6997 + 36.7483$(unemployment rate)   **Equation 15.6**

Equation 15.6 can be used to calculate the predicted value of the burglary rate, given a value for the unemployment rate. For example, if a county had an unemployment rate of 2.5, we would predict from our model that the burglary rate would be about 610.57.

W orking It Out

Burglary rate $= 518.6997 + 36.7483$(unemployment rate)
$$= 518.6997 + (36.7483)(2.5)$$
$$= 610.5705$$

For a county with an unemployment rate of 4.2, we would predict a burglary rate of about 673.04.

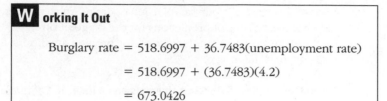

> ## W orking It Out
>
> Burglary rate = 518.6997 + 36.7483(unemployment rate)
>
> = 518.6997 + (36.7483)(4.2)
>
> = 673.0426

And for a county that had an unemployment rate of 7.5, we would predict a burglary rate of about 794.31.

> ## W orking It Out
>
> Burglary rate = 518.6997 + 36.7483(unemployment rate)
>
> = 518.6997 + (36.7483)(7.5)
>
> = 794.3120

How well our regression line fits the data is illustrated in Figure 15.4, which presents the regression line in the scatterplot of the data. Overall, it looks as though the regression line captures the relationship between unemployment rates and burglary rates reasonably well—the values for burglary rate tend to cluster near the regression line.

Figure 15.4   *Scatterplot and Regression Line Showing the Relationship Between Unemployment Rate and Burglary Rate for California Counties, 1999*

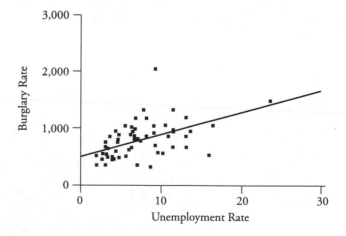

Choosing the Best Line of Prediction Based on Regression Error

One question we might ask is whether the regression line we identify is the best one that could be drawn, given the data available to us. In order to answer this question, we must first decide on the criteria that we will use for defining the best line. In regression, as in many of the statistical techniques we have examined, we use the criterion of minimizing error.

Regression error (e) is defined as the difference between the actual values of Y and the predicted values of Y, or $\hat{Y}$, as shown in Equation 15.7.

$$e = Y - \hat{Y} \qquad \text{\textbf{Equation 15.7}}$$

In Table 15.2, the actual values of Y and the predicted values ($\hat{Y}$) are contrasted for the 15 subjects in our example of age and number of arrests. Subject 8, for example, had four arrests over the last year. The predicted value for arrests based on our regression equation is 6.6080, so the error in this case is -2.6080. In other words, the actual value of Y is made up of both our prediction and some amount of error. The equation form of this relationship gives the basic **regression model** for our example. This model may be expressed either in terms of a theoretical model describing the relationships in the population or in terms of the observed relationships found in our sample. For a population model, we use Greek letters to represent the parameters. So for our example, the population model would be

$$Y = \beta_0 + \beta(\text{age}) + \epsilon$$

Table 15.2

Contrast of the Predicted Values for Y, or $\hat{Y}$, and the Actual Values for Y

SUBJECT	AGE X	NUMBER OF ARRESTS Y	$\hat{Y}$	$Y_i - \hat{Y}_i$
1	14	0	2.1046	-2.1046
2	13	1	1.2039	-0.2039
3	15	1	3.0053	-2.0053
4	13	2	1.2039	0.7961
5	14	2	2.1046	-0.1046
6	14	3	2.1046	0.8954
7	17	3	4.8066	-1.8066
8	19	4	6.6080	-2.6080
9	21	4	8.4093	-4.4093
10	19	6	6.6080	-0.6080
11	16	8	3.9060	4.0940
12	18	9	5.7073	3.2927
13	20	9	7.5086	1.4914
14	21	10	8.4093	1.5907
15	22	11	9.3100	1.6900

$$\sum_{i=1}^{N}(Y_i - \hat{Y}_i) = 0.0000$$

The model for the example would be expressed as

$$Y = b_0 + b(\text{age}) + e$$

By looking at one of our 15 subjects, we can see this relationship in practice. Subject 3's age is 15. The difference between the predicted value for arrests and the actual number of arrests, or the error (e), for Subject 3 is -2.0053. If we add the Y-intercept, the subject's age times the coefficient b, and the error, we obtain a value of 1.

W orking It Out

$$Y = b_0 + b(\text{age}) + e$$
$$= -10.5053 + 0.9007(15) + (-2.0053)$$
$$= -10.5053 + 13.5105 + (-2.0053)$$
$$= 1$$

As we see from Table 15.2, this subject's actual value for Y is also 1 arrest over the last year.

In using error as a criterion for choosing the best line, we are forced to base our decision not on the sum of errors in our equation, but on the sum of the squared errors. This is because the deviations above and below the regression line cancel each other out (see Table 15.2). In regression, as in deviations from the mean, the sum of the deviations of $\hat{Y}$ from Y are always equal to 0.

Squaring the deviations of $\hat{Y}$ from Y provides estimates with only positive signs and allows us to assess the amount of error found. The regression line we have constructed is the best line in terms of the criteria of squared deviations of $\hat{Y}$ from Y. In mathematical language, the regression line is the line for which the sum of the squared errors is a minimum (Equation 15.8).

$$\sum_{i=1}^{N} (Y_i - \hat{Y})^2 = \text{minimum}$$

Equation 15.8

For this reason, we call this approach **ordinary least squares regression analysis,** or **OLS regression.** We hope you remember that we first introduced the concept of the least squares property when we discussed the mean in Chapter 4. As is often the case in statistics, ideas learned early on continue to be important in understanding more complex statistics.

Evaluating the Regression Model

Having noted that OLS regression provides the best line in terms of the least squares criteria for error, we may still ask how well this line predicts the dependent variable. Does the regression model add to our ability to predict number of arrests in our sample? Researchers commonly use a measure called the percent of variance explained to answer this question.

Percent of Variance Explained

The **percent of variance explained,** or R^2, in regression is analogous to eta squared in analysis of variance. With eta squared, we examine the proportion of the total sum of squares accounted for by the between (or explained) sum of squares. In the case of regression, the explained sum of squares (ESS) is calculated from the difference between the predicted value of Y, or $\hat{Y}$, and the mean of Y, or $\overline{Y}$: $(\hat{Y}_i - \overline{Y})^2$. The total sum of squares (TSS) is represented by the difference between Y and the mean of Y: $(Y_i - \overline{Y})^2$. R^2 for regression, like eta squared for analysis of variance, is the ratio of the explained to the total sum of squares (Equation 15.9).

$$R^2 = \frac{\text{ESS}}{\text{TSS}} = \frac{\sum_{i=1}^{N} (\hat{Y}_i - \overline{Y})^2}{\sum_{i=1}^{N} (Y_i - \overline{Y})^2}$$

Equation 15.9

Why do we define the explained and total sums of squares in terms of the mean? If we did not have our regression model, but had only the raw data in our sample, our best single prediction of Y would be the mean of Y. The question answered by R^2 is "How much additional knowledge have we gained by developing the regression line?" This is illustrated in Figure 15.5, where we take one subject from our analysis of the effect of age on number of arrests, Subject 13, and plot that subject's score relative to the regression line and the mean of Y. The distance between the predicted value of Y and the mean of Y represents the explained deviation, $(\hat{Y} - \overline{Y})$. The distance from the mean of Y to the actual score for the subject is the total deviation from the mean, $(Y - \overline{Y})$. The explained deviation thus represents the improvement in predicting Y that the regression line provides over the mean.

To calculate the explained sum of squares for our example, we simply take the difference between the predicted score for arrests and the mean for arrests, square that value, and sum the outcomes across the 15 subjects. This is done in column 5 of Table 15.3, where our final result is 112.7041. For the total sum of squares, we subtract the mean of arrests for the sample from each subject's actual number of arrests. This value is

Figure 15.5   *The Explained, Unexplained, and Total Deviations*
from the Mean for Subject 13 (Age = 20; Arrests = 9)

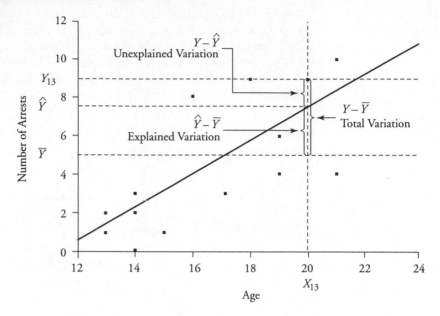

squared, and the 15 outcomes are added together (see Table 15.3, column 7). The total sum of squares for our example is 187.7333.

To obtain the percent of variance explained, or R^2, we take the ratio of these two values. The percent of variance explained beyond the mean in our regression model is 0.60.[4]

---

[4]In the case of multivariate regression analysis (described in detail in Chapter 16), where there are multiple independent variables, some statisticians advise using an adjusted measure of R^2. Commonly referred to as adjusted R^2, it is routinely provided by most statistical software programs. Adjusted R^2 is calculated using the following formula:

$$\text{Adjusted } R^2 = 1 - (1 - R^2)\left(\frac{N-1}{N-k-1}\right)$$

where k equals the number of independent variables and N is the number of observations in the sample.

Adjused R^2 can prevent a misleading interpretation of the strength of prediction of a model, because it offsets the artificial inflation in the statistic that is created with every additional variable added to a regression model. Nonetheless, the adjustment represents a transformation of the R^2 value and thus alters the simple meaning of the statistic. We do not advise using the adjusted R^2 value unless it differs substantially from the simple R^2 value.

Working It Out

$$R^2 = \frac{\text{ESS}}{\text{TSS}} = \frac{\sum_{i=1}^{N}(\hat{Y}_i - \overline{Y})^2}{\sum_{i=1}^{N}(Y_i - \overline{Y})^2}$$

$$= \frac{112.7041}{187.7333}$$

$$= 0.6003$$

Is an R^2 of 0.6003 large or small? As noted in earlier chapters, determining whether a relationship is large or small inevitably involves a value judgment. In deciding on the strength of your prediction, you would likely compare your results to those of other research on the same or related topics. As a general rule in criminal justice, regression models seldom result in R^2 values greater than 0.40. If your R^2 is larger than 0.40, you can usually assume that your prediction model is a powerful one. The percent of variance explained in our model accordingly suggests a very high level of prediction. Conversely, when the percent of variance explained is less than 0.15 or 0.20, the model is likely to be viewed as relatively weak in terms of prediction.

Table 15.3 Calculations for R^2 Values for 15 Young Offenders

X (1)	Y (2)	$\hat{Y}$ (3)	$\hat{Y}_i - \overline{Y}$ (4)	$(\hat{Y}_i - \overline{Y})^2$ (5)	$Y_i - \overline{Y}$ (6)	$(Y_i - \overline{Y})^2$ (7)
14	0	2.1046	−2.7621	7.6292	−4.8667	23.6848
13	1	1.2039	−3.6628	13.4158	−3.8667	14.9514
15	1	3.0053	−1.8614	3.4649	−3.8667	14.9514
13	2	1.2039	−3.6628	13.4158	−2.8667	8.2180
14	2	2.1046	−2.7621	7.6292	−2.8667	8.2180
14	3	2.1046	−2.7621	7.6292	−1.8667	3.4846
17	3	4.8066	−0.0601	0.0036	−1.8667	3.4846
19	4	6.6080	1.7413	3.0320	−0.8667	0.7512
21	4	8.4093	3.5426	12.5501	−0.8667	0.7512
19	6	6.6080	1.7413	3.0320	1.1333	1.2844
16	8	3.9060	−0.9607	0.9230	3.1333	9.8176
18	9	5.7073	0.8406	0.7066	4.1333	17.0842
20	9	7.5086	2.6419	6.9798	4.1333	17.0842
21	10	8.4093	3.5426	12.5501	5.1333	26.3508
22	11	9.3100	4.4433	19.7427	6.1333	37.6174

$\overline{X} = 17.0667$ $\quad \sum_{i=1}^{N}(\hat{Y}_i - \overline{Y})^2 = 112.7041 \quad \sum_{i=1}^{N}(Y_i - \overline{Y})^2 = 187.7333$

Percent of Variance Explained:
Unemployment Rates and Burglary Rates in California

Returning to our example of unemployment rates and burglary rates, we can similarly examine how well unemployment rates help to explain burglary rates in California counties. The two key pieces of information we need are the explained sum of squares and the total sum of squares. The first column of Table 15.4 presents the burglary rates, and the second column presents the predicted value of the burglary rate for each county. The third and fourth columns present the calculations to obtain the explained sum of squares. Column 3 displays the difference between the predicted value of the burglary rate $(\hat{Y}_i)$ and the mean of the burglary rate $(\overline{Y})$, while column 4 presents the squared difference between the predicted value and the mean. The explained sum of squares, which has a value of 1,364,425.7358 (see the bottom of column 4), is the sum of the squared differences between the predicted value of the burglary rate and the mean of the burglary rate. The calculations for the total sum of squares are presented in columns 5 and 6. The fifth column represents the difference between the observed burglary rate (Y_i) and the mean of the burglary rate $(\overline{Y})$, while the sixth column contains the squared differences between the observed burglary rate and the mean of the burglary rate. The total sum of squares, which has a value of 5,659,404.5114 (located at the bottom of column 6), is the sum of the squared differences between the observed burglary rate and the mean of the burglary rate.

To obtain the value of R^2, we again use Equation 15.9, inserting our values for the explained and total sums of squares.

***

W orking It Out

$$
R^2 = \frac{\text{ESS}}{\text{TSS}} = \frac{\sum\limits_{i=1}^{N} (\hat{Y}_i - \overline{Y})^2}{\sum\limits_{i=1}^{N} (Y_i - \overline{Y})^2}
$$

$$
= \frac{1,364,425.7358}{5,659,404.5114}
$$

$$
= 0.2411
$$

***

Our R^2 of 0.2411 indicates that about 24% of the variance in burglary rates in California counties is explained by the unemployment rate.

Table 15.4

Calculations for R^2 Values for Unemployment
Rates and Burglary Rates in California Counties

Y (1)	$\hat{Y}$ (2)	$\hat{Y}_i - \overline{Y}$ (3)	$(\hat{Y}_i - \overline{Y})^2$ (4)	$Y_i - \overline{Y}$ (5)	$(Y_i - \overline{Y})^2$ (6)
837.89	647.3188	−143.5720	20,612.9048	46.9993	2,208.9342
2,037.49	853.1092	62.2185	3,871.1455	1,246.5993	1,554,009.8148
818.55	687.7419	−103.1488	10,639.6791	27.6593	765.0369
865.04	768.5881	−22.3026	497.4042	74.1493	5,498.1187
989.76	772.2630	−18.6277	346.9923	198.8693	39,548.9985
520.06	1,102.9977	312.1070	97,410.7607	−270.8307	73,349.2681
664.73	628.9446	−161.9461	26,226.5393	−126.1607	15,916.5222
1,200.91	812.6861	21.7954	475.0395	410.0193	168,115.8264
509.87	662.0181	−128.8726	16,608.1548	−281.0207	78,972.6338
924.10	1,011.1269	220.2362	48,503.9926	133.2093	17,744.7176
845.29	930.2807	139.3900	19,429.5609	54.3993	2,959.2838
1,027.79	753.8888	−37.0019	1,369.1391	236.8993	56,121.2783
1,526.40	1,378.6099	587.7192	345,413.8816	735.5093	540,973.9304
511.12	728.1650	−62.7257	3,934.5122	−279.7707	78,271.6446
960.18	937.6303	146.7396	21,532.5161	169.2893	28,658.8671
649.22	1,000.1024	209.2117	43,769.5480	−141.6707	20,070.5872
1,333.21	801.6616	10.7709	116.0125	542.3193	294,110.2232
361.24	775.9378	−14.9529	223.5892	−429.6107	184,599.7240
610.28	735.5147	−55.3760	3,066.5047	−180.6107	32,620.2250
929.32	941.3052	150.4145	22,624.5068	138.4293	19,162.6711
526.98	588.5215	−202.3692	40,953.3053	−263.9107	69,648.8576
775.92	790.6371	−0.2536	0.0643	−14.9707	224.1219
843.92	764.9133	−25.9774	674.8248	53.0293	2,812.1067
1,214.69	1,007.4521	216.5614	46,898.8356	423.7993	179,605.8467
325.08	831.0603	40.1695	1,613.5927	−465.8107	216,979.6082
957.95	764.9133	−25.9774	674.8248	167.0593	27,908.8097
570.14	871.4834	80.5927	6,495.1801	−220.7507	48,730.8716
477.54	639.9691	−150.9216	22,777.3324	−313.3507	98,188.6612
455.37	669.3677	−121.5230	14,767.8322	−335.5207	112,574.1401
464.52	614.2453	−176.6454	31,203.6044	−326.3707	106,517.8338
646.12	636.2943	−154.5964	23,900.0593	−144.7707	20,958.5556
1,030.58	849.4344	58.5437	3,427.3648	239.6893	57,450.9605
1,049.18	717.1405	−73.7502	5,439.0891	258.2893	66,713.3625
925.61	673.0426	−117.8481	13,888.1841	134.7193	18,149.2898
845.75	812.6861	21.7954	475.0395	54.8593	3,009.5428
883.02	695.0915	−95.7992	9,177.4791	92.1293	8,487.8079
539.82	632.6194	−158.2713	25,049.7949	−251.0707	63,036.4964
744.81	628.9446	−161.9461	26,226.5393	−46.0807	2,123.4309
896.85	842.0847	51.1940	2,620.8297	105.9593	11,227.3733
540.79	636.2943	−154.5964	23,900.0593	−250.1007	62,550.3601
355.82	592.1963	−198.6944	39,479.4646	−435.0707	189,286.5140
444.07	662.0181	−128.8726	16,608.1548	−346.8207	120,284.5979
347.57	628.9446	−161.9461	26,226.5393	−443.3207	196,533.2430
647.73	750.2140	−40.6767	1,654.5947	−143.1607	20,494.9860
823.95	775.9378	−14.9529	223.5892	33.0593	1,092.9173
699.71	856.7841	65.8934	4,341.9349	−91.1807	8,313.9201
575.09	897.2072	106.3165	11,303.1960	−215.8007	46,569.9421
769.30	687.7419	−103.1488	10,639.6791	−21.5907	466.1583
555.44	617.9201	−172.9706	29,918.8250	−235.4507	55,437.0321
1,057.99	904.5569	113.6661	12,919.9937	267.0993	71,342.0361
859.11	996.4276	205.5369	42,245.4173	68.2193	4,653.8729
816.55	764.9133	−25.9774	674.8248	25.6593	658.3997
676.23	941.3052	150.4145	22,624.5068	−114.6607	13,147.0761
1,047.32	1,125.0467	334.1560	111,660.1989	256.4293	65,755.9859
908.79	757.5637	−33.3270	1,110.6923	117.8993	13,900.2449
491.86	695.0915	−95.7992	9,177.4791	−299.0307	89,419.3595
591.28	676.7174	−114.1733	13,035.5447	−199.6107	39,844.4316
1,366.76	944.9800	154.0893	23,743.5062	575.8693	331,625.4507

$$\sum_{i=1}^{N}(\hat{Y}_i - \overline{Y})^2 = 1,364,425.7358 \qquad \sum_{i=1}^{N}(Y_i - \overline{Y})^2 = 5,659,404.5114$$

Statistical Significance of the Regression Coefficient:
The Case of Age and Number of Arrests

In assessing the statistical significance of the regression coefficient, we once again use the t distribution, introduced in Chapter 10.

Assumptions:

Level of Measurement: Interval scale.

Population Distribution: Normal distribution of Y around each value of X (must be assumed because N is not large).

Homoscedasticity.

Linearity.

Sampling Method: Independent random sampling.

Sampling Frame: Youth in one U.S. city.

Hypotheses:

H_0: Age does not predict the number of arrests over the last year in the population of young offenders ($\beta = 0$).

H_1: Age does predict the number of arrests over the last year in the population of young offenders ($\beta \neq 0$).

To test the significance of a regression coefficient, we assume that both variables are measured at the interval level. Because this is a parametric test of significance, we must also make assumptions regarding the population distribution. For tests of statistical significance with b, we must assume that for each value of X the scores of Y are normally distributed around the regression line. We must also assume that the variances of the distribution of Y scores around each value of X are equal. This is the assumption of homoscedasticity, described in Chapter 14. Researchers generally rely on the central limit theorem to relax assumptions of normality. As with analysis of variance and correlation, we are generally concerned only with marked violations of the homoscedasticity assumption.

To visualize these assumptions in the case of regression, it is once again useful to look at a scatterplot. Suppose Figure 15.6 represents the scatterplot of the population of scores for age and number of arrests in the city examined. Like Figure 14.7, which we used to examine these assumptions in terms of the correlation coefficient, this figure illustrates a joint distribution between X and Y that both is normal in form and meets the assumption of homoscedasticity. But here, our imaginary line is actually the regression line. When we examine points above and below the regression line, we see that there is a clustering of points close to the line. Farther from the line, there are fewer points. This distribution is basically normal in that the scores of Y for every value of X form a bell

Figure 15.6   *Scatterplot Showing Normal Distribution and Homoscedasticity*

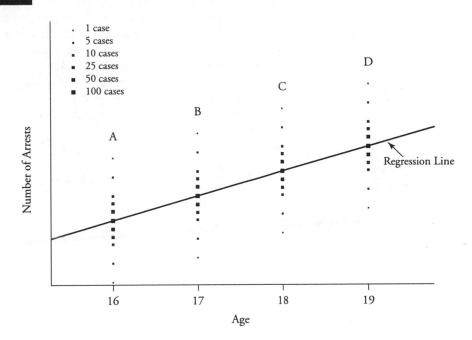

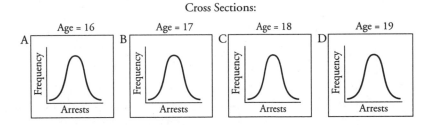

shape that is highest on the regression line and then slopes down in normal form away from the line. This is illustrated in the cross section for each age group.

Also, the points around the regression line have about equal variances (homoscedasticity). That is, the spread of the Y scores around each X in this distribution is about equal, whether we look at the cases associated with the youngest subjects (on the left side of the scatterplot), those associated with average-age subjects (in the middle of the scatterplot), or those associated with the oldest offenders (on the right side of the scatterplot).

In contrast, the scatterplot in Figure 15.7 shows a case that violates—rather than meets—the assumptions for our *t*-test. In this scatterplot, the points are not normally distributed around the regression line. Indeed, they form a type of bimodal distribution with peaks above and below the regression line (see the cross section for each age group). As discussed in Chapter 14, heteroscedasticity refers to unequal variances around the regression line. The scatterplot in Figure 15.7 also shows a distribution with unequal variances. For subjects aged 17 and 19, the scores of *Y* are scattered widely around the regression line. For subjects

Figure 15.7   *Scatterplot Showing Nonnormal Distribution and Heteroscedasticity*

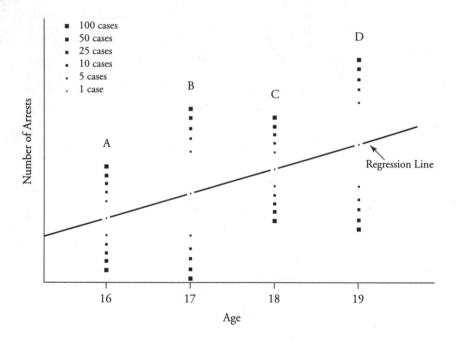

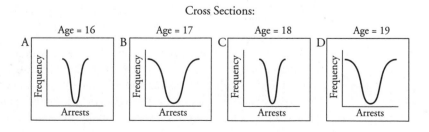

aged 16 and 18, however, the scores of Y are tightly clustered around the regression line.

In our example, we have only 15 cases, and thus we cannot invoke the central limit theorem. As in the case of Pearson's correlation coefficient, we recommend that the N of cases be at least 30 before this is done. Accordingly, our test results cannot be relied on unless the assumption of a normal distribution of Y around each value of X is true for the population to which we infer. Of course, we cannot make this assumption without some prior knowledge of the population distribution of scores. With regard to the assumption of homoscedasticity, as we noted in Chapter 14, researchers generally use the scatterplot of sample cases as an indication of the form of the population distribution. Based on the scatterplot shown in Figure 14.1, we concluded earlier that there was not evidence of serious violations of this assumption.

We also must assume linearity, which we examined in our scatterplot of the relationship between age and number of arrests . Finally, our null hypothesis is that age does not influence number of arrests over the last year for the population of young offenders from which our sample was drawn ($\beta = 0$). Our research hypothesis is that age does influence number of arrests in that population ($\beta \neq 0$).

The Sampling Distribution   The sampling distribution is t, with $N - 2$ degrees of freedom. For our example, df $= 15 - 2 = 13$.

Significance Level and Rejection Region   With a two-tailed 0.05 significance threshold, the critical value for the t-test (with 13 degrees of freedom) is 2.160 (see Appendix 4). We will reject the null hypothesis if the t-score is greater than 2.160 or less than -2.160.

The Test Statistic   The t-test for the significance of the regression coefficient is performed by taking the difference between the observed value of b and the hypothesized value β and then dividing that result by the standard error of b, or $\hat{\sigma}_b$. The formula for the t-statistic is shown in Equation 15.10.

$$t = \frac{b - \beta}{\hat{\sigma}_b}$$ **Equation 15.10**

where b is the estimated regression coefficient, β is the hypothesized population value, and $\hat{\sigma}_b$ is the standard error of b. In practice, this formula can simply be written as b divided by the standard error of b, since the null hypothesis for β ordinarily is that it is equal to 0.

To determine the standard error of b in a **bivariate regression model** (one with one dependent and one independent variable), we use Equation 15.11.[5]

$$\hat{\sigma}_b = \sqrt{\frac{\sum_{i=1}^{N}(Y_i - \hat{Y}_i)^2/(N-2)}{\sum_{i=1}^{N}(X_i - \overline{X})^2}}$$

Equation 15.11

where the numerator represents the sum of the squared differences between the observed value of the dependent variable (Y_i) and the predicted value of the dependent variable ($\hat{Y}_i$) divided by the number of observations (N) minus 2. The denominator is the measure of variability for the independent variable, X.

Table 15.5 presents the values for age and number of arrests for 15 offenders and illustrates the calculations necessary for obtaining the standard error of b. In the fourth column, we have calculated the difference between the observed value for number of arrests (Y_i) and the predicted value ($\hat{Y}_i$).

Table 15.5

Calculations for the Standard Error of b for Age and Number of Arrests for 15 Young Offenders

X (1)	Y (2)	$\hat{Y}$ (3)	$Y_i - \hat{Y}_i$ (4)	$(Y_i - \hat{Y}_i)^2$ (5)	$X_i - \overline{X}$ (6)	$(X_i - \overline{X})^2$ (7)
14	0	2.1046	−2.1046	4.4294	−3.0667	9.4046
13	1	1.2039	−0.2039	0.0416	−4.0667	16.5380
15	1	3.0053	−2.0053	4.0211	−2.0667	4.2712
13	2	1.2039	0.7961	0.6337	−4.0667	16.5380
14	2	2.1046	−0.1046	0.0109	−3.0667	9.4046
14	3	2.1046	0.8954	0.8017	−3.0667	9.4046
17	3	4.8066	−1.8066	3.2639	−0.0667	0.0044
19	4	6.6080	−2.6080	6.8015	1.9333	3.7376
21	4	8.4093	−4.4093	19.4420	3.9333	15.4708
19	6	6.6080	−0.6080	0.3696	1.9333	3.7376
16	8	3.9060	4.0940	16.7612	−1.0667	1.1378
18	9	5.7073	3.2927	10.8419	0.9333	0.8710
20	9	7.5086	1.4914	2.2242	2.9333	8.6042
21	10	8.4093	1.5907	2.5303	3.9333	15.4708
22	11	9.3100	1.6900	2.8562	4.9333	24.3374

$\overline{X} = 17.0667$ $\sum_{i=1}^{N}(Y_i - \hat{Y}_i)^2 = 75.0293$ $\sum_{i=1}^{N}(X_i - \overline{X})^2 = 138.9326$

[5]It is important to note that this equation for the standard error of b is appropriate *only* if we have a bivariate regression model. If we have two or more independent variables, then a modified equation is necessary to calculate the standard error of the regression coefficients.

Column 5 shows the squares of the differences, which are then summed at the bottom of the column. We find the sum of the squared deviations between the observed value for number of arrests (Y_i) and the predicted value ($\hat{Y_i}$) to be 75.0293. The deviations between age and mean age appear in column 6, while the squared deviations between age and mean age appear in column 7. The sum of the squared deviations between age and mean age is 138.9326 (see the bottom of column 7). We insert these values into Equation 15.11 to calculate the standard error for b, which has a value of 0.2038.

Working It Out

$$\hat{\sigma}_b = \sqrt{\frac{\sum_{i=1}^{N} (Y_i - \hat{Y_i})^2/(N-2)}{\sum_{i=1}^{N} (X_i - \overline{X})^2}}$$

$$= \sqrt{\frac{75.0293/(15-2)}{138.9326}}$$

$$= 0.2038$$

Once we have calculated the standard error of b, we can return to Equation 15.10 and calculate a t-score for b to obtain our test statistic. The test statistic is 4.4195 for our example.[6]

Working It Out

$$t = \frac{b - \beta}{\hat{\sigma}_b}$$

$$= \frac{0.9007}{0.2038}$$

$$= 4.4195$$

---

[6]Except for rounding error, this result is the same as the one we obtained in testing the significance of the correlation coefficient for this relationship (4.4195 vs. 4.4188). In practice, you could use the correlation coefficient significance test result for defining the statistical significance of the regression coefficient. Indeed, in many texts only one formula is provided for both coefficients.

The Decision　As 4.4195 is greater than our critical value of t (2.160), we reject the null hypothesis that age does not predict number of arrests. We conclude that there is a statistically significant relationship between age and number of arrests in the population of young offenders. However, because we cannot strongly support the assumption of normality in this test or relax that assumption because N is large, we cannot place strong reliance on our test result.

Testing the Statistical Significance of the Regression Coefficient for Unemployment Rates and Burglary Rates in California

Let's assess the statistical significance of the regression coefficient in our example concerning unemployment rates and burglary rates from California counties. We again begin by stating the assumptions and hypotheses of our test.

Assumptions:

Level of Measurement: Interval scale.

Population Distribution: Normal distribution of Y around each value of X (relaxed because N is large).

Homoscedasticity.

Linearity.

Sampling Method: Independent random sampling (all counties are included in one year).

Sampling Frame: Counties in California.

Hypotheses:

H_0: Unemployment rates do not influence burglary rates in California counties ($\beta = 0$).

H_1: Unemployment rates do influence burglary rates in California counties ($\beta \neq 0$).

The Sampling Distribution　The sampling distribution is the t distribution, with df $= 58 - 2 = 56$.

Significance Level and Rejection Region　Since the research hypothesis is nondirectional, we use a two-tailed test of statistical significance and set the significance level at 0.05. The critical values for the t-test with 56 degrees of freedom are about -2.003 and 2.003, meaning that we will reject the null hypothesis if the test statistic is less than -2.003 or greater than 2.003.

The Test Statistic　To test the statistical significance of our regression coefficient b, we again use Equation 15.11 to determine the standard error of b and Equation 15.10 to calculate the t-score. Table 15.6

Table 15.6 Calculations for the Standard Error of b for Unemployment Rates and Burglary Rates for 58 California Counties

X (1)	Y (2)	$\hat{Y}$ (3)	$Y_i - \hat{Y}_i$ (4)	$(Y_i - \hat{Y}_i)^2$ (5)	$X_i - \bar{X}$ (6)	$(X_i - \bar{X})^2$ (7)
3.5	837.89	647.3188	190.5712	36,317.4013	−3.9069	15.2639
9.1	2,037.49	853.1092	1,184.3808	1,402,757.8083	1.6931	2.8666
4.6	818.55	687.7419	130.8081	17,110.7643	−2.8069	7.8787
6.8	865.04	768.5881	96.4519	9,302.9613	−0.6069	0.3683
6.9	989.76	772.2630	217.4970	47,304.9581	−0.5069	0.2569
15.9	520.06	1,102.9977	−582.9377	339,816.3271	8.4931	72.1327
3.0	664.73	628.9446	35.7854	1,280.5949	−4.4069	19.4208
8.0	1,200.91	812.6861	388.2239	150,717.7965	0.5931	0.3518
3.9	509.87	662.0181	−152.1481	23,149.0352	−3.5069	12.2983
13.4	924.10	1,011.1269	−87.0269	7,573.6848	5.9931	35.9172
11.2	845.29	930.2807	−84.9907	7,223.4123	3.7931	14.3876
6.4	1,027.79	753.8888	273.9012	75,021.8564	−1.0069	1.0138
23.4	1,526.40	1,378.6099	147.7901	21,841.9077	15.9931	255.7792
5.7	511.12	728.1650	−217.0450	47,108.5364	−1.7069	2.9135
11.4	960.18	937.6303	22.5497	508.4881	3.9931	15.9448
13.1	649.22	1,000.1024	−350.8824	123,118.4797	5.6931	32.4114
7.7	1,333.21	801.6616	531.5484	282,543.6909	0.2931	0.0859
7.0	361.24	775.9378	−414.6978	171,974.2653	−0.4069	0.1656
5.9	610.28	735.5147	−125.2347	15,683.7226	−1.5069	2.2707
11.5	929.32	941.3052	−11.9851	143.6438	4.0931	16.7535
1.9	526.98	588.5215	−61.5415	3,787.3525	−5.5069	30.3259
7.4	775.92	790.6371	−14.7171	216.5936	−0.0069	0.0000
6.7	843.92	764.9133	79.0067	6,242.0571	−0.7069	0.4997
13.3	1,214.69	1,007.4521	207.2379	42,947.5513	5.8931	34.7286
8.5	325.08	831.0603	−505.9803	256,016.0134	1.0931	1.1949
6.7	957.95	764.9133	193.0367	37,263.1637	−0.7069	0.4997
9.6	570.14	871.4834	−301.3434	90,807.8327	2.1931	4.8097
3.3	477.54	639.9691	−162.4291	26,383.2093	−4.1069	16.8666
4.1	455.37	669.3677	−213.9977	45,795.0284	−3.3069	10.9356
2.6	464.52	614.2453	−149.7253	22,417.6595	−4.8069	23.1063
3.2	646.12	636.2943	9.8257	96.5452	−4.2069	17.6980
9.0	1,030.58	849.4344	181.1456	32,813.7284	1.5931	2.5380
5.4	1,049.18	717.1405	332.0395	110,250.2163	−2.0069	4.0276
4.2	925.61	673.0426	252.5674	63,790.3117	−3.2069	10.2842
8.0	845.75	812.6861	33.0639	1,093.2215	0.5931	0.3518
4.8	883.02	695.0915	187.9285	35,317.1061	−2.6069	6.7959
3.1	539.82	632.6194	−92.7994	8,611.7342	−4.3069	18.5494
3.0	744.81	628.9446	115.8654	13,424.7909	−4.4069	19.4208
8.8	896.85	842.0847	54.7653	2,999.2337	1.3931	1.9407
3.2	540.79	636.2943	−95.5043	9,121.0637	−4.2069	17.6980
2.0	355.82	592.1963	−236.3763	55,873.7552	−5.4069	29.2346
3.9	444.07	662.0181	−217.9481	47,501.3612	−3.5069	12.2983
3.0	347.57	628.9446	−281.3746	79,171.6655	−4.4069	19.4208
6.3	647.73	750.2140	−102.4840	10,502.9682	−1.1069	1.2252
7.0	823.95	775.9378	48.0122	2,305.1713	−0.4069	0.1656
9.2	699.71	856.7841	−157.0741	24,672.2603	1.7931	3.2152
10.3	575.09	897.2072	−322.1172	103,759.4841	2.8931	8.3700
4.6	769.30	687.7419	81.5581	6,651.7269	−2.8069	7.8787
2.7	555.44	617.9201	−62.4801	3,903.7641	−4.7069	22.1549
10.5	1,057.99	904.5569	153.4332	23,541.7315	3.0931	9.5673
13.0	859.11	996.4276	−137.3176	18,856.1233	5.5931	31.2828
6.7	816.55	764.9133	51.6367	2,666.3478	−0.7069	0.4997
11.5	676.23	941.3052	−265.0752	70,264.8351	4.0931	16.7535
16.5	1,047.32	1,125.0467	−77.7267	6,041.4321	9.0931	82.6845
6.5	908.79	757.5637	151.2263	22,869.4089	−0.9069	0.8225
4.8	491.86	695.0915	−203.2315	41,303.0589	−2.6069	6.7959
4.3	591.28	676.7174	−85.4374	7,299.5476	−3.1069	9.6528
11.6	1,366.76	944.9800	421.7800	177,898.3853	4.1931	17.5821

$\bar{X} = 7.4069$ $\qquad \sum_{i=1}^{N}(Y_i - \hat{Y}_i)^2 = 4,294,978.7756 \qquad \sum_{i=1}^{N}(X_i - \bar{X})^2 = 1,010.3570$

presents the calculations necessary for calculating the standard error of b. Column 4 of Table 15.6 provides the difference between the observed burglary rate (Y_i) and the predicted burglary rate $(\hat{Y_i})$. Column 5 shows the square of each of the differences; the squares are then summed at the bottom of the column. We find the sum of the squared deviations between the observed burglary rate and the predicted burglary rate to be 4,294,978.7756. The deviations between observed unemployment (X_i) and mean unemployment appear in Column 6, while the squared deviations between unemployment and mean unemployment appear in Column 7. The sum of the squared deviations between age and mean age is 1,010.3570 (see the bottom of Column 7). After inserting these values into Equation 15.11, we calculate a value of 8.7126 for the standard error for b.

W orking It Out

$$\hat{\sigma}_b = \sqrt{\frac{\sum\limits_{i=1}^{N} (Y_i - \hat{Y_i})^2/(N-2)}{\sum\limits_{i=1}^{N} (X_i - \overline{X})^2}}$$

$$= \sqrt{\frac{4,294,978.7756/(58-2)}{1,010.3570}}$$

$$= 8.7126$$

The t-statistic is then calculated by inserting our values for b and the standard error of b into Equation 15.10. For our example, the test statistic is 4.2178.

W orking It Out

$$t = \frac{b - \beta}{\hat{\sigma}_b}$$

$$= \frac{36.7483 - 0}{8.7126}$$

$$= 4.2178$$

The Decision Our test statistic of 4.2178 is greater than our critical *t*-value of 2.003, leading us to reject the null hypothesis that unemployment rates do not influence burglary rates in California counties and conclude that there is a statistically significant relationship between unemployment rates and burglary rates.

The *F*-Test for the Overall Regression

In regression analysis, we can carry out a second type of test of statistical significance to evaluate whether the overall regression model contributes significantly to our understanding of the dependent variable. This test is particularly useful when we have more than one independent variable in our model, a situation we will examine in Chapter 16. For this second test of statistical significance, we draw on the logic we used in developing the measure of percent of variance explained, or R^2.

Percent of variance explained tells how much our model improves our predictions beyond what can be learned from the mean. But another question is whether we can conclude from our sample R^2 that R^2 is in fact different from 0 in the population. This is the test of statistical significance for the regression model overall. The assumptions for this test are the same as those described in the previous section.

To test this hypothesis, we use analysis of variance, which was introduced in Chapter 12. Again, the *F*-test is based on a ratio of the explained variance to the unexplained variance. The explained and unexplained variance estimates are obtained by dividing the explained sum of squares (ESS) and unexplained sum of squares (USS) by their appropriate degrees of freedom, as shown in Equation 15.12.

$$F = \frac{\text{ESS/df}}{\text{USS/df}}$$

Equation 15.12

The explained sum of squares was discussed above. The unexplained sum of squares is simply the sum of the squared errors of the regression:

$$\text{USS} = \sum_{i=1}^{N} (Y_i - \hat{Y}_i)^2$$

Age and Number of Arrests
The total sum of squares can be partitioned into its explained and unexplained components. The total sum of squares for our example of age and number of arrests is 187.7333, which is equivalent to the explained

sum of squares (112.7041) plus the unexplained sum of squares, or error sum of squares of the regression (75.0292).

W orking It Out

$$TSS = ESS + USS$$

$$\sum_{i=1}^{N} (Y_i - \overline{Y})^2 = \sum_{i=1}^{N} (\hat{Y}_i - \overline{Y})^2 + \sum_{i=1}^{N} (Y_i - \hat{Y}_i)^2$$

$$187.7333 = 112.7041 + 75.0292$$

The number of degrees of freedom for the ESS (df_1) is k, or the number of variables in the regression. In our example, the regression includes only one independent variable—age—and thus the number of degrees of freedom for the ESS is 1. For the USS, the number of degrees of freedom (df_2) is equal to $N - k - 1$. In the case of our example of number of arrests and age, it is equal to $15 - 1 - 1$, or 13. The F-statistic for our regression is thus calculated by dividing the ratio of the explained variance (112.7041/1) by that of the unexplained variance (75.0292/13), obtaining $F = 19.53$.

W orking It Out

$$F = \frac{ESS/df}{USS/df}$$

$$= \frac{112.7041/1}{75.0292/13}$$

$$= \frac{112.7041}{5.7715}$$

$$= 19.5278$$

Setting a 5% significance threshold, we can see in the F table in Appendix 5 that the critical value associated with 1 and 13 degrees of freedom is 4.67. If our F-statistic is larger than this value, then our observed significance level is less than the criterion significance level we set for our test. Our test statistic of 19.53 is much larger than this value, and thus we would reject the null hypothesis that the percent of variance explained by the regression line in the population to which we infer is 0.[7]

Unemployment Rates and Burglary Rates in California

The *F*-test may also be used to assess the overall regression for the relationship between unemployment rates and burglary rates in California. We reported in our calculations of R^2 that the value for the total sum of squares is 5,659,404.5114 and the value for the explained sum of squares is 1,364,425.7358, which means that the value for the unexplained sum of squares is 4,294,978.7756.

W orking It Out

$$TSS = ESS + USS$$

$$5,659,404.5114 = 1,364,425.7358 + 4,294,978.7756$$

The number of degrees of freedom for the ESS (df_1) is $k = 1$, and the number of degrees of freedom for the USS (df_2) is $N - k - 1$, which is $58 - 1 - 1 = 56$. The *F*-statistic for our regression of burglary rates on unemployment rates is calculated by dividing the ratio of the explained variance (1,364,425.7358/1) by that of the unexplained variance (4,294,978.7756/56), which gives us $F = 17.7900$.

W orking It Out

$$F = \frac{ESS/df}{USS/df}$$

$$= \frac{1,364,425.7358/1}{4,294,978.7756/56}$$

$$= \frac{1,364,425.7358}{76,696.0496}$$

$$= 17.7900$$

---

[7]We have likely violated the normality assumption of our test because we do not have knowledge about the shape of the joint distribution of age and number of arrests in the population and $N = 15$ cases is not enough to safely invoke the central limit theorem.

If we set a 5% significance threshold, we see in the F table (Appendix 5) that the critical value associated with 1 and 56 degrees of freedom is not given in the table. Interpolating from the values for 40 degrees of freedom (4.008) and 60 degrees of freedom (4.000) for df_2, we estimate a critical value of 4.002. Our test statistic of 17.79 is much larger than the critical value, so we reject the null hypothesis that the percent of variance explained by the regression line in the population to which we infer is 0.

Chapter Summary

The **regression coefficient b** tells us how much one variable **(the independent variable, X)** influences another variable **(the dependent variable, Y)**. The regression coefficient is expressed in specific units of the dependent variable and is interpreted as follows: A change of one unit in X produces a change of b units in the estimated value of Y.

A researcher cannot predict values of Y using the regression coefficient alone. The additional piece of information required is the **Y-intercept (b_0)**. The b_0 coefficient may be interpreted as the expected value of Y when $X = 0$. The predicted value of Y for other values of X can be calculated by adding b_0 to the product of the regression coefficient and X. **Regression error** is the difference between the predicted and actual values of Y. The **regression line** is the line for which the sum of the squared errors is at a minimum—hence the name **ordinary least squares regression (OLS).** OLS regression is a solid basis for prediction within, but not beyond, the sample range.

The **R^2** statistic is the proportion of the total sum of squares $(Y - \overline{Y})^2$ accounted for by the explained sum of squares $(\hat{Y} - \overline{Y})^2$. This proportion represents the improvement in predicting Y that the regression line provides over the mean of Y.

The t distribution may be used to test statistical significance for the regression coefficient b. It is assumed that the variables examined are measured on an interval scale. There is also an assumption of normality and a requirement of homoscedasticity. These assumptions relate to the distribution of Y around each value of X. The researcher must also assume linearity. The F-test for the overall regression determines whether the researcher can conclude from the sample R^2 that R^2 is different from 0 in the population.

Key Terms

bivariate regression A technique for predicting change in a dependent variable using one independent variable.

dependent variable (Y) The variable assumed by the researcher to be influenced by one or more independent variables.

independent variable (X) A variable assumed by the researcher to have an impact on the value of the dependent variable, Y.

OLS regression See *ordinary least squares regression analysis*.

ordinary least squares regression analysis A type of regression analysis in which the sum of squared errors from the regression line is minimized.

percent of variance explained (R^2) A measure for evaluating how well the regression model predicts values of Y. It represents the improvement in predicting Y that the regression line provides over the mean of Y.

regression coefficient b A statistic used to assess the influence of an independent variable, X, on a dependent variable, Y. The regression coefficient b is interpreted as the estimated change in Y that is associated with a one-unit change in X.

regression error (e) The difference between the predicted value of Y and the actual value of Y.

regression line The line predicting values of Y. The line is plotted from knowledge of the Y-intercept and the regression coefficient.

regression model The hypothesized statement by the researcher of the factor or factors that define the value of the dependent variable, Y. The model is normally expressed in equation form.

Y-intercept (b_0) The expected value of Y when $X = 0$. The Y-intercept is used in predicting values of Y.

Symbols and Formulas

b_0	Y-intercept
β_0	Y-intercept for population model
b	Regression coefficient
β	Regression coefficient for the population
X	Independent variable
Y	Dependent variable
e	Error
ϵ	Error for population model
ESS	Explained sum of squares

USS   Unexplained sum of squares

TSS   Total sum of squares

k Number of variables in the overall regression model

$\hat{\sigma}_b$ Standard error of the regression coefficient

To determine the value of the Y-intercept:

$$b_0 = \overline{Y} - b\overline{X}$$

To predict values of the dependent variable, Y:

$$\hat{Y} = b_0 + bX$$

To identify the regression error:

$$e = Y - \hat{Y}$$

To show that the sum of squared error in an OLS regression line is a minimum:

$$\sum_{i=1}^{N} (Y_i - \hat{Y}_i)^2 = \text{minimum}$$

A bivariate regression model for a sample:

$$Y = b_0 + bX + e$$

A bivariate regression model for a population:

$$Y = \beta_0 + \beta X + \epsilon$$

To calculate the percent of explained variance:

$$R^2 = \frac{\text{ESS}}{\text{TSS}} = \frac{\sum_{i=1}^{N} (\hat{Y}_i - \overline{Y})^2}{\sum_{i=1}^{N} (Y_i - \overline{Y})^2}$$

To calculate the value of t for the regression coefficient b:

$$t = \frac{b - \beta}{\hat{\sigma}_b}$$

To calculate the standard error of the regression coefficient:

$$\hat{\sigma}_b = \sqrt{\frac{\sum_{i=1}^{N} (Y_i - \hat{Y}_i)^2/(N - 2)}{\sum_{i=1}^{N} (X_i - \overline{X})^2}}$$

To calculate the value of F for the overall regression:

$$F = \frac{\text{ESS/df}}{\text{USS/df}} = \frac{\sum\limits_{i=1}^{N} (\hat{Y}_i - \overline{Y})^2/k}{\sum\limits_{i=1}^{N} (Y_i - \hat{Y}_i)^2/(N - k - 1)}$$

Exercises

15.1 A researcher carries out a series of regression analyses for different studies. The results of three of the studies are given below. In each case, explain what the results mean in plain English.

 a. $X =$ number of prior driving offenses; $Y =$ fine in dollars imposed by magistrate; $b = 72$.

 b. $X =$ number of times a household has been broken into prior to purchase of first burglar alarm; $Y =$ amount of money in dollars spent by homeowner on first burglar alarm; $b = 226$.

 c. $X =$ number of times subject has been involved in a car accident; $Y =$ estimated average speed of subject when driving on a freeway in miles per hour; $b = -8.5$.

15.2 Nine adolescents are interviewed about the number of hours per week they work and the number of times they have smoked marijuana in the last year. The results are recorded as follows:

 X: Number of hours worked per week 0 10 10 15 5 30 20 40 15

 Y: Number of times smoked marijuana
   in the last year   1 3 2 5 0 13 10 20 25

 a. Calculate the regression coefficient b, and explain what it means in plain English.

 b. Calculate the value of the Y-intercept, b_0.

 c. Calculate a test of statistical significance for the regression coefficient b.

15.3 A study of sentencing decisions hypothesized that judges would become increasingly lenient with drug offenders as they accumulated more years of experience. To test this hypothesis, researchers gathered data on a sample of 12 drug offenders. The data included information on number of years on the bench for the judge and length of the sentence (in months). The results were recorded as follows:

X: Number of years as a judge   3 1 0 1 2 5 9 13 17 0 6 2

Y: Length of sentence (months)   14 22 24 20 15 12 3 6 18 18 10 18

a. Calculate the regression coefficient b, and explain what it means in plain English.

b. Calculate the value of the Y-intercept, b_0.

c. Calculate a test of statistical significance for the regression coefficient b.

15.4   Ten police officers are asked how many promotions they have received and how many years they have served on the force. The results are recorded below:

X: Years on the force   7 1 5 3 12 2 4 1 9 6

Y: Number of promotions   5 1 3 1 8 1 2 0 7 2

a. Calculate the regression coefficient b.

b. Calculate the value of the Y-intercept, b_0.

c. How many promotions would you predict for an officer who had served 10 years on the force?

d. What is the regression error in predicting the number of promotions for an officer who has served 12 years on the force?

15.5   Ten prosecutors were asked what percentage of their cases ended in guilty pleas and how many years of experience each had as a prosecutor. The results were recorded as

X: Number of years of experience
as a prosecutor   10 12 8 1 0 2 7 20 5

Y: Percentage of cases resulting in
a guilty plea   93 90 87 72 70 70 82 97 94

a. Calculate the regression coefficient b, and explain what it means in plain English.

b. Calculate the value of the Y-intercept, b_0.

c. Calculate a test of statistical significance for the regression coefficient b.

d. If a prosecutor had six years of experience, what would be the predicted percentage of guilty pleas?

15.6   A study exploring the link between aggression and crime reported aggression scores and number of arrests for six individuals who participated in the study. The values for aggression and number of arrests are as follows:

X: Aggression score   92 63 77 29 51 10

Y: Number of arrests   6 2 3 1 2 0

a. Calculate the regression coefficient b, and explain what it means in plain English.

b. Calculate the value of the Y-intercept, b_0.

c. Calculate a test of statistical significance for the regression coefficient b.

d. What would be the predicted number of arrests for a person with an aggression score of 75?

e. What would be the predicted number of arrests for a person with an aggression score of 25?

15.7 For the last ten convicts released from Wilmslow Prison, Joan recorded the percentage of their initial sentence from which they were excused. She also recorded the number of times each convict was called before a disciplinary committee over the course of his sentence. The scores of each subject on these two variables are listed below:

X: Number of disciplinary hearings   0 5 2 1 6 4 4 0 5 3

Y: Percentage of sentence not served   33 5 18 32 0 10 5 30 0 17

a. Calculate the regression coefficient b.

b. Calculate the value of the Y-intercept, b_0.

c. Using the data provided, show that the sum of the error on either side of the regression line equals 0:

$$\sum_{i=1}^{N} (Y_i - \hat{Y}) = 0$$

d. Using the data provided, show that

$$\sum_{i=1}^{N} (Y_i - \hat{Y})^2$$

is less than

$$\sum_{i=1}^{N} (Y_i - \overline{Y})^2$$

e. Explain in plain English the meaning of what you showed in part d for the regression model.

15.8 In running a small pilot study for a large-scale research project, George gathers data on the average number of homicides monthly for five U.S. cities. While he is looking for a good predictor of the different homicide rates, he stumbles across the following set of data on the number of theaters in each of the cities:

X: Number of theaters   1   3   6   7   8

Y: Homicides monthly   10   14   23   26   32

a. Calculate the regression coefficient b.

b. Calculate the value of the Y-intercept, b_0.

c. According to this regression model, how many homicides would a city with ten theaters expect per month?

d. Why is this model misleading?

15.9   Lee is investigating six recent cases of vandalism in the local shopping mall. She compares the amount of damage done in each case with the number of vandals involved in each incident. Her findings are as follows:

X: Number of vandals   3   2   6   4   1   2

Y: Damage done (\$)   1,100   1,850   3,800   3,200   250   1,200

a. Calculate the regression coefficient b.

b. Calculate the value of the Y-intercept, b_0.

c. Plot the scores on a scatterplot, and draw the regression line where you think it should go.

d. Calculate the value of R^2. What does this tell you about the model?

15.10 Refer to the data from Exercise 15.2.

a. Calculate the value of R^2. What does it tell you about the model?

b. Run an F-test for the overall regression. Remember to outline all of the steps required in a test of statistical significance, including any violations of your assumptions. Can you conclude that the percent of explained variance (R^2) is different from 0 for the population?

15.11 Refer to the data from Exercise 15.5.

a. Calculate the value of R^2. What does it tell you about the model?

b. Run an F-test for the overall regression. Remember to outline all of the steps required in a test of statistical significance, including any violations of your assumptions. Can you conclude that the percent of explained variance (R^2) is different from 0 for the population?

15.12 Refer to the data from Exercise 15.9.

a. Calculate the value of R^2. What does it tell you about the model?

b. Run an F-test for the overall regression. Remember to outline all of the steps required in a test of statistical significance, including any violations of your assumptions. Can you conclude that the percent of explained variance (R^2) is different from 0 for the population?

Computer Exercises

Obtaining Regression Results in SPSS

Ordinary least squares regression analyses are performed with the linear regression command in SPSS (Analyze → Regression → Linear). After you execute the command, a window will appear, listing all the variables in the data file in a box on the left. On the right will be self-explanatory boxes for the dependent and independent variables. To run a regression analysis, simply move the names of the variables to the appropriate box and click on "OK" to run the command.

There are three tables of results that contain the statistics discussed in this chapter. The first table of results, labeled "Model Summary," presents the value for R^2.

The second table of results, labeled "ANOVA," contains the ANOVA table that was originally discussed in Chapter 12. In this table, you will find the values for the explained, unexplained, and total sums of squares; the F-statistic; and the observed significance level of F. Please note, however, that the labels for the sums of squares are different. The explained sum of squares is labeled "Regression," and the unexplained sum of squares is labeled "Residual."

The third table of results presents the regression coefficients, the standard errors of the coefficients, the t-statistic for each coefficient, and the observed significance level for each regression coefficient. Note, too, that there is a distinction between unstandardized and standardized regression coefficients. The unstandardized coefficients are the regression coefficients presented in this chapter. We discuss standardized regression coefficients in Chapter 16.

It is also possible to have SPSS calculate predicted values and residuals for each observation in the data file. To obtain one or both of these values, click on the "Statistics" button after entering the variables into the dependent and independent variable boxes. In the new window that opens, click on the box next to "Unstandardized" under the "Predicted Values" and/or "Residuals" labels. Click on "Continue" to return to the window listing the variables. Click on "OK" to run the command. The predicted values and residuals will appear as new variables in your data file with the names pre_1 (for the predicted values) and res_1 (for the residuals). We will return to this command in the computer exercises for Chapter 16.

1.   Open the ***caucr_99.sav*** data file, which contains the data presented in Table 14.8. Run the linear regression command in SPSS, using burglary rate as the dependent variable and unemployment rate as the independent variable. Note that the values reported in the three tables of results match those reported in the text.

2.   Enter the data from Exercise 15.2.

   a. Run the linear regression command, using number of times smoked marijuana as the dependent variable and number of hours worked per week as the independent variable.

   b. Compare your answers to Exercises 15.2 and 15.10 with the results produced by SPSS.

3. Enter the data from Exercise 15.3.

    a. Run the linear regression command, using sentence length as the dependent variable and number of years as a judge as the independent variable.

    b. What is the value of R^2?

    c. Perform an F-test for the overall regression. Outline all of the steps required in a test of statistical significance, including any violations of your assumptions. Can you conclude that the percent of explained variance (R^2) is different from 0 for the population?

4. Enter the data from Exercise 15.7.

    a. Run the linear regression command, using percentage of sentence not served as the dependent variable and number of disciplinary hearings as the independent variable.

    b. What is the value of R^2?

    c. Perform an F-test for the overall regression. Outline all of the steps required in a test of statistical significance, including any violations of your assumptions. Can you conclude that the percent of explained variance (R^2) is different from 0 for the population?

5. Open the *nys_1.sav* data file into SPSS. Use the linear regression command and run regression analyses for the pairs of variables listed below. Do the following for each pair of variables:

    — Explain the regression coefficient in plain English.

    — Perform a t-test for the regression coefficient.

    — Report the value of R^2.

    — Perform an F-test for the overall regression.

    a. Age (X) and number of thefts valued at less than $5 in the last year ($Y$).

    b. Number of times drunk (X) and number of thefts valued at $5 to $50 in the last year ($Y$).

    c. Frequency of marijuana use (X) and number of times the youth has hit other students in the last year (Y).

    d. Number of times the youth has hit a parent (X) and number of thefts valued at more than $50 in the last year ($Y$).

    e. Number of times the youth has been beaten up by a parent (X) and number of times the youth has hit a teacher in the last year (Y).

Multivariate Regression

ONE OF THE STATISTICAL TOOLS most commonly used in criminal justice and criminology is regression modeling. A regression model allows the researcher to take a broad approach to criminological research problems. It is based not simply on understanding the relationships among variables, but on specifying why changes occur and what factors are directly responsible for these changes. In a regression model, the researcher tries to disentangle the various potential factors that have an impact on the dependent variable, in order to provide an accurate picture of which variables are in fact most important in causing change.

In this chapter, we discuss why it is generally necessary to take into account more than just one independent variable in building a regression model. Previous chapters have focused on bivariate statistical analysis, in which we relate two variables—nominal, ordinal, or interval—to each other. This chapter introduces multivariate analysis, in which the researcher takes into account a series of independent variables within one statistical model.

The Importance of Correct Model Specifications

The most important assumption we make in regression modeling is that the model we have estimated is specified correctly. A **correctly specified regression model** is one in which the researcher has taken into account all of the relevant predictors of the dependent variable and has measured them accurately. This requirement of regression modeling is the most difficult one that researchers face. Its importance is linked both to prediction of the dependent variable and to correct estimation of regression coefficients.

Errors in Prediction

Predictions of Y in regression are based on the factors that are included in a regression model. So far, we have examined bivariate regression models, in which one independent variable is used to predict values of Y. But in the real world it is unlikely that only one variable will influence the dependent measure you are examining. Most often, it will be necessary to take into account a number of independent variables. Regression analysis that takes into account more than one independent variable is called **multivariate regression** analysis. The regression model we have discussed so far can be extended to the multivariate case simply by adding a term for each new variable. For example, to include years of education in the model predicting number of arrests presented earlier, we would express our regression equation as follows:

$$Y_{\text{arrests}} = b_0 + b_1(\text{age}) + b_2(\text{education}) + e$$

The population model for this equation would be written as

$$Y_{\text{arrests}} = \beta_0 + \beta_1(\text{age}) + \beta_2(\text{education}) + \epsilon$$

Sometimes, when examining multiple independent variables, researchers find it tedious to include the names of the variables in subscripts. Accordingly, they will often use a general form of the regression equation and then define each variable in a table or in their description of results. For example, the above equation could be expressed in terms of the population parameters as

Model 1: $Y = \beta_0 + \beta_1 X_1 + \beta_2 X_2 + \epsilon$

where Y = arrests
   X_1 = age
   X_2 = years of education

In theory, you could define all relevant predictors of Y and include them all in your regression model. This correctly specified model would also provide the most accurate predictions of Y. Conversely, a misspecified model, or one that does not include all relevant predictors, will provide **biased** predictions of Y.

Let's say, for example, that family median income is also an important predictor of arrests. In this case, the corrected population regression equation would be written as follows:

Model 2: $Y = \beta_0 + \beta_1 X_1 + \beta_2 X_2 + \beta_3 X_3 + \epsilon$

where Y = arrests
   X_1 = age
   X_2 = years of education
   X_3 = family median income

By adding this additional variable, we improve our predictions of Y over those provided by Model 1. Because we have taken into account the influence of family income on arrests, we have added to our ability to correctly predict the dependent variable. By implication, our predictions of Y will be less trustworthy when we do not include a factor that influences the dependent variable.

Sometimes, statisticians express this fact in terms of an assumption about the error term in the population regression model. The error term, ϵ, should represent only random fluctuations that are related to the outcomes (Y) that you are examining. For this reason, we also call the errors residuals, since they are in theory what is left over once you have taken into account all systematic causes of Y. However, if you fail to include an important predictor of Y as an independent variable, then by implication it moves to your error term. The error term now is not made up only of random—or what statisticians sometimes call stochastic—variation in Y, but rather includes the systematic variation that can be attributed to the excluded variable. For example, in Model 1, the effect of median family income is not taken into account, and thus the systematic relationship between median family income and number of arrests is found in the error term for that regression equation. When a model is not correctly specified, the error term will not represent only random or stochastic variation, as is required by the assumptions of regression analysis; it will be systematically related to the dependent variable.

Correctly Estimating the Effect of *b*

Failure to correctly specify a regression model may also lead the researcher to present biased estimates of the effects of specific independent variables. Suppose, for example, that a bivariate regression is defined in which number of years in prison is identified as influencing number of arrests after prison:

$$Y_{rearrests} = b_0 + b_1(\text{years in prison}) + e$$

In estimating this relationship from the data presented in Table 16.1, we find that the regression coefficient based on this model is 1.709. That is, every additional year of imprisonment produces about a 1.709 increase in our prediction of number of subsequent arrests.

W orking It Out

$$b = \frac{\sum_{i=1}^{N}(X_i - \overline{X})(Y_i - \overline{Y})}{\sum_{i=1}^{N}(X_i - \overline{X})^2}$$

$$= \frac{31.7}{18.55}$$

$$= 1.7089$$

Our model for subsequent arrests states that the only causal factor influencing arrests is years of imprisonment. This, of course, is a questionable statement, because common sense tells us that this model is not

| Table 16.1 | | Number of Rearrests (Y) and Years Spent in Prison (X) for 20 Former Inmates | | | | |

| | REARRESTS | | YEARS SPENT IN PRISON | | | |
SUBJECT	Y	$Y_i - \bar{Y}$	X	$X_i - \bar{X}$	$(X_i - \bar{X})^2$	$(X_i - \bar{X})(Y_i - \bar{Y})$
1	0	−3.1	2	−1.15	1.3225	3.565
2	0	−3.1	3	−0.15	0.0225	0.465
3	1	−2.1	1	−2.15	4.6225	4.515
4	1	−2.1	2	−1.15	1.3225	2.415
5	1	−2.1	3	−0.15	0.0225	0.315
6	1	−2.1	3	−0.15	0.0225	0.315
7	2	−1.1	4	0.85	0.7225	−0.935
8	2	−1.1	2	−1.15	1.3225	1.265
9	2	−1.1	2	−1.15	1.3225	1.265
10	3	−0.1	3	−0.15	0.0225	0.015
11	3	−0.1	3	−0.15	0.0225	0.015
12	3	−0.1	3	−0.15	0.0225	0.015
13	4	0.9	3	−0.15	0.0225	−0.135
14	4	0.9	4	0.85	0.7225	0.765
15	4	0.9	4	0.85	0.7225	0.765
16	4	0.9	4	0.85	0.7225	0.765
17	5	1.9	4	0.85	0.7225	1.615
18	6	2.9	4	0.85	0.7225	2.465
19	7	3.9	5	1.85	3.4225	7.215
20	9	5.9	4	0.85	0.7225	5.015
	$\bar{Y} = 3.1$		$\bar{X} = 3.15$		$\sum_{i=1}^{N}(X_i - \bar{X})^2$ $= 18.55$	$\sum_{i=1}^{N}(X_i - \bar{X})(Y_i - \bar{Y})$ $= 31.7$

Bivariate Regression Model:

Dependent Variable: Subsequent Rearrests
Independent Variable: Years in Prison
Regression Coefficient: b(years in prison) = 31.7/18.55 = 1.7089

correctly specified. There are certainly other factors that influence arrests. Some of those factors, in turn, may also be related to the number of years that an offender serves in prison. If this is true—that relevant factors related to years of imprisonment have been omitted from the model—then the regression coefficient may provide a very misleading estimate of the effect of imprisonment on arrests.

Judges, for example, are likely to impose longer prison sentences on offenders with more serious prior records. Using the sample data in Table 16.2, we can look at the correlations among these three variables (see Table 16.3). The number of prior arrests is strongly related ($r = 0.63$) to the length of prison term served. Prior arrests are even more strongly related to subsequent arrests ($r = 0.76$). This suggests, first of all, that prior record is a relevant factor that should be included if our model is to be correctly specified. But it also raises a very important concern: How do we know that our finding that "years in prison" increases reoffending is not simply a result of the fact that those who serve longer prison terms generally have more serious prior records of offending?

| Table 16.2 | Number of Rearrests, Years Spent in Prison, and Number of Prior Arrests for 20 Former Inmates |

SUBJECT	REARRESTS	YEARS IN PRISON	PRIOR ARRESTS
1	0	2	4
2	0	3	2
3	1	1	2
4	1	2	3
5	1	3	3
6	1	3	2
7	2	4	3
8	2	2	3
9	2	2	1
10	3	3	2
11	3	3	3
12	3	3	3
13	4	3	4
14	4	4	3
15	4	4	4
16	4	4	5
17	5	4	4
18	6	4	5
19	7	5	5
20	9	4	6
	$\overline{Y} = 3.10$	$\overline{X} = 3.15$	$\overline{X} = 3.35$
	$s = 2.300$	$s = 0.9631$	$s = 1.2360$

In an ideal world, our comparisons of the impact of imprisonment would be made with subjects who were otherwise similar. That is, we would want to be sure that the offenders with longer and shorter prison sentences were comparable on other characteristics, such as the seriousness of prior records. In this case, there would be no relationship between prior arrests and length of imprisonment, and thus we would not have to be concerned with the possibility that the effect of length of imprisonment actually reflects the influence of prior arrests on reoffending.

In criminal justice, this approach is taken in the development of **randomized experiments.**[1] A randomized study of the impact of

| Table 16.3 | Correlation Coefficients for the Variables Years in Prison, Prior Arrests, and Subsequent Rearrests Based on Data from 20 Former Inmates |

	YEARS IN PRISON	PRIOR ARRESTS
Prior Arrests	$r = 0.6280$	
Subsequent Rearrests	$r = 0.7156$	$r = 0.7616$

[1]For a discussion of experimental methods in criminal justice, see E. Babbic and M. Maxfield, *The Practice of Social Research in Criminal Justice* (Belmont, CA: Wadsworth, 1995). For a comparison of experimental and nonexperimental methods, see D. Weisburd, C. Lum, and A. Petrosino, "Does Research Design Affect Study Outcomes in Criminal Justice?" *The Annals* 578 (2001): 50–70.

length of imprisonment on reoffending would be one in which the researcher took a sample of offenders and assigned them to treatment and control conditions at random. For example, the researcher might define a sentence of 6 months as a control condition and a sentence of 1 year as an experimental condition. In this case, the researcher could examine the effects of a longer versus a shorter prison sentence on rearrests without concern about the confounding influences of other variables. Random allocation of subjects to treatment and control conditions allows the researcher to assume that other traits, such as prior record, are randomly scattered across the treatment and control conditions. Our problem in criminal justice is that it is often impractical to develop experimental research designs. For example, it is highly unlikely that judges would allow a researcher to randomly allocate prison sanctions. The same is true for many other research problems relating to crime and justice.

Fortunately for criminal justice researchers, a correctly specified regression model will take into account and control for relationships that exist among the independent variables included in the model. So, for example, the inclusion of both length of imprisonment and prior arrests in one regression model will provide regression coefficients that reflect the specific impact of each variable, once the impact of the other has been taken into account. This is illustrated in Equation 16.1, which describes the calculation of a multivariate regression coefficient in the case of two independent variables (X_1 and X_2). Equation 16.2 applies Equation 16.1 to the specific regression model including both length of imprisonment and prior arrests. The model can be described as follows:

$$Y = b_0 + b_1X_1 + b_2X_2 + e$$

where Y = subsequent rearrests
X_1 = years in prison
X_2 = prior arrests

Here we calculate the multivariate regression coefficient b_1 for length of imprisonment.

$$b_{X_1} = \left(\frac{r_{Y,X_1} - (r_{Y,X_2}r_{X_1,X_2})}{1 - r_{X_1,X_2}^2} \right)\left(\frac{s_Y}{s_{X_1}} \right) \qquad \text{Equation 16.1}$$

$$b_{X_1} = \left(\frac{r_{Y,YP} - (r_{Y,PA}r_{YP,PA})}{1 - r_{YP,PA}^2} \right)\left(\frac{s_Y}{s_{YP}} \right) \qquad \text{Equation 16.2}$$

In Equations 16.1 and 16.2, the bivariate correlations among the three measures examined, as well as the standard deviations of years in prison and rearrests, are used to calculate the multivariate regression coefficients. The three correlations for our specific example are (1) $r_{Y,YP}$, or the correlation between subsequent rearrests and years in prison; (2) $r_{Y,PA}$, or the correlation between subsequent rearrests and prior arrests; and (3) $r_{YP,PA}$, or the correlation between years in prison and prior arrests.

What is most important to note in Equation 16.2 is that the numerator (in the first part) takes into account the product of the relationship between prior arrests and subsequent rearrests and that of prior arrests and years in prison. This relationship is subtracted from the simple correlation between years in prison and subsequent arrests. In this way, multivariate regression provides an estimate of b that takes into account that some of the impact of years in prison may be due to the fact that longer prison terms are associated with more serious prior records. This estimate is now purged of the bias that was introduced when prior record was not included in the regression model. The multivariate regression coefficient for years in prison when prior record is included in the regression model (0.936) is considerably smaller than the estimate calculated earlier in the bivariate regression (1.709).

W orking It Out

$$b_{X_1} = \left(\frac{r_{Y,YP} - (r_{Y,PA} r_{YP,PA})}{1 - r_{YP,PA}^2} \right) \left(\frac{s_Y}{s_{YP}} \right)$$

$$= \left(\frac{0.7156 - (0.7616)(0.6280)}{1 - (0.6280)^2} \right) \left(\frac{2.300}{0.9631} \right)$$

$$= \left(\frac{0.2373152}{0.605616} \right) (2.388122)$$

$$= 0.9358$$

With the same information, we can calculate the multivariate regression coefficient for prior arrests. We find the value for b_2 to be 0.9593 (see working it out, page 468). The bivariate regression coefficient for prior arrests is calculated in the box on page 467 so that you can compare the results. As you can see, the value of b when we take into account years in prison (0.96) is much smaller than that in the bivariate case (1.4).

Calculation of Bivariate Regression Coefficient for Number of Rearrests (Y) and Number of Prior Arrests (X) for 20 Former Inmates

SUBJECT	REARRESTS Y	$Y_i - \bar{Y}$	PRIOR ARRESTS X	$X_i - \bar{X}$	$(X_i - \bar{X})^2$	$(X_i - \bar{X})(Y_i - \bar{Y})$
1	0	−3.1	4	0.65	0.4225	−2.015
2	0	−3.1	2	−1.35	1.8225	4.185
3	1	−2.1	2	−1.35	1.8225	2.835
4	1	−2.1	3	−0.35	0.1225	0.735
5	1	−2.1	3	−0.35	0.1225	0.735
6	1	−2.1	2	−1.35	1.8225	2.835
7	2	−1.1	3	−0.35	0.1225	0.385
8	2	−1.1	3	−0.35	0.1225	0.385
9	2	−1.1	1	−2.35	5.5225	2.585
10	3	−0.1	2	−1.35	1.8225	0.135
11	3	−0.1	3	−0.35	0.1225	0.035
12	3	−0.1	3	−0.35	0.1225	0.035
13	4	0.9	4	0.65	0.4225	0.585
14	4	0.9	3	−0.35	0.1225	−0.315
15	4	0.9	4	0.65	0.4225	0.585
16	4	0.9	5	1.65	2.7225	1.485
17	5	1.9	4	0.65	0.4225	1.235
18	6	2.9	5	1.65	2.7225	4.785
19	7	3.9	5	1.65	2.7225	6.435
20	9	5.9	6	2.65	7.0225	15.635

$$\bar{Y} = 3.10 \qquad \bar{X} = 3.35 \qquad \sum_{i=1}^{N}(X_i - \bar{X})^2 = 30.55 \qquad \sum_{i=1}^{N}(X_i - \bar{X})(Y_i - \bar{Y}) = 43.30$$

Bivariate Regression Model:

Dependent Variable: Subsequent Rearrests
Independent Variable: Prior Arrests
Regression Coefficient: b(Prior Arrests) = 43.30/30.55 = 1.4173

> **W** orking It Out
>
> $$b_{X_2} = \left(\frac{r_{Y,PA} - (r_{Y,YP}r_{YP,PA})}{1 - r_{YP,PA}^2}\right)\left(\frac{s_Y}{s_{PA}}\right)$$
>
> $$= \left(\frac{0.7616 - (0.7156)(0.6280)}{1 - (0.6280)^2}\right)\left(\frac{2.300}{1.2360}\right)$$
>
> $$= \left(\frac{0.3122032}{0.605616}\right)(1.8608)$$
>
> $$= 0.9593$$

The fact that the results are different when we examine the effects of years in prison and prior arrests in the multivariate regression model shows that the bivariate regression coefficients were indeed biased. In both cases, the estimate of the effect of b provided by the bivariate regression coefficient was much too high. These differences also reflect a difference in interpretation between the multivariate regression coefficient and the bivariate regression coefficient. In the bivariate case, the regression coefficient represents the estimated change in Y that is produced by a one-unit change in X. In the multivariate case, b represents the estimated change in Y associated with a one-unit change in X when *all other independent variables in the model are held constant.* Holding prior arrests constant leads to a reduction in the impact of years in prison. Holding years in prison constant leads to a reduction in the estimate of the effect of prior arrests. These differences may be seen as the bias introduced by misspecifying the regression model through the exclusion of prior arrests.

We can also identify this bias in terms of assumptions related to the error term in regression. It is assumed not only that the errors in the regression are stochastic, but also that there is no specific systematic relationship between the error term and the independent variables included in the regression. If there is such a relationship, the regression coefficient will be biased. While this may seem like a new concept, it is really a restatement of what you learned above.

Let's use our model predicting rearrest as a substantive example. We saw that if we estimated the regression coefficient for years in prison without taking into account prior arrests, the regression coefficient would be biased—in this case, overestimated. What happens in theory to the error term in this case? As we discussed earlier in the chapter, when we exclude an independent variable, the effect of that variable moves to the error term. In our case, the population model including both independent variables may be stated as follows:

$$Y = \beta_0 + \beta_1 X_1 + \beta_2 X_2 + \epsilon$$

where Y = subsequent rearrests
X_1 = years in prison
X_2 = prior arrests

When we take into account only one independent variable, the model includes only the term X_1:

$$Y = \beta_0 + \beta_1 X_1 + \epsilon$$

where Y = subsequent rearrests
X_1 = years in prison

In the latter model, number of prior arrests is included by implication in the error term. But what does this mean regarding the relationship in this model between the error term and years in prison? Our sample data suggest that the number of prior arrests is related to years in prison (as was shown in Table 16.3) and is now found in the error term, or residual, the error term is now related to years in prison as well. By implication, since number of prior arrests is now found in the error term, the error term can now be assumed to be related to years in prison as well. Accordingly, if we leave prior arrests out of our equation, then we violate the assumption that there is no systematic relationship between the error term and the independent variables in the equation.

By looking at bias in terms of the error term, we can also specify when excluding an independent variable will not lead to bias in our estimates of the regression coefficients of other variables. If the excluded variable is unrelated to other variables included in the regression, it will not cause bias in estimates of b for those specific variables. This is the case because when there is no systematic relationship between the excluded variable and the included variable of interest, its exclusion does not lead to a systematic relationship between the error term and the variable of interest.

For example, if years in prison and prior arrests were not systematically related (e.g., the correlation between the variables was 0), it would not matter whether we took into account prior arrests in estimating the regression coefficient for years in prison.[2] In this case, the exclusion of prior arrests would not lead to a systematic relationship between the error term

[2]It is important to note that bias can be caused by a nonlinear relationship between the excluded and the included variable. The assumption is that there is no systematic relationship of any form.

and years in prison, because there is no systematic relationship between prior arrests and years in prison. However, it is important to remember that the exclusion of prior arrests will still cause bias in our estimate of Y. In this situation, we continue to violate the assumption that the error term is stochastic. It now includes a systematic predictor of Y, prior arrests.

Comparing Regression Coefficients Within a Single Model: The Standardized Regression Coefficient

A multivariate regression model allows us to specify the impact of a specific independent variable while holding constant the impact of other independent variables. This is a very important advantage of multivariate regression analysis over bivariate regression analysis. However, when we include multiple variables in the same model, it is natural to want to compare the impact of the different variables examined. For example, in our case, does years in prison have a stronger effect on subsequent rearrests than number of prior arrests does? Or does number of prior arrests have a stronger effect than years in prison? The ordinary regression coefficient b does not allow us to answer this question, since it reports the effect of a variable in its original units of measurement. Accordingly, the regression coefficient for years in prison reports the predicted change in subsequent rearrests for each year change in years in prison. The regression coefficient for number of prior arrests reports the predicted change in subsequent rearrests for each change in number of prior arrests. Though the interpretation of the regression coefficients in these cases is straightforward, we cannot directly compare them.

Another statistic, called the **standardized regression coefficient** or **Beta,** allows us to make direct comparisons. Beta weights take the regression coefficients in an equation and standardize them according to the ratio of the standard deviation of the variable examined to the standard deviation of the dependent variable. Beta is expressed mathematically in Equation 16.3:

$$\text{Beta} = b\left(\frac{s_X}{s_Y}\right)$$

Equation 16.3

The interpretation of the standardized coefficient is similar to that of b (the unstandardized coefficient), except that we change the units. We interpret Beta as the expected amount of change in the standard deviation of the dependent variable, given a one-unit change in the standard deviation of the independent variable.

For years in prison in our example, we take the regression coefficient of 0.9358 and multiply it by the ratio of the standard deviation of years in prison (0.9631) and subsequent rearrests (2.3000). The result is 0.3919, which tells us that an increase of one standard deviation in years in prison is expected to result in an increase of 0.392 standard deviation in rearrests.

W orking It Out

$$\text{Beta} = b\left(\frac{s_X}{s_Y}\right)$$

$$= 0.9358\left(\frac{0.9631}{2.3000}\right)$$

$$= 0.3919$$

For prior arrests, we begin with our regression coefficient of 0.9593. Again, we standardize our estimate by taking the ratio of the standard deviation of prior arrests (1.2360) and subsequent rearrests (2.3000). Our estimate of Beta here is 0.5155, which indicates that an increase of one standard deviation in prior arrests is expected to result in an increase of 0.516 standard deviation in rearrests.

W orking It Out

$$\text{Beta} = b\left(\frac{s_X}{s_Y}\right)$$

$$= 0.9593\left(\frac{1.2360}{2.3000}\right)$$

$$= 0.5155$$

In our example, the Beta weight for prior arrests is larger than that for years in prison. According to this estimate, the number of prior arrests has a greater impact on subsequent rearrests than the number of years in prison does. The standardized regression coefficient thus provides us with an answer to our original question regarding which of the independent variables examined has the most influence on the dependent variable. As you can see, the standardized regression coefficient is a useful tool for comparing the effects of variables measured differently within a single regression model. However, because standardized regression coefficients are based on the standard deviations of observed samples, they are generally considered inappropriate for making comparisons across samples.

Correctly Specifying the Regression Model

The previous section illustrated the importance of a correctly specified regression model. If a regression model is not correctly specified, then the predictions that are made and the coefficients that are estimated may provide misleading results. This raises important theoretical as well as practical questions for criminal justice research.

In criminal justice research, we can seldom say with assurance that the models we develop include all relevant predictors of the dependent variables examined. The problem is often that our theories are not powerful enough to clearly define the factors that influence criminal justice questions. Criminal justice is still a young science, and our theories for explaining crime and justice issues often are not well specified. This fact has important implications for the use of criminal justice research in developing public policy. When our predictions are weak, they do not form a solid basis on which to inform criminal justice policies.[3]

One implication of our failure to develop strongly predictive models in criminal justice is that our estimates of variable effects likely include some degree of bias. We have stressed in this chapter the importance of controlling for relevant predictors in regression modeling. The cost of leaving out important causes is not just weaker prediction but also estimates of variable effects that include potentially spurious components. This fact should make you cautious in reporting regression analyses and critical in evaluating the research of others. Just because regression coefficients are reported to the fifth decimal place on a computer printout does not mean that the estimates so obtained are solid ones.

The fact that regression models often include some degree of misspecification, however, should not lead you to conclude that the regression approach is not useful for criminal justice researchers. As in any sci

---

[3]Mark Moore of Harvard University has argued, for example, that legal and ethical dilemmas make it difficult to base criminal justice policies about crime control on models that still include a substantial degree of statistical error. See M. Moore, "Purblind Justice: Normative Issues in the Use of Prediction in the Criminal Justice System," in A. Blumstein, J. Cohen, A. Roth, and C. A. Visher (eds.), *Criminal Careers and "Career Criminals,"* Vol. 2 (Washington, DC: National Academy Press, 1986).

ence, the task is to continue to build on the knowledge that is presently available. The researcher's task in developing regression models is to improve on models that were developed before. With each improvement, the results we gain provide a more solid basis for making decisions about criminal justice theory and policy. This, of course, makes the practical task of defining the correct model for the problem you are examining extremely important. How then should you begin?

Defining Relevant Independent Variables

Importantly, model specification does not begin with your data. Rather, it starts with theory and a visit to the library or other information systems. To build a regression model, you should first identify what is already known about the dependent variable you have chosen to study. If your interest, for example, is in the factors that influence involvement in criminality, you will need to carefully research what others have said and found regarding the causes of criminality. Your regression model should take into account the main theories and perspectives that have been raised by others.

If you do not take prior research and theory into account, then those reviewing your work will argue that your predictions and your estimates of variable effects are biased in one way or another. Just as the exclusion of prior record from our example led to a misleading estimate of its impact on length of imprisonment, so too the exclusion of relevant causal factors in other models may lead to bias. The only way to refute this potential criticism is to include such variables in your regression model.

Taking into account the theories and perspectives of others is the first step in building a correctly specified regression model. However, in most research we seek to add something new to existing knowledge. In regression modeling, this usually involves the addition of new variables. Sometimes, such new variables are drawn from an innovative change in theory. Other times, they involve improvements in measurement. Often, the finding that these new or transformed variables have an independent impact above and beyond those of variables traditionally examined by researchers leads to important advances in criminal justice theory and policy.

Taking into Account Ordinal- and Nominal-Scale Measures in a Multivariate Regression

Until now, we have assumed that ordinary least squares regression analysis requires an interval level of measurement, both for the dependent and for the independent variables. However, criminal justice researchers will sometimes use this approach with ordinal-level dependent variables when there are a number of categories and there is good reason to assume that the intervals for the categories are generally similar. In practice, you should be cautious in using OLS regression when your dependent variable is not interval level. Moreover, as will be explained in Chapter 17, the use of OLS regression in the case of a binary dependent variable is inappropriate.

What about the inclusion of non–interval-level independent variables? Such variables often are important in explaining criminal justice outcomes. If we are required to include all relevant causes of Y in order to correctly specify our model, how can we exclude ordinal- and nominal-level measures? Fortunately, we do not have to. In multivariate regression, it is acceptable to include ordinal- and nominal-level independent variables as long as there is at least one interval-level independent variable also included in the analysis.

But even though you can include ordinal- and nominal-level variables, you need to take into account the specific interpretation used by regression analysis for interpreting the effects of one variable on another. Including an ordinal-level measure in a multivariate regression is relatively straightforward. This is done in Table 16.4, which presents a standard SPSS printout for a regression analysis. The data used are drawn from a national sample of police officers developed by the Police Foundation.[4] The dependent variable in this analysis is hours worked per week. There are two independent variables. One, years with the department, is measured at the interval level. The second, level of education, is on an ordinal scale with eight levels, ranging from some high school to doctoral degree. We can see that both of these variables have a significant impact on hours worked per week—the observed significance levels ("Sig." in the

Table 16.4 SPSS Printout for Regression Analysis of the Police Officer Example

Coefficients

Model		Unstandardized Coefficients B	Std. Error	Standardized Coefficients Beta	t	Sig.
1	(Constant)	44.968	.749		60.031	.000
	YEARS WITH DEPARTMENT	−7.354E-02	.026	−.092	−2.816	.005
	LEVEL OF EDUCATION	.456	.173	.086	2.636	.009

a Dependent Variable: HOURS PER WEEK WORKED

[4]David Weisburd et al., *The Abuse of Authority: A National Study of Police Officers' Attitudes* (Washington, DC: The Police Foundation, 2001).

SPSS table) are less than the conventionally applied significance level of 0.05 we would likely use in this case. This result, as in most statistical packages, is calculated for a two-tailed test of statistical significance (generally the default option). For years with the department, we can see that the impact is negative. When we control for the impact of level of education, each year with the department is associated with an average decrease of about 0.074 hour in number of hours worked each week.

But what is the meaning of the effect of level of education? Here, what we have is not an interval scale but a group of ordered categories. For the regression, this ordinal-level scale is treated simply as an interval-level scale. It is assumed that the categories must be roughly similar in value, or that each level increase in that scale is related in a linear manner to the dependent variable. Thus, our interpretation of this regression coefficient is that for every one-level increase in education level, there is, on average, a 0.456 increase in the number of hours worked (once we have taken into account years with the department). In this case, the standardized regression coefficient is very useful. It appears from the size of the coefficients that the overall effect of years with the department is less than that of level of education. However, the standardized regression coefficients (represented by Beta) show that the two variables have about the same effect.

This example illustrates how we can include an ordinal-level variable in a multivariate regression. The inclusion of an ordinal variable is straightforward, and its interpretation follows that of an interval-level independent variable. But when we include a nominal-level variable, we have to adjust our interpretation of the regression coefficient.

Table 16.5 reports the results of a regression with a single interval-level variable and a binary nominal-level variable. We use the same

Table 16.5 | **SPSS Printout for Regression Analysis with an Interval-Level and Nominal-Level Variable**

Coefficients

Model		Unstandardized Coefficients B	Std. Error	Standardized Coefficients Beta	t	Sig.
1	(Constant)	48.550	.977		49.672	.000
	YEARS WITH DEPARTMENT	$-7.737\text{E-}02$	.026	$-.097$	-2.943	.003
	RESPONDENT GENDER	-1.669	.803	$-.068$	-2.077	.038

a Dependent Variable: HOURS PER WEEK WORKED

dependent variable and data examined in our prior example. To make our example easier, we include only two measures in predicting number of hours worked. Again, we have an interval-level measure, years with the department. A binary independent variable, gender, is also included.

In regression analysis, a binary nominal-level independent variable is generally called a **dummy variable.** Our first problem is to give numbers to this dummy variable. Multivariate regression analysis does not recognize qualitative categories. By convention, we give one category a value of 0 and the other a value of 1. It is generally good practice to give the category with the largest number of cases a value of 0 because, as we will illustrate in a moment, that category becomes the reference category. Since this sample included many more men than women, we assigned men the value 0 and women the value 1.

Again, we can see that both variables have a statistically significant impact on hours worked per week. The observed significance level for years with the department is 0.003, and that for gender is 0.038. But how can we interpret the dummy variable regression coefficient of -1.669? One way to gain a better understanding of the interpretation of dummy variable regression coefficients is to see how they affect our regression equation. Let's begin by writing out the regression equation for our example:

$$Y = b_0 + b_1X_1 + b_2X_2$$

where Y = hours worked per week
X_1 = years with the department
X_2 = gender of officer

As a second step, let's insert the coefficients gained in our regression analysis:

$$Y = 48.550 + (-0.077)X_1 + (-1.669)X_2$$

or

$$Y = 48.550 - 0.077X_1 - 1.669X_2$$

What happens if we try to write out the regression equations for men and women separately? For men, the regression equation is

$$Y = 48.550 - 0.077X_1 - 1.669(0)$$

or

$$Y = 48.550 - 0.077X_1$$

Because men are coded as 0, the second term of the equation falls out. But what about for women? The second term in the equation is a constant because all of the women have a value of 1. If we write it out, we have the following result:

$$Y = 48.550 - 0.077X_1 - 1.669(1)$$

or

$$Y = 48.550 - 0.077X_1 - 1.669$$

We can simplify this formula even more, because the two constants at the beginning and the end of the equation can be added together:

$$Y = 46.881 - 0.077X_1$$

What then is the difference between the regression equations for men and women? In both cases, the slope of the regression line is given by the term $-0.077X_1$. The difference between the two equations lies in the Y-intercept, as illustrated in Figure 16.1. As you can see, men and women have parallel regression lines. However, the women's line intersects the Y-axis about 1.7 hours lower than the men's line. This provides us with the interpretation of our coefficient. Women police officers, on

Figure 16.1   *Regression Lines for Men and Women Police Officers*

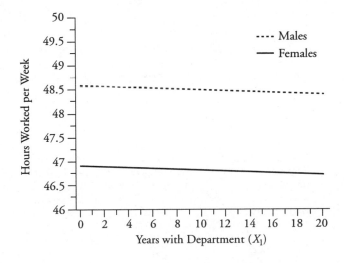

average, work about 1.669 hours a week less than men police officers, taking into account years with the department.

This example also suggests why it is generally recommended that you place the category with the largest number of cases as the 0 category of a binary dummy variable. The category men, in this case, is the reference category, meaning that the coefficient for gender gives us the estimate of the female category in reference to the male category. We want our reference category to be as stable as possible, and a large number of cases makes this category more stable.

But how can we assess the impact of a nominal variable that has multiple categories? In fact, multiple-category nominal variables create a good deal more complexity for the researcher than do ordinal or binary nominal variables. In this case, you must create a separate variable for each category in your analysis. For example, the Police Foundation study divided the United States into four regions: North Central, Northeast, South, and West. In practice, you would need to create a separate variable for each of these regions. In other words, you would define a variable North Central, which you would code 1 for all those officers in the North Central region and 0 for all other officers. You would repeat this process for each of the other regional categories.

As with the binary independent variable, you must choose one of the categories to be a reference category. In this case, however, the reference category is excluded from the regression. Again, it is generally recommended that you choose as the reference category the category with the largest number of cases.[5] In our example, the largest number of officers is drawn from the South. Suppose that we include only one interval-level variable in our equation: years with the department. Table 16.6 presents the results from an analysis in which years with the department and region are used to predict number of hours worked.

In this example, we included in the regression a single interval-level variable and three region measures: North Central, Northeast, and West. While South is not included as a variable, it is in fact the reference cate-

---

[5]There may be times when you want to choose a category that does not include the largest number of cases as the reference. For example, if you wanted to compare a series of treatments to a no-treatment, or control, condition, it would make sense to have the control condition as the excluded category, even if it did not include the largest *N*. However, if the excluded category has a small number of cases, it may lead to instability in the regression estimates.

| Table 16.6 | SPSS Printout for Regression Analysis with Multiple-Category Nominal Variable |

Coefficients

Model		Unstandardized Coefficients		Standardized Coefficients	t	Sig.
		B	Std. Error	Beta		
1	(Constant)	47.654	.470		101.435	.000
	YEARS WITH DEPARTMENT	−6.138E-02	.026	−.077	−2.352	.019
	NORTH CENTRAL	−2.335	.610	−.141	−3.825	.000
	NORTHEAST	−1.758	.573	−.114	−3.067	.002
	WEST	−.846	.616	−.050	−1.372	.170

a Dependent Variable: HOURS PER WEEK WORKED

gory. If we again write out our regression equation, we can see why this is the case:

$$Y = b_0 + b_1X_1 + b_2X_2 + b_3X_3 + b_4X_4$$

where Y = hours worked per week
X_1 = years with department
X_2 = North Central
X_3 = Northeast
X_4 = West

Using the results for this model presented in Table 16.6, we can write the results in equation form as follows:

$$Y = 47.654 - 0.061X_1 - 2.335X_2 - 1.758X_3 - 0.846X_4$$

In this case, we can also write out a separate regression equation for each of the four regions. Since the South is our reference category, those from the South are coded 0 on the three included variables. Thus, our equation is simply the Y-intercept and the variable years with the department. For officers from the North Central region, the equation includes the Y-intercept, b_1X_1, and b_2X_2. The other parameters are set to 0, since those in the North Central region have 0 values on X_3 and X_4. Similarly, for both the Northeast and the West, only one of the three dummy variables is included. For each equation, we can once again add the constant for the dummy variable to the Y-intercept:

Officers from the South:

$$Y = 47.654 - 0.061X_1$$

Officers from the North Central:

$$Y = 47.654 - 0.061X_1 - 2.335X_2 \quad \text{or} \quad Y = 45.319 - 0.061X_1$$

Officers from the Northeast:

$$Y = 47.654 - 0.061X_1 - 1.758X_3 \quad \text{or} \quad Y = 45.896 - 0.061X_1$$

Officers from the West:

$$Y = 47.654 - 0.061X_1 - 0.846X_4 \quad \text{or} \quad Y = 46.808 - 0.061X_1$$

Once again, we can gain a better conceptual understanding of our results if we plot them, as in Figure 16.2. In this case, each of the included categories is found to have a Y-intercept lower than that of the excluded

Figure 16.2   *Plot of Hours Worked and Years with Department, by Region*

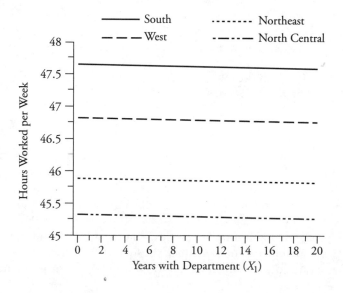

category, the South. This means that, on average, officers work fewer hours in all of the other regions. The least number of hours worked per week is found in the North Central region. Here, officers work, on average, about 2.335 hours less than they do in the South, once we have taken into account years with the department. In the Northeast, officers work about 1.758 hours less and in the West about 0.846 hour less a week.

Are these differences statistically significant? It is important to note that the significance statistic reported for each coefficient tells us only whether the category is significantly different from the reference category. This is one reason it is so important to be clear about the definition of the reference category. In our example, the North Central and Northeast regions are significantly different from the South, using a 5% significance threshold and a two-tailed significance test (the default option in SPSS). The West, however, is not significantly different from the South, using this threshold.

If you wanted to determine whether region overall as a variable had a statistically significant impact on hours worked per week, you would have to run an additional significance test based on the F-test for the regression model, introduced in Chapter 15. The F-test for multiple-category dummy variables in regression compares the R^2 statistic gained with the dummy variables included in the regression to the R^2 statistic gained without those variables. In practice, you must run two separate regressions, although most computer programs now provide this statistic directly. First, you calculate the regression without the new dummy variable categories (referred to as the reduced model) and identify its R^2. In our case, the regression without the dummy variables produces an R^2 of only 0.008. You then compute the regression with the dummy variables, as we did earlier (referred to as the full model). In this case, R^2 is 0.023. The F-test formula is presented in Equation 16.4.

$$F = \frac{(R^2_{fm} - R^2_{rm})/(k_{fm} - k_{rm})}{(1 - R^2_{fm})/(N - k_{fm} - 1)}$$

Equation 16.4

To apply Equation 16.4 to our example, we first subtract the R^2 of the reduced model (R^2_{rm}) from the R^2 of the full model (R^2_{fm}) and then divide this quantity by the number of variables in the full model (k_{fm}) minus the number of variables in the reduced model (k_{rm}), which is 3. The denominator is found by subtracting the R^2 of the full model from 1, and then dividing this quantity by $N - k_{fm} - 1$. For this sample, N is 923 and k_{fm} is 4. Our final result is $F = 4.55$. Looking at the F-distribution (see

Appendix 5) with 3 and 918 degrees of freedom, we can see that our result is statistically significant at the 0.05 level.

W **orking It Out**

$$F = \frac{(R^2_{\text{fm}} - R^2_{\text{rm}})/(k_{\text{fm}} - k_{\text{rm}})}{(1 - R^2_{\text{fm}})/(N - k_{\text{fm}} - 1)}$$

$$= \frac{(0.023 - 0.008)/(4 - 1)}{(1 - 0.023)/(923 - 4 - 1)}$$

$$= \frac{(0.015/3)}{(0.977/918)} = \frac{0.005}{0.0011}$$

$$= 4.5455$$

One final question we might ask is whether we can use the standardized regression coefficient to compare dummy variables to ordinal- and interval-level measures. In general, statisticians discourage such use of standardized regression coefficients, since they are based on standard deviations and the standard deviation is not an appropriate statistic for a nominal-level variable. Additionally, for a nominal-level variable, the standardized regression coefficient refers only to the difference between the reference category and the dummy variable category examined. This may sometimes make sense in the case of a binary dummy variable, since we can say that one category is Beta standard deviations higher or lower on the dependent variable. But it can be extremely misleading in the case of multicategory nominal-level variables, such as region in our example. The size of the standardized regression coefficient, like the size of the coefficient itself, will depend on which category is excluded. In general, you should exercise caution when interpreting standardized regression coefficients for dummy variables in a multivariate regression analysis.

The Problem of Multicollinearity

In trying to build correctly specified regression models, researchers are faced with an ironic statistical problem. Even though multivariate regression was developed in part to take into account the interrelationships among variables that predict Y, when independent variables in a regression model are too strongly related to one another, regression estimates become unstable. This problem is called **multicollinearity.**

In criminal justice, the independent variables examined are generally multicollinear, or correlated with one another. Indeed, this correlation is one reason it is so important to use multivariate techniques in criminal justice research. When variables are intercorrelated, as in the case of our example of years in prison and prior arrests, it is important to control for the potential confounding influences of one variable on the other. Failure to do so is likely to lead to bias in our estimates of the effects of specific regression coefficients. However, the irony of multicollinearity is that when variables become too correlated, or highly multicollinear, the regression estimates become unreliable.

Multicollinearity can be identified in one of two ways. A common method is to look at the intercorrelations among the independent variables included in your model. Very high correlations between independent variables are likely to lead to multicollinearity problems. What is considered a very high correlation? As with many other definitions in statistics, there is no absolute number at which multicollinearity is considered serious. As a general rule, a correlation between two independent variables of greater than 0.80 should be seen as a warning that serious multicollinearity may be evident in your model.

Multicollinearity between two variables occurs less often than multicollinearity across a series of variables. To diagnose this type of multicollinearity, we use a statistic that is usually defined as **tolerance.** Tolerance measures the extent of the intercorrelations of each independent variable with all other independent variables. It is defined as 1 minus the percent of variance in X explained by the other independent variable examined (Equation 16.5).

$$\text{Tolerance} = 1 - R_X^2 \qquad \text{Equation 16.5}$$

Calculation of tolerance is generally provided as an option in standard statistical computing packages, but it also can be calculated by taking each independent variable as the dependent variable in a regression that includes all other independent variables. This value is then subtracted from 1. For example, let's say we defined a model for explaining arrests that included three independent variables:

$$Y_{\text{rearrests}} = b_0 + b_1(\text{age}) + b_2(\text{age at first arrest}) + b_3(\text{education}) + e$$

R_X^2 for age would be estimated by calculating a regression in which age was the dependent variable and education and age at first arrest were the independent variables. You would then take this R^2 and subtract it from 1. Similarly, to get R_X^2 for education, you would regress age and age at first arrest on education and then subtract the resulting R^2 from 1.

A very small tolerance statistic suggests that the model is likely to include a high level of multicollinearity. Again, there is no clear yardstick for defining a level of tolerance that is likely to lead to estimation problems. In general, however, a tolerance level of less than 0.20 should be taken as a warning that serious multicollinearity may exist in your model.

Beyond these diagnostic procedures for multicollinearity, there are warning signs that can be observed in the regressions that are estimated. Sometimes when multicollinearity is present, the percent of explained variance in a model is high, but the regression coefficients overall fail to reach conventional thresholds of statistical significance. Sometimes multicollinearity inflates coefficients to unrealistic sizes or produces coefficients in a direction contrary to conventional wisdom. One problem in diagnosing multicollinearity is that it may have such varied effects in your model that you may have difficulty distinguishing a misleading result that is due to multicollinearity from one that represents a new and interesting finding.

When there are indications of serious multicollinearity, you can take a number of alternative corrective measures. The simplest is to exclude the variable or variables that are contributing most to multicollinearity. The drawback of this approach is that the exclusion of such measures is likely to lead to model misspecification and may result in biased estimates of other regression coefficients that remain in the model. This approach makes sense only when other variables that remain in the model measure the same concept or theory. An approach that achieves a similar result, without excluding specific measures, is to create new indices from clusters of variables that are multicollinear. For example, if a group of measures all relating to social status are multicollinear, you may decide to create a new composite measure defined as social status and use it as an independent variable in subsequent regressions.

Chapter Summary

In a **bivariate regression model,** there is only one independent variable, and it must be an interval-level measure. Importantly, the researcher can rarely be sure that the change observed in the dependent variable is due to one independent variable alone. And if variables that have an impact on the dependent measure are excluded, the predictions of Y gained in a regression will be biased. If the excluded variables are related to the included factor, then the estimate of b for the included factor will also be biased. **Randomized experiments,** which scatter different traits at random, offer a solution to the latter problem, but they are often impractical in criminal justice research. A statistical solution that enables us to correct for both types of bias is to create a **multivariate regression model.**

In a multivariate regression model, there may be several independent variables, only one of which needs to be interval level. Such a model considers the effect of each independent variable, while holding all the other variables constant. A binary nominal-level variable included in a regression model is called a **dummy variable.** Regression coefficients measured using different scales may be compared with a **standardized regression coefficient (Beta).** A regression model is **correctly specified** if the researcher has taken into account and correctly measured all of the relevant predictors of the dependent variable. Existing literature and prior research are suitable places to start.

Multicollinearity occurs when independent variables in a regression model are too strongly related. It leads to unstable results. The problem may be diagnosed by checking the bivariate correlations between the variables and by measuring **tolerance.** Multicollinearity may be dealt with either by excluding specific variables altogether or by merging several similar variables into one composite index.

Key Terms

biased Describing a statistic when its estimate of a population parameter does not center on the true value. In regression analysis, the omission of relevant independent variables will lead to bias in the estimate of Y. When relevant independent variables are omitted and those measures are related to an independent variable included in regression analysis, then the estimate of the effect of that variable will also be biased.

correctly specified regression model A regression model in which the researcher has taken into account all of the relevant predictors of the dependent variable and has measured them correctly.

dummy variable A binary nominal-level variable that is included in a multivariate regression model.

multicollinearity Condition in a multivariate regression model in which independent variables examined are very strongly intercorrelated. Multicollinearity leads to unstable regression coefficients.

multivariate regression A technique for predicting change in a dependent variable, using more than one independent variable.

randomized experiment A type of study in which the effect of one variable can be examined in isolation through random allocation of subjects to treatment and control, or comparison, groups.

standardized regression coefficient (Beta) Weighted or standardized estimate of b that takes into account the standard deviation of the independent and the dependent variables. The standardized regression coefficient is used to compare the effects of independent variables measured on different scales in a multivariate regression analysis.

tolerance A measure of the extent of the intercorrelations of each independent variable with all other independent variables. Tolerance may be used to test for multicollinearity in a multivariate regression model.

Symbols and Formulas

k Number of independent variables in the overall regression model

r_{Y,X_1} Correlation coefficient for Y and X_1

r_{Y,X_2} Correlation coefficient for Y and X_2

r_{X_1,X_2} Correlation coefficient for X_1 and X_2

s_Y Standard deviation for Y

s_{X_1} Standard deviation for X_1

R^2_{fm} R^2 obtained for the full regression model

R^2_{rm} R^2 obtained for the reduced regression model

k_{fm} Number of independent variables in the full regression model

k_{rm} Number of independent variables in the reduced regression model

R^2_X R^2 obtained when an independent variable is treated as a dependent variable in a test for tolerance

To calculate a multivariate regression coefficient for two independent variables:

$$b_{X_1} = \left(\frac{r_{Y,X_1} - (r_{Y,X_2} r_{X_1,X_2})}{1 - r^2_{X_1,X_2}} \right) \left(\frac{s_Y}{s_{X_1}} \right)$$

and

$$b_{X_2} = \left(\frac{r_{Y,X_2} - (r_{Y,X_1} r_{X_1,X_2})}{1 - r^2_{X_1,X_2}} \right) \left(\frac{s_Y}{s_{X_2}} \right)$$

A sample multivariate regression model with three independent variables:

$$Y = b_0 + b_1 X_1 + b_2 X_2 + b_3 X_3 + e$$

A population multivariate regression model with three independent variables:

$$Y = \beta_0 + \beta_1 X_1 + \beta_2 X_2 + \beta_3 X_3 + \epsilon$$

To calculate the standardized coefficient (Beta):

$$\text{Beta} = b \left(\frac{s_X}{s_Y} \right)$$

To calculate an F-test on a subset of variables in a regression model:

$$F = \frac{(R_{fm}^2 - R_{rm}^2)/(k_{fm} - k_{rm})}{(1 - R_{fm}^2)/(N - k_{fm} - 1)}$$

To calculate tolerance:

$$\text{Tolerance} = 1 - R_X^2$$

Exercises

16.1 Consider the following regression model, which purports to predict the length of sentence given to convicted thieves:

$$Y = b_0 + bX + e$$

where Y = length of sentence

X = number of prior sentences

a. List the variables you might wish to include in a more comprehensive model. Include a brief statement about why each additional variable should be included.

b. Present your model in equation form.

16.2 In an article in the newspaper, a researcher claims that low self-esteem is the cause of crime. Upon closer inspection of the results in the paper, you learn that the researcher has computed a bivariate model using self-reported theft as the dependent variable (Y) and self-esteem as the one independent variable (X).

a. List the variables you might wish to include in a more comprehensive model. Include a brief statement about why each additional variable should be included.

b. Present your model in equation form.

16.3 A researcher has built a multivariate regression model to predict the effect of prior offenses and years of education on the length of sentence received by 100 convicted burglars. He feeds the data into a computer package and obtains the following printout:

Dependent Variable (Y): Length of Sentence (months)

Independent Variable (X1): Number of Prior Offenses

Independent Variable (X2): Years of Education

F sig = 0.018

R Square = 0.16

X1: b = +0.4   Sig t = 0.023

X2: b = −0.3   Sig t = 0.310

Evaluate the results, taking care to explain the meaning of each of the statistics produced by the computer.

16.4   An analysis of the predictors of physical violence at school produced the following results:

Independent Variable	b	Beta
Age (Years)	0.21	0.05
Sex (Female = 1, Male = 0)	−3.78	0.07
Race (White = 1, Nonwhite = 0)	−1.34	0.06
Number of friends arrested	1.96	0.33
Number of times attacked by others	3.19	0.24
Number of times hit by parents	2.05	0.27

Explain what each regression coefficient (b) and standardized regression coefficient (Beta) means in plain English.

16.5   Danny has obtained figures on the amount of drugs seized per month at a seaport over the course of two years. He wishes to explain variations in the amount of drugs seized per month and runs a regression analysis to check the effect of his independent variable—the total number of customs officers on duty for each month—on the quantity of drugs seized. The resulting regression coefficient is +4.02. Danny is worried, however, that his bivariate model might not be correctly specified, and he decides to add another variable—the number of ships that arrive at the port each month. He calculates the correlations between the three pairs of variables, and the results are as follows:

Y (drugs seized), X_1 (customs officers): +0.55

Y (drugs seized), X_2 (ships arriving): +0.60

X_1 (customs officers), X_2 (ships arriving): +0.80

The standard deviations for the three variables are 20 kg (quantity of drugs seized per month), 1.6 (number of customs officers on duty), and 22.5 (number of ships arriving).

a. Calculate the regression coefficient for customs officers.

b. Calculate the regression coefficient for ships arriving.

c. How do you account for the difference between your answer to part a and the regression coefficient of +4.02 that Danny obtained earlier?

16.6   A study of prison violence examined the effects of two independent variables—percent of inmates sentenced for a violent crime (X_1) and average amount of space per inmate (X_2)—on the average number of violent acts per day (Y). All variables were measured for a random selection of cell blocks in three prisons. The researcher reported the following results:

$$r_{Y,X_1} = 0.20$$

$$r_{Y,X_2} = 0.41$$

$$r_{X_1,X_2} = 0.05$$

$$s_Y = 0.35$$

$$s_{X_1} = 10.52$$

$$s_{X_2} = 2.64$$

a. Calculate the regression coefficients for the effects of X_1 and X_2 on Y. Explain what these coefficients mean in plain English.

b. Calculate the standardized regression coefficients for the effects of X_1 and X_2 on Y. Explain what these coefficients mean in plain English.

c. Which one of the variables has the largest effect on prison violence? Explain why.

16.7 A study of recidivism classified offenders by type of punishment received: prison, jail, probation, fine, or community service. A researcher interested in the effects of these different punishments analyzes data on a sample of 967 offenders. She computes two regression models. In the first, she includes variables for age, sex, race, number of prior arrests, severity of the last conviction offense, and length of punishment. The R^2 for this model is 0.27. In the second model, she adds four dummy variables for jail, probation, fine, and community service, using prison as the reference category. The R^2 for this model is 0.35. Explain whether the type of punishment had an effect on recidivism (assume a 5% significance level).

16.8 A public opinion poll of 471 randomly selected adult respondents asked about their views on the treatment of offenders by the courts. Expecting race/ethnicity to be related to views about the courts, a researcher classifies respondents as African American, Hispanic, and white. To test for the effect of race/ethnicity, he computes one regression using information about the age, sex, income, and education of the respondents and finds the R^2 for this model to be 0.11. In a second regression, he adds two dummy variables for African American and Hispanic, using white as the reference category. The R^2 for this second model is 0.16. Explain whether the race/ethnicity of the respondent had a statistically significant effect on views about the courts (assume a 5% significance level).

16.9 Rachel collects police data on a series of burglaries and wishes to determine the factors that influence the amount of property stolen in each case. She creates a multivariate regression model and runs a test of tolerance for each of the independent variables. Her results are as follows, where Y = Amount of property stolen (\$):

Independent Variable	Scale	Tolerance
X_1: Time of robbery (A.M. or P.M.)	Nominal	0.98
X_2: Accessibility of property	Ordinal	0.94
X_3: Number of rooms in house	Interval	0.12
X_4: Size of house	Interval	0.12
X_5: Joint income of family	Interval	0.46

Would you advise Rachel to make any changes to her model? Explain your answer.

16.10 A researcher examining neighborhood crime rates computes a regression model using the following variables:

Y = crime rate (per 100,000)

X_1 = percent living in poverty

X_2 = percent unemployed

X_3 = median income

X_4 = percent of homes being rented

The researcher finds the F-statistic for the overall model to be statistically significant (with $\alpha = 0.05$), but the results for each variable are as follows:

Independent Variable	b	Sig.	Tolerance
Percent living in poverty	52.13	0.17	0.15
Percent unemployed	39.95	0.23	0.07
Median income	22.64	0.12	0.19
Percent of homes being rented	27.89	0.33	0.05

a. Explain why the researcher found a statistically significant regression model, but no significant regression coefficients.

b. What would you recommend the researcher do in this case?

Computer Exercises

Multivariate Regression Analysis

In Chapter 15, we explored the basic features of the regression command in SPSS in the computation of a bivariate regression model. To compute a multivariate regression model, we simply add additional independent variables to the independent variables box. The following exercises illustrate some of the additional features of the regression command.

Standardized Regression Coefficients (Betas)

The standardized regression coefficients (Betas) are part of the standard output for SPSS's regression command. In the table of results presenting the coefficients, the standardized coefficients are located in the column following those presenting the values for the regression coefficients (b) and the standard errors of b. Nothing else is required to obtain the standardized coefficients.

F-Test for a Subset of Variables

There are two ways to obtain an F-test on a subset of variables in SPSS, neither of which is particularly convenient. The only direct way to obtain an F-test on a subset of variables requires use of SPSS syntax—the SPSS programming language. Since we have focused on the use of menus in SPSS, we will not discuss this command. However, should you have an interest in pursuing this option through the use of the syntax language, assistance is available through the SPSS help command.

You can obtain all the information you need for an F-test in a relatively straightforward manner, however, and then enter the values into Equation 16.4. The process involves entering what SPSS refers to as blocks of variables. When you are prompted for independent variables, note the reference to "Block 1 of 1" above the independent variables box. To obtain the R^2 results needed for an F-test, you begin by entering the variables in the reduced model into the first block of variables. After entering these variables into the independent variable list, you click on the "Next" button to enter a second block of variables. Your second group of variables (i.e., the second block of variables), which might include a group of dummy variables indicating a multicategory nominal variable, is entered into the independent variables box.

After you click on "OK" to run the regression command with two blocks of independent variables, note that the output window now contains expanded tables for Model Summary, ANOVA, and Coefficients. In the first row of each table, you will find the results for the reduced model: the model with only the variables entered in the first block of independent variables. The second row of each table presents the results for the full model.

To calculate an F-statistic for a subset of variables, use the values for R^2 presented in the Model Summary table. The R^2 for the reduced model (i.e., R^2_{rm}) is given in the first row, and the R^2 for the full model (i.e., R^2_{fm}) is given in the second row. The numbers of independent variables in the two models (k_{fm} and k_{rm}) are indicated by the df for the regression model and presented in the ANOVA table. The sample size used in the analysis is given by adding 1 to the total df given in the ANOVA table. You would then enter these values into Equation 16.4 to calculate the value of F.

Collinearity Diagnostics

SPSS's regression command will produce an assortment of collinearity statistics, including the tolerance statistic discussed earlier. To obtain the collinearity diagnostics, click on the "Statistics" button when you enter the variable names for the dependent and independent variables. In the middle of the new window that opens, you will see an option for "Collinearity diagnostics." Select this item to have SPSS compute collinearity statistics.

After the regression command is run, the collinearity output is split across two tables. The tolerance statistics are presented in the Coefficients table, where you will also find the regression coefficients. Recall from the previous discussion that a tolerance statistic of less than about 0.20 is indicative of collinearity problems in a regression model.

Residual Analysis

It is also possible with the regression command to analyze residuals in ways ranging from simple to complex. Perhaps the most straightforward way of analyzing residuals is graphically, through the use of a residual plot that SPSS can produce. To obtain this graph, click on the "Plots" button in the regression window. In the new window that opens, you will be presented with several different ways of graphing residuals. The most straightforward plot is listed in the lower left corner of this window under "Standardized Residual Plots." The "Histogram" option will generate a simple histogram of residuals for your analysis and overlay a normal curve so that you can see how closely the residuals approximate a normal distribution. If the residuals do not resemble a normal distribution, this is often an indication of a problem with the regression model, such as one or more relevant independent variables having been omitted from the analysis.

1.   Enter the data from Table 16.2. Run the regression command to reproduce the unstandardized and standardized regression coefficients presented in this chapter.

   a. Have SPSS compute the tolerance statistics for the two independent variables in the analysis. What can you conclude about collinearity with these data?

   b. Compute two bivariate regression models, using years in prison as the independent variable in one regression and prior arrests as the independent variable in the second regression. Generate a histogram of the residuals for each regression model. What does the pattern of results in this plot suggest to you about the distribution of error terms?

   c. Compute the multivariate model, and generate a histogram of the residuals for this regression model. How has the pattern of error terms changed relative to the two histograms produced in part b?

Open the **nys_1.sav** data file into SPSS to do Exercises 2 through 5.

2.   Compute a multivariate regression model, using number of times the student hit other students as the dependent variable. From the variables included in the data file, select at least five independent variables that you think have some relationship to hitting other students.

   a. Compute the tolerance statistic for each of the independent variables. Does it appear that there are problems with collinearity in this regression model? Explain why.

b. Generate a histogram of the residuals for this regression model. What does the pattern of results in this plot suggest to you about the distribution of error terms?

3. Compute a multivariate regression model, using number of times something worth $5 or less has been stolen as the dependent variable. From the variables included in the data file, select at least five independent variables that you think have some relationship to stealing something worth $5 or less.

   a. Compute the tolerance statistic for each of the independent variables. Does it appear that there are problems with collinearity in this regression model? Explain why.

   b. Generate a histogram of the residuals for this regression model. What does the pattern of results in this plot suggest to you about the distribution of error terms?

4. Compute a multivariate regression model, using number of times the student cheated on exams as the dependent variable. From the variables included in the data file, select at least five independent variables that you think have some relationship to cheating on exams.

   a. Compute the tolerance statistic for each of the independent variables. Does it appear that there are problems with collinearity in this regression model? Explain why.

   b. Generate a histogram of the residuals for this regression model. What does the pattern of results in this plot suggest to you about the distribution of error terms?

5. Compute a multivariate regression model, using number of times drunk as the dependent variable. Use age, sex, race, employment status, hours spent studying per week, grade point average, and number of friends who use alcohol as the independent variables.

   a. Use an F-test to test whether demographic characteristics—age, sex, and race—affect drinking behavior.

   b. Use an F-test to test whether academic characteristics—hours spent studying per week and grade point average—affect drinking behavior.

   c. Compute the tolerance statistic for each of the independent variables. Does it appear that there are problems with collinearity in this regression model? Explain why.

   d. Generate a histogram of the residuals for this regression model. What does the pattern of results in this plot suggest to you about the distribution of error terms?

c h a p t e r   s e v e n t e e n

Logistic Regression

logistic regression as a tool
for examining a dichotomous dependent variable

Why Is It Inappropriate to Use OLS Regression for a Dichotomous
Dependent Variable?

What Shape Does the Logistic Model Curve Take?

How Is the Outcome Altered in a Logistic Regression Model?

interpreting logistic regression coefficients

Why Is It Difficult to Interpret the Logistic Regression Coefficient?

What Is an Odds Ratio and How Is It Interpreted?

What Is the Derivative at Mean and How Is It Interpreted?

comparing logistic regression
coefficients within a single model

How Can Probability Estimates Be Used to Compare the Strength of Logistic
Regression Coefficients?

What Is the Standardized Logistic Regression Coefficient and How Is It
Interpreted?

evaluating the logistic regression model

How Is the Percent of Correct Predictions Interpreted?

What Is Pseudo R^2 and How Is It Interpreted?

testing for statistical significance

What Is the Test of Statistical Significance for the Overall Logistic Regression
Model?

What Is the Test of Statistical Significance for the Logistic Regression Coefficient?

What Is the Test of Statistical Significance for a Multicategory Nominal Variable?

O RDINARY LEAST SQUARES REGRESSION is a very useful tool for identifying how one or a series of independent variables affects an interval-level dependent variable. As noted in Chapter 16, this method may also be used—though with caution—to explain dependent variables that are measured at an ordinal level. But what should the researcher do when faced with a binary or dichotomous dependent variable? Such situations are common in criminology and criminal justice. For example, in examining sentencing practices, the researcher may want to explain why certain defendants get a prison sentence while others do not. In assessing the success of a drug treatment program, the researcher may be interested in whether offenders failed a drug test or whether they returned to prison within a fixed follow-up period. In each of these examples, the variable that the researcher seeks to explain is a simple binary outcome. It is not appropriate to examine binary dependent variables using the regression methods that we have reviewed thus far.

This chapter introduces a type of regression analysis that allows us to examine a dichotomous dependent variable. Called logistic regression analysis, it has become one of the analysis tools most frequently used in crime and justice research. We begin the chapter by explaining why the OLS regression approach described in Chapters 15 and 16 is not appropriate when the dependent variable is binary. We then describe the logistic regression approach and the logic underlying it. Finally, we illustrate the interpretation of logistic regression statistics in the context of a substantive criminal justice research example. In this chapter, as in Chapter 16, our focus will be more on explaining how logistic regression can be used in research than on describing the mathematical properties that underlie the computations used to develop logistic regression statistics.

Why Is It Inappropriate to Use OLS Regression for a Dichotomous Dependent Variable?

In Chapter 16, you saw that we could use not only interval-level variables, but also ordinal- and nominal-level variables, as independent measures in a multivariate ordinary least squares regression. While we emphasized that the assumptions regarding measurement of the dependent variable are much more stringent in OLS regression, even in the case of the dependent variable the researcher may sometimes decide to use ordinal- as well as interval-level variables. But applying the OLS regression approach is inappropriate when the dependent variable is nominal, as is the case with a binary or dichotomous dependent variable.

Why do we state this rule so unequivocally? One reason is that the logic underlying our explanation of a dichotomous dependent variable is at odds with the models that we build using the OLS regression approach. In order to expand on this idea, we need to return to how predictions are developed using OLS regression. In the simple linear model—the OLS model—we predict the value of Y based on an equation that takes into account the values of a Y-intercept (b_0) and one or a series of independent variables (e.g., b_1X_1). This model is represented below for a bivariate regression example in which we seek to explain the yearly budget of police departments based on the number of officers employed.

$$Y = b_0 + b_1X_1$$

where Y = yearly police department budget in dollars

          X_1 = number of sworn officers

This is an additive model, in which we predict the value of Y—in this case, the yearly police department budget in dollars—by adding the value of the Y-intercept to the value of the regression coefficient times the value of X_1 (the number of sworn officers in a department).

Let's say that a representative sample of police agencies were surveyed and analysis of the responses yielded the following regression equation:

$$Y = 100,000 + 100,000X_1$$

This equation suggests that for each additional officer employed, the department budget is expected to increase by $100,000. For a police agency with 100 officers, we would expect a budget of about $10,100,000:

> **W** orking It Out
>
> $Y = 100,000 + 100,000X_1$
>
> $= 100,000 + 100,000(100)$
>
> $= 100,000 + 10,000,000$
>
> $= 10,100,000$

For a police agency with 1,000 officers, we would expect a budget of about \$100,100,000:

> **W** orking It Out
>
> $Y = 100,000 + 100,000X_1$
>
> $= 100,000 + 100,000(1,000)$
>
> $= 100,000 + 100,000,000$
>
> $= 100,100,000$

This model, like other OLS regression models, assumes that there is no real limit to the value that the dependent variable can attain. With each additional officer comes an expected increase in the departmental budget. Our model suggests that the increase is about \$100,000 for each additional officer. While this logic makes very good sense when we are speaking about interval-scale measures, such as the budget of a police agency, does it make sense when we are dealing with a dichotomous dependent variable, such as whether a parolee has failed a drug test?

Let's say that we surveyed 30 parolees who had been tested for drug use. Our independent variable is prior drug arrests. The data in Table 17.1 report whether a parolee failed the drug test and also give the number of prior drug arrests for each parolee. We have coded a failed drug test as 1 and a successful drug test as 0. Table 17.2 provides the OLS regression results for our example. The OLS regression suggests a very strong relationship between prior drug arrests and failing the drug test. But if we look more closely at the regression model, we can see that this approach may lead to outcomes that are not consistent with the processes we seek to understand.

Figure 17.1 shows the data points for our example in a scatterplot, as well as the regression line drawn from the outcomes in Table 17.2. It is

Table 17.1

Drug Testing Results and Prior Drug Arrests for 30 Parolees

DRUG TEST RESULT	DRUG TEST SCORE	NUMBER OF DRUG ARRESTS
Pass	0	0
Pass	0	0
Pass	0	0
Pass	0	0
Pass	0	0
Fail	1	0
Pass	0	1
Pass	0	1
Pass	0	1
Pass	0	1
Pass	0	1
Pass	0	1
Fail	1	2
Fail	1	2
Fail	1	2
Fail	1	2
Fail	1	2
Fail	1	3
Fail	1	3
Pass	0	3
Fail	1	4
Fail	1	4
Fail	1	4
Fail	1	5
Fail	1	5
Fail	1	5
Fail	1	6
Fail	1	6
Fail	1	7
Fail	1	8

Table 17.2

OLS Regression Results for Example
of Drug Testing and Prior Drug Arrests

Model		Unstandardized Coefficients		Standardized Coefficients	t	Sig.
		B	Std. Error	Beta		
1	(Constant)	.211	.104		2.025	.052
	Drug Arrests	0.148	.030	.681	4.921	.000

a Dependent Variable: FAILURE ON DRUG TEST

| Figure 17.1 | *Scatterplot of Example of Drug Testing with the Predicted Regression Line* |

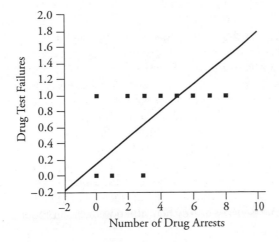

Note: In this scatterplot (produced using SPSS), the points sometimes represent more than one observation.

clear that the OLS regression approach leads to predicted outcomes that are not possible, given our dependent variable. For example, for a parolee with six drug arrests, our model predicts that Y will have a value of 1.099:

W orking It Out

$$Y = 0.211 + 0.148X$$
$$= 0.211 + 0.148(6)$$
$$= 0.211 + 0.888$$
$$= 1.099$$

For a parolee with eight drug arrests, our model predicts that Y will have a value of 1.395:

W orking It Out

$$Y = 0.211 + 0.148X$$
$$= 0.211 + 0.148(8)$$
$$= 0.211 + 1.184$$
$$= 1.395$$

But in our example, the predicted value of Y should logically be no greater than 1 or no less than 0. A value of 1 means that the parolee failed the drug test, and a value of 0 means that the parolee passed the drug test. Predicting values greater than 1 or less than 0 just does not make sense given the possible outcomes of a binary dependent variable.

This example, then, illustrates a logical problem in using OLS methods to gain estimates for cases where the dependent variable is dichotomous. The OLS approach assumes that there is no limit to the predicted value of the dependent variable. But in the case of a dichotomous dependent variable, there are limits—the values 0 and 1. While this assumption of predictions within the limits of the possible outcomes of the dependent variable is also violated when OLS regression is used for an ordinal-level dependent variable and sometimes when it is applied to specific interval-level measures, the violation is most extreme in the case of a binary dependent variable, such as drug testing failures. It does not make sense to analyze such situations with a model that allows the value of Y to increase at a constant rate for each change in the value of X. For our analysis to be consistent with the problem we are examining, it must provide predictions that are constrained to values between 0 and 1.

Figure 17.1 illustrates additional problems that arise in using the OLS method in a case where the dependent variable is dichotomous. In our discussion of excluded variables in Chapter 16, we noted that a central assumption of the regression approach is that there is no systematic relationship between the error term and the independent variables included in the regression. When a systematic relationship exists, estimates of the regression coefficients are likely to be biased. But if you look at parolees for whom the value of prior drug arrests is greater than 5 (see Figure 17.1), you can see that there is a consistent relationship between the regression error and the independent variable. Because the actual value of Y cannot be greater than 1, and the predicted values continue to increase in a linear fashion (as evidenced by the regression line), the regression error increases in the negative direction as the number of prior drug arrests increases. This means that as the number of prior drug arrests gets larger and larger, we will make larger and larger negative errors in prediction. When OLS regression is used to examine a binary dependent variable, we are very likely to have a systematic relationship between the independent variable and the errors we make in predicting Y, because Y-values are constrained to 0 and 1 and predicted values of Y have no limit.

Figure 17.1 also illustrates why, when we examine a dichotomous dependent variable, we violate assumptions important to making statistical inferences with OLS regression. We noted in Chapter 15 that two parametric assumptions of our tests of statistical significance in regression are that the values of X are normally distributed around the regression line and that they meet an assumption of homoscedasticity (equal variances around the regression line). The normality assumption is clearly violated when we have a dichotomous dependent variable. As Figure 17.1 shows, the shape of the distribution of X around Y will be bimodal because the observed values of our dependent variable are constrained in practice to 0 and 1. However, if our sample is large enough, we generally allow violations of this assumption. Our problem in regard to homoscedasticity is more serious. We noted in Chapter 15 that violations of the assumption of homoscedasticity must be large before they become a concern. In the case of a binary dependent variable, heteroscedasticity (violation of the homoscedasticity assumption) is likely to be large. As shown in Figure 17.1 for our distribution of drug testing failures, the distribution of the scores of X around the regression line is likely to vary widely in form, depending on the scores of the independent variable.

Logistic Regression

While the application of OLS regression methods to a dichotomous dependent variable raises a number of substantive and statistical concerns, there are many advantages to the basic form of the regression approach introduced in previous chapters. For example, the effect of each b was constant. That is, we could define a single constant effect for each variable in the regression model. That effect took into account the other variables in the model. And we could add all of these effects and the Y-intercept to get a predicted value for Y. Because of the utility of the regression approach, statisticians have developed alternative methods for conducting regression analysis with dichotomous dependent variables that do not violate basic assumptions but allow us to continue to use the overall regression approach. Perhaps the most widely used of these methods is **logistic regression analysis.**[1] Logistic regression analysis is

[1] A method called generalized least squares might also be used to deal with violations of our assumptions, though logistic regression analysis is generally the preferred method. See E. A. Hanushek and J. E. Jackson, *Statistical Methods for Social Scientists* (New York: Academic Press, 1977) for a comparison of these approaches. See also David W. Hosmer and Stanley Lemeshow, *Applied Regression Analysis*, 2nd ed. (New York: Wiley, 2000). Another method, probit regression analysis, is very similar to that presented here, though it is based on the standard normal distribution rather than the logistic model curve. The estimates gained from probit regression are likely to be very similar to those gained from logistic regression. Because logistic regression analysis has become much more widely used and is available in most statistical software packages, we focus on logistic regression in this chapter.

based on a transformation of the regression model that allows the outcomes of the regression equation to vary without limit, but constrains the predictions of the dependent variable to values between 0 and 1. At the same time, the inferential statistics used in logistic regression do not rely on assumptions regarding the population distribution of scores.

In fitting the data that are analyzed, logistic regression analysis uses the logic of a curve rather than that of a straight line. Figure 17.2 shows the **logistic model curve** for the probability that $Y = 1$. While the logistic regression curve follows the linear model in the middle of its distribution, it does not allow values below 0 or above 1. Indeed, as the logistic curve approaches 0 or 1, it begins to flatten, so it keeps coming closer to—but never actually reaches—either of these two values. The logistic curve thus satisfies our primary objection to the linear OLS regression method. That is, it does not allow predictions greater than or less than the actual values of the distribution of scores that we are trying to predict.

The logistic model curve provides a solution to the problem of predictions beyond the observed distribution. However, in order to gain the desired property of outcomes between 0 and 1, we have to alter the form of our regression equation. Using OLS regression, we represent our equation for the prediction of Y with one independent variable as follows:

$$Y = b_0 + b_1 X_1$$

As noted earlier, this approach may yield values that are greater than 1 or less than 0, as was the case in our drug testing example.

Figure 17.2   *The Logistic Model Curve*

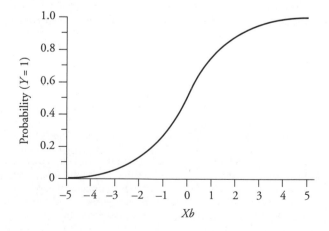

In logistic regression, we alter the form of what we are trying to predict. Rather than predicting Y, as in OLS regression, we now predict the natural logarithm (ln) of the odds of getting a 1 on the dependent variable. Although this sounds very imposing, it is simply a transformation of the equation presented above. Equation 17.1 represents the prediction equation for a bivariate logistic regression:

$$\ln\left(\frac{P(Y=1)}{1-P(Y=1)}\right) = \ln\left(\frac{P(Y=1)}{P(Y=0)}\right) = b_0 + b_1 X_1 \qquad \text{Equation 17.1}$$

There is no change on the right side of this equation. We have the constant b_0 and the regression coefficient b_1 that reflects a constant effect for the independent variable examined. Moreover, the outcome of this formula has no limit. But on the left side of the equation, we now have **the natural logarithm of the odds of Y,** or what statisticians call the **logit of Y.** A **logarithm,** or log, is the exponent of the power to which a fixed number (called a base) must be raised to produce another number. So, for example, if the base is 10, the logarithm of 100 is 2. That is, if we take 10 to the 2nd power (10^2), we get 100. In logistic regression, we do not use a base of 10, which is associated with what is called the common logarithm; rather, we use a base of 2.71828, which is associated with what is called the natural logarithm and is represented in symbol form as ln. The base of the natural logarithm, 2.71828, is also known as Euler's constant and is denoted by the symbol e. What this means is that $\ln(x)$ is the power to which e must be raised to get x.

What about the notation $P(Y=1)/[1-P(Y=1)]$ in Equation 17.1? This represents the odds of getting an outcome of 1, rather than 0, on the dependent variable. The odds are determined by dividing the probability of getting a 1 [$P(Y=1)$] by the probability of not getting a 1 [$1-P(Y=1)$]. In our drug testing example, this would be the odds of failing a drug test divided by those of not failing the test. If an individual had an 80% predicted likelihood of failing the drug test, then the odds would be 0.80/0.20, or 4 to 1.

W orking It Out

$$\text{Odds} = \frac{P(Y=1)}{1-P(Y=1)}$$

$$= \frac{0.80}{0.20}$$

$$= 4.0$$

We begin with the specification of the logistic regression model:

$$\ln\left(\frac{P(Y=1)}{1-P(Y=1)}\right) = b_0 + b_1 X_1$$

To simplify, we let

$$Xb = b_0 + b_1 X_1$$

and

$$P - P(Y=1) \Rightarrow 1 - P(Y=1) = 1 - P$$

Using these simplifications, we can rewrite the logistic regression equation as

$$\ln\left(\frac{P}{1-P}\right) = Xb$$

If we exponentiate both sides of the equation (i.e., take the value of e to the power of both sides of the equation), we obtain

$$e^{\ln[P/(1-P)]} = e^{Xb}$$

Then, $\ln\left(\frac{P}{1-P}\right)$ is the power to which we must raise e to get $\frac{P}{1-P}$; that is,

$$e^{\ln[P/(1-P)]} = \frac{P}{1-P}$$

If we transform this equation further, we see that it gives us the property we are looking for. That is, the predicted values of Y produced by our regression equation will vary between 0 and 1, despite the fact that the outcomes in our regression equation can reach any value between plus and minus infinity. In the box above, we show how to transform the equation so that the outcome is the probability that Y will be 1. The

This leads to rewriting the logistic regression equation as

$$\frac{P}{1-P} = e^{Xb}$$

We multiply both sides of the equation by $(1 - P)$:

$$P = e^{Xb}(1 - P) = e^{Xb} - Pe^{Xb}$$

Then we add Pe^{Xb} to both sides of the equation:

$$P + Pe^{Xb} = e^{Xb}$$

Next we rewrite the equation to pull out the common factor, P:

$$P(1 + e^{Xb}) = e^{Xb}$$

Now we divide both sides of the equation by $(1 + e^{Xb})$ to solve for P:

$$P = \frac{e^{Xb}}{1 + e^{Xb}} = \frac{1}{\left(\dfrac{1 + e^{Xb}}{e^{Xb}}\right)} = \frac{1}{\left(\dfrac{1}{e^{Xb}} + 1\right)}$$

$$= \frac{1}{1 + e^{-Xb}}$$

Since, as noted above, $P = P(Y = 1)$,

$$P(Y = 1) = \frac{1}{1 + e^{-Xb}}$$

end result is a simple equation that can be calculated on a hand calculator with a natural log function. This equation is often called the **cumulative logistic probability function.**

$$P(Y = 1) = \frac{1}{1 + e^{-(b_0 + b_1 X_1)}}$$

Equation 17.2

By using the term Xb to represent the right side of the regression equation, we may write Equation 17.2 more generally to take into account any number of independent variables:

$$P(Y = 1) = \frac{1}{1 + e^{-Xb}}$$

Equation 17.3

What this equation does is divide 1 by the sum of 1 and e (the value 2.71828) taken to the $-Xb$ power. The process of taking a number to some power is referred to as exponentiation. Here we exponentiate e to the power $-Xb$. Exponentiation may also be familiar to you as the antilog or inverse log.[2]

Table 17.3

Illustration of the Fact That $P(Y = 1)$ Will Not Exceed 1 or Be Less Than 0

Xb	$P(Y = 1)$
−25	0.000000000014
−20	0.000000002061
−15	0.000000305902
−10	0.000045397669
−5	0.006692850924
−4	0.017986209962
−3	0.047425873178
−2	0.119202922022
−1	0.268941421370
0	0.500000000000
1	0.731058578630
2	0.880797077978
3	0.952574126822
4	0.982013790038
5	0.993307149076
10	0.999954602131
15	0.999999694098
20	0.999999997939
25	0.999999999986

[2]Your calculator likely has a button labeled "e^x," which performs this operation. If there is no e^x button, then you should be able to locate a button labeled "INV" and another for the natural logarithm, ln. By pushing "INV" and then "ln" (the inverse or antilog), you will be able to perform this operation.

Importantly, whatever the value associated with Xb, the value of $P(Y = 1)$ will always be between 0 and 1. The value of $P(Y = 1)$ can get closer and closer to 1 or to 0, but it will never exceed that number. This is illustrated in Table 17.3, where we take very large negative and positive values of Xb. As the values get very large, the gain for each increase in Xb becomes smaller and smaller. Logistic regression, then, allows us to use the traditional regression format in which the outcome, Xb, can achieve any size without limit. However, since we have converted what we are predicting to the logit of Y, our predictions of Y are bounded by 0 and 1.

Use of the natural logarithm of the odds of Y, or the logit of Y, has allowed us to develop a regression model in which the predicted outcomes of Y are constrained between 0 and 1. But what does a prediction between the values 0 and 1 mean? As we have already noted, the observed outcomes for a dichotomous dependent variable have a score of either 0 or 1. For example, in our drug testing example, either parolees failed the drug test (coded as 1) or they passed the test (coded as 0). When we examined the regression approach in previous chapters, the predicted value of Y was simply one of the possible values in the distribution of scores on our interval-level measure. With a dichotomous dependent variable, our interpretation must be different. The predicted value of Y in this case is the predicted probability of getting an outcome of 1. So, for example, a value of 0.50 in our drug testing example would mean that, according to our model, an individual was predicted to have about an equal chance of failing and not failing drug testing. A value of 0.90 would suggest that an individual was highly likely to have a drug testing failure.

To estimate the coefficients of a logistic regression, we use a much more complex mathematical process than was used in OLS regression. It is based on **maximum likelihood estimation (MLE)** techniques. Using these techniques, we try to maximize the probability that our regression estimates will produce a distribution similar to that of the observed data. With this approach, we do not simply derive a single mathematical solution for obtaining the regression estimates.[3] Rather, we begin by identifying a tentative solution, which we then try to improve upon. Our criterion for improvement is termed a likelihood function. A likelihood function measures the probability of observing the

---

[3]It should be noted, however, that maximum likelihood techniques do not always require an iterative process.

results in the sample, given the coefficient estimates in our model. By convention in logistic regression, we use -2 times the natural logarithm of the likelihood function (or **−2LL**), which is defined as the **log likelihood function.** We repeat this process again and again, until the change in the likelihood function is considered negligible. Each time we repeat the process and reestimate our coefficients is called an **iteration.** Logistic regression is said to be an iterative procedure, because it tries a number of solutions before arriving at a final result—or, in statistical terms, converging.

Most packaged statistical programs set a default limit on the number of iterations that can be tried. In SPSS, that limit is 20 iterations. **Lack of convergence** in a standard number of iterations may indicate some type of problem in the regression model. Often, it occurs when the number of variables examined is large relative to the number of cases in the study. John Tukey, a noted statistician who taught at Princeton University, has suggested a rule for logistic regression: that there be at least five cases and preferably at least ten in the smaller category of the dependent variable for each independent variable examined.[4] Whatever the cause, if you receive a message from a packaged statistical analysis program that your regression has failed to converge, you should look carefully at your model and your measures.

We have now looked at the basic logic of the logistic regression model. While the logistic regression model differs from the OLS regression model in the outcome predicted, the basic form of the additive linear model has been maintained. The right side of the equation remains an additive function of the Y-intercept and the independent variables (multiplied by their associated regression coefficients). The effect of each independent variable remains its independent effect, with the other variables in the model controlled. We also continue to be constrained by the same regression assumptions regarding correct model specification. Excluding variables from the regression will lead to bias, either in our prediction of Y or in our estimates of specific regression coefficients. The models are also sensitive to problems of multicollinearity. These concepts were reviewed in Chapter 16, but you should remember that they apply to our discussion of logistic regression.

---

[4]See John Tukey, *Report to the Special Master*, p. 5; *Report to the New Jersey Supreme Court* 27 (1997).

A Substantive Example: Adoption of Compstat in U.S. Police Agencies

Application of logistic regression to a substantive problem will help you to understand the use of logistic regression, as well as the different coefficients associated with the technique. The example we use is drawn from a Police Foundation survey of U.S. police agencies, begun in 1999 and completed in the year 2000.[5] The Police Foundation surveyed all police agencies with more than 100 sworn officers ($N = 515$) and got a response rate of 86%. A main concern of the survey was whether Compstat, a management system first developed in New York City in order to reduce crime and improve quality of life, had been widely adopted in some form by other U.S. police agencies. It was theorized that Compstat would be much more likely to be adopted by larger police agencies. Using logistic regression analysis, we will examine whether this hypothesis is supported by the Police Foundation data.

The dependent variable in our analysis is dichotomous, measuring whether the department claimed to have adopted a "Compstat-like program." The main independent variable is the number of sworn officers serving in the department at the time of survey.[6] We also include, as a second independent variable, region, which divides the country into four regions: South, West, North Central, and Northeast. For this multicategory nominal variable, we use three dummy variables to represent region and define the North Central region as the reference, or excluded, category. Our regression model (Xb) is represented in Equation 17.4:

$$Xb = b_0 + b_1X_1 + b_2X_2 + b_3X_3 + b_4X_4 \qquad \textbf{Equation 17.4}$$

where X_1 = number of sworn officers
X_2 = Northeast
X_3 = South
X_4 = West

---

[5]For a description of this study, see David Weisburd, Stephen Mastrofski, Ann Marie McNally, and Rosann Greenspan, *Compstat and Organizational Change* (Washington, DC: The Police Foundation, 2001).

[6]Departments with 1,300 or more officers were coded in our example as 1,300 officers. This transformation was used in order to take into account the fact that only 5% of the departments surveyed had more than this number of officers and their totals varied very widely relative to the overall distribution. Another solution that could be used to address the problem of outliers is to define the measure as the logarithm of the number of sworn officers, rather than the raw scores. We relied on the former solution for our example because interpretation of the coefficients is more straightforward. In an analysis of this problem, a researcher would ordinarily want to compare different transformations of the dependent variable in order to define the one that best fit the data being examined.

Table 17.4	Iteration History Using SPSS's Logistic Regression Program

Iteration History

		−2 Log likelihood	Coefficients				
Iteration			Constant	NOREAST	SOUTH	WEST	NMSWORN
Step 1	1	493.418	−1.555	.258	.629	.308	.001
	2	492.515	−1.783	.351	.795	.419	.002
	3	492.513	−1.795	.359	.805	.428	.002

a Method: Enter
b Constant is included in the model.
c Initial −2 Log Likelihood: 528.171
d Estimation terminated at iteration number 3 because log likelihood decreased by less than .010 percent.

Table 17.4 shows the iteration history for estimating this regression. As you can see, it took only three iterations to achieve convergence. The convergence criterion used in this SPSS run was that the log likelihood function declined by less than 0.010%. As noted earlier, we use −2 times the natural logarithm of the likelihood function (−2LL) to define the log likelihood function. The final coefficients listed in this table are the same as the regression coefficients (B) reported in the summary of the regression results provided in Table 17.5.

Table 17.5	Summary of the Logistic Regression Coefficients Using SPSS's Logistic Regression Program

Variables in the Equation

		B	S.E.	Wald	df	Sig.	Exp(B)
Step 1	NORTHEAST	.359	.372	.931	1	.335	1.432
	SOUTH	.805	.332	5.883	1	.015	2.237
	WEST	.428	.367	1.360	1	.244	1.534
	#SWORN	.002	.000	24.842	1	.000	1.002
	Constant	−1.795	.311	33.378	1	.000	.166

a Variable(s) entered on step 1: NORTHEAST, SOUTH, WEST, #SWORN.

We can now express our regression equation in terms of the outcomes of our analysis. Above, we defined our regression model using the term Xb:

$$Xb = b_0 + b_1X_1 + b_2X_2 + b_3X_3 + b_4X_4$$

where X_1 = number of sworn officers
  X_2 = Northeast
  X_3 = South
  X_4 = West

Inserting the values from our regression analysis, we can express the equation as follows (note that the constant in the SPSS printout is the Y-intercept, b_0):

$$Xb = -1.75 + 0.002X_1 + 0.359X_2 + 0.805X_3 + 0.428X_4$$

We can also develop predictions of Y from this model, as in the case of the OLS model. However, as explained above, our predictions of Y are not the direct outcome of our additive regression model. Rather, the probability of Y occurring was expressed in Equation 17.3 for the cumulative logistic probability function:

$$P(Y = 1) = \frac{1}{1 + e^{-Xb}}$$

For example, let's say that we want to predict the probability of a Compstat-like program in a department with 1,000 officers in the North Central region. Our first task is to define the value of Xb. We do that by applying coefficients gained in our logistic regression analysis. Because North Central is the reference category, the equation contains only the Y-intercept and the effect of the number of sworn officers:

W orking It Out

$$\begin{aligned}
Xb &= b_0 + b_1X_1 + b_2X_2 + b_3X_3 + b_4X_4 \\
&= -1.795 + 0.002(1000) + 0.359(0) + 0.805(0) + 0.428(0) \\
&= -1.795 + 0.002(1000) \\
&= -1.795 + 2 \\
&= 0.205
\end{aligned}$$

where X_1 = number of sworn officers
  X_2 = Northeast
  X_3 = South
  X_4 = West

Applying this result to our equation, we see that, according to our regression model, the probability of having a Compstat-like program in such a department is about 55%.

W orking It Out

$$P(Y = 1) = \frac{1}{1 + e^{-Xb}}$$

$$= \frac{1}{1 + e^{-0.205}}$$

$$= \frac{1}{1 + 0.8146}$$

$$= 0.55$$

For a police department in the South with 1,000 officers, the predicted probability of having a Compstat-like program is fully 73%:

W orking It Out

$$Xb = b_0 + b_1 X_1 + b_2 X_2 + b_3 X_3 + b_4 X_4$$

$$= -1.795 + 0.002(1000) + 0.359(0) + 0.805(1) + 0.428(0)$$

$$= -1.795 + 0.002(1000) + 0.805(1)$$

$$= -1.795 + 2 + 0.805$$

$$= 1.01$$

And,

$$P(Y = 1) = \frac{1}{1 + e^{-Xb}}$$

$$= \frac{1}{1 + e^{-1.01}}$$

$$= \frac{1}{1 + 0.3642}$$

$$= 0.7330$$

If we apply our prediction model to smaller departments, we see that they are less likely, according to our estimates, to have a Compstat-like program. For example, our model suggests that a police agency with only 100 officers from the South would have a probability of only 31% of having a Compstat-like program:

W orking It Out

$$Xb = b_0 + b_1X_1 + b_2X_2 + b_3X_3 + b_4X_4$$
$$= -1.795 + 0.002(100) + 0.359(0) + 0.805(1) + 0.428(0)$$
$$= -1.795 + 0.002(100) + 0.805(1)$$
$$= -1.795 + 0.2 + 0.805$$
$$= -0.79$$

And,

$$P(Y = 1) = \frac{1}{1 + e^{-Xb}}$$
$$= \frac{1}{1 + e^{-(-0.79)}}$$
$$= \frac{1}{1 + 2.2034}$$
$$= 0.3122$$

Interpreting Logistic Regression Coefficients

Using Table 17. 5, we can also define the specific effects of the variables in our model. In this case, the logistic regression coefficients are listed in the column labeled B. As expected, the coefficient for the number of sworn officers (#SWORN) is positive; that is, as the number of sworn officers increases, the likelihood of having a Compstat-like program also increases. The three dummy variables included for region also have a positive impact relative to the North Central region, which is the excluded category. This means that in the Police Foundation sample, police departments in the Northeast, West, and South regions were more likely to claim to have a Compstat-like program than those in the North Central region.

What about the exact interpretation of the logistic regression coefficient? Here, we can see the price we pay for developing a regression model in which the predictions of the probability of Y are constrained between 0 and 1. In the OLS regression case, the interpretation of b is in reference to units of measurement of Y. In the multivariate case, b represents the estimated change in Y associated with a unit change in X, when all other independent variables in the model are held constant. So a b of 2 in an OLS regression suggests that a unit increase in X is associated with a two-unit increase in Y (all other included independent variables held constant).

The interpretation of the **logistic regression coefficient** is not as straightforward. Our regression equation is predicting not Y, but the logarithm of the odds of getting a 1—or, in our example, the log of the odds of having a Compstat-like program. In a multivariate logistic regression, b represents the estimated change in the log of the odds of Y occurring when all other independent variables are held constant. The coefficient for number of sworn officers is 0.002, meaning that each additional officer increases by 0.002 the log of the odds of having a Compstat-like program. While some researchers may have an intuitive understanding of the change in the log of the odds, the transformation of the outcome measure in the logistic regression model has made the regression coefficients very difficult to explain or interpret in a way that nonstatisticians will understand.

The Odds Ratio

To make results easier to understand, statisticians have developed other methods of interpreting logistic regression coefficients. An approach commonly used is to report the regression coefficient in terms of its odds ratio. The **odds ratio,** sometimes called the exponent of B, is reported as Exp(B) in the SPSS printout in Table 17.5. The odds ratio represents the impact of a one-unit change in X on the ratio of the probability of an event occurring to the probability of the event not occurring. Equation 17.5 defines the odds ratio in terms of the calculation of the odds for two events separated by a change of one unit in X:

$$\text{Odds ratio} = \frac{\left[\dfrac{P(Y=1)}{1-P(Y=1)}\right]_X}{\left[\dfrac{P(Y=1)}{1-P(Y=1)}\right]_{X-1}} \qquad \textbf{Equation 17.5}$$

where $P(Y=1) = \dfrac{1}{1+e^{-Xb}}$

An odds ratio greater than 1 indicates that the odds of getting a 1 on the dependent variable *increase* when the independent variable *increases*. An odds ratio less than 1 indicates that the odds of getting a 1 on the dependent variable *decreases* when the independent variable *increases*. For our example, an odds ratio greater than 1 indicates that as the independent variable increases, the odds of having a Compstat-like program also increase. If the odds ratio were 3, for example, then a one-unit change in

X would make the event Y about three times as likely to occur. An odds ratio less than 1 would suggest that the likelihood of having a Compstat-like program decreased as the independent variable increased.

To calculate the odds ratio, we need to define the probability of getting a 1 [i.e., $P(Y = 1)$] on our dependent variable at two values, X and $X - 1$. We can choose any two consecutive values of the independent variable; our odds ratio will be the same, no matter what consecutive values we choose. Let's start with number of sworn officers. For simplicity, we will take 101 and 100 as X and $X - 1$ and we will calculate the probabilities when a department is in the North Central region. We first need to work out the odds of getting a Compstat-like program from our model for the case of 101 sworn officers. As shown below, the result is 0.2034.

W orking It Out   Number of Sworn Officers = 101

Step 1: Defining the probability of $Y = 1$.

$$Xb = b_0 + b_1X_1 + b_2X_2 + b_3X_3 + b_4X_4$$

$$= -1.795 + 0.002(101) + 0.359(0) + 0.805(0) + 0.428(0)$$

$$= -1.795 + 0.002(101)$$

$$= -1.795 + 0.202$$

$$= -1.593$$

where X_1 = number of sworn officers
X_2 = Northeast
X_3 = South
X_4 = West

Step 2: Defining $P(Y = 1)$.

$$P(Y = 1) = \frac{1}{1 + e^{-Xb}}$$

$$= \frac{1}{1 + e^{-(-1.593)}}$$

$$= \frac{1}{1 + 4.9185}$$

$$= 0.1690$$

Step 3: Defining the odds.

$$\left[\frac{P(Y = 1)}{1 - P(Y = 1)} \right]_X = \frac{0.1690}{0.8310}$$

$$= 0.2034$$

We then need to follow the same procedure for 100 sworn officers. As shown below, the odds in the case of 100 sworn officers in the North Central region are 0.2029.

W **orking It Out**   **Number of Sworn Officers = 100**

Step 1: Defining the probability of $Y = 1$.

$$Xb = b_0 + b_1X_1 + b_2X_2 + b_3X_3 + b_4X_4$$

$$= -1.795 + 0.002(100) + 0.359(0) + 0.805(0) + 0.428(0)$$

$$= -1.795 + 0.002(100)$$

$$= -1.795 + 0.2$$

$$= -1.595$$

where X_1 = number of sworn officers

X_2 = Northeast

X_3 = South

X_4 = West

Step 2: Defining $P(Y = 1)$.

$$P(Y = 1) = \frac{1}{1 + e^{-Xb}}$$

$$= \frac{1}{1 + e^{-(-1.595)}}$$

$$= \frac{1}{1 + 4.9283}$$

$$= 0.1687$$

Step 3: Defining the odds.

$$\left[\frac{P(Y = 1)}{1 - P(Y = 1)} \right]_{X-1} = \frac{0.1687}{0.8313}$$

$$= 0.2029$$

Finally, using these two odds, we can estimate our odds ratio, which is simply the ratio of these two numbers, or 1.002:

W **orking It Out**

$$\text{Odds ratio} = \frac{\left[\dfrac{P(Y=1)}{1-P(Y=1)}\right]_X}{\left[\dfrac{P(Y=1)}{1-P(Y=1)}\right]_{X-1}}$$

$$= \frac{0.2034}{0.2029}$$

$$= 1.002$$

Of course, it would be a lot easier to just look at your computer print-out, which provides the same outcome. You will probably not calculate odds ratios by hand outside your statistics class. But working out the odds ratio gives you a better understanding of what it is and where it comes from.

In Table 17.5, we see that $b = 0.002$ and Exp(B) $= 1.002$ for number of sworn officers. Instead of working through the three steps above, we can move directly from the logistic regression coefficient to the odds ratio by exponentiating the value of the coefficient b. As noted earlier in the chapter, when we exponentiate the value of the coefficient b, we take e—the value 2.71828—to the power of the coefficient b. For number of sworn officers, it is $e^{(0.002)} = 1.002$. What this means is that for any logistic regression analysis, all we need to do is exponentiate the logistic regression coefficient to calculate the odds ratio. SPSS, like most other statistical software, will automatically report the odds ratios for each of the independent variables included in the analysis.

It is important to keep in mind that the odds ratio provides an estimate for only a *single* one-unit increase in the independent variable. The odds ratio is *not* a linear function of the coefficients; thus, we cannot say that for each one-unit increase in the independent variable, the odds increase by some amount. If we are interested in a change of more than one unit in our independent variable—say 2, 5, 10, or 100 units— we multiply that number by our coefficient b and then exponentiate that value. For example, returning to the number of sworn officers, suppose we are interested in the odds of adopting a Compstat-like program for a department that added 100 officers. We multiply our coefficient of 0.002 by 100, getting a value of 0.2, and then take *e* to the power of 0.2, which gives us a value of 1.2214.

W orking It Out

Odds ratio $= e^{(0.002)(100)} = e^{(0.2)} = 1.2214$

This odds ratio tells us that the odds of adopting a Compstat-like program increase by a factor of 1.22 for a department with 100 additional officers. As an exercise, take the odds of adopting a Compstat-like program for a department with 100 officers in the North Central region (0.2029; see page 516) and calculate the odds for a department with 200 officers. Then take the ratio of these two odds—it will equal 1.2214.

Our focus on the number of sworn officers illustrates another feature of logistic regression coefficients that is easily overlooked. There are times—usually for an interval-level independent variable— when the logistic regression coefficient will appear to have a small value. Yet, when we begin to account for the range of the independent variable and start to look at increases of 10, 100, or even 1,000 in the independent variable, we may find that the odds increase by a substantial amount.

For our regional dummy variables, it should be remembered that the three measures are compared to the reference category, the North Central region. Because working out the odds ratio is tedious, we will carry out the calculations only for the South. According to the results presented in Table 17.5, the South has an associated odds ratio of 2.237, meaning that being in the South region of the country, as opposed to the North Central region, more than doubles the odds of having a Compstat-like program. As with our number of sworn officers coefficient, we get a value of 2.2367 by taking *e* to the power of 0.805, which is the logistic regression coefficient for the South region.

W orking It Out

Odds ratio $= e^{(0.805)} = 2.2367$

Alternatively, we can work through the calculation of the odds ratio to arrive at the same conclusion. Setting the number of sworn officers at 100, we will calculate the odds ratio of a Compstat-like program for the case where a department is in the South versus the case where it is in the North Central region.

W orking It Out   **Departments in the South**

Step 1: Defining the probability of $Y = 1$.

$$Xb = b_0 + b_1X_1 + b_2X_2 + b_3X_3 + b_4X_4$$

$$= -1.795 + 0.002(100) + 0.359(0) + 0.805(1) + 0.428(0)$$

$$= -1.795 + 0.002(100) + 0.805(1)$$

$$= -1.795 + 0.200 + 0.805$$

$$= -0.790$$

where X_1 = number of sworn officers
X_2 = Northeast
X_3 = South
X_4 = West

Step 2: Defining $P(Y = 1)$.

$$P(Y = 1) = \frac{1}{1 + e^{-Xb}}$$

$$= \frac{1}{1 + e^{-(-0.790)}}$$

$$= \frac{1}{1 + 2.2033}$$

$$= 0.3122$$

Step 3: Defining the odds.

$$\left[\frac{P(Y = 1)}{1 - P(Y = 1)}\right]_X = \frac{0.3122}{0.6878}$$

$$= 0.4539$$

W orking It Out   **Departments in the North Central Region**

Step 1: Defining the probability of $Y = 1$.

$$Xb = b_0 + b_1X_1 + b_2X_2 + b_3X_3 + b_4X_4$$
$$= -1.795 + 0.002(100) + 0.359(0) + 0.805(0) + 0.428(0)$$
$$= -1.795 + 0.002(100)$$
$$= -1.795 + 0.2$$
$$= -1.595$$

where X_1 = number of sworn officers
X_2 = Northeast
X_3 = South
X_4 = West

Step 2: Defining $P(Y = 1)$.

$$P(Y = 1) = \frac{1}{1 + e^{-Xb}}$$
$$= \frac{1}{1 + e^{-(-1.595)}}$$
$$= \frac{1}{1 + 4.9283}$$
$$= 0.1687$$

Step 3: Defining the odds.

$$\left[\frac{P(Y = 1)}{1 - P(Y = 1)}\right]_{X-1} = \frac{0.1687}{0.8313}$$
$$= 0.2029$$

W orking It Out

$$\text{Odds ratio} = \frac{\left[\dfrac{P(Y=1)}{1 - P(Y=1)}\right]_{X}}{\left[\dfrac{P(Y=1)}{1 - P(Y=1)}\right]_{X-1}}$$
$$= \frac{0.4539}{0.2029}$$
$$= 2.2367$$

Turning to the odds comparing the West and Northeast regions with the North Central region, we can see that the differences are smaller (see Table 17.5). Like the South region statistic, these coefficients are positive, meaning that departments in these regions have a higher likelihood of reporting a Compstat-like program. The odds ratios for both regions are about 1.5. A police department in these regions is about 1.5 times as likely to have a Compstat-like program as a department in the North Central region.

The Derivative at Mean

Another measure that sometimes makes it easier to understand the logistic regression coefficient (but that is not reported in SPSS) is the **derivative at mean (DM)**. The derivative at mean converts the nonlinear logistic regression coefficient into a simple linear regression coefficient. Accordingly, it has the advantage of having the same interpretation as the result would have had if OLS regression had been appropriate to the problem. The disadvantage of the derivative at mean is that it calculates the regression coefficient as if it had a constant effect over the entire distribution of predicted values of Y, based on the change observed when the predicted value of Y is at its mean. In fact, the logistic curve in Figure 17.2 shows that the impact of the parameters will change in absolute terms, depending on where in the distribution they are calculated. The derivative at mean will be largest when the mean of the dependent variable is close to the middle of the logistic curve. As the mean of the distribution moves closer to the tails of the logistic curve, the derivative will be smaller.

The interpretation of the derivative at mean is similar to that of the OLS regression coefficient. The derivative at mean may be defined as the change in Y associated with a unit change in X at the mean value of the dependent variable. The derivative at mean is defined mathematically in Equation 17.6:

$$DM = \overline{Y}(1 - \overline{Y})b_i \qquad \text{Equation 17.6}$$

where $\overline{Y}$ is the mean of the dependent variable (i.e., the proportion of cases having a value of 1 for the dependent variable).

Table 17.6 provides the derivative at mean for each of the coefficients in our regression model. Since about 33% of the sample claimed to have implemented a Compstat-like program, the derivative at mean is calculated for a mean of Y of 0.33. If we look at the derivative at mean for the dummy variables associated with region, we can see the advantage of this approach. Taking the South region, for which the difference

Table 17.6	Derivative at Mean for Each of the Regression Coefficients in the Compstat Example

VARIABLE	b	$DM = \bar{Y}(1 - \bar{Y})b_i$
Northeast	0.359	$(0.33)(0.67)(0.359) = 0.0794$
South	0.805	$(0.33)(0.67)(0.805) = 0.1778$
West	0.428	$(0.33)(0.67)(0.428) = 0.0946$
Number of Sworn Officers	0.002	$(0.33)(0.67)(0.002) = 0.0004$

from the excluded category is largest, we calculate the derivative at mean below:

W orking It Out

$$DM = \bar{Y}(1 - \bar{Y})b_i$$
$$= (0.33)(1 - 0.33)(0.805)$$
$$= (0.33)(0.67)(0.805)$$
$$= 0.1778$$

We can interpret this coefficient much as we interpreted the dummy variable regression coefficients in Chapter 16. If a police department is located in the South as opposed to the North Central region, its outcome on the dependent variable is about 0.1778 unit higher. Since the dependent variable has values ranging between 0 and 1, we can interpret this coefficient in terms of percentages. Departments in the South have, on average, about an 18 percentage-point higher chance of claiming to have a Compstat-like program when Y is at its mean.

The derivative at mean for number of sworn officers is about 0.0004. This suggests that for each additional officer, there is a 0.0004 increase in the value of Y. According to the derivative at mean, an increase in 100 officers would lead to a 4 percentage-point increase in the likelihood of having a Compstat-like program. An increase of 1,000 officers would lead to a 40 percentage-point increase.

W orking It Out

$$DM = \bar{Y}(1 - \bar{Y})b_i$$
$$= (0.33)(1 - 0.33)(0.002)$$
$$= (0.33)(0.67)(0.002)$$
$$= 0.0004$$

Comparing Logistic Regression Coefficients

In Chapter 16, you saw how standardized regression coefficients could be used to compare the magnitude of regression coefficients measured on different scales. There is no widely accepted method for comparing the magnitude of the coefficients in logistic regression. When variables are measured on the same scale, we can rely on comparisons of the statistics we have reviewed so far. For example, if our model includes two binary dummy variables, we can easily gain a sense of the impact of each variable by comparing the size of each odds ratio.

Let's say that we are interested in predicting the likelihood of getting a prison sentence for a sample of convicted burglars. We include two binary dummy variables in our analysis. The odds ratio for the first variable, gender (0 = female; 1 = male), is 1.5. The odds ratio for the second, whether a gun was used in the burglary (0 = no; 1 = yes), is 2.0. In this case, we could say that use of a weapon has a larger effect on the likelihood of getting a prison sentence than does gender. In the case of gender, being a male as opposed to a female increases the odds of getting a prison sentence by about 50%. However, according to these estimates, using a gun in the burglary doubles the odds of getting a prison sentence.

Using Probability Estimates to Compare Coefficients

If variables are measured on very different scales, comparing the magnitude of effects from one variable to another is often difficult. One easily understood and transparent method for doing this is to rely on the predicted probabilities of Y. In a study using logistic regression, Wheeler, Weisburd, and Bode were confronted with a large number of statistically significant independent variables measured on very different scales.[7] They decided to calculate probability estimates for measures at selected intervals when the scores of all other predictors were held at their mean. They also calculated a range of predictions computed from the 5th to 95th percentile scores for the measure of interest. The table they developed is reproduced in Table 17.7.

The study examined factors that explained whether or not white-collar offenders convicted in federal courts were sentenced to prison. The table gives the reader a sense of how changes in the independent variable affect changes in the dependent variable, as well as a general idea (using the range) of the overall influence of the measure examined. For example, the amount of "dollar victimization" in an offense (variable 2) and "role in offense" (variable 13) are both ordinal-level variables but are measured with a different number of categories. Looking at the table,

---

[7]See Stanton Wheeler, David Weisburd, and Nancy Bode, "Sentencing the White Collar Offender: Rhetoric and Reality," *American Sociological Review* 47 (1982): 641–659.

Table 17.7	Selected Probability Estimates and Calculated Range for Significant Variables in Wheeler, Weisburd, and Bode's Study of White-Collar-Crime Sentencing

INDEPENDENT VARIABLES	PROBABILITY ESTIMATES[a]	RANGE[b]	INDEPENDENT VARIABLES	PROBABILTY ESTIMATES[a]	RANGE[b]
I. *Act-Related Variables*			10) Criminal Background: Most Serious Prior Conviction		20
1) Maximum Exposure to Prison		44	None	37	
1 day–1 year	32		Minor Offense	46	
1 year & 1 day–2 years	35		Low Felony	52	
4 years & 1 day–5 years	45		Moderate Felony	57	
14 years & 1 day–15 years	76		13) Role in Offense		24
2) Dollar Victimization		41	Minor	26	
$101–$500	27		Missing	33	
$2,501–$5,000	38		Single/Primary	50	
$10,001–$25,000	47		III. *Legal Process Variables*		
$25,001–$100,000	51		16) Statutory Offense Category		39
over $2,500,000	68		Antitrust Violations	28	
3) Complexity/Sophistication		27	Bribery	30	
4	32		Bank Embezzlement	36	
6	38		False Claims	36	
8	45		Postal Fraud	38	
10	52		Lending/Credit Fraud	45	
12	59		SEC Violations	65	
4) Spread of Illegality		21	Tax Violations	69	
Individual	40		IV. *Other Variables*		30
Local	47		17) Sex		
Regional	54		Male	50	
National/International	61		Female	20	
II. *Actor-Related Variables*			18) Age		____[c]
7) Social Background: Duncan S.E.I.		29	22	42	
15.1	28		30	48	
49.4	41		39	50	
62.0	47		48	46	
66.1	49		61	32	
84.0	57		21) District		28
8) Social Background: Impeccability		17	Northern Georgia	34	
7	54		Southern New York	34	
11	49		Central California	43	
14	45		Western Washington	43	
17	42		Maryland	50	
21	37		Northern Illinois	53	
9) Criminal Background: Number of Arrests		22	Northern Texas	62	
0	37				
1	43				
2	45				
5	51				
9	59				

[a]Estimated likelihood of imprisonment when scores on all other variables are held at their mean.
[b]Range computed from 5th to 95th percentile score.
[c]Because of the curvilinear effect measured here, the range is not relevant.

we can see that a person playing a minor role in an offense had a predicted probability of imprisonment of about 26%, while someone playing a primary role had a 50% likelihood of imprisonment, according to the model estimated (and holding all other independent variables constant at their mean). A crime involving less than $500 in victimization led to an estimated likelihood of imprisonment of 27%. A crime netting over $2,500,000 led to an estimated likelihood of imprisonment of 68%. If we compare the range of predicted values between the 5th and 95th percentile scores for each variable, our calculation suggests that dollar victimization (with a range of 41%) has a much larger impact than role in an offense (with a range of 24%). Of course, the choice of the 5th and 95th percentiles is arbitrary. And this method also arbitrarily holds every other independent variable to its mean. Nonetheless, the advantage of this approach is that it provides a method of comparison that is straightforward and easy for the nonstatistician to understand.

To apply this method to our data, we need information on the mean for each independent variable. For our data, the means are

Northeast: 0.225

South: 0.373

West: 0.229

Number of sworn officers: 334.784

In the box on pages 526–527, the calculations are carried out according to the method employed by Wheeler, Weisburd, and Bode. Table 17.8 describes the results. Using this table, we can see that there are very large differences in the predicted probabilities of a Compstat-like program for departments of varying size. This illustrates a point made earlier, when we noted that the odds ratio for each change in number of sworn officers was small. Though the change per unit change in X is small in this case (because departments differ widely in size), the predicted change can be very large. Under this approach, the range variable suggests a larger impact for number of sworn officers than for region of country.

Table 17.8	Table of Selected Probability Estimates and Range for the Compstat Model

VARIABLE	PROBABILITY ESTIMATE	RANGE
Number of sworn officers:		
100 (5th percentile)	0.2468	0.53
500	0.4217	
1,300 (95th percentile)	0.7831	
Northeast	0.4090	——
South	0.4647	——
West	0.4216	——

For all of the following calculations,

X_1 = number of sworn officers
X_2 = Northeast
X_3 = South
X_4 = West

Probability estimate for number of sworn officers:

$$Xb = b_0 + b_1 X_1 + b_2 \overline{X}_2 + b_3 \overline{X}_3 + b_4 \overline{X}_4$$
$$= -1.795 + 0.002 X_1 + 0.359(0.225) + 0.805(0.373) + 0.428(0.229)$$
$$= -1.795 + 0.002 X_1 + 0.0808 + 0.3003 + 0.0980$$
$$= -1.3159 + 0.002 X_1$$

$P(Y = 1)$ for number of sworn officers:

$$P(Y = 1) = \frac{1}{1 + e^{-(-1.3159 + 0.002 X_1)}}$$

$P(Y = 1)$ for 100 officers:

$$P(Y = 1) = \frac{1}{1 + e^{-[-1.3159 + (0.002)(100)]}} = \frac{1}{1 + e^{-(-1.1159)}} = 0.2468$$

$P(Y = 1)$ for 500 officers:

$$P(Y = 1) = \frac{1}{1 + e^{-[-1.3159 + (0.002)(500)]}} = \frac{1}{1 + e^{-(-0.3159)}} = 0.4217$$

$P(Y = 1)$ for 1,300 officers:

$$P(Y = 1) = \frac{1}{1 + e^{-[-1.3159 + (0.002)(1300)]}} = \frac{1}{1 + e^{-(1.2841)}} = 0.7831$$

"Standardized" Logistic Regression Coefficients

Some statistical software programs list the **standardized logistic regression coefficient** Beta, which is analogous to the standardized regression coefficient. Like the standardized regression coefficient, the standardized logistic regression coefficient can be interpreted relative to changes

Probability estimate for Northeast:

$$Xb = b_0 + b_1\overline{X}_1 + b_2X_2 + b_3\overline{X}_3 + b_4\overline{X}_4$$
$$= -1.795 + 0.002(334.784) + 0.359X_2 + 0.805(0.373) + 0.428(0.229)$$
$$= -1.795 + 0.6696 + 0.359X_2 + 0.3003 + 0.0980$$
$$= -0.7271 + 0.359X_2$$

$P(Y = 1)$ for Northeast:

$$P(Y = 1) = \frac{1}{1 + e^{-(-0.7271 + 0.359X_2)}} = \frac{1}{1 + e^{0.3681}} = 0.4090$$

Probability estimate for South:

$$Xb = b_0 + b_1\overline{X}_1 + b_2X_2 + b_3X_3 + b_4\overline{X}_4$$
$$= -1.795 + 0.002(334.784) + 0.359(0.225) + 0.805X_3 + 0.428(0.229)$$
$$= -1.795 + 0.6696 + 0.0808 + 0.805X_3 + 0.0980$$
$$= -0.9466 + 0.805X_3$$

$P(Y = 1)$ for South:

$$P(Y - 1) = \frac{1}{1 + e^{-(-0.9466 + 0.805X_3)}} = \frac{1}{1 + e^{0.1416}} = 0.4647$$

Probability estimate for West:

$$Xb = b_0 + b_1\overline{X}_1 + b_2\overline{X}_2 + b_3\overline{X}_3 + b_4X_4$$
$$= -1.795 + 0.002(334.784) + 0.359(0.225) + 0.805(0.373) + 0.428X_4$$
$$= -1.795 + 0.6696 + 0.0808 + 0.3003 + 0.428X_4$$
$$= -0.7443 + 0.428X_4$$

$P(Y = 1)$ for West:

$$P(Y = 1) = \frac{1}{1 + e^{-(-0.7443 + 0.428X_4)}} = \frac{1}{1 + e^{0.3163}} = 0.4216$$

(measured in standard deviation units) in the independent variable. The magnitude of the standardized logistic regression coefficient allows us to compare the relative influence of the independent variables, since a larger value for the standardized coefficient means that a greater change in the log of the odds is expected. In contrast to the standardized regression coefficients for linear regression models, the Beta calculated for logistic regression models does not fall between 0 and 1, but can take on any value.[8] Some statisticians warn that such coefficients should be interpreted with caution.[9] Nonetheless, they can provide a method for gaining a general sense of the strength of coefficients in logistic regression. The standardized logistic regression coefficient is calculated using Equation 17.7:

$$\text{Beta}_i = b_i s_i$$

Equation 17.7

where b_i is the unstandardized coefficient for variable i from the original logistic regression model and s_i is the standard deviation for variable i. We interpret Beta as the change in the log of the odds of $P(Y = 1)$ relative to changes (measured in standard deviation units) in the independent variable. For example, a Beta of 0.4 implies that for a one-standard-deviation change in the independent variable, the log of the odds is expected to increase by 0.4. Alternatively, if Beta $= -0.9$, a one-standard-deviation change in the independent variable is expected to result in a decrease of 0.9 in the log of the odds that $P(Y = 1)$.

Returning to our example using the Compstat data, we find the standardized coefficient for number of sworn officers to be 0.6616.

W orking It Out

Beta $= b_i s_i$

$= (0.002)(330.797)$

$= 0.6616$

In Table 17.9, we calculate Beta for all four of the coefficients in the model and present the accompanying unstandardized logistic regression coefficients. Though the unstandardized logistic regression coefficient for the South (0.805) seems very large relative to that for number of sworn

---

[8]Some researchers have proposed alternative ways of calculating standardized logistic regression coefficients that allow for interpretations related to changes in probabilities. See, for example, Robert L. Kaufman, "Comparing Effects in Dichotomous Logistic Regression: A Variety of Standardized Coefficients," *Social Science Quarterly* 77 (1996): 90–109.

[9]For example, see Andy Field, *Discovering Statistics Using SPSS for Windows* (London: Sage Publications, 2000).

Table 17.9	Beta and Associated Logistic Regression Coefficients for the Compstat Model

VARIABLE	STANDARD DEVIATION	b	BETA
Number of sworn officers	330.797	0.002	(330.797)(0.002) = 0.6616
Northeast	0.416	0.359	(0.416)(0.359) = 0.1493
South	0.484	0.805	(0.484)(0.805) = 0.3896
West	0.421	0.428	(0.421)(0.428) = 0.1802

officers (0.002), the reverse relationship is found when we look at the standardized coefficients. The standardized coefficient for number of sworn officers is 0.662, while that for the South is 0.390. This is consistent with our analysis of the probability estimates. Both of these methods take into account the fact that the scales of measurement for these measures differ widely. While you should use caution in relying on standardized logistic regression coefficients, here, as in other cases, they can provide a general yardstick for comparing the relative strength of coefficients within regression models.[10]

Evaluating the Logistic Regression Model

In OLS regression, to assess how well our model explains the data, we use a straightforward measure of the percent of variance explained beyond the mean (R^2). There is no equivalent statistic in logistic regression. Nonetheless, a number of measures have been proposed for assessing how well a model predicts the data.

Percent of Correct Predictions

One widely accepted method for assessing how well a logistic regression model predicts the dependent variable is to compare the values of Y predicted by the model to those that would be obtained simply by taking the observed distribution of the dependent variable. This statistic is commonly described as the **percent of correct predictions**. Table 17.10

---

[10]As with standardized regression coefficients in OLS regression, you should not compare standardized logistic regression coefficients across models. Moreover, while we report standardized regression coefficients for the dummy variables included in the model, you should use caution in interpreting standardized coefficients for dummy variables. See Chapter 16, pages 471–472, for a discussion of this problem.

Table 17.10 Percent of Correct Predictions
for the Logistic Regression of the Compstat Data

Classification Table

			Predicted		
			COMPSTAT		Percentage Correct
	Observed		.00	1.00	
Step 1	COMPSTAT	.00	264	19	93.3
		1.00	106	30	22.1
	Overall				70.2

a The cut value is .500.

shows the percent of correct predictions for our Compstat example. The formula for percent of correct predictions is presented in Equation 17.8.

$$\text{Percent of correct predictions} = \left(\frac{N_{\text{corrrect predictions}}}{N_{\text{total}}}\right) \times 100 \qquad \textbf{Equation 17.8}$$

The observed predictions in our example represent the observed proportion of departments that report having a Compstat-like program. As we noted before, this number is about 0.33 (or 33%). We add the 106 and 30 cases in Table 17.7 where the observed value is 1 and then divide this number by the total number of cases in the analysis ($N = 419$). The predicted values are drawn from Equation 17.3. But, importantly, in order to compare these predicted values with the observed values, we must assign each case a 0 or a 1. The decision as to whether to define the predicted value as a 1 or a 0 is based on a set cut-off point. Herein lies the main drawback of this approach: The point at which you determine that the prediction is a 1 is arbitrary. In SPSS, as in other standard software packages, 0.50 is used as a natural cut-off point. That is, if we get a predicted probability of 0.50 or greater for a case in our study, it will be counted as a prediction of 1. Remember that a 1 in our case means that the department has a Compstat-like program. In this analysis, if the prediction is 0.495, the case is given a 0. Clearly, by using a single and arbitrary cut-off point, we are losing a good deal of information about how well the model fits the data.

The proportion of correct predictions is worked out below, using Equation 17.8. The N of correct predictions is found by taking each case for which the actual and predicted values are the same. In 264 cases, the actual and predicted values are 0. In only 30 cases are the actual and predicted values equal to 1. These are the correct predictions in our analysis, so the total number of correct predictions is $264 + 30 = 294$. The percent of correct predictions is 70.2. This seems like a very high level of prediction. However, to interpret this statistic, we must compare it with the level we would have reached if we had not used our regression model. In that case, we would have had information only on the split in the dependent variable. As noted earlier, 33% of the departments claim to have implemented a Compstat-like program. Knowing only this, our best bet would have been to predict that every department did not have a Compstat-like program. If we did this, we would be correct about 67% of the time. Thus, our model did not improve our prediction very much over what we would have predicted with knowledge of only the outcomes of the dependent variable.

Working It Out

$$\text{Percent of correct predictions} = \left(\frac{N_{\text{correct predictions}}}{N_{\text{total}}} \right) \times 100$$

$$= \left(\frac{294}{419} \right) \times 100$$

$$= (0.7017) \times 100$$

$$= 70.17$$

Pseudo R^2

While there is no direct R^2 measure for logistic regression, a number of what may be termed **pseudo R^2** measures have been proposed. Like standardized logistic regression coefficients, these measures are not well accepted and must be used with caution. Nonetheless, by providing a general sense of the prediction level of a model, they can add information to other statistics, such as the percent of correct predictions. A commonly used pseudo R^2 measure is **Cox and Snell's R^2**.[11] As with other pseudo R^2 statistics, a main component of this measure is the log likelihood function $(-2LL)$. It makes good sense to rely on the log likelihood function, since it measures the degree to which a proposed model predicts the data examined. In this case, we compare the difference between the $-2LL$ estimate

---

[11]D. R. Cox and E. J. Snell, *The Analysis of Binary Data,* 2nd ed. (London: Chapman and Hall, 1989).

| Table 17.11 | Pseudo R^2 Statistics as Reported in SPSS |

Model Summary

Step	−2 Log likelihood	Cox & Snell R Square	Nagelkerke R Square
1	492.513	.082	.114

obtained when no independent variables are included (the null model) and the −2LL estimate obtained when all the independent variables are included (the full model). The −2LL value for the null model (528.171) is given in Table 17.4. The −2LL value for the full model (492.513) is given in the model summary statistics provided in Table 17.11. Equation 17.9 provides the method of calculation for Cox and Snell's R^2.

$$R^2 = 1 - e^{-[(-2LL_{\text{null model}}) - (-2LL_{\text{full model}})]/N}$$

Equation 17.9

While this equation looks intimidating, it can be solved in two easy steps. First, we calculate the number that appears above e, or the exponent of the natural log:

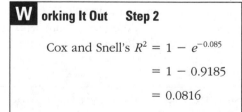

W orking It Out   Step 1

$$-[(-2LL_{\text{null model}}) - (-2LL_{\text{full model}})]/N$$

$$= -[(528.171) - (492.513)]/419$$

$$= -35.658/419$$

$$= -0.085$$

We then take e to the power of −0.085, which, as we noted earlier, can be done simply on a basic scientific calculator. We next subtract this number from 1:

W orking It Out   Step 2

$$\text{Cox and Snell's } R^2 = 1 - e^{-0.085}$$

$$= 1 - 0.9185$$

$$= 0.0816$$

Rounding 0.0816 to three decimal places gives a result of 0.082, which is identical to that produced in the SPSS printout.

Like the percent of correct predictions, Cox and Snells R^2 suggests that our model does not provide for a very strong level of prediction. SPSS produces another R^2 statistic: the Nagelkerke R^2. This statistic corrects for the fact that Cox and Snell's estimate, as well as many other pseudo R^2 statistics, often have a maximum value of less than 1 (which would indicate that all of the variance in the dependent variable was explained by the independent variables included in the model). Nagelkerke's R^2 is thus generally larger than Cox and Snell's R^2, which—especially with large values—will be too conservative.[12] Other pseudo R^2 statistics will give estimates similar to those produced here. None of these values should be seen as an exact representation of the percent of variance explained in your model. But they can give you a rough sense of how well your model predicts the outcome measure.

Statistical Significance in Logistic Regression

Statistical significance for a logistic regression can be interpreted in much the same way as it was for the regression models discussed in Chapters 15 and 16. However, a chi-square distribution is used, and thus we do not have to be concerned with assumptions regarding the population distribution in our tests. For the overall model, there is a general test, based on the difference between the $-2LL$ statistics for the full and null models. The chi-square formula for the overall model in logistic regression is represented in Equation 17.10.

$$\text{Model chi-square} = (-2LL_{\text{null model}}) - (-2LL_{\text{full model}})$$ **Equation 17.10**

For our example, the model chi-square is 35.657 (see working it out, next page). The number of degrees of freedom is determined by the number of independent variables included in the model estimated. In our case, there are three regression coefficients for the variable region and the measure number of sworn officers. The number of degrees of freedom thus equals 4. Looking at Appendix 2, we can see that a chi-square statistic of greater than 18.465 is needed for a statistically significant result at the 0.001 level. Because our chi-square statistic is much larger than this, our observed significance level is less than 0.001. Using

---

[12]See N. J. D. Nagelkerke, "A Note on a General Definition of the Coefficient of Determination, *Biometrika* 78 (1991): 691–692.

conventional significance criteria, we would reject the null hypothesis and conclude that the model estimated provides significant improvement over that without any independent variables.

W orking It Out

Model chi-square $= (-2LL_{\text{null model}}) - (-2LL_{\text{full model}})$

$$= 528.171 - 492.513$$

$$= 35.658$$

In testing the statistical significance of individual parameters, statistical software packages ordinarily provide the **Wald statistic.** This statistic also has a chi-square distribution, and so the statistical significance of a result may be checked in a chi-square table. The Wald statistic takes the ratio of the logistic regression coefficient to its standard error (see Equation 17.11). The standard error of the logistic regression coefficient is provided in the SPSS printout (see Table 17.12). For the comparison of the South and North Central regions (the latter being the excluded category), we take the logistic regression coefficient of 0.805 and divide it by the reported standard error of 0.332. To get the Wald statistic, we square this number. The result is 5.879.[13]

$$W^2 = \left(\frac{b}{SE_b}\right)^2$$

Equation 17.11

W orking It Out   **South Region Measure**

$$W^2 = \left(\frac{b}{SE_b}\right)^2$$

$$= \left(\frac{0.805}{0.332}\right)^2$$

$$= 5.879$$

---

[13]The difference between our result and that shown in Table 17.12 is due to rounding error.

| Table 17.12 | SPSS Printout with B, SE of B, and Wald Statistics[14] |

Variables in the equation

		B	S.E.	Wald	df	Sig.	Exp(B)
Step 1	NORTHEAST	.359	.372	.931	1	.335	1.432
	SOUTH	.805	.332	5.883	1	.015	2.237
	WEST	.428	.367	1.360	1	.244	1.534
	#SWORN	.002	.000	24.842	1	.000	1.002
	Constant	−1.795	.311	33.378	1	.000	.166

a Variable(s) entered on step 1: NORTHEAST, SOUTH, WEST, #SWORN.

To determine whether this coefficient is statistically significant, we can refer to the chi-square table for 1 degree of freedom. The number of degrees of freedom for an individual variable in a logistic regression will always be 1. Looking at Appendix 2, we see that a chi-square of 10.827 is required for a result to be statistically significant at the 0.001 level. A chi-square of 6.635 is required at the 0.01 level, and a chi-square of 5.412 at the 0.02 level. Our observed significance level can therefore be defined as falling between 0.01 and 0.02. The SPSS printout gives the exact observed significance level as 0.015. Using conventional levels of statistical significance, we would conclude that we can reject the null hypothesis that there is no difference in the reported implementation of Compstat-like programs in the South versus the North Central region.

Looking at the significance statistics column in Table 17.12, we can see that the number of sworn officers is also statistically significant—in this case, at greater than the 0.001 level. It is important to note that the statistics reported in this table, as well as in most statistical software, are for two-tailed significance tests. We mentioned at the outset that there was a strong hypothesis that larger departments are more likely to report a Compstat-like program. If we wanted to use a directional test of statistical significance, we would simply divide the observed significance level in our test by 2.

Looking at the other region dummy variables, we can see that there is not a statistically significant difference between the Northeast and North Central regions or between the West and North Central regions. But, as noted in Chapter 16, it is important to ask whether the variable region overall contributes significantly to the regression. To test this hypothesis, we can conduct a **likelihood ratio chi-square test,** which compares the

---

[14]This printout is identical to that in Table 17.5. It is reproduced here for easy reference as you work through the computations presented in this section.

| Table 17.13 | **Model Summary for the Reduced Model** |

Model Summary

Step	−2 Log likelihood	Cox & Snell R Square	Nagelkerke R Square
1	499.447	.066	.092

log likelihood function of the model with the multicategory nominal variable (the full model) with the log likelihood function of the model without the multicategory nominal variable (the reduced model). Equation 17.12 details the likelihood ratio chi-square test. The number of degrees of freedom is defined as the number of dummy variables added by the multicategory nominal variable. In our case, it is 3 for the three included regions.

$$\text{Likelihood ratio chi-square test} = (-2LL_{\text{reduced model}}) - (-2LL_{\text{full model}})$$

Equation 17.12

We can get the statistics for the test by running two separate regressions. The reduced model regression excludes the dummy variables associated with region. The $-2LL$ for this model is shown in the model summary from an SPSS printout in Table 17.13. The second regression is the full model—the model we have been using throughout the chapter, with the region dummy variables included. The model statistics were reported in Table 17.11.

Below, we work out the likelihood ratio chi-square using these two estimates. The likelihood ratio chi-square for the region variable is 6.934, with 3 degrees of freedom (the number of dummy variable measures included in the model). Looking at Appendix 2, we can see that with 3 degrees of freedom, a chi-square of 7.815 would be needed to reject the null hypothesis of no relationship between region and a reported Compstat-like program at the 0.05 significance threshold. Because our chi-square statistic is smaller than this number, we cannot conclude that there is overall a statistically significant relationship between region and claimed development of a Compstat-like program.

W orking It Out

$$\text{Likelihood ratio chi-square test} = (-2LL_{\text{reduced model}}) - (-2LL_{\text{full model}})$$
$$= 499.447 - 492.513$$
$$= 6.934$$

Chapter Summary

Ordinary least squares regression is not an appropriate tool for analyzing a problem in which the dependent variable is dichotomous. In such cases, OLS regression is likely to predict values that are greater than 1 and less than 0 and thus outside the observed distribution of Y. Using the OLS approach in this case will also lead to violations of parametric assumptions required for associated statistical tests. **Logistic regression analysis** uses a **logistic model curve,** rather than a straight line, to predict outcomes for Y in the case of a dichotomous dependent variable. This constrains predictions to between 0 and 1.

While the logistic model curve provides a solution to predictions beyond the observed distribution, the outcome variable is transformed into the **natural logarithm of the odds of Y,** or the **logit of Y.** Through use of the **cumulative logistic probability function,** the logistic regression equation may be used to predict the likelihood of Y occurring. **Maximum likelihood techniques** are used to estimate the coefficients in a logistic regression analysis. In this approach, we begin by identifying a tentative solution, which we then try to improve upon. Our criterion for improvement is termed the **log likelihood function** ($-2LL$). We repeat this process again and again until the change in the likelihood function is considered negligible. Each time we repeat the process and reestimate our coefficients is called an **iteration. Lack of convergence** in a standard number of iterations indicates some type of problem in the regression model that is being estimated.

The multivariate **logistic regression coefficient,** b, may be interpreted as the increase in the log of the odds of Y associated with a one-unit increase in X (with all other independent variables in the model held constant). The **odds ratio,** or **Exp(B),** and the **derivative at mean, DM,** provide more easily interpreted representations of the logistic regression coefficient. The odds ratio represents the impact of a one-unit change in X on the ratio of the probability of Y. Like an ordinary regression coefficient, the derivative at mean may be interpreted as the change in Y associated with a unit change in X. The DM will change depending on the mean value of Y in the problem examined.

There is no widely accepted method for comparing logistic regression coefficients measured on different scales. One method is to compare probability estimates at selected intervals. Standardized regression coefficients have been suggested for logistic regression, though they should be interpreted with caution. There is no single widely accepted statistic for assessing how well the logistic regression model predicts the observed data. An approach commonly used is to calculate the **percent of correct predictions.** This method establishes an arbitrary decision point (usually 0.50) for deciding when a predicted value should be set at 1. These predictions are then compared to the observed data. **Pseudo R^2** statistics have also been developed, though they remain a subject of debate.

Statistical significance for the overall logistic regression model is assessed through computation of the **model chi-square**. Statistical significance for individual regression coefficients is evaluated with the **Wald statistic**. A **likelihood ratio chi-square test** can be used to calculate the statistical significance of a multicategory nominal variable.

Key Terms

Cox and Snell's R^2 A commonly used pseudo R^2 measure whose main component, as in other pseudo R^2 statistics, is the log likelihood function ($-2LL$).

cumulative logistic probability function A transformation of the logistic probability function that allows computation of the probability that Y will occur, given a certain combination of characteristics of the independent variables.

derivative at mean (DM) A measure that converts the nonlinear logistic regression coefficient to a simple linear regression coefficient, which may be interpreted as the change in Y associated with a unit change in X.

iteration Each time we identify another tentative solution and reestimate our logistic regression coefficients.

lack of convergence Failure of a logistic regression analysis to reach a result that meets the criterion of reduction in the log likelihood function.

likelihood ratio chi-square test A test for statistical significance that allows the researcher to examine whether a subset of independent variables in a logistic regres-

sion is statistically significant. It compares $-2LL$ for a full model to $-2LL$ for a reduced model.

log likelihood function A measure of the probability of observing the results in the sample, given the coefficient estimates in the model. In logistic regression, the log likelihood function ($-2LL$) is defined as -2 times the natural logarithm of the likelihood function.

logarithm The power to which a fixed number (the base) must be raised to produce another number.

logistic model curve The form of the predicted outcomes of a logistic regression analysis. Shaped like an S, the logistic curve begins to flatten as it approaches 0 or 1, so it keeps coming closer to—but never actually reaches—either of these two values.

logistic regression analysis A type of regression analysis that allows the researcher to make predictions about dichotomous dependent variables in terms of the log of the odds of Y.

logistic regression coefficient The coefficient b produced in a logistic regression analysis. It may be interpreted as the increase in the log of the odds of Y associated with a one-unit increase in X.

maximum likelihood estimation A technique for estimating the parameters or coefficients of a model that maximizes the probability that the estimates obtained will produce a distribution similar to that of the observed data.

model chi-square The statistical test used to assess the statistical significance of the overall logistic regression model. It compares the $-2LL$ for the full model with the $-2LL$ calculated without any independent variables included.

Nagelkerke R^2 A pseudo R^2 statistic that corrects for the fact that Cox and Snell's estimates, as well as many other pseudo R^2 statistics, often have a maximum value of less than 1.

natural logarithm of the odds of Y (logit of Y) The outcome predicted in a logistic regression analysis.

odds ratio [Exp(B)] A statistic used to interpret the logistic regression coefficient. It represents the impact of a one-unit change in X on the ratio of the probability of Y.

percent of correct predictions A statistic used to assess how well a logistic regression model explains the observed data. An arbitrary decision point (usually 0.50) is established for deciding when a predicted value should be set at 1, and then the predictions are compared to the observed data.

pseudo R^2 The term generally used for a group of measures used in logistic regression to create an approximation of the OLS regression R^2. They are generally based on comparisons of $-2LL$ for a full model and a null model (without any independent variables).

standardized logistic regression coefficient A statistic used to compare logistic regression coefficients that use different scales of measurement. It is meant to approximate Beta, the standardized regression coefficient in OLS regression.

Wald statistic A statistic used to assess the statistical significance of coefficients in a logistic regression model.

Symbols and Formulas

e	Base of the natural logarithm
ln	Natural logarithm
$-2LL$	-2 times the log likelihood function

The natural logarithm of the odds of $P(Y = 1)$ to $P(Y = 0)$:

$$\ln \left(\frac{P(Y = 1)}{1 - P(Y = 1)} \right) = \ln \left(\frac{P(Y = 1)}{P(Y = 0)} \right) = b_0 + b_1 X_1$$

To calculate the probability that $Y = 1$:

$$P(Y = 1) = \frac{1}{1 + e^{-Xb}}$$

To calculate the odds ratio for $P(Y = 1)$, given a one-unit change in the independent variable X:

$$\text{Odds ratio} = \frac{\left[\dfrac{P(Y=1)}{1 - P(Y=1)}\right]_X}{\left[\dfrac{P(Y=1)}{1 - P(Y=1)}\right]_{X-1}} = \text{Exp(B)}$$

To calculate the derivative at mean:

$$DM = \overline{Y}(1 - \overline{Y})b_i$$

To calculate the standardized logistic regression coefficient:

$$\text{Beta}_i = b_i s_i$$

To calculate the percent of correct predictions:

$$\text{Percent correct} = \left(\frac{N_{\text{corrrect predictions}}}{N_{\text{total}}}\right) \times 100$$

To calculate Cox and Snell's R^2:

$$R^2 = 1 - e^{-[(-2LL_{\text{null model}}) - (-2LL_{\text{full model}})]/N}$$

To calculate the model chi-square:

$$\text{Model chi-square} = (-2LL_{\text{null model}}) - (-2LL_{\text{full model}})$$

To calculate the Wald statistic:

$$W^2 = \left(\frac{b}{SE_b}\right)^2$$

To calculate the likelihood ratio chi-square statistic for a subset of independent variables:

$$\text{Likelihood ratio chi-square test} = (-2LL_{\text{reduced model}}) - (-2LL_{\text{full model}})$$

Exercises

17.1 As part of a research project for a class, a student analyzed data on a sample of adults who had been asked about their decision to report being assaulted to the police. Their decision was coded as 1 = assault reported to the police, 0 = assault not reported to the police. The student used ordinary least squares regression to estimate the effects of age (in years), sex (0 = male, 1 = female), and race (0 = white, 1 = nonwhite). The student reported the regression results as

Variable	b
Age	0.01
Sex	0.5
Race	−0.2
Constant	−0.1

a. Calculate the predicted values for each of the following persons:

— A 65-year-old white female

— A 25-year-old nonwhite male

— A 40-year-old white male

— A 30-year-old nonwhite female

b. Should any of the student's predicted values lead the student to question the use of ordinary least squares regression? Explain why.

17.2 A research institute concerned with raising public attention about the use of force by school children calculates the following effects on the likelihood of hitting another child at school, using logistic regression analysis:

Variable	b
Sex (0 = girl, 1 = boy)	0.7
Grade in school	−0.1
Constant	−0.4

Hitting another child was coded as 1; no hitting was coded as 0.

a. Interpret the effects of sex and grade in school on the log of the odds that $P(Y = 1)$.

b. Calculate and interpret the odds ratios for the effects of sex and grade in school on use of force.

17.3 Supervision of defendants on pretrial release is thought to reduce the chance that defendants will flee the community. A government agency funds a small study to examine whether supervision affects pretrial flight (flight = 1, no flight = 0) and reports the following logistic regression results:

Variable	b	Standard Error of b
Age (years)	−0.01	0.02
Sex (1 = male, 0 = female)	0.67	0.25
Severity of offense scale (0 to 10)	0.21	0.03
Number of prior felony convictions	0.35	0.09
Number of contacts with supervision caseworker	−0.13	0.03
Constant	−0.52	

a. Calculate and interpret the odds ratio for each of the independent variables.

b. Can the government agency conclude that supervision in the form of contact with a caseworker has a statistically significant effect on pretrial flight? Explain why.

c. If the agency reports that the $-2LL_{\text{null model}}$ is 653.2 and the $-2LL_{\text{full model}}$ is 597.6, can it conclude that the model is statistically significant? Explain why.

17.4 A survey of adolescents indicated that 17% had used marijuana in the last year. In addition to standard demographic predictors of drug use, a researcher expects that school performance also affects the likelihood of marijuana use. The researcher's table of results follows.

Variable	Mean	Standard Deviation	b	Standard Error of b
Age (years)	14.6	3.1	0.07	0.03
Sex (1 = male, 0 = female)	0.55	0.50	0.36	0.15
Race (1 = white, 0 = nonwhite)	0.75	0.43	−0.42	0.30
Grade point average	2.76	1.98	−0.89	0.24
Think of self as a good student (1 = yes, 0 = no)	0.59	0.49	−0.65	0.33
Constant			−0.87	

a. Calculate the predicted probability of marijuana use for each of the following persons:

— A 14-year-old white male who does not think of himself as a good student and has a GPA of 3.07.

— A 17-year-old nonwhite female who thinks of herself as a good student and has a GPA of 3.22.

— A 15-year-old white female who thinks of herself as a good student and has a GPA of 2.53.

b. Calculate the standardized coefficient for each of the independent variables in the model. Which variable appears to have the largest effect on marijuana use?

c. Calculate the derivative at mean for each of the independent variables in the model. Which variable appears to have the largest effect on marijuana use?

d. Compare your answers for parts b and c. How do you explain this pattern?

17.5 After losing a court battle over a requirement that it reduce its jail population, a county conducted an analysis to predict which offenders would pose the greatest threat of committing a violent offense if released early. A random sample of 500 inmates released from the jail in the last three years was analyzed to see what factors predicted arrest for a violent crime in the 12 months after release. For the final model, which included five predictors of violent arrest, the county reported the following statistics:

$-2LL_{\text{null model}} = 876.5$

$-2LL_{\text{full model}} = 861.3$

	Predicted No Violent Arrest	Predicted Violent Arrest
Observed No Violent Arrest	439	19
Observed Violent Arrest	27	15

a. Calculate the percent correctly predicted for this model. What does this statistic indicate about the county's prediction model?

b. Calculate the model chi-square for this model. Interpret this statistic.

c. Calculate Cox and Snell's R^2 for this model. Interpret this statistic.

d. How do you explain the difference in the results for parts a through c?

17.6 Hopeful that media attention to wrongful convictions has increased public opinion in favor of abolishing the death penalty, an abolitionist organization conducts a study to assess public support for abolishing the death penalty. Overall, the organization finds that 35% would support abolishing the death penalty if offenders could be sentenced to life without the option of parole (coded as 1 = abolish the death penalty, 0 = do not abolish the death penalty). In a logistic regression model examining the effects of respondent characteristics on support, the organization finds the following:

Variable	Mean	Standard Deviation	b	Standard Error of b
Age (years)	41.2	15.4	−0.01	0.01
Sex (1 = male, 0 = female)	0.44	0.50	−0.42	0.19
Race (1 = white, 0 = nonwhite)	0.76	0.43	−0.24	0.09
Political conservative (1 = yes, 0 = no)	0.33	0.47	−1.12	0.22
Region of Country:				
South	0.23	0.42	−0.19	0.11
West	0.31	0.46	−0.09	0.04
North (omitted = Central)	0.27	0.44	0.27	0.12
Constant			0.11	

a. Which variable has a relatively greater impact on support for abolishing the death penalty? Explain why.

b. If $-2LL_{reduced\ model} = 376.19$ and $-2LL_{full\ model} = 364.72$ when region variables are omitted from the analysis, do the region variables have a statistically significant effect on support for abolishing the death penalty?

Computer Exercises

Obtaining Logistic Regression Results in SPSS

Logistic regression analyses are performed in SPSS with the binary logistic command (Analyze → Regression → Binary Logistic). After you execute the command, a window appears in which all the variables in the data file are listed on the left. On the right side of the window are self-explanatory boxes for the dependent and independent variables. To run a logistic regression analysis, simply move the names of the variables to the appropriate box and click on "OK" to run the command.

Much of the output from running this command has been discussed in this chapter. The difference between the linear regression command and the logistic regression command is that the output from a logistic regression presents information for the model that includes only the intercept and is labeled "Block 0" in the SPSS output. The next section of output is labeled "Block 1," and it contains the results discussed above: Omnibus Tests of Model Coefficients, Model Summary, Classification Table, and Variables in the Equation.

It is possible to have SPSS calculate the predicted probability and residual for each observation in the data file. To obtain one or both of these values, click on the "Save" button after entering the variables into the dependent and independent variable boxes. In the new window that opens, click on the box next to "Probabilities" under the "Predicted Values" label and/or the box next to "Unstandardized" under the "Residuals" label. Click on "Continue" to return to the window listing the variables. Click on "OK" to run the command. The predicted values and residuals will appear as new variables in your data file with the names pre_1 (for the predicted values) and res_1 (for the residuals).

1. Open the ***compstat.sav*** data file. These are the data analyzed in this chapter. Run the binary logistic regression command in SPSS, using Compstat as the dependent variable and number of sworn officers, Northeast, South, and West as the independent variables. Note that the values reported in the SPSS output match those reported in the text in Tables 17.4, 17.5, 17.10, and 17.11.

2. Open the ***nys_1.sav*** data file into SPSS. Using the binary logistic regression command, run an analysis for each of the measures of delinquency below. As in the computer exercises in Chapter 16, you will need to select a set of independent variables that you think are related to the dependent variable. Note that each of the delinquency items will need to be recoded as 0 or 1 to represent whether or not the act was committed. Do the following for each analysis:

    — Explain the logistic regression coefficients in plain English.

    — Explain the odds ratios in plain English.

    — Interpret the results of the Wald statistic for each of the logistic regression coefficients.

    — Interpret the value of Cox and Snell's R^2.

    — Perform a chi-square test for the overall regression model.

    a. Number of thefts valued at less than $5 in the last year; convert to any thefts in the last year.

    b. Number of times drunk in the last year; convert to any times drunk in the last year.

    c. Number of times the youth has hit other students in the last year; convert to any times the youth has hit other students in the last year.

    d. Number of times the youth has hit a parent in the last year; convert to any times the youth has hit a parent in the last year.

Special Topics: Confidence Intervals

O NE OF THE MAIN CONCERNS of this text has been to define how we make inferences from samples to populations. This is also one of the main concerns of researchers, since in most cases they must make decisions about population parameters on the basis of sample statistics. Our approach has been to use the logic of statistical inference, which begins with the creation of a null hypothesis. Importantly, the logic of statistical inference we have reviewed so far is concerned primarily with the decision as to whether to reject or fail to reject the null hypothesis. This means in practice that we have relied on a logic that allows us to make a statement about where the population parameter is *not*.

This approach has enabled us to come to concrete decisions about population parameters on the basis of sample statistics. When we reject the null hypothesis on the basis of a statistical test, we conclude that the relationship we have examined is statistically significant. For example, when we reject the null hypothesis on the basis of our sample statistics in a statistical test of the difference of means, we have confidence that there is a difference between the means of the two populations. When we reject the null hypothesis that there is not a linear correlation between two variables, we have confidence that there is in fact a linear correlation between these two variables in the population. But the logic we have used so far does not allow us to zero in on the value of the population parameter. When we find that the relationship between two variables in a sample is statistically significant, we conclude that there is likely to be a relationship in the population from which the sample was drawn. But this decision does not provide us with an estimate of the size of that relationship in the population.

In this chapter, we turn to an approach to statistical inference that leads us to make specific statements about population parameters from sample statistics. The logic used in this approach is very similar to that described in earlier chapters. However, we do not make a single decision about the null hypothesis. Rather, we create an interval of values within which we can be fairly confident that the true parameter lies. Of course, without data on the population itself, we can never be certain of the value of the population parameter. This interval is generally called a confidence interval. In this chapter, we begin by explaining the logic behind confidence intervals and how they are used. We then illustrate how confidence intervals are constructed for the main statistics reviewed in this text.

Confidence Intervals

In the statistical tests presented in earlier chapters, we began by setting a null hypothesis. Our null hypothesis made a statement about the value of the population parameter. In practice, the null hypothesis generally stated that a statistic had a value of 0. For example, for the difference of means test, the null hypothesis generally stated that the difference between two population means was 0; for the correlation coefficient, that the population correlation had a value of 0; or for the regression coefficient, that the population regression coefficient had a value of 0. When the results of our statistical test indicated that we should reject the null hypothesis, we concluded that it was unlikely that the population parameter had the value stated in the null hypothesis. Since the null hypothesis was generally 0 or no difference, we rejected the hypothesis that the population parameter had this null value.

We can use similar logic to make a very different statement about population parameters. In this case, we ask where the population parameters are likely to be found. In statistics, the interval of values around the sample statistic within which we can be fairly confident that the true parameter lies is called a **confidence interval.** A confidence interval makes it possible for us to state where we think the population parameter is likely to be—that is, the range of values within which we feel statistically confident that the true population parameter is likely to be found. Importantly, the fact that we are confident does not mean that the population parameter actually lies in that range of values. As in tests of statistical significance, we rely on probabilities in making our decisions.

One common illustration of confidence intervals comes from newspaper articles and television news programs reporting the results from public opinion polls. In addition to stating that some percentage of the population supports a particular political candidate in an upcoming election or a particular policy, more thorough accounts of these kinds of survey results typically make reference to a range of values. For example, a poll might indicate that 60% of adults in the United States favor using the death penalty for convicted murderers, ±4% (plus or minus 4 percent).

The value of 60% is often described in statistics as a **point estimate.** Absent knowledge of the population parameter, the statistic we obtain for our sample is generally used as an estimate—in statistical terms, a point estimate—of the population parameter. The range of values represented by ±4% is sometimes described as the **margin of error** of a poll. In statistics, we prefer to call this margin of error a confidence interval. Based on a very specific set of statistical assumptions, it is the interval within which the true population value is expected to fall.

Confidence intervals are based on the same statistical logic as tests of statistical significance. It will be easier to understand the relationship between tests of statistical significance and the construction of confidence intervals if we start with an example that—although it is very unusual—allows us to make a straightforward link between these two concepts. Let's say that we gather data on attitudes toward the death penalty using an interval-scale measure that has both positive values, indicating support for the death penalty, and negative values, indicating opposition to the death penalty. We use an independent random sampling method to draw our sample from the population of all adult Americans. After completing our study, we find that the mean score for attitudes toward the death penalty is 0.

In determining a confidence interval, we rely on the same basic assumptions that we use for tests of statistical significance. If we were going to compare the mean in our sample to some hypothesized population mean, we would use a t-test as our test of statistical significance. This means that the t-test also underlies our confidence interval. Accordingly, we have to assume an interval level of measurement and make parametric assumptions regarding the population distribution. Let's assume that our sample is very large, so we can relax the assumption of a normal population distribution. We have already noted that the sampling method meets the requirements of a t-test.

If we intended to conduct a test of statistical significance for this example, we would have stated a null hypothesis and an alternative hypothesis and set a level of statistical significance. Let's say that the null hypothesis is that Americans are neutral regarding the death penalty. This means that H_0 for our example will be 0.0, as the scale is divided between positive attitudes greater than 0 and negative attitudes less than 0. There is no reason to posit a directional research hypothesis, so our test will be two-tailed. We will use a standard 0.05 significance level.

Figure 18.1 illustrates the t-test for this example. The rejection region begins at a t- value of 1.96 either above or below the null hypothesis of 0. In order to reject the null hypothesis, we need an observed value of t for our sample that is greater than 1.96 or less than -1.96. Since our observed value of the measure is 0, the value of t will also be 0. Clearly, we would not reject the null hypothesis in this case.

Figure 18.1	*The 5% Rejection Region and 95% Confidence Interval on a Normal Frequency Distribution (where $\overline{X}$ and $H_0 = 0$)*

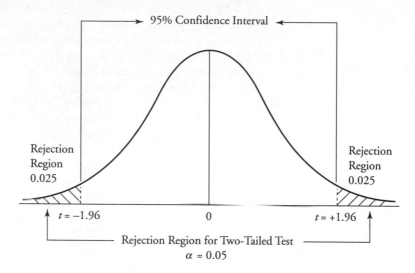

But what would a confidence interval for this example look like? With a confidence interval, we are not concerned about whether the population parameter is *not* at a specific value (for example, the null hypothesis); rather, we are concerned about specifying a range of values within which we can be fairly confident (though not certain) that the population parameter lies. How do we choose this range of values? Clearly, we want to make the interval large enough that, given the observed statistic in our sample, the population parameter is unlikely to lie outside it. As in tests of statistical significance, our choice is based on convention. With a test of statistical significance, it is common to set a threshold of 5% for the risk we are willing to take of falsely rejecting the null hypothesis. With confidence intervals, we define the width of the interval so that we can be very confident that the true population value lies within it. The confidence interval most commonly used is a 95% confidence interval. Figure 18.1 illustrates the 95% confidence interval for our example. As you can see, the confidence interval extends until the rejection region begins. It is, in this sense, the flip side of the rejection region.

Thus, a 95% confidence interval and a 5% significance level are directly related. In our example, the 5% significance rejection region represents values far enough away from the null hypothesis that we are confident in rejecting it. The 95% confidence interval represents values close enough to our observed statistic, or point estimate, that we are confident that the population parameter lies within that interval.

Of course, in practical examples it is very unlikely that our observed sample statistic will be the same as the population parameter hypothesized by the null hypothesis. A more common situation is that of the opinion poll described earlier. What would the confidence interval look like for our opinion poll? We have all the information we need to illustrate that example, except that the level of confidence of the interval was not specified. Let's assume that a 95% confidence interval was used in arriving at the margin of error. The observed statistic, or point estimate, of 60% will be the mean of the distribution. We would use a z-test rather than a t-test because we are concerned with only a single proportion. Let's assume that the other assumptions of the test were met. The margin of error of the test, or size of the confidence interval, is 4%. Figure 18.2 shows the confidence interval relative to the z distribution. As you can see, the interval ranges between 56% and 64%.

But how does this confidence interval relate to a test of statistical significance? First, we need to identify a null hypothesis. Suppose we make the null hypothesis for our test that the population is evenly divided in their attitudes toward the death penalty. In this case, the H_0 takes on a value of 0.50, meaning that about half of the population to which the sample infers are for and half against the use of the death penalty for

Figure 18.2   *95% Confidence Interval for the Public Opinion Poll Example*

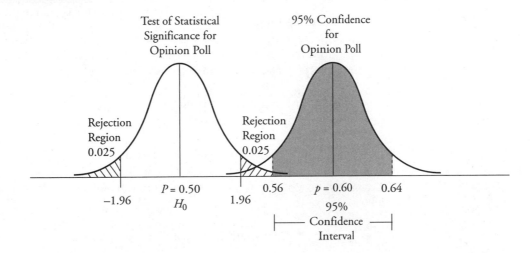

convicted murderers. Note that this value is very far outside the confidence interval that we have defined for our example.

Figure 18.2 shows the sampling distribution for our example. As you can see, our point estimate of 0.60 falls much to the right of the critical value ($t = \pm 1.96$) of our test of statistical significance. As a general rule, if the null hypothesis for a test of statistical significance lies outside the confidence interval for the statistic (and the confidence interval and the significance level represent opposite parts of the same criterion—for example, 0.95 and 0.05; 0.99 and 0.01), then you may assume that the result is statistically significant. This again points to the close relationship between tests of statistical significance and confidence intervals.

While we use the logic of confidence intervals to define where a population parameter is likely to be found, the confidence interval has a very specific statistical interpretation. Were we to draw repeated samples of a specific sample size from the same population, using a 95% confidence interval, we would expect that in 95% of these samples the confidence interval would include the population parameter. That is, we would expect that in only 5 out of every 100 samples would the parameter lie outside the confidence interval. As in tests of statistical significance, we must be aware at the outset that we are only making an informed decision about the value of the population parameter. Using a 95% confidence interval, we will make the wrong decision about 5 in a 100 times.

Constructing Confidence Intervals

Confidence intervals for many different sample statistics can be constructed using the same basic equation. To illustrate how we construct a confidence interval, we use the example of a t-statistic. The most general equation for calculating a t-statistic for a sample statistic is written as follows:

$$t = \frac{\text{sample statistic} - \text{population parameter}}{\text{standard error of sampling distribution}}$$

To construct a confidence interval, we adjust this equation so that we can solve it for the population parameter. We can do this through simple algebra. Solving for the population parameter produces the following equation:

$$\text{Population parameter} = \left(\begin{array}{c} \text{sample} \\ \text{statistic} \end{array} \right) + t \left(\begin{array}{c} \text{standard error of} \\ \text{sampling distribution} \end{array} \right)$$

In setting the boundaries for the confidence interval, we will use the positive and negative values associated with a two-tailed t-test to provide the upper and lower boundaries, respectively (see Figure 18.1). After we account for the positive and negative t-values, our confidence interval is given by Equation 18.1.

$$\text{Confidence limit} = \left(\begin{array}{c}\text{sample}\\\text{statistic}\end{array}\right) \pm t \left(\begin{array}{c}\text{standard error of}\\\text{sampling distribution}\end{array}\right) \qquad \textbf{Equation 18.1}$$

The t-value in the equation coincides with the level of confidence we require (i.e., the critical t-value). Following our earlier logic, this t-value is the flip side of the significance threshold. For a 95% confidence interval, we use a t-value associated with a two-tailed 0.05 significance level. For a 99% confidence interval, we use a t-value associated with a two-tailed 0.01 significance level. In general, if α is our significance level for a two-tailed test, then we can construct a confidence interval for $100 \times (1 - \alpha)$ using the same critical t-values.

Confidence Intervals for Sample Means

Let's start by constructing a confidence interval for a sample mean $(\overline{X})$. If we rewrite Equation 18.1 to replace the general terms with the mean and the standard error, we have Equation 18.2.

$$\text{Confidence limit} = \overline{X} \pm t \left(\frac{s}{\sqrt{N - 1}}\right) \qquad \textbf{Equation 18.2}$$

where $\overline{X}$ is the sample mean, s is the sample standard deviation, N is the sample size, and t is the critical t-value associated with a given significance level. To determine our critical t, we use df $= N - 1$, as in the single-sample t-test (see Chapter 10).

For an illustration of the calculation of a confidence interval for a sample mean, consider a recent study of fear of crime among Korean Americans living in the Chicago area.[1] The investigators constructed a fear of crime instrument that was measured on an interval scale and ranged in value from 11.00 to 110.00. The mean fear of crime score for the 721 respondents was 81.05, with a standard deviation of 23.41.

To calculate a 99% confidence interval for the fear of crime instrument, we use the t-value associated with a 0.01 significance level and 720 degrees of freedom (df $= 721 - 1$). Using the last line of the t distribution table in Appendix 4, we find the corresponding critical t-value to be 2.576.

---

[1]Min Sik Lee and Jeffery T. Ulmer, "Fear of Crime Among Korean Americans in Chicago Communities," *Criminology* 38:4 (2000): 1173–1206.

A 99% confidence interval for the fear of crime instrument has the following values:

W **orking It Out**

Confidence limit $= \overline{X} \pm t\left(\dfrac{s}{\sqrt{N-1}}\right)$

$= 81.05 \pm 2.576\left(\dfrac{23.41}{\sqrt{721-1}}\right)$

$= 81.05 \pm 2.25$

The result of ± 2.25 indicates that the 99% confidence interval includes values ranging from a low of 78.80 (81.05 − 2.25) to a high of 83.30 (81.05 + 2.25). By using a 99% confidence interval, we can be very confident that the population mean lies somewhere between 78.80 and 83.30. In statistical terms, if we were to observe repeated samples of this size drawn from this population and calculate a confidence interval for each of them, only about 1 in 100 would fail to include the true population parameter.

Confidence Intervals for Sample Proportions We can apply the same type of logic to calculating a confidence interval for a sample proportion, modifying Equation 18.1 by replacing the critical t-value with the critical z-value. To calculate a confidence interval for a sample proportion, we use Equation 18.3:

$$\text{Confidence limit} = p \pm z\left(\sqrt{\frac{pq}{N}}\right)$$

Equation 18.3

where p is the sample proportion, q is $1-p$, N is the sample size, and z is the critical z-value associated with a given significance level.

In their study of fear of crime among Korean Americans in the Chicago area, the investigators also included a question about the respondent's victimization experiences. Specifically, respondents were asked whether they had experienced any kind of victimization in the past three years. Included in this global indicator of victimization were violent as well as property crime victimizations. The investigators reported that 27% of the 721 respondents had experienced some form of victimization during this time period.

Knowing that the sample proportion is 0.27 and the z-score is 1.96, we can calculate a 95% confidence interval for this proportion. We insert our values for p, q, and N into Equation 18.3.

W orking It Out

$$\text{Confidence limit} = p \pm z \sqrt{\frac{pq}{N}}$$

$$= 0.27 \pm 1.960 \sqrt{\frac{(0.27)(1 - 0.27)}{721}}$$

$$= 0.27 \pm 1.960(0.0165)$$

$$= 0.27 \pm 0.03$$

The 95% confidence interval is $\pm$3% around the sample mean of 27%. It suggests that we can be confident that the percentage of Korean Americans living in and around Chicago who experienced some form of criminal victimization within the three-year period lies between 24% and 30%.

Confidence Intervals for a Difference of Sample Means In Chapter 11, we discussed calculating t-statistics to test for significant differences between two sample means. Another way of calculating a confidence interval for the difference of two sample means is by modifying Equation 18.1 to replace the sample mean with the difference of sample means and insert the appropriate standard error for the difference of two sample means. Recall from Chapter 11, however, that there are two methods for calculating the standard error of the sampling distribution: the separate variance method and the pooled variance method (see pages 260–263). Equations 18.4a and 18.4b present formulas for calculating a confidence interval for a difference of two sample means, using either the separate variance method or the pooled variance method.

$$\text{Confidence limit} = (\overline{X}_1 - \overline{X}_2) \pm t \sqrt{\frac{s_1^2}{N_1 - 1} + \frac{s_2^2}{N_2 - 1}}$$

Equation 18.4a Separate Variance Method

$$\text{Confidence limit} = (\overline{X}_1 - \overline{X}_2) \pm t \left(\sqrt{\frac{N_1 s_1^2 + N_2 s_2^2}{N_1 + N_2 - 2}} \sqrt{\frac{N_1 + N_2}{N_1 N_2}} \right)$$

Equation 18.4b Pooled Variance Method

In both equations, $\overline{X}_1$ and $\overline{X}_2$ represent the two sample means, s_1^2 and s_2^2 represent the two sample variances, N_1 and N_2 represent the two sample sizes, and t is the critical t-value associated with a given significance level. As with the two-sample t-test (see Chapter 11), the number of degrees of freedom for determining the critical t-value will be df = $N_1 + N_2 - 2$.

Chapter 11 presented a test for differences in bail amounts required of African American and Hispanic defendants in Los Angeles County. A sample of 1,121 African Americans were required to post a mean bail amount of $50,841 ($s$ = 115,565), while a sample of 1,798 Hispanics were required to post a mean bail amount of $66,552 ($s$ = 190,801). The difference in the two sample means is $15,711, where Hispanics were required to post higher bail amounts, on average.

Using Equations 18.4a and 18.4b, we can calculate a 95% confidence interval for this difference of sample means. For both equations, we use the t-value associated with a 0.05 significance level and 2,917 degrees of freedom. From the last line of the t distribution table in Appendix 4, we find that critical t = 1.960.

W orking It Out   **Separate Variance Method**

$$\text{Confidence limit} = (\overline{X}_1 - \overline{X}_2) \pm t \sqrt{\frac{s_1^2}{N_1 - 1} + \frac{s_2^2}{N_2 - 1}}$$

$$= (50{,}841 - 66{,}552) \pm 1.960 \sqrt{\frac{115{,}565^2}{1{,}121 - 1} + \frac{190{,}801^2}{1{,}798 - 1}}$$

$$= -15{,}711 \pm 1.960(5{,}673.02)$$

$$= -15{,}711 \pm 11{,}119.12$$

W orking It Out   **Pooled Variance Method**

$$\text{Confidence limit} = (\overline{X}_1 - \overline{X}_2) \pm t \left(\sqrt{\frac{N_1 s_1^2 + N_2 s_2^2}{N_1 + N_2 - 2}} \sqrt{\frac{N_1 + N_2}{N_1 N_2}} \right)$$

$$= (50{,}841 - 66{,}552)$$

$$\pm 1.960 \left(\sqrt{\frac{(1{,}121)(115{,}565^2) + (1{,}798)(190{,}801^2)}{1{,}121 + 1{,}798 - 2}} \sqrt{\frac{1{,}121 + 1{,}798}{(1{,}121)(1{,}798)}} \right)$$

$$= -15{,}711 \pm 1.960(6{,}319.07)$$

$$= -15{,}711 \pm 12{,}385.38$$

Using the separate variance method, we find that the confidence interval is ±11,119.12 around the difference of sample means of 15,711. This interval suggests that we can be confident, based on our sample findings, that the average bail amounts posted in Los Angeles by African Americans were from $4,591.88 to $26,830.12 *less* than the average bail amounts required of Hispanics. The pooled variance method provides very similar results, indicating that the confidence interval is ±12,385.38 around the difference of sample means. Again, this interval suggests that we can be fairly confident that African Americans were required to post average bail amounts from $3,325.62 to $28,096.38 *less* than those required of Hispanics.

Confidence Intervals for Pearson's Correlation Coefficient, *r*

The calculation of confidence intervals for Pearson's correlation coefficient, *r*, relies on a similar logic, but requires an additional step. In contrast to that for sample means, sample proportions, or differences of means, the sampling distribution for Pearson's *r* is not normal or even approximately normal.[2] Consequently, we need to convert *r* into another statistic, Z^*, that does have a normal distribution. The conversion of *r* is known as the Fisher *r*-to-Z^* transformation.[3] After calculating the standard error for Z^*, we can then modify Equation 18.1 to calculate a confidence interval for Z^*. Since the values for Z^* are not directly interpretable, we will then convert the confidence limits back into values of *r*.

The Fisher *r*-to-Z^* transformation is given in Equation 18.5. In this equation, we take the natural logarithm of 1 plus *r* divided by 1 minus *r* and multiply this value by $\frac{1}{2}$.

$$Z^* = \frac{1}{2} \times \ln\left(\frac{1 + r}{1 - r}\right)$$

Equation 18.5

Values for Z^* for correlation coefficients ranging in value from 0.000 to 1.000 are given in Appendix 8. Note that the correlations given in the appendix are all positive. If *r* is negative, then Z^* will also be negative.

In Chapter 14, we reported that the correlation between unemployment rates and burglary rates for 58 counties in California was 0.491. If

---

[2]The sampling distribution for *r* will generally be normal and symmetric only for the case where *r* = 0, which is what allowed us to use the *t* distribution to test whether r_p = 0 (i.e., the null hypothesis) in Chapter 14. When *r* ≠ 0, the sampling distribution is not symmetric around *r*, so we cannot calculate a confidence interval for *r* in the same way we did for sample means or the difference of sample means.

[3]Ronald A. Fisher, *Statistical Methods for Research Workers*, 14th ed. (New York: Hafner, 1970).

we locate $r = 0.491$ in Appendix 8, we find Z^* to be 0.5374. We obtain the same value for Z^* if we use Equation 18.5.

W orking It Out

$$Z^* = \frac{1}{2} \times \ln \left(\frac{1 + r}{1 - r} \right)$$

$$= \frac{1}{2} \times \ln \left(\frac{1 + 0.491}{1 - 0.491} \right)$$

$$= 0.5374$$

The standard error of Z^*, which is based on the size of the sample (N), is presented in Equation 18.6.

$$\sigma_{sd(Z^*)} = \frac{1}{\sqrt{N - 3}}$$ **Equation 18.6**

In our example concerning unemployment rates and burglary rates for California counties, we have 58 observations, so the standard error of Z^* is 0.1348.

W orking It Out

$$\sigma_{sd(Z^*)} = \frac{1}{\sqrt{N - 3}}$$

$$= \frac{1}{\sqrt{58 - 3}}$$

$$= 0.1348$$

We can now modify Equation 18.1 by inserting Z^* as the sample statistic, a critical z-value (since Z^* is approximately normally distributed), and the equation for the standard error of Z^*. The formula for the confidence interval for Z^* is given in Equation 18.7.

$$\text{Confidence limit} = Z^* \pm z \left(\frac{1}{\sqrt{N - 3}} \right)$$ **Equation 18.7**

where Z^* is based on the Fisher r-to-Z^* transformation, N is the sample size, and z is the critical z-value associated with a given significance level.

Continuing our example for $Z^* = 0.5374$ and $N = 58$, we calculate a 95% confidence interval for Z^* by using critical $z = 1.960$ and inserting the values into Equation 18.7.

W orking It Out

$$\text{Confidence limit} = Z^* \pm z \left(\frac{1}{\sqrt{N-3}} \right)$$

$$= 0.5374 \pm 1.960 \left(\frac{1}{\sqrt{58-3}} \right)$$

$$= 0.5374 \pm 0.2642$$

The confidence interval is ± 0.2642 around $Z^* = 0.5374$, indicating that the range for Z^* is 0.2732 to 0.8016. Since we are unable to directly interpret values of Z^*, we should convert the values of Z^* back to values of r, using Appendix 8. The conversion of Z^* back to r will provide us with the confidence interval for r. For $Z^* = 0.2732$, we find that $r = 0.267$. For $Z^* = 0.8016$, we find that $r = 0.665$. For both values of Z^*, we used the closest Z^*-value reported in Appendix 8 to determine the values for r, since an exact match could not be found. These results suggest that we can be confident that the population value for the correlation coefficient falls between 0.267 and 0.665. Note that the upper and lower confidence limits are not symmetric around r—the lower limit is farther away from $r = 0.491$ than is the upper limit.

Confidence Intervals for Regression Coefficients

Confidence intervals for regression coefficients are nearly identical in form to confidence intervals for sample means. The formula for calculating confidence intervals for regression coefficients is given in Equation 18.8.

$$\text{Confidence limit} = b \pm t\hat{\sigma}_b \qquad \qquad \textbf{Equation 18.8}$$

where b is the regression coefficient, $\hat{\sigma}_b$ is the standard error of b, and t is the critical t-value associated with a given level of significance. The number of degrees of freedom for the critical t will be equal to $N - k - 1$, where N is the sample size and k is the number of independent variables in the regression model.

In Chapter 15, we reported that the regression coefficient representing the effect of unemployment rates on burglary rates in California was 36.7483 and the standard error for b was 8.7126 (see page 446). If we calculate a 99% confidence interval, the number of degrees of freedom will be 56 (df = 58 − 1 − 1 = 56), so the critical t we will use is 2.669 (see Appendix 4).

W **orking It Out**

$$\text{Confidence limit} = b \pm t\hat{\sigma}_b$$
$$= 36.7483 \pm 2.669(8.7126)$$
$$= 36.7483 \pm 23.2539$$

The result of ±23.2539 indicates that the 99% confidence interval includes values ranging from a low of 13.4944 to a high of 60.0022. The 99% confidence interval suggests that we can be very confident that the population value of the regression coefficient representing the effect of unemployment rates on burglary rates lies somewhere between 13.4944 and 60.0022.

Confidence Intervals for Logistic Regression Coefficients and Odds Ratios

Confidence intervals for logistic regression coefficients are calculated in exactly the same way as logistic regression coefficients (Equation 18.8). The number of degrees of freedom for determining the critical t-value also equals $N - k - 1$.

In addition to being able to calculate confidence intervals for the original logistic regression coefficients, we can also refer to confidence intervals for odds ratios. As noted in Chapter 17, we can convert our logistic regression coefficients into odds ratios by exponentiating the coefficient b. This means that we can take the lower and upper limits of our confidence interval for b and convert them to odds ratios. We can then discuss the confidence interval relative to the odds, rather than the untransformed coefficients, which are difficult to interpret.

An illustration of the use of confidence intervals for logistic regression coefficients is provided by a recent study examining the link between mental disorders and violent victimization for a sample of 747 adults.[4] The dependent variable measured whether the individual had reported a

---

[4] Eric Silver, "Mental Disorder and Violent Victimization: The Mediating Role of Involvement in Conflicted Social Relationships," *Criminology* 40 (2002): 191–212.

violent victimization in the preceding ten weeks. One of the nine inde-pendent variables used by the researcher was the level of neighborhood disadvantage, which was an interval-level instrument that combined eco-nomic indicators, such as poverty rate, unemployment rate, and income. The effect of neighborhood disadvantage was positive ($b = 0.33$), mean-ing the greater the level of neighborhood disadvantage, the more likely the individual was to have experienced a violent victimization. The stan-dard error for b was reported to be 0.09.

To calculate a 99% confidence interval for b, we use critical $t = 2.576$, since df = $747 - 9 - 1 = 737$, and insert the values into Equation 18.8.

W orking It Out

Confidence limit $= b \pm t\hat{\sigma}_b$

$$= 0.33 \pm 2.576(0.09)$$

$$= 0.33 \pm 0.23$$

The result of ± 0.23 tells us that the 99% confidence interval includes values ranging from a low of 0.10 to a high of 0.56. If we exponentiate the lower and upper limits of the confidence interval for b, we will have the lower and upper limits of the confidence interval for the odds ratio. The lower limit of the confidence interval for the odds ratio is 1.105 [Exp(0.10)], and the upper limit of the confidence interval for the odds ratio is 1.751 [Exp(0.56)]. These results suggest that we can be very confi-dent that the population value of the odds ratio lies somewhere between 1.105 and 1.751. If we took repeated random samples of the size exam-ined here and calculated a confidence interval for each, then in only about 1 in 100 cases would that interval fail to include the true odds ratio.

Chapter Summary

In tests of statistical significance, we make a statement about where the population parameter is *not*. In this chapter, we turned to an approach to statistical inference that leads us to make a very different type of state-ment about population parameters. The logic used in this approach is similar to that described in earlier chapters. However, we do not make a single decision about the null hypothesis. Rather, we create an interval of values within which we can be fairly confident that the true parameter lies—although, without data on the population itself, we can never be certain of the value of the population parameter. This interval is generally called a **confidence interval.**

A confidence interval makes it possible for us to say where we think the population parameter is likely to be—that is, the range of values within which we feel statistically confident that the true population parameter is likely to be found. A confidence interval is generally constructed around the observed statistic of interest, commonly called a **point estimate.** Absent knowledge of the population parameter, the statistic we obtain for our sample is generally used as an estimate—in statistical terms, a point estimate—of the population parameter. The size of the confidence interval is often referred to as the **margin of error.**

Confidence intervals may be constructed at any level of confidence. By convention, we use 95% and 99% confidence levels, which are based on 5% and 1% significance thresholds. While it is commonly said, when using a confidence interval, that the researcher is confident that the true parameter lies in the interval defined, confidence intervals have a specific statistical interpretation. Suppose we find, using a 95% or 99% criterion, that a confidence interval is of a certain size. If we were to draw repeated samples of the same size, using the same methods, and calculate a confidence interval for each sample, then in only 5 in 100 (for a 95% interval) or 1 in 100 (for a 99% interval) of these samples would the interval fail to include the true population parameter.

Key Terms

confidence interval An interval of values around a statistic (usually a point estimate). If we were to draw repeated samples and calculate a 95% confidence interval for each, then in only 5 in 100 of these samples would the interval fail to include the true population parameter. In the case of a 99% confidence interval, only 1 in 100 samples would fail to include the true population parameter.

margin of error The size of the confidence interval for a test. A margin of error of ±3% in an opinion poll means that the confidence interval ranged between 3% above and 3% below the point estimate or observed statistic.

point estimate An estimate of the population parameter. Absent knowledge of the population parameter, the statistic we obtain for a sample is generally used as an estimate—or, in statistical terms, a point estimate—of the population parameter.

Symbols and Formulas

To calculate the confidence interval for a sample mean:

$$\text{Confidence limit} = \overline{X} \pm t\left(\frac{s}{\sqrt{N-1}}\right)$$

To calculate the confidence interval for a sample proportion:

$$\text{Confidence limit} = p \pm z\left(\sqrt{\frac{pq}{N}}\right)$$

To calculate the confidence interval for a difference of sample means, using the separate variance method:

$$\text{Confidence limit} = (\overline{X}_1 - \overline{X}_2) \pm t\sqrt{\frac{s_1^2}{N_1 - 1} + \frac{s_2^2}{N_2 - 1}}$$

To calculate the confidence interval for a difference of sample means, using the pooled variance method:

$$\text{Confidence limit} = (\overline{X}_1 - \overline{X}_2) \pm t\left(\sqrt{\frac{N_1 s_1^2 + N_2 s_2^2}{N_1 + N_2 - 2}}\sqrt{\frac{N_1 + N_2}{N_1 N_2}}\right)$$

To convert r to Z^* (Fisher r-to-Z^* transformation):

$$Z^* = \frac{1}{2} \times \ln\left(\frac{1+r}{1-r}\right)$$

To calculate the confidence interval for Z^*:

$$\text{Confidence limit} = Z^* \pm z\left(\frac{1}{\sqrt{N-3}}\right)$$

To calculate the confidence interval for a regression or logistic regression coefficient:

$$\text{Confidence limit} = b \pm t\hat{\sigma}_b$$

Exercises

18.1 In a study of self-reported marijuana use, a sample of high school students were asked how many times they had smoked marijuana in the last month. Researchers reported that the average for the sample was

2.4 times, with a 95% confidence interval of ±1.3. Explain what this result means in plain English.

18.2 Following a revolution, the new leadership of the nation of Kippax intends to hold a national referendum on whether the practice of capital punishment should be introduced. In the buildup to the referendum, a leading army general wishes to gauge how the people are likely to vote so that he can make a public statement in line with popular feeling on the issue. He commissions Greg, a statistician, to carry out a secret poll of how people plan to vote. The results of Greg's poll are as follows: The sample proportion in favor of introducing capital punishment is 52%; the sample has a 95% confidence interval of ±10%. How should Greg explain these results to the army general?

18.3 Concerned that taxpayers were not reporting incomes honestly, a state department of revenue commissioned an independent study to estimate the number of times people had cheated on their tax returns in the last five years. The researchers interviewed a random sample of 121 adults and found that the mean number of times they had cheated on their income taxes in the last five years was 2.7, with a standard deviation of 1.1.

   a. Calculate a 95% confidence interval for this sample mean.

   b. Explain what this result means.

18.4 The country of Mifflin is preparing for an upcoming presidential election. A random sample of 200 likely voters in Mifflin indicates that 57% are going to vote for the Hawk Party candidate, while the remaining 43% are planning on voting for the Gopher Party candidate.

   a. Calculate a 95% confidence interval for the proportion voting for the Hawk Party candidate.

   b. Calculate a 99% confidence interval for the proportion voting for the Hawk Party candidate.

   c. Which of the two confidence intervals provides a better indicator of who will win the election? Who do you predict will win the election?

18.5 A long-running disagreement between science and humanities professors at Big Time University focuses on which department has the smarter students. As evidence supportive of the contention that science students are smarter, a physics professor shows that the mean grade point average for a random sample of 322 recent science graduates was 3.51 ($s = 1.2$). Asserting that there is no meaningful difference, a history professor shows that the mean grade point average for a sample of 485 recent humanities graduates was 3.36 ($s = 1.6$). Construct a 99% confidence interval for this difference of means, and explain which professor appears to be more correct.

18.6   Interested in the effects of income and poverty on robbery rates, a student selected a random sample of 125 cities and correlated average income and percentage of persons living in poverty with the robbery rate. She reported the following correlations:

Income and robbery: $r = -0.215$
Poverty and robbery: $r = 0.478$

a. Calculate a 95% confidence interval for each correlation.

b. Explain what these results mean.

18.7   Delinquency researchers at DP Institute interviewed a sample of 96 adolescents about their behavior. The researchers estimated a regression model, using number of delinquent acts in the last year as the dependent variable. The table of results follows:

Variable	b	Standard Error
Intercept	−0.21	0.15
Age	−0.02	0.01
Number of friends arrested	2.56	0.73
Number of hours per week studying	−0.17	0.08
Number of hours per week working	0.09	0.03
Self-esteem	−1.05	0.51

a. Calculate a 95% confidence interval for each of the independent variable regression coefficients.

b. Explain what these results mean.

18.8   In a follow-up to the analysis reported in Exercise 18.7, the researchers recoded delinquency as 0 = no delinquency and 1 = one or more delinquent acts. They estimated a logistic regression model and found the following:

Variable	b	Standard Error
Intercept	0.05	0.04
Age	−0.12	0.05
Number of friends arrested	1.86	0.57
Number of hours per week studying	−0.23	0.09
Number of hours per week working	0.44	0.17
Self-esteem	−0.79	0.38

a. Calculate a 95% confidence interval for each of the independent variable regression coefficients.

b. Explain what these results mean.

Computer Exercises

Many of the statistical procedures available in SPSS allow for the calculation of confidence intervals. Four of the confidence intervals discussed in this chapter—sample mean, difference of means, regression, and logistic regression—may be computed easily in SPSS. There is no option in SPSS at this time for computing confidence intervals for Pearson's r.

To obtain the confidence interval for a sample mean, use the "One Sample T Test" command (Analyze → Compare Means → One Sample T Test). Click on the "Options" button located in the lower right corner of the window. The next window that opens will allow you to specify the size of the confidence interval. The default value is a 95% confidence interval.

To obtain the confidence interval for a difference of means t-test, use the "Independent Samples T Test" command (Analyze → Compare Means → Independent Samples T Test). Click on the "Options" button in the lower right corner of the window. As with the single-sample command, the next window that opens will allow you to specify the size of the confidence interval. The default value is again 95%.

For regression coefficients, use the linear regression command (Analyze → Regression → Linear). In the window that allows you to specify the dependent and independent variables, click on the "Statistics" button in the lower left section. Select the box next to "Confidence Intervals"—this will produce 95% confidence intervals for the independent variables included in the regression model. Note that there is no option to specify a different confidence interval for the regression coefficients.

The logistic regression command (Analyze → Regression → Binary Logistic) also allows for the computation of confidence intervals. After you execute the command, you will be presented with a window in which to enter the dependent and independent variables. Click on the "Options" button in the lower right corner. In the next window that opens, select the box next to "CI for Exp(B)." You may specify a confidence interval other than 95% at this time. Please note that the confidence interval SPSS will compute is for the odds ratio [Exp(B)], not the original coefficient (B).

Open the ***nys_1.sav*** data file to answer the following questions.

1. For each of the following measures of delinquency, compute a 95% confidence interval and explain what it means.

    a. Number of times the youth has stolen something valued at less than $5.

    b. Number of times the youth has cheated on exams at school.

    c. Number of times the youth has been drunk.

2. For each of the following difference of means tests, compute a 95% confidence interval and explain what it means.

    a. Does the number of times the youth has taken something valued at less than $5 differ for males and females?

b. Does the number of times the youth has hit his or her parents differ for whites and African Americans?

c. Does the number of times the youth has cheated on exams differ for students earning mostly Bs and students earning mostly Cs?

3. Rerun two of the regression models you estimated in the Chapter 16 computer exercises (see page 493). For each model, compute the confidence intervals for the regression coefficients and explain what each result means.

4. Rerun two of the logistic regression models you estimated in the Chapter 17 computer exercises (see page 545). For each model, compute the confidence intervals for the odds ratios and explain what each result means.

Special Topics: Statistical Power

As WE HAVE SEEN in earlier chapters, criminal justice researchers place a strong emphasis on statistical inference and its use in making decisions about population parameters from sample statistics. In statistical significance, we focus on the problem of Type I, or alpha, error: the risk of falsely rejecting the null hypothesis. Paying attention to the statistical significance of a finding keeps researchers honest, because it provides a systematic approach for deciding when the observed statistics are convincing enough for the researcher to state that they reflect broader processes or relationships in the general population from which the sample was drawn. If the threshold of statistical significance is not met, then the researcher cannot reject the null hypothesis and cannot conclude that a relationship exists.

But there is another type of error that should concern the researcher developing or evaluating research studies. This is Type II error, originally introduced in Chapter 6. A Type II error occurs when, based on sample statistics, the researcher fails to reject the null hypothesis when it is false in the population of interest. A study that has a high risk of Type II error is very likely to mistakenly conclude that treatments are not worthwhile or that a relationship does not exist when in fact it does.

Traditionally, researchers in criminal justice, as in other fields, have placed much more emphasis on statistical significance than on statistical power, the area of statistics concerned with estimating the risk of Type II error. However, recently researchers and those who fund research have begun to pay a good deal more attention to this problem and its implications for research studies. In this chapter, we introduce the concept of statistical power and explain why it is important to those who design and evaluate criminal justice research. We also examine the different factors that affect statistical power and the methods used to increase the power of a test.

Statistical Power

The most common way to assess the risk of a Type II error in a study is to measure its level of **statistical power.** Statistical power may be defined as $1 - P$(Type II error), or one minus the probability of falsely failing to reject the null hypothesis. In contrast to statistical significance, which identifies for the researcher the risk of stating that factors are related when they are not, statistical power questions how often one would fail to identify a relationship that in fact exists in the population.

As the statistical power of a study gets higher, the risk of making a Type II error, or failing to identify a relationship, gets smaller. For example, a study with a statistical power level of 0.90 has only a 10% probability of failing to reject the null hypothesis when it is false. Conversely, as the power level of a study gets lower, the risk of making a Type II error gets larger. A study in which the statistical power level is only 0.10 has a 90% probability of falsely failing to reject the null hypothesis.

Sometimes statistical power is defined as the probability that a test will lead to rejection of the null hypothesis. If the power of a test is high and the null hypothesis is false for the population under study, then it is very likely that the researcher will reject the null hypothesis and conclude that there is a statistically significant finding. If the power of a test is very low, it is unlikely to yield a statistically significant finding even if the research hypothesis is in fact true. Studies with very low statistical power are sometimes described as being "designed for failure," because a study that is underpowered is unlikely to yield a statistically significant result even when the outcomes observed are consistent with the research hypothesis.

Think for a moment of the implications for theory and practice in criminal justice of a study that has low statistical power. For example, let's say that a promising new program has been developed for dealing with spouse assault. If you evaluate that program with a study that has very low statistical power, you are very likely to fail to reject the null hypothesis based on your sample statistics, even if the program does indeed have the potential for reducing spouse assault. Although you are likely to say that the program does not have a statistically significant impact on spouse assault, this is not because the program is not an effective one, but because you have designed your study in such a way that it is unlikely to be able to identify program success. The same problem applies in the case of establishing a relationship between two theoretically important variables. Even if a relationship exists in the population, a study with low statistical power is unlikely to conclude that the relationship is statistically significant.

One might assume that researchers in criminal justice would work very hard to develop statistically powerful studies because such studies are more likely to support the research hypothesis proposed by the investigators. In fact, however, statistical power is often ignored by criminal justice researchers, and thus criminal justice studies often have a low level of statistical power.[1]

It is generally recommended that a statistical test have a power level greater than 0.50, meaning that it is more likely than not to show a significant result if the null hypothesis is false in the population under study. But it is generally accepted that the most powerful studies seek a power level of 0.80 or above. Such studies are highly likely to evidence a significant finding based on sample statistics if there is an effect or relationship in the population to which the researcher seeks to infer.

Statistical Significance and Statistical Power

In Chapter 6, we adjusted the levels of statistical significance used to take into account both Type I and Type II errors in our statistical tests. Indeed, the most straightforward way to increase the statistical power of a test is to change the significance level used.

A significance level of 0.05 results in a more powerful test than a significance level of 0.01 because it is easier to reject the null hypothesis using more lenient significance criteria. A 0.20 level of significance would, of course, make it even easier to reject the null hypothesis, as illustrated in Table 19.1. It would take a z-value greater than 1.282 or less than -1.282 to reject the null hypothesis in a two-tailed test with $\alpha = 0.20$, a z-value greater than 1.960 or less than -1.960 with $\alpha = 0.05$, and a z-value greater than 2.576 or less than -2.576 with $\alpha = 0.01$. Clearly, it is much easier to reject the null hypothesis with a 0.20 significance threshold than with a 0.01 significance threshold.

This method for increasing statistical power is direct, but it means that any benefit we gain in reducing the risk of a Type II error is offset by an

| Table 19.1 | The z-Score Needed to Reject H_0 in a Two-Tailed Significance Test at Different Levels of Statistical Significance |

α	0.20	0.10	0.05	0.01	0.001
z	1.282	1.645	1.960	2.576	3.291

[1] See S. E. Brown "Statistical Power and Criminal Justice Research," *Journal of Criminal Justice* 17 (1989): 115–122. However, criminal justice researchers are not very different from researchers in other areas of social science; see also D. Weisburd "Design Sensitivity in Criminal Justice Experiments," *Crime and Justice* 17 (1991): 337–379.

increase in the risk of a Type I error. By setting a less strict significance threshold, we do indeed gain a more statistically powerful research study. However, the level of statistical significance of our test also declines. Moreover, as has been pointed out throughout this book, norms concerning statistical significance are strongly established in criminal justice. Generally, a 0.05 significance level is expected in research. When significance thresholds that make it easier to reject the null hypothesis are used, the researcher is expected to carefully explain this departure from established convention.

A related method for increasing the statistical power of a study is to limit the direction of the research hypothesis. A one-tailed test provides greater power than a two-tailed test for the same reason that a less stringent level of statistical significance provides more power than a more stringent one. By choosing a one-tailed test, the researcher reduces the value of the test statistic needed to reject the null hypothesis. Once again, we can see this in practice with the z-test. Table 19.2 lists the z-values needed to reject the null hypothesis in one- and two-tailed tests for five different levels of statistical significance.

At each level, as in other statistical tests, the test statistic required to reject the null hypothesis is smaller in the case of a one-tailed test. For example, at the 0.05 level, a z-value greater than or equal to 1.960 or less than or equal to -1.960 is needed to reject the null hypothesis in a two-tailed test, whereas in a one-tailed test z need only be greater than or equal to 1.645. At the 0.01 level, a z-value greater than or equal to 2.576 or less than or equal to -2.576 is needed to reject the null hypothesis in a two-tailed test, whereas in a one-tailed test z need only be greater than or equal to 2.326. As discussed in earlier chapters, in a one-tailed test all of the rejection region is on one side of the sampling distribution; thus, the rejection region is larger, and it is easier to reject the null hypothesis.

Although the researcher can increase the statistical power of a study by using a directional, as opposed to a nondirectional, research hypothesis, there is a price for shifting the rejection region to one side of the sampling distribution. Once a one-directional test is defined, a finding in the direction opposite to that originally predicted cannot be recognized. To do otherwise would bring into question the integrity of the assumptions of the statistical test you have defined.

Table 19.2   The z-Score Needed to Reject H_0 in One-Tailed and Two-Tailed Tests of Significance

α	0.20	0.10	0.05	0.01	0.001
z-Score, one-tailed test	0.842	1.282	1.645	2.326	3.090
z-Score, two-tailed test	1.282	1.645	1.960	2.576	3.260

Effect Size and Statistical Power

Effect size (ES) is a component of statistical power that is unrelated to the criteria for statistical significance used in a test. Effect size measures the difference between the actual parameters in the population and those hypothesized in the null hypothesis. Its relationship to statistical power is clear. When the population parameters differ strongly from the null hypothesis, you are more likely to observe a significant difference in a particular sample.

In defining effect size, statisticians take into account both the raw differences between scores and the degree of variability found in the measures examined. Taking into account variability in effect size is a method of standardization that allows comparison of effects between studies that use different scales or different types of measures. Generally, effect size is defined as in Equation 19.1.

$$ES = \frac{\text{Parameter} - H_0}{\sigma}$$

Equation 19.1

Effect size will increase either as the difference between the actual parameter and the hypothesized parameter under the null hypothesis increases or as the variability in the measure examined decreases. Variability is generally defined as the pooled or common standard deviation of the outcome measures in the two populations (see Chapter 11). For example, for a difference of means test, effect size is calculated by first subtracting the population difference as stated in the null hypothesis ($H_0\mu_1 - H_0\mu_2$) from the difference between the true means in the population ($\mu_1 - \mu_2$). This value is then divided by the common standard deviation for the two populations studied (see Equation 19.2).[2]

$$ES = \frac{(\mu_1 - \mu_2) - (H_0\mu_1 - H_0\mu_2)}{\sigma}$$

Equation 19.2

Because the null hypothesis for a difference of means test is ordinarily that the two population means are equal, we can simplify this formula and include only the difference between the actual population parame-

---

[2]Effect size can also be calculated for observed differences in a study. This is a common approach in meta-analysis, where a large group of studies are summarized for a single analysis. For example, in calculating effect size for a randomized experiment with one treatment and one control group, the researcher would substitute the outcome scores for both groups in the numerator of the ES equation, and the pooled standard deviation for the two outcome measures in the denominator. For a more detailed discussion of effect size and its use generally for comparing effects across different studies, see Mark Lipsey and David Wilson, *Practical Meta-Analysis*, Applied Social Research Methods Series 49 (Thousand Oaks, CA: Sage, 2001).

ters. Thus, ES for a difference of means test may be defined simply as the raw difference between the two population parameters divided by their common standard deviation, as shown in Equation 19.3.

$$ES = \frac{\mu_1 - \mu_2}{\sigma}$$ **Equation 19.3**

As Equation 19.3 illustrates, when the difference between the population means is greater, ES for the difference of means will be larger. Also, as the variability of the scores of the parameters grows, as represented by the standard deviation of the estimates, ES will get smaller.

Table 19.3 shows the relationship between effect size and statistical power in practice. It presents the number of statistically significant outcomes expected in 100 t-tests (using a 0.05 significance threshold and a nondirectional research hypothesis, $\sigma_1 = \sigma_2$), each with 100 cases per sample, under six different scenarios. In the first three scenarios, the mean differences between the two populations are varied and the standard deviations for the populations are the same. In the last three scenarios, the mean differences are the same and the standard deviations differ.

As Table 19.3 shows, the largest number of statistically significant outcomes is expected in either the comparisons with the largest differences between mean scores or the comparisons with the smallest standard deviations. As the differences between the population means grow (scenar-

Table 19.3   Number of Statistically Significant Outcomes Expected in 100 Two-Sample t-Tests for Six Different Scenarios

GROUP A: MEANS DIFFER; STANDARD DEVIATIONS HELD CONSTANT

SCENARIO	μ_1	μ_2	σ	EXPECTED SIGNIFICANT OUTCOMES
1	0.3	0.5	2	10
2	0.3	0.9	2	56
3	0.3	1.3	2	94

GROUP B: MEANS HELD CONSTANT; STANDARD DEVIATIONS DIFFER

SCENARIO	μ_1	μ_2	σ	EXPECTED SIGNIFICANT OUTCOMES
4	0.3	0.5	0.5	80
5	0.3	0.5	1	29
6	0.3	0.5	2	10

Note: Each test has 100 cases per sample, a 0.05 significance threshold, and a nondirectional research hypothesis ($\sigma_1 = \sigma_2$).

ios 1, 2, and 3), so too does the likelihood of obtaining a statistically significant result. Conversely, as the population standard deviations of the comparisons get larger (scenarios 4, 5, and 6), the expected number of significant outcomes decreases.

As this exercise illustrates, there is a direct relationship between the two components of effect size and statistical power. Studies that examine populations in which there is a larger effect size will, all else being equal, have a higher level of statistical power. Importantly, the relationship between effect size and statistical power is unrelated to the significance criteria we use in a test. In this sense, effect size allows for increasing the statistical power of a study (and thus reducing the risk of Type II error) while minimizing the risk of Type I error (through the establishment of rigorous levels of statistical significance).

Even though effect size is often considered the most important component of statistical power,[3] it is generally very difficult for the researcher to manipulate in a specific study. Ordinarily, a study is initiated in order to determine the type of relationship that exists in a population. In many cases, the researcher has no influence at all over the raw differences, or the variability of the scores on the measures examined. For example, if the researcher is interested in identifying whether men and women police officers have different attitudes toward corruption, the nature of these attitudes, or their variability, is a given that the researcher does not influence.

Nonetheless, particularly in evaluation research—in which the study attempts to evaluate a specific program or intervention—the researcher can influence the effect size of a study and thus minimize the risk of making a Type II error. There is growing recognition, for example, of the importance of ensuring the strength and integrity of criminal justice interventions.[4] Many criminal justice evaluations fail to show a statistically significant result simply because the interventions are too weak to have the desired impact or the outcomes are too variable to allow a statistically significant finding.

Statistical power suggests that researchers should be very concerned with the effect size of their evaluation studies if they want to develop a fair test of the research hypothesis. First, the interventions should be strong enough to lead to the expected differences in the populations under study. Of course, the larger the differences expected, the greater

[3]See M. W. Lipsey, *Design Sensitivity: Statistical Power for Experimental Research* (Newbury Park, CA: Sage, 1990).
[4]For example, see J. Petersilia "Randomized Experiments: Lessons from BJA's Intensive Supervision Project," *Evaluation Review* 13 (1989): 435–458; and D. Weisburd, "Design Sensitivity in Criminal Justice Experiments,"*Crime and Justice* 17 (1991): 337–379.

the statistical power of an investigation. Second, interventions should be administered in ways that maximize the homogeneity of outcomes. For example, interventions applied differently to each subject will likely increase the variability of outcomes and thus the standard deviation of those scores. Finally, researchers should recognize that the heterogeneity of the subjects studied (and thus the heterogeneity of the populations to which they infer) will often influence the statistical power of their tests. Different types of people are likely to respond in different ways to treatment or interventions. If they do respond differently, the variability of outcomes will be larger, and thus the likelihood of making a Type II error will grow.

Sample Size and Statistical Power

The method used most often to manipulate statistical power in social science research is to vary sample size. Like effect size, sample size can be manipulated without altering the risk of a Type I error in a test. In contrast to effect size, the number of subjects included in an investigation is—in most circumstances—under the control of the researcher.

The relationship between statistical power and sample size is straightforward. Larger samples, all else being equal, provide more stable estimates than do smaller samples. As discussed in Chapter 7, this makes intuitive sense. One would not be too surprised to throw a successive run of heads in three tosses of an honest coin. However, getting 25 heads in 25 coin tosses would lead even the most trusting person to doubt the fairness of the coin. In statistics, we have a more formal measure for assessing the reliability of results in a study—the standard error. When the standard error is smaller, reliability is greater. Importantly, as the number of cases studied increases, the standard error of the sampling distribution used in a test decreases. This relationship can be illustrated simply by looking at the calculation for the standard error in the single-sample t-test:

$$\sigma_{sd} = \frac{\sigma}{\sqrt{N}}$$

The standard error for this distribution is obtained by dividing the standard deviation of the population parameter by the square root of N. As N gets larger, irrespective of the value of the standard deviation itself, the standard error of the estimate gets smaller. For example, when the standard deviation is 10, Table 19.4 shows that the standard error with 25 cases is twice as large as it is with a sample of 100.

As the standard error of a test declines, the likelihood of achieving statistical significance grows, because the test statistic for a test of statistical significance is calculated by taking the ratio of the observed differ-

Table 19.4	Changes in the Standard Error of the Sampling Distribution for the Single Sample t-Test as Sample Size Increases, $\sigma = 10$

SAMPLE SIZE	STANDARD ERROR OF SAMPLING DISTRIBUTION
10	3.16
25	2.00
75	1.15
100	1.00
200	0.71
500	0.45

ence from the null hypothesis to the standard error of that difference. For example, in the t-test for two independent samples (see Equation 19.4), the value of the t-statistic is obtained by dividing the difference between the observed means minus the difference between the population means under the null hypothesis (generally 0) by the standard error of the estimates ($\hat{\sigma}_{sd(\bar{X}_1 - \bar{X}_2)}$).

$$t = \frac{(\bar{X}_1 - \bar{X}_2) - (\mu_1 - \mu_2)}{\sigma_{sd(\bar{X}_1 - \bar{X}_2)}}$$

Equation 19.4

For the difference of means test, as for other statistical tests of significance, as the standard error gets smaller, the test statistic grows. Accordingly, there is a relationship between sample size and statistical power, because larger samples lead to smaller standard errors and smaller standard errors lead to larger test statistics. Of course, a larger test statistic will lead to a larger likelihood of rejecting the null hypothesis.

Table 19.5 illustrates the relationship between sample size and statistical power in practice. The number of statistically significant outcomes expected in 100 two-sample t-tests in which there is a mean difference

Table 19.5	Number of Statistically Significant Outcomes Expected in 100 Two-Sample t-Tests for Four Different Scenarios

SCENARIO	SAMPLE SIZE (PER GROUP)	$\mu_1 - \mu_2$	σ	EXPECTED SIGNIFICANT OUTCOMES
1	35	0.2	1	13
2	100	0.2	1	29
3	200	0.2	1	51
4	1,000	0.2	1	99

Note: The parameters are held constant but the sample size varies. The tests have a 0.05 significance threshold and a nondirectional research hypothesis.

of two arrests between groups ($\sigma = 1$) is examined for four different scenarios (using a 5% significance threshold and a two-tailed test). In the first scenario, the sample size for each group is only 35 cases; in the second scenario, the sample size is 100; in the third, 200; and in the fourth, fully 1,000. Table 19.5 shows that the likelihood of rejecting the null hypothesis changes greatly with each of these scenarios, even though the population parameters remain the same. Under the first scenario, we would expect only about 13 statistically significant outcomes in 100 tests. In the second scenario, 29 significant outcomes would be expected; and in the third, 51. In the final scenario of samples of 1,000, nearly every test (99 out of 100) would be expected to lead to a significant result.

Sample size is often a primary concern in statistical power analysis because (1) it is directly related to statistical power, (2) it is a factor usually under the control of the researcher, and (3) it can be manipulated without altering the criteria for statistical significance of a study.

In most cases, researchers maximize the statistical power of a study by increasing sample size. However, sometimes adding cases to a study can have unanticipated consequences on other factors that influence statistical power.[5] This is most likely to occur in evaluation research. For example, let's say that a researcher has developed a complex and intensive method for intervening with high-risk youth. The impact of the treatment is dependent on the subjects' receiving the "full dosage" of the treatment for a six-month period. If the researcher were to increase the sample size of this study, it might become more difficult to deliver the treatments in the way they were intended. More generally, when increasing the sample size of a study, you should be careful not to decrease the integrity or dosage of the interventions that are applied.[6]

---

[5]For a review of this issue in criminal justice experiments, see D. Weisburd, "Design Sensitivity in Criminal Justice Experiments," *Crime and Justice* 17 (1991): 337–379.
[6]Increasing the size of a sample may also affect the variability of study estimates in other ways. For example, it may become more difficult to monitor implementation of treatments as a study grows. It is one thing to make sure that 100 people or places receive a certain intervention, but quite another to ensure consistency of interventions across hundreds or thousands of subjects. Also, studies are likely to include more heterogeneous groups of subjects as sample size increases. For example, in one intensive probation study, eligibility requirements were continually relaxed in order to meet project goals regarding the number of participants; see J. Petersilia, "Randomized Experiments: Lessons from BJA's Intensive Supervision Project," *Evaluation Review* 13 (1989): 435–458. As noted earlier, as the heterogeneity of treatments or subjects in a study grows, it is likely that the standard deviations of the outcomes examined will also get larger. This, in turn, leads to a smaller effect size for the study and thus a lower level of statistical power.

Parametric versus Nonparametric Tests

Before we turn to methods for calculating the statistical power of a test, it is important to note that the type of statistical test used in a study can affect its statistical power. The differences in power of various tests (assuming that the tests are equally appropriate for making statistical inferences from the data) are usually relatively small. However, in the case of one general group of comparisons, differences can often be more meaningful: As a general rule, parametric tests are more statistically powerful than nonparametric tests. This is one reason researchers generally prefer to use parametric tests, even though they require more assumptions than do their nonparametric counterparts.

Why do parametric tests lead to a smaller risk of Type II error? The answer lies in a principle stated much earlier in the book: If all else is equal, researchers should give preference to statistics that take advantage of more information. This is why interval measures are generally preferred over ordinal measures, and ordinal measures over nominal measures. Parametric tests generally involve comparisons among interval-level measures. Nonparametric tests make comparisons based on nominal- or ordinal-level data—for example, groupings or rankings in a distribution. Because parametric tests take into account more information in arriving at a conclusion about the statistical significance of findings, they are more statistically powerful, or more sensitive, tests of hypotheses.

Estimating Statistical Power: What Size Sample Is Needed for a Statistically Powerful Study?

A number of texts have been written that provide detailed tables for defining the statistical power of a study.[7] You can also calculate the statistical power of specific examples by hand, although this can be a very tedious exercise. Calculation of specific power estimates is beyond the scope of this text. Nonetheless, it is possible to develop some basic rules for statistical power analysis that rely on standardized estimates of effect size.

---

[7]For example, see Jacob Cohen, *Statistical Power Analysis for the Behavioral Sciences* (Hillsdale, NJ: Lawrence Erlbaum, 1988); M. W. Lipsey, *Design Sensitivity: Statistical Power for Experimental Research* (Newbury Park, CA: Sage, 1990); and H. C. Kraemer and S. Thiemann, *How Many Subjects: Statistical Power Analysis in Research* (Newbury Park, CA: Sage, 1987). There also are software packages for computing statistical power; for example, see M. Borenstein and J. Cohen, *Statistical Power Analysis: A Computer Program* (Hillsdale, NJ: Lawrence Erlbaum, 1988).

Statistical power analysis is generally used to define the sample size needed to achieve a statistically powerful study. We have already noted that increasing the size of a sample can sometimes affect other features of statistical power. Thus, in using increased sample size to minimize Type II error, we must consider the potential consequences that larger samples might have on the nature of interventions or subjects studied. Nonetheless, sample size remains the tool most frequently used for adjusting the power of studies because it can be manipulated by the researcher and does not require changes in the significance criteria of a test.

To define how many cases should be included in a study, we must conduct power analyses before the study is begun. However, we can also use the methods described here to evaluate whether studies already conducted have acceptable levels of statistical power.

To define the sample size needed for a powerful study, we must first clearly define each of the components of statistical power other than sample size. These include

1. The statistical test

2. The significance level

3. The research hypothesis (whether directional or nondirectional)

4. The effect size

The first three of these elements are familiar and based on our assumptions made in developing tests of hypotheses. The statistical test is chosen based on the type of measurement and the extent to which the study can meet certain assumptions. For example, if we want to compare three sample means, we will likely use analysis of variance as our test. If we are comparing means from two samples, we will likely use a two-sample t-test.

To calculate statistical power, we must also define the significance level of a test and its research hypothesis. By convention, we generally use a 0.05 significance threshold, and thus we are likely to compute statistical power estimates based on this criterion. The research hypothesis defines whether a test is directional or nondirectional. Again, in most circumstances, we choose a nondirectional test to take into account the different types of outcomes that can be found in a study. If we were evaluating an existing study, we would use the decisions as stated by the researchers in assessing its level of statistical power.

The fourth element, defining effect size, is more difficult. How can we estimate the effect size in the population? It is perhaps better to define this criterion a bit differently. The purpose of a power analysis is to see whether our study is likely to detect an effect of a certain size. Usually we define that effect in terms of what is a meaningful outcome in a study. A power analysis, then, tells us whether our study is designed in a way that is likely to detect that outcome (i.e., reject the null hypothesis on the basis of our sample statistics). This is one of the reasons why statistical power is sometimes defined as **design sensitivity.** It assesses whether our study is designed with enough sensitivity to be likely to reject the null hypothesis if an effect of a certain size exists in the population under study.

Statisticians have made the task of defining effect size easier by identifying broad categories of effect size. That is, they have developed a general scale for comparing effect size within and across studies. Jacob Cohen has suggested one widely used measure that simply divides effect size into small, medium, and large.[8] For example, for a proportion, Cohen defines a difference of 0.50 versus 0.40 between the two populations under study as a small effect, a difference of 0.65 versus 0.40 as a medium effect, and a difference of 0.78 versus 0.40 as a large effect. Cohen has developed similar estimates for other statistical tests, trying to use a similar standard in each of the cases. Regarding these standardized estimates of effect size, he states,

Although arbitrary, the proposed conventions will be found to be reasonable by reasonable people. An effort was made in selecting these operational criteria to use levels of ES which accord with a subjective average of effect sizes such as are encountered in behavioral sciences. "Small" effect sizes must not be so small that seeking them amidst the inevitable operation of measurement and experimental bias and lack of fidelity is a bootless task, yet not so large as to make them fairly perceptible to the naked observational eye. . . . In contrast, large effects must not be defined as so large that their quest by statistical methods is wholly a labor of supererogation, or to use Tukey's delightful term "statistical sanctification." That is, the difference in size between apples and pineapples is of an order which hardly requires an approach via statistical analysis. (p. 13)

Put simply, Cohen suggests that his estimates make good common sense. As we have emphasized throughout this text, common sense is at the root of most statistics.

---

[8]Jacob Cohen, *Statistical Power Analysis for the Behavioral Sciences* (Hillsdale, NJ: Lawrence Erlbaum, 1988).

Table 19.6	Sample Size per Group Required to Achieve a Statistical Power Level of 0.80 for a Two-Sample t-Test of Means

EFFECT SIZE	REQUIRED SAMPLE SIZE
Small ES	393
Medium ES	64
Large ES	25

Using standardized measures of effect size, Table 19.6 illustrates the importance of sample size in statistical power. The sample sizes needed to achieve a statistical power level of 0.80 or above, under assumptions of small, medium, and large effect size, are provided for a two-sample t-test of means. Table 19.6 is based on a test with a 5% significance threshold and a nondirectional research hypothesis.

If we define the effect size for the test as large, it does not take a very large sample to achieve a power level of 0.80. Only 25 cases are needed in each group. To achieve the same threshold with a moderate effect size, we must have 64 cases in each group. If the effect size in the population is small, then fully 393 cases are needed in each group. This example shows how important effect size is in statistical power. When effects are assumed to be large, it is relatively easy to design a powerful study. However, if we seek to identify a relationship with a small effect size, a very large number of cases will be required.

These standardized estimates of effect size allow us to identify the size sample needed to achieve a statistically powerful study, given a specific set of assumptions. They also enable us to assess the statistical power of a study that has been conducted by another researcher. Was the study designed in a way that would enable the detection of moderate or small effects? Certainly, if a study was underpowered for detecting large effects, you would want to be cautious in interpreting a finding that was not statistically significant.

Table 19.7 provides similar statistical power estimates for some commonly used statistical tests of significance. In each case, we use a 0.05 significance threshold and a nondirectional test. For each test, Table 19.7 provides the number of cases needed to achieve a statistical power level of 0.80. As noted earlier, this is the threshold generally used for defining a powerful study. Estimates are given for small, medium, and large effects.

You can get a general sense of the requirements of sample size from Table 19.7, although you should use caution in applying it to specific cases. In general, if you are trying to identify small effects, your overall sample will have to be very large. For example, in a two-sample t-test,

| Table 19.7 | Overall Sample Size Required to Achieve a Statistical Power Level of 0.80 for Selected Statistical Tests |

	EFFECT SIZE		
	Small ES	Medium ES	Large ES
Binomial	783	85	30
Chi-square*	964	107	39
Two-sample z-test[†]	784	126	50
Two-sample t-test[†]	786	128	50
ANOVA (3 Groups)[†]	945	156	63
t-Test for correlation and regression[†]	780	84	28

* df = 2 (e.g., a 3-by-2 table).
[†] Equal group sizes assumed; significance level set at 5%; two-tailed test.

you will need 786 cases (393 cases per group) to achieve a statistical power level of 0.80. In a chi-square test with 3 columns and 2 rows (2 degrees of freedom), you will need more than 960 cases in your total sample to achieve the same level of statistical power.

In contrast, for large effects you can generally use very small samples and still have a statistically powerful study. For example, only 28 cases are needed for a t-test for a correlation or regression coefficient. Fifty cases (25 per group) would be required to achieve a similar threshold of statistical power in a t-test for means. The sample sizes needed for a statistically powerful study for medium effect size do not fall midway between the estimates for large and small effect size but are generally much closer to the sample size required for large effects. For the difference of means test, for example, 128 cases (64 per group) would be required, and for the chi-square test (with 2 degrees of freedom), 107 cases would be required.

Summing Up: Avoiding Studies Designed for Failure

The statistical power of a test can be compared to the sensitivity of a radiation meter. A very sensitive meter will be able to identify even the smallest deposits of radioactivity. A meter that is not very sensitive will often miss such small deposits, although it likely will detect very large radiation signals from areas rich in radioactivity. Similarly, a statistically sensitive study will be able to identify even small effects. This is usually because the researcher has increased the sample size of the study to make it more statistically powerful. Conversely, a study that has little sensitivity is unlikely to yield a statistically significant result even when relatively large differences or program impacts are observed. Such studies may be seen as "designed for failure," not because of inadequacies in the theories or programs evaluated, but because the investigator failed to consider statistical power at the outset of the study.

You might question why we would even bother to define the size of the sample needed for statistically powerful studies. Why not just collect 1,000 or more cases in every study and be almost assured of a statistically powerful result? The simple answer is that although you should try to sample as many cases as you can in a study, there are generally constraints in developing samples. These constraints may be monetary, related to time, or associated with access to subjects. It is often important to know the minimum number of cases needed to achieve a certain threshold of statistical power so that you can try, within the constraints of the research setting, to reach an adequate level of statistical power in your study. It is also important to be able to assess whether studies that you read or evaluate were designed in such a way that they are reasonable tests of the hypotheses presented. If such studies are strongly underpowered, then you should have much less confidence in findings that do not support the research hypothesis.

Chapter Summary

A statistically powerful test is one for which there is a low risk of making a Type II error. **Statistical power** can be defined as 1 minus the probability of falsely accepting the null hypothesis. A test with a statistical power of 0.90 is one for which there is only a 10% probability of making a Type II error. If the power of a test is 0.10, the probability of a Type II error is 90%. A minimum statistical power level of at least 0.50 is recommended. However, it is generally accepted that in better studies, the level of statistical power will be at least 0.80. A study with a low level of statistical power can be described as "designed for failure," as it is unlikely to produce a statistically significant result even if the expected effect exists in the population under study.

There are several ways in which statistical power can be maximized. First, we may raise the significance threshold. Doing so, however, also increases the risk of a Type I error. Second, we may limit the direction of the research hypothesis and conduct a one-tailed test. Doing so, though, will necessarily ignore outcomes in the opposite direction. Third, we may try to maximize the **effect size.** The greater the differences between the populations and the smaller the variability of those differences, the larger the population effect size will be. Effect size, however, is usually beyond the control of the researcher. Fourth, we may increase the sample size. A larger sample produces a smaller standard error for the sampling distribution and a larger test statistic. The larger the sample, all else being equal, the greater the chance of rejecting the null hypothesis.

Sample size is generally the most useful tool for maximizing statistical power. A power analysis before a study is begun will define the number of cases needed to identify a particular size effect—small, medium, or large. A power analysis of an existing study will help to identify whether it was well designed to assess the questions that were examined. To identify a small effect size, the overall sample must be very large. For a large effect size, a much smaller sample will suffice.

Key Terms

design sensitivity The statistical power of a research study. In a sensitive study design, statistical power will be maximized, and the statistical test employed will be more capable of identifying an effect.

effect size (ES) A standardized measure derived by taking the effect size (e.g., the difference between two populations), measured in the raw units of the outcome measure examined, and dividing it by the pooled or common standard deviation of the outcome measure.

statistical power One minus the probability of a Type II error. The greater the statistical power of a test, the less chance there is that a researcher will mistakenly fail to reject the null hypothesis.

Symbols and Formulas

ES   Effect size

To calculate effect size:

$$ES = \frac{Parameter - H_0}{\sigma}$$

To calculate the effect size for a difference of means test:

$$ES = \frac{(\mu_1 - \mu_2) - (H_0\mu_1 - H_0\mu_2)}{\sigma}$$

Exercises

19.1 Emma wishes to run a series of statistical tests comparing samples drawn from two different populations. She devises four scenarios:

Scenario 1: One-tailed test, 0.01 significance level
Sample size = 100 each
$\mu_1 = 15, \mu_2 = 10, \sigma = 2$

Scenario 2: One-tailed test, 0.05 significance level
Sample size = 100 each
$\mu_1 = 15, \mu_2 = 10, \sigma = 2$

Scenario 3: Two-tailed test, 0.01 significance level
Sample size = 100 each
$\mu_1 - 15, \mu_2 - 10, \sigma = 2$

Scenario 4: Two-tailed test, 0.05 significance level
Sample size = 100 each
$\mu_1 = 15, \mu_2 = 10, \sigma = 2$

a. What is the effect size for each of the four scenarios?

b. In which of these scenarios would the test have the highest level of statistical power? Explain your answer.

19.2 A joint Swedish-U.S. research foundation wishes to sponsor research to investigate whether parents in the two countries have different ways of disciplining their children. Four researchers—Anna, Bert, Christina, and Dave—have each submitted a proposal. The researchers intend to run a two-tailed test of statistical significance, except for Anna, who proposes a one-tailed test. The researchers intend to set a 5% level of significance, except for Dave, who proposes a 1% level. Anna and Bert propose samples of 400 Swedish parents and 400 U.S. parents, Christina proposes samples of 70 each, and Dave proposes samples of 40 each. Each of the researchers expects a moderate size effect from his or her test.

a. Do any of these proposals appear to you to be "designed for failure"? Explain your answer.

b. Which researcher's proposal would you recommend for acceptance? Explain your answer.

19.3 Fiona wishes to run a series of statistical tests comparing samples drawn from two different populations. She devises four scenarios.

Scenario 1: Two-tailed test, 0.05 significance level
Sample size = 100 each
$\mu_1 = 15, \mu_2 = 14, \sigma = 5$

Scenario 2: Two-tailed test, 0.05 significance level

Sample size = 100 each

$\mu_1 = 13, \mu_2 = 16, \sigma = 5$

Scenario 3: Two-tailed test, 0.05 significance level

Sample size = 100 each

$\mu_1 = 8, \mu_2 = 10, \sigma = 5$

Scenario 4: Two-tailed test, 0.05 significance level

Sample size = 100 each

$\mu_1 = 11.5, \mu_2 = 9, \sigma = 5$

a. What is the effect size for each of the four scenarios?

b. In which of these scenarios would the test have the highest level of statistical power? Explain your answer.

19.4 Philip is studying the attitudes of members of a newly formed police precinct toward drug offenders. He has prepared a 45-minute film, in which offenders talk frankly about their backgrounds and how they came to be involved in crime, as well as a questionnaire, which should take about 15 minutes to complete. He has been given permission to show the film and distribute the questionnaire in a one-hour lunch break on a specific day only, in a lecture room that holds no more than 25 people.

For the planned study, Philip intends to draw two independent random samples of 25 officers. Both groups will be asked to complete a questionnaire assessing their attitudes toward drug offenders. One group (the research group) will have seen the film; the other (the control group) will not. The researcher plans to check for differences between the research and control groups by running a two-sample *t*-test and making a decision about his null hypothesis on the basis of a two-tailed test of statistical significance, setting the significance threshold at 0.05. He is worried, however, about the statistical power of the test.

Philip's assistant suggests three different ways of increasing the statistical power of the test. Discuss the merits and pitfalls of each suggestion.

a. Run a one-tailed test of statistical significance instead of a two-tailed test.

b. Increase the size of the rejection region by changing the significance threshold from 0.05 to 0.10.

c. Double the size of each sample to 50. Because of limitations on time and space, the film would have to be shown in two sittings. The research group would have to be split into two subgroups of 25. Each subgroup would watch the first 20 minutes of the 45-minute film and then spend 10 minutes filling in the questionnaire.

19.5   Caroline wishes to run a series of statistical tests comparing samples drawn from two different populations. She devises four scenarios.

Scenario 1: Two-tailed test, 0.05 significance level

Sample size = 50 each

$\mu_1 = 16, \mu_2 = 10, \sigma = 2$

Scenario 2: One-tailed test, 0.05 significance level

Sample size = 150 each

$\mu_1 = 16, \mu_2 = 10, \sigma = 2$

Scenario 3: Two-tailed test, 0.05 significance level

Sample size = 150 each

$\mu_1 = 16, \mu_2 = 10, \sigma = 2$

Scenario 4: Two-tailed test, 0.05 significance level

Sample size = 100 each

$\mu_1 = 16, \mu_2 = 10, \sigma = 2$

a. What is the standard error of the sampling distribution for each of the four scenarios?

b. In which of these scenarios would the test have the highest level of statistical power? Explain your answer.

19.6   Robert drew an independent random sample of 100 men and 100 women from Chaos Town and questioned them about their fear of crime, scoring each one on an index from 0 to 20 and then comparing the sample means using a two-sample *t*-test.
    A few months later, he decided to repeat the experiment, but this time by comparing a random sample of youngsters under the age of 18 with a random sample of adults aged 18 or older.
    Assume that for his first experiment the population mean for men was 11 and for women was 14 (with a common standard deviation of 6). For his second experiment, assume that the population mean for the youngsters was 10 and for the adults was 14 (with a common standard deviation of 8).

a. If the sample sizes in the second experiment were the same as those in the first experiment, would the statistical power of the two tests be the same?

b. How large would the samples need to be in the second experiment for the standard error of the sampling distributions in both tests to be the same?

19.7   In an analysis of after-school supervision programs, a group of researchers reported the following proportions for self-reported delinquency of youth under supervision and those not under supervision by time of day:

Time Period	Unsupervised		Supervised		
	Proportion	N	Proportion	N	s
Before school	0.14	199	0.01	97	0.295
During school	0.18	203	0.03	98	0.313
End of school through 6 P.M.	0.15	199	0.03	98	0.308
6 P.M. through 12 A.M.	0.14	200	0.04	97	0.313
12 A.M. through 6 A.M.	0.07	198	0.01	97	0.214
Weekends	0.24	200	0.04	97	0.370

Source: D. C. Gottfredson, G. D. Gottfredson, and S. A. Weisman, "The Timing of Delinquent Behavior and Its Implications for After-School Programs," *Criminology and Public Policy* 1 (2001): 79.

a. On average, was this study designed to have a high level of statistical power to identify medium ES? What about small ES?

b. If you assumed that the observed differences between the samples were reflective of the population differences, which comparison would have the highest level of statistical power? Explain why.

Factorials

$0! = 1$
$1! = 1$
$2! = 2$
$3! = 6$
$4! = 24$
$5! = 120$
$6! = 720$
$7! = 5,040$
$8! = 40,320$
$9! = 362,880$
$10! = 3,628,800$
$11! = 39,916,800$
$12! = 479,001,600$
$13! = 6,227,020,800$
$14! = 87,178,291,200$
$15! = 1,307,674,368,000$
$16! = 20,922,789,888,000$
$17! = 355,687,428,096,000$
$18! = 6,402,373,705,728,000$
$19! = 121,645,100,408,832,000$
$20! = 2,432,902,008,176,640,000$
$21! = 51,090,942,171,709,440,000$
$22! = 1,124,000,727,777,607,680,000$
$23! = 25,852,016,738,884,976,640,000$
$24! = 620,448,401,733,239,439,360,000$
$25! = 15,511,210,043,330,985,984,000,000$

Critical Values of χ^2 Distribution

df	α					
	0.20	0.10	0.05	0.02	0.01	0.001
1	1.642	2.706	3.841	5.412	6.635	10.827
2	3.219	4.605	5.991	7.824	9.210	13.815
3	4.642	6.251	7.815	9.837	11.341	16.268
4	5.989	7.779	9.488	11.668	13.277	18.465
5	7.289	9.236	11.070	13.388	15.086	20.517
6	8.558	10.645	12.592	15.033	16.812	22.457
7	9.803	12.017	14.067	16.622	18.475	24.322
8	11.030	13.362	15.507	18.168	20.090	26.125
9	12.242	14.684	16.919	19.679	21.666	27.877
10	13.442	15.987	18.307	21.161	23.209	29.588
11	14.631	17.275	19.675	22.618	24.725	31.264
12	15.812	18.549	21.026	24.054	26.217	32.909
13	16.985	19.812	22.362	25.472	27.688	34.528
14	18.151	21.064	23.685	26.873	29.141	36.123
15	19.311	22.307	24.996	28.259	30.578	37.697
16	20.465	23.542	26.296	29.633	32.000	39.252
17	21.615	24.769	27.587	30.995	33.409	40.790
18	22.760	25.989	28.869	32.346	34.805	42.312
19	23.900	27.204	30.144	33.687	36.191	43.820
20	25.038	28.412	31.410	35.020	37.566	45.315
21	26.171	29.615	32.671	36.343	38.932	46.797
22	27.301	30.813	33.924	37.659	40.289	48.268
23	28.429	32.007	35.172	38.968	41.638	49.728
24	29.553	33.196	36.415	40.270	42.980	51.179
25	30.675	34.382	37.652	41.566	44.314	52.620
26	31.795	35.563	38.885	42.856	45.642	54.052
27	32.912	36.741	40.113	44.140	46.963	55.476
28	34.027	37.916	41.337	45.419	48.278	56.893
29	35.139	39.087	42.557	46.693	49.588	58.302
30	36.250	40.256	43.773	47.962	50.892	59.703

Source: From Table IV of R. A. Fisher and F. Yates, *Statistical Tables for Biological, Agricultural and Medical Research* (London: Longman Group Ltd., 1974). (Previously published by Oliver & Boyd, Edinburgh.) Reprinted by permission of Pearson Education Ltd.

Appendix 3

Areas of the Standard Normal Distribution

The entries in this table are the proportion of the cases in a standard normal distribution that lie between 0 and z.

SECOND DECIMAL PLACE IN z

z	0.00	0.01	0.02	0.03	0.04	0.05	0.06	0.07	0.08	0.09
0.0	0.0000	0.0040	0.0080	0.0120	0.0160	0.0199	0.0239	0.0279	0.0319	0.0359
0.1	0.0398	0.0438	0.0478	0.0517	0.0557	0.0596	0.0636	0.0675	0.0714	0.0753
0.2	0.0793	0.0832	0.0871	0.0910	0.0948	0.0987	0.1026	0.1064	0.1103	0.1141
0.3	0.1179	0.1217	0.1255	0.1293	0.1331	0.1368	0.1406	0.1443	0.1480	0.1517
0.4	0.1554	0.1591	0.1628	0.1664	0.1700	0.1736	0.1772	0.1808	0.1844	0.1879
0.5	0.1915	0.1950	0.1985	0.2019	0.2054	0.2088	0.2123	0.2157	0.2190	0.2224
0.6	0.2257	0.2291	0.2324	0.2357	0.2389	0.2422	0.2454	0.2486	0.2517	0.2549
0.7	0.2580	0.2611	0.2642	0.2673	0.2704	0.2734	0.2764	0.2794	0.2823	0.2852
0.8	0.2881	0.2910	0.2939	0.2967	0.2995	0.3023	0.3051	0.3078	0.3106	0.3133
0.9	0.3159	0.3186	0.3212	0.3238	0.3264	0.3289	0.3315	0.3340	0.3365	0.3389
1.0	0.3413	0.3438	0.3461	0.3485	0.3508	0.3531	0.3554	0.3577	0.3599	0.3621
1.1	0.3643	0.3665	0.3686	0.3708	0.3729	0.3749	0.3770	0.3790	0.3810	0.3830
1.2	0.3849	0.3869	0.3888	0.3907	0.3925	0.3944	0.3962	0.3980	0.3997	0.4015
1.3	0.4032	0.4049	0.4066	0.4082	0.4099	0.4115	0.4131	0.4147	0.4162	0.4177
1.4	0.4192	0.4207	0.4222	0.4236	0.4251	0.4265	0.4279	0.4292	0.4306	0.4319
1.5	0.4332	0.4345	0.4357	0.4370	0.4382	0.4394	0.4406	0.4418	0.4429	0.4441
1.6	0.4452	0.4463	0.4474	0.4484	0.4495	0.4505	0.4515	0.4525	0.4535	0.4545
1.7	0.4554	0.4564	0.4573	0.4582	0.4591	0.4599	0.4608	0.4616	0.4625	0.4633
1.8	0.4641	0.4649	0.4656	0.4664	0.4671	0.4678	0.4686	0.4693	0.4699	0.4706
1.9	0.4713	0.4719	0.4726	0.4732	0.4738	0.4744	0.4750	0.4756	0.4761	0.4767
2.0	0.4772	0.4778	0.4783	0.4788	0.4793	0.4798	0.4803	0.4808	0.4812	0.4817
2.1	0.4821	0.4826	0.4830	0.4834	0.4838	0.4842	0.4846	0.4850	0.4854	0.4857
2.2	0.4861	0.4864	0.4868	0.4871	0.4875	0.4878	0.4881	0.4884	0.4887	0.4890
2.3	0.4893	0.4896	0.4898	0.4901	0.4904	0.4906	0.4909	0.4911	0.4913	0.4916
2.4	0.4918	0.4920	0.4922	0.4925	0.4927	0.4929	0.4931	0.4932	0.4934	0.4936
2.5	0.4938	0.4940	0.4941	0.4943	0.4945	0.4946	0.4948	0.4949	0.4951	0.4952
2.6	0.4953	0.4955	0.4956	0.4957	0.4959	0.4960	0.4961	0.4962	0.4963	0.4964
2.7	0.4965	0.4966	0.4967	0.4968	0.4969	0.4970	0.4971	0.4972	0.4973	0.4974
2.8	0.4974	0.4975	0.4976	0.4977	0.4977	0.4978	0.4979	0.4979	0.4980	0.4981
2.9	0.4981	0.4982	0.4982	0.4983	0.4984	0.4984	0.4985	0.4985	0.4986	0.4986
3.0	0.4987	0.4987	0.4987	0.4988	0.4988	0.4989	0.4989	0.4989	0.4990	0.4990
3.1	0.4990	0.4991	0.4991	0.4991	0.4992	0.4992	0.4992	0.4992	0.4993	0.4993
3.2	0.4993	0.4993	0.4994	0.4994	0.4994	0.4994	0.4994	0.4995	0.4995	0.4995
3.3	0.4995	0.4995	0.4995	0.4996	0.4996	0.4996	0.4996	0.4996	0.4996	0.4997
3.4	0.4997	0.4997	0.4997	0.4997	0.4997	0.4997	0.4997	0.4997	0.4997	0.4998
3.5	0.4998	0.4998	0.4998	0.4998	0.4998	0.4998	0.4998	0.4998	0.4998	0.4998
3.6	0.4998	0.4998	0.4999	0.4999	0.4999	0.4999	0.4999	0.4999	0.4999	0.4999
3.7	0.4999									
4.0	0.49997									
4.5	0.499997									
5.0	0.4999997									

Source: R. Johnson, *Elementary Statistics* (Belmont, CA: Duxbury Press, 1996).

Appendix 4

Critical Values of Student's *t* Distribution

One-tailed value

Two-tailed value

Degrees of Freedom	ONE-TAILED VALUE					
	0.25	0.10	0.05	0.025	0.01	0.005
	TWO-TAILED VALUE					
	0.50	0.20	0.10	0.05	0.02	0.01
1	1.000	3.078	6.314	12.706	31.821	63.657
2	0.816	1.886	2.920	4.303	6.965	9.925
3	0.765	1.638	2.353	3.182	4.541	5.841
4	0.741	1.533	2.132	2.776	3.747	4.604
5	0.727	1.476	2.015	2.571	3.365	4.032
6	0.718	1.440	1.943	2.447	3.143	3.707
7	0.711	1.415	1.895	2.365	2.998	3.499
8	0.706	1.397	1.860	2.306	2.896	3.355
9	0.703	1.383	1.833	2.262	2.821	3.250
10	0.700	1.372	1.812	2.228	2.764	3.169
11	0.697	1.363	1.796	2.201	2.718	3.106
12	0.695	1.356	1.782	2.179	2.681	3.055
13	0.694	1.350	1.771	2.160	2.650	3.012
14	0.692	1.345	1.761	2.145	2.626	2.977
15	0.691	1.341	1.753	2.131	2.602	2.947
16	0.690	1.337	1.746	2.120	2.583	2.921
17	0.689	1.333	1.740	2.110	2.567	2.898
18	0.688	1.330	1.734	2.101	2.552	2.878
19	0.688	1.328	1.729	2.093	2.539	2.861
20	0.687	1.325	1.725	2.086	2.528	2.845
21	0.686	1.323	1.721	2.080	2.518	2.831
22	0.686	1.321	1.717	2.074	2.508	2.819
23	0.685	1.319	1.714	2.069	2.500	2.807
24	0.685	1.318	1.711	2.064	2.492	2.797
25	0.684	1.316	1.708	2.060	2.485	2.787
26	0.684	1.315	1.706	2.056	2.479	2.779
27	0.684	1.314	1.703	2.052	2.473	2.771
28	0.683	1.313	1.701	2.048	2.467	2.763
29	0.683	1.311	1.699	2.045	2.462	2.756
30	0.683	1.310	1.697	2.042	2.457	2.750
31	0.682	1.309	1.696	2.040	2.453	2.744
32	0.682	1.309	1.694	2.037	2.449	2.739
33	0.682	1.308	1.692	2.035	2.445	2.733
34	0.682	1.307	1.691	2.032	2.441	2.728
35	0.682	1.306	1.690	2.030	2.438	2.724
40	0.681	1.303	1.684	2.021	2.423	2.704
45	0.680	1.301	1.680	2.014	2.412	2.690
50	0.680	1.299	1.676	2.008	2.403	2.678
55	0.679	1.297	1.673	2.004	2.396	2.669
60	0.679	1.296	1.671	2.000	2.390	2.660
70	0.678	1.294	1.667	1.994	2.381	2.648
80	0.678	1.293	1.665	1.989	2.374	2.638
90	0.678	1.291	1.662	1.986	2.368	2.631
100	0.677	1.290	1.661	1.982	2.364	2.625
120	0.677	1.289	1.658	1.980	2.358	2.617
>500	0.674	1.282	1.645	1.960	2.326	2.576

Source: "Table D, The *t* Table" adapted from SCIENTIFIC TABLES, published by Ciba-Geigy, in WAYS AND MEANS OF STATISTICS by Leonard Tashman and Kathleen Lamborn, Copyright © 1979 by Harcourt Brace & Company, *reprinted by permission of Harcourt Brace & Company.*

Critical Values of the F-Statistic

($\alpha = 0.05$)

NUMERATOR DEGREES OF FREEDOM

df₂ \ df₁	1	2	3	4	5	6	8	12	24	∞
1	161.4	199.5	215.7	224.6	230.2	234.0	238.9	243.9	249.0	254.3
2	18.51	19.00	19.16	19.25	19.30	19.33	19.37	19.41	19.45	19.50
3	10.13	9.55	9.28	9.12	9.01	8.94	8.84	8.74	8.64	8.53
4	7.71	6.94	6.59	6.39	6.26	6.16	6.04	5.91	5.77	5.63
5	6.61	5.79	5.41	5.19	5.05	4.95	4.82	4.68	4.53	4.36
6	5.99	5.14	4.76	4.53	4.39	4.28	4.15	4.00	3.84	3.67
7	5.59	4.74	4.35	4.12	3.97	3.87	3.73	3.57	3.41	3.23
8	5.32	4.46	4.07	3.84	3.69	3.58	3.44	3.28	3.12	2.93
9	5.12	4.26	3.86	3.63	3.48	3.37	3.23	3.07	2.90	2.71
10	4.96	4.10	3.71	3.48	3.33	3.22	3.07	2.91	2.74	2.54
11	4.84	3.98	3.59	3.36	3.20	3.09	2.95	2.79	2.61	2.40
12	4.75	3.88	3.49	3.26	3.11	3.00	2.85	2.69	2.50	2.30
13	4.67	3.80	3.41	3.18	3.02	2.92	2.77	2.60	2.42	2.21
14	4.60	3.74	3.34	3.11	2.96	2.85	2.70	2.53	2.35	2.13
15	4.54	3.68	3.29	3.06	2.90	2.79	2.64	2.48	2.29	2.07
16	4.49	3.63	3.24	3.01	2.85	2.74	2.59	2.42	2.24	2.01
17	4.45	3.59	3.20	2.96	2.81	2.70	2.55	2.38	2.19	1.96
18	4.41	3.55	3.16	2.93	2.77	2.66	2.51	2.34	2.15	1.92
19	4.38	3.52	3.13	2.90	2.74	2.63	2.48	2.31	2.11	1.88
20	4.35	3.49	3.10	2.87	2.71	2.60	2.45	2.28	2.08	1.84
21	4.32	3.47	3.07	2.84	2.68	2.57	2.42	2.25	2.05	1.81
22	4.30	3.44	3.05	2.82	2.66	2.55	2.40	2.23	2.03	1.78
23	4.28	3.42	3.03	2.80	2.64	2.53	2.38	2.20	2.00	1.76
24	4.26	3.40	3.01	2.78	2.62	2.51	2.36	2.18	1.98	1.73
25	4.24	3.38	2.99	2.76	2.60	2.49	2.34	2.16	1.96	1.71
26	4.22	3.37	2.98	2.74	2.59	2.47	2.32	2.15	1.95	1.69
27	4.21	3.35	2.96	2.73	2.57	2.46	2.30	2.13	1.93	1.67
28	4.20	3.34	2.95	2.71	2.56	2.44	2.29	2.12	1.91	1.65
29	4.18	3.33	2.93	2.70	2.54	2.43	2.28	2.10	1.90	1.64
30	4.17	3.32	2.92	2.69	2.53	2.42	2.27	2.09	1.89	1.62
40	4.08	3.23	2.84	2.61	2.45	2.34	2.18	2.00	1.79	1.51
60	4.00	3.15	2.76	2.52	2.37	2.25	2.10	1.92	1.70	1.39
120	3.92	3.07	2.68	2.45	2.29	2.17	2.02	1.83	1.61	1.25
>500	3.84	2.99	2.60	2.37	2.21	2.09	1.94	1.75	1.52	1.00

DENOMINATOR DEGREES OF FREEDOM

($\alpha = 0.01$)
NUMERATOR DEGREES OF FREEDOM

df₂	1	2	3	4	5	6	8	12	24	∞
1	4052	4999	5403	5625	5764	5859	5981	6106	6234	6366
2	98.49	99.01	99.17	99.25	99.30	99.33	99.36	99.42	99.46	99.50
3	34.12	30.81	29.46	28.71	28.24	27.91	27.49	27.05	26.60	26.12
4	21.20	18.00	16.69	15.98	15.52	15.21	14.80	14.37	13.93	13.46
5	16.26	13.27	12.06	11.39	10.97	10.67	10.27	9.89	9.47	9.02
6	13.74	10.92	9.78	9.15	8.75	8.47	8.10	7.72	7.31	6.88
7	12.25	9.55	8.45	7.85	7.46	7.19	6.84	6.47	6.07	5.65
8	11.26	8.65	7.59	7.01	6.63	6.37	6.03	5.67	5.28	4.86
9	10.56	8.02	6.99	6.42	6.06	5.80	5.47	5.11	4.73	4.31
10	10.04	7.56	6.55	5.99	5.64	5.39	5.06	4.71	4.33	3.91
11	9.65	7.20	6.22	5.67	5.32	5.07	4.74	4.40	4.02	3.60
12	9.33	6.93	5.95	5.41	5.06	4.82	4.50	4.16	3.78	3.36
13	9.07	6.70	5.74	5.20	4.86	4.62	4.30	3.96	3.59	3.16
14	8.86	6.51	5.56	5.03	4.69	4.46	4.14	3.80	3.43	3.00
15	8.68	6.36	5.42	4.89	4.56	4.32	4.00	3.67	3.29	2.87
16	8.53	6.23	5.29	4.77	4.44	4.20	3.89	3.55	3.18	2.75
17	8.40	6.11	5.18	4.67	4.34	4.10	3.79	3.45	3.08	2.65
18	8.28	6.01	5.09	4.58	4.25	4.01	3.71	3.37	3.00	2.57
19	8.18	5.93	5.01	4.50	4.17	3.94	3.63	3.30	2.92	2.49
20	8.10	5.85	4.94	4.43	4.10	3.87	3.56	3.23	2.86	2.42
21	8.02	5.78	4.87	4.37	4.04	3.81	3.51	3.17	2.80	2.36
22	7.94	5.72	4.82	4.31	3.99	3.76	3.45	3.12	2.75	2.31
23	7.88	5.66	4.76	4.26	3.94	3.71	3.41	3.07	2.70	2.26
24	7.82	5.61	4.72	4.22	3.90	3.67	3.36	3.03	2.66	2.21
25	7.77	5.57	4.68	4.18	3.86	3.63	3.32	2.99	2.62	2.17
26	7.72	5.53	4.64	4.14	3.82	3.59	3.29	2.96	2.58	2.13
27	7.68	5.49	4.60	4.11	3.78	3.56	3.26	2.93	2.55	2.10
28	7.64	5.45	4.57	4.07	3.75	3.53	3.23	2.90	2.52	2.06
29	7.60	5.42	4.54	4.04	3.73	3.50	3.20	2.87	2.49	2.03
30	7.56	5.39	4.51	4.02	3.70	3.47	3.17	2.84	2.47	2.01
40	7.31	5.18	4.31	3.83	3.51	3.29	2.99	2.66	2.29	1.80
60	7.08	4.98	4.13	3.65	3.34	3.12	2.82	2.50	2.12	1.60
120	6.85	4.79	3.95	3.48	3.17	2.96	2.66	2.34	1.95	1.38
>500	6.64	4.60	3.78	3.32	3.02	2.80	2.51	2.18	1.79	1.00

DENOMINATOR DEGREES OF FREEDOM

$$(\alpha = 0.001)$$
NUMERATOR DEGREES OF FREEDOM

df₁ df₂	1	2	3	4	5	6	8	12	24	∞
1	405284	500000	540379	562500	576405	585937	598144	610667	623497	636619
2	998.5	999.0	999.2	999.2	999.3	999.3	999.4	999.4	999.5	999.5
3	167.5	148.5	141.1	137.1	134.6	132.8	130.6	128.3	125.9	123.5
4	74.14	61.25	56.18	53.44	51.71	50.53	49.00	47.41	45.77	44.05
5	47.04	36.61	33.20	31.09	29.75	28.84	27.64	26.42	25.14	23.78
6	35.51	27.00	23.70	21.90	20.81	20.03	19.03	17.99	16.89	15.75
7	29.22	21.69	18.77	17.19	16.21	15.52	14.63	13.71	12.73	11.69
8	25.42	18.49	15.83	14.39	13.49	12.86	12.04	11.19	10.30	9.34
9	22.86	16.39	13.90	12.56	11.71	11.13	10.37	9.57	8.72	7.81
10	21.04	14.91	12.55	11.28	10.48	9.92	9.20	8.45	7.64	6.76
11	19.69	13.81	11.56	10.35	9.58	9.05	8.35	7.63	6.85	6.00
12	18.64	12.97	10.80	9.63	8.89	8.38	7.71	7.00	6.25	5.42
13	17.81	12.31	10.21	9.07	8.35	7.86	7.21	6.52	5.78	4.97
14	17.14	11.78	9.73	8.62	7.92	7.43	6.80	6.13	5.41	4.60
15	16.59	11.34	9.34	8.25	7.57	7.09	6.47	5.81	5.10	4.31
16	16.12	10.97	9.00	7.94	7.27	6.81	6.19	5.55	4.85	4.06
17	15.72	10.66	8.73	7.68	7.02	6.56	5.96	5.32	4.63	3.85
18	15.38	10.39	8.49	7.46	6.81	6.35	5.76	5.13	4.45	3.67
19	15.08	10.16	8.28	7.26	6.61	6.18	5.59	4.97	4.29	3.52
20	14.82	9.95	8.10	7.10	6.46	6.02	5.44	4.82	4.15	3.38
21	14.59	9.77	7.94	6.95	6.32	5.88	5.31	4.70	4.03	3.26
22	14.38	9.61	7.80	6.81	6.19	5.76	5.19	4.58	3.92	3.15
23	14.19	9.47	7.67	6.69	6.08	5.65	5.09	4.48	3.82	3.05
24	14.03	9.34	7.55	6.59	5.98	5.55	4.99	4.39	3.74	2.97
25	13.88	9.22	7.45	6.49	5.88	5.46	4.91	4.31	3.66	2.89
26	13.74	9.12	7.36	6.41	5.80	5.38	4.83	4.24	3.59	2.82
27	13.61	9.02	7.27	6.33	5.73	5.31	4.76	4.17	3.52	2.75
28	13.50	8.93	7.19	6.25	5.66	5.24	4.69	4.11	3.46	2.70
29	13.39	8.85	7.12	6.19	5.59	5.18	4.64	4.05	3.41	2.64
30	13.29	8.77	7.05	6.12	5.53	5.12	4.58	4.00	3.36	2.59
40	12.61	8.25	6.60	5.70	5.13	4.73	4.21	3.64	3.01	2.23
60	11.97	7.76	6.17	5.31	4.76	4.37	3.87	3.31	2.69	1.90
120	11.38	7.31	5.79	4.95	4.42	4.04	3.55	3.02	2.40	1.56
>500	10.83	6.91	5.42	4.62	4.10	3.74	3.27	2.74	2.13	1.00

(Left margin vertical label: DENOMINATOR DEGREES OF FREEDOM)

Source: From Table IV of R. A. Fisher and F. Yates, *Statistical Tables for Biological, Agricultural and Medical Research* (London: Longman Group Ltd., 1974). (Previously published by Oliver & Boyd, Edinburgh.) Reprinted by permission of Pearson Education Ltd.

Appendix 6

Critical Value for P (P_{crit}), Tukey's HSD Test

LEVEL OF SIGNIFICANCE ($\alpha = 0.05$)
k = THE NUMBER OF MEANS OR
NUMBER OF STEPS BETWEEN ORDERED MEANS

df_w	2	3	4	5	6	7	8	9	10	12	15	20
1	17.97	26.98	32.82	37.08	40.41	43.12	45.40	47.36	49.07	51.96	55.36	59.56
2	6.08	8.33	9.80	10.88	11.74	12.44	13.03	13.54	13.99	14.75	15.65	16.77
3	4.50	5.91	6.82	7.50	8.04	8.48	8.85	9.18	9.46	9.95	10.52	11.24
4	3.93	5.04	5.76	6.29	6.71	7.05	7.35	7.60	7.83	8.21	8.66	9.23
5	3.64	4.60	5.22	5.67	6.03	6.33	6.58	6.80	6.99	7.32	7.72	8.21
6	3.46	4.34	4.90	5.30	5.63	5.90	6.12	6.32	6.49	6.79	7.14	7.59
7	3.34	4.16	4.68	5.06	5.36	5.61	5.82	6.00	6.16	6.43	6.76	7.17
8	3.26	4.04	4.53	4.89	5.17	5.40	5.60	5.77	5.92	6.18	6.48	6.87
9	3.20	3.95	4.41	4.76	5.02	5.24	5.43	5.59	5.74	5.98	6.28	6.64
10	3.15	3.88	4.33	4.65	4.91	5.12	5.30	5.46	5.60	5.83	6.11	6.47
11	3.11	3.82	4.26	4.57	4.82	5.03	5.20	5.35	5.49	5.71	5.98	6.33
12	3.08	3.77	4.20	4.51	4.75	4.95	5.12	5.27	5.39	5.61	5.88	6.21
13	3.06	3.73	4.15	4.45	4.69	4.88	5.05	5.19	5.32	5.53	5.79	6.11
14	3.03	3.70	4.11	4.41	4.64	4.83	4.99	5.13	5.25	5.46	5.71	6.03
15	3.01	3.67	4.08	4.37	4.59	4.78	4.94	5.08	5.20	5.40	5.65	5.96
16	3.00	3.65	4.05	4.33	4.56	4.74	4.90	5.03	5.15	5.35	5.59	5.90
17	2.98	3.63	4.02	4.30	4.52	4.70	4.86	4.99	5.11	5.31	5.54	5.84
18	2.97	3.61	4.00	4.28	4.49	4.67	4.82	4.96	5.07	5.27	5.50	5.79
19	2.96	3.59	3.98	4.25	4.47	4.65	4.79	4.92	5.04	5.23	5.46	5.75
20	2.95	3.58	3.96	4.23	4.45	4.62	4.77	4.90	5.01	5.20	5.43	5.71
24	2.92	3.53	3.90	4.17	4.37	4.54	4.68	4.81	4.92	5.10	5.32	5.59
30	2.89	3.49	3.85	4.10	4.30	4.46	4.60	4.72	4.82	5.00	5.21	5.47
40	2.86	3.44	3.79	4.04	4.23	4.39	4.52	4.63	4.73	4.90	5.11	5.36
60	2.83	3.40	3.74	3.98	4.16	4.31	4.44	4.55	4.65	4.81	5.00	5.24
120	2.80	3.36	3.68	3.92	4.10	4.24	4.36	4.47	4.56	4.71	4.90	5.13
∞	2.77	3.31	3.63	3.86	4.03	4.17	4.29	4.39	4.47	4.62	4.80	5.01

Source: From *Comprehending Behavioral Statistics*, by R. T. Hurlburt, Copyright © 1994, Brooks/Cole Publishing Company, Pacific Grove, CA 93950, a division of International Thomson Publishing Inc. By permission of the publisher. *Adapted from Biometrika Tables for Statisticians*, vol. 1, 3rd ed., E. S. Pearson and H. O. Hartley (eds.). Copyright © 1966, Cambridge University Press for Biometrika Trust. By permission of the Biometrika Trust.

Critical Values for Spearman's Rank-Order Correlation Coefficient

	LEVEL OF SIGNIFICANCE (α) FOR ONE-TAILED TEST			
	0.05	0.025	0.01	0.005
	LEVEL OF SIGNIFICANCE (α) FOR TWO-TAILED TEST			
n	0.10	0.05	0.02	0.01
5	0.900	—	—	—
6	0.829	0.886	0.943	—
7	0.714	0.786	0.893	0.929
8	0.643	0.738	0.833	0.881
9	0.600	0.700	0.783	0.833
10	0.564	0.648	0.745	0.794
11	0.536	0.618	0.709	0.818
12	0.497	0.591	0.703	0.780
13	0.475	0.566	0.673	0.745
14	0.457	0.545	0.646	0.716
15	0.441	0.525	0.623	0.689
16	0.425	0.507	0.601	0.666
17	0.412	0.490	0.582	0.645
18	0.399	0.476	0.564	0.625
19	0.388	0.462	0.549	0.608
20	0.377	0.450	0.534	0.591
21	0.368	0.438	0.521	0.576
22	0.359	0.428	0.508	0.562
23	0.351	0.418	0.496	0.549
24	0.343	0.409	0.485	0.537
25	0.336	0.400	0.475	0.526
26	0.329	0.392	0.465	0.515
27	0.323	0.385	0.456	0.505
28	0.317	0.377	0.448	0.496
29	0.311	0.370	0.440	0.487
30	0.305	0.364	0.432	0.478

Source: From *Comprehending Behavioral Statistics*, by R. T. Hurlburt, Copyright © 1994, Brooks/Cole Publishing Company, Pacific Grove, CA 93950, a division of International Thomson Publishing Inc. By permission of the publisher.

Appendix 8 Fisher *r*-to-*Z** Transformation

The entries in this table are the *Z*-values for correlations ranging from 0.000 to 0.999.

r	0.000	0.001	0.002	0.003	0.004	0.005	0.006	0.007	0.008	0.009
				THIRD DECIMAL PLACE IN *r*						

r	0.000	0.001	0.002	0.003	0.004	0.005	0.006	0.007	0.008	0.009
0.00	0.0000	0.0010	0.0020	0.0030	0.0040	0.0050	0.0060	0.0070	0.0080	0.0090
0.01	0.0100	0.0110	0.0120	0.0130	0.0140	0.0150	0.0160	0.0170	0.0180	0.0190
0.02	0.0200	0.0210	0.0220	0.0230	0.0240	0.0250	0.0260	0.0270	0.0280	0.0290
0.03	0.0300	0.0310	0.0320	0.0330	0.0340	0.0350	0.0360	0.0370	0.0380	0.0390
0.04	0.0400	0.0410	0.0420	0.0430	0.0440	0.0450	0.0460	0.0470	0.0480	0.0490
0.05	0.0500	0.0510	0.0520	0.0530	0.0541	0.0551	0.0561	0.0571	0.0581	0.0591
0.06	0.0601	0.0611	0.0621	0.0631	0.0641	0.0651	0.0661	0.0671	0.0681	0.0691
0.07	0.0701	0.0711	0.0721	0.0731	0.0741	0.0751	0.0761	0.0772	0.0782	0.0792
0.08	0.0802	0.0812	0.0822	0.0832	0.0842	0.0852	0.0862	0.0872	0.0882	0.0892
0.09	0.0902	0.0913	0.0923	0.0933	0.0943	0.0953	0.0963	0.0973	0.0983	0.0993
0.10	0.1003	0.1013	0.1024	0.1034	0.1044	0.1054	0.1064	0.1074	0.1084	0.1094
0.11	0.1104	0.1115	0.1125	0.1135	0.1145	0.1155	0.1165	0.1175	0.1186	0.1196
0.12	0.1206	0.1216	0.1226	0.1236	0.1246	0.1257	0.1267	0.1277	0.1287	0.1297
0.13	0.1307	0.1318	0.1328	0.1338	0.1348	0.1358	0.1368	0.1379	0.1389	0.1399
0.14	0.1409	0.1419	0.1430	0.1440	0.1450	0.1460	0.1471	0.1481	0.1491	0.1501
0.15	0.1511	0.1522	0.1532	0.1542	0.1552	0.1563	0.1573	0.1583	0.1593	0.1604
0.16	0.1614	0.1624	0.1634	0.1645	0.1655	0.1665	0.1676	0.1686	0.1696	0.1706
0.17	0.1717	0.1727	0.1737	0.1748	0.1758	0.1768	0.1779	0.1789	0.1799	0.1809
0.18	0.1820	0.1830	0.1841	0.1851	0.1861	0.1872	0.1882	0.1892	0.1903	0.1913
0.19	0.1923	0.1934	0.1944	0.1955	0.1965	0.1975	0.1986	0.1996	0.2007	0.2017
0.20	0.2027	0.2038	0.2048	0.2059	0.2069	0.2079	0.2090	0.2100	0.2111	0.2121
0.21	0.2132	0.2142	0.2153	0.2163	0.2174	0.2184	0.2195	0.2205	0.2216	0.2226
0.22	0.2237	0.2247	0.2258	0.2268	0.2279	0.2289	0.2300	0.2310	0.2321	0.2331
0.23	0.2342	0.2352	0.2363	0.2374	0.2384	0.2395	0.2405	0.2416	0.2427	0.2437
0.24	0.2448	0.2458	0.2469	0.2480	0.2490	0.2501	0.2512	0.2522	0.2533	0.2543
0.25	0.2554	0.2565	0.2575	0.2586	0.2597	0.2608	0.2618	0.2629	0.2640	0.2650
0.26	0.2661	0.2672	0.2683	0.2693	0.2704	0.2715	0.2726	0.2736	0.2747	0.2758
0.27	0.2769	0.2779	0.2790	0.2801	0.2812	0.2823	0.2833	0.2844	0.2855	0.2866
0.28	0.2877	0.2888	0.2899	0.2909	0.2920	0.2931	0.2942	0.2953	0.2964	0.2975
0.29	0.2986	0.2997	0.3008	0.3018	0.3029	0.3040	0.3051	0.3062	0.3073	0.3084
0.30	0.3095	0.3106	0.3117	0.3128	0.3139	0.3150	0.3161	0.3172	0.3183	0.3194
0.31	0.3205	0.3217	0.3228	0.3239	0.3250	0.3261	0.3272	0.3283	0.3294	0.3305
0.32	0.3316	0.3328	0.3339	0.3350	0.3361	0.3372	0.3383	0.3395	0.3406	0.3417
0.33	0.3428	0.3440	0.3451	0.3462	0.3473	0.3484	0.3496	0.3507	0.3518	0.3530
0.34	0.3541	0.3552	0.3564	0.3575	0.3586	0.3598	0.3609	0.3620	0.3632	0.3643
0.35	0.3654	0.3666	0.3677	0.3689	0.3700	0.3712	0.3723	0.3734	0.3746	0.3757
0.36	0.3769	0.3780	0.3792	0.3803	0.3815	0.3826	0.3838	0.3850	0.3861	0.3873
0.37	0.3884	0.3896	0.3907	0.3919	0.3931	0.3942	0.3954	0.3966	0.3977	0.3989
0.38	0.4001	0.4012	0.4024	0.4036	0.4047	0.4059	0.4071	0.4083	0.4094	0.4106
0.39	0.4118	0.4130	0.4142	0.4153	0.4165	0.4177	0.4189	0.4201	0.4213	0.4225
0.40	0.4236	0.4248	0.4260	0.4272	0.4284	0.4296	0.4308	0.4320	0.4332	0.4344
0.41	0.4356	0.4368	0.4380	0.4392	0.4404	0.4416	0.4428	0.4441	0.4453	0.4465
0.42	0.4477	0.4489	0.4501	0.4513	0.4526	0.4538	0.4550	0.4562	0.4574	0.4587
0.43	0.4599	0.4611	0.4624	0.4636	0.4648	0.4660	0.4673	0.4685	0.4698	0.4710
0.44	0.4722	0.4735	0.4747	0.4760	0.4772	0.4784	0.4797	0.4809	0.4822	0.4834
0.45	0.4847	0.4860	0.4872	0.4885	0.4897	0.4910	0.4922	0.4935	0.4948	0.4960
0.46	0.4973	0.4986	0.4999	0.5011	0.5024	0.5037	0.5049	0.5062	0.5075	0.5088
0.47	0.5101	0.5114	0.5126	0.5139	0.5152	0.5165	0.5178	0.5191	0.5204	0.5217
0.48	0.5230	0.5243	0.5256	0.5269	0.5282	0.5295	0.5308	0.5321	0.5334	0.5347

	THIRD DECIMAL PLACE IN r								
r	0.000	0.001	0.002	0.003	0.004	0.005	0.006	0.007	0.008	0.009
0.49	0.5361	0.5374	0.5387	0.5400	0.5413	0.5427	0.5440	0.5453	0.5466	0.5480
0.50	0.5493	0.5506	0.5520	0.5533	0.5547	0.5560	0.5573	0.5587	0.5600	0.5614
0.51	0.5627	0.5641	0.5654	0.5668	0.5682	0.5695	0.5709	0.5722	0.5736	0.5750
0.52	0.5763	0.5777	0.5791	0.5805	0.5818	0.5832	0.5846	0.5860	0.5874	0.5888
0.53	0.5901	0.5915	0.5929	0.5943	0.5957	0.5971	0.5985	0.5999	0.6013	0.6027
0.54	0.6042	0.6056	0.6070	0.6084	0.6098	0.6112	0.6127	0.6141	0.6155	0.6169
0.55	0.6184	0.6198	0.6213	0.6227	0.6241	0.6256	0.6270	0.6285	0.6299	0.6314
0.56	0.6328	0.6343	0.6358	0.6372	0.6387	0.6401	0.6416	0.6431	0.6446	0.6460
0.57	0.6475	0.6490	0.6505	0.6520	0.6535	0.6550	0.6565	0.6580	0.6595	0.6610
0.58	0.6625	0.6640	0.6655	0.6670	0.6685	0.6700	0.6716	0.6731	0.6746	0.6761
0.59	0.6777	0.6792	0.6807	0.6823	0.6838	0.6854	0.6869	0.6885	0.6900	0.6916
0.60	0.6931	0.6947	0.6963	0.6978	0.6994	0.7010	0.7026	0.7042	0.7057	0.7073
0.61	0.7089	0.7105	0.7121	0.7137	0.7153	0.7169	0.7185	0.7201	0.7218	0.7234
0.62	0.7250	0.7266	0.7283	0.7299	0.7315	0.7332	0.7348	0.7365	0.7381	0.7398
0.63	0.7414	0.7431	0.7447	0.7464	0.7481	0.7498	0.7514	0.7531	0.7548	0.7565
0.64	0.7582	0.7599	0.7616	0.7633	0.7650	0.7667	0.7684	0.7701	0.7718	0.7736
0.65	0.7753	0.7770	0.7788	0.7805	0.7823	0.7840	0.7858	0.7875	0.7893	0.7910
0.66	0.7928	0.7946	0.7964	0.7981	0.7999	0.8017	0.8035	0.8053	0.8071	0.8089
0.67	0.8107	0.8126	0.8144	0.8162	0.8180	0.8199	0.8217	0.8236	0.8254	0.8273
0.68	0.8291	0.8310	0.8328	0.8347	0.8366	0.8385	0.8404	0.8423	0.8441	0.8460
0.69	0.8480	0.8499	0.8518	0.8537	0.8556	0.8576	0.8595	0.8614	0.8634	0.8653
0.70	0.8673	0.8693	0.8712	0.8732	0.8752	0.8772	0.8792	0.8812	0.8832	0.8852
0.71	0.8872	0.8892	0.8912	0.8933	0.8953	0.8973	0.8994	0.9014	0.9035	0.9056
0.72	0.9076	0.9097	0.9118	0.9139	0.9160	0.9181	0.9202	0.9223	0.9245	0.9266
0.73	0.9287	0.9309	0.9330	0.9352	0.9373	0.9395	0.9417	0.9439	0.9461	0.9483
0.74	0.9505	0.9527	0.9549	0.9571	0.9594	0.9616	0.9639	0.9661	0.9684	0.9707
0.75	0.9730	0.9752	0.9775	0.9798	0.9822	0.9845	0.9868	0.9892	0.9915	0.9939
0.76	0.9962	0.9986	1.0010	1.0034	1.0058	1.0082	1.0106	1.0130	1.0154	1.0179
0.77	1.0203	1.0228	1.0253	1.0277	1.0302	1.0327	1.0352	1.0378	1.0403	1.0428
0.78	1.0454	1.0479	1.0505	1.0531	1.0557	1.0583	1.0609	1.0635	1.0661	1.0688
0.79	1.0714	1.0741	1.0768	1.0795	1.0822	1.0849	1.0876	1.0903	1.0931	1.0958
0.80	1.0986	1.1014	1.1042	1.1070	1.1098	1.1127	1.1155	1.1184	1.1212	1.1241
0.81	1.1270	1.1299	1.1329	1.1358	1.1388	1.1417	1.1447	1.1477	1.1507	1.1538
0.82	1.1568	1.1599	1.1630	1.1660	1.1692	1.1723	1.1754	1.1786	1.1817	1.1849
0.83	1.1881	1.1914	1.1946	1.1979	1.2011	1.2044	1.2077	1.2111	1.2144	1.2178
0.84	1.2212	1.2246	1.2280	1.2315	1.2349	1.2384	1.2419	1.2454	1.2490	1.2526
0.85	1.2562	1.2598	1.2634	1.2671	1.2707	1.2745	1.2782	1.2819	1.2857	1.2895
0.86	1.2933	1.2972	1.3011	1.3050	1.3089	1.3129	1.3169	1.3209	1.3249	1.3290
0.87	1.3331	1.3372	1.3414	1.3456	1.3498	1.3540	1.3583	1.3626	1.3670	1.3714
0.88	1.3758	1.3802	1.3847	1.3892	1.3938	1.3984	1.4030	1.4077	1.4124	1.4171
0.89	1.4219	1.4268	1.4316	1.4365	1.4415	1.4465	1.4516	1.4566	1.4618	1.4670
0.90	1.4722	1.4775	1.4828	1.4882	1.4937	1.4992	1.5047	1.5103	1.5160	1.5217
0.91	1.5275	1.5334	1.5393	1.5453	1.5513	1.5574	1.5636	1.5698	1.5762	1.5826
0.92	1.5890	1.5956	1.6022	1.6089	1.6157	1.6226	1.6296	1.6366	1.6438	1.6510
0.93	1.6584	1.6658	1.6734	1.6811	1.6888	1.6967	1.7047	1.7129	1.7211	1.7295
0.94	1.7380	1.7467	1.7555	1.7645	1.7736	1.7828	1.7923	1.8019	1.8117	1.8216
0.95	1.8318	1.8421	1.8527	1.8635	1.8745	1.8857	1.8972	1.9090	1.9210	1.9333
0.96	1.9459	1.9588	1.9721	1.9857	1.9996	2.0139	2.0287	2.0439	2.0595	2.0756
0.97	2.0923	2.1095	2.1273	2.1457	2.1649	2.1847	2.2054	2.2269	2.2494	2.2729
0.98	2.2976	2.3235	2.3507	2.3796	2.4101	2.4427	2.4774	2.5147	2.5550	2.5987
0.99	2.6467	2.6996	2.7587	2.8257	2.9031	2.9945	3.1063	3.2504	3.4534	3.8002

Note: Values were computed using the equation for the Fisher r-to-Z^* transformation.

Glossary

analysis of variance (ANOVA) A parametric test of statistical significance that assesses whether differences in the means of several samples (groups) can lead the researcher to reject the null hypothesis that the means of the populations from which the samples are drawn are the same.

arrangements The different ways events can be ordered and yet result in a single outcome. For example, there is only one arrangement for gaining the outcome of ten heads in ten tosses of a coin. There are, however, ten different arrangements for gaining the outcome of nine heads in ten tosses of a coin.

assumptions Statements that identify the requirements and characteristics of a test of statistical significance. These are the foundations on which the rest of the test is built.

bar chart A graph in which bars represent frequencies, percentages, or proportions for the categories or values of a variable.

between sum of squares (BSS) A measure of the variability between samples (groups). The between sum of squares is calculated by taking the sum of the squared deviation of each sample mean from the grand mean multiplied by the number of cases in that sample.

biased Describing a statistic when its estimate of a population parameter does not center on the true value. In regression analysis, the omission of relevant independent variables will lead to bias in the estimate of Y. When relevant independent variables are omitted and those measures are related to an independent variable included in regression analysis, then the estimate of the effect of that variable will also be biased.

binomial distribution The probability or sampling distribution for an event that has only two possible outcomes.

binomial formula The means of determining the probability that a given set of binomial events will occur in all its possible arrangements.

bivariate regression A technique for predicting change in a dependent variable using one independent variable.

cells The various entries in a table, each of which is identified by a particular row and column. When we use a table to compare two variables, it is convenient to refer to each combination of categories as a cell.

central limit theorem A theorem that states: "If repeated independent random samples of size N are drawn from a population, as N grows large, the sampling distribution of sample means will be approximately normal." The central limit theorem enables the researcher to make inferences about an unknown population using a normal sampling distribution.

chi-square distribution A sampling distribution that is used to conduct tests of statistical significance with binary or multicategory nominal variables. The distribution is nonsymmetrical and varies according to degrees of freedom. All the values in the distribution are positive.

chi-square statistic The test statistic resulting from applying the chi-square formula to the observed and expected frequencies for each cell. This statistic tells us how much the observed distribution differs from that expected under the null hypothesis.

classification The process whereby data are organized into categories or groups.

coefficient of relative variation A measure of dispersion calculated by dividing the standard deviation by the mean.

concordant pairs of observations Pairs of observations that have consistent rankings on two ordinal variables.

confidence interval An interval of values around a statistic (usually a point estimate). If we were to draw repeated samples and calculate a 95% confidence interval for each, then in only 5 in 100 of these samples would the interval fail to include the true population parameter. In the case of a 99% confidence interval, only 1 in 100 samples would fail to include the true population parameter.

convenience sample A sample chosen not at random, but according to criteria of expedience or accessibility to the researcher.

correctly specified regression model A regression model in which the researcher has taken into account all of the relevant predictors of the dependent variable and has measured them correctly.

correlation A measure of the strength of a relationship between two variables.

covariation A measure of the extent to which two variables vary together relative to their respective means. The covariation between the two variables serves as the numerator for the equation to calculate Pearson's r.

Cox and Snell's R^2 A commonly used pseudo R^2 measure whose main component, as in other pseudo R^2 statistics, is the log likelihood function ($-2LL$).

Cramer's _V_ A measure of association for two nominal variables that adjusts the chi-square statistic by the sample size. _V_ is appropriate when at least one of the nominal variables has more than two categories.

critical value The point at which the rejection region begins.

cumulative logistic probability function A transformation of the logistic probability function that allows computation of the probability that _Y_ will occur, given a certain combination of characteristics of the independent variables.

curvilinear relationship An association between two variables whose values may be represented as a curved line when plotted on a scatter diagram.

data Information used to answer a research question.

degrees of freedom A mathematical index that places a value on the extent to which a particular operation is free to vary after certain limitations have been imposed. Calculating the degrees of freedom for a chi-square test determines which chi-square probability distribution we use.

dependent variable (_Y_) The variable assumed by the researcher to be influenced by one or more independent variables; the outcome variable; the phenomenon that we are interested in explaining. It is dependent on other variables in the sense that it is influenced—or we expect it to be influenced—by other variables.

derivative at mean (DM) A measure that converts the nonlinear logistic regression coefficient to a simple linear regression coefficient, which may be interpreted as the change in _Y_ associated with a unit change in _X_.

descriptive statistics A broad area of statistics that is concerned with summarizing large amounts of information in an efficient manner. Descriptive statistics are used to describe or represent in summary form the characteristics of a sample or population.

design sensitivity The statistical power of a research study. In a sensitive study design, statistical power will be maximized, and the statistical test employed will be more capable of identifying an effect.

deviation from the mean The extent to which each individual score differs from the mean of all the scores.

directional hypothesis A research hypothesis that indicates a specific type of outcome by specifying the nature of the relationship that is expected.

discordant pairs of observations Pairs of observations that have inconsistent rankings on two ordinal variables.

distribution-free tests Another name for nonparametric tests.

dummy variable A binary nominal-level variable that is included in a multivariate regression model.

effect size (ES) A standardized measure derived by taking the effect size (e.g., the difference between two populations), measured in the raw units of the outcome measure examined, and dividing it by the pooled or common standard deviation of the outcome measure.

eta A measure of the degree of correlation between an interval-level and a nominal-level variable.

eta squared The proportion of the total sum of squares that is accounted for by the between sum of squares. Eta squared is sometimes referred to as the percent of variance explained.

expected frequency The number of observations one would predict for a cell if the null hypothesis were true.

explained sum of squares (ESS) Another name for the between sum of squares. The explained sum of squares is the part of the total variability that can be explained by visible differences between the groups.

external validity The extent to which a study sample is reflective of the population from which it is drawn. A study is said to have high external validity when the sample used is representative of the population to which inferences are made.

factorial The product of a number and all the positive whole numbers lower than it.

frequency The number of times that a score or value occurs.

frequency distribution An arrangement of scores in order from the lowest to the highest, accompanied by the number of times each score occurs.

gamma (_γ_) PRE measure of association for two ordinal variables that uses information about concordant and discordant pairs of observations within a table. Gamma has a standardized scale ranging from −1.0 to 1.0.

Goodman and Kruskal's tau (_τ_) PRE measure of association for two nominal variables that uses information about the proportional distribution of cases within a table. Tau has a standardized scale ranging from 0 to 1.0. For this measure, the researcher must define the independent and dependent variables.

grand mean The overall mean of every single case across all of the samples.

heteroscedasticity A situation in which the variances of scores on two or more variables are not equal. Heteroscedasticity violates one of the assumptions of the parametric test of statistical significance for the correlation coefficient.

histogram A bar graph used to represent a frequency distribution.

homoscedasticity A statement that the variances and standard deviations of two or more populations are the same.

honestly significant difference (HSD) test A parametric test of statistical significance, adjusted for making pairwise comparisons. The HSD test defines the difference between the pairwise comparisons required to reject the null hypothesis.

independent Describing two events when the occurrence of one does not affect the occurrence of the other.

independent random sampling A form of random sampling in which the fact that one subject is drawn from a population in no way affects the probability of drawing any other subject from that population.

independent variable (X) A variable assumed by the researcher to have an impact on or influence the value of the dependent variable, Y.

index of qualitative variation A measure of dispersion calculated by dividing the sum of the possible pairs of observed scores by the sum of the possible pairs of expected scores (when cases are equally distributed across categories).

inferential, or inductive, statistics A broad area of statistics that provides the researcher with tools for making statements about populations on the basis of knowledge about samples. Inferential statistics allow the researcher to make inferences regarding populations from information gained in samples.

interval scale A scale of measurement that uses a common and standard unit and enables the researcher to calculate exact differences between scores, in addition to categorizing and ordering data.

iteration Each time we identify another tentative solution and reestimate our logistic regression coefficients.

Kendall's τ_b PRE measure of association for two ordinal variables that uses information about concordant pairs, discordant pairs, and pairs of observations tied on both variables examined. τ_b has a standardized scale ranging from -1.0 to 1.0 and is appropriate only when the number of rows equals the number of columns in a table.

Kendall's τ_c A measure of association for two ordinal variables that uses information about concordant pairs, discordant pairs, and pairs of observations tied on both variables examined. τ_c has a standardized scale ranging from -1.0 to 1.0 and is appropriate when the number of rows is not equal to the number of columns in a table.

Kruskal-Wallis test A nonparametric test of statistical significance for multiple groups, requiring at least an ordinal scale of measurement.

lack of convergence Failure of a logistic regression analysis to reach a result that meets the criterion of reduction in the log likelihood function.

lambda (λ) PRE measure of association for two nominal variables that uses information about the modal category of the dependent variable for each category of the independent variable. Lambda has a standardized scale ranging from 0 to 1.0.

least squares property A characteristic of the mean whereby the sum of all the squared deviations from the mean is a minimum—it is lower than the sum of the squared deviations from any other fixed point.

levels of measurement Types of measurement that make use of progressively larger amounts of information.

likelihood ratio chi-square test A test for statistical significance that allows the researcher to examine whether a subset of independent variables in a logistic regression is statistically significant. It compares $-2LL$ for a full model to $-2LL$ for a reduced model.

linear relationship An association between two variables whose joint distribution may be represented in linear form when plotted on a scatter diagram.

log likelihood function A measure of the probability of observing the results in the sample, given the coefficient estimates in the model. In logistic regression, the log likelihood function ($-2LL$) is defined as -2 times the natural logarithm of the likelihood function.

logarithm The power to which a fixed number (the base) must be raised to produce another number.

logistic model curve The form of the predicted outcomes of a logistic regression analysis. Shaped like an S, the logistic curve begins to flatten as it approaches 0 or 1, so it keeps coming closer to—but never actually reaches—either of these two values.

logistic regression analysis A type of regression analysis that allows the researcher to make predictions about dichotomous dependent variables in terms of the log of the odds of Y.

logistic regression coefficient The coefficient b produced in a logistic regression analysis. It may be interpreted as the increase in the log of the odds of Y associated with a one-unit increase in X.

margin of error The size of the confidence interval for a test. A margin of error of $\pm 3\%$ in an opinion poll means that the confidence interval ranged between 3% above and 3% below the point estimate or observed statistic.

marginal The value in the margin of a table that totals the scores in the appropriate column or row.

maximum likelihood estimation A technique for estimating the parameters or coefficients of a model that maximizes the probability that the estimates obtained will produce a distribution similar to that of the observed data.

mean A measure of central tendency calculated by dividing the sum of the scores by the number of cases.

mean deviation A measure of dispersion calculated by adding the absolute deviation of each score from the mean and then dividing the sum by the number of cases.

measurement The assignment of numerical values to objects, characteristics, or events in a systematic manner.

measures of central tendency Descriptive statistics that allow us to identify the typical case in a sample or population. Measures of central tendency are measures of typicality.

measures of dispersion Descriptive statistics that tell us how tightly clustered or dispersed the cases in a sample or population are. They answer the question "How typical is the typical case?"

median A measure of central tendency calculated by identifying the value or category of the score that occupies the middle position in the distribution of scores.

mode A measure of central tendency calculated by identifying the score or category that occurs most frequently.

model chi-square The statistical test used to assess the statistical significance of the overall logistic regression model. It compares the $-2LL$ for the full model with the $-2LL$ calculated without any independent variables included.

multicollinearity Condition in a multivariate regression model in which independent variables examined are very strongly intercorrelated. Multicollinearity leads to unstable regression coefficients.

multiplication rule The means for determining the probability that a series of events will jointly occur.

multivariate regression A technique for predicting change in a dependent variable, using more than one independent variable.

multivariate statistics Statistics that examine the relationships among variables while taking into account the possible influences of other confounding factors. Multivariate statistics allow the researcher to isolate the impact of one variable from others that may distort his or her results.

Nagelkerke R^2 A pseudo R^2 statistic that corrects for the fact that Cox and Snell's estimates, as well as many other pseudo R^2 statistics, often have a maximum value of less than 1.

natural logarithm of the odds of Y (logit of Y) The outcome predicted in a logistic regression analysis.

nominal scale A scale of measurement that assigns each piece of information to an appropriate category without suggesting any order for the categories created.

nondirectional hypothesis A research hypothesis that does not indicate a specific type of outcome, stating only that there is a relationship or a difference.

nonparametric tests Tests of statistical significance that make no assumptions as to the shape of the population distribution.

normal curve A normal frequency distribution represented on a graph by a continuous line.

normal frequency distribution A bell-shaped frequency distribution, symmetrical in form. Its mean, mode, and median are always the same. The percentage of cases between the mean and points at a measured distance from the mean is fixed.

null hypothesis A statement that reduces the research question to a simple assertion to be tested by the researcher. The null hypothesis normally suggests that there is no relationship or no difference.

observed frequency The observed result of the study, recorded in a cell.

observed significance level The risk of Type I error associated with a specific sample statistic in a test. When the observed significance level is less than the criterion significance level in a test of statistical significance, the researcher will reject the null hypothesis.

odds ratio [Exp(B)] A statistic used to interpret the logistic regression coefficient. It represents the impact of a one-unit change in X on the ratio of the probability of Y.

OLS regression See *ordinary least squares regression analysis*.

one-tailed test of significance A test of statistical significance in which the region for rejecting the null hypothesis falls on only one side of the sampling distribution. One-tailed tests are based on directional research hypotheses.

ordinal scale A scale of measurement that categorizes information and assigns it an order of magnitude without using a standard scale of equal intervals.

ordinary least squares regression analysis A type of regression analysis in which the sum of squared errors from the regression line is minimized.

outlier(s) A single or small number of exceptional cases that substantially deviate from the general pattern of scores.

overall mean See *grand mean*.

pairwise comparisons Comparisons made between two sample means extracted from a larger statistical analysis.

parameter A characteristic of the population—for example, the mean number of previous convictions for all U.S. prisoners.

parametric tests Tests of statistical significance that make assumptions as to the shape of the population distribution.

Pearson's correlation coefficient See *Pearson's r*.

Pearson's *r* A commonly used measure of association between two variables. Pearson's *r* measures the strength and direction of linear relationships on a standardized scale from −1.0 to 1.0.

percent of correct predictions A statistic used to assess how well a logistic regression model explains the observed data. An arbitrary decision point (usually 0.50) is set for deciding when a predicted value should be set at 1, and then the predictions are compared to the observed data.

percent of variance explained (1) R^2, a measure for evaluating how well the regression model predicts values of Y; it represents the improvement in predicting Y that the regression line provides over the mean of Y. (2) η^2, the proportion of the total sum of squares that is accounted for by the explained sum of squares.

percentage A relation between two numbers in which the whole is accorded a value of 100 and the other number is given a numerical value corresponding to its share of the whole.

phi (ϕ) A measure of association for two nominal variables that adjusts the chi-square statistic by the sample size. Phi is appropriate only for nominal variables that each have two categories.

pie chart A graph in which a circle (called a pie) is cut into wedges to represent the relative size of each category's frequency count.

point estimate An estimate of the population parameter. Absent knowledge of the population parameter, the statistic we obtain for a sample is generally used as an estimate—or, in statistical terms, a point estimate—of the population parameter.

pooled variance A method of obtaining the standard error of the sampling distribution for a difference of means test. The pooled variance method requires an assumption of homoscedasticity.

population The universe of cases that the researcher seeks to study. The population of cases is fixed at a particular time (e.g., the population of the United States). However, populations usually change across time.

population distribution The frequency distribution of a particular variable within a population.

probability distribution A theoretical distribution consisting of the probabilities expected in the long run for all possible outcomes of an event.

proportion A relation between two numbers in which the whole is accorded a value of 1 and

the other number is given a numerical value corresponding to its share of the whole.

proportional reduction in error (PRE) The proportional reduction in errors made when the value of one measure is predicted using information about the second measure.

pseudo R^2 The term generally used for a group of measures used in logistic regression to create an approximation of the OLS regression R^2. They are generally based on comparisons of −2LL for a full model and a null model (without any independent variables).

random sampling Drawing samples from the population in a manner that ensures every individual in that population an equal chance of being selected.

randomized experiment A type of study in which the effect of one variable can be examined in isolation through random allocation of subjects to treatment and control, or comparison, groups.

range A measure of dispersion calculated by subtracting the smallest score from the largest score. The range may also be calculated from specific points in a distribution, such as the 5th and 95th percentile scores.

rank-order test A test of statistical significance that uses information relating to the relative order, or rank, of variable scores.

ratio scale A scale of measurement identical to an interval scale in every respect except that, in addition, a value of zero on the scale represents the absence of the phenomenon.

regression coefficient *b* A statistic used to assess the influence of an independent variable, X, on a dependent variable, Y. The regression coefficient b is interpreted as the estimated change in Y that is associated with a one-unit change in X.

regression error (*e*) The difference between the predicted value of Y and the actual value of Y.

regression line The line predicting values of Y. The line is plotted from knowledge of the Y-intercept and the regression coefficient.

regression model The hypothesized statement by the researcher of the factor or factors that define the value of the dependent variable, Y. The model is normally expressed in equation form.

rejection region The area of a sampling distribution containing the test statistic values that will cause the researcher to reject the null hypothesis.

relaxing an assumption Deciding that we need not be concerned with that assumption. For example, the assumption that a population is normal may be relaxed if the sample size is sufficiently large to invoke the central limit theorem.

reliability The extent to which a measure provides consistent results across subjects or units of study.

representative sample A sample that reflects the population from which it is drawn.

research hypothesis The antithesis of the null hypothesis. The statement normally answers the initial research question by suggesting that there is a relationship or a difference.

research question The question the researcher hopes to be able to answer by means of a study.

sample A set of actual observations or cases drawn from a population.

sample distribution The frequency distribution of a particular variable within a sample drawn from a population.

sample statistic A characteristic of a sample—for example, the mean number of previous convictions in a random sample of 1,000 prisoners.

sampling distribution A distribution of all the results of a very large number of samples, each one of the same size and drawn from the same population under the same conditions. Ordinarily, sampling distributions are derived using probability theory and are based on probability distributions.

sampling frame The universe of eligible cases from which a sample is drawn.

sampling with replacement A sampling method in which individuals in a sample are returned to the sampling frame after they have been selected. This raises the possibility that certain individuals in a population may appear in a sample more than once.

scale of measurement Type of categorization used to arrange or assign values to data.

scatter diagram See *scatterplot*.

scatterplot A graph whose two axes are defined by two variables and upon which a point is plotted for each subject in a sample according to its score on the two variables.

separate variance A method of obtaining the standard error of the sampling distribution for a difference of means test. The separate variance method does not require an assumption of homoscedasticity.

significance level The level of Type I error a researcher is willing to risk in a test of statistical significance.

single-sample *t*-test A test of statistical significance that is used to examine whether a sample is drawn from a specific population with a known or hypothesized mean. In a *t*-test, the standard deviation of the population to which the sample is being compared is unknown.

single-sample *z*-test A test of statistical significance that is used to examine whether a sample is drawn from a specific population with a known or hypothesized mean. In a *z*-test, the standard deviation of the population to which the sample is being compared either is known

or—as in the case of a proportion—is defined by the null hypothesis.

skewed Describing a spread of scores that is clearly weighted to one side.

Somers' *d* PRE measure of association for two ordinal variables that uses information about concordant pairs, discordant pairs, and pairs of observations tied on the independent variable. Somers' *d* has a standardized scale ranging from -1.0 to 1.0.

Spearman's correlation coefficient See *Spearman's r*.

Spearman's *r* (r_s) A measure of association between two rank-ordered variables. Spearman's *r* measures the strength and direction of linear relationships on a standardized scale between -1.0 and 1.0.

standard deviation A measure of dispersion calculated by taking the square root of the variance.

standard deviation unit A unit of measurement used to describe the deviation of a specific score or value from the mean in a *z* distribution.

standard error The standard deviation of a sampling distribution.

standard normal distribution A normal frequency distribution with a mean of 0 and a standard deviation of 1. Any normal frequency distribution can be transformed into the standard normal distribution by using the *z* formula.

standardized logistic regression coefficient A statistic used to compare logistic regression coefficients that use different scales of measurement. It is meant to approximate Beta, the standardized regression coefficient in OLS regression.

standardized regression coefficient (Beta) Weighted or standardized estimate of *b* that takes into account the standard deviation of the independent and the dependent variables. The standardized regression coefficient is used to compare the effects of independent variables measured on different scales in a multivariate regression analysis.

statistical inference The process of making generalizations from sample statistics to population parameters.

statistical power One minus the probability of a Type II error. The greater the statistical power of a test, the less chance there is that a researcher will mistakenly fail to reject the null hypothesis.

statistically significant Describing a test statistic that falls within the rejection region defined by the researcher. When this occurs, the researcher is prepared to reject the null hypothesis and state that the outcome or relationship is statistically significant.

sum of squares The sum of squared deviations of scores from a mean or set of means.

tails of the distribution The extremes on the sides of a sampling distribution. The events represented by the tails of a sampling distribution are those deemed least likely to occur if the null hypothesis is true for the population.

test of statistical significance A test in which a researcher makes a decision to reject or to fail to reject the null hypothesis on the basis of a sample statistic.

test statistic The outcome of the study, expressed in units of the sampling distribution. A test statistic that falls within the rejection region will lead the researcher to reject the null hypothesis.

tied pairs of observations (ties) Pairs of observations that have the same ranking on two ordinal variables.

time series data Repeated measures of the same variable over some regularly occurring time period, such as days, months, or years.

time series plot A line graph that connects repeated measures of the same variable over some regularly occurring time period, such as days, months, or years.

tolerance A measure of the extent of the intercorrelations of each independent variable with all other independent variables. Tolerance may be used to test for multicollinearity in a multivariate regression model.

total sum of squares (TSS) A measure of the total amount of variability across all of the groups examined. The total sum of squares is calculated by summing the squared deviation of each score from the grand mean.

***t*-test for dependent samples** A test of statistical significance that is used when two samples are not independent.

two-sample *t*-test A test of statistical significance that examines the difference observed between the means or proportions of two samples.

two-tailed test of significance A test of statistical significance in which the region for rejecting the null hypothesis falls on both sides of the sampling distribution. Two-tailed tests are based on nondirectional research hypotheses.

Type I error Also known as alpha error. The mistake made when a researcher rejects the null hypothesis on the basis of a sample statistic (i.e., claiming that there is a relationship) when in fact the null hypothesis is true (i.e., there is actually *no* such relationship in the population).

Type II error Also known as beta error. The mistake made when a researcher fails to reject the null hypothesis on the basis of a sample statistic (i.e., failing to claim that there is a relationship) when in fact the null hypothesis is false (i.e., there actually *is* a relationship).

unexplained sum of squares (USS) Another name for the within sum of squares. The unexplained sum of squares is the part of the total variability that cannot be explained by visible differences between the groups.

universe The total population of cases.

validity The extent to which a variable accurately reflects the concept being measured.

variable A trait, characteristic, or attribute of a person/object/event that can be measured at least at the nominal-scale level.

variance (s^2) A measure of dispersion calculated by adding together the squared deviation of each score from the mean and then dividing the sum by the number of cases.

variation ratio A measure of dispersion calculated by subtracting the proportion of cases in the modal category from 1.

Wald statistic A statistic used to assess the statistical significance of coefficients in a logistic regression model.

within sum of squares (WSS) A measure of the variability within samples (groups). The within sum of squares is calculated by summing the squared deviation of each score from its sample mean.

***Y*-intercept (b_0)** The expected value of Y when $X = 0$. The Y-intercept is used in predicting values of Y.

***z*-score** Score that represents standard deviation units for a standard normal distribution.

Index